NEGATIVE COMPARATIVE LAW

Written under the sign of Beckett, this book addresses comparative law's commitment to the deterritorialization of the legal and its attendant claim for the normative relevance of foreign law locally in the fabrication of statutory determinations, judicial opinions, or academic reflections. Wanting to withstand the law's persistent tendency towards nationalist retrenchment and counter comparative law's institutional marginalization, the fifteen essays at hand impart radical and discerning intellectual equipment in order to foster the valorization of the legally foreign and the comparative motion. In particular, the critique informing this manifesto examines pre-eminent topics like culture and difference, understanding and translatability, objectivity and truth, invention and tracing. Harnessing insights from a range of disciplinary discourses, this book contends that comparatists must boldly desist from their field's dominant epistemology and embrace a practice much better attuned to the study of foreignness.

PIERRE LEGRAND teaches comparative law at the Sorbonne.

CAMBRIDGE STUDIES IN INTERNATIONAL AND COMPARATIVE LAW: 167

Established in 1946, this series produces high quality, reflective and innovative scholarship in the field of public international law. It publishes works on international law that are of a theoretical, historical, cross-disciplinary or doctrinal nature. The series also welcomes books providing insights from private international law, comparative law and transnational studies which inform international legal thought and practice more generally.

The series seeks to publish views from diverse legal traditions and perspectives, and of any geographical origin. In this respect it invites studies offering regional perspectives on core *problématiques* of international law, and in the same vein, it appreciates contrasts and debates between diverging approaches. Accordingly, books offering new or less orthodox perspectives are very much welcome. Works of a generalist character are greatly valued and the series is also open to studies on specific areas, institutions or problems. Translations of the most outstanding works published in other languages are also considered.

After seventy years, Cambridge Studies in International and Comparative Law sets the standard for international legal scholarship and will continue to define the discipline as it evolves in the years to come.

A list of books in the series can be found at the end of this volume.

NEGATIVE COMPARATIVE LAW

A Strong Programme for Weak Thought

PIERRE LEGRAND

CAMBRIDGE
UNIVERSITY PRESS

CAMBRIDGE
UNIVERSITY PRESS

Shaftesbury Road, Cambridge CB2 8EA, United Kingdom

One Liberty Plaza, 20th Floor, New York, NY 10006, USA

477 Williamstown Road, Port Melbourne, VIC 3207, Australia

314–321, 3rd Floor, Plot 3, Splendor Forum, Jasola District Centre, New Delhi – 110025, India

103 Penang Road, #05–06/07, Visioncrest Commercial, Singapore 238467

Cambridge University Press is part of Cambridge University Press & Assessment, a department of the University of Cambridge.

We share the University's mission to contribute to society through the pursuit of education, learning and research at the highest international levels of excellence.

www.cambridge.org
Information on this title: www.cambridge.org/9781009054867

DOI: 10.1017/9781009051910

First published 2022
First paperback edition 2024

A catalogue record for this publication is available from the British Library

ISBN 978-1-316-51197-8 Hardback
ISBN 978-1-009-05486-7 Paperback

Enfin sorti de l'étroite prison, j'ai voyagé jusqu'à l'étiolement.
Aujourd'hui, j'habite le pays que tu m'as festonné
et notre insolente solitude me comble.
Je n'ai pas les mots pour faire ton éloge
ou dire notre emmêlement somptueux.
Je m'émerveille.
Mais voici donc ces tissures, ces vestiges,
pendant qu'ailleurs on s'affiche sûr.
Dotés d'étangs camarguais,
de tes vifs chevaux blancs aux crinières vaporeuses
(Mein Muppie et Der Züße),
avantagés des arcades de ton vieux cloître arlésien,
des chemins rocailleux du massif mistralé aussi,
signalant avec ardeur leur regimbement,
tu as voulu qu'ils s'élancent, Compagne.

'[I]n this great worry around the manner of governing
and in research on the manners of governing, one detects
a perpetual question that would be: "how not to be governed *like that*,
by them, in the name of these principles, with a view to such objectives
and by the means of such processes, not like that, not for that, not by them?" . . . .
[I]t seems that one could place on that side pretty much what one would call
the critical attitude . . . as a manner to be wary [of the arts of governance],
to recuse them, to limit them, to find them a just measure, to transform them,
to seek to escape these arts of governance or, at any rate,
to displace them, by way of essential reticence, but also and thereby
as a line of development of the arts of governance . . .,
[what] I would call quite simply . . .
the art of not being governed like that and at that price.'

DISCONTENTS

I

Raising My Game – To Fail Better

I envisage *Negative Comparative Law: A Strong Programme for Weak Thought* (*NCL*) as a manifesto in favour of a radically different approach to research in foreign law, such material practice operating under the technical and institutional label 'comparative law'. Given my circumstances – I refer both to my predilections and the opportunities that have presented themselves to me – I must offer a Eurocentric critique of comparative law as a Eurocentric intellectual pursuit. Fortunately, there remains significant epistemic value in this introspection, not least because it demurs Eurocentrism. I wish I could write insightfully about the Cambodian or Ethiopian law-worlds, Bolivian or Ugandan legal cultures, the law of Mongolia on the status of foreign legal nationals or of India on general secondary education in the state language. Alas, no creditable endeavour along these lines is possible.

Negative Comparative Law targets an Establishment, a settled theoretical model articulating comparative law that I name 'positivism'. This framework casts foreign law as a textual invariant and assumes the possibility of immaculate interpretive and representative access to it – not least through method, long the favoured technology of entry. Positivism has demonstrably exercised strong dominance over comparatists-at-law, whether in classrooms or law reviews, keynotes or monographs. Now, the epistemic occlusions and delusions informing the idea of a stable foreign law and the feasibility of impeccable readerly contact with it has contributed to the stigmatization of comparative law within the wider academic world and led to the inferior placement of comparison in the hierarchy of scholarly enterprises. Not only has the immaturity of the comparatist's epistemic instruments tainted comparability in the eyes of jurists, but the hold of positivist research has pre-empted the emergence of a more sophisticated theoretical arrangement within the field of comparative law. In particular, positivism's unexamined attraction to objectivity and truth (two artifices assuming the quiddity of foreign law-texts); its infatuation to the wifty ideas of equivalence or commonality and the allegedly unbroken chains of likenesses across laws that would extend through the centuries and planetwide; and its disciplinary confinement to purportedly exclusively 'legal' themes – if with an occasional sprinkling of anthropological, philosophical, or sociological evocations – have eschewed a searching critique of the cognitive conditions pursuant to which the comparison of laws has been effectively unfolding and must be developing as, soberly to point the irrefutable, a report on foreign law is *made* – it is a composition, a bricolage. Not coincidentally, this striking absence of (self-)critique has favoured the lame ideologies that one associates with the depoliticization and naturalization of the status quo.

Because they have generated substantial epistemic, ethico-political, and institutional damage, positivists who crowd the field of comparative law must be exposed and their philistinism discarded. Positivism's decidedly exiguous and stealthily neophobic approach to the comparison of laws requires to be replaced by a far more incisive theoretical and practical model heralding in convincing terms what is epistemically desirable and plausible as one appreciates foreign law, that is, a paradigm effectively advancing one's understanding of what it means to understand foreign law and the comparison of laws. Specifically, this alternative strategy must efface any idea of a foreign law that would exist as a fixed entity docilely awaiting its comparatist and eliminate any appeal to an objective or true representative access to foreign law-texts. A substitute programme also requires to emphasize the comparatist's ethical responsibilities and political commitments, if only because the question of speaking for the other (which is what the comparatist emphatically does) is very vexed terrain indeed. Primordially, the different disposition I defend demands that comparison be apprehended as interpretation understood as transformation;[1] that foreign law therefore be regarded as intrinsically variable according to the intelligibilities and interests of the interpreting comparatist whose interpretation of foreignness fashions something new in the very act of interpretation; and that the comparatist accordingly be considered an inevitable part of any intervention into foreign law and of any reporting outcome arising

[1] cf F Moretti, 'The Roads to Rome' (2020/124) New Left R 125, 136: 'Interpretation *transforms* all it touches.'

from such an intervention – which means that any dichotomy along the lines of subject and object must be forsaken.

As I seek to deconstruct a general economy of comparative law – to dismantle the Positivist Machine and refute its pre-lapsarian ontological indistinction isolating law from every other discursive formation – and as I aim to abandon the presumptuous Cartesian fable of an idealized and autonomous mind (a myopic vision informing an occidental metaphysics obsessed with individual rationality and agential subjectivity), I argue for an individual of limited mind-sovereignty framed through preceding determinative cultural forces – structures of emergence and becoming – into which he is inextricably entwined, not least by way of language (but also on account of socialization and institutionalization).[2] My ethical/political dissolution and reconstitution of the comparative project denying the primacy of (liberal) human subjectivity demands not merely new manners of thinking and reading, but a different attitude, another way of perceiving and being, too. Basically, I ask the comparatist to accept that his place (or his displacement) is invariably 'between' rather than 'within', which means that foreign law's reality lies beyond where the comparatist can reach even as he remains too close to be able to detach himself from it. In other words, access to foreignness's full meaning – the foreign's meaning *as it is*, if you will – must be persistently deferred to another day (and must insistently differ according to its specific interpreter), no matter how sophisticated the cognitive assemblage the comparatist is able to deploy towards the ascription of sense to foreignness. There being no meaning grounding foreign law here and now, *the* meaning of foreignness always-already pertains to fiction. What there is, then, is a comparatist standing on the verge of foreignness facing both the irreducible unknowability of foreign law's meaning and its attendant proliferation.

As a matter of creditability, I claim that the comparison of laws necessitates to manifest itself as the material practice indivisibly legal and cultural – legal/cultural – that it is: the jurist comparing laws is encultured (a fact that the comparatist must acknowledge by visibly inscribing himself and his report into the interpretive existence of the foreign law-text), and the foreign law being interpreted is encultured, too.

[2] I am reminded of Fernand Braudel's exclamation in his sprawling study of the Mediterranean Sea: 'Thus am I always tempted, before a human being, to see him imprisoned within a destiny that he barely fashions': F Braudel, *La Méditerranée*, vol 3 (2nd edn, Colin 2017 [1966]) 314. As regards the vexed decussation of language and gender, I address the matter presently.

In this epistemological vein, I hold that one's value-commitments are available for assessment only as regards their internal coherence, there being no transcultural or universally valid criteria by which one can move beyond contestation to Rational or Reasonable consensus. Any evaluation of foreign means and ambitions can only be critique from the standpoint of one's own. Still, the course of inquiry and mode of experience that is comparison hold forth as important vehicles of change of the self(-in-the-law) through the other(-in-the-law) as opposed, say, to mere solipsism. To be sure, in the comparison no one becomes the other, but no one remains who one was before engaging the other. Just as the comparatist's interpretation of foreign law affects its existence as foreign law and impacts its iteration in the comparative report and elsewhere, the comparatist finds himself being changed by virtue of his comparative work. Picture a movement of co-constitution of meaning arising out of the interchange between the comparatist and the foreign law-text.

*

Because the fifteen essays I have assembled as this book – an extended skiagraphy – seek to contradict the orthodox ideology presiding over comparative law, it follows that they struggle against a master scenario that prohibits, silences, condemns, outcasts, or exiles counter-discourses (readily deemed inutilious, belligerent, or strident), a segregation that is institutionally prescribed and ceaselessly inscribed within the comparison of laws. As it chastises this 'powerful gesture of protection and containment', this 'Cartesian gesture',[3] my argument delineates an engagement with activism that resists the dominant explanation of foreign law-worlds, foreign legal cultures, and foreign law-texts informed by an authoritarian model positing the right way to think about comparative law, the proper method to practise comparison-at-law, and the existence of the correct meaning of foreign law. Since such autarchic epistemology (not in the least apolitical) interrupts the democratic negotiation with otherness-in-the-law, it must be interrupted in its turn to promote the relativization of the comparative enterprise. As I interpret the field and respond to its discursive and repressive utterances, as I aim to remove comparative law from the grip of the posited and the positers, from the clasp of that *mindset*, affectivity figures significantly in my address, which is above all a refusal quietly to acquiesce to the field's deceptive theoretical and practical schemes. The epistemic complacency on display within comparative law disappoints me. And it makes me anxious, not to say irate.

[3] J Derrida, *L'Ecriture et la différence* (Editions du Seuil 1967) 85.

But the fact is that no hegemony is hermetic. Every discursive space, no matter how seemingly entrenched, features gaps – that is, from the point of view of those who contest the orthodox enterprise, latitude. I wish to harness such epistemic crevices as I can discern in the citadel so as to oppose ideas that I regard as inimical to scholarly inquiry, but also that I consider dangerous – dangerous to comparatists on account of the disabling epistemic dependence they have instilled and installed (not least in the newly educated, eager for accreditation and therefore susceptible to levelling and conformist tendencies), dangerous to the field, but also dangerous to the foreign law-worlds or legal cultures or law-texts themselves that are being investigated under impoverished epistemic auspices. Effectively, I am doing what it seems other comparatists-at-law do not want to be doing, which is to revisit the epistemologically indefensible claims that so many appear willing to take in their stride without due probing.[4] My wager is that these received ideas can be examined and challenged to the comparatist's benefit, to the field's advantage, and to foreignness's profit also. In the process, I hope to put pressure on my own comparatism, too; indeed, I want to push myself further, to be more demanding of myself, to responsibilize myself in order to act more critically tomorrow and the day after.

From their various angles, the following essays therefore call on comparative law to confront its positivist heritage (largely a German legacy, although not exclusively so), which it must now recognize as a deficient intellectual configuration inasmuch as this approach eschews profound understanding of foreignness and fails to generate deep understanding of what the comparatist does when he addresses foreignness. Crucially, the texts I collate reveal new problems and new ways of conceiving problems and suggest addressing these challenges with sharpened tools. As they advocate for different themes, modalities, sensitivities, and perspectives – at least in the sense that such topics and outlooks have been conspicuously absent from the controlling texts in the field of comparative law – these essays squarely situate themselves within contemporary critical theory. (I mean *genuine* critique, not Kantian critique.[5]) Defying the nationalist conviction long invested in the idea that local-law-is-ultimately-the-only-law-that-matters, thus making the case (and the normative argument) for more-than-one-law permeating

[4] cf L Wittgenstein, *Vermischte Bemerkungen* in *Über Gewißheit* (GEM Anscombe ed, Suhrkamp 1984 [1948]) 543: 'Where others keep going, there I stop.'

[5] For remarks on this important distinction, see BE Harcourt, *Critique and Praxis* (Columbia University Press 2020) 541n1.

legal argumentation in its various aspects, this work's militancy in favour of legal analyses comprising diverse laws also addresses the ever-increasing and seemingly ubiquitous marketization of life-in-the-law, which within comparative law has entailed the development of agendas in favour of standardization or normalization, tactics going under designations like unification, uniformization, or harmonization – all processes consisting of making-laws-look-equivalent or making-laws-look-common, all instances of concoction of sham-equivalence or sham-commonality. In a significant way, my contention thus purports to resist the pervasive neo-liberal rationality suffusing the 'economization' of comparative law under layers of positivist shellac.

*

The leitmotiv informing this monograph is epistemic, five times.

First, the writings I appose oppose any Hegelian-style theory or vision contemplating anything like a state of eventual oneness as the most developed stage of human consciousness in which a higher homeostatic wholeness would be achieved through individual finite selves somehow being tied together within a condition of spiritual recognition of each other – unless, of course, this mutuality should take place within the form of free-market fundamentalism. Hegel's idealism swallows contingencies and smothers singularities. In the end, it is indifferent to the concrete world. To refute the idea that totality can/must surpass plurality does not mean, however, that I defend identity groups understood as separate, distinct, self-contained units featuring an 'inner something' common to all members, insulated and inaccessible to outsiders. But my rejection of essentialism does not detract from the fact that the homogeneity of, say, French legal culture (I am not writing of its unchanging nature), while neither pristine nor pure, is not spurious either, even less so vis-à-vis, say, English legal culture. Yes: French legal culture exists, and it exists meaningfully. And yes, French legal culture differs from English legal culture, and it differs meaningfully. (For positivists, one of the main difficulties pertaining to culture is that it cannot be grasped directly. The fact that any theory or conceptualization of culture must rest on its individual manifestations prompts positivism, in effect, to confine culture to a mere rhetorical figure – an ostracization that amounts to the unsustainable denial of non-genetic axiological or attitudinal patterns informing the law and its capillarian instantiations.)

Secondly, these essays want to stand as a forceful objection to Hans Kelsen as he writes that '[t]he law counts only as positive law, that is, as legislated law';[6] as he maintains that purity poses 'the limits within which cognition must remain, and these limits are, especially for legal science, *very narrow*';[7] and as he proclaims, 'I consider the law as a self-standing . . . system.'[8] Bearing in mind that Kelsen's construction easily qualifies as the only theory benefitting from any kind of entitlement to serious long-standing intellectual consideration across the entire European legal scene, not to mention Europe's colonial emanations,[9] my opposition extends to Kelsenians of all hues and Kelsenisms of all shades, including the most diffuse or insidious manifestations of science fetishism in the form of a drive for an ever-purer theory of posited law (or an ever-purer posited law) – even as I tell myself that the 'purity' model is ultimately too ludicrous to mislead.[10] Again, each of my texts wants to promote the epistemic invalidation of positivism's complacency – to foster a less reductive, more sophisticated, less mysophobic, more complex understanding of the legal. Indeed, I claim that the legal empirically exists not only as what is posited by the legislature (which, tautologically, bases itself on the right to posit the law that is conferred to it by. . . the posited law), but as a cultural intervention, as a modality of culture, as culture speaking legally. The law – say, this statute or that appellate judicial decision – exists as culture, which means that, for example, it conceals, more or less subterraneously, economic, historical, philosophical, political, or sociological dimensions. Observe that it is emphatically not the case that law *reflects* culture, an idea that would suffer at the very least from the suggestion that law operates as a different discourse from culture instead of working as an exemplification of it. Law exists *as* a cultural formation, so that when a French statute prohibits certain religious attire in public schools or a US Supreme Court decision sanctions an individual right to use weapons at home, the law-text is indissociable from the cultural commitments

6 H Kelsen, *Reine Rechtslehre* (Deuticke 1934) 64.

7 H Kelsen, *Das Problem der Souveränität und die Theorie des Völkerrechts* (Mohr Siebeck 1920) v [my emphasis].

8 ibid.

9 I do not exclude the common law tradition altogether. Eg: P Troop, 'Why Legal Formalism Is Not a Stupid Thing' (2018) 31 Ratio Juris 428; T Smith, *Judicial Review in an Objective Legal System* (Cambridge University Press 2015).

10 For an authoritative discussion of purity in Kelsen's theory, see SL Paulson, 'The Purity Thesis' (2018) 31 Ratio Juris 276. Stanley Paulson insists that for Kelsen, '[t]he limits of the jurist's competence are set by purity': ibid 280.

of which it is but the legal expression. There is much more to a law-text than its graphematic inscription, and it behoves the comparatist to apply an enriched appreciation of textuality with a view to tracing the text to the cultural claims (say, Islamophobia or conservatism) that lurk between the lines, encrypted in the text's fabric. Such enciphering indicates that culture is not to be relegated to the law's context either – a conclusion that deprives positivism of the facile retort that being circumambient vis-à-vis law, culture would be located somewhere beyond the law-box.[11] In fact, the law-text is in the world, and the world is in the law-text also.

Now, everything that there is being situated, the jurist – say, the comparatist-at-law – exists as culture, too. Not unlike a law-text, then, a comparatist-at-law stands as a cultural formation, an encultured entity. This statement does not mean to suggest that the individual would be but the passive support of supereminent forces somehow mechanically deploying themselves in line with an autotelic logic: no one is a normative zombie, and there is no question of a collective brain either. The idea is rather that comparatists have inherited, through education and interaction, schemes of understanding, judgement, and performance that structure their lives-in-the-law, that delineate the thinkable and predispose the thought, these configurations being neither strictly individualistic nor completely deterministic. If you will, the body is in the world, but the world is in the body also.

Meanwhile, positivism, having sought to ignore the empirical fact of cultural imbrication, has been promoting absurd conceptual distinctions separating culture from both law-texts and the law's interpreters and thereby promoting the cultureless character of foreign law and of the comparatist. I reject positivism's mutilating scissions, the organized abdication of the enterprise that would seek to explain why the law exists as it does and why the comparatist apprehends it as he does. I earnestly refute positivism's false rigours, and I chastise its conceited cultural unmattering.

Thirdly, the studies I regroup all disclose, each in its own way, how the comparatist's work on foreign legal cultures or law-texts implies 'a

[11] The argument from culture-as-context proves particularly vulnerable to a positivist exclusionary rejoinder when its unfurling is marred by sustained confusion as in U Kischel, *Rechtsvergleichung* (Beck 2015) passim. For a critique, see P Legrand, 'Kischel's Comparative Law: *Fortschritt ohne Fortschritt*' (2020) 15(2) J Comp L 292, 293n11, 296n23, and 327–36 (review article of U Kischel, *Comparative Law* [A Hammel tr, Oxford University Press 2019]).

relation of relationlessness',[12] an *irrelation* – how the comparative endeavour supposes at once that the comparatist ought to access the other law or other-in-the-law *and* that such access cannot be had not only because the self cannot be the other, but also since 'the uttered otherness is already no longer a "true" otherness'.[13] Indeed, no description features absolute deixis, and to evoke is to revoke. Yet, a comparatist wagers that even though comparison is structurally unable ever to grasp otherness – the other law or other-in-the-law is not at hand, not present; rather it is not-at-hand, not-present – the comparative motion can unfold as a productive practice. Resolutely, comparison-at-law claims to be able to attest to a strong interpretive yield despite the epistemic aporia in which it finds itself mired.

Fourthly, the different texts I colligate as *NCL* want to indicate that no configuration being reasonably styled 'foreign' can meaningfully exist without a comparatist-at-law ascribing meaning to it in 'his' language – language thereby imposing its law unto him and compelling him to do violence to foreignness accordingly. Even acknowledging the remarkable achievement that seeing far into foreign law must involve, it remains that to find words in one's language to express what one thinks one has seen into foreign law is impossible (it is trite to recall that there are no semantic equivalences or commonalities across languages). It follows that the comparatist-at-law must frame the foreign in a language that is, perforce, alien to foreignness.[14] Paradoxically, the comparatist has no choice: so as to ascertain the other law, he must configure it in terms of 'his' language – and even though he can inflect the linguistic equipment available to him in order to attune it so that it can account for otherness as felicitously or justly as possible, the most audacious neologisms (only procurable within certain semantic limits, in any event) still depend on 'his' language.[15] No matter how excellent the comparatist's work, his comparison is therefore fated to be unable to move beyond the realm of the approximate or hypothetical: it cannot but operate asymptotically vis-à-vis the foreignness that there is there. As it necessarily finds itself

[12] R Jaeggi, *Entfremdung* (Suhrkamp 2016) 20 [emphasis omitted].

[13] L Bonoli, *Lire les cultures* (Kimé 2008) 61.

[14] 'Heterology and violence' is thus a heading in R Barthes, *Roland Barthes par Roland Barthes* in *Œuvres complètes*, vol 4 (2nd edn, E Marty ed, Editions du Seuil 2002 [1975]) 678.

[15] cf J Derrida, *De la grammatologie* (Editions de Minuit 1967) 227: '[T]he writer writes *in* a language and *in* a logic the very own system, the laws, and the life of which, by definition, his discourse cannot absolutely dominate.'

overwhelmed by an excess of foreign aspects, surfaces, and remainders, the comparatist's account is thus destined to differ from the foreign legal culture or law-text that he has made into the focus of his investigation and report. In this important sense, comparative law thus affirms the breach between the laws – the self's and the other's – even as it promises to draw a bridge across them.

Fifthly, the essays I defend want to implement to the fullest possible extent the regime of authenticity that befits comparative law. These texts therefore aim to shield the comparatist-at-law's interventions from the specious authority of objectivity and truth. Instead, they activate a programme of *invention* – etymologically, the term straddles the ideas of finding and fashioning (the comparatist comes to the foreign law-texts that he finds there, which he then moves to articulate, to fashion, by way of his report). In effect, 'the concept of invention distributes its two essential values between the two poles of the constative (to discover or disclose ...) and the performative (to produce, institute, transform)', there being an 'infinitely rapid oscillation' between the two situations.[16] Invention? The comparatist *inventing* foreign law? Precisely. Yes.

Meanwhile, I strongly condemn the view that the only or most worthy enunciation within comparative law would be an objective or true statement regarding the foreign. Although I maintain that I am offering sophisticated inquiries and not mere sophistry, my contribution to the comparative conversation refuses to make any argument in favour of its objectivity, and it rejects the idea that it would be propounding any truth-claim. While it exists as a characteristic discursive formation outside the comparatist, foreignness – foreign law – can only be thought and experienced by the comparatist through the comparatist's thought and experience. As comparatist-at-law, my dealing and understanding, my alloying and writing – all of it in 'my' words – are thus informed by aesthetic, rhetorical, practical, or cognitive considerations that are inherently contingent and firmly limit my comparative work to

[16] Eg: see J Derrida, *Psyché*, vol 1 (2nd ed, Galilée 1998 [1987]) 23 and 25. Jacques Derrida is right to claim that 'one would not say today that Christopher Columbus has invented America .... [U]sage or the system of certain modern, relatively modern conventions would prohibit us from speaking of an invention whose object would be an existence as such': ibid 41. Yet, in the Roman liturgical rite, there was long celebrated on 3 May the Invention of the Holy Cross (*Inventio Sancta Crucis*), that is, St Helena's *discovery* of the Cross in 326. Having been abolished by Pope John XXIII in 1960, the feast of the *Inventio* remains important for the Church of the East on 13 September. As one applies oneself to repair comparative law, 'one must today reinvent invention': ibid 37.

interpretation-as-transformation. It is not that my circumstances act as an impairment to reading, but that they intervene as a medium of intelligibility and also as a salutary corrective to foundationalist ways of thinking. In this regard, although no doubt immodestly, I hold that the interpretations I propose carry over those I contest on account of their stronger yield: quite simply, an appreciation of law-as-culture is able to generate much more relevant information about the foreign than any conceptualization of the legal as pure-law-as-rules can ever evince. If you will, even as the comparatist-at-law ought not to aspire to objectivity or truth, I believe that an understanding of law-as-culture can allow him to safeguard more reliably against arbitrariness or falsehood.

It is thus the case – and this assertion can easily stand as a sixth epistemic postulate – that I argue in favour of a theory and practice of comparative law deploying itself for the other not in any dogmatic way, but attentively, sensibly, and, yes, tenaciously and courageously (indeed, the other's ways can well appear impolitic). Because the approach I espouse marks a decisive rupture with positivism-as-orthodox-comparative-law – not to mention, evidently, age-old nationalist configurations – I find myself advocating for 'the force of non-participation' vis-à-vis both arrangements.[17] The heterogeneous fabric of this collection of essays, which I have not wanted to erase and probably remains unerasable, thus comes – visibly and legibly – to underline my critical engagement in favour of *heteronomy*.

*

Treatises – meta-narratives of all kinds – have grown dated. The idea of a comprehensive asseveration and its accompanying attempt to achieve fixation of data (and of belief) is ill-formed to meet the moment, which is pluralistic and polyphonic – which harbours, in fact, the very *fluidity* that a treatise wishes in principle to surmount. It has become awkward to imagine how a well-schooled undergraduate student, upon being asked to contend with *A Theory of Justice*, would not nowadays ask 'whose justice?'. Because the mode of writing informs, concentrates, and constrains the contents of thought, an aggregation of essays – a configuration thus lying somewhere between the fully integrated, overarching master recitation and the chaotic mass of wordy debris – assists me in resisting any drive I might feel towards anything like a total or exhaustive discourse, a finished or achieved statement, what would want to be

[17] TW Adorno, 'Erziehung nach Auschwitz' in *Gesammelte Schriften*, vol 10(2) (R Tiedemann ed, Suhrkamp 1977 [1966]) 679.

a veridictive and therefore secure enunciation.[18] Rather, these texts are a gathering (indeed, a singular gathering) denouncing gathering, since they disseminate ideas widely, not least through the range of topics they pursue and because they show that, its numerous words notwithstanding, *NCL* is not in the least done with the potentialities that comparative law – and that writing about comparative law – can convey. Even as I attempt to develop a continuous and cumulative argument from essay to essay, which means that my claim is not as scattered or digressive as may appear at first blush, *NCL* is definitely intended to intervene by way of opening rather than closing. As regards structural unfinishedness, Martin Heidegger (1889–1976) and Theodor Adorno (1903–69) meet for the first time within the confines of this project: Heidegger introduced many of his inquiries as meandering explorations,[19] and Adorno emphatically preferred the essay to the treatise.[20]

In the sense in which it stands as an extended anacoluthon, as a discontinuous association, as an 'ill-jointed marquetry',[21] *NCL* thus prudently refrains from defending any grand theory or *grand récit* (an inflection showing that there are writerly situations where *nomen non est omen*). And I am comforted in my diffidence as I read Homi Bhabha's self-assessment of his *Location of Culture*, which I wholeheartedly appropriate: 'In the narrative grafting of my chapter[s], I have attempted no general theory, only a certain productive tension of the perplexity of language in various locations of living.'[22] No fake uniformity or harmony, then: no fragment to be understood as a text featuring a closed unity,[23] not 'a beautiful unity of tone and treatment' throughout the book

[18] For a famous challenge to wholeness, see Letter from WB Yeats to V Hunt in *The Collected Letters of WB Yeats*, vol 3 (J Kelly and R Schuchard eds, Oxford University Press 1994 [20 February 1902]) 155: 'Nothing has life except the incomplete.'

[19] Eg: M Heidegger, *Holzwege* (Klostermann 2015 [1950]); M Heidegger, *Wegmarken* (Klostermann 2013 [1967]); M Heidegger, *Der Feldweg* (Klostermann 2006 [1949]); M Heidegger, *Unterwegs zur Sprache* (Neske 1959).

[20] See TW Adorno, 'Der Essay als Form' in *Noten zur Literatur* (R Tiedemann ed, Suhrkamp 1974 [1958]) 9–33. For a noteworthy argument in praise of Adorno's essay-writing, see PA Bové, *Love's Shadow* (Harvard University Press 2021) 135–84. For an excellent general discussion, see B Dillon, *Essayism* (Fitzcarraldo 2017).

[21] Montaigne, *Les Essais* (J Balsamo et al eds, Gallimard 2007 [1595†]) bk 3, ch 9, 1008.

[22] HK Bhabha, *The Location of Culture* (Routledge 1994) 170.

[23] For a well-known rebuttal of the idea of unity with specific reference to an exploration at once brief and scrupulous of the essay form, see WC Williams, 'An Essay on Virginia' in *Imaginations* (W Schott ed, New Directions 1970 [1925]) 323: 'Unity is the shallowest, the cheapest deception of all composition. In nothing is the banality of the intelligence more clearly manifested.'

that would have 'as it were, embalmed the whole'[24] – nothing from what I am fond of styling the epistemic bargain basement. Instead, I suggest idiorhythmic efforts aiming optimally to express this or that idea even as I accept that strictly speaking my array of scripting initiatives is fated to founder, since writing-as-language is unable to capture foreignness, the ultimate matter to assess then concerning the magnitude of the failure. And because my topography is full of loops and curves, of turns and deviations, not to mention frictions and no doubt a few contradictions,[25] the segments that follow this prologue hardly resemble the fabric of a law-book in the conventional sense of the term except from a material standpoint (I am thinking of the covers, the spine, or the binding). My composition is interruptive, if not tangential: words, sentences, ideas emerge, subside, and re-emerge as I do not advance towards my goal through a straight road and as I cannot bring myself artificially to force my thoughts into a linear course. Despite the edification of an oft-refined sequential exposition, I can only show a reflection under the form of fragments, which I have sought to order while remaining aware how the demarcation I have entered between the different parts comports, on each occasion, an insurmountable indeterminacy – this or that passage could easily have been featured in a different essay – and how the contents of any given text remain enmeshed in the provisional and unfinished – this or that paragraph could assuredly have been formulated differently, in all likelihood improved, perhaps profitably omitted. In other terms, I envisage *NCL*'s pieces as an ambagious series of beginnings that never offer closure, since there is always something more (hazardous) to come. And the matter is not simply one of form: 'Thinking develops differently when pursued through the essay.'[26]

To press the term 'fragments' into service nearly a century after Virginia Woolf heralded 'an age of fragments',[27] to answer the fragmentary exigency still, is for me to find myself returning to a word I already marshalled more than two decades ago when I very reluctantly – and, I now appreciate, mistakenly – succumbed to undue institutional

[24] S Beckett, 'Proust in Pieces' in *Disjecta* (R Cohn ed, Grove 1984 [1934]) 64.

[25] After all, 'any contradiction is likely to have some sensible interpretations': W Empson, *Seven Types of Ambiguity* (2nd edn, Chatto & Windus 1947) 197.

[26] JT Lysaker, *Philosophy, Writing, and the Character of Thought* (University of Chicago Press 2018) 34.

[27] V Woolf, 'How It Strikes a Contemporary' in *The Common Reader (First Series)* (A McNeillie ed, Harcourt 1984 [1925]) 234: 'It is an age of fragments.'

pressure (to institutional bullying, really) and produced a short monograph by way of legacy, of trace, to coincide with the termination of my five years of occupancy of a research chair in the Netherlands.[28] I then intended, and I still do in *NCL*, '[a] series of tries, goes, bashes, cracks and shots',[29] self-consciously hesitant statements, openly unsure of their direction or success, resisting the narrative arc of the traditional academic text. If I had to produce *NCL*,[30] I wanted a book where 'each piece suffices to itself, and nonetheless it is ever but the interstice between its neighbours'.[31] As I finally contemplate my specific, selective, and restricted complex of writings as a remedy to the hubris animating a full or complete model, I am keen to return to the idea of possibility: 'A fragment is not a ruin. It is much rather a seed.'[32] I am a fragmentist, then – so much so that the pieces I collocate as *NCL* are not fragments of an antecedent whole, but fragments *tout court*. If you will, I always-already begin with fragmentation, and no totality ever existed.

I do not regret that the inscription of each of these fifteen texts as irreducibly autobiographical events – *that time in that place, that place at that time* – should neutralize any hope I might have so fleetingly nurtured of the various writings produced and collected as *NCL* making systematic sense. And I realize that, once printed and published, once circulating, these essays, as they undertake to mean what meaning their readership ascribes to them, are destined to live beyond any exercise of interpretive control I might wish to apply over them. I accept they will generate worldly interpretive effects overflowing any conscious intention I may have had as I wrote them, that they will effectively plunge me in the midst of interpretive potencies I could not have anticipated and will be unable to master. (Using words in a certain way, no matter how meticulously, can never cause my meaning to be faithfully construed.) As they harbour traces of anterior texts, these texts will trace their way into subsequent texts through trajectories that will materialize irrespective

[28] See P Legrand, *Fragments on Law-as-Culture* (Tjeenk Willink 1999).

[29] S Wood, *Without Mastery* (Edinburgh University Press 2014) 26.

[30] Of course, the question squarely arises whether I ultimately had to proceed. Is it not a matter of some effrontery to author a book? Samuel Beckett formulated better than I ever could the most honest answer I can give to justify my audacity: 'If you ask me why the canvas does not stay white, I can invoke only this unintelligible need, forever without cause, to ejaculate colour on it, be it by vomiting one's being on it': Letter from S Beckett to G Duthuit in *The Letters of Samuel Beckett*, vol 2 (G Craig et al eds, Cambridge University Press 2009 [9 March 1949]) 137.

[31] Barthes (n 14) 671.

[32] J Rancière, *La Parole muette* (Fayard 2010) 59.

of me,[33] before they eventually descend into irremediable obsolescence. For the present, I submit these disquisitions to my reader as so many singular testimonies of the entangled fluctuations in my thinking. For Herder, '[i]t lies in the weakness of human nature always to want to erect a system'.[34] I am very glad I have been able to overcome this infirmity.[35]

*

While over the years I have pictured *NCL* differently at different junctures (ultimately, the text I wrote is not the one I meant to write), I was always clear, then, that the essays should read independently from one another. This book does not have a beginning, middle, and end. Rather, throughout *NCL* the argument is 'a beginning again and again and again and again': it is 'more and more beginning and beginning and beginning'.[36] As I recurrently address certain themes, points, or issues from different slants (or as I occasionally return to my topics from a perspective already examined), *NCL* is inter alia disjunctive or repetitive, self-assertive or self-cancelling, anecdotal or aphoristic. My essays refrain from presenting a comprehensive account of the highways and byways within the field – which is what a book written by a devotee of a system of thought would purport to achieve – but instead do what a sceptical account must do, that is, critically to examine the order of significance it rejects, in other words, challenge the logic of the central problems and claims that have given comparative law its typical quality and constitute its major thrust.[37] That *NCL* stands thus means, crucially, that it is not a survey. Accordingly, it does not style itself as a conspectus that would be listing a series of chapters on the different laws of the world (Hebraic, Islamic, and the like) or the different study-areas such as company law, contract law, or constitutional law. Nor does it cast itself as a compilation of the writers having researched comparative law

[33] cf Montaigne (n 21) 1115: 'There is always room for a follower.'

[34] JG Herder, 'Von Baumgartens Denkart in seinen Schriften' in *Werke*, vol 1 (U Gaier et al eds, Deutscher Klassiker 1985 [1767]) 657.

[35] cf S Sangral, *Préface à ce livre* (Galilée 2019) 76: 'I do not believe, in any case I believe not to believe, in any system: not only can my writing therefore only be fragmented, but my idea according to which my writing can only be fragmented can therefore be, also, only fragmented.'

[36] G Stein, 'Composition as Explanation' in *Writings 1903–1932* (CR Stimpson and H Chessman eds, Library of America 1998 [1926]) 528 and 525.

[37] For this reason, the established order's response may well take the form of silence. But wilful blindness can confer potency to critique, too.

who could be said to be defining or influencing the field at this writing.[38] What, then, does this work aspire to be?

*

Preeminently, *NCL* wishes to exist as an unapologetic theoretical exertion, comparative law being envisioned as 'a kind of *anamorphosis* of legal theory'.[39]

I am interested above all in theoretical dramatization, in the staging of theory with a view to ameliorating practice. I therefore choreograph

[38] In the spirit of Edward Said – 'the whole point is to be embarrassing, contrary, even unpleasant' (EW Said, *Representations of the Intellectual* [Pantheon 1994] 12) – and in line with George Steiner – '[t]here are questions we must be tactless and undiplomatic enough to raise if we are to stay honest with ourselves and our students' (G Steiner, *Language and Silence* [Faber & Faber 1967] 61–62) – I find important to indicate that published surveys within the field of comparative law have proved deficient. For my critique of the first edition of *The Oxford Handbook of Comparative Law* (a second edition – *immer in guten Händen* – was released in 2019), see P Legrand, 'Book Review' (2007) 2(2) J Comp L 253. And for my rejoinder to *The Cambridge Companion to Comparative Law*, see P Legrand, 'Jameses at Play: A Tractation on the Comparison of Laws' (2017) 65 Am J Comp L [Special Issue] 1, 11n27 [hereinafter 'Jameses']. The other survey I want to mention is R Leckey, 'Review of Comparative Law' (2017) 26 Social & Legal Stud 3. Like the *Oxford* and *Cambridge* panoramas, this appraisal suffers from serious deficits, not least the author's obvious decision to promote friends and colleagues (present or former, permanent or visiting, alive or dead), boasting a connection with the institution where he himself is based. It is particularly disconcerting that the reporter, being entrusted with an inspection of the *field*, should be extolling Patrick Glenn's work while omitting to refer to the collective review that appeared in the *Journal of Comparative Law* where, over more than one hundred pages, twelve comparatists (and a thirteenth one) raised numerous and momentous creditability issues with respect to HP Glenn, *Legal Traditions of the World* (2nd edn, Oxford University Press 2004). See NHD Foster (ed), 'A Fresh Start for Comparative Legal Studies?' (2006) 1(1) J Comp L 100; BS Jackson, 'Internal and External Comparisons of Religious Law: Reflections from Jewish Law' (2006) 1(1) J Comp L 177. Given repeated evidence in his survey that the author is conversant with the *Journal of Comparative Law*'s scholarly existence and on the understanding that not all thirteen commentators can be cavalierly dismissed as 'vituperative' or 'shril[l]' (Leckey, 9), the reasonable assumption is that the thirteen inconvenient critics were suppressed – a strategic erasure aiming to confer immunity from critique to a specific individual, who happens to be fulsomely acknowledged at the end of the study as someone having long taught at the same law school as the reviewer's. In sum, the reader in search of an account of comparative law that would do justice to its key quandaries, salient texts, and noteworthy people – that would be *responding* to the field – instead of indulging parochialism and nationalism, matriotism and patriotism, must be kept waiting. I am aware of JM Smits (ed), *Elgar Encyclopedia of Comparative Law* (2nd edn, Elgar 2014); E Örücü and D Nelken (eds), *Comparative Law: A Handbook* (Hart 2007).

[39] P Richard, *Le Jeu de la différence: réflexions sur l'épistémologie du droit comparé* (Presses de l'Université Laval 2007) 15.

comparative thought at work, in the process of inventing itself, as it discovers its materials and designs its reports, as it forges its equipment, too (say, its concepts or tools). Now, the ideas I articulate in these fifteen essays are the precipitate of the theoretical investigations that have pre-occupied and occupied me for twenty-five years or so – a way of inhabiting the planet I have found agreeable, that has operated largely rewardingly for me. Yet, *NCL* is not in the least an anthology of all the publications I have in print nor is it an attempt to give an account of all my concerns as comparatist-at-law (I leave to one side my additional identities). In other words, I do not regard these texts as the summation of my career as comparatist-at-law (and I certainly do not contemplate them as an aggregate of my life). In fact, the very idea of a final synthesis that would somehow unify all prior insights and arguments into a single whole is, to me, as unattractive as it appears to be unsustainable. I come to my publications obliquely. My book builds on some only of my published work, and it excerpts some only of the reasons informing my earlier texts into the narratives that I re-present as *NCL*. This limited exercise in intertextuality combines with incalculable further readings to produce the precipitate at hand: studies seeking in many ways to revise, sharpen, complement, or contradict – to emend and amend – my prior research (including some of the translations I suggested over time). Meanwhile, other monographs were (and remain) possible. And other works will in fact be written – certainly by other comparatists-at-law, which is as it should be, and plausibly by me, too. In any event, there must be no intimation whatsoever that this collection of essays represents anything like the last word or my last word on any given issue.

As must be readily apparent, *NCL* is emphatically not about comparative climate-change law or comparative anti-terrorism law or comparative Internet law or the comparative law of the status of autonomous robots or comparative blockchain law with specific reference to health care. Audaciously, no doubt, I have written on themes meant to provide those who pursue any or all of these endeavours, or any other comparative enterprise in the law for that matter, with sound theoretical equipment purporting to orient their practice in a way destined to generate a stronger, more creditable interpretive yield, with a view to making comparative research most advantageously edifying.

Greek etymology reminds one that the theorist journeys in order to see and learn. In Ancient Greece, a *theoros* (*θεωρός*) travelled beyond the boundaries of his city-state, perhaps to improve his education or consult an oracle. Occasionally, as an official emissary, a *theoros* attended events such as religious celebrations or spectacles like athletic competitions. Having witnessed these festivities – that is, having practised *theoria* – the traveller returned home, sometimes to engage in discussion with his 'community'.[40] Historically, the *theoros* is thus a foreigner in a foreign land. First and foremost, he requires to understand what he witnesses – which, to be sure, he can only do in terms of the meanings that constitute knowledge in his own 'community' and that have shaped his enculturation (the meanings he has in-corporated or em-bodied and that have therefore travelled with him, as him).[41] Having translated foreignness to himself, the *theoros* proceeds to (re-)translate it to others in his 'community' upon his return home. Always, the *theoros* expresses himself with the explicit purpose of making sense. (Observe that he seeks to 'make' sense of what he observes, which means that there is fabrication of meaning.) Specifically, as he refers to what he has found there, the *theoros* fashions the description and significance of it – a finding/fashioning approach properly pointing to an act of invention on his part. Strictly speaking, the *theoros* is inventing what he has seen. Yes. As he remains sensitive to the singularity of otherness and aware of the fact that he cannot occupy the other's horizon on account of his own singularity, as he appreciates that he cannot therefore eschew a misunderstanding of the other,[42] he brings to bear a critical mind. Of course, the very act of

[40] See AW Nightingale, *Spectacles of Truth in Classical Greek Philosophy* (Cambridge University Press 2004) 3–5, 40–71, and passim.

[41] The concept of 'community' must pertain to constructivism, since in fine there are only individuals – 'there are only islands': J Derrida, *La Bête et le souverain*, vol 2 (M Lisse et al eds, Galilée 2010 [2002]) 31. To frame the question in Derrida's terms, '[w]ho can ever dare an "us" without trembling?': J Derrida, *Chaque fois unique, la fin du monde* (P-A Brault and M Naas eds, Galilée 2003) 259. Perhaps it is permissible for me to bring into play 'my' two principal languages to show that 'community' is never other than (and is never more than) an entity looking like a unity, appearing as a unity, an 'as-unity', a '*comme*-unity' – an entity that, strictly speaking, is therefore not a unity. To be 'as one' or '*comme-un*' is still not to be 'one'. It would therefore make sense to write ~~community~~, the Heideggerian rature inscribing the unsurmountable semantic inadequacy of the term being mobilized. Alternatively, and less distractingly, one can put the word in quotation marks, which is the strategy I adopt throughout *NCL*. Observe also that for many (like myself), '[t]he authority of the *togetherness* will always be the first threat to any "living together"': J Derrida, *Le Dernier des Juifs* (Galilée 2014 [2001]) 21. Indeed, 'community' can readily mean a constraint from which one necessitates an emancipatory rupture. cf Letter from S Beckett to T McGreevy in *The Letters of Samuel Beckett*, vol 1 (MD Fehsenfeld and LM Overbeck eds, Cambridge University Press 2009 [6 June 1939]) 660: 'All groups are horrible.'

[42] cf J Caputo, *Hermeneutics* (Penguin 2018) 50: 'The pre-understanding summons the misunderstanding before itself.'

interpretation/translation is inherently critical – and in this sense, it rightly qualifies as an exercise of epistemic power or violence over otherness. Otherwise said, even the most straightforward imputation of meaning cannot be dissociated from an act of (encultured) supremacy: it simply cannot be appreciated without it for the decisory character of culture is genuine. If more than one *theoros* had been attending a certain foreign event, the event would have differed according to the different translations/interpretations of it – and such would have been the case even if all *theoroses* had hailed from a particular city-state and had all sought to describe or interpret what they had seen in the plainest language possible. For the comparatist-at-law, a *homo viator* involved in critical deterritorialization with a view to returning home in order to educate his 'community' in ways foreign, it makes good sense to work as a *theoros*. After all, '[a]ny form of comparison must always be informed by at least a minimum of theory'.[43] Incidentally, my theoretical concentration readily allows the various essays in *NCL* to be steeped in examples, in 'anecdata'. Working as a theoretician does not prevent me from operating as an 'anecdatagrapher'.

*

I note that the theoretico-practical order prevailing within the field of comparative law acts on the basis of a series of epistemic presuppositions in the form of theses that aim to structure comparative interventions *in advance* – and that have largely succeeded in so doing. A key dimension of the predilections thus informing and sustaining the epistemic regime in place is *evidentiary*. The proper way to compare has indeed become evident – it has acquired the status of what goes without saying and, of course, without discussing. The right comparison thus ultimately finds its warrant in a belief that procures amongst comparatists-at-law a sense of confidence, even of certainty, at once immediate and tacit. In fact, the degree of conviction is such that the processes of socialization and institutionalization (of *epistemologization*) that translate into the mental structures governing the field will not be questioned. Inasmuch as it generates its own reality, with reference to which the governing epistemic premisses acquire value, the orthodoxy's epistemology thus proves powerfully realistic. Arguably, the prevailing epistemic model is so compelling that the belief it generates within comparative law no longer thinks of itself as belief at all. In particular, the orthodoxy's empire

[43] AA Yengoyan, 'Comparison and Its Discontents' in AA Yengoyan (ed), *Modes of Comparison* (University of Michigan Press 2006) 154.

extends to comparatists-at-law who leave unthought the predispositions informing their thinking. Now, one of the crucial markers of the orthodoxy's epistemic authority concerns how it excludes ex ante the history of its own epistemic genesis thereby suggesting acclimatization or submission to a spontaneous intellectual alignment, a form of naturalization. Responding to analogous manifestations in other fields, Pierre Bourdieu spoke of 'clandestine persuasion',[44] while Maurice Merleau-Ponty remarked on a 'silent persuasion'.[45] As it happens, the principal beneficiaries of this strategy are precisely those individuals enjoying a dominant position within the field whose interest is to extend the epistemic supremacy of the orthodoxy and claim that what is, in fact, a contingent regime of domination (not least a political one) pertains to an indubitable epistemic order.

The orthodox disposition's emergence is therefore not evident at all. Instead, the doxa has imposed its matrix of appreciations and propensions as the outcome of epic epistemic battles amongst comparatists-at-law defending competing visions of a comparative intervention's status and merit, opposite understandings of the cognitive constraints such an enterprise must face, and contested postulations of the cognitive achievements comparison can muster. A governing configuration that has been constructed and instituted only as the result of confrontations with other models, the orthodox episteme stands as a structured structure deploying itself as a structuring structure. It is an edified framework unfolding as an arrangement that frames practice in its turn – for instance, that channels the evaluative work of peers or publishers as they are asked to pronounce on whether what they are reading counts as *good* comparison. Even as the orthodoxy unfurls a capital of intellectual authority pretending to be entirely disinterested, strictly 'scientific' (whatever this term is taken to mean), it acts in effect as a form of censorship: it proceeds as a decreed and decreeing discipline. Somewhat unfathomably, the desire to know that would have informed the orthodox comparatist's endeavour at the inception of his professional trajectory can be seen to have progressively merged with the desire to exercise power.

Comparative law's orthodoxy therefore stands at once as sedimented experience and generator of schemes of perception, appreciation, and action – properly speaking, it operates as a *savoir-faire*. Observe that the

[44] P Bourdieu and L Wacquant, *Invitation à la sociologie réflexive* (Editions du Seuil 2014 [1991]) 222.

[45] M Merleau-Ponty, 'Notes de travail' in *Le Visible et l'invisible* (C Lefort ed, Gallimard 1964†) 263.

orthodoxy frames the comparatist in bodily terms, too. The comparatist literally in-corporates the doxa, he em-bodies its tenets. Since the corpus or body is the place where the doxa is ingested and digested as information, where it is assimilated, where it is individually lived or experienced as normativity, and where it is turned into a permanent disposition in the form of a (corporeal or bodily) enactment of culture, there is thus a phenomenon of incorporated or embodied significance manifesting itself. (Thought demands a body, the shared materialism of body and thought constitutively cancelling the Cartesian mind/body split.) In other terms, the individual is in possession of his world and carries it within him, as him. But he is possessed by it, too. To be sure, there is no crude (and mysterious) mechanistic determinism unravelling, because the individual also makes a personal investment into his world (hence the singularity of each comparatist-at-law), but there is no full subjectivity either, since the individual is invested by his world (hence the enculturation of each comparatist-at-law). One must think in terms of 'ontological complicity'.[46]

Even as I countenance that the orthodox inclination within comparative law conceals an extraordinary capacity of resistance to interrogation – its abiding ambition being to ensure the accomplishment of practices that avoid most reflection and spare themselves most questioning and thereby promote unchallenged validation, legitimation, and confirmation of their epistemic accoutrements – I find it necessary to denounce the implicit contract of adhesion with the established epistemic order that one must agree to sign as a right of entry into the field of comparative law. I accept that the cognitive subversion I recommend therefore stands as an act of *political* resistance. Indeed, I require my argument to entail a conversion of the governing *Weltanschauung*, a change of paradigm. It is not, however, that I want to challenge every single epistemic stake characterizing the field – for example, the fact of pleading in favour of legal deterritorialization or the further fact of ascribing normative value to foreign law. Rather, I dispute the understanding of what constitutes good comparison-at-law, that is, I revisit structures of epistemic domination within comparative law that connect to long-standing stances working advantageously from the standpoint of those who are now installed as authorities on the basis of these very schemes that have served them so well even as such scenarios' epistemic impostures can readily be demonstrated.

[46] Bourdieu and Wacquant (n 44) 176. The words are Bourdieu's.

What *NCL* aims to do, then, is primarily to release myself and others from comparative law's epistemic shackles. In this regard, I do not harbour Bernard Harcourt's reservations about inviting fellow comparatists to accept my line of reasoning, and I readily approach *NCL* as a protreptic designed to alter the behaviour of its readership. Accordingly, I purposefully exhort my readers to embark on a certain course of comparative action – one of comparative law's crucial components being that of outreach.[47] My ambition is therefore to suspend the application of what I argue is effectively an unexamined model that, upon scrutiny, proves utterly unsatisfactory from an epistemological standpoint. I thus want to interrupt the adherence or attachment of comparatists-at-law to the settled epistemic order. In particular, I strongly object to the idea that there can be an immediate knowledge of foreign law on the basis that the foreign would exist in a state of utter steadfastness while awaiting interpretive harvesting and on the further basis that an individual could mobilize and demobilize cognitive resources consciously and purposefully, disinterestedly and 'scientifically', allowing him to make contact with the foreign as such. *It is not so, twice.*

A crucial feature of the reconsideration that I defend concerns the self. As I encourage thinking about the comparing self, I mean specifically the self-as-encultured-entity. At least from the perspective of comparative law, there is no meaningful incarnation of the self apart from its cultural inscription. It is enculturation, as a kind of mediator between exteriority and interiority, that delineates for a comparatist what it is conceivable to think and enunciates what lies beyond the limits of what is thinkable (beyond the mental hurdles that must inevitably confine one's comparative intervention). Now, any worthy examination of the epistemic dynamics at work must reveal not only the cultural conditions of feasibility of the individual's thought, but also the way in which foreign law as encultured entity restricts the thinking that can take place. Otherwise said, the ambition must be for the comparatist-at-law to understand himself as a cultural entity studying a cultural entity. Call it an exercise in epistemic vigilance vis-à-vis the self's (the comparatist's) and the other's (the foreign law-text's) cultural conditioning. In *NCL*, I pursue the aim of overcoming the forgetting of culture that positivism has wanted to generate, to surmount positivism's deliberate amnesia in favour of a culturalist *anamnesis* (which, as the prefix indicates, is

[47] The reluctance to mandate is a recurring theme in Harcourt (n 5).

precisely the opposite of an amnesia). The idea, then, is for the comparatist to re-appropriate culture by conjuring the positivist effacement of culture (even as one may not spontaneously experience oneself or foreign law as cultural beings). In comparative law, every claim to knowledge has to be cultural, and every claim to knowledge must be of the cultural – although enculturation often manifests itself infraconsciously at best. Once one admits these two claims, the comparative game changes drastically, and the stakes rise exponentially: there is now meaningful *play*. The tracing strategy I defend – for the encultured comparatist to trace the encultured foreign law-text to its cultural components in order to make optimal sense of the legal – shows how the comparison of laws cannot be strictly structuralist; indeed, there is a comparatist, here. And it also reveals how comparison-at-law cannot be exclusively phenomenological either, for there is a foreign text, there. If you will, tracing neither cancels structuralism and phenomenology nor does it synthesize them. Rather, it overtakes them by assuming epistemic priority over them: it is at once hyperagential (remember that this agency is thoroughly encultured) and hypertextual (recall that this textuality is thoroughly encultured, too).

*

Why would I take the comparative venture so seriously – why would I bring such urgency to my intellectual quest – and why would I devote so much time and effort to attempting the epistemological overhaul I am seeking? Ultimately, the answer must be personal. Comparative law has offered me a way to make the realm of law, of law teaching, and of law teachers, in which I found myself living and later having to live, more or less acceptable, more or less bearable. To reflect on my socialization and institutionalization (on my epistemologization) – to consider my enculturation – has also helped me to understand certain things about myself. Comparative law has therefore acted as a sort of personal therapy, as a consolation of a sort. For me, there has been a *consolatio comparationis*. In this sense, in the sense of what comparison has done for me, I think of comparative law as having served not unlike an analytical cure. Of course, it would be illusory to assume that awareness is enough for complete emancipation. Discernment drives home the weight of the *acquis*, of the predispositions that saddle one. It thus clarifies how little one owes to oneself, and how much one is affected by otherness. On the subject-matter of obligation, I find that I am beholden to comparative law – which, I think, is justification enough for me to want to improve the theory and practice of it. I hope the concepts and tools I have sought to fabricate for myself in the course of an academic career spent comparing laws and thinking about comparing laws, all instruments devised with a view to achieving more honest thinking about comparative law generally and more integrity in the implementation of my comparative research in particular, can also assist others and thus the field.

*

In terms of the theory that speaks to me, that interpellates me – for Ronald de Sousa, 'the broad lines of every philosoph[ical] positio[n] are determined by innate temperament'[48] – I find that I am mostly obligated to Heidegger's post-phenomenology (even as I am aware of his Nazism and anti-Semitism) and Adorno's critical theory (even as I appreciate his cultural elitism),[49] these two intellectual pursuits having supplied excellent philosophical resources that allowed me to ascertain the shallowness of the dominant epistemological assumptions within the field of comparative law and challenge these deplorable premisses. I have found my struggles with Heidegger and Adorno immensely edifying. I hasten to add that I am not spellbound and do not purport slavishly to follow either Heidegger or Adorno. (In any event, I would resist the thought that there is one 'correct' reading of Heidegger or 'the' right understanding of Adorno.) Rather, while I am most careful to apply full interpretive integrity, I seek to deploy these thinkers to my own critical ends, to ply their discourses to my own intellectual strivings. According to my informed interpretations of them (*to my informed interpretations of their interpretations*), I want unashamedly to put Heidegger and Adorno to work with a view to furthering my own project: to bring to

[48] R de Sousa, *Emotional Truth* (Oxford University Press 2011) 139.

[49] I hold that the constructive spirit in which I draw from Heidegger's work – neither wistfully apologetic nor dogmatically denunciatory, neither taking the view that his Nazism and anti-Semitism lie at the core of his philosophy nor that they have nothing whatsoever to do with it – is thoughtfully expressed in ER Wolfson, *The Duplicity of Philosophy's Shadow* (Columbia University Press 2018); J Cohen and R Zagury-Orly, *L'Adversaire privilégié* (Galilée 2021). Contra: A Knowles, *Heidegger's Fascist Affinities* (Stanford University Press 2019). And I agree with Richard Rorty, who maintained that 'attempts to dismiss Heidegger as "a Nazi philosopher" resemble the Nazis' attempt to dismiss Einstein's theory of relativity as "Jewish physics"': R Rorty, 'Diary' *London Review of Books* (8 February 1990) 21. Irrespective of how one appreciates Heidegger's (and Adorno's) allegiances, it must be clear that comparative law primordially disallows the entrenchment of rigid identity categories and that the comparative venture, as it emphasizes the connection between human achievement, human finitude, and human situatedness, must stand firmly opposed to any manifestation of cultural denigration (or extolment).

bear on the study of foreign law-worlds, legal cultures, or law-texts a way of thinking, reading, and writing so as to achieve a more profound understanding of foreignness and of what it means to understand foreignness.[50]

*

Given the spectacular discrepancies in the two philosophers' responses to the ascendancy of Nazism in Germany in the 1930s – Heidegger was an early card-carrying member of the Nazi party, which he remained throughout the Second World War, while Adorno was a Jewish refugee (his name at birth was Theodor Wiesengrund) forced into a fifteen-year exile in England and the United States from 1934 to 1949[51] – it cannot come as a surprise that these two individuals never worked together in any sense of the term. Indeed, they met only once when the then twenty-five-year-old Adorno was introduced to Heidegger after a presentation the senior philosopher had given in Frankfurt in 1929 (Heidegger was thirty-nine at the time). The perfunctory conversation was followed by a lifelong 'refusal of communication' with not so much as a single exchange of correspondence.[52] Heidegger ignored Adorno, and Adorno wrote solitarily, if most combatively, against Heidegger.[53] Yet, despite a steadfast indifference, on one hand, and a soliloquent display of hostility, on the other, Heidegger and Adorno shared latent preoccupations, and they defended converging 'negative' philosophical projects – Fred Dallmayr refers to 'an almost

[50] I keep in mind Michel Foucault's remarks on the thought of Nietzsche. He says that it is incumbent on one 'to use it, to deform it, to make it squeal, scream'. He adds that 'whether commentators say if one is or not faithful, this has not any interest': M Foucault, 'Entretien sur la prison: le livre et sa méthode' in *Dits et écrits*, vol 1 (D Defert and F Ewald eds, Gallimard 1994 [1975]) 753.

[51] For Adorno's Jewishness, see R Geuss, *Changing the Subject* (Harvard University Press 2017) 275.

[52] I borrow the expression from the title of Hermann Mörchen's detailed record of the interaction between Heidegger and Adorno: H Mörchen, *Adorno und Heidegger: Untersuchung einer philosophischen Kommunikationsverweigerung* (Klett-Cotta 1981). Mörchen holds that the 'brief encounter' between the two philosophers took place on 24 January 1929: ibid 13.

[53] 'Adorno maintained a relentless opposition to Heidegger's work and lavished on it an unending stream of political venom, a practice aggravated by personal distance': F Dallmayr, 'Adorno and Heidegger' (1989) 19 Diacritics 82, 82. Yet, Heidegger always remained someone to whom Adorno 'addresse[d] himself seriously': S Gandesha, 'Leaving Home: On Adorno and Heidegger' in T Huhn (ed), *The Cambridge Companion to Adorno* (Cambridge University Press 2004) 103.

involuntary complicity'[54] – that I find crucially relevant to my own intellectual endeavours.[55]

Specifically, both thinkers challenge the overbearing assumptions inaugurated by the Cartesian cogito, consolidated by the advances of mathematical physics and technology, and confirmed as a process of (purportedly) complete explanatory calculability (allegedly) leading to the full management of the planet and the attendant prioritization of instrumentalization, assimilation, appropriation, uniformization, and totalization – what Heidegger styles '*Machenschaft*', a pejorative term aiming to capture the idea of modernity's obsession with an imperious way of making the planet fit for wilful machination, an infatuation with 'makeability'.[56] Although Adorno's objection to scientism focussed principally on the manner in which a one-dimensional perspective reducing worldly phenomena to empirical givenness was complicit with political and social domination, he also deplored how positivism atrophied philosophical reflection.

As Heidegger and Adorno both moved away from the primacy of metaphysical foundationalism (abandoning, for example, the subject-object correlation) in order to argue that the co-being between humans and their world should be understood in an alternative guise (which should acknowledge how the individual, far from operating within a safe zone of self-appropriation, loses oneself in the experience of worldliness), they insisted on the need to acknowledge the ultimate intractability of the world by the mind.[57] In line with this decentering of subjectivity, the two philosophers thus objected to the idea of language as a transparent medium of representation: there could be no presentation of pure immediacy without its mediators, and those mediators were fated to be cultural beings with all the representational limitations that that fact entailed. In other terms, both Heidegger and Adorno maintained that there must be a tension between one's desire to work with words optimally adequate to the world that one is trying (failingly) to describe and the linguistic

[54] Dallmayr (n 53) 83.

[55] Eg: M Heidegger, 'Die Negativität' in *Gesamtausgabe*, vol 68 (I Schüßler ed, Klostermann 1993 [1938–39]) 1–61; TW Adorno, *Negative Dialektik* (Suhrkamp 1966). See generally I Macdonald and K Ziarek (eds), *Adorno and Heidegger* (Stanford University Press 2008); AG Düttmann, *Das Gedächtnis des Denkens: Versuch über Heidegger und Adorno* (Suhrkamp 1991).

[56] Eg: M Heidegger, *Beiträge zur Philosophie* (2nd edn) in *Gesamtausgabe*, vol 65 (F-W von Herrmann ed, Klostermann 1994 [1936–38]) 38–41 and 126–34.

[57] I closely track F Dallmayr, 'Adorno and Heidegger on Modernity' in I Macdonald and K Ziarek (eds), *Adorno and Heidegger* (Stanford University Press 2008) 174–80.

medium through which one must necessarily express oneself. For Heidegger and Adorno, we are not yet thinking adequately about this problematique, and 'we have to find a way of thinking that is attentive to the event of withdrawal, a way of comportment that addresses what is absent as something present in thinking'.[58] Thought must appreciate language's limits, that is, it must realize there is only so much language can do when it entrusts to itself the task of making sense of a world. And until it adjusts its epistemic sights, thought will remain deluded – in the way in which it has shown itself to be at least since Descartes – into thinking that language can reign supreme over a world.[59]

The primordial question – a basic parallel between Heidegger and Adorno's philosophical pursuits – then becomes how thought can regain its integrity vis-à-vis its focus of study (for instance, the foreign legal culture or law-text), which it has lost under the spell of what would be the subject's meaning-imposing or meaning-representing authority concerning a world that it regards as an object. Thus, Adorno: 'Philosophy has, at this historical situation, its true interest . . . in nonconceptuality, individuality, and particularity; in that which since Plato has been dismissed as transitory and insignificant.'[60] It follows that the epistemic goal must be to surmount the alienation of reason from the target of knowledge, which (post-Enlightenment) synthetic reductionism has promoted. The triumphalism of Rationality notwithstanding, there is, as a matter of fact, a stubborn excess of world over charts. Regardless of the modern epistemological cogito proclaiming itself, after Descartes, to be the maker and master of all things, the idea must now be, against the backdrop of the temporality and finitude of human experience, to allow things or entities (say, foreign legal cultures or law-texts) to be given a genuine hearkening. In other terms, one must resist annexation of otherness and, on the understanding that the self cannot be the other, allow epistemic room for difference even in proximity. Consider Jacques Derrida: 'The fine ear is an ear that hears finely, that perceives differences . . . . To perceive differences is to convey, precisely, the distinction between things apparently similar.'[61] Heidegger and Adorno's philosophical programmes therefore intersect to favour experience-

[58] M Wenning, 'Adorno, Heidegger, and the Problem of Remembrance' in I Macdonald and K Ziarek (eds), *Adorno and Heidegger* (Stanford University Press 2008) 156.

[59] It is this delusion that Adorno had in mind when he wrote that '[i]n the mental omnipotence of the subject its real impotence has its echo': Adorno (n 55) 181.

[60] ibid 19–20.

[61] J Derrida, *L'Oreille de l'autre* (C Lévesque and CV McDonald eds, VLB Editeur 1982) 70.

informed interventions, necessarily encultured and thus inevitably situated, with a view to doing justice to the differentiated law-worlds under examination (say, foreign legal cultures or law-texts), necessarily encultured and thus inevitably situated.[62]

After Adorno, who defends the priority of things or entities (that is, the idea that no thing or entity can be equalled either by way of words or through the mobilization of a concept, that every thing or entity is more than what it is said or conceptualized to be), and after Heidegger, whose *Sein und Zeit* recasts the very idea of subject as '*Dasein*' with a view to emphasizing the primordial 'thereness' of being ('*da*' means 'there' in German),[63] I hold that the comparatist-at-law must recognize and abide the priority of the other over the self inasmuch as otherness resists selfness's attempt at full interpretation, to the extent that otherness ultimately keeps its secret: '[T]he differentiated persists as the foreign, the distant, and the different – even in communication and consensus', a fact that Adorno found to be 'decisive'.[64] And as the comparatist thinks of himself as being-in-the-world (it is not that he cannot make choices, but that he makes them as an encultured individual), the contrarian challenge becomes to tame what Merleau-Ponty styles, phenomenologically, the 'fundamental narcissism of all vision'.[65]

Adorno's instructions to the comparatist-at-law would be that he must bring to bear to his comparative interventions a 'lingering look',[66] which has need of 'patience with regard to the matter at hand',[67] not to mention a willingness 'not to swim with one's own current'[68] – say, not to go along with a positivist reading of foreign law. All importantly, the comparatist

[62] See I Macdonald and K Ziarek, 'Introduction' in I Macdonald and K Ziarek (eds), *Adorno and Heidegger* (Stanford University Press 2008) 3.

[63] See M Heidegger, *Sein und Zeit* (Niemeyer 2006 [1927]) passim. There is a reference to this 'agonistic motif' in J Früchtl, 'The Struggle of the Self Against Itself: Adorno and Heidegger on Modernity' in I Macdonald and K Ziarek (eds), *Adorno and Heidegger* (Stanford University Press 2008) 149.

[64] U Guzzoni, '"Were Speculation About the State of Reconciliation Permissible...": Reflections on the Relation Between Human Beings and Things in Adorno and Heidegger' in I Macdonald and K Ziarek (eds), *Adorno and Heidegger* (Stanford University Press 2008) 127. Guzzoni refers to Adorno (n 55) 192.

[65] M Merleau-Ponty, *Le Visible et l'invisible* in *Œuvres* (C Lefort ed, Gallimard 2010 [1964†]) 1764.

[66] Adorno (n 55) 38.

[67] TW Adorno, *Stichworte: Kritische Modelle 2* in *Kulturkritik und Gesellschaft*, vol 2 (R Tiedemann et al eds, Suhrkamp 2003 [1965]) 602.

[68] ibid 604. I am accordingly delighted to have been afforded the opportunity to contribute a monograph in Portuguese (Brazil) with *Editora Contracorrente*, a text written exclusively for this intrepid contrarian São Paulo publisher and its valorous founder, Rafael

must not appropriate the thing or entity towards which he is turning his gaze, which means that he must generate 'nearness within farness'.[69] Indeed, if one contents oneself with an 'undiminished, ... already attained nearness', then 'the denial of foreignness inflicts extreme injustice upon the other ... , "adds it up", incorporates it to the inventory of possession'.[70] The convergence with Heidegger's thought is apparent in such a Heideggerian formulation as '[n]earness draws the far near specifically *as the far*'.[71] Heidegger also refers to 'the nearness to farness'.[72] Ute Guzzoni's analysis of Heidegger's concept of '*Gelassenheit*', or releasement, clearly evokes Adorno's articulation of the uncircumventable priority of world over word:

> Releasement characterizes a thinking that involves itself with what it has to think and does so by letting itself be determined by it. ... This releasement stands in radical opposition to the calculating relation of humans to the whole of the world .... Released thinking ... is neither the grasping of the modern subject, which attempts to get things into its grip; nor does it exercise a mere disinterested spectatorship. Instead, it originates out of an attentive questioning and listening and a sensitive reflection.[73]

Now, consider Adorno: '[T]he foreign ... remains in the granted nearness, the distant and the different, beyond the heterogeneous and the own.'[74]

Both Heidegger and Adorno maintain in effect that the thing or entity (say, the foreign legal culture or law-text), even as it is held apart from the comparatist, must be located within a frame of togetherness with the comparatist. It is only within the space of this relation as *irrelation* – the space where recognition towards otherness and respect for otherness can intervene – that the dynamics between the comparatist and foreign law can take place.[75] But this interpretive motion is negative inasmuch as it is structurally unable to account for a world as it exists, there, as such. If you will, word fails world, if by one letter only. The togetherness is therefore not-togetherness, and *interpretation cannot be representation*. I maintain

Valim. See P Legrand, *Como ler o direito estrangeiro* (DW Hachem tr, Editora Contracorrente 2018).

69 TW Adorno, *Minima Moralia* (R Tiedemann ed, Suhrkamp 2003 [1951]) 100.

70 ibid 207.

71 M Heidegger, *Vorträge und Aufsätze* in *Gesamtausgabe*, vol 7 (F-W von Herrmann ed, Klostermann 2000 [1954]) 179 [my emphasis].

72 M Heidegger *Gelassenheit* (Neske 1959) 69.

73 Guzzoni (n 64) 136.

74 Adorno (n 55) 192.

75 Consider Jaeggi (n 12).

that comparative law must accept, primordially, that it *cannot* tame otherness. Comparatists must harness this limitation and apply to comparative interventions a 'mastery of non-mastery',[76] which one can understand as 'a braiding together of activity and passivity, agency and patiency, the development of a capacity to be acted upon, even as one acts'.[77] Again, the comparatist stands between selfness and otherness: he is sort of going beyond selfness so as to sort of access otherness. But, of course, he does *not* leave himself and does *not* reach the other.

I regard negativity understood in Heidegger's and Adorno's sense (there are other semantic extensions to be addressed also) as a transversal orientation requiring to inform the very heart of the theoretical matrix according to which the practice of comparative law must unfold.

*

Not least because, within comparative law, the orthodox episteme – the subject–object or thought–matter dualism – can straightforwardly be connected to Descartes's philosophy,[78] I find it apposite to emphasize the epistemic significance that must attach to Heidegger's decisive critique of the Cartesian project,[79] that pertains to the 'idiomaticity of the Heideggerian gesture'.[80] Heidegger's drastic divergence from Cartesianism found a well-known public expression on the occasion of the disputation he held with neo-Kantian philosopher Ernst Cassirer (1874–1945) in Davos (Switzerland), a philosophical conversation that took place in March 1929 consisting of seven lectures (three by Heidegger, four by Cassirer) and a debate.[81] This 'epic'

[76] R Barthes, *Fragments d'un discours amoureux* in *Œuvres complètes*, vol 5 (2nd edn, E Marty ed, Editions du Seuil 2002 [1977]) 258.

[77] Paper Boat Collective, 'Archipelagos, A Voyage in Writing' in A Pandian and S McLean (eds), *Crumpled Paper Boat* (Duke University Press 2017) 17.

[78] For a demonstration, see P Legrand, 'Paradoxically, Derrida: For a Comparative Legal Studies' (2005) 27 Cardozo LR 631, 645–54. While Descartes's contribution can in all likelihood be traced to ancient Greece, it introduced a more radical and significantly more influential version of the dichotomies I mention.

[79] For an outstanding exposition of Heidegger's philosophical challenge, see J Richardson, *Existential Epistemology* (Oxford University Press 1986).

[80] J Derrida, *Geschlecht III* (G Bennington, K Chenoweth, and R Therezo eds, Editions du Seuil 2018 [1985]) 153.

[81] For a definitive account of the Davos confrontation, see PE Gordon, *Continental Divide* (Harvard University Press 2010). For the transcript of the Davos discussion, see OF Bollnow and J Ritter (eds), 'Davos Disputation zwischen Ernst Cassirer und Martin Heidegger' in M Heidegger, *Kant und das Problem der Metaphysik* (Klostermann 2010 [1929]) 274–96. Heidegger's *Kant-Buch* was issued within months of the Davos meeting.

Auseinandersetzung immediately assumed great intellectual importance.[82] It continues to be viewed in philosophical memory as a defining argumentative moment.[83] On one hand, the conversation cast a classical world-view positing the primacy of human agency and, on the other, an innovative understanding of the human being confining him to a largely receptive position. In other words, Davos contrasted the ideas of 'human creativity, or spontaneity', an understanding 'aligned . . . with philosophical trends born from the Enlightenment', and the 'restor[ation] [of] human being to a deepened recognition of its thrownness in historical time' – in Heidegger's own words, to 'the hardness of his fate'.[84] Cassirer and Heidegger stood for two countervailing models of man and the extent to which man is conditioned by his worldliness.[85] They epitomized two apprehensions of the degree to which human finitude is to be envisaged as 'a permanent and incorrigible feature' of the constitutive condition of human beings.[86]

Ever since it was staged, the Davos encounter has been seen to have marked an epistemological break in continental thought. Nearly sixty years after attending, Emmanuel Levinas (1906–95) recalled that '[a] young student could have the impression that he was attending the creation and the end of the world. . . . Cassirer represented an order that was going to be defeated. . . . Heidegger heralded a world that was

It contains the elaboration of his radically ingenious Davos lectures, which explains why it was found convenient to publish the transcript of the Davos disputation as an appendix to that volume. For another learned account of the Davos event, see G Waite, 'On Esotericism: Heidegger and/or Cassirer at Davos' (1998) 26 Political Theory 603. See also D Kaegi and E Rudolph (eds), *Cassirer-Heidegger: 70 Jahre Davoser Disputation* (Meiner 2002).

82 RB Brandom, in PE Gordon, *Continental Divide* (Harvard University Press 2010) book jacket, back cover.

83 Eg: M Jay, in PE Gordon, *Continental Divide* (Harvard University Press 2010) book jacket, back cover, who refers to 'the aftershocks that continue to reverberate to this day'; JP McCormick, in PE Gordon, *Continental Divide* (Harvard University Press 2010) book jacket, back cover, who observes that 'the historical and philosophical ramifications of Davos '29 are even more profound than previously understood'.

84 Gordon (n 81) 214. The quotation from Heidegger's is in the Davos record: Bollnow and Ritter (n 81) 291. The idea of 'thrownness' ('*Geworfenheit*') is a key Heideggerian motif. One is always-already thrown ('*geworfen*') into a world, proclaims Heidegger. See eg Heidegger (n 63) 383–84. Heidegger's 'thrownness' percipiently captures the idea that one is delivered over to a factical existence in the public space, which is not a life of one's own making or under one's control. Specifically, one is thrown into the constitutive features of one's prejudicial fore-structure such as language, religion, morality, forms of politeness – or law.

85 Gordon (n 81) 363.

86 ibid 76.

going to be upset' – although the two speakers were, in fact, only fifteen years apart.[87] Reminiscing half a century after the event, Otto Bollnow (1903–91), one of the two editors responsible for the Davos transcript, concurred wholeheartedly: 'From here and now arises a new epoch of world-history.'[88] In the words of Steven Schwarzschild (1924–89), a US Professor of Philosophy and Judaic Studies thoroughly conversant in the German language and German philosophical culture, '"Davos" was like a medieval morality-play, in which each of the two antagonists represented great ideas or virtues.'[89] Peter Gordon remarks that 'for several critics, the difference of historical and philosophical perspective was so immense that it prohibited genuine dialogue'.[90] In this regard, Gordon notes that 'each [philosopher] spoke a unique language with terminology so distinct as to defy the possibility of mutual translation',[91] while Levinas discerned 'an unsurpassable antinomy'.[92] In the *Frankfurter Zeitung*, Hermann Herrigel (1888–1973), a German journalist writing for the newspaper's university supplement ('*Hochschule und Jugend*'), held that the *Internationale Davoser Hochschulkurse*, the host-organization, '[i]nstead of seeing two worlds collide', had effectively witnessed two individuals who 'talked monologues'.[93]

The controversy between the two philosophers, who were then amongst the leading thinkers in Europe, touched upon the most urgent questions in the history of philosophy through the lenses of two theoretical paradigms strikingly at variance with one another: interpretation, over-interpretation (*Überdeutung*), disclosure, representation, understanding, experience, imagination, facticity, subjectivity, culture, world-view (*Weltanschauung*), values, finitude, incommensurability, relativism, difference, aporia, translation, communication, language, objectivity, scientificity, methodological formalism, transcendence, truth,

87 F Poirié, *Emmanuel Levinas: qui êtes-vous?* (La Manufacture 1987) 78. The words are Levinas's, which he spoke in an interview with François Poirié in 1986.

88 OF Bollnow, 'Gespräche in Davos' in G Neske (ed), *Erinnerung an Martin Heidegger* (Neske 1977) 28. In 1929, Bollnow was a student of Heidegger's, while his co-editor Joachim Ritter was Cassirer's pupil. For the circumstances surrounding the preparation of the transcript, see Gordon (n 81) 104–9.

89 S Schwarzschild, 'Franz Rosenzweig and Martin Heidegger: The German and the Jewish Turns to Ethnicism', unpublished typescript, no date, 2 [on file]. The typescript consists of eighty-three pages.

90 Gordon (n 81) 330.

91 ibid 189.

92 Poirié (n 87) 77. The words are Levinas's.

93 [H Herrigel], 'Denken dieser Zeit: Fakultäten und Nationen treffen sich in Davos, I' *Frankfurter Zeitung*, '*Hochschule und Jugend*' supplement (22 April 1929) 4.

knowledge, and ethics.[94] Comparatists-at-law will immediately recognize how these concerns are very much comparative law's central epistemic preoccupations.

*

With specific reference to his work on textuality and the self/other dynamics, Derrida (1930–2004) remains paramount for me. In Derrida's audacious and courageous philosophical work, I find many crucial insights bringing not-together aspects of Heidegger's and Adorno's discerning projects.[95] Along the way, I have also derived assistance in some key respects from the writings of Hans-Georg Gadamer (1900–2002), in particular from his philosophical hermeneutics, although I have come decisively to arbitrate the hermeneutics/deconstruction debate in favour of Derrida's insurgent interpretive ways over Gadamer's unduly conservative, at times reactionary motions.[96] (One of the main limitations of Gadamer's undertaking is the monocultural character of his philosophical model, an impediment that qualifies in important respects his framework's relevance for comparatists-at-law.[97]) Even as I appreciate that Derrida's thought readily provokes the fear and anxiety of the extra-ordinary, which is typically met by repression (rather than by any attempt at serious engagement), I conjure the spectre of deconstruction to commend a radical re-evaluation of comparative law's strategies for reading, thinking, and writing about the foreign and about what it means to study the foreign. Michel Foucault (1926–84), Bourdieu (1930–2002), Ludwig

[94] For an extensive thematic account, see Gordon (n 81) 136–214.

[95] Derrida exclaims, 'Nothing of what I am attempting would have been possible without the opening of Heideggerian questions': J Derrida, *Positions* (Editions de Minuit 1972) 18. In 2001, Derrida received the 'Theodor-W-Adorno' prize, which is bestowed every three years. For the text of Derrida's acceptance speech, see J Derrida, *Fichus* (Galilée 2002).

[96] See P Legrand, 'Derrida's Gadamer' in S Glanert and F Girard (eds), *Law's Hermeneutics: Other Investigations* (Routledge 2017) 144–67. Even partisans of hermeneutics acknowledge its foibles. Eg: M Lambek, 'The Hermeneutics of Ethical Encounters' (2015) 5 Hau: J Ethnographic Theory 227, 230.

[97] A good example of Gadamer's monoculturalism is his assertion that 'understanding is more original than misunderstanding': H-G Gadamer, 'Sprache und Verstehen' in *Gesammelte Werke*, vol 2 (Mohr Siebeck 1986 [1970]) 187. For a thorough examination of the intercultural shortcomings of Gadamerian hermeneutics, see S Glanert, 'The Interpretation of Foreign Law: How Germane Is Gadamer?' in S Glanert and F Girard (eds), *Law's Hermeneutics: Other Investigations* (Routledge 2017) 63–79. See also X Zhang, 'Comparison Paradox, Comparative Situation and Inter-Paradigmaticity: A Methodological Reflection on Cross-Cultural Philosophical Comparison', (2010) 1 Comp Philosophy 90, 99n7: 'Gadamer is blind at what is really needed for a cross-cultural comparative understanding.' Contra: LC Simpson, *Hermeneutics as Critique* (Columbia University Press 2021) 54–80.

Wittgenstein (1889–1951), and Roland Barthes (1915–80) have also supplied me with many pivotal insights.[98] I repeat that the main disposition informing my work is determinedly anti-Cartesian.[99]

*

It remains to mention Samuel Beckett, very much the foremost tutelary intellectual presence informing *NCL*'s various lines of reasoning, a man who travelled in realms to which most people do not want to be introduced, much less explore. Over the many years that I have spent taking an assiduous interest in Beckett (in his work and in the demeanour of his life, too), I have been struck, no doubt impertinently, by how my understanding of comparative law tallies with his insights – often, very often, to the point of uncanny resonances. I have long derived much reassurance and encouragement from these frequent correlations. As it unfolds in the course of the ensuing essays, my argument repeatedly evokes and invokes Beckett as it discloses a number of the Beckettian connections I have ascertained. Suffice it to mention at this early stage a few general observations undergirding the many references that follow. For my comparative and epistemological purposes, perhaps Beckett's most elemental enunciation is his declaration to the effect that 'anyone nowadays who pays the slightest attention to his own experience finds it the experience of a non-knower, a non-can-er'.[100] Applying Beckett's contention to the specific case of foreign law, this statement entails that 'any attempt to utter or eff it is doomed to fail, doomed, doomed to fail'.[101] Indeed, it is one of *NCL*'s salient claims that the concept of comparison harbours within itself a generative *irrelating* that must ultimately entail a structural unknowing.[102]

[98] While I have sought assistance from Levinas in some of my earlier work and although I am not adverse to occasional references (I particularly value Levinas's appreciation of the ethical priority of otherness vis-à-vis selfhood), I have become impatient with the pervasive mysticism informing his philosophy, especially with the relentless allusions to suffering, expiation, culpability, and persecution, not to mention an overall kerygmatic tone. I experience an analogous difficulty with respect to Søren Kierkegaard (1813–55). Despite my affinity with various aspects of Kierkegaardian thought (I have in mind the idea of singularity or the insight to the effect that one cannot really understand another), I find the heavy and relentless theological strain in his writing unattractive.

[99] For a thoughtful critique of Cartesianism, see R Fortin, *L'Anti-Descartes* (Liber 2016).

[100] I Shenker, 'An Interview with Beckett' in L Graver and R Federman (eds), *Samuel Beckett: The Critical Heritage* (Routledge 1979 [1956]) 148. For further information on this conversation, see D Bair, *Samuel Beckett* (Harcourt Brace Jovanovich 1978) 651n22.

[101] S Beckett, *Watt* (CJ Ackerley ed, Faber & Faber 2009 [1953]) 53.

[102] Those who value coherence, who resent comparatists-at-law changing their minds (a German colleague once took me to task in print for having amended my view over a twenty-three-year period) will be relieved to note that nowhere in the extensive perusal

Beckett is emphatic about the paramountcy of nescience. First, there can be no systematization or conceptualization of any kind that can exist free of tangible connections to an experienced or lived-in world. One of Beckett's numerous utterances in this regard comes from his private correspondence: '[F]orgive all this gossip from the only source I have, the only source of reference, my own bloody self.'[103] Secondly, there is the further fact that worldly meaning is properly irreducible to any linguistic configuration. In Beckett's own words, '[t]he most ideal tautology . . . involves only an approximate identification, and by asserting unity denies unity'.[104] Crucially, the incapacity for any exactness – the impossibility of representative achievement, strictly speaking – must lead one to restrain one's epistemic claims. The unfailing failure to understand (in the profound sense of the verb) must prompt, instead of any flight into metaphysical or other transcendental narratives falsely pretending to be able to deliver congruity between word and world (think of objectivity or truth) even as 'mind and world come asunder in irreparable dissociation',[105] as one must 'feel kept at word's length',[106] an abiding measure of self-negating epistemic humility.

Fascinatingly, Beckett never puts his work ahead of his experience: he always shows how the act of writing authentically can never be outside the writer's frame of reference. He thus consistently short-circuits the old demarcation between subject and object, the fundamental dualism upon which narrative, indeed language, has been constructed, certainly ever

I devote to comparative law's epistemological conundrums in the *American Journal of Comparative Law* do I claim that the comparatist can acquire knowledge of foreign law. See Legrand, 'Jameses' (n 38). Throughout my argument, I assert that what there is, and all there can be, is a construction or deeming of knowledge – if you will, there is knowledge *as* foreign law rather than knowledge *of* foreign law. Given the fact that the self cannot be the other, this predicament is inexorable. Yet, even if he does not know what he thinks he knows, the orthodox comparatist typically behaves *as if* he had knowledge of foreign law (and as if foreign law existed, but this is another matter altogether to which I return elsewhere in *NCL*).

103 Letter from S Beckett to T McGreevy in *The Letters of Samuel Beckett*, vol 1 (MD Fehsenfeld and LM Overbeck eds, Cambridge University Press 2009 [14 November 1930]) 55.

104 S Beckett, *Proust* in *The Grove Centenary Edition*, vol 4 (P Auster and JM Coetzee eds, Grove 2006 [1931]) 542.

105 S Beckett, 'The Essential and the Incidental' in *Disjecta* (R Cohn ed, Grove 1984 [1934]) 82.

106 Letter from S Beckett to N Rawson in *The Letters of Samuel Beckett*, vol 4 (G Craig et al eds, Cambridge University Press 2016 [14 February 1976]) 422. cf R Musil, *Der Mann ohne Eigenschaften* (A Frisé ed, Rowohlt 1978 [1930]) bk 1, s 105, 503–4: 'A word is able of much, but there is much more!'

since Descartes. Because he finds that this neat delineation is simply not available to him, Beckett relinquishes any protection the narrator's purported separation from the narrative might offer, any succour the myths of objectivity or truth would supply. Beckett's greatest gift to his readership may be his modest reminder that writing is not about representation, his proclamation of the art of non-representation, a negativity that is precisely the opposite of nothingness or emptiness. Disregarding easy gratification, Beckett abjures all theory that pretends to be *able*.

After Beckett, *NCL* very much seeks to *discontent* comparative law – it wants to make comparatists appreciate how they must not rest content that the self can produce neat duplications of the other, if only it will work harder, if only it will engage in enough scratchings and rewritings, if only it will implement a syntax that will be better attuned to otherness or more symmetrical vis-à-vis it. Beckett is adamant, and so is *NCL*: there will be no stability to the self's account of otherness, and there will be no satiability either. Also, when he claims that '[t]he only fertile research is excavatory',[107] Beckett is effectively urging one to engage in the investigation of the story underwriting the seemingly evident narrative. I do, too – and I call my strategy 'tracing'. (I have already addressed this complexifier at length.[108]) Still focussing on the matter of knowledge from a basic standpoint, Beckett teaches one that although one must resign oneself to one's cognitive limits, one's resignation cannot take the form of an abdication. In other words, even as the comparatist's 'knowledge' of otherness-in-the-law is structurally doomed to vagueness, the comparatist must persist in seeking knowledge, ever more sophisticated knowledge of otherness-in-the-law. One must seek to generate an ever-stronger interpretive yield. In Beckett's own arresting formulation, one must, incessantly, '[f]ail better'.[109] In other terms, the most battle-hardened comparatist's inevitable defeat notwithstanding, one must 'keep on keeping on',[110] one must *compare on*. The limitations regarding the self-in-the-law's language being no more deniable than the urgent

[107] Beckett (n 104) 539.

[108] See eg P Legrand, 'Siting Foreign Law: How Derrida Can Help' (2011) 21 Duke J Comp & Int'l L 595.

[109] S Beckett, *Worstward Ho* in *Company/Ill Seen Ill Said/Worstward Ho/Stirrings Still* (D Van Hulle ed, Faber & Faber 2009 [1983]) 81.

[110] Letter from S Beckett to T McGreevy in *The Letters of Samuel Beckett*, vol 1 (MD Fehsenfeld and LM Overbeck eds, Cambridge University Press 2009 [19 August 1936]) 368.

need to articulate otherness-in-the-law, I agree. And I do 'keep on keeping on'. And I do *compare on.*

*

It appeared improbable to assemble a book on comparative law (a practice involving unceasing interaction with otherness) without my texts closely engaging with an extensive range of othernesses – whether, for example, with other comparatists-at-law, other languages, or other disciplines. In the course of preparing *NCL*'s various essays, I implemented my commitment in a number of different regards, for instance, through quotation, translation, interpretation, re-signification, rescription, and discussion. Unabatingly, I wrote my way through my work with the words of others, and I invited the words of others to write their way through my work.[111]

Nothing is more foreign to my thought or to my life than the idea of closure – whether it be, say, territorial or disciplinary closure, hence my long-standing interest in comparative law and, more precisely, in a resolutely open-textured approach to comparative law. The objection that Jürgen Habermas addresses to Adorno, Derrida, and Foucault (all three being expressly named) thus strikes me as bizarre. For Habermas, the three intellectuals he attacks are to be condemned, since '[they] elude ... those categories according to which modern knowledge, by no means accidentally, has differentiated itself, and which nowadays underlies our understanding of texts'.[112] In Habermas's view, it is a serious problem, as one considers Adorno's, Derrida's, and Foucault's writings, that '[t]hey let themselves be clearly attributed neither to philosophy or science, nor to moral and legal theory, nor to literature and art'.[113] Indeed, '[s]uch discourses unsettle the institutionalized standards of fallibilism'.[114] As I read Habermas, he thinks that the legitimacy of scholarly work depends on the relevant text fitting neatly within received categories of knowledge, which he appears to invest with the transcendental aura of essential or natural delineations. I earnestly disagree, and I hold that insightful and progressive scholarship must depend in significant part on the innovative reconfiguration of disciplinary lines – on work developing as a re-rationalization of each disciplinary domain and

[111] Meaningfully for me, Harry Collins, a leading sociologist, recommends 'the extensive use of quotations': H Collins, *Forms of Life* (MIT Press 2019) 19. See also ibid 101.

[112] J Habermas, *Der philosophische Diskurs der Moderne* (Suhrkamp 1983) 390.

[113] ibid.

[114] ibid 390–91.

as a re-configuration of the modes of scholarly presentation traditionally on offer. Yes.

Now, I easily favour *indiscipline* over interdisciplinarity, and I readily distinguish the demand for comparatists-at-law to mobilize pro tanto non-law discourses such as continental philosophy (if this designation be sustainable), literary criticism, translation studies, anthropology, or sociology, for example, from any requirement to claim expertise in any of these fields. To be clearer still, I am not suggesting that in order to do comparative law, one has to be well-versed in multiple disciplines, each heralding its own canons and controversies. In my determination to fight silo-thinking (an expression from early-1990s management speech), I lift quotations, texts, ideas, and references from these various fields and, by way of a massive subacting process, I proceed to connect these materials to comparative law. *I make them connect.* Indeed, *I force them to connect.* And I can creditably compel such connections, because of the signal relevance of these other discursive endeavours to the salient theoretical questions that (must) detain comparative law as the classical and tired positivist paradigm desperately calls to be cancelled in so many elementary respects. Note that, for me, indiscipline is not about the accumulation of information so much as it concerns the deployment of insights with a view innovatively to foster a new, enriched appreciation of what foreign law can mean and of what it must mean to research foreign law.[115] Being based in France, I am moved incidentally to observe that I have found myself referring to French legal thought very rarely, because of its excessively formalist and parochial focus.[116]

*

Negative Comparative Law is principally destined for academics taking a professional interest in foreign law. I suspect the argument may spontaneously appeal to the contracentric, egregious comparatist-at-law, to the disobedient and the transgressor, to the dissentient and the subversive. Meanwhile, I appreciate that *NCL* could only aim to be understood by devoted positivists if it spoke their language, which it does not and does not purport to do. Even if I can envisage how the curious and sedulous positivist might nonetheless want to be a reader, I expect that he would be impatient, perhaps fearful, certainly eager to annul this

[115] Eg: A Mercescu, *Pour une comparaison des droits indisciplinée* (Helbing Lichtenhahn 2018).

[116] For my purposes, I am aware of one outstanding work only, which is Richard (n 39). This monograph was published in Canada.

claim, to invalidate it, wanting to bring the matter back to his dogmatic fallacies, unwilling to retrace his steps – a bad reader. Beyond these entrenchments, though, *NCL* eagerly addresses the postgraduate student wishing to incorporate comparison-at-law into a planned dissertation, that is, the individual having a serious stake in the future of the discipline who can be expected to be familiar with the themes I discuss, well-versed in the debates within the field of comparative law surrounding the topics I raise, and, of course, someone who would not have fully succumbed to comparative law's orthodoxy and its positivist-analytical stratagems. This is mostly the reader I want to provoke, impress, engage, and convince. This is the reader I can still hope to sway. I trust that this reader may find in *NCL* a new account of the discipline's present situation, an argument that strikes him as troubling enough so as to get him to agree that comparatists need to do comparative law differently in future, that they must operate otherwise and other-wise – that is, differently and in a manner alert to the epistemic demands that otherness makes on one. At the very least, I wish that after getting acquainted with *NCL*, comparatists-at-law who are willing to attend to the argument (not, then, those animated by defensive resentment or philistine indifference or those coming to the matter with condescension, half-heartedness, or meagerness of outlook) will be better equipped to appreciate that the positivist norms they have been implementing as they have been conducting their research into some aspect or other of a foreign legal culture or law-text – in all likelihood the norms that dissertation supervisors or journal editors have been compelling them to apply – are profoundly contestable, deserve to be ardently disputed, and indeed call to be abandoned. Along the way, although I make no deliberate attempt at esoterism, I purposefully avoid the demotic (no plebeianization of comparative law for me, *please*).

*

Even as aspiration to English and capability in English have become indicators of 'world-readiness',[117] I resolutely wanted my sources to range beyond English materials. Accordingly, in the course of researching *NCL* I consistently sought to interfere with the hegemony of publications in English by making copious reference to texts in other languages, in particular to writings in French or German. Inevitably, my proclivity for these two other languages had much to do with the linguistic possibilities and primary sources at my disposal. But my

[117] D Gramling, *The Invention of Monolingualism* (Bloomsbury 2016) 93.

decision to focus on French and German texts was also the result of the remarkable influence that French and German intellectuals have exercised throughout the modern era, say, since 1600, not least as regards an extensive range of theoretical issues that crucially matter to comparatists-at-law. (Needless to add, as I refer to the noteworthy impact of French and German thought, I do not have in mind jurists so much as philosophers and sociologists, not to mention literary critics.) Also, I was determined that my sources should not be saddled with published English translations. In this regard, I faced a paradox. While the very topic of this book – comparative law – exists as translation (every exercise in comparison is a translation, if only because it entails a transportation or transversion of legal/cultural entities across law-worlds, a rewording from otherness to selfness or across othernesses), I elected to operate with source-texts and source-quotations, which is my own concession to 'originalism' (albeit my version is of a very different kind than the one my US friends are supporting). In fact, I have sought to proceed in this way almost uncompromisingly. Throughout, I have been keen to let the authors whom I discuss circumvent their published translators' voices, which I have found regularly to disserve them, at times significantly so. Apart from rare instances, I have therefore supplied my own Englishing. Unless attributed, then, all translations are mine (and so are their imperfections).

Although both the localization of source-materials and the inscription of my own English translations with respect to hundreds upon hundreds of passages, short or long, forthright or complicated, implied considerable work over a number of years, these fleeting intimations of dwelling-in-otherness have allowed me a personal engagement with foreign writers that, I think, has benefitted me and my work – and, I hope, them and their work. Along the way, I have not been concerned with accuracy or exactness or correctness, but with justness: I have sought to be just vis-à-vis the source-texts – I have wanted to do them *justice*. To be sure, I appreciate that I cannot erase the difference between the source-text and my re-writing of it, that there is no possible equivalence or commonality across languages, every language affording its own signifying modulations. And I accept that the only strategy available to me is therefore *assignment* of equivalence or commonality (in effect, the machination and imposition of sham-equivalence or sham-commonality), a process consisting of making-languages-look-equivalent or making-languages-look-common – an illustration of the epistemic power or violence that translation necessarily visits on the translated.

Because translation is inevitably transformative, I have consistently been keen to offer responsible translations, that is, translations that *respond* to the source-text before all else, and I mean translations that are more interested in adhering to the formulation of the source-text than in opting for a re-arrangement permitting the source-text to read fluently and, yes, easily, in the host-language (that is, as regards *NCL*, English). If you will, by prioritizing the source-text and compelling my English translation to 'track' it, I have crafted 'other-oriented' translations – if at the cost of a de-standardization of standard English. I firmly maintain that '[c]ultural translation is not simply about moving the source culture into the target culture but about translating the target culture into a new form'.[118] To apply Stanley Cavell's, as translators we are 'educations' for our readers.[119] To be sure, this approach is neither for the lazy nor for those in haste to publish. As befits serious comparative work and for the sake of translative accountability, I indicate the source-texts in extenso on my website.[120] If my intuition is sound and if my strategy is indeed beneficial to the foreign texts with which I have concerned myself, I hold that this approach ought ultimately to profit my readership also, even though I am effectively asking my readers to leave their linguistic comfort zone and make the effort to touch base with the source-text and to do so, to a certain extent at least, on the source-text's own terms. Otherwise said, although my translations discontinue or interrupt – or supplement – the language in which a passage was first written, they *recognize* and *respect* that language, which is why I translate while always keeping a gimlet eye on the source-texts and why I make them available to my readership. Although some of my translations may prove less than

118 RJC Young, 'The Dislocations of Cultural Translation' (2017) 132 PMLA 186, 192. Along analogous lines, Homi Bhabha encourages one 'to perform the act of cultural translation' by way of an 'apprehension of difference', that is, 'to inscribe the specific locality of cultural systems – their incommensurable differences': Bhabha (n 22) 164. The undertaking to help do justice to the other-in-the-law through the foreignization of the host-language is readily traceable to Walter Benjamin's seminal essay. See W Benjamin, 'Die Aufgabe des Übersetzers' in *Illuminationen: Ausgewählte Schriften*, vol 1 (S Unseld ed, Suhrkamp 1977 [1923]) 61: 'The basic error of the translator is that he clings to the contingent state of his own language instead of letting it be moved powerfully by the foreign language.' Famously, Benjamin contends that 'our [German] translations, even the best, start from a false tenet[:] they want to germanize the Hindi, Greek, English, instead of Hindianizing, Graecizing, Anglicizing the German': ibid.

119 S Cavell, *Conditions Handsome and Unhandsome* (University of Chicago Press 1991) 31.

120 See <www.pierre-legrand.com>, where the relevant page is 'Originalism'.

optimally fluent in idiomatic English, I trust that my foreignizing English-in-translation will keep foreignness present in my anglophone reader's mind. This has been my goal: to ensure that as I invite my anglophone reader to ponder Heidegger or Derrida, Adorno or Foucault, he does not forget that he is reading a foreign text – hence the idea of generating the discomfort zone I address.

Even as I fully accept that '[t]ranslators do not become authors',[121] without my translations, without this affirmation of (limited) sovereignty on my part, *NCL* would not be mine in the way it must be.[122] And without the source-texts, which I make a determined point of inscribing, *NCL* would not be the foreign authors' in the way it must be. In the end, the comparatist's foreignizing translation coupled with the reproduction of the source-text show the comparative dynamic as I am fervently of the view that it should be cast. (In passing, let me say that I also harbour this feeling as regards the disciplinary and linguistic *diversity* of source-materials: this pluralism, too, befits a text on comparative law.) A fellow comparatist-at-law once pointed to the use of source-texts in the scholarship of one of our colleagues as evidence of arrogance on that individual's part, perhaps being led astray by our colleague's demonstrable propensity for affectation. Be our colleague's personality as it may, I must vehemently contest the verdict bearing upon the scholarly practice on display: comparative law cannot exist in English only, and it must not, and every attempt that is made to move comparative law away from an all-English disposition deserves to be lauded. For my part, the manner in which I purport to evoke source-texts through my foreignizing translations and the further way in which I supply source-texts both allow me to indicate my commitment to ultimate untranslatability. Crucially, then, I approach my English translations in *NCL* not as substitutions for the source-texts, but as *articulations* of them.

*

Perhaps bearing in mind that 'nice' derives from the Latin '*nescius*', which may signify 'foolish', *NCL* does not mean to be *nice*. Given the disciplinary pressure, gentle or not so gentle, to nod, smile, and agree – or at least to keep quiet – no doubt some readers will claim to find in the text too much verve and torque. I cannot fairly pretend such assessments to be devoid of any merit whatsoever, and I confess that I have not sought to propitiate anyone

121 A Pym, *The Moving Text* (Benjamins 2004) 109.

122 For a rewarding passage on the translator's (limited) sovereignty, see J-L Nancy, *La Déclosion* (Galilée 2005) 159.

by way of my dulciloquence, since I very much regard any standard of agreeability as intrinsically dangerous to the amelioration of the ideas that must matter within the field of comparative law. Given the epistemological predicament I address, I fear that discordance is long overdue. I willingly own my dissensus, then; indeed, I wear it as a mark of integrity, a manifestation of my inveterate instinct to earnestness, a habit of withering intensity that I can do little to tame, even if I was minded to attempt to do so. There are, I have to say, no misgivings or scruples, but rather a deeply felt sense of vocation (not, I know, a popular disposition and one in fact likely to attract derision or be mistaken as *épatisme*). But why write critique if it is so banal as not to carry a cost?[123] Why content oneself with being a docile writer, whose words pertain 'to a revision of or addition to a preexisting and accepted narrative' and thus 'always remai[n] within the rules and boundaries of the discursive "tradition" the field has set'?[124]

When I write critically, I am *on duty*. However, this 'I' requires to be problematized, because there is me and, then, there is me-as-writer. Specifically, the latter feels compelled to make statements that the former might prefer to withhold. To re-signify a term from Gilles Deleuze's, I work *dividually*, I write as a *dividual*.[125] I therefore claim a uniquely writerly voice, and I do make my essays very 'voicey'. Meanwhile, I feel confident that I do not judge anyone harder than I judge myself (people close to me point to a surfeit of self-abrasion).[126] Yet, no matter how much I regret this fact in my more introvertive moments, I cannot incessantly practice incorruptible scrutiny given that some comparatists-at-law are my friends and others close colleagues. And the will to a certain blindness that seems an essential part of friendship (and perhaps of close collegiality) brings to bear a different mode of reading, less sharply critical – still insightful, I think, but unduly concerned not to be unkind, distressing, or hurtful. At times, the proximity I discuss also leads to a deliberate closing of the eyes. Let me simply say, therefore, that throughout *NCL* I have tried hard to contain such factical interferences with critical freedom.

123 cf R Char, 'A la santé du serpent' in *Fureur et mystère* in *Œuvres complètes* (J Roudaut ed, Gallimard 1983 [1948]) 263: 'What comes to the world to trouble nothing deserves neither regard nor patience.' Taking the long historical view, the cost of critique has occasionally been dramatically high. See generally C Bradatan, *Dying for Ideas* (Bloomsbury 2015).

124 WB Hallaq, *Restating Orientalism* (Columbia University Press 2018) 172.

125 See G Deleuze, *Pourparlers* (Editions de Minuit 1990) 240–47.

126 cf TS Eliot, 'The Function of Criticism' in *Selected Essays 1917–1932* (Harcourt, Brace 1932 [1923]) 18: 'I maintain even that the criticism employed by a trained and skilled writer on his own work is the most vital, the highest kind of criticism.'

Taking his cue from André Gide, Derrida proclaims his singularity, his keen desire to maintain his independence.[127] As I apply his declaration to my own circumstances, I, too, attest that I am not-belonging, that I am not one of anyone's. Derrida adds that not to be part of a group or school must be 'a commitment'.[128] Convinced that '[a] writer who aspires to be impregnable has no friends',[129] I have long and steadfastly tried to uphold Derrida's pledge, which has meant, as I have understood his pronouncement, deliberately, as much as has been reasonably possible at any rate, to stand well outside the orthodox paradigmatic structure and away from the various institutional manifestations that conscript one, perhaps unwittingly, into the system of epistemic power. Subversion, if it is to prove honest, must assume optimal unburdenment from the sensitivities that are bound to arise from sharing a conference panel, drinks, or dinner with a colleague or from being co-opted into other forms of collegial intimacy such as contributing to a *Festschrift* or accepting any form whatsoever of institutional recompense. Whether familiarity breeds contempt may be debatable, but the fact that it stifles academic critique seems very difficult to dispute.[130] Inevitably, though, wilful seclusion has its limits.

*

Negative Comparative Law's essays, then, rebel against the unquestioned 'attainments' on which orthodox comparative law has been smugly relying. They say no to these 'accomplishments'. They thus defend negative comparative law. If only because they arise in a society characterized by the 'fetishization of the positive',[131] these texts are

[127] See J Derrida, *Points de suspension* (E Weber ed, Galilée 1992) 352. See also J Derrida and M Ferraris, *Le Goût du secret* (A Bellantone and A Cohen eds, Hermann 2018 [1993]) 34–36. The passage is Derrida's.

[128] Derrida and Ferraris (n 127) 35. The words are Derrida's.

[129] Lysaker (n 26) 90. cf Beckett (n 104) 539: 'For the artist, who does not deal in surfaces, the rejection of friendship is not only reasonable, but a necessity.'

[130] I accept that even my forceful attachment to subversion does not exempt me from all the trappings of power, for instance, on account of an institutional affiliation that connects me with one of the most prestigious names in the world of higher education. cf AC Hutchinson, *Law, Life, and Lore* (Cambridge University Press 2018) 26: 'There is no place of exile to which the intellectual (or anyone else) can retire which is beyond the reach or influence of prevailing power structures and norms.' Further, I appreciate that without institutional relays like the Sorbonne – or the *American Journal of Comparative Law* – '[I] will not be able to bring about any significant changes in the structures of power': C Mouffe, *Agonistics* (Verso 2013) 77.

[131] TW Adorno, *Vorlesung über Negative Dialektik* (R Tiedemann ed, Suhrkamp 2007 [1965]) 34.

always-already contrarian. As an exercise in negativity (again, largely *sans* Hegel despite his resounding call for 'the tremendous power of the negative' as 'the energy of thought'),[132] my argument can accurately be read as an attempt to lead comparatists to go where they have not gone, and where most of them have not wanted to go.[133] Because *NCL* aims to destabilize a hegemonic state of affairs – to change the conceptual furniture, to transform the agential epistemics – the irritation of those destined to be disrupted is expectable. And I fully presume such aggravation. I am at ease with the idea that the claims I make must be asserted and with the fact that orthodox comparatists-at-law would prefer them not to be uttered.

*

I take into account the documentation I could consult until 21 March 2022. All references to websites were correct on that date, when I last accessed electronic sources. Although I have strived to link to persistent or stable URLs, I have thought it best nonetheless to download and file certain documents, which I indicate in the notes as appropriate. All along, I have sought to refer to the most scholarly and authoritative editions of the works I array. Unless I enter an indication to the contrary, all emphases in quotations belong to the source-texts.

Except when I mention a female author or choose to insert a female protagonist in my narrative, I deliberately use the masculine gender as I do not feel entitled to express myself as if I were a woman (or other), and I certainly do not pretend to be writing neutrally.

I draw the book's epigraph from Foucault's.[134]

*

Abidingly, *NCL* attests to the fact that I remain motivated to expend considerable energy in deploying the case for the comparison of laws and that I continue to be determined to instil in fellow jurists, whether through my teaching, conferences, or publications, a keen sense of the

[132] GWF Hegel, *Phänomenologie des Geistes* (E Moldenhauer and KM Michel eds, Suhrkamp 1986 [1807]) 36.

[133] I am heartened to learn that as influential a contrarian thinker as Bourdieu regarded his intellectual enterprise as a 'negative philosophy': P Bourdieu, *Méditations pascaliennes* (Editions du Seuil 1997) 15 [emphasis omitted].

[134] M Foucault, 'Qu'est-ce que la critique?' in *Qu'est-ce que la critique? – La Culture de soi* (H-P Fruchaud and D Lorenzini eds, Vrin 2015 [1978]) 36–37 ©Librairie Philosophique J Vrin (French)/©University of Chicago Press (English). I am grateful to copyright holders for kindly allowing me to quote this French excerpt in my English translation.

comparative enterprise's intellectual and moral worth. If you will, being a comparatist-at-law is part of my self-schema. Comparative law is something I do every day for many hours a day, not unlike the professional pianist who plays the piano quotidianly for hours on end. For me, to live the life of a comparatist is to assume an identity carrying with it core normative commitments to a set of claims revolving around the valorization of otherness and otherness-in-the-law and providing reasons to act in particular ways consonantly with this motion. *Negative Comparative Law* – the collage that I call *NCL* – is also an expression of my desire to become both a better comparatist-at-law and a better writer-in-English-as-a-second-language, these two ambitions ultimately not having so much to do with any reader as with the imperative not to trick myself. And yet, even as I resolve not to cheat, the published version of *NCL* hides the errors, missteps, and setbacks, the dead-ends – all these debacles, large or small, and all the time wasted, too. And it also conceals the illnesses and injuries, the major life crises, not to mention the inopportune breakdowns of laptops and printers.

Out, then, comes *NCL*, a collection of essays in purposive revendication of comparative law and in steadfast defence of a different comparative law, apertures spurting – a bit of a grandiose gesture, really. Permit me, or forgive me.

II

Sniffing the Wind

It smells, or perhaps it stinks.

To be fair to Shakespeare, his term of choice is not nearly as pungent, and in *Much Ado About Nothing* he has the hapless Constable Dogberry call comparisons 'odorous'.[1] Now, the bungling character's malapropr-ism was as flagrant as fragrant, and the late-sixteenth-century audience would have instantly recognized the mishap, since by 1599 the statement that comparisons are odious had become familiar prose. It seems that John Lydgate (c 1370–c 1451), a monk and prolific poet (he admired Chaucer and befriended his son), initiated the disparagement. In his 'Hors, Goose and Shepe' (there would be many variations on this title over the years), a poem apparently penned around 1440 and first printed posthumously circa 1477, Lydgate's seventy-sixth stanza opens with the verse, 'Odyous of olde been comparisonis'.[2] This stylistic arrangement would not be repeated. The form closer to modern usage appears attrib-utable to Robert Greene (1558–92), a popular Elizabethan dramatist and pamphleteer who, in his *Mamillia* (1583), writes: 'I will not make com-parisons, because they be odious.'[3] Later, possibly in 1601, John Donne (1572–1631) appropriated the expression in one of his elegies (suitably entitled 'The Comparison'). Having graphically metaphorized the full range of his lady's bodily fluids, he eventually winced and declared that '[s]he and comparisons are odious'.[4] In subsequent years, many other

[1] W Shakespeare, *Much Ado About Nothing* (1598–99), act 3, scene 5.

[2] J Lydgate, 'Horse, goose and sheep' (c 1477†) <https://archive.org/stream/lydgateshorse goo0lydggoog#page/n86/mode/2up> [on file].

[3] R Greene, *Mamillia* in *The Life and Complete Works in Prose and Verse of Robert Greene*, vol 2 (AB Grosart ed, 1881 [1583]) <www.forgottenbooks.com/en/books/TheLifeandCompleteWorksinProseandVerseofRobertGreeneMA_10464195> 52 [on file].

[4] J Donne, *The Major Works* (2nd edn, J Carey ed, Oxford University Press 2000 [1688†]) 63. According to John Carey, the relevant elegy was written in 1601: see ibid 433.

writers would mobilize the saying, not least Cervantes (1547–1616). In the second instalment of his *Don Quijote*, which he released in 1615, the renowned novelist has his ingenious nobleman utter 'comparisons . . . are always odious'.[5] In 1621, Robert Burton (1577–1640) also rehearsed the formulation in his *Anatomy of Melancholy* as he compared women. 'Comparisons are odious', he proclaimed.[6] Closer to law, John Fortescue (c 1395–c 1477), the major English political theorist, marshalled the expression in *De Laudibus Leges Angliae*, which he wrote between 1468 and 1471 while in exile in France. Even as he proved determined to enthuse about the laws of England and cast them as more advanced than their French or Roman counterparts, Fortescue issued a warning. According to the current English translation, he exclaimed: '[C]omparisons ... are reputed odious, and so I am not fond of making them.'[7]

*

Beyond the stench, then, it would be a matter of overcoming the obnoxious character of the comparative motion. In sum, to harness a term perhaps conveniently capturing at once the ideas of effluvium and repugnance, one would have to surmount the *nauseousness* that comparison fosters – how disgusting or offensive it is. But why would the act of comparison – the gnosiological operations pertaining to comparative judgement – have long evoked repellence even as '[c]omparison is an inevitable mode of human cognition'?[8] As regards law, the principal

[5] M [de] Cervantes, *El ingenioso caballero Don Quijote de la Mancha* (1615) <https://es.wikisource.org/wiki/Don_Quijote,_Segunda_Parte:_Cap%C3%ADtulo_I> pt 2, ch 1 [on file].

[6] R Burton, *The Anatomy of Melancholy*, vol 3 (NK Kiessling et al eds, Oxford University Press 1994 [1621]) pt 3, s 3, memb 1, sub-s 2, 282.

[7] J Fortescue, *In Praise of the Laws of England* in *On the Laws and Governance of England* (S Lockwood ed and tr, Cambridge University Press 1997) ch 19, 29. Shelley Lockwood presents his translation as an amended version of SB Chrimes's 1942 English text. The first translation from the Latin appeared in 1567.

[8] SS Friedman, 'Why Not Compare?' in R Felski and SS Friedman (eds), *Comparison* (Johns Hopkins University Press 2013) 43. See also B Lincoln, *Apples and Oranges* (University of Chicago Press 2018) 109: '[W]e have no alternatives to comparison, since no knowledge is possible without it'; D Caramani, *Introduction to the Comparative Method with Boolean Algebra* (Sage 2009) 1: 'Comparison ... is ... a basic element of everyday life. It is a spontaneous mental process .... Daily we compare lines in shops (shorter or longer), the weather from one day to the next (better or worse), the size of clothing articles (larger or smaller), the arrival of trains (earlier or later). ... With classification ..., comparison is one of the crucial conceptual processes making the world intelligible.' For Guy Swanson, '[t]hinking without comparisons is unthinkable': GE Swanson, 'Frameworks for Comparative Research: Structural Anthropology and the Theory of Action' in I Vallier

focus of *NCL*, very much has to do, I want to claim, with the way in which comparatists have been readily branding comparison as a sure foundation of knowledge, a methodological warrant of cognitive discovery. Typical assertions are that comparison is in a position to generate conclusions resting on a 'realistic basis',[9] that it is able to deliver 'scientific exactitude and objectivity'.[10] As far as I can discern, the confidence underlying such pronouncements arises largely from the long-rehearsed postulate that any good comparative investigation is fated to confirm the existence of equivalences or commonalities across the assortment of legal entities under comparison, these recurrences effectively validating the model being reproduced. If you will, and not unlike what takes place in a biochemistry laboratory, the very fact of duplication is deemed to supply a guarantee of correctness or rightness, reliability and veracity being further enhanced through sheer accumulation of exemplary instances. Consider a characteristic formulation from the standpoint of the comparison of laws: 'Legal problems in each country are of the same type. One can address the same questions and apply the same standards to each legal order in the world.'[11] Again: 'Different legal orders come, as regards the same questions of life, often down to details, to the same or at least perplexingly similar solutions.'[12] In other words, '[d]ifferences are in truth not relevant'.[13]

Such an intemperate effort to efface otherness-in-the-law from the comparative perspective – in this sense, a strategy properly marked as odious – suggests a recoilment in the face of the relativization that acknowledgement of difference would instigate. Because the other's singularity, if it were effectively attested, would question selfhood, possibly in a challenging or disturbing manner, one readily expresses a preference for the neutralization of otherness through processes of appropriation or invalidation, of assimilation or annihilation. Pursuant

(ed), *Comparative Methods in Sociology* (University of California Press 1971) 145. cf WD Mignolo, 'On Comparison: Who Is Comparing What and Why?' in R Felski and SS Friedman (eds), *Comparison* (Johns Hopkins University Press 2013) 99: '"Comparison" … is a field of investigation into the neurology of cognition.' In Ben Hutchinson's terms, 'comparison is hard-wired into the very ways that we think': B Hutchinson, *Comparative Literature* (Oxford University Press 2018) 2.

9 K Zweigert and H Kötz, *Einführung in die Rechtsvergleichung* (3rd edn, Mohr Siebeck 1996) 32.

10 ibid 44.

11 ibid 45.

12 ibid 38.

13 ibid 60.

to this catabolism, difference is branded either as superfluous (although perhaps intriguing) or threatening. This insight is readily applicable to the legal scene: to the self-in-the-law, the legal other's conflictual ways of occupation of legal space from one territory to the next have traditionally appeared either as immaterial (however potentially fascinating) or ominous.[14]

I find that juristic assurance in the likeness of laws – in their equivalence or commonality – must be correlated to the way in which comparative law's doxa has long been committed to an understanding of the legal that can fairly be termed 'positivist-analytical' or 'positivist' *tout court*.[15] Not least because of its volubility, the governing epistemic type

[14] In particular, jurists hailing from the so-called 'civil law' tradition have shown themselves to be steadfast proponents of the idea of one-law, a pursuit that assumes the praising of indistinction and the correlative silencing of differentiation. While Zweigert and Kötz offer a well-known contemporary illustration of this predilection (supra 49), the attitude I mention is deeply ingrained. Observe how, as early as 1900, Louis Josserand suggested a 'universal common law' on the occasion of the Paris congress devoted to comparative law, the first such large-scale institutional gathering: L Josserand, 'Conception générale du droit comparé' in Congrès international de droit comparé, *Procès-verbaux des séances et documents*, vol 1 (LGDJ 1905) 243. Josserand's view has been widely shared. Eg: H Lévy-Ullmann, *Vers le droit mondial du XXe siècle* (Rousseau 1923); R Demogue, *L'Unification internationale du droit privé* (Rousseau 1927). As comparatists-at-law aim to re-inscribe the law bereft of any spatio-temporal facticity, they adopt one of two perspectives. Thus, they may assume the idea of a 'higher' law, which postulates a brand of transcendentalization I style 'celestial'. Contrariwise, they can use a 'tellurian' approach and refer to a 'common-core' enterprise the designation of which suggests the idea of a nucleus or kernel undergirding what are then taken to be superficial or surface differences across laws. Eg: RB Schlesinger, 'Introduction' in RB Schlesinger (ed), *Formation of Contracts: A Study of the Common Core of Legal Systems*, vol 1 (Oceana 1968) 9 and 35. cf M Bussani and U Mattei, 'The Common Core Approach to European Private Law' (1997–98) 3 Columbia J Euro L 339, 340: '[C]ommon core research is a very promising tool for *unearthing* deeper analogies hidden by formal differences' [my emphasis]. For a scathing (if justified) critique of Schlesinger's endeavours, see W Ewald, 'Comparative Jurisprudence (I): What Was It Like to Try a Rat?' (1995) 143 U Pennsylvania LR 1889, 1978–82. John Merryman has linked the manifestations of these totalizing intellectual and moral schemes to the so-called '*jus commune*'. For him, '[t]he idealization of . . . the *jus commune* is at the bottom of a special attitude which might be called "the nostalgia of the civil lawyer". It refers to a desire to reestablish a *jus commune* – a common law of mankind – in the West. . . . [A] similar nostalgia is not a part of the culture of the common law': JH Merryman and DS Clark, *Comparative Law: Western European and Latin American Legal Systems* (Bobbs-Merrill 1978) 104–5. See generally P Legrand, 'Are Civilians Educable?' (1998) 18 Legal Stud 216.

[15] '[A]nalytical jurisprudence' and 'positivism' are 'interchangeable labels': BZ Tamanaha, 'The Contemporary Relevance of Legal Positivism' (2007) 32 Australian J Legal Phil 1, 38. Given positivism's currency, it is noteworthy that some leading positivists would abandon the term. Frederick Schauer explains this (defensive) posture both on the ground that

ought to be immediately familiar to readers of specialized journals and expert books as it features comparatists steadfastly focussing on statutes or cases and propounding the juxtaposition of substantive or adjectival laws within formalized classificatory schemes (including the preposterous categorization going under the anthropomorphic label of 'legal families' – which, in the manner it connects legal form with the attendant ideas of indistinguishability and substitutability, has first and foremost the ideological effect of obscuring historical relations of colonial or military domination and the socio-economic fact of uneven or stalled development).[16] Predictably (and not unlike the doctrine of positivism itself), the field of comparative law harbours many positivist variations – even as socialization or institutionalization into the disciplinary matrix that is positivism is mainly an implicit process, which means that comparatists-at-law may not be fully aware of their position and of the hegemonic character of the stance they adopt. Indeed, positivism is not expressly taught in law school: no lecturer announces to his students that he will be teaching them a positivist version of property or administrative law. Rather, positivism infiltrates itself into the learning of law surreptitiously.

'attempts to characterize positivism often degenerate into caricature' and because of 'excess dichotomization of perspectives into positivist and nonpositivist (or antipositivist)': F Schauer, *The Force of Law* (Harvard University Press 2015) 179n17. Ought one to surrender oppositions as a matter of course given the risk of 'excess dichotomization'? Along with Gilles Deleuze and Félix Guattari, I maintain that 'all dualisms . . . are the enemy, but the enemy quite necessary': G Deleuze and F Guattari, *Mille plateaux* (Editions de Minuit 1980) 31. See also C Levine, *Forms* (Princeton University Press 2015) 9.

[16] The idea that for comparatists-at-law who remain transfixed by organizational schemes the optimal classificatory scenario should be articulated around the theme of 'parent', 'offspring', and 'sibling' laws strikes me as very naive, to say the least. Yet, these are the words one finds in U Kischel, *Rechtsvergleichung* (Beck 2015) 221. Now, Kim Scheppele properly observes that '[m]etaphors matter in shaping thought, and so it is crucial to get the metaphors right for highlighting key features of the matter under discussion': KL Scheppele, 'The Migration of Anti-Constitutional Ideas: The Post-9/11 Globalization of Public Law and the International State of Emergency' in S Choudhry (ed), *The Migration of Constitutional Ideas* (Cambridge University Press 2006) 347. For my part, I distinctly recall the late Bernard Rudden, my Oxford supervisor, instructing me that the common law had never been adopted voluntarily anywhere in the world. How, then, do imperialism, conquest, and colonization relate to the cosy rhetoric that terms like 'families', 'parent', 'offspring', and 'siblings' readily summon – *and are meant to connote*? To claim, as does Uwe Kischel, that the notion of legal families has a 'clear place' and a 'clear justification' as regards the classification of the world's laws is, in effect, to remain wilfully blind to 500 years of geo-politics: ibid 228.

One can distinguish, if somewhat schematically, between the porous positivisms practised in the United States and the hermetic variations to be found in continental Europe (or Latin America and Southeast Asia), where positivism continues to prevail as reverentially hypostasized dogma. Yet, the diverse renditions of the positivist agenda share a certain number of basic characteristics. Thus, all positivisms are primarily concerned with analytics, that is, with legal technique and the rationalization of legal technique. They foster legal dogmatics, to transpose a German phrase, inasmuch as they aim to arrange the law as an orderly, coherent, and systematic articulation of the different rules in force applying at the behest of the state. All positivist investigations therefore remain squarely set on rules – on what has been posited by authorized officials as 'what the law is' – and on the formulation of institutional accounts of these rules, whether judicial or academic, that are heralded as veritistic. In Frederick Schauer's terms, 'the description of law' stands 'at the heart of the positivist outlook', which is staunchly averse to any form of speculation.[17]

Because they are effectively engaged in realizing a description of the law, positivists readily assume an investment in method and its clockworky ways as opposed, say, to experience, which is taken to be striking an unduly personalized and unreliable chord. Accordingly, method must count for almost everything, while the individual who deploys the method must count for almost nothing – unless, perhaps, as an obstacle to the proper use of the right method meant to allow for an objective revelation of the truth about the object of research and foster its doctrinal taming.[18] Specifically, positivists earnestly refuse to accept that there is 'a political act that precedes, exceeds, and conditions the use of methodologies'.[19] According to positivist tenets, interpretation must optimally apply as a kind of *écriture blanche*. Ideally, it ought to act exegetically, assiduously so, or, if you will, as psittacistically as is feasible.

It follows that from the standpoint of positivism broadly understood, a commentary must optimally be required to manifest itself in a rigidly deciphering way, obeying as much as possible the dictates of (assertional) textual repetition. The investment of a statute, say, with any meaning that would be considered exterior to it would be taken to involve a re-creation of the legislative text that would be regarded as tantamount to a

17 Schauer (n 15) 12.

18 I track B de Sousa Santos, *The End of the Cognitive Empire* (Duke University Press 2018) 136.

19 ibid.

wreck-creation of it and, in any event, to an inadmissible recreation on the part of the judge or textbook writer meant to be acting as loyal institutional expositor. In other words, as they seek to promote an interpretive commentary on the legal provisions in force that would be determinedly conceptual and rational, explain the law-texts' reach and their potential, eliminate or reduce the texts' apparent technical flaws, conceptual obscurities, semantic hiatuses, or textual contradictions, positivists adhere to a brand of writing purporting to deploy itself in a largely unproblematic and unsituated mode so that, showing impermeability to the range of existential vagaries liable to afflict interpretation, it can be harnessed to foster exact, correct, or accurate (that is, non-perspectival or non-horizoned) statements about 'what the law is'. It is a crucial assumption of positivism, particularly in continental Europe and former European colonies, that political commitment or personal investment on the part of interpretive authorities should be minified so as not to contaminate the *scientific* attitude, which Europositivists and their scions regard as determinant, and in order not to prevent *scientific* access to law-texts-as-they-are, which Europositivists and their scions deem achievable.[20] Confident that any difficulty addressed scientifically can be resolved scientifically, this positivist streak incessantly strives for the brand of fixity or invariance of meaning that is more readily associated with the Pythagorean theorem or the laws on thermodynamics. Over time, deferential reprises of law-texts through judicial decisions or textbooks must install the stabilization of the meaning of law as *the* meaning of law, thus supplying the kind of reassuring fixity that accompanies fundamental immobility.

For positivism, therefore, whether of the porous or hermetic kind, law must be independently identifiable and knowable *as such*. Moreover, it must be properly expressed in terms that would preferably be strictly confined to a sheer description of it. In the end, though, positivism probably most famously propugns the succinct proposition that *what counts as law is only what is binding as law*.[21] Indeed, Schauer insists on 'analytic jurisprudence's concern for legal validity'.[22] '[H]av[ing]

[20] cf E Cassirer, *An Essay on Man* (Yale University Press 1944) 286: '[O]ne of the principal aims of scientific thought is the elimination of all personal and anthropomorphic elements.'

[21] '[T]he core of legal positivism is the view that the validity of any law can be traced to an objectively verifiable source': R Wacks, *Philosophy of Law* (2nd edn, Oxford University Press 2014) 25. Etymologically, the Latin term '*positivus*' refers to what is imposed. See JB Murphy, *The Philosophy of Positive Law* (Yale University Press 2005) 18.

[22] Schauer (n 15) 157.

invested hard, painful labor into the mastery of . . . maddeningly intricate grids', not to mention 'the construction of endless legal mazes, the piling on of endless legal distinctions, the excruciating refinement of ever more precise doctrinal taxonomies', which they relentlessly proceed 'to integrate . . . into extremely massive and intricate . . . compendiums and commentaries',[23] positivists rigorously abide by the normative position that 'law is only that which is binding'.[24]

Positivism's insistence on bindingness had traditionally meant that for positivists, law – whether national, regional, or international – was to be stringently equated with the law in force *within a given jurisdiction*. And since its institutional emergence in the first part of the nineteenth century, it is one of comparative law's convulsive epistemic initiatives to have extended the range of positivist pertinence so as to include within the legitimate province of law as a focus of study *foreign* positivisms, mostly manifesting themselves at the national level, despite the obvious fact that foreign law does not enjoy any binding character locally. It is precisely this approach that accounts, say, for the US Supreme Court taking an interest in European law and valorizing European law as a (nebulous) source of relevant normative information within US legal adjudication in decisions like *Lawrence v Texas, Roper v Simmons*, or *Lozano v Montoya Alvarez*.[25] (But there remains recalcitrance, and Swiss

[23] P Schlag, *The Enchantment of Reason* (Duke University Press 1998) 11, 144, and 144.

[24] C von Bar and O Lando, 'Communication on European Contract Law: Joint Response of the Commission on European Contract Law and the Study Group on a European Civil Code' (2002) 10 Euro R Private L 183, 232. Ole Lando and Christian von Bar assumed temporary visibility in Europe in the 1990s and 2000s on account of their self-appointment at the helm of hand-picked task forces erstwhile loquaciously devoted to the drafting of Principles of European Contract Law (Lando) or of a European Civil Code (von Bar) that would have applied across Member States within the European Union.

[25] *Lawrence v Texas* (2003) 539 US 558; *Roper v Simmons* (2005) 543 US 551; *Lozano v Montoya Alvarez* (2014) 572 US 1. In *Roper*, Justice Anthony Kennedy, writing for a majority of the US Supreme Court, held that foreign law, 'while not controlling our outcome, does provide respected and significant confirmation for our own conclusions': ibid 578. Although Justice Kennedy appeared willing to grant a measure of normative purchase to foreign law, therefore going beyond mere paraffles, the extent of the persuasiveness of this allegedly persuasive authority remains unspecified. The Kennedy opinion refers to a 'significant confirmation', which means that the foreign input would be meaningful, that it would bring to bear an important measure of legitimation to the US Supreme Court's decision. But why is there a need for the Supreme Court to have its opinions validated at all? Is the Supreme Court not supreme? And, in point of constitutional theory, how can foreign law, issuing from a normative source located beyond national borders and not institutionally rooted in the national constitutional order, contribute to the ascertainment of the command of the US sovereign and thus supply a ratification making the US judicial decision normatively weightier? Note that in

or Brazilian law faculties, for example, still regard references to foreign law as decorative self-indulgence and largely refuse to teach comparative law as part of the official institutional curriculum.) In the main, however, the decentring I discuss has been confined to the geographical sense of the term and failed to embrace the kind of decentring of the mind, so to speak, that would have led comparatists to develop a primary understanding of law more adequate to the task of cross-border studies. Instead, comparatists, unable to escape the epistemological system into which they had been socialized and institutionalized 'at home', have found themselves projecting unto the international scene the positivism they had been used to practise locally. Nowadays, comparatists occupying the supranational stage thus continue for the most part as unrepentant positivists devoted as ever to a conception of the law separated from anything along the lines of cultural justification. The vaunted deterritorialization of the law having largely limited itself to a physical instead of a cerebral reterritorialization of the legal (although committed to peripateticism, the comparatist mostly continues to think *habitually*), the comparative foray in the direction of a practice acting as an antidote to a strictly local understanding of law therefore reveals the strong gravitational attraction of the positivist structuring structure and demonstrates how '[t]he force and efficacy of the system, precisely, transform regularly transgressions into "false exits"'.[26] In the words of John Merryman, the regretted distinguished US comparatist,

> most academic comparative law teaching and scholarship centers on rules of law and related texts. ... Still today, the works of leading theorists of comparative law exhibit a strong tendency to treat rules as the primary substance of their work. ... Thus comparative law, despite ... some comparative lawyers trying to free their work from the confinement of rule-comparison, still is rule-dominated. ... [The study of rules] is their paradigm, what they and others with whom they identify have learned to do. ... There is no clearly posed alternative, no apparent clash of competing paradigms, no perceived necessity of choice.[27]

Graham v Florida (2010) 560 US 48, Justice Kennedy wrote about foreign law offering the US Supreme Court 'respected reasoning to support it[s] [rationale]': ibid 82. I suggest that the ideas of 'confirmation' (as in *Roper*) and 'support' (as in *Graham*) must be distinguished, a fact further confusing the institutional dynamics between US judicial decision-making and foreign law.

26 J Derrida, *Marges* (Editions de Minuit 1972) 162.

27 JH Merryman, 'The Loneliness of the Comparative Lawyer' in *The Loneliness of the Comparative Lawyer and Other Essays in Foreign and Comparative Law* (Kluwer 1999) 5–7. Eg: M Bogdan, 'On the Value and Method of Rule-Comparison in Comparative Law'

Comparative law has been proceeding on the basis of a firm epistemological consensus, an agreement broad and solid enough at any rate to constitute a Kuhnian paradigm (in the loose sense in which the term has come to be used, that is, as a designation for a discrete set of thought patterns, including theories, methods, and standards allowing for the identification of referential contributions to any scholarly enterprise, whether scientific or not).[28] Now, there cannot be many academic fields where the stock of orthodox theoretical assumptions has continued in the grip of as demonstrably indigent an epistemology – a composition at once muzzy and janky – as has been the case in comparative law for decades on end. (One has the very uneasy feeling that given the angustation of comparative law, an attendee at the 1900 Paris congress who had time-travelled to 2020 would have found little cause for puzzlement or disputation.) At this juncture, comparative law persists as a discourse disappointingly plagued by uninvestigated, jejune, and, well, irritating arguments regarding the construction of what is readily branded as foreign legal knowledge. To imagine someone holding forth on astrophysics whose only acquaintance with the subject-matter is *The Oxford Illustrated Science Dictionary* gives a good idea of what it feels like to read orthodox comparatists-at-law on epistemology.

After the early post-modernity had witnessed their protracted servitude to the barren classifications, fallacious correspondences, and meagre interpretive return of *Les Grands systèmes* – a predicament that, implausibly, endures in countries as diverse as Egypt, France, and Russia – law's comparatists began taking their epistemological orders from Hamburg and the Hamburgher diaspora. For fifty years or so at this writing, they have been gorged on a diet of *Rechtsdogmatik*, scientism, objectivity, neutrality, truth, and assorted shibboleths. Since the 1960s, the formalistic agenda having informed the training and publication programmes at the *Max-Planck-Institut für ausländisches und internationales Privatrecht an der Elbe* is liable for the normalization of bromides that, no matter how epistemically unsustainable, have oriented comparative practice and

in H-P Mansel et al (eds), *Festschrift für Erik Jayme* (Sellier 2004) 1233, 1235: 'This author finds the scientific comparison between legal rules belonging to different legal systems to be of such obvious value and use that it is almost embarrassing having to defend it.'

[28] In the body text, my intimation of Thomas Kuhn is, of course, a reference to TS Kuhn, *The Structure of Scientific Revolutions* (2nd edn, University of Chicago Press 1970) passim. Margaret Masterman holds that the word 'paradigm' carries twenty-one different meanings in Kuhn's book. See M Masterman, 'The Nature of a Paradigm' in I Lakatos and A Musgrave (eds), *Criticism and the Growth of Knowledge* (Cambridge University Press 1970) 59.

characterized what has been deemed to count as good comparison – even as the old ackamarackus was stymieing the comparatist-at-law's sense-making. Indeed, the institute's wealth has allowed it, in a remarkable display of epistemological proselytism, to sponsor '*Dogmatisierung über alles*' through the incessant fabrication of disciples-as-doctors (or is it doctors-as-disciples?) and by way of the sustained promotion of conferences, journals, and books inter se. As if these epistemic chimeras were not ensnaring enough, the lame French model was eventually revived, although it was tweaked to focus on traditions instead of systems.[29]

[29] In 1964, René David rebranded his 1950 *Traité élémentaire de droit civil comparé* as *Les Grands systèmes de droit contemporains*, the most recent English version having been released in 1985, in John EC Brierley's translation, as *Major Legal Systems in the World Today* (Stevens). While *Les Grands systèmes* strikes me as epistemologically very troublesome, I do not seek to deny David's audacity when he left a professorial post in France to become a law student in Cambridge. See P Legrand, 'René David: la contre-allée (1906–1990)' in L Cadiet et al (eds), *L'Ecole de droit de la Sorbonne dans la cité* (2nd edn, IRJ Sorbonne Editions 2016) 233–37. In 2000, Patrick Glenn startlingly sought to breathe new life into David's model by releasing his *Legal Traditions of the World* (Oxford University Press). A commentator remarked that it was 'as if one ha[d] been upgraded from an ordinary package tour to a luxury cruise ship with a more sophisticated guide to the standard sights': W Twining, 'Glenn on Tradition: An Overview' (2006) 1 J Comp L 107, 108. A digest of the world's laws appears to entice comparatists like pheromone draws bees, and it seems to have become an unassailable institutional fact of life in comparative law that one feels able and entitled to hold forth on any heliocentric law whatsoever irrespective of competence or expertise. Consider Kischel's panorama of laws in his *Rechtsvergleichung*. I can only surmise that this largely superfluous accumulation of information is allowed to fill roughly two-thirds of the book in compliance with the orthodox, if profoundly disturbing, expectation within comparative law that a comparatist must effectively act as a summulist: see Kischel (n 16) 243–944. cf G Tusseau, *Contentieux constitutionnel comparé* (LGDJ 2021), where the back cover proudly indicates how, '[f]rom Afghanistan to Zimbabwe' ('*[d]e l'Afghanistan au Zimbabwe*'), the book addresses 'nearly 200 systems' ('*près de 200 systèmes*'). (That one should be at intellectual ease with such an announcement is a wonder to behold.) It beggars belief that comparative law didactics repeatedly generates the hubristic compulsion to produce such planetary surveys – which, like any purported *totum simul*, are structurally fated to evoke innocence or arrogance and to provoke endless litanies of pernicious superficialities, not to mention evidently erratic pronouncements. Can one even begin to fathom an introduction to comparative literature featuring successive chapters on the literatures from Africa, Asia, Latin-America, and so forth? The very idea! (Suffice it to refer to D Damrosch, *Comparing the Literatures* [Princeton University Press 2020].) And what of the matter of authority? If I am going to read, say, a German jurist expounding on African or Latin-American laws, I properly expect him to address me on the basis of close experience of the subject-matter at hand. With particular reference to treatise or textbook writing, I find it difficult to imagine any other way in which an argument can claim a credentialed status.

Seasoned researchers into foreign law will be cognizant of some of the most preposterous claims having afflicted comparative scholarship on account of their formulation in Konrad Zweigert and Hein Kötz's *Einführung in die Rechtsvergleichung*, alternatively (and better) known as *Introduction to Comparative Law* – which even the lamented Tony Weir's elegant translation from the German has not managed to emancipate from an epistemic concludency as shallow as it is unconvincing.[30] Now, '[w]hatever one makes of it, one must begin by hearing the canon'.[31] If one writes as a comparatist-at-law – not therefore as an individual simply seeking to assuage his cognitive inquisitiveness, but as a jurist attaching normative value to foreign law (again, the claim is evidently not that foreign law matters because it would be binding beyond its local circumstances, but that it is valuable since it can act as persuasive authority in other settings than its own) – the canon, for instance, the book imposing a benchmark of judgement or authority, the writing attracting the largest credencive following, is uncontrovertibly Zweigert and Kötz's text. While the delineation of one's situation is not always easily achieved – in fact, Jacques Derrida observes that it can be expected to induce 'vertigo'[32] – the field of comparative law makes the identification of the locus of textual governance, epistemic authority, and scholarly subjugation remarkably easy on account of the fact that it has not changed in any meaningful way since the 1970s.

When I somewhat timidly entered comparative law in the 1980s as an ill-equipped Oxford postgraduate student, the pre-constituted reigning discourse and theoretical framework, the epistemic governmentality in force, were therefore emphatically Zweigert and Kötz's – and comparatists were heeding their words. Forty years later, comparatists still pay allegiance to Zweigert and Kötz's model, an adhesion attesting to this theory's 'determining imprint', that is, to the fact that Zweigert and Kötz's contribution has modified key aspects of the prevailing discursivity and dominant structure of epistemic attitudes within the field of comparative law.[33] (Observe that an orthodoxy is a co-creation, no

[30] See K Zweigert and H Kötz, *Introduction to Comparative Law* (3rd edn, T Weir tr, Oxford University Press 1998).

[31] J Derrida, *Résistances* (Galilée 1996) 98. Note the close connection between the canon and the institution. Eg: GC Spivak, *Outside in the Teaching Machine* (Routledge 1993) 270: 'Canons secure institutions as institutions secure canons.'

[32] J Derrida (with C Malabou), *La Contre-allée* (La Quinzaine littéraire 1999) 147.

[33] For an important observation emphasizing Zweigert and Kötz's enduring influence, see G Frankenberg, '"Rechtsvergleichung" – A New Gold Standard?' (2016) 76 Zeitschrift für ausländisches öffentliches Recht und Völkerrecht 1001, 1002. Even canonical works tend to undergo discursive revisions, qualifications, subtractions, or accretions, that is, ameliorations.

matter how asymmetrical: the disciples and their incessant acts of faith, their veneration, also shape the doxa inasmuch as their credenciveness moulds the conditions of felicity allowing a certain discourse to reign orthodoxically.[34]) Rather than fall into the trap of adulation, as an Italian colleague once expressly invited me to do (it was in Capri, in June 1999), I firmly believe that every generation of comparatists has to take hold of the intellectual capital that its predecessors have accumulated and critically re-invest it to productive epistemic ends – that is, in a way that will allow the field to generate stronger interpretive yields. Such, then, is how I envisage my situation within the call-and-response structure that I see canonical work to be heralding. And the monumental knowledge I have been facing, this disciplinary inheritance, is clearly Zweigert and Kötz's textbook. This, then, is where I must start.[35] One must *play it as it lays*.[36]

However, Zweigert and Kötz have remained fervently dedicated to the static iteration of their central doctrines over many decades. Elsewhere, I have had occasion to trace *verbatim* all of these authors' major theoretical statements – I count two dozens of them or so – from the third (German 1996; English 1998) to the second (German 1985; English 1987) to the first (German 1969; English 1977) edition of their leading book (see Zweigert and Kötz [n 9 and n 30]). For more specific information on this tracing exercise, see P Legrand, 'Paradoxically, Derrida: For a Comparative Legal Studies' (2005) 27 Cardozo LR 631, 642–43. The expression I quote in the body text is from EW Said, *Orientalism* (Vintage 1994 [1978]) 23. Within the orthodoxy, one can ascertain central and perimetric discursive spheres. For example, when Basil Markesinis enjoins the comparatist to apply himself to 'how similar [laws] can be made to look with the help of some skilful (and well-meaning) *manipulation*', such contemnible discourse, although falling firmly within the bounds of the orthodoxy, is nonetheless demarcating itself in its open willingness to favour dishonesty: BS Markesinis, 'Why a Code Is Not the Best Way to Advance the Cause of European Legal Unity' (1997) 5 Euro R Private L 519, 520 [my emphasis]. I find it very hard to fathom how even charitable interpretation can salvage this exhortation.

34 On the subject-matter of discipleship, I appreciate that there are new-generation comparatists who are unfamiliar with Zweigert and Kötz's text and do not feel that it interpellates them. And I accept further that there are comparative law practices unfolding without any conscious connection with the strategies Zweigert and Kötz have been promoting. As one assesses the limits of Zweigert and Kötz's epistemic reach, one would have to consider the fact, however, that influence can manifest itself through a process of tacit validation – or is it that there exists an epistemic disciplinary unconscious? I am struck, for instance, to see that Vicki Jackson feels able to write how '[f]unctional comparison is appealing and seductive' without entering any reference to Zweigert and Kötz's work (despite extensive endnotes running to nearly 200 pages): VC Jackson, *Constitutional Engagement in a Transnational Era* (Oxford University Press 2010) 182 and passim.

35 cf J Derrida, *De la grammatologie* (Editions de Minuit 1967) 233: 'We must begin *somewhere where we are*', '*[s]omewhere where we are*: within a text already where we believe that we are.' See also S Fish, *Is There a Text in This Class?* (Harvard University Press 1980) 350: '[T]he space in which a critic works has been marked out for him by his predecessors.'

36 I have in mind J Didion, *Play It as It Lays* (Farrar, Straus & Giroux 1970).

*

Consider some of the controlling ideas that Zweigert and Kötz, who between them directed Hamburg's Max-Planck comparative law institute from 1963 to 2000, initially assembled in the first German edition of their book and have proceeded to repeat since 1969.[37] According to Zweigert and Kötz, then, '[comparatists] must cut themselves loose from their own doctrinal and juridical preconceptions and liberate themselves from their own cultural context in order to discover "neutral" concepts with which to describe ... problems'.[38] Their 'eradicat[ion]' enterprise needs to engender 'pure and disinterested' research into foreign law and requires the formulation of reports that will be 'objective, that is, free from any critical evaluation'.[39] In effect, since for Zweigert and Kötz comparatists cannot but aspire to 'scientific exactitude and objectivity',[40] comparative law has to operate like 'physics', 'microbiology', or 'geology'.[41] To be sure, in order for comparative research to make itself into a '*science pure*',[42] thus into an 'international legal science' or 'universal legal science',[43] it must focus exclusively on those aspects of the law deemed (by Zweigert and Kötz themselves) to be 'relatively "unpolitical"' and therefore 'leave aside the topics which are heavily impressed by moral views or values'.[44] This delineation prompts the co-authors to posit a '*præsumptio similitudinis*' to the effect that 'the legal problems of all countries are the same',[45] to declare that laws are common 'even as to detail',[46] and to proclaim the existence of 'a unitary sense of justice'.[47] Zweigert and Kötz add that 'if one poses one's questions properly ... and if one investigates a legal system in its entirety, ... differences are really immaterial'.[48] They

[37] By way of modest homage to the late Tony Weir and in fond appreciation of the numerous congenial and intellectually rewarding moments I was privileged to spend in his witty company in Cambridge over many years, I purposefully quote from his English translation throughout the passage that follows in the body text. Elsewhere in *NCL*, I generally refer to the German source-text and supply my own English version.

[38] Zweigert and Kötz (n 30) 10.

[39] ibid 35, 34, and 43.

[40] ibid 45.

[41] ibid 15.

[42] ibid 6.

[43] ibid 45 and 46.

[44] ibid 40.

[45] ibid 40 and 46.

[46] ibid 39.

[47] ibid 3.

[48] ibid 62. For these claims' published antecedents, see eg K Zweigert, 'Die "praesumptio similitudinis" als Grundsatzvermutung rechtsvergleichender Methode' in M Rotondi (ed), *Inchieste di diritto comparato*, vol 2 (Cedam 1973) 735–58; K Zweigert, 'Des

further endorse a return to 'the era of natural law'.[49] Consistently, they maintain 'the ultimate goal of discovering the truth'[50] – that is, of ascertaining the correct, the right, the 'better' law[51] – comparative law thus being cast as an *'école de vérité'* (*en français dans le texte*).[52] Ultimately, comparative law wants to 'promote international trade and advance the general standard of living'.[53] Methodologically speaking, the achievement of these goals demands that 'the solutions [that comparatists] find in the different jurisdictions must be cut loose from their conceptual context and stripped of their national doctrinal overtones'.[54]

It is very strange that this farrago of unsubstantiated peremptories – this epistemic mush – should have achieved a position of dominance in comparative legal thought. Moreover, it has aptly been remarked how '[i]t is odd that it took so long for anyone to object to th[is] … vision'.[55] Yet, a critique chastising the deficit of threadbare Hanseatic

solutions identiques par des voies différentes' (1966) Revue internationale de droit comparé 5.

49 Zweigert and Kötz (n 30) 45. cf RA Posner, 'A Political Court' (2005) 119 Harvard LR 32, 86: 'To cite foreign decisions or precedents is indeed to flirt with the idea of universal natural law.' What Richard Posner overlooks is that the equation between comparative law and natural law is not in the least necessary. Not only is comparatism compatible with different outcomes, but the comparison of laws sophisticatedly understood assumes difference across laws. Eg: S Fredman, 'Foreign Fads or Fashions: The Role of Comparativism in Human Rights Law' (2015) 64 Int'l & Comp LQ 631.

50 Zweigert and Kötz (n 30) 3.

51 ibid 8.

52 ibid 15. Conforming to the German formulation (see Zweigert and Kötz [n 9] 14), this expression is not italicized in the English translation.

53 ibid 3–4.

54 ibid 44. See also infra 60.

55 R Hyland, *Gifts* (Oxford University Press 2009) 63. To my astonishment, Zweigert and Kötz's text has been hailed as '[c]risp, specific, complete, and reliable', and it has been commended for its 'rich and focused material': BS Markesinis, 'A Matter of Style' (1994) 110 LQR 607, 607. Perhaps the commentator has in mind such spectacular ethnocentric or juricentric projection as this pronouncement: 'The basic unity of legal science in the Anglo-American world still exists': Zweigert and Kötz (n 30) 14. cf P Stein, 'The Tasks of Historical Jurisprudence' in N MacCormick and P Birks (eds), *The Legal Mind* (Oxford University Press 1986) 293: 'In Britain and in the English-speaking world generally law is not treated as a science.' For a well-known concurring observation, see JH Merryman, *The Civil Law Tradition* (2nd edn, Stanford University Press 1985) 66: 'Legal science is a creation of the professors – it smells of the lamp – and our judge-dominated [common] law is fundamentally inhospitable to it.' This edition was the last to appear under Merryman's signature. The view that the common law is *Unwissenschaftlichkeit* boasts a long history. Eg: OW Holmes, 'Codes, and the Arrangement of the Law' (1931) 44 Harvard LR 725, 728: 'Law is not a science, but is essentially empirical.' This article first appeared in 1870.

knowledge-claims began to emerge in the 1980s. In a pioneering and justifiably opinionated essay, Günter Frankenberg offered a detailed – and, to my mind, wholly convincing – rebuttal of Zweigert and Kötz's unexamined epistemological postulates.[56] Frankenberg thus observed that 'the fictitious neutrality stabilizes the influence and authority of the comparatist's own perspective, and nurtures the good conscience with which comparatists deploy their self-imposed dichotomies, distinctions and systematizations'.[57] And he argued how '[i]nstead of pretending to the posture of a neutral, objective, and disinterested observer, the comparatist has to regard herself as being involved: involved in an ongoing, particular social practice constituted and pervaded by law; involved in a given legal tradition (a peculiar story of law); and involved in a specific mode of thinking and talking about law'.[58] For Frankenberg, 'critical comparisons require a greater sensitivity to the relationship between the self and the other .... Instead of continuing the endless search for a neutral stance and objective status, comparatists have to recognize that they are participant observers, therefore their studies have to be self-reflective and self-critical.'[59]

I confess that I find it ever more interesting that Frankenberg's sharp indictment, although it appeared in the United States, should have been produced under the counter-signature of a jurist originating from the land of *Rechtswissenschaft*, of seemingly relentless legal conceptualism and systematization, of apparently incessant categorical thinking, the country where one appreciates being told that one is a good dogmatician, the mysophobic abode of '*der Jurist als solcher*' (or is it '*der Universaljurist*'?).[60] Indeed, on account of his outstanding decimation of the received theory and practice of comparative law, Frankenberg has long been a notable participant in my intellectual life. Like some other comparatists who entered comparative law in the 1980s or 1990s – a socio-intellectual arena where jurists commit to the intellectual

[56] G Frankenberg, 'Critical Comparisons: Re-thinking Comparative Law' (1985) 26 Harvard Int'l LJ 411.

[57] ibid 425.

[58] ibid 443.

[59] ibid 441.

[60] The first German expression I report in the body text is in B Windscheid, 'Die Aufgaben der Rechtswissenschaft' in *Gesammelte Reden und Abhandlungen* (Duncker & Humblot 1904 [1884]) 111. The 'jurist-as-such' ensures that the study of law will not be defiled by 'ethical, political, [or] economic considerations': ibid 112. Bernhard Windscheid was a professor of law who made an exceptional contribution to the drafting of the 1896 German civil code and continues to be ascribed institutional eminence in Germany.

deterritorialization of the legal and claim the normative relevance of foreign law locally, for example, in the formulation of statutory choices, judicial opinions, or academic views – I was drawn to fashion a critical sensitivity in response to the field's stifling epistemological orthodoxy. In particular, I felt very uneasy about my scholarly existence being constituted according to the dominating positivism – the narrow, rigid, and frankly soul-crushing ideology that, scanting interpretive opportunities, was obsessed with the technical carapace of the law to the exclusion of the legal's cultural significance. The infinite patience required to learn so unproductive a mindset as positivism simply did not make sense to me. Basically taking the view that '[t]he law is only a matter of what legal institutions ... have decided in the past', established comparatists assumed that 'questions of law c[ould] always be answered by looking in the books where the records of institutional decisions are kept'.[61] I was unwilling to accept what was a principally mimeographic approach to the legal promoting an ivory-tower conceptual unity and coherence that sought to hide the cultural fact of dispersal and disjunction across laws.[62] And I could not countenance how prominent comparatists, unwilling to enhance their viewing of foreign law and even less prepared to enhance their viewing of themselves viewing foreign law, blatantly ignored the constraints associated with knowledge-making and operated as if these limits were inexistent (either out of distressing naiveté or deplorable dishonesty). I was struck by the fact that positivism's disingenuousness extended to an aversion on its part to recognize that far from escaping culturalism's reach, it was unfolding as a thoroughly encultured perspective on the law rather than as anything like 'the law' (indeed, Zweigert and Kötz's positivism – in effect a hyperpositivism, that is, a positivism having sought to make itself more compelling

[61] R Dworkin, *Law's Empire* (Harvard University Press 1986) 7.

[62] The subordination of the comparative endeavour to the logic of equivalence or commonality is deeply embedded and manifests itself even in situations where institutional trajectories or affiliations and scholarly themes combine to generate an expectation of particular sensitivity. Eg: H Murav, 'Justice as Translation', in A Sarat, M Anderson, and CO Frank (eds), *Law and the Humanities* (Cambridge University Press 2010) 399: '[I]n the era of globalization, ... the differences between cultures pale before the overwhelming similarities produced by the mobility of labor and capital and global insecurity.' See also S Seppänen, 'After Difference: A Meta-Comparative Study of Chinese Encounters with Foreign Comparative Law' (2020) 68 Am J Comp L 186. For Samuli Seppänen, the construction of an equivalence or commonality irrespective of the differend that is effectively the case across laws would be redeemable by reference to the ideological project being pursued. I assume Markesinis would concur: see Markesinis (n 33).

through internationalization – is emphatically a culturalism, if an uninvestigated one).[63]

Frankenberg's article proved crucial to me inasmuch as it offered that most magnetic of epistemic, ethical, and political space: a *possibility*.[64] Inscribing itself in the very long shadow of the field's orthodoxy, Frankenberg's text demonstrated that another brand of comparative law was conceivable, a comparatism that, most significantly, could build on defensible epistemological premisses and allow for a meaningful interpretive yield, for an improved and valorized understanding of foreign law – the law of the other – and ultimately for greater justice being visited on the other. Also, Frankenberg's critique supplied important epistemological equipment for an enhanced appreciation of the interpretive dynamics governing local law, the law of the self. In the years that followed its publication, even when orthodox comparative law was busily financing its shrivelled way into the law lists of major university presses or filling the pages of law journals with an unceasing output of 'black-letter' recrement, even when it was massively subsidizing research initiatives or large conferences to promote its ideologically cloistered view of law and world, to foster its cryptonormativity (for it much preferred a commitment to silent rather than explicitly articulated values), even when orthodox comparative law, then, appeared to be commandeering almost the entire stage – although without ever being able to overcome the persistent failure of institutional tenability that reinforced local distrust towards references to the laws of other countries – comparatists yearning for sophisticated comparative law and hoping for heightened intellectual standing could turn to Frankenberg's article. (On the matter of silence, observe that whether doctrinal or political, positivism's choices are deliberately invisibilized as positivists claim to embody the voice of obviousness and as outcomes are presented in the rational language and assured tone of technical self-evidence rather than as the distributive elections they effectively are, such distributive elections being, in fact, endemic to any formulation of the legal.[65])

63 A key leitmotiv informing Zweigert and Kötz's argument is that law cannot claim to be genuinely scientific as long as it remains mired in nationalism. Eg: Zweigert and Kötz, supra 60.

64 I recall a comment to the effect that '[h]igher than actuality stands *possibility*': M Heidegger, *Sein und Zeit* (Niemeyer 2006 [1927]) 38.

65 For a critique of comparatists-as-positivists' determination to shelter their politics, see D Kennedy, 'The Politics and the Methods' in P Legrand and R Munday (eds), *Comparative Legal Studies: Traditions and Transitions* (Cambridge University Press 2003) 345–433.

Frankenberg's accomplished argument provided a reminder that hope for better epistemic days, for enriched interpretive times, could legitimately stay alive, that there might yet emerge a comparatism other-wise. Such heteronomic strategy would feature research into foreign law that would be at once different from what it had been and more attuned to the place of otherness-in-the-law, to the epistemological challenges and opportunities arising from the insistent presence of the other's law. Of course, to desire a new kind of thinking, to want to disclose a narrative space allowing for foreign law to be encountered with respect to its mode of existence (and with respect *for* its mode of existence) can be risky. To counter positivism as it seeks to assert its relation to the world by simultaneously propounding its estrangement from the world and to maintain instead that a separation of the legal from the world is an unsustainable separation of the legal from its effects, for it is only in the world that the law can have consequences, to defend such a stance, then, can be perilous, so fraught with danger in fact that the critical comparatist may at any moment be confined to one kind of muteness or another by any of the field's 'gatekeepers' (a stillness that, unless he is *irrepressible*, may in turn prompt the deepest part of him also to fall quiet).

I first encountered Frankenberg's work as an Oxford postgraduate student (although, I hasten to add, I then had no scope to apply his insights not only given the fact that I was coming to the very end of my dissertation, but because Oxford simply did not afford the critical environment that would have been needed for me to deploy Frankenberg's objection – a situation, incidentally, that still very much obtains, the condition of critique as regards comparative law at Oxford having, if anything, noticeably deteriorated since the late 1990s as *Rechtswissenschaft* has found itself repeatedly invited to achieve Oxonian inroads, arguably on account of a woefully siderosous local attitude). Since I began to publish my own critical work on comparative law in the 1995 edition of the *Modern Law Review*,[66] I have, in many

[66] Eg: P Legrand, 'Comparative Legal Studies and Commitment to Theory' (1995) 58 Modern LR 262. Later publications include P Legrand, 'On the Singularity of Law' (2006) 47 Harvard Int'l LJ 517; P Legrand, 'Siting Foreign Law: How Derrida Can Help' (2011) 21 Duke J Comp & Int'l L 595; P Legrand, 'Foreign Law: Understanding Understanding' (2011) 6(2) J Comp L 67 [hereinafter 'Understanding']; P Legrand, 'Law's Translation, Imperial Predilections and the Endurance of the Self' (2014) 20 The Translator 290; P Legrand, 'Foreign Law as Self-Fashioning' (2017) 12(2) J Comp L 6 [hereinafter 'Self-Fashioning']; P Legrand, 'Jameses at Play: A Tractation on the Comparison of Laws' (2017) 65 Am J Comp L [Special Issue] 1; P Legrand, 'What Is That, To Read Foreign Law?' (2019) 14(2) J Comp L 294. In parallel, in a minor key so to speak, I sought over many years to pursue a scholarly career in my

respects, consciously been treating Frankenberg's scholarship as exemplary. And the fact that our respective (and mostly respectful) critiques of comparative law's orthodoxy have been framed from different vantage points has not diminished my admiration for Frankenberg's contribution. Again, it has come to be especially meaningful for me, and for some of my colleagues, that Frankenberg's critical objection should have come from a *German* comparatist. After all, it is German comparatists (and their staunchly Germanophile friends) who, more than any others, have led comparative law's orthodoxy into the epistemic impasse that has long incapacitated it.[67] And it is German comparatists (and their staunchly Germanophile friends again) who, more than anyone else, continue to inform the field's orthodoxy. It therefore remains encouraging that one can see such a forceful epistemic critique as Frankenberg's emerging out of the very scholarly milieu that, above all others, has been structuring established comparative law so deficiently.

A few years after Frankenberg, and very much like him, Jonathan Hill noted that 'comparatists cannot avoid the fact that their perception of the merits and demerits of different legal systems will be based on a range of (often unarticulated) value-judgments'.[68] Hill proceeded to chastise Zweigert and Kötz's enterprise as 'stumbl[ing] upon the broader theoretical issues only by accident, and randomly'.[69] According to Hill, Zweigert and Kötz's endeavour is, in effect, 'atheoretical'.[70] Other illustrations of critical retorts include Susan Millns's. Remarking that Zweigert and Kötz's work 'does not engage with the contribution made by those comparatists who have sought to haul comparative legal studies into the twenty-first

native language. For representative publications in French, see P Legrand, *Pour la relevance des droits étrangers* (IRJ Sorbonne Editions 2014); P Legrand, *Le Droit comparé* (5th & final ed, Presses Universitaires de France 2015). Adde: P Legrand, *Como ler o direito estrangeiro* (DW Hachem tr, Editora Contracorrente 2018); P Legrand, *Direito Comparado: compreendendo a compreendê-lo* (R Spindola tr, Editora Contracorrente 2021). In fact, I can claim a further, early incarnation as a Canadian positivist. While this initial instantiation of my legal self lasted twelve years or so and is forever inscribed in the Supreme Court of Canada law reports, I do not care to recollect its publicized manifestations (even though not all were pitiably gullible).

67 For a good example of the dross I have in mind, see J Basedow, 'Comparative Law and Its Clients' (2014) 62 Am J Comp L 821, 853.

68 J Hill, 'Comparative Law, Law Reform and Legal Theory' (1989) 9 Oxford J Legal Stud 101, 106.

69 ibid 111.

70 ibid 112.

century',[71] Millns (properly) refers to the co-authors' 'deception' as they introduce a 'closed, black-letter presentation of comparative law'.[72] Meanwhile, George Fletcher and Simone Glanert have focussed on method.

Fletcher's 'target' is Zweigert and Kötz's only recommended method, their exclusive and exclusionary procedure seemingly demanding cult-like loyalty.[73] Calling for '[a] little sophistication about legal argument',[74] Fletcher sensitively warns against 'an extraordinary form of political naivete'.[75] Underlining that '[t]he nexus between language and legal culture is far stronger than we ordinarily assume in teaching and writing about comparative law',[76] Fletcher holds that '[l]egal cultures are embedded, more than we realize, in particular languages'.[77] Taking the view that '[l]anguage shapes cultural identity',[78] Fletcher foregrounds 'the close connection between language, on the one hand, and legal argument and legal theory, on the other'.[79] It follows that 'there are differences in detail that are so profound they call into question the extent of a shared foundation of legal thought'.[80] Even as Zweigert and Kötz remain completely silent on the questions of language and translatability, while giving pride of place to their concocted '*præsumptio similitudinis*' (arguably, to relegate laws to an assumed equivalence or commonality demands *wilfully* to ignore the language-singularity of thought specifically and the culture-singularity of thought generally), Fletcher insightfully defends 'an approach to comparative law that takes ... linguistic particularities as the starting point for an analysis of our divergent legal cultures'.[81]

71 S Millns, 'Book Review' (1999) 48 Int'l & Comp LQ 982, 982–83 (review of K Zweigert and H Kötz, *Introduction to Comparative Law* [3rd edn, T Weir tr, Oxford University Press 1998]).

72 ibid 983.

73 GP Fletcher, 'The Universal and the Particular in Legal Discourse' (1987) Brigham Young U LR 335, 335. For the exclusory methodological claim I mention, see Zweigert and Kötz (n 9) 33: 'The basic methodological principle of all comparative law is that of *functionality*'; 'The initial question of every comparative work must ... be posed purely functionally.'

74 Fletcher (n 73) 337.

75 ibid.

76 ibid 340.

77 ibid.

78 ibid 341.

79 ibid.

80 ibid 342.

81 ibid 350. When Markesinis salutes Zweigert and Kötz for having been 'quick to emphasise similarities of result even methodology', it is easy to retort that the problem is precisely that these comparatists have proceeded much *too* rapidly: Markesinis (n 55) 607.

Glanert shares with Fletcher not only a keen appreciation for the untranslatability of law and an understanding of the ensuing theoretical or practical implications,[82] but she concurs with his indictment of Zweigert and Kötz's methodological assumptions. As I read her, Glanert would agree with Boaventura de Sousa Santos that 'all knowledge created by humans, including scientific knowledge, is ultimately amethodical' in the sense at least that there is no heuristic process that is not politically overdetermined.[83] Otherwise said, '[e]verything we know is known by us; we can't eliminate ourselves from the picture. Defining methods, choosing which ones to use, deciding how to use them, understanding what they produce: each of these acts is fundamentally interpretive.'[84] If you will, the comparatist is therefore the measure of all things (with apologies to Protagoras) and also the measure of all the measures that comparative law has at its disposal. Contending that every method, by its very character, brings to bear a certain invasive disposition – in its striving for appropriation and order, it engages in a hostile take-over of facts – and observing that it unfolds as a single, unified, all-encompassing, exhaustive form, which as regards comparative law is precisely what is profoundly wrong with it, Glanert's critique thoughtfully (and bravely) contests the very premiss that comparative research must operate according to a method.[85] In her words, she aims 'to challenge the ideology of method prevailing in the field of comparative law, which, epistemologically speaking, cannot be sustained as it proves to be more of a severe epistemological obstacle than a fertile source of epistemological opportunities'.[86] In sum, Glanert wants 'to show that method cannot be approached strictly as a solution, but that it must also be envisaged as a problem'.[87]

Meanwhile, even such a discerning comparatist as Bernhard Großfeld appears to have fallen under the spell of the '*præsumptio similitudinis*'. See B Großfeld, *Kernfragen der Rechtsvergleichung* (Mohr Siebeck 1996) 283. The overarching theme is, of course, the comparatist-at-law's 'serious reduction of [his] cognitive possibilities', the way in which 'shallow forms of thought [have] become the organizational frame' within comparative law: Schlag (n 23) 143–44 and 144.

[82] Eg: S Glanert, *De la traductibilité du droit* (Dalloz 2011).

[83] Sousa Santos (n 18) 188.

[84] J Riskin, 'Just Use Your Thinking Pump!' *The New York Review of Books* (2 July 2020) 50.

[85] See S Glanert, 'Method?' in PG Monateri (ed), *Methods of Comparative Law* (Elgar 2012) 61–81.

[86] ibid 81.

[87] ibid.

Even as the governing textual system continued to withstand wholesale epistemological reconsideration, some other critics writing in the course of the 1990s and 2000s contributed a limited heterodoxization of the mainstream discourse within comparative law, although in most cases their influence has been limited to the occasional noise. These various contrapuntal arguments approached the orthodox discourse obliquely, questioning or nuancing it in some ways, at times inscribing a more significant contestation, while consolidating received doctrinal tenets in other respects.[88] Certainly, none of these expressions of mild occasional resistance to Zweigert and Kötz's disappointing epistemic enterprise has been prepared to express such forthrightness as Lawrence Rosen's rejoinder. Rosen, the eminent legal anthropologist, was reacting to the following passage (and, in particular, to the words I italicize): 'Convinced, *perhaps from living by the sea*, that life will controvert the best-laid plans, the Englishman is more at home with case-law proceeding cautiously step-by-step than with legislation that purports to lay down rules for the solution of all future cases.' Rosen's ironical retort shows how the emperor has, quite simply, no epistemic clothes: 'I had thought if comparative studies had demonstrated anything it was that the perverse attachment by the British to the common law was, in fact, due to a surfeit of marmite at a formative stage of youth, combined with the restricted blood flow to the brain that comes from wearing rubber wellies and fingerless gloves!'[89] *Touché.*

[88] For examples of the not inconsiderable array of disquisitions, some of them enchiridia, that stand, in my view, as so many variations on the orthodoxy, a few purporting to distend the net a little further, see M Adams and J Bomhoff (eds), *Practice and Theory in Comparative Law* (Cambridge University Press 2012); J Husa, *A New Introduction to Comparative Law* (Hart 2015); M Siems, *Comparative Law* (3rd edn, Cambridge University Press 2022); C Valcke, *Comparing Law* (Cambridge University Press 2018); B Fekete, *Paradigms in Modern European Comparative Law* (Hart 2021); SP Donlan and J Mair (eds), *Comparative Law* (Routledge 2019); M Bogdan, *Concise Introduction to Comparative Law* (Europa Law 2013). I sense that Geoffrey Samuel scores the best citation impact. Eg: G Samuel, *An Introduction to Comparative Law Theory and Method* (Hart 2014). The commitment to critique has ranged from the strikingly equivocal (eg: W Ewald, 'Comparative Jurisprudence [II]: The Logic of Legal Transplants' [1995] 43 Am J Comp L 489) to the more compelling (eg: 'Symposium: New Approaches to Comparative Law' [1997] Utah LR 255; GP Fletcher, 'Comparative Law as a Subversive Discipline' [1998] 46 Am J Comp L 683).

[89] L Rosen, 'Beyond Compare' in P Legrand and R Munday (eds), *Comparative Legal Studies: Traditions and Transitions* (Cambridge University Press 2003) 494. Rosen refers to the English version of Zweigert and Kötz (n 30) 70 [my emphasis]. I discuss the impact Rosen's statement had on me in G Samuel and P Legrand, 'A Conversation on Comparative Law' (2020) 15(2) J Comp L 371, 372–73. Reading Rosen, I am reminded

*

Noteworthily, there are comparatists who, as I read them, have applied a strategy of defiance vis-à-vis the orthodoxy without engaging in a fully fledged theoretical exercise. Such expositions have shown how the comparison of laws could beneficially be implemented well away from the '*præsumptio similitudinis*' and what not. In this regard, Teemu Ruskola's *Legal Orientalism* impresses me as exemplary.[90] (I hasten to add that I claim no expertise in Chinese law, and I focus on the 'how' rather than the 'what'.) In significant ways, Ruskola's abiding concern is epistemological: he is interested in 'the construction of China as an object of legal knowledge'.[91] This mindset prompts him to valorize difference. It is not that there is no law in China – '[o]nly the most negligent observer could miss the fact that imperial China boasted dynastic legal codes going back to the Tang dynasty (618–907 CE)'[92] – but that there is no 'law' as the concept is understood, say, in the United States, that is, in the sense of 'a liberal legal order that constrains the state in a particular way'.[93] As he accentuates the differend across laws, Ruskola is keen to avoid a simplistic hierarchization whereby he would be staging one law as the 'better' one of the two. Indeed, *Legal Orientalism* cogently refuses to be tricked into the kind of ethnocentric or juricentric move pursuant to which the enlightened, 'the US legal subject', would be systematically elevated by reference to the benighted, 'the Chinese nonlegal nonsubject',[94] so that 'the universal subjects of history' would be incessantly opposed to 'undifferentiated ... masses ... , witless myrmidons living under the tyranny of history'.[95] Ruskola is justifiably emphatic: '[T]here is no cross-cultural standard that would help us arrive at a universal definition of law.'[96] Accordingly, *Legal Orientalism* 'seek[s] to universalize neither China nor the United States'.[97] *Given* (I use the word advisedly) the intransigence of difference across local legal

of HP Glenn, *Legal Traditions of the World* (5th edn, Oxford University Press 2014) 141–42: 'There was resistance [to the *ius commune*] ... in Scandinavia, the enlightenment idea losing some of its allure on entering "the cooler climate of the North"' [my emphasis].

90 T Ruskola, *Legal Orientalism* (Harvard University Press 2013).

91 ibid 10.

92 ibid 12.

93 ibid.

94 ibid 23.

95 ibid.

96 ibid 59.

97 ibid.

knowledges, any notion of 'universal law' is a major contradiction in terms. In other words, 'common humanity is a trap since it defines divergence as secondary'.[98]

One of *Legal Orientalism*'s most significant lessons is therefore that law primordially exists as culture and requires to be studied as culture. For example, Ruskola writes that '[l]aw only exists in concrete historical and political conjunctures and cannot be evaluated apart from them'.[99] And he adds that 'even the seemingly most natural legal categories are ultimately cultural artifacts'.[100] Still on the topic of culture, *Legal Orientalism* warns against the inclination to assume stasis or autarky. For instance, Ruskola insists on how 'it is a singular historical fact that no state has ever produced as much organizational, procedural, and substantive law as quickly as China has since 1978'.[101] Also, he observes that 'China's uniqueness cannot but be circumscribed by its profound linkages with other localities and other histories'.[102] Ruskola's insightful understanding of law-as-culture spontaneously leads him to illustrate to excellent effect how a serious comparative legal study must construct itself as an indisciplined investigation. Specifically, *Legal Orientalism*'s geo-political argument addresses at the minimum American studies, Chinese studies, comparative law, international law, glocalization, and post-colonial studies – although Ruskola reminds his readership that China was never colonized.[103]

Throughout, *Legal Orientalism* reveals the importance of promoting 'an antifoundationalist model of comparison',[104] that is, of acknowledging the impossibility of anything like a neutral or veridictive account of otherness. Crucially, Ruskola contends that '[t]here are only different ways of reading China, some surely more rewarding than others, but none "right" to the exclusion of all others'.[105] A further insight is for *Legal Orientalism* to foster the preservation of negativity as a 'resource'.[106] In fact, major chapters entitled 'Canton Is Not Boston' and 'The District of China Is Not the District of Columbia' implement this commitment to

98 I Stengers, 'Comparison as a Matter of Concern' (2011) 17 Common Knowledge 48, 62–63.
99 Ruskola (n 90) 21.
100 ibid 59.
101 ibid.
102 ibid 256.
103 See ibid 198–235.
104 ibid 25.
105 ibid 50.
106 J Derrida, *L'Ecriture et la différence* (Editions du Seuil 1967) 381 [emphasis omitted].

excellent effect.[107] Ruskola thus warns comparatists how '[t]he danger is in the neatness of identifications',[108] effectively urging them to avoid the contrivance of bogus equivalences or commonalities. Significantly, too, *Legal Orientalism* stands *for* the other – arguably one of the book's most hortative virtues. Now, the adoption of this ethical attitude means more than salvaging otherness from weirdness. In his determination to convey his conviction that one can *learn* from the other-in-the-law, Ruskola refers to the fact that China experienced economic growth 'unrivaled by any economy on the planet' over three decades.[109] And he notes that China long performed without a law of property – which, in effect, did not appear on the local legal scene until 2007.[110] Still on the subject of learning from the other, Ruskola boldly asks: 'Why couldn't the study of China generate *primary* knowledge – theory itself – rather than merely secondary data to confirm or disprove theories developed elsewhere?'[111]

With *Legal Orientalism*, Ruskola offers his readership a deeply personal text. I find that this work is profoundly informed by its author's intellectual trajectory, notably by experience of increasing attunement to Chinese culture over time, but also by greater (critical) implication in US culture as Ruskola has found himself spending more and more years living and working away from his native Europe. An apposite illustration of the way in which the comparatist comes to his intervention as an encultured being, Ruskola's book is intensely autobiographical, not least as it proves itself *hospitable* to the Chinese other-in-the-law and willing to *provincialize* the US self-in-the-law.[112] Not for Ruskola, then, the kind of Cartesian intellectual terrorism that would disqualify one's culture as a vector for the channelling of one's attunement to the

107 See Ruskola (n 90) 108–51 and 152–97.

108 S Beckett, 'Dante. . . Bruno. Vico.. Joyce' in *Disjecta* (R Cohn ed, Grove 1984 [1929]) 19.

109 Ruskola (n 90) 220.

110 See ibid 219–20.

111 ibid 221. cf AR Mufti, 'Global Comparativism' (2005) 31 Critical Inquiry 472, 486: '"[T]hey" have literatures and other modes of cultural expression that are worthy of consideration, but only "we" have theory, the inclination to think in abstract and conceptual terms about language, culture, and the world and about the conditions of possibility of such knowledge itself.'

112 cf R Radhakrishnan, 'Why Compare?' in R Felski and SS Friedman (eds), *Comparison* (Johns Hopkins University Press 2013) 25: '[N]o direct access to the other is possible; but what is indeed eminently possible is rigorous autocritique and autodefamiliarization in coeval response to the presence of the other.'

world.[113] Ruskola is not in front of his text, but in the midst of it – he is of it, and it is of him.[114] But Ruskola's preoccupation for authenticity and scholarly integrity also reveals itself as he draws extensively on Chinese texts with a view to letting the other speak in otherness's singular voice – to allow the other to enter the comparison, to make an appearance in the fabric of the comparative text, to assert visibility within it, to *compear*. For example, the discussion on the current state of legal theory in China features extensive excerpts from Chinese works.[115] In sum, if '[t]here is the good comparison that acknowledges the other, and the bad comparison that seeks to outdo and undo him',[116] I know precisely where to locate *Legal Orientalism*.

*

It remains that neither Hill, Millns, Fletcher, Glanert, nor the other comparatists I address have elected to produce a primordial and comprehensive theoretical attack on the established set of epistemological assumptions governing the field of comparative law with a view to generating *a new regime of comparability*.[117] While diversely notable, the variously concurring or dissenting stances I indicate qualify as so many theoretical 'false exits', to borrow once more Derrida's distinctly useful expression.[118] In sum, 'mainstream views of comparative law . . . continue to dominate the vast majority of all work done in the field'.[119]

113 See Descartes, *Discours de la méthode* in *Œuvres philosophiques*, vol 1 (F Alquié ed, Garnier 1997 [1637]) II, 583–84. Descartes is adamant: he cannot accept that there would exist nothing more epistemologically trustworthy than the power of one's enculturation, that one's understanding of one's world would fall prey to the fact that one has been raised with 'the French', 'the Germans', 'the Chinese', or 'the Cannibals'. Famously, Descartes maintains that the remedy to the cognitive predicament whereby 'it is much more custom and example that persuade us than any certain knowledge' would lie in the use of method: ibid 584.

114 This claim must concern every comparative law text – not least Zweigert and Kötz's oh-so-discernibly-German book even as these comparatists appear to proclaim Kant's 1787 Baconian mantra, '*De nobis ipsis silemus*' ('About ourselves we are silent'). In Beckett's characteristically apt words, though, 'it is always oneself that one chooses': Letter from S Beckett to M Arnaud in *The Letters of Samuel Beckett*, vol 1 (MD Fehsenfeld and LM Overbeck eds, Cambridge University Press 2009 [10 June 1940]) 684.

115 See Ruskola (n 90) 222–29.

116 H Saussy, 'Axes of Comparison' in R Felski and SS Friedman (eds), *Comparison* (Johns Hopkins University Press 2013) 70.

117 I return to Frankenberg presently.

118 Supra 55.

119 U Kischel, 'Critical Legal Studies, Postmodernism, and the Contextual Method in Comparative Law – A Reply to Günter Frankenberg' (2016) 76 Zeitschrift für ausländisches öffentliches Recht und Völkerrecht 1009, 1010.

It is nothing short of amazing that comparative law's orthodoxy has been able to govern for so long unencumbered by any epistemic challenge whose monographic exposition would have decidedly assumed competing eminence.[120] The release of an English translation of Uwe Kischel's *Rechtsvergleichung* evinces how this peculiar state of affairs is set to continue.[121] Indeed, it is metastasizing. In the meantime, although it is probably excessive to talk of a pariah discipline, the field continues to languish on the periphery of the law-school curriculum even as the issues that comparative legal scholarship addresses, ranging from the reconciliation of a normative role for foreign law with the idea of constitutional sovereignty to the communicational dynamics between legal selfhood and legal otherness to the tensions surrounding the operationalization of concepts such as representation or agency, could hardly prove more epistemologically (and politically) momentous.

*

I hold that Günter Frankenberg's *Comparative Law as Critique*, in compelling respects an account at once capital and extensive, comes closest to a comprehensive interruption of the long-standing deployment of comparative law's mainstream theoretical imposture.[122] Frankenberg's refutation is thus well worth iterating, and the report that follows wishes loyally to apply itself to this important re-presentative task, not least by affording the author much latitude to express himself in his own voice. Although, in my view, a close examination of Frankenberg's text must show that it still fails to escape the dominant thought-system's epistemological orbit, it deserves consideration as being the most sophisticated extant attempt to think comparison-at-law differently, to provide it with the ecdysis it so badly requires.[123]

120 At this writing, the latest recalcitrance hails from S Glanert, A Mercescu, and G Samuel, *Rethinking Comparative Law* (Elgar 2021).

121 See U Kischel, *Comparative Law* (A Hammel tr, Oxford University Press 2019). While Kischel's text offers by far the most thoroughgoing theoretical exposition to have appeared since Zweigert and Kötz's book, it unstintingly defends the received approach to comparative law as emerges clearly from the following exchange: Frankenberg (n 33); Kischel (n 119). In his own words, Kischel contends that 'the basic line of thought' informing Zweigert and Kötz's theoretical model deserves to be approved in 'unreserved' fashion: Kischel (n 16) 187. I formulate a detailed critique of Kischel's argument in P Legrand, 'Kischel's Comparative Law: *Fortschritt ohne Fortschritt*' (2020) 15(2) J Comp L 292, where I also list an array of Kischel's tributes to Zweigert and Kötz ransacking the lexicon of admiration. See ibid 309.

122 See G Frankenberg, *Comparative Law as Critique* (Elgar 2016).

123 For an extensive review reaching this conclusion (and yet avoiding the trap of the favourable notice churning platitudinous reviewerese), see S Glanert and P Legrand,

Frankenberg's disquisition begins with a detailed theoretical statement which, by the author's own admission, adopts the form neither of a 'treatise' nor of a 'textbook' on comparative law, not even of a 'comprehensive introduction' to the subject-matter.[124] Frankenberg also contributes a meticulous application of his manifesto through a chapter on religious attire, while adding two essays on human rights and access to justice – '[all] experiment[s] in how [critique] can be done',[125] critique involving 'non-scientistic theorizing; non-traditional theory; oppositional spirit; and, if possible, transformative vision',[126] that is, 'mean[ing] more than the random and vague expression of doubt, dissent or discontent'.[127] Although the book does not expressly fashion its argument around a ternary structure, the epistemological claim it advances – its strategy to 'creat[e] an anarchic moment in knowledge production by disrupting the established routines and, in particular, what is considered "good comparative practice"' or '"good disciplinary practice"'[128] – discernibly features three recurring counterpoints.

First, Frankenberg castigates comparative law's 'Anglo-Eurocentrism' and maintains the correlative need to 'provincialize Western law'.[129] Even as one may express surprise that comparatists should stand accused of falling prey to unwarrantable ethnocentrism or juricentrism, to a self-centredness going beyond what arguably inevitably burdens one, it bears recalling Derrida's warning to the effect that '[o]ne will apparently be avoiding ethnocentrism at the very moment when it will have already operated in depth, silently imposing its ongoing concepts of speech and of writing'.[130]

Secondly, the author censures law's comparatists for hiding 'the relations between knowledge and power'.[131] Specifically, Frankenberg attacks what he styles comparative law's 'posture of innocence' and its obsession with 'cognitive control'.[132] He thus decries comparatists for 'comfortably

'Law, Comparatism, Epistemic Governance: There Is Critique and Critique' (2017) 18 German LJ 701. As I draw on this essay, I am in Simone Glanert's debt for graciously extending me her permission to do so.

124 Frankenberg (n 122) x.
125 ibid 22.
126 ibid 31.
127 ibid.
128 ibid 33 and 17.
129 ibid x.
130 Derrida (n 35) 178.
131 Frankenberg (n 122) 41.
132 ibid ix and 13.

accept[ing] the traditional object-subject conception of comparison',[133] for pursuing 'what they believ[e] to be an "objective" access to the reality of foreign law',[134] for being 'bent on determining what the law *is* in another country, *the law* as contained in statutes and court decisions and accompanied by scholarly commentary',[135] therefore excluding 'all extralegal incursions – notably politics, ethics, culture and the economy – on law-making and law-deciding'.[136] Frankenberg rejects this '[b]oundary-work' and the ensuing 'reduc[tion] [of comparative law] to a mere technicality',[137] not unlike engineering,[138] holding that 'a discipline defined by its techniques is almost invariably complemented by tales of its *scientific* nature'[139] – as is the case with comparative law, historically marked by the 'ambition to promote [itself] to a science'.[140] Moreover, Frankenberg contradicts the comparatists' 'similarity disposition', and he castigates 'the moral deficit that comes with the routine management of similarities'.[141] In this regard, directing his attention to comparative law's typical 'unitary projects',[142] he percipiently notes that 'the universal does not exist independently from the particular perspective from which it is seen'.[143] In sum, Frankenberg reproves comparative law's 'logocentric, positivist . . . course',[144] its understanding of 'the legal vocabulary and grammar as an autonomous body of rules and decisions, arguments and doctrines',[145] as a 'narrow cognitive operation' marred by an 'astonishing aloofness from methodological and epistemological battles'.[146]

133 ibid 6.
134 ibid.
135 ibid 15.
136 ibid 6.
137 ibid 8 and 40.
138 See ibid 40.
139 ibid 38. Meanwhile, '[t]here are no transhistorical and transcultural criteria to define science and to distinguish it unambiguously from other, nonscientific kinds of knowledge': Sousa Santos (n 18) 47. Indeed, 'it doesn't seem possible to stipulate a set of characteristics defining, unequivocally and consensually, a particular item of knowledge as scientific': ibid 45. For one thing, there is 'behind the rigor of scientific inquiries, the silenced presence of the "lifeworld"': WD Mignolo, *The Politics of Decolonial Investigations* (Duke University Press 2021) 458.
140 Frankenberg (n 122) 46.
141 ibid ix and 88.
142 ibid 44.
143 ibid 98.
144 ibid 14.
145 ibid 5.
146 ibid 37 and 78.

Thirdly, Frankenberg, determined to move beyond comparative law's 'unbearable formalism, barrenness and mechanistic style',[147] attends to 'the ethical and political implications of locating, studying and comparing the foreign'.[148] He thus propounds a strategy 'for recognizing the other – foreign legal systems, cultures, institutions – in its own right',[149] which he articulates around 'the twin operations of *distancing* and *differencing*',[150] each motion an occurrence of performativity,[151] of constructivism also.[152] For Frankenberg, '*distancing/differencing* calls on the comparatist to decenter her worldview and to consciously establish subjectivity and context in the comparative space, that is, to take into account the observer's perspective'.[153] In other terms, 'comparatists operate and observe within the boundaries of a *particular* context and interpret what they see within a *particular* matrix provided by a specific cultural context that constitutes law and is also constituted by law'.[154] According to Frankenberg, '[b]oth operations encompass the willingness and capability to cope with preconceptions and stereotypes, biases and rationalist assumptions that fall within the analytical framework and normative matrix of one's own (legal) education and experience'.[155]

As he proceeds to enunciate his theoretical engagement, Frankenberg entwines his claims with a panorama of the discourses having successively dominated the field's epistemological scene over the years. Specifically, he identifies four principal (and overlapping) phases, which he names 'universalism'[156] – the 1900 Paris conference, the quest for a *droit commun législatif*, and the configuration of law as a *science universelle*, these uniformizing pursuits having been driven by 'a rhetoric of truth and objectivity';[157] 'taxonomy' – the age of legal systems (or families);[158] 'functionalism'[159] – 'the categorical imperative of comparative reason',[160] effectively 'an analytical device introduced ... [for]

147 ibid 288.
148 ibid 41.
149 ibid 6.
150 ibid 42.
151 See ibid ix and 111.
152 See ibid ix and x.
153 ibid 74.
154 ibid 72.
155 ibid 83.
156 See ibid 42–47.
157 ibid 45.
158 See ibid 47–52.
159 See ibid 52–59.
160 ibid 52.

the narrow purpose of comparative legal problem-solving',[161] but a practice 'not likely to either recognize or respect, let alone relish, significant differences' across laws;[162] and 'factualism'[163] – the self-indulgent, rambling, untheorized, and ultimately inconsequential 'common-core' initiative hailing from Trento in the 1990s and having developed under two tutelary deities, Rodolfo Sacco and Rudolf Schlesinger, the former committed to 'structuralist positivism',[164] the latter to comparison 'in terms of precise and narrow rules' that would 'carry the same meaning to lawyers brought up in various legal systems'.[165] Bringing together what he identifies as the four current epistemological strands within comparative law,[166] contributing his own distancing/differencing rejoinder, Frankenberg also produces a master grid where the diverse positions are correlated and contrasted through cursory inscriptions in the various quadrants.[167] (Interestingly, Frankenberg's diagram, perhaps heeding the theological quip that one begins to err as one begins to count, is silent on two insistent configurations of comparative legal knowledge, both revealing a peculiar understanding of the planet as 'flat' and both disclosing seemingly unalloyed faith in numbers: econometric or indicator-based research adopting the paradigm of 'standard rational conduct', on one hand, and 'empirical' surveys aiming to accumulate epigrams about the laws of fourteen, twenty-six, seventy-nine, one hundred and thirty-four, or... one hundred and eighty countries, on the other.[168])

Frankenberg's theoretical critique finds its most detailed exemplification by way of a study relative to religious attire, an inquiry featuring a reprise of the master grid with specific reference to the range of opinions on 'Muslim veiling'.[169] In particular, Frankenberg discusses the 2004 French statute that prohibits attire (the untranslatable French

161 ibid 54–55.
162 ibid 57.
163 See ibid 59–70 and 94–95.
164 ibid 63.
165 Schlesinger (n 14) 9. See also RB Schlesinger, 'The Common Core of Legal Systems: An Emerging Subject of Comparative Study' in KH Nadelmann et al (eds), *Twentieth Century Comparative and Conflicts Law: Legal Essays in Honor of Hessel E Yntema* (Sijthoff 1961) 78.
166 See Frankenberg (n 122) 85–112.
167 See ibid 84.
168 William Ewald refers to 'the "telephone-book approach" to comparative law' and notes how 'the animating spirit of comparative law has been the Muse Trivia – the same Goddess who inspires stamp collectors, accountants, and the hoarders of baseball statistics': Ewald (n 14) 1983 and 1992.
169 Frankenberg (n 122) 118. For the full discussion, see ibid 117–64.

word is '*tenues*') 'ostensibly' ('*ostensiblement*') demonstrating a religious belonging in public primary and secondary schools. While Frankenberg introduces the law in force in Germany, the United Kingdom, or the United States – he also refers to various European Court of Human Rights decisions – French legislation remains his principal focus. In effect, Frankenberg contrasts 'the French brand of … militant Republican secularism'[170] – an exercise in 'social-cultural hygiene' allowing no room for any 'displace[ment] [of] the power of the hegemonic culture, its beauty criteria and loyalty claims'[171] – with the recognition of something like a 'human right to veiling'.[172]

Although many apprehend the issue of religious attire by readily mobilizing an ethnocentric, controlling, assimilationist, appropriationist, imperialist, crusading, proselytizing, or universalizing frame of mind – all tactics reminiscent of comparative law's 'equivalizers' and 'commonalizers' and their time-honoured arrangements purporting to show foreign laws basically to exist as re-enactments of one another – certain comparatists-at-law, like Frankenberg, defy a 'reductionist understanding of … practices of dress'.[173] Boldly channelling a distancing/differencing standpoint, Frankenberg withstands 'the denial of Muslim women and their complex identity construction'.[174] As he stigmatizes 'the colonial obsession with unveiling, uncovering and unmasking',[175] the refusal to respect the fact that 'the covered Muslim woman chooses to be sexually unavailable',[176] Frankenberg disputes the unexamined occidental view

170 ibid 130.

171 ibid 150 and 142.

172 ibid 138.

173 ibid 143–44.

174 ibid 143.

175 ibid 148. See also K Brayson, 'Of Bodies and Burkinis: Institutional Islamophobia, Islamic Dress, and the Colonial Condition' (2019) 46 J L & Society 55, 62, where the author holds that '[t]he defensiveness demonstrated by the French state through criminalizing Islamic dress evidences the attachment of the colonial past to the present and future; it is a manifestation of the failure of the historical project of French colonialism'. Further in her excellent critique, Kimberley Brayson observes that 'Islamic dress and the presence of colonial subjects in French public space on their own terms are … an affront to the fundamental pillars of the republic …. Colonial subjects are being punished for their failure to assimilate': ibid 63. Attire is order.

176 Frankenberg (n 122) 148. Frankenberg repeatedly quotes Frantz Fanon, a psychiatrist and philosopher who settled in Algeria from his native Martinique. See ibid 150–51. Fanon is best known for his analysis of colonialism and decolonization, which established him as a leading anti-colonial thinker. On the subject of veiling, Fanon writes as follows: 'This [Algerian] woman who sees without being seen frustrates the colonizer. There is no reciprocity. She does not surrender herself, does not give herself, does not

that postulates 'the liberatory meaning of skin showing',[177] allying himself with politist Wendy Brown, whom he quotes.[178] He thus defends a robust comparative practice embracing '[the] ethics and politics of skepticism',[179] challenging the view that 'legislative bans or administrative measures (by school principals) will help to find answers to the complex problems of integration in immigration societies'.[180] It is, as Frankenberg explains, about 'accept[ing] the otherness of the "other" without *othering* it',[181] that is, safeguarding foreignness and saving foreignness from marginalization or effacement or 'cannibaliz[ation]' by 'the ... power of the sovereign self'.[182]

Drawing on contemporary ethnography, Frankenberg's bracing conclusive remarks enter a plea for 'thick' comparison, for narrativized comparative work that is 'open to local knowledge and context sensitive',[183] 'interested in restoring and rehabilitating law's detail',[184] keen to 'transmit the richness of law's events ... with their cultural background as well as their political, economic and social ramifications'.[185] And the 'thickness' that Frankenberg commends enjoins an acute awareness that 'the comparatist is *always already* anchored in a specific, particular legal tradition, culture and experience',[186] that he is culturally encumbered, then, not at all a *solus ipse*.

offer herself. ... The European [man] facing the Algerian [woman] wants to see. He reacts in an aggressive way before this limitation to his perception': F Fanon, *L'an V de la révolution algérienne* in *Œuvres* (La Découverte 2011 [1959]) 281. But it was not only men who wanted to unveil Algerian women. 'During the Algerian war (1954–62), French women settlers staged unveiling ceremonies for Muslim women to identify their liberation with the French cause': JW Scott, *Sex and Secularism* (Princeton University Press 2018) 57. For a complementary investigation of the cultural dynamics between French women and their North-African counterparts, see JA Boittin, 'Feminist Mediations of the Exotic: French Algeria, Morocco and Tunisia, 1921–39' (2010) 22 Gender & History 131.

177 Frankenberg (n 122) 162.

178 W Brown, *Regulating Aversion* (Princeton University Press 2006) 189, where the author castigates 'the nearly compulsory baring of skin' prevailing in occidental countries.

179 Frankenberg (n 122) 159 [capitals omitted].

180 ibid 161.

181 ibid 71.

182 ibid 225 and 71.

183 ibid 227.

184 ibid 228.

185 ibid.

186 ibid 230.

Eruditely invigorating, Frankenberg's critical aspirations are nonetheless insufficiently far-reaching, his oppositional edge not sharp enough to operate as comparative law's governing epistemological practice. Inasmuch as it eschews a consideration of the primordiality and magnitude of the epistemological hurdles that present themselves to the comparatist, Frankenberg's critique is not as resolute as mine. It is less *radical* than mine (I use the term etymologically), and it is also less anacoluthic. Reading Frankenberg, one may be led to conclude that comparative law would ultimately *work*, if only it could escape the orthodoxy's stultifying epistemic chains by including some consideration of law's context, showing enhanced awareness of the comparatist-at-law's ethnocentric or juricentric bias, or embracing methodological pluralism. But not even Frankenberg's incisive indictment of orthodox cognitive assumptions addresses the underlying fact that comparative law is epistemologically doomed, since the comparatist must always-already *fail* to access or recount foreign law as it exists in advance of his interpretive assay. Like me, Frankenberg has pondered Samuel Beckett's poetics of ameliorative failure – 'Ever tried. Ever failed. No matter. Try again. Fail again. Fail better.'[187] Unlike me, he refuses to follow the playwright to his uncompromisingly dissensual conclusion, to the Derridean view that '[t]here is no world, [that] there are only islands',[188] that 'the worlds in which we live are different to the point of the monstrosity of the unrecognizable, of the un-similar, of the unbelievable, of the non-similar, of the non-resembling or resemblable, of the non-assimilable, of the untransferable',[189] and that neither awareness of context or bias nor method (not to mention translation) can ever overcome this separation. Let me be clear, though, that to assert how one must reckon with comparative law's structural failure to account for the other law or the other-in-the-law – how one must earnestly overcome 'the confusion of . . . identifying the description with what is described' and thus pursue the 'rhetoric of dissimilation'[190] – is not in the

[187] S Beckett, *Worstward Ho* in *Company/Ill Seen Ill Said/Worstward Ho/Stirrings Still* (D Van Hulle ed, Faber & Faber 2009 [1983]) 81. For Frankenberg's reference to Beckett, see Frankenberg (n 122) 20. cf S Firestein, *Failure* (Oxford University Press 2016) 63–69, where the author discusses 'the integrity of failure' [capitals omitted].

[188] J Derrida, *La Bête et le souverain*, vol 2 (M Lisse et al eds, Galilée 2010 [2002]) 31. cf S Fish, *Doing What Comes Naturally* (Duke University Press 1989) 136: '[P]ersons embedded within *different* discursive systems will not be able to hear the other's reasons *as* reasons, but only as errors or even delusions.'

[189] Derrida (n 188) 367.

[190] Mignolo (n 139) 225; N Melas, *All the Difference in the World* (Stanford University Press 2007) 65.

least to disqualify comparatism as a necessary intellectual pursuit. Quite apart from the fact that the very existence of foreign law interpellates one, makes a claim on one, solicits one's recognition and respect,[191] its normative relevance as persuasive authority abidingly prevails over exclusionary national or territorial arguments (in the obvious way in which materialism must carry over solipsism, colloquy over soliloquy, openness over closure). And even as any scrutiny of foreign law has to accept the presence of an epistemic gap that the comparatist cannot bridge and must acknowledge that the comparatist and the foreign law will therefore never *meet*, that comparative law inevitably promotes the unravelling (the disentanglement *and* the annulment) of the foreign, comparison – *la comparaison quand même* – remains the only brand of interpretation that can prove excentrically edifying despite the fact that/because of how the comparatist must ultimately abide distant reading.

Since sheer duplication of foreign law by the comparatist is of no interest in any event, interpretive enrichment requires a comparative text that tells foreign law otherwise than foreign law's own telling of itself. Only, then, by means of the comparatist's trials, sallies, shots, goes, and shies at somehow bringing 'elsewhere within here',[192] can there be a conversation, a deliberation, or a negotiation across laws of the kind that may allow for an amelioration of the attentive and lucid not-understanding of the other (and of the self) that is feasible, for the development of 'the best way, the most respectful and the most grateful, the most giving also, of correlating oneself with the other and of correlating the other with oneself'.[193] As it affords a more significant interpretive *yield* – as it informs the realization that 'the *commitment* to [comparative law] means that one can never become a [*comparatist*]'[194] – inadequacy is opportunity. The comparative advantage, if you will, is 'to write about a foreign legal system the way no native would write about it'.[195]

[191] To my knowledge, the best study on interpellation is J-J Lecercle, *De l'interpellation* (Editions Amsterdam 2019). In this book, the author examines at length the philosophical, linguistic, and ideological ramifications of this concept, which Louis Althusser (1918–90) initially developed.

[192] Eg: TT Minh-ha, *Elsewhere, Within Here* (Routledge 2011).

[193] J Derrida, *Points de suspension* (E Weber ed, Galilée 1992) 296.

[194] DN Rodowick, *Philosophy's Artful Conversation* (Harvard University Press 2015) 306 [my emphasis]. I adopt David Rodowick's observation regarding 'his' discipline, and I apply it to 'mine'.

[195] Fletcher (n 88) 691.

*

Frankenberg's critique prompts me to address comparative law's spectacular expansion into constitutional studies, even as Zweigert and Kötz – by way of a remarkable attempt to impose the German model's historical prioritization – have expressly, and repeatedly, sought to confine the field to private law only, indeed to a configuration that would stand as '"apolitical" private law' (if one can begin to fathom such an arrangement).[196] Yet, a remarkable explosion of scholarship in comparative constitutional law finally emerged in the course of the 2000s – the sheer abundance of which appears to withstand any meaningful exercise in nomination or enumeration – traceable to Vicki Jackson and Mark Tushnet's prominent devisement of the subject-matter.[197] (Evidently, comparative constitutionalism's history extends much further back in time.[198]) Given the profusion of intellectual activity surrounding the comparison of constitutional laws, it seems hard to believe that the 2019 edition of *The Oxford Handbook of Comparative Law* should be content to devote to the topic, out of 1,400 pages of text or so, *less* than the mere 35-page chapter it had allocated in 2006.[199] In the meantime, one observes the release of an ever-burgeoning list of compendiums, collections of essays, and monographs – some of them seeking to extend the reach of constitutionalism beyond the foundational territorial confines of the nation-state and thus to supplement traditional understandings.[200]

196 Zweigert and Kötz (n 9) 39. For Frankenberg's own contribution to comparative constitutional law, see eg G Frankenberg, *Comparative Constitutional Studies* (Elgar 2018) [hereinafter *Studies*]. Adde: G Frankenberg, 'Constitutional Transfer: The IKEA Theory Revisited' (2010) 8 Int'l J Constitutional L 563.

197 VC Jackson and M Tushnet (eds), *Comparative Constitutional Law* (Foundation 1999). An earlier book is SE Finer, V Bogdanor, and B Rudden, *Comparing Constitutions* (Oxford University Press 1995).

198 For a helpful (Eurocentric) historical overview, see M Rosenfeld and A Sajó, 'Introduction' in M Rosenfeld and A Sajó (eds), *The Oxford Handbook of Comparative Constitutional Law* (Oxford University Press 2012) 3–8.

199 Compare M Tushnet, 'Comparative Constitutional Law' in M Reimann and R Zimmermann (eds), *The Oxford Handbook of Comparative Law* (2nd edn, Oxford University Press 2019) 1193–1221; and M Tushnet, 'Comparative Constitutional Law' in M Reimann and R Zimmermann (eds), *The Oxford Handbook of Comparative Law* (Oxford University Press 2006) 1225–58.

200 For optimal access to an extensive range of issues, see M Rosenfeld and A Sajó (eds), *The Oxford Handbook of Comparative Constitutional Law* (Oxford University Press 2012). Adde: R Masterman and R Schütze (eds), *The Cambridge Companion to Comparative Constitutional Law* (Cambridge University Press 2019); P Dann et al, *The Global South and Comparative Constitutional Law* (Oxford University Press 2020); R Dixon and T Ginsburg (eds), *Comparative Constitutional Law in Asia* (Elgar 2014); DS Law (ed),

Moreover, comparative constitutional law features its own professional societies, journals, chairs, conferences, research centres or institutes, courses, and postgraduate programmes – all the markers indicating the constitution of a discrete field in point of sociological or institutional fact.

An important issue regarding the problematique of field emergence, although not determinative, has to do with whether agents – in this instance, constitutionalists – collectively perceive themselves as a group sharing interests and practices distinct from the patterns of scholarly behaviour they associate with comparative law, this understanding itself depending on the character, extent, and intensity of the social interaction between participants in what would be the new meaning system and on whether these dynamics would have revealed a specific desire to exploit an opportunity for epistemological differentiation. If a re-configuration of the comparative scene has indeed manifested itself along the lines I discuss, it would mean that Zweigert and Kötz's dogmatic strategy would effectively have proved successful and that, in this particular respect, the legal tradition known to anglophones as the 'civil law' would have been able to export beyond its epistemological confines its long-cherished delineation between private and public law. And it would also entail that one could now engage in a comparison of two modalities of comparative law. If you will, one could proceed to articulate a study in comparative comparative law.

Even as I duly take cognizance of the substantial effort that has been informing the deterritorialization of constitutional law, I cannot but recall a conversation with a distinguished internationalist during a teaching visit at Georgetown University in 2011. 'It's such a throwback', she exclaimed by way of response to my observations regarding the effervescence surrounding comparative constitutionalism. From a theoretical standpoint, there is cause for concern. For example, Ruti

Constitutionalism in Context (Cambridge University Press 2022). The view that a range of non-state forms of political authority, whether on the international scene or within the private sector, should also be understood as sites of constitutionalism is mostly associated with Gunther Teubner's model of 'societal constitutionalism'. Eg: G Teubner, 'The Project of Constitutional Sociology: Irritating Nation-State Constitutionalism' (2013) in D Göbel (ed), *Critical Theory and Legal Autopoiesis* (Manchester University Press 2019) 302–16. Teubner draws on D Sciulli, *Theory of Societal Constitutionalism* (Cambridge University Press 1992). I find that a thoughtfully analytical point of entry into this wide-ranging topic is GW Anderson, 'Beyond "Constitutionalism Beyond the State"' (2012) 39 J L & Society 359. For an insightful critique, see A Duval, 'The Olympic Charter: A Transnational Constitution Without a State?' (2018) 45 J L & Society S245.

Teitel is right, I think, to refer to a prominent streak of comparative constitutional law as 'neo-functionalist',[201] and she is correct to discern within comparative constitutionalism 'a contemporary revival and extension of the functionalist school of thought'.[202] As Teitel observes, 'functionalists downplay any differences among constitutional democracies',[203] which effectively means that they 'abstract constitutional problems from their contexts'.[204] This brand of comparative constitutionalism 'sets out the goal of universal constitutionalism',[205] 'comparative analysis [being conceived] in terms of a timeless legal convergence' and 'systematizing broadly across cultures and world history'.[206] Percipiently, Teitel concludes that 'the functionalist project is of limited value because the functionalist comparative constitutional analysis tends to elide political, economic, and social realities in its quest to identify legal regimes that can be transplanted across national lines'.[207] For instance, 'neo-functionalist logic does not offer a way to fully elucidate normative constitutional evolution',[208] the insertion of the adverb being, in my opinion, superfluous.

*

Within the ever-expanding discursive space that comparative constitutional law has been occupying, Ran Hirschl's extensive theoretization in his *Comparative Matters: The Renaissance of Comparative Constitutional Law* deserves especial attention.[209] At first blush, Hirschl's gambit strikes a determinedly critical note: '[C]omparative constitutional studies rides on a fuzzy and rather incoherent epistemological and methodological matrix.'[210] It is plagued, he writes, by 'considerable confusion about its aims and purposes, and even about its subject'.[211] Indeed, 'self-professed

201 R Teitel, 'Comparative Constitutional Law in a Global Age', (2004) 117 Harvard LR 2570, 2573n14.
202 ibid 2595.
203 ibid 2576.
204 ibid 2578.
205 ibid 2592.
206 ibid.
207 ibid 2581.
208 ibid 2584.
209 R Hirschl, *Comparative Matters: The Renaissance of Comparative Constitutional Law* (Oxford University Press 2014) [hereinafter *Comparative Matters*]. For a summary of key aspects of this argument, see R Hirschl, 'Judicial Review and the Politics of Comparative Citations: Theory, Evidence and Methodological Challenges' in EF Delaney and R Dixon (eds), *Comparative Judicial Review* (Elgar 2018) 403–22.
210 Hirschl, *Comparative Matters* (n 209) 5.
211 ibid 4.

"comparativism" sometimes amounts to little more than a passing reference to the constitution of a country other than the scholar's own'.[212] Given the fact that '[s]election biases abound',[213] it soon emerges that 'purportedly universal insights are based on a handful of frequently studied and not always representative settings or cases'.[214] Because of 'the prevalence of "armchair" constitutional research carried out with little or no fieldwork or systematic data collection',[215] 'the outcome is a loose and under-defined epistemic and methodological framework that seems to be held together by a rather thin intellectual thread: interest of some sort or another in the constitutional law of polity or polities other than the observer's own'.[216] I agree.

Hirschl identifies three justifications for engagement with other constitutional laws. An interest in foreign constitutions may thus arise out of *necessity* – the word being accorded a rather generous semantic extension, since the term might be taken more readily to connote, say, the imperative to maintain a minimal body temperature in order to survive. But Hirschl claims, precisely, that '[s]urvival instincts may push minority communities to develop a matrix for selective engagement with the laws of others in order to maintain their identity in the face of powerful convergence pressures'.[217] Another motivation for addressing the foreign involves *inquisitiveness*. For instance, '[i]ntellectual curiosity may drive scholars to investigate new constitutional settings and develop novel concepts, arguments, and ideas with respect to the constitutional universe'.[218] And then, there is *politics*: 'Comparative engagement may also be – indeed, often is – driven by a desire to advance a concrete political agenda or an ideological outlook.'[219] For Hirschl, this third explanation, as it accounts for strategic constitutional self-positioning, is 'crucial'.[220] He forcefully argues – convincingly, in my view – that 'comparative constitutional inquiries are as much a political enterprise as they are a scholarly or a jurisprudential one'.[221] Hirschl observes that 'the specific scope and nature of engagement with the constitutive laws of

[212] ibid.
[213] ibid.
[214] ibid 4–5.
[215] ibid 5.
[216] ibid.
[217] ibid 7.
[218] ibid.
[219] ibid.
[220] ibid.
[221] ibid.

others in a given polity at a given time cannot be meaningfully understood independent of the concrete sociopolitical struggles, ideological agendas, and "culture wars" shaping that polity at that time'.[222]

In this regard, the work of the Supreme Court of Israel, which Hirschl explores at some length, would offer a compelling illustration of the significance of 'the sociopolitical context within which constitutional courts and judges operate'[223] – an 'infrequently acknowledged feature, a background setting that may seem to be invisible unless it is brought to the fore'.[224] Why, then, do leading Israeli judges refer to foreign judicial decisions and scholarly commentary? Importantly, Hirschl remarks that these mentions of other laws are highly selective. While a country like India shares with Israel 'a similar experience of deep identity and ethnic-religious rifts',[225] it is absent from Israeli Supreme Court opinions. And although countries like Pakistan, Turkey, or Malaysia feature 'tensions between secularism and religiosity . . . [which] resemble tensions embedded in Israel's self-definition as a "Jewish and democratic" state',[226] they do not appear in judgments of the Supreme Court of Israel either. These omissions can be explained by reference to 'the "identity" dimension' pertaining to comparative constitutionalism.[227] In effect, references to foreign law partake of an 'attempt to define who "we" are as a political community, and to articulate in a public way what "our image" or "our place" in the world is or should be'.[228] The fact that Israeli Supreme Court judges prefer to turn to jurisdictions like the United States, Canada, or the United Kingdom thus asserts a 'desire to be included in the liberal-democratic club of nations'.[229] Incidentally, this resolve explains why 'Israeli secular judges (who make up the vast majority of those appointed to the bench) hardly ever treat Jewish law as a relevant source of comparative insight'.[230] (Fascinatingly, this is the case even though, pursuant to a 1980 Israeli statute, Jewish law is 'actually the sole source to which the law refers judges when they encounter a lacuna'.[231]) In sum, '[v]oluntary

222 ibid.
223 ibid 8.
224 ibid 7.
225 ibid 9.
226 ibid.
227 ibid.
228 ibid.
229 ibid.
230 ibid.
231 ibid.

reference to foreign precedents is at least as much a political phenomenon as it is a juridical one'.[232]

While I value Hirschl's historical account of engagement with constitutional otherness,[233] I remain particularly interested in his extensive discussion of salient theoretical issues. In this regard, Hirschl raises three specific concerns: the formalization of comparative constitutional studies (that he bemoans); the universalizability of constitutional law (that he appears to want to promote); and the design of comparative inquiry (that he would scientificize). The detailed treatment of these three questions in *Comparative Matters* warrants that I should address them in turn.

Hirschl's lament concerning the excessively formal character of comparative constitutionalism is legitimate, and I wholeheartedly support his call for a more eminent approach to the practice of comparison. Hirschl justifiably contests the pattern to the effect that '[t]wo dozen court rulings from South Africa, Germany, Canada, and the European Court of Human Rights alongside a more traditional set of landmark rulings from the United States and Britain and an occasional tribute to India or Australia, now form an unofficial canon of "global constitutionalism" that informs comparative constitutional law syllabi throughout much of the English-speaking world'.[234] Such a 'court-centric focus' ignores the fact that 'constitutions neither originate nor operate in a vacuum'.[235]

[232] ibid 10.

[233] Still, Hirschl's referencing practice raises an important difficulty, which his treatment of Montesquieu exemplifies. See Hirschl, *Comparative Matters* (n 209) 125–33. One can only be delighted that Montesquieu, a French comparatist *avant la lettre*, should have earned Hirschl's attention and retained it over nearly eight pages of discussion. Alas, the notes reveal references to four commentators only, the citations being on the whole sketchy and dated. One cannot help but think that Hirschl is not doing justice to the interpretive literature on Montesquieu in English. Moreover, if one excepts Durkheim-in-translation, there is not a single reference to French publications, which is surprising since Montesquieu has predictably attracted substantial critical attention from leading French anthropologists, sociologists, and politists. While I am not fixated on the matter of quantity, there comes a point, I think, where the lack of pertinent references becomes a problem. With respect to the treatment of Montesquieu, this point may well have been reached. If one is not careful, one promptly starts to look like a comparatist who would write on Chinese law without any reading proficiency in Mandarin, on Islamic law without being able to make sense of Arabic, on Japanese law without access to Japanese primary materials, and on Jewish law without any competence in Hebrew (possibly all in one book, too). In sum, I wish to enter a cautionary note regarding minimum assertional thresholds, an issue concerning the field of comparative law generally and thus going well beyond Hirschl's text.

[234] Hirschl, *Comparative Matters* (n 209) 163.

[235] ibid 163 and 152.

Indeed, '[a]ny attempt to portray the constitutional domain as predominantly legal, rather than imbued in the social or political arena, is destined to yield thin, ahistorical, and overly doctrinal or formalistic accounts of the origins, nature, and consequences of constitutional law'.[236] Interestingly, Hirschl reminds his readership that comparative constitutional law's 'disciplinary identity' was not always understood so narrowly.[237] In effect, 'the epistemological difference between the comparative constitutionalism of the early 20th century and that of the 21st century is substantial'.[238] Hirschl thus reports that even Dicey's brand of comparatism addressed, in Dicey's own words, 'the conceptions or ideas which underlie political arrangements, [rather] than [the] study [of] the actual mechanism of politics'.[239] Although it is hard to envisage a topic that would not be beneficially informed by the tracing of the constitutional law-text to its constitutive cultural elements (ideological, political, sociological, and otherwise), the need for such archaeological or genealogical work can prove particularly relevant in situations where there is a strong discrepancy between the official law-text and local practice, for instance, when constitutions in countries like India, Turkey, and the United States defend the idea of a secular polity in the face of an ascertainably strong popular commitment to religiosity. Under such circumstances, the tracing process discloses the expression of a political will at variance with popular sentiment and raises the issue of what can perhaps economically be called a constitutional democratic deficit.

Also as regards the urgent need for comparative constitutional scholarship to decloister itself, Hirschl offers five reasons to underwrite his call to action. The last of these arguments concerns what *Comparative Matters* styles comparative constitutionalism's 'amorphous methodological matrix'.[240] This claim connects with the third facet of Hirschl's theoretical argument, where he enters a plea for increased scientificization. As I return to the issue of scientificization momentarily, suffice it to say at this juncture that I can understand how someone who believes in method – as Hirschl does, and as I do not – would subscribe to

236 ibid 152.
237 ibid 190n108.
238 ibid 157.
239 ibid. The reference is to AV Dicey, 'Introduction' in *Lectures on Comparative Constitutionalism* (JWF Allison ed, Oxford University Press 2013 [1894]) 6. I have added a few words of Dicey's to Hirschl's quotation.
240 Hirschl, *Comparative Matters* (n 209) 186 [emphasis omitted].

'causality-oriented exercise[s]' in search of 'valid inferences'.[241] But how Hirschl can expressly link the idea of method with the practice of a 'hermeneutic [comparative constitutional inquiry]' baffles me.[242] If Hans-Georg Gadamer's pioneering work has taught us anything, it is precisely that hermeneutics decidedly moves away from method, indeed that 'faith in method' risks 'an actual deformation of knowledge'.[243] Gadamer could hardly be clearer: 'The hermeneutic phenomenon is originally not a problem of method at all.'[244] More generally, I deplore *Comparative Matters*'s unwillingness to engage philosophical hermeneutics at any length. To be sure, Hirschl makes a fleeting allusion to Martin Heidegger's 'fore-structure of understanding' – which is so rapid, in fact, that it remains unsourced.[245] But the desultory character of this intimation cannot even begin to do justice to what is arguably, at least if one is willing to follow Heidegger's insight through to its deconstructive ramifications (that is, until Derrida), *the* key intuition purporting to inform post-Kantian philosophy and, specifically, *the* most important contention claiming to make sense of interpretation's sense-making, of what it means to make sense of a text.

With respect to the question of universalism – Hirschl's second major theoretical preoccupation – I do not read *Comparative Matters* to be questioning either the idea or its value. I find little in Hirschl's argument that could persuasively identify him as a critic of universalism or a refuter of the view that constitutional processes (or the comparatist's interpretation thereof) ought to be striving towards universalization. In point of fact, Hirschl appears to defend the position that comparative constitutional law has not been universal *enough*. As long as comparatists continue to focus practically exclusively on what he names the 'global north' and persist in excluding more or less reflexively the 'global south' or the 'constitutional south',[246] Hirschl holds that any claim that comparative constitutionalism might be advancing in favour of universalism would be greatly exaggerated. Hirschl's main consideration, then, seems to be that

241 ibid 187.

242 ibid 186.

243 H-G Gadamer, *Wahrheit und Methode* (5th edn, Mohr Siebeck 1986) 306.

244 ibid 1. See also H-G Gadamer, 'A Classical Text – A Hermeneutic Challenge' (F Lawrence tr) in S Kresic (ed), *Contemporary Literary Hermeneutics and Interpretation of Classical Texts* (University of Ottawa Press 1981 [1978]) 328: '[H]ermeneutics . . . is not itself a method.' This text has appeared in English only.

245 Hirschl, *Comparative Matters* (n 209) 188. Nowhere in his monograph does Hirschl supply any reference to Heidegger.

246 See ibid 205–23.

the habitual selection of laws under comparative examination is insufficiently broad to warrant a persuasive claim in favour of universalism. For Hirschl, the problem at stake is therefore first and foremost one of representativity: comparative constitutional law as it has been unfolding remains discordant in terms of the extant variety of polities all over the planet. It is not that there would be something epistemically wrong with universalism, then, but rather that comparative constitutional law must be prevented from making any claim to universalism as long as it remains epistemologically mired in its septentrionic ways. In sum, Hirschl's argument is that it is problematic to pretend to universalism on the basis of inadequate information. As I read *Comparative Matters*, Hirschl wants comparative constitutionalism to re-organize itself and engage on an epistemological course of action allowing it creditably to reach conclusions that could legitimately brand themselves as universal.

Now, I regard Hirschl's assumption that universalism is at once achievable and desirable, if only comparative constitutional law could broaden its geographical reach, as eminently contestable. Part of the difficulty is that Hirschl's argument for universalism remains under-theorized. My threshold objection thus concerns the superficiality of Hirschl's pronouncements on universalism. For instance, Hirschl writes in the most general terms that '[d]espite striking differences in socioeconomic conditions and cultural particularities, modern states paradoxically adopt similar policies and institutions', adding that 'in many countries that do not share common characteristics, national constitutions outlaw ethnic and racial discrimination, embrace similar understandings of rights, and call for largely similar commitments to justice and equality'.[247] To focus on a few of these words only, there would exist across polities 'similar understandings of rights' and 'largely similar commitments to justice and equality'.

Why, then, does the Supreme Court of Canada, in a 2006 unanimous decision, allow a twelve-year-old Sikh boy to wear his ceremonial metal dagger at school,[248] while a 2004 French statute, having garnered the support of ninety-three per cent of parliamentarians in each of France's two legislative houses (and thus cutting well across political lines), prohibits attire ('*tenues*') 'ostensibly' ('*ostensiblement*') demonstrating a religious belonging in public primary and secondary schools?[249] And

[247] See ibid 53–54.

[248] *Multani v Commission scolaire Marguerite-Bourgeoys* [2006] 1 SCR 256.

[249] Statute no 2004-228 of 15 March 2004 enframing, in application of the principle of laicity, the wearing of signs or attire demonstrating a religious belonging in public

why is the French constitution so much easier to amend than the US constitution? And why is the Australian courts' interpretation of the word 'commerce' as regards the Trade and Commerce Power in the Australian constitution so different from the US courts' interpretation of the word 'commerce' pursuant to the Commerce Clause in the US constitution? Is 'commerce' not 'commerce'? The difficulty with Hirschl's argument in favour of 'similar understandings of rights' and 'largely similar commitments to justice and equality' – elsewhere in his book, he refers to 'copious similarity'[250] – is that the three examples I adduce are... exemplary. In other terms, these three illustrations offer but three typical manifestations of what is the case, that is, of *differential* constitutionalism. Meanwhile, a seemingly infinite number of instances could easily be mobilized to press the descriptive case against universalism.[251]

For Hirschl to claim 'a considerable convergence of constitutional structures, institutions, texts, and interpretive methods ... over the past few decades' as 'undisputed' (incidentally without adducing any supporting case study) cannot be satisfactory.[252] Not only is the contention about 'considerable convergence' disputed, but it is readily disputable. The 'copious similarity' that Hirschl purports to identify, which he attributes in significant part to the willingness of an elite caste of academics (*Comparative Matters* calls them 'constitutional "engineers"'[253]) to be 'ready to hop on a plane to any of the four corners of the world to provide expert advice as to how to draft a constitution',[254] is not established. Nor can it be (which is perhaps why, elsewhere in his monograph, Hirschl contests 'the sweeping global convergence claim' and argues that 'because ... divergence [with respect to economic and social rights] reflects lasting determinants such as legal tradition and region, it is likely

primary and secondary schools, art 1 <www.legifrance.gouv.fr/loda/id/JORFTEXT000000417977/ > [on file].

250 Hirschl, *Comparative Matters* (n 209) 205.

251 Eg: J Greene, 'Rights as Trumps?' (2018) 132 Harvard LR 28, where different constitutional understandings of rights in various countries are discussed. However, epistemic reflexes such as Hirschl's, no doubt depending on the reflector's enculturation, reveal confounding resilience so that as astute a participant observer of the international scene as Gráinne de Búrca, for example, still feels able to write how 'it is true that human rights law and practice are animated by essentially universally oriented values that are neither partisan nor particular': G de Búrca, *Reframing Human Rights in a Turbulent Era* (Oxford University Press 2021) 6. I must accept that optical illusions do not vanish even when empirical information proves them to be illusions.

252 Hirschl, *Comparative Matters* (n 209) 205.

253 ibid 203.

254 ibid 203–4.

to persist').[255] Frenetic plane-hopping (and earnest air-miles collecting) notwithstanding, the fact is that such constitutional iterations as are ascertainable across polities can most aptly be envisaged as instances of glocalization rather than as illustrations of 'globalization'.[256] To quote Bernard Harcourt: '[T]here are no universals'.[257] Otherwise said, universalism is nullibiquitous. Allow me to sustain this argument by reference to the appraisal of the constitutional validity of legislative acts, what US lawyers know as 'judicial review', a designation impertinent in France where the responsible body is the *Conseil constitutionnel* – not a court – whose members are, well, 'members' ('*membres*') – not judges, hence the local designation '*contrôle de constitutionnalité*' (literally, 'control of constitutionality'). While the defenders of the convergence thesis within comparative constitutional law have been harnessing this topic in support of their position (although conveniently dispensing with detailed argumentation along the way),[258] such claim is unsustainable as the following précis ought to make clear.

On 1 March 2010, France introduced fully fledged constitutional review. To be sure, French law had featured a form of constitutional review before then on account of the text of the 1958 Constitution and a major 1974 constitutional amendment. Indeed, since 1974 the constitutionality of a statute has been impugnable *before* its coming into force, but only at the behest of the President of the Republic, the Prime Minister, the President of the *Assemblée nationale* (the lower house of Parliament), the President of the Senate (the upper house of Parliament), or a group of sixty members of the *Assemblée* or the Senate. Since March 2010, not only is constitutional review also possible as regards statutes having been promulgated into force, but any litigant can now

255 ibid 273. Note that even as Hirschl objects to 'the sweeping global convergence claim', he writes, somewhat confusingly, that '[w]ithout doubt, the sweeping worldwide convergence toward constitutional rights and judicial review has brought about tremendous advances': ibid 179.

256 For a more detailed treatment of 'glocalization', see infra 120–28.

257 BE Harcourt, *Critique and Praxis* (Columbia University Press 2020) 436. See also Mignolo (n 139) 228: 'There is nothing behind the claim to universality other than the apparatus of enunciation that claims it.' cf A MacIntyre, *Whose Justice? Whose Rationality?* (University of Notre Dame Press 1988) 346: '[T]here is no place for appeals to a practical-rationality-as-such or a justice-as-such to which all rational persons would by their very rationality be compelled to give their allegiance. There is instead only the practical-rationality-of-this-or-that-tradition and the justice-of-this-or-that-tradition.' MacIntyre is sounding a warning against the tyranny of the capital letter (think Rationality or Justice).

258 Eg: Jackson (n 34) 1.

interrupt a lawsuit by way of a 'prioritary constitutional question' ('*question prioritaire de constitutionnalité*') to challenge the constitutionality of an in-force statute pertaining to the legal dispute at hand. After undergoing two filtering assessments attesting to its novelty, relevance to the litigation, and inherent seriousness – whether by private law or public law 'judges' (there are two discrete adjudicative 'pyramids' in France) – the file is conveyed to the *Conseil constitutionnel*, which must decide on the constitutional matter within three months.[259] Meanwhile, the ex ante procedure continues to be available to politicians in line with the 1958/1974 scheme. Such cursory observations should suffice to demonstrate that French constitutional review remains at considerable variance with, say, the US institution. And they should be enough to show that the French amendments simply cannot be pointing to transnational convergence of constitutional laws.[260] Indeed, '[f]or better or for worse, the reform does not erase French exceptionalism or "anomalies"'.[261] The singularity of the French configuration *lives on*.

In terms of comparative constitutional law, the difficulty I see arising in this instance, as so often, is that 'the comparati[st] presumes similarities between different jurisdictions in the very act of searching for

259 Eg: M Guillaume, *Question prioritaire de constitutionnalité* (Dalloz 2019); D Rousseau and P Pasquino (eds), *La Question prioritaire de constitutionnalité* (Mare & Martin 2019).

260 Eg: Legrand, 'Understanding' (n 66) 98–103. More generally, I object to the promotion of comparative constitutional analysis because different countries would be facing 'similar problems' or 'similar social, political, and legal challenges': Greene (n 251) 36 and 132. Mary Ann Glendon is right to discard such an unsubstantiated allegation as 'casual' and 'disquieting' and to rebuke this postulation as not addressing the complexity of 'comparability': MA Glendon, 'Comparative Law in the Age of Globalization' (2014) 52 Duquesne LR 1, 16. Glendon specifically refers to S Breyer, 'Keynote Address' (2003) 97 Am Society Int'l L Proceedings 265. Justice Stephen Breyer's imprisonment of singular modes of being-in-the-law into superficial patterns of standardization prompts him to maintain, for example, that '[j]udges in different countries increasingly apply somewhat similar legal phrases to somewhat similar circumstances' (ibid 266) and that there are 'cross-country results that resemble each other more and more' so that there can be discerned 'growing institutional and substantive similarities' across constitutional laws (ibid 267). Justice Breyer's constitutional simplism is far from being an isolated occurrence of comparative reductionism.

261 M Hunter-Hénin, 'Constitutional Developments and Human Rights in France: One Step Forward, Two Steps Back' (2011) 60 Int'l & Comp LQ 167, 172. For another argument, by a leading French constitutionalist, to the effect that the 2010 revision has not had a significant impact on the ways of the *Conseil constitutionnel*, see D Baranger, 'French Constitutional Law' in R Masterman and R Schütze (eds), *The Cambridge Companion to Comparative Constitutional Law* (Cambridge University Press 2019) 107.

them',[262] that there takes place yet another attempt to fit the square peg of equivalence or commonality into the round hole of singularity not least on account of (repressive) institutional forces imposing restrictive and determinate forms on comparative modes of thinking and imagining. However, one would want a comparatist-at-law to implement precisely the opposite disposition, that is, show recognition of the singularity of local legal knowledge and demonstrate respect for it as a matter of the epistemic justice owed to it as there takes place an attempted representation of it, in effect, a substitution for it – a contention that has nothing to do with an essentialist understanding of legal identity and a strategy that does not in the least call into question the merits of comparative inquiry. As Hirschl himself appositely underlines, 'even the most in-depth, single-case-study works may, and in fact often do, carry theoretical insights that travel well beyond the specific setting studied'.[263]

Despite the ascertainable migration, circulation, and dissemination of legal ideas (this diffusion being noticeably more prevalent than was the case, say, 100 years ago at a time when national laws were not nearly as leachy as some of them have become) – despite laws' traffic – difference across constitutional laws holds. No matter how organizational forms or rhetorical idioms have been spreading planetarily, each situation inevitably features adaptation to local knowledge, which takes the form of a specific assemblage with indigeneity. To return to my illustration, what the observant comparatist can see happening in France is a singular assemblage bringing together in a singular configuration, at the minimum, what is in all likelihood an idea ultimately emerging from the United States, on one hand, with French local knowledge, on the other (no doubt the enmeshment of the constitutive parts of the assemblage – its texture – being extraordinarily complicated). To reframe the matter more philosophically, what the observant comparatist can see happening in France is the French self-in-the-law re-signifying itself through the incorporation into its 'body legal' of an infusion of 'otherness-in-the-law'. The self thus becomes a revised self on account of the other. But although it is now affected by the other, it is still a self, *it is still its self* – which is to say that it continues as itself and has emphatically not become the other. In sum, the outcome remains a French constitutional self, which it would be superficial to dilute into a purportedly universal configuration called (in English!) 'judicial review', which would now

[262] J Vining, *The Authoritative and the Authoritarian* (University of Chicago Press 1986) 65.
[263] Hirschl, *Comparative Matters* (n 209) 189.

obtain everywhere, if with slight variations rapidly to be deemed secondary or even irrelevant. The empirical fact of the matter is that there is not convergence around a single, originally occidental (or US) pattern of institutions and the cultural understanding thereof, but an irreducible multiplicity of irreducibly singular institutional patterns and cultural models – some of which actually stand as strong expressions of resistance to uniformization processes. Again, what there is, there, is not universalism, but something like *diversalism*. And if I may indulge an additional philosophical thought, ultimately this result ought not to prove surprising as one reminds oneself of Leibniz's Law,[264] which I would rephrase thus: if there is more than one in co-presence, there must be difference.

As I read Hirschl, I am uncomfortably reminded of other uncreditable epistemological theses advocating for 'generic law' or a 'global constitutional gene pool'.[265] In betraying a misconception of the agonistic constitutional processes that have been unfolding, these expressions negate difference for the sake of positing a sham-equivalence or sham-commonality. Admittedly operating from a different angle, the idiosyncratic vantage point of autopoietic theory (a uniquely formalistico-mechanistic, abstracto-speculative, and rigidly analytico-categorical perspective), Gunther Teubner (whom Hirschl does not mention) cogently maintains that '[i]f one wishes to conceive at all of a "global constitution", the only possible blueprint is that of particular constitutions for each of these global fragments – nations, transnational regimes, regional cultures – connected to each other in a constitutional conflict of laws'.[266]

264 See [GW] Leibniz, *Discours de métaphysique* in *Die philosophischen Schriften von Gottfried Wilhelm Leibniz*, vol 4 (CI Gerhardt ed, Olms 1965 [1686]) s 9, 433: '[I]t is not true that two substances resemble each other entirely.' See also [GW] Leibniz, *Nouveaux essais sur l'entendement* in *Die philosophischen Schriften von Gottfried Wilhelm Leibniz*, vol 5 (CI Gerhardt ed, Olms 1965 [1764†]) 49: '[B]y virtue of imperceptible variations, two individual things cannot be perfectly similar, and . . . they must always differ.'

265 DS Law, 'Generic Constitutional Law' (2005) 89 Minnesota LR 652; C Saunders, 'Towards a Global Constitutional Gene Pool' (2009) 4(3) Nat'l Taiwan U LR 1. In A Jakab et al (eds), *Comparative Constitutional Reasoning* (Cambridge University Press 2017), my computer counts 404 references to 'generic' law. Adde: M Tushnet, 'Can There Be Autochthonous Methods of Constitutional Interpretation?' in F Gárdos-Orosz and Z Szente (eds), *Populist Challenges to Constitutional Interpretation in Europe and Beyond* (Routledge 2021) 64, where the author refers to 'provisions generically common in constitutions' and raises the matter of a 'generic relationship'.

266 G Teubner, *Constitutional Fragments* (Oxford University Press 2012) 14.

Now, from a resolutely epistemological perspective I must dispute Hirschl's claim that 'there is not much sense in comparing things that are perfectly identical',[267] the basic fact of the matter being that if there are 'things' (that is, more than one thing), there cannot be 'perfec[t] identi[ty]'. Such is precisely Leibniz's crucial philosophical insight. In effect, Hirschl's formulation therefore displays an oxymoron. Either there are 'things' or there is 'perfec[t] identi[ty]'. Another difficulty is Hirschl's further observation to the effect that, well, in the end there is not much to distinguish the upholders of universalism from those who deny its existence: we all exaggerate, do we not? Thus: 'Proponents of universalism tend to overemphasize cross-national similarities, while advocates of contextualism tend to over-emphasize differences.'[268] And, also, 'comparability requires unity *and* plurality'.[269] I argue that these parallels or amalgams are misleading simplifications.

The primordial fact undergirding any comparison is that in order to compare there has to be more than one entity in co-presence, which means that there has to be difference.[270] And the further structural fact is that as long as there is more than one entity in co-presence, difference is 'irreducible'.[271] As long as there is more than one – say, more than one polity, more than one law, more than one constitution – *the differend is what is the case*. Any purported equivalence or commonality, meanwhile, is the result of the comparatist's own input. It is the outcome of what one might call a process of 'equivalization' or 'commonalization', of making-look-equivalent or making-look-common, a sham-equivalence or sham-commonality. In other words, any alleged/fake equivalence or commonality is the product of the comparatist's construction, which will have been undertaken to further some political agenda or other. (Note, however, that even the vaunted equivalence or commonality effectively fails to overcome difference.[272] If entity A is said to be equivalent or common to entity B, a statement assuming more than one entity, entity A must be and remain different from entity B. Heidegger formulates the matter succinctly and clearly: 'In the identical, the difference

[267] Hirschl, *Comparative Matters* (n 209) 204.
[268] ibid 203.
[269] ibid 204 .
[270] Eg: J Derrida, *La Vérité en peinture* (Flammarion 1993) 429: '[T]o compare[:] [t]hen again, there must be a difference permitting it' [emphasis omitted]; Hutchinson (n 8) 11: '[T]o compare presupposes the ability to contrast.'
[271] J Derrida, *Limited Inc* (E Weber ed, Galilée 1990) 253.
[272] See also infra 234–35.

disappears. In the same, the difference appears.'[273]) The constructivism I discuss explains why Hirschl is mistaken as he asserts that '[c]learly, an old water well and the concept of infidelity are hardly comparable'.[274] Strictly speaking, it is not that the well and infidelity are not comparable, for they are. The threshold challenge is not so much the act of comparison, which can take place, as the fact that the comparison to be deployed, because it must contend with incommensurability, requires the comparatist himself to delineate an interface allowing a point of entry into his comparative intervention – a 'cue-equivalence' or 'cue-commonality'. Again, though, it is certainly not the case that incommensurability should constitute an unsurmountable obstacle to comparison.[275]

Consider the old well and infidelity. Could a comparatist not retain 'tangibility' by way of notion bringing not-together these two entities? Through a comparison around the notion of tangibility, the old well would be shown to be more tangible than infidelity, and infidelity less tangible than the old well. Observe that it is very much the comparatist himself who is constructing the interface allowing him to compare the old well and infidelity. If you will, tangibility remains the speculative outcome of the comparatist's own translations/transactions. It is therefore the comparatist himself – and only him – who is forcing the old well and infidelity to converse, to engage in a *negotiation* within the structure – tangibility – that he himself is articulating and to which he is assigning the entities under examination. At the outset, it might have appeared that the old well and infidelity had nothing to say to each other lest each entity rehearse its own story in a language that the other could only imagine itself understanding. However, the comparatist can change this situation.

[273] M Heidegger, *Identität und Differenz* (Neske 1957) 35.

[274] Hirschl, *Comparative Matters* (n 209) 204.

[275] Within comparative law, incommensurability has been misapprehended as incomparability: see HP Glenn, 'Are Legal Traditions Incommensurable?' (2001) 49 Am J Comp L 133, 135. But see eg TS Kuhn, 'Commensurability, Comparability, Communicability' in J Conant and J Haugeland (eds), *The Road Since Structure* (University of Chicago Press 2000 [1982]) 36: 'No more in its metaphorical than its literal form does incommensurability imply incomparability.' See also U Eco, *Dire quasi la stessa cosa* (Bompiani 2003) 41: '[I]ncommensurability does not mean incomparability' [emphasis omitted]; H von Sass, 'Incomparability' in A Epple et al (eds), *Practices of Comparing* (Bielefeld University Press 2020) 98: '[I]ncommensurability … is compatible with comparability.' For an illustration, see J Baggini, 'How to Compare Fruit' *The Times Literary Supplement* (25 May 2018) 8: '[Y]ou *can* compare apples and oranges. Oranges have thicker, less edible skins, are more juicy, have a different colour and so on. What you can't do is measure the quality of an apple and the orange using the same scale. What makes a good orange is not what makes a good apple, and vice versa. This is incommensurability.'

Through his delineation of a point of entry into his comparative intervention, he can get the old well and infidelity to 'relate' even as this 'relation' effectively consists of an ascribed and therefore contrived 'relation' – actually, of an *irrelation*. Still, irrespective of the connections a word like tangibility may suggest, the 'negotiation of incommensurable differences' intervening in the space of the interface that the comparatist has now specified (call it the third space)[276] – what effectively stands as a 'negoti[ation] [with] the non-negotiable'[277] – must ultimately fail to engender an economy of equivalence or commonality in terms of what is the case. In other words, there are limits to what the comparatist's construction can *really* achieve: irrelation holds.

Indeed, the framed interface must fail to efface the differend. Ultimately, what can be said about the two entities is that '[they have] in common [that they have] nothing in common' (the word 'nothing' referring to the interval in-between).[278] When Hirschl suggests that an old well and infidelity are 'hardly comparable', I therefore take him not to mean literally that no comparison can be had, for one *can* compare,[279] but that a comparison featuring these two entities will not afford the kind of interpretive yield warranting the comparative trouble, so to speak. Accordingly, the matter is not so much a question of comparability as it is one of interpretive yield. The fact is that to compare an old well and infidelity in terms of their tangibility will, in all likelihood, simply not afford an interesting, rewarding, or productive interpretive output. As Hirschl moves from the old well and infidelity to 'broccoli' and a 'manual transmission gearbox',[280] he himself remarks that the key issue is a matter of 'the analytical or theoretical yield'.[281]

And then, Hirschl's theoretical statement in *Comparative Matters* involves a third instalment on the design of comparative constitutional research. In the fifty pages or so pertaining to the insights that comparative constitutionalism can helpfully derive from social science studies,[282]

[276] HK Bhabha, *The Location of Culture* (Routledge 1994) 218.

[277] J Derrida, *Etats d'âme de la psychanalyse* (Galilée 2000) 83.

[278] J Derrida and M Ferraris, *Le Goût du secret* (A Bellantone and A Cohen eds, Hermann 2018 [1994]) 71. The words are Derrida's. To anthropomorphize the matter, there are no 'shared thoughts': RB Brandom, *Making It Explicit* (Harvard University Press 1994) 562.

[279] cf A Epple and W Erhart, 'Practices of Comparing' in A Epple et al (eds), *Practices of Comparing* (Bielefeld University Press 2020) 15: '[Y]ou truly can compare everything with everything.'

[280] Hirschl, *Comparative Matters* (n 209) 205.

[281] ibid 204.

[282] See ibid 224–81.

Hirschl suggests a typology of the different '[m]odes of comparative inquiry' that can be conducted.[283] Specifically, he refers to the '[s]ingle-country study';[284] investigations 'geared toward self-reflection or betterment through analogy, distinction, and contrast';[285] research 'emphasizing the broad similarity of constitutional challenges and functions across many relatively open, rule-of-law polities';[286] and analyses that 'ai[m] to engage in theory-testing and explanation through causal inference'.[287] In line with his wish to favour the scientificization of comparative constitutional law – the words 'scientific inquiry' appear more than once throughout this part of the argument and are expressly linked to the matter of 'intellectual integrity'[288] – Hirschl emphasizes what he styles 'inference-oriented' comparative studies out of a concern for 'clearly articulated methodological principles'.[289] He thus identifies comparative research being variously configured around '[t]he "most similar cases" principle';[290] '[t]he "most different cases" principle';[291] '[t]he "prototypical cases" principle';[292] '[t]he "most difficult" case principle';[293] or '[t]he "outlier cases" principle'[294] – all 'small-N' studies, that is, all instances of research examining a small number of cases.[295] And then, there are 'large-N' projects, 'analyses of large sets of observations'.[296] These would involve, in the case of comparative constitutionalism, all the constitutions of the world (what the author calls – most surprisingly, to my mind – 'a manageable number' of instances).[297] In terms of 'large-N' research, the governing idea must be to 'go beyond the clichés, heuristics, and biases that emanate from the decades-long over-study of a handful of cases to actually test some of the canonical insights of constitutional theory or shed new light on causal links within

[283] ibid 232.
[284] ibid [emphasis omitted].
[285] ibid 235 [emphasis omitted].
[286] ibid 238.
[287] ibid 242 [emphasis omitted].
[288] ibid 228.
[289] ibid.
[290] ibid 245 [emphasis omitted].
[291] ibid 253 [emphasis omitted].
[292] ibid 256 [emphasis omitted].
[293] ibid 260 [emphasis omitted].
[294] ibid 262 [emphasis omitted].
[295] See ibid 244.
[296] ibid 267.
[297] ibid.

the constitutional universe'.[298] Hirschl's insistence on analytics, causality, and method – his focus on science – is not without reminding me of the bizarre epistemic tenets that Zweigert and Kötz have long defended in their leading text, which expressly advocates for the scientificization of comparative law, not least through an accentuation of analytics and method.[299] (To his credit, Hirschl favours 'methodological pluralism and well-thought-out analytical eclecticism',[300] thus distancing himself from Zweigert and Kötz's excessive claim in favour of methodological monism, indeed, of 'pure' methodological monism.[301])

One would not tell from Hirschl's treatment of comparative-law-as-science that this brand of comparatism has been (wisely) regarded as epistemically unsustainable.[302] How can the epistemological framework guiding a laboratory experiment in, say, biochemistry, prove of any meaningful relevance as regards the protocols governing the interpretation of a foreign law-text? It is not as if interpretation of foreign law consisted of some technique that could be readily replicated from one interpreter to the next or from one law to the next. Quite simply, the transposition I critique involves an 'improper extension of [scientism] to domains of cultural activity to which it does not and cannot apply'.[303] There takes place an 'illicit' projection.[304] In any event, the territory of science is also a cultural space – a fact that, in my experience, comparatists-at-law largely fail to appreciate.[305] Reading Hirschl, one gets the general sense of an argument for comparative-law-as-science that remains largely unexamined. Illustrations of the reigning confusion

[298] ibid 268–69.

[299] Supra 60–61.

[300] Hirschl, *Comparative Matters* (n 209) 280. For updated summaries of Hirschl's methodological views, see R Hirschl, 'Methodology and Research Design' in DS Law, *Constitutionalism in Context* (Cambridge University Press 2022) 41–58; R Hirschl, 'Comparative Methodologies' in R Masterman and R Schütze (eds), *The Cambridge Companion to Comparative Constitutional Law* (Cambridge University Press 2019) 11–39.

[301] Supra 60.

[302] Eg: Teitel (n 201) passim.

[303] Rodowick (n 194) 55.

[304] PMS Hacker, 'Wittgenstein and the Autonomy of Humanistic Understanding' in R Allen and M Turvey (eds), *Wittgenstein, Theory and the Arts* (Routledge 2001) 42.

[305] Eg: K Chemla and EF Keller (eds), *Cultures Without Culturalism: The Making of Scientific Knowledge* (Duke University Press 2017). Adde: K Knorr-Cetina, *The Manufacture of Knowledge: An Essay on the Constructivist and Contextual Nature of Science* (Pergamon 1981); B Latour and S Woolgar, *Laboratory Life: The Construction of Scientific Facts* (2nd edn, Princeton University Press 1986); A Pickering, *Constructing Quarks: A Sociological History of Particle Physics* (University of Chicago Press 1984).

include the presence on at least one occasion of the expression 'quasi-scientific',[306] not to mention the author's treatment of 'causal inference' and 'deep understanding' as synonyms,[307] the latter formulation, however, being more spontaneously evocative of humanistic ventures informed by a cultural sensibility like Clifford Geertz's. As is well known, Geertz famously wrote of 'thick understanding', and he also published a famous essay entitled 'Deep Play: Notes on the Balinese Cockfight'.[308]

Meanwhile, the detailed survey of comparative constitutional scholarship on offer, as *Comparative Matters* introduces the various voices within the field, is marred by a profound contradiction – which, I suggest, undermines the text's creditability. Hirschl's panorama thus advances critical reflections to the effect that law's comparative constitutionalism 'lacks theoretical elevation and coherence',[309] a theme that is very much the leitmotiv of the entire book. Specifically, Hirschl objects to 'the field's ambivalence, if not outright reluctance, with respect to theory-building through causal inference'.[310] He adds that 'comparative constitutional law often overlooks (or is unaware of) the methodological principles of controlled comparison, research design, and case selection deployed in the human sciences'.[311] At the end of his demonstration, some fifty-four pages later, Hirschl formulates his principal critique again: '[C]omparative constitutional law, as a method and a project, remains under-theorized and blurry.'[312] Indeed, 'the field of comparative constitutional law remains quite eclectic, and continues to lack coherent methodological and epistemological foundations'.[313] Strangely, though, Hirschl offers not a single example of the work that he so insistently chastises. Even more perplexingly, Hirschl variously terms the texts that he discusses '[g]reat', 'thoughtful', 'effective', 'detailed', 'seminal', 'carefu[l]', 'meticulous', 'carefully crafted', and 'thorough'. Some, he writes, offer a 'good substantive illustration', others 'a most valuable contribution'. Yet others are 'well-executed', 'enrich[ing]', 'successfu[l]', 'nuanced', 'high-quality', 'useful', 'ample', 'impressive', 'exemplar[y]',

306 Hirschl, *Comparative Matters* (n 209) 280.
307 ibid 224.
308 C Geertz, *The Interpretation of Cultures* (Basic Books 1993 [1973]) 5–10 and 412–53.
309 Hirschl, *Comparative Matters* (n 209) 224.
310 ibid.
311 ibid.
312 ibid 278.
313 ibid.

'majestic', 'impressive' (again), 'most sophisticated', 'effective', 'effective' (again), 'effective' (yet again), 'innovativ[e]', 'effective' (once more), 'thorough' (one more time), 'detailed' (*bis*), 'successful' (again), 'methodologically astute', 'most influential', 'influential', 'most prominent', 'powerful', 'notable', and 'pioneering'. One text constitutes 'a major development', another is 'impressive' (once more), while yet another is 'open[ing] up entirely new possibilities'. Finally, two works are 'captivating' and, yes, 'effective'.[314] As I elucidate this fissure in the proposed theoretical model, as I engage in fissure-disclosure, I want to invite the rewriting of the system of knowledge being proffered well beyond the concealing course of action that is effectively on display. Arguing from the fissure, I summon enhanced intrepidity and integrity.[315]

Although I have dissented in a number of respects from what remains, to underscore my preliminary claim, comparative constitutional law's leading theoretical statement at this juncture,[316] I want to underscore how edifying I find Hirschl's call for a turn 'from comparative constitutional law to comparative constitutional studies'.[317] While directed at constitutionalists, this bracing injunction conveys all comparatists to adjust their mindsets. Even as the label 'comparative constitutional law' itself can be expected to prevail, the substantive difference between 'law' and 'studies' raises the vexed matter of names.

[314] All the words, expressions, or phrases I quote are at ibid 232–77.

[315] For a sophisticated treatment of fissures (including recondite crevices) and their potentially empowering role as dynamic spaces of reformulation, see GE Anzaldúa, *Light in the Dark, Luz en lo oscuro: Rewriting Identity, Spirituality, Reality* (A Keating ed, Duke University Press 2015) 16–17, 45, 71–73, and 95.

[316] My *proxime accessit* award goes to Frankenberg, *Studies* (n 196).

[317] Hirschl, *Comparative Matters* (n 209) 151 [capitals omitted].

III

Onomastics, Very Briefly

I long contended that when it came to indicate what comparatists-at-law do, the designation 'comparative legal studies' should replace 'comparative law'. And I applied my preference in the titles of various articles or chapters I wrote and to name a book I co-edited.[1] Even as I felt it disappointing that the comparative enterprise in law remained beset with such a terminological debate, I found it hard to circumvent the problem. Why, after all, ought *error communis* be allowed to govern? It seemed clear to me that one had to do all one could in order to contribute to the de-positivization of the field of comparative law, and I thought the word 'law' thus deserved to be displaced as it was unduly suggestive of an exclusive focus on rules (or at least, it could legitimately be taken to indicate a predilection for a 'black-letter' approach informing comparative interventions). In this regard, I was easily reminded of Samuel Beckett's warning about 'those little phrases that seem so innocuous and, once you let them in, pollute the whole of speech'.[2] The late Peter Stein usefully expands on Beckett's exhortation with reference to the academic world in general and law in particular:

> The labelling of any area of study may be crucially important to the way in which it is regarded and the respect in which it is held. . . . Labelling is also important within the area of legal studies themselves, where the

[1] Eg: P Legrand, 'Comparative Legal Studies and Commitment to Theory' (1995) 58 Modern LR 262; P Legrand, 'John Henry Merryman and Comparative Legal Studies: A Dialogue' (1999) 47 Am J Comp L 3; P Legrand, 'The Return of the Repressed: Moving Comparative Legal Studies Beyond Pleasure' (2001) 75 Tulane LR 1033; P Legrand, 'Paradoxically, Derrida: For a Comparative Legal Studies' (2005) 27 Cardozo LR 631; P Legrand, 'Comparative Legal Studies and the Matter of Authenticity' (2006) 1(2) J Comp L 365; P Legrand, 'Word/World (Of Primordial Issues for Comparative Legal Studies)' in H Petersen et al (eds), *Paradoxes of European Legal Integration* (Routledge 2008) 185–233. The book I have in mind is P Legrand and R Munday (eds), *Comparative Legal Studies: Traditions and Transitions* (Cambridge University Press 2003).

[2] S Beckett, *Malone Dies* (P Boxall ed, Faber & Faber 2010 [1956]) 17.

> acceptance of a particular form of enquiry as respectable may depend on the attribution of an appropriate title. Labelling can work to the disadvantage of a subject, if it cannot free itself from the disfavour which a certain line of enquiry has attracted.[3]

In effect, 'comparative law' always struck me as an embarrassing misnomer that, because it sowed confusion about the focus of comparative legal research (how can 'law' be 'comparative'? What is *that*? What does that *mean*?), made the practice discernibly more vulnerable from an institutional standpoint. If a specification does not readily denote an intelligible referent in the eyes of the various beholders (including the suspicious ones), if the very name of the field does not meet the threshold test of elementary sense-making, it is not hard to imagine how scholarly discredit should follow in short order.

Consider Harold Gutteridge's observations (while the excerpt I want to quote is long and despite the fact that I regard the author's insistence on law-as-rules as unduly reductionist, I find this passage helpful with respect to the argument I am making about nomenclature):

> [I]t is obvious that there can be no such thing as 'comparative' law. . . . The process of comparing rules of law taken from different systems does not result in the formulation of any independent rules for the regulation of human relationships or transactions. Not only are there no 'comparative' rules of law but there are no transactions or relationships which can be described as comparative. When we speak, for instance, of the comparative law of marriage this does not mean that comparative lawyers have devised a new set of rules to govern the relations between husband and wife; it merely indicates that the marriage laws of several countries have been subjected to a process of comparison in order to ascertain how far, and in what respects, they may differ from one another. There is no 'comparative' branch or department of the law in the sense in which a lawyer speaks of 'Family Law' or 'Maritime Law' or the other departments into which law is conventionally divided for the purpose of indicating the particular type of subject-matter with which each department deals.[4]

In the light of his remarks on the denomination 'comparative law', Gutteridge reaches an uncompromising conclusion regarding '[t]he emptiness of the phrase'.[5] (In passing, I must applaud Gutteridge's explanation to the effect that the comparison of laws 'from *different*

[3] P Stein, 'The Tasks of Historical Jurisprudence' in N MacCormick and P Birks (eds), *The Legal Mind* (Oxford University Press 1986) 293.

[4] HC Gutteridge, *Comparative Law* (2nd edn, Cambridge University Press 1949) 1.

[5] ibid.

systems' is deployed 'in order to ascertain how far, and in what respects, [laws] may *differ* from one another'.)

To be sure, the difficulty I address is not exclusive to law (there is 'comparative literature', for instance),[6] and it is not specific to the English language either. French ('*droit comparé*'), Portuguese ('*direito comparado*'), Romanian ('*drept comparat*'), Italian ('*diritto comparato*'), and Spanish ('*derecho comparado*'), to confine myself to these five illustrations, fare only marginally better.[7] (The reason for the small improvement over the English designation is that one can argue that 'law compared' – the literal English translation for the Romance expressions I adduce – features more clarity than 'law comparative', since it evokes sentences such as 'the law that is compared' or 'the law being compared'.[8]) In this regard, the German and Dutch languages, for instance, largely manage to escape critique as words like '*Rechtsvergleichung*' and '*Rechtsverjelijking*' emphasize the idea of process rather than problematically directing attention to a substantive and rule-based orientation, that is, to a positivist inclination in the treatment of the legal. The German and Dutch formulations helpfully remain 'free from any implication of the existence of a body of rules forming a separate branch or department of the law'.[9]

But, notwithstanding how incessant and steadfast the commitment I harboured over many years, I eventually deferred to pragmatics. *J'ai viré ma cuti.* No matter how significant the implications, how frequent the reservations, how persuasive the claims in favour of an alternative designation, it became apparent to me that the 'regimen' (if I may be allowed this convenient shorthand to refer to the mighty forces of institutional inertia, that I often personally experienced, ranging from law faculties to law publishers, from journal editors to directors of research institutes,

6 cf B Johnson, 'Bad Writing' in J Culler and K Lamb (eds), *Just Being Difficult?* (Stanford University Press 2003) 162–63, where Barbara Johnson asks why not 'comparable literature' instead of 'comparative literature' – the latter expression being, in the author's view, an 'od[d] name' for the field.

7 By way of example, the French specification '*droit comparé*' has long been the focus of fierce objections from comparatists writing in the French language. Eg: R David, *Traité élémentaire de droit civil comparé* (LGDJ 1950) 3–4; P Arminjon et al, *Traité de droit comparé*, vol 1 (LGDJ 1950) 10; M Ancel, *Utilité et méthodes du droit comparé* (Ides et Calendes 1971) 31; L-J Constantinesco, *Traité de droit comparé*, vol 1 (LGDJ 1972) 6; HA Schwarz-Liebermann von Wahlendorf, *Droit comparé* (LGDJ 1978) 171–72.

8 Of course, it cannot do to have 'law' in the singular as comparison *entails* more than one law.

9 Gutteridge (n 4) 1.

from scholars steeped in tradition and reflexively wary of change to the small army of indifferent positivists) will easily withstand calls for a label modification, an alteration it readily apprehends as an unwarranted dislocation rather than a timely amelioration – after all, 'liberation depends on the consciousness of servitude'[10] – hence my mentimutation.

In his seminal critique, Günter Frankenberg, addressing 'the complaint that the term [comparative law] has little or no meaning',[11] writes as follows: '[D]efinitions and redefinitions have not silenced the doubts that there is something basically wrong with comparative law. Instead of providing the ultimate definition, I propose that we do not bother with changes in terminology but deal with the doubts instead.'[12] While I initially disagreed with Frankenberg's sanguine reaction to the terminological mess I discuss, I now concede, if with marked reluctance, the wisdom there is in refraining from investing time and effort in a battle that must ultimately be regarded as almost integrally futile. The economy of the 'regimen' will prevail, and I must abdicate: comparative law is an ugly expression, and comparative law, which deserved better, is saddled with it. But I renounce *in name only*, and I continue to think of comparative *legal studies*, to encourage a determinently *studenty* attitude vis-à-vis the legal, to foster the dedicated *study* of the foreign. In other words, my capitulation cannot prevent me from contesting, *as I work*, the positivist semantic extension of the word 'law' with a view, well, to the de-position of the orthodox comparative enterprise, which therefore continues as *NCL*'s abiding endeavour.

Drawing once more on Gutteridge, who allows that 'the employment of the phrase "comparative law" is now too deeply rooted to be dislodged and that no great harm will result from it *so long as it is not permitted to exercise any restrictive influence*',[13] I, too, remain eager to move comparative law beyond '[t]he flat presentation of bankable findings' along the lines of phillumeny,[14] beyond, that is, the inscription of research into foreign law that 'seems simpl[e] and ... straightforward, comforting, knowledge as it is supposed to look'[15] – 'comforting' to jurists immersed

[10] H Marcuse, *One-Dimensional Man* (2nd edn, Routledge 1991 [1964]) 9.

[11] G Frankenberg, 'Critical Comparisons: Re-thinking Comparative Law' (1985) 26 Harvard Int'l LJ 411, 411n1.

[12] ibid.

[13] HC Gutteridge, 'Comparative Law and the Law of Nations' (1944) 21 British Yearbook Int'l L 1, 1 [my emphasis].

[14] C Geertz, *After the Fact* (Harvard University Press 1995) 62.

[15] ibid.

into positivism, that is. Indeed, I aim to do much more in *NCL* than rearrange the deck chairs on what I regard as an epistemological undertaking not only stinking, but sinking. To quote Jacques Derrida, what I want to accomplish is 'at the outset to put into question a certain scene of reading and of evaluation, with its comforts, its interests, its programmes of all kind'.[16] Yes. I am aware that it is already very late: comparative law, my learned Cambridge colleague and friend pronounced solemnly in July 2018, is 'a dying subject'. But there are stirrings still – with thanks to Beckett for lending an apt form of words – at least if one is willing to accord significance to the sheer mass of materials currently issuing from constitutional law specialists and also to heed other movements, such as the development of transnational law and the comparativization of international law, as, I think, one must resolutely do.

[16] J Derrida, *Points de suspension* (E Weber ed, Galilée 1992 [1983]) 124.

IV

More Comparative Law

What is 'transnational' law, and how does it concern the comparison of laws? Economically stated, the modish word, in effect a variation on the theme of 'interlegality',[1] purports to capture legal regulations as they concern individuals, corporations, or governments operating over legal borders.[2] (To distinguish the transnational from the international, it has been helpfully suggested that the former term should be reserved for cross-border situations involving at least one non-governmental agent.[3]) Uncontroversial examples of transnational law include international commercial contracts, foreign investment, conflict of laws, the Internet, and market regulation broadly understood. Dispute-resolution mechanisms such as commercial arbitration are also deemed to fall within the new

[1] I derive the expression from B de Sousa Santos, *Toward a New Legal Common Sense* (3rd edn, Cambridge University Press 2020) 519. The term embraces 'not the legal pluralism of traditional legal anthropology, in which the different legal orders are conceived as separate entities coexisting in the same political space, but rather, the conception of different legal spaces superimposed, interpenetrated and mixed in our minds, as much as in our actions'. cf J Klabbers and G Palombella (eds), *The Challenge of Inter-Legality* (Cambridge University Press 2019). For a critique of the label 'transnational', see F Werro, 'Is There Such a Thing as Transnational Law? Insights for Defining the Object of Transnational Legal Studies' in S Keller and S Wiprächtiger (eds), *Recht zwischen Dogmatik und Theorie* (Dike 2012) 311–28.

[2] For a noteworthy argument, see R Schmidt, *Regulatory Integration Across Borders* (Cambridge University Press 2018). See also TC Halliday and G Shaffer (eds), *Transnational Legal Orders* (Cambridge University Press 2015); M Maduro et al (eds), *Transnational Law* (Cambridge University Press 2014). For an impressive collection of documents and annotations, see DE Childress et al (eds), *Transnational Law and Practice* (2nd edn, Wolters Kluwer 2020).

[3] T Hale and D Held, 'Mapping Changes in Transnational Governance' in T Hale and D Held (eds), *Handbook of Transnational Governance* (Polity 2012) 4.

categorization.[4] (Note that such subject-matters existed long before transnational law became a fashionable slogan.[5])

While it aptly challenges the classical or 'Westphalian' idea that the only law that would matter normatively would be state law, and even as it fittingly underscores the normative significance of regimes of legal governance featuring non-state forms or decentralized models, the transnational, whether it addresses climate change, nanotechnologies, or immigration, remains anchored to the core concept of the nation-state (the space of flows – the flows of information, technology, and finance, for example – does not replace the space of places). Unsurprisingly, then, transnational scholarship retains an important role for the state to play as it refutes any idea that the transborder patterns under consideration would amount to anything remotely resembling a universal law – a claim that does not at all entail a reactionary emphasis on nations and nationalism.[6] As Robert Wai explains in an excellent assessment making specific reference to international commercial contracts, complexity and pluralism have to be seen as defining characteristics of these alternative normative schemes, each and every one of them consisting in an intricate and singular legal assemblage.[7] Crucially from the standpoint of comparative law – to maintain the disappointingly uncontested

[4] See generally D Lehmkuhl, 'Transnational Commercial Arbitration' in T Hale and D Held (eds), *Handbook of Transnational Governance* (Polity 2012) 138–47.

[5] For a noteworthy argument seeking to 'update' a field and move it from its classical preoccupations to new or contemporary ones, see H Muir Watt, 'Private International Law Beyond the Schism' (2011) 2 Transnational Legal Theory 347; H Muir Watt, 'When Societal Constitutionalism Encounters Private International Law: Of Pluralism, Distribution, and "Chronotopes"' (2018) 45 J L & Society S185; H Muir Watt, *Discours sur les méthodes du droit international privé (des formes juridiques de l'inter-altérité)* (Brill 2019) [hereinafter *Discours*]. In the latter text, the transcript of her 2017 course before the Hague Academy of International Law, Horatia Muir Watt specifically argues for the renaming of 'private international law' as 'law of inter-alterity' ('*droit de l'inter-altérité*'): Muir Watt, *Discours*, 22n21 and passim.

[6] Eg: LC Backer, 'Governance Without Government: An Overview' in G Handl et al (eds), *Beyond Territoriality: Transnational Legal Authority in an Age of Globalization* (Brill 2012) 111–12, where the author observes that states still produce 'an important good – regulation – that can be characterised as a cost of operations'.

[7] R Wai, 'The Interlegality of Transnational Private Law' (2008) 71(3) L & Contemporary Problems 107 [hereinafter 'Interlegality']. For further emphasis on transnationalism and legal pluralism, see R Wai, 'Beyond Normal Trade Law?' in A Santos et al (eds), *World Trade and Investment Law Reimagined* (Anthem 2019) 107–17. Observe that my argument about assemblages shows well that '[t]o think in terms of singularities . . . is *not* to make a claim against the demonstrable and documentable permeability of cultures and languages': D Chakrabarty, *Provincializing Europe* (2nd edn, Stanford University Press 2008) 83.

misnomer – Wai observes that the transnational private ordering he addresses stands as 'a regime of ... conditional cosmopolitan hospitality'.[8] This remark deserves to be generalized: processes of transnationalization are emphatically not to be confused with patterns of unification or uniformization – and this conclusion obtains whether transnational legal operations are to be regarded as constituting a new field or not,[9] and whether they are understood as strengthening or weakening democratic sovereignty.[10] More precisely, '[t]ransnationalism is ... a process of de- and renationalization in which new forms of interconnectedness are established as passing resolutions of the contradictions between place and non-place, place and flow'.[11]

Transnational law thus remains law-in-situation, even when it features a normative de-situationalization from traditional state structures and even when that normative de-situationalization purports to be extensive – which means that transnational law invites comparative analysis in ways not at all dissimilar to what the more traditional or state-based regulatory frameworks have long encouraged. Indeed, '[a] study of law which crosses "systems" *compels* a comparative analysis'.[12] Just as one can engage in a comparative investigation of Italian and Dutch corporate-governance laws, then, one can proceed to compare how the Organization for Economic Co-operation and Development (OECD)'s corporate-governance principles (first stated in 1999 and later revised)[13] – a typical non-binding intergovernmental initiative – are being interpreted locally, that is, how they apply in practice in specific national jurisdictions. Given that '[t]he principles are intended and designed to be sufficiently broad, or ambiguous, to avoid suffocating national cultures',[14] such comparative research will, in fact, prove essential.

[8] Wai, 'Interlegality' (n 7) 125.

[9] Eg: R Cotterrell, 'What Is Transnational Law?' (2012) 37 L & Social Inquiry 500.

[10] Eg: S Benhabib, 'The New Sovereigntism and Transnational Law: Legal Utopianism, Democratic Scepticism and Statist Realism' (2016) 5 Global Constitutionalism 109.

[11] P Osborne, 'On Comparability: Kant and the Possibility of Comparative Studies' (2005) 32(2) *boundary 2* 3, 20.

[12] C Menkel-Meadow, 'Why and How to Study "Transnational" Law?' (2011) 1 UC Irvine LR 97, 111 [my emphasis]. See also D Roth-Isigkeit, *The Plurality Trilemma* (Palgrave Macmillan 2018) 34–41.

[13] See Organization for Economic Co-operation and Development, *G20/OECD Principles of Corporate Governance* (2015) <www.oecd.org/corporate/principles-corporate-governance.htm>.

[14] A Baker, 'Global Corporate Governance Principles' in T Hale and D Held (eds), *Handbook of Transnational Governance* (Polity 2012) 277.

I find it important to emphasize that no one, I think, would deny the ascertainable existence of economic forces in the widest sense – let us say, transnational configurations – being at work beyond the local and conditioning the local. Consider transnationalization processes whereby production is displaced beyond local borders, for instance, through subcontracting. To be sure, this articulation of production is not entirely new. But recent technologies have endowed capital and production with enhanced mobility. In particular, they have stretched spatial extension to unprecedented levels. Along the way, capital has sought maximum advantage against labour, that is, it has managed to emancipate itself as much as possible from local social and political fetters. In the era of technological capitalism, production is now often heavily concentrated in the transnational corporation, which implies that the power of any government to engage in territorial regulation of the economy is limited. (Meanwhile, any regulation of the international economic order emerges as an even more daunting challenge.) In fact, the transnationalization of production is the source, at once, of unprecedented international congruity (think of economic homogenization) and of unprecedented fragmentation (consider how the production process breaks into subnational regions and localities). In this regard, observe that even societies having historically been non-capitalist now make their own claims to capitalism. Envisage the conciliation of the so-called 'Confucian' values prevailing in East-Asian societies with capitalism, and note how a local account is thereby being re-articulated into a capitalist narrative (not, of course, into 'the' capitalist narrative, since Confucianism emphasizes values more communitarian than the individualism that, in its various declensions, has characterized Eurocentrism).[15]

Irrespective of how transnational legal governance has developed and of the prevalence it has assumed, it is the case that every framework must ultimately resolve itself as a series of situated applications, which means that every transnational regulatory regime finds concrete expression somewhere, that every meaningful application is 'grounded' in the form of a singular assemblage between non-local and local facets.[16] To be sure,

[15] Eg: T Ruskola, 'People, Inc.? Law, Economic Enterprise, and the Development of Inequality in China' (2019) 67 Am J Comp L 383.

[16] It seems odd, then, for the title of a book to refer to 'comparative and transnational law' as in M Fenwick et al (eds), *The Shifting Meaning of Legal Certainty in Comparative and Transnational Law* (Hart 2017). It is not that there is 'the comparative' and 'the transnational', but that the transnational's instantiations invite comparative analysis, that the transnational exists *comparatively*.

ICANN (or the Internet Corporation for Assigned Names and Numbers) has been a fully transnational regulatory agency since October 2016 (it had previously been subject to US government oversight). But the transnational dimension hardly makes for legal unification or uniformization, and one can profitably engage in a comparative study of the management of IP (Internet Protocol) numbers and of the DNS (Domain Name System) involving, say, the laws of Canada and Germany, the latter now featuring the European Union's General Data Protection Regulation that was implemented on 25 May 2018. In effect, the expansion of the transnational offers infinite opportunities for further comparative scholarship, that is, for comparative research reaching beyond the classical juxtaposition of state laws. In this crucial sense, the transnational properly stands as a further vehicle for the deployment of comparative law's agenda, whether the comparatist is interested in any one of the more than 2,000 intergovernmental organizations, the more than 3,000 multilateral treaties, or the more than 27,000 bilateral agreements in existence at this writing.[17] And this is not even to mention non-governmental organizations (NGOs), firms, or individuals ranging from Human Rights Watch to Greenpeace, from Médecins Sans Frontières to The Body Shop, and from Apple to the Gates Foundation and its work on health care in developing countries.

If, for instance, one's focus is the International Association of Insurance Supervisors and its promotion, since 1994, of standards regarding the improved supervision of the insurance industry for the protection of policyholders, one will want to operate in the knowledge that 'there is still a broad difference among countries in respect of the level of implementation of the international standards'.[18] Meanwhile, if one is concerned with the work of the World Commission on Dams, which was established in 1998 in order to formulate internationally acceptable criteria for the development of dams (including their financing), one will ensure to bear in mind how the standards have prompted a wide range of national governments' and private banks' reactions.[19] And anyone interested in Rugmark, the certification for hand-made carpets produced in India, Nepal, and Pakistan that developed from 1994 to 1997 with a view to attesting that no child labour is involved,

[17] See Hale and Held (n 3) 5.

[18] D Masciandaro, 'International Association of Insurance Supervisors' in T Hale and D Held (eds), *Handbook of Transnational Governance* (Polity 2012) 78–79.

[19] See NK Dubash, 'World Commission on Dams' in T Hale and D Held (eds), *Handbook of Transnational Governance* (Polity 2012) 204–5.

will be well-advised to remain aware that local effectiveness varies.[20] Being structurally constituted to take legal analysis beyond state borders, comparative law thus always-already stands not only as an inherent problematization of legal nationalism, but also of the legal nationalism that inevitably survives manifestations of the transnational – which means that the development of transnational models proceeds to *reinforce* the comparative claim.

*

The relevance of comparative law also finds itself enhanced through what I style 'the comparativization of international law'. It is trite to recall that, in terms of one of the very raisons d'être of the field in which they toil (comparison depends on there being more than one law in co-presence), comparatists, lest they lose themselves in cognitive dissonance, cannot be sharing in the aspiration to one-law that characterizes international law. Even as '[i]nternational law aspires to be a universal field',[21] comparatists have long applied their disciplinary orientation towards the view that international law cannot be unified or uniform, that there will potentially be as many different versions of a certain formulation of international law as there are polities, and that international law in its various local declensions therefore readily lends itself to comparison. In this vein, a comparatist like Joachim Zekoll goes so far as to write of 'public international law' as an 'aspec[t] of comparative law'.[22] Be the 'aspectual' characterization as it may, some internationalists have long concurred in the differential argument. For instance, David Kennedy has realistically observed that 'international law is different in different places'.[23]

[20] See M Koenig-Archibugi, 'Rugmark' in T Hale and D Held (eds), *Handbook of Transnational Governance* (Polity 2012) 335–36.

[21] A Roberts, *Is International Law International?* (Oxford University Press 2017) 321.

[22] J Zekoll, 'Kant and Comparative Law – Some Reflections on a Reform Effort' (1996) 70 Tulane LR 2719, 2733. cf HC Gutteridge, 'Comparative Law and the Law of Nations' (1944) 21 British Yearbook Int'l L 1, 10, where the author argues that comparative law's 'value as an instrument for the development of the law of nations is undoubted'.

[23] D Kennedy, 'The Disciplines of International Law and Policy' (1999) 12 Leiden J Int'l L 9, 17. 'Reservations' offer a ready illustration of the differentiation Kennedy addresses. Eg: A Aust, *Modern Treaty Law and Practice* (Cambridge University Press 2013) 114–44; R Kolb, *The Law of Treaties* (Elgar 2016) 63–88; M Bowman, 'Treaty Obligations, Universalized Norms and Differentiated Responsibilities' in MJ Bowman and D Kritsiotis (eds), *Conceptual and Contextual Perspectives on the Modern Law of Treaties* (Cambridge University Press 2018) 392–439.

While the claim for a differentialist approach to international law has repeatedly been made over the years,[24] one witnesses a resurgence of interest in this thesis as internationalists, rather than focus on whether international law is law, have taken to asking whether international law is international.[25] And internationalists, as they advocate for internationalist introspection regarding the effective limits of the international's internationalization, are supplying a resounding 'no' by way of answer to their self-addressed question. Thus:

> On issues from treaty interpretation to the content of customary international law, different states and international bodies may set forth different interpretations of the same rules, sometimes strategically, other times unaware of the differences. In some cases, these varying interpretations may subsist with minimal attention, while in others they may change or destabilize the international rules themselves.[26]

In addition, an extensive array of figures and statistics establishes that there are strong local variations as regards the manner in which international law is inscribed in textbooks and casebooks, not to mention the institutional profiles of academics specializing in the teaching of international law across diverse jurisdictions – the predictable implication involving the dissemination of different information to different students in different countries concerning the matter 'international law' (this very expression actually featuring a different semantic reach from, say, '*droit international*', '*derecho internacional*', and so forth).[27] While the accumulation of data in favour of the non-international character of international law is impressive, it behoves a seasoned comparatist to observe that the exercise is marred by

[24] Eg: M Koskenniemi, 'The Case for Comparative International Law' (2009) 20 Finnish Yearbook Int'l L 1; BN Mamlyuk and U Mattei, 'Comparative International Law' (2011) 36 Brooklyn J Int'l L 385; A Roberts, 'Comparative International Law? The Role of National Courts in Creating and Enforcing International Law' (2011) 60 Int'l & Comp LQ 57; 'Symposium: Exploring Comparative International Law' (2015) 109 Am J Int'l L 467.

[25] See Roberts (n 21).

[26] A Roberts et al, 'Conceptualizing Comparative International Law' in A Roberts et al (eds), *Comparative International Law* (Oxford University Press 2018) 4.

[27] For the claim concerning the differentiation of materials across local textbooks or casebooks, see Roberts (n 21) 129–208. For an analogous contention emphasizing differentiation with respect to law professors, see ibid 51–128.

unfortunate simplifications.[28] Also, it is afflicted by undue reliance on clichés.[29]

[28] Consider textbooks, which figure prominently in Anthea Roberts's study. While the matter of 'what it means to be a textbook of "international law"' is properly addressed (ibid 130), the question, arguably more primordial, of what it means to be a *textbook* is ignored. Consequently, a US textbook is deemed to be epistemologically commensurate with a German textbook, both works being, well, textbooks and therefore fit for statisticization. Suffice it to recall Mary Ann Glendon's insights in MA Glendon, *Rights Talk* (Free Press 1991) 169. Glendon thus remarks that in the United States, a treatise 'can never substitute for immersion in a line of cases'. She warns that European jurists are 'apt to regard American scholarly works as more complete and authoritative than their authors mean them to be'. Indeed, says Glendon, '[t]he authors of [US] treatises typically do not exhibit the same mania for thoroughness of coverage, or striving for balanced evaluation, that characterizes European books bearing similar titles'. For Glendon, '[US treatises] tend to be more imaginative than their continental counterparts, but also more idiosyncratic'. An important conclusion ensues: '[E]ven excellent works on American constitutional law risk being misunderstood by readers who have been schooled to regard a treatise as a comprehensive treatment of a subject by an author striving to be objective.' What would be the US term for the French word '*doctrine*'? And what would be the US label for the German expressions '*herrschende Lehre*' or '*Lehrmeinung*'? I suggest that the reductionism on display in Roberts's compilation is problematic. At the very least, Roberts's reader is entitled to be told more about what the materials that detain her mean to their respective legal constituencies and on what basis she feels entitled to collocate certain materials existing differently in different legal 'communities' for comparative and statistical purposes. Analogous comments could deservedly be made as regards law reviews. Glendon is also helpful in this respect. See ibid. For a sustained contestation of the commensurability being reflexively assumed by internationalists professing to take comparison seriously, see J d'Aspremont, 'Comparativism and Colonizing Thinking in International Law' (2020) 57 Canadian Yearbook Int'l L 89.

[29] It is pernicious to entitle a sub-section 'German Excellence in Doctrinalism', and it is even more detrimental to proceed to quote a German jurist asserting that 'German doctrinal scholarship will always be superior to that of other countries': Roberts (n 21) 218 and 219. It so happens that Franz Werro and I had occasion to reply to that very German jurist's very self-serving assertion. Given that our rejoinder, despite the fact that it appeared on a prominent law blog, does not seem to have come to Roberts's attention (unless it simply happened to stand in the way of her argument), I am pleased to rehearse what I regard as the relevant segment: '[The German jurist's] assertion is as implausible as if he maintained that "French literary criticism will always be superior to that of other countries" or that "Japanese aesthetics will always be superior to that of other countries" or for that matter that "the Spanish language will always be superior to that of other countries". The ascertainable fact is that German legal scholarship, French literary criticism, Japanese aesthetics, or the Spanish language – to the extent that such entities can be persuasively delineated – are cultural formations. They are made, fabricated, constructed by women and men interacting in a certain place and at a certain time. They are artefacts. It is not then that there would be something like "cultural excellence" *an sich*, for all to see. Rather, the quality of excellence is ascribed by an ascertainable constituency of individuals who appreciate "excellence" according to local criteria. For example, the matter of "excellence" in legal scholarship will be attributed by a group of jurists who have been trained to deem certain scholarly forms to be "excellent", that is, who have been inducted into

Although readily presenting itself as 'a newly emerging field',[30] comparative international law appears to want to draw, most awkwardly for what purports to stand as a novel scholarly province, on decidedly obsolescent comparative law. While acknowledging in the most cursory terms the textual existence of a critique of this unpersuasive brand of comparatism, comparative international law seems to have chosen to hitch its epistemic wagon to the woefully under-theorized and unsophisticated theoretical model that persists as orthodox comparative law – an orientation presumably suggesting a strong positivist inclination on the part of its internationalist partisans.[31] It remains that the new/old thinking within international law is *reinforcing* the relevance and visibility of comparative law – if of an epistemologically impoverished configuration of the comparative endeavour.

*

Another initiative, evidently informed by more subtle epistemological insights than comparative international law has sought fit to convene, pertains to 'comparative foreign relations law', what would be 'a new field of study and teaching'.[32] In this regard, the presiding ambition is to

appreciating certain scholarly practices and socialized into favoring certain scholarly values. To be sure, German scholarly undertakings will often, perhaps typically, adopt a conceptual form and eschew the candid policy concerns that are familiar to US academics. And the reader of German legal scholarship can therefore expect more on systemics and less on patriarchy, more on categories and less on externalities, more on subsumption and less on critical race theory. But none of these German predilections is intrinsically "excellent" or "superior" to prevailing perspectives in other countries. In other words, scholarly excellence very much lies in the eye of the beholder. In the end, there is neither more nor less to be said for or against the "excellence" of German legal scholarship – which, if we are willing to assume such a configuration, illustrates but one way among others to approach the study of law, no matter how influential. Lest influence be confused with rightness or truthfulness, let us emphasize that it is not because German legal scholarship enjoys a substantial and long-standing following that it can claim any particular entitlement to being right or true. Nor is it the case that the tiresome repetition on the part of so many German jurists that their scholarly model is best can, in time, somehow elevate it to the exalted status of universal yardstick by which other forms of scholarship would be assessed. Needless to add, these precise reservations must be entered as regards United States legal scholarship, which must also confine any claim to excellence it may wish to hold to a specifiable horizon.' I am grateful to Franz Werro for allowing me to reproduce this excerpt. For the complete entry, see P Legrand and F Werro, 'When It Would Have Been Better Not to Talk About a Better Model' (*PrawfsBlog*, 2 March 2014) <http://prawfsblawg.blogs.com/prawfsblawg/2014/03/legrand-and-werro-on-the-doctrinewars.html> [on file].

30 Roberts et al (n 26) 6.

31 See ibid 12–16.

32 CA Bradley, 'Preface' in CA Bradley (ed), *The Oxford Handbook of Comparative Foreign Relations Law* (Oxford University Press 2019) vii.

'compar[e] and contras[t] how nations, and also supranational entities such as the European Union, structure their decisions about matters such as entering into and exiting from international agreements, engaging with international institutions, and using military force, as well as how they incorporate treaties and customary international law into their domestic legal systems'.[33] Even a cursory acquaintance with what must uncontroversially qualify as one of the foundational texts in this emerging field shows how scholarly authorities are keenly aware that with respect to foreign relations law, the comparatist must expect 'significant differences among countries in institutional structures'.[34] Otherwise said, it is readily appreciated that '[c]omparison does not imply similarity or harmonization'.[35] In fact, comparatists are expressly warned that '[a]s [they] compare practices across states, it can sometimes be easy to lose sight of ... differences'.[36] Accordingly, they are advised that 't[he] engage[ment] in comparative foreign relations law should ... not be understood as an effort to identify outliers and encourage conformity'.[37] Moreover, comparatists are reminded that 'quantitative analysis ... is not a substitute for in-depth nuanced assessment of practices' or for 'more detailed understandings of the multitude of institutional dynamics states have employed'.[38] Indeed, 'individual legal rules and practice on particular legal topics ... are necessarily embedded in and intertwined with a given state's unique legal, historical, political context'. Using slightly different wording, another statement buttresses this claim: '[A]ny comparative analysis ... should be approached with caution. Each country's laws and practices are embedded within that

[33] ibid.

[34] CA Bradley, 'What Is Foreign Relations Law?' in CA Bradley (ed), *The Oxford Handbook of Comparative Foreign Relations Law* (Oxford University Press 2019) 19.

[35] K Knop, 'Foreign Relations Law' in CA Bradley (ed), *The Oxford Handbook of Comparative Foreign Relations Law* (Oxford University Press 2019) 49. Karen Knop's sub-title is 'Comparison as Invention': ibid 45. While, throughout *NCL*, I deploy 'invention' in a different sense than Knop's (see supra 10 and infra 175–76 and 303), I find the semantic coincidence worthy of emphasis.

[36] OA Hathaway, 'A Comparative Foreign Relations Law Agenda' in CA Bradley (ed), *The Oxford Handbook of Comparative Foreign Relations Law* (Oxford University Press 2019) 96.

[37] ibid. See also T Ginsburg, 'Constitutions and Foreign Relations Law: The Dynamics of Substitutes and Complements' (2017) 111 Am J Int'l L Unbound 326, 330, where the author, recommending the 'search for an account of variation', invites comparatists to ask '[w]hy is it that countries differ in their constitutional arrangements and doctrine' and to seek 'to understand the consequences of different arrangements'.

[38] Hathaway (n 36) 84 and 87–88.

country's particular legal culture, political system, and historical tradition.'[39] (Indeed, one is forewarned that practice may prove 'substantially different' from 'formal written law'.[40]) As it is conceded with becoming modesty that 'there is much that we still do not know about foreign relations laws and practices around the world',[41] as it is notably claimed that comparative foreign relations law must address 'states that are less well represented in scholarship and academic circles',[42] one senses that the comparative sensibility on display, certainly in the passages I have indicated, is heralding not only further comparative law, but a brand of comparison featuring decidedly auspicious epistemological awareness. Crucially, it is also acknowledged that 'comparison is necessarily generative',[43] an observation percipiently emphasizing the comparatist's *productive* role in the enunciation of information regarding foreignness (which means that such information, far from being objective or true, must be seen to bear, necessarily, the interpretive – the *inventive* – mark of the comparatist arranging and inscribing it, this badge never being innocent and always heralding a commitment).

*

Beyond the transnational and the international, and in addition to the case of foreign affairs, every attempt at the enactment of a unified or uniform law – every allegedly regionalizing or universalizing strategy – is destined, ipso facto so to speak, also to amplify the comparison of laws' relevance. To reformulate my point, I maintain that the more the unification or uniformization of laws is pursued, the more there will be a remarkable role for comparative law to play, since not even the most purportedly unifying or uniformizing legal initiative, whether on account of an international convention or any other legal instrument, can avoid its ultimate resolution in terms of localization. The fact of the matter is that none of the presumed panopticons I address can efface spatial disjuncture.[44] Indeed, the gathering of more than one law into a form

[39] CA Bradley, 'US War Powers and the Potential Benefits of Comparativism' in CA Bradley (ed), *The Oxford Handbook of Comparative Foreign Relations Law* (Oxford University Press 2019) 765.
[40] Bradley (n 34) 19.
[41] Bradley (n 32) ix.
[42] Hathaway (n 36) 85–86.
[43] Knop (n 35) 45.
[44] Eg: PS Berman, 'The Inevitable Pluralism Within Universal Harmonization Regimes: The Case of the CISG' (2016) 21 Uniform LR 23; PB Stephan, 'The Futility of Unification and Harmonization in International Commercial Law' (1999) 39 Virginia J Int'l L 743. See also eg S Zwingel, *Translating International Women's Rights* (Palgrave Macmillan 2016);

that would now be 'the one' cannot overcome the empirical determination that, formalist pirouettes notwithstanding, difference across laws is what there is in the co-presence of more than one law, such difference remaining irreducible. Not even the most express positing of formal unity can withstand the persistent manifestation of the manifold. Through unified or uniform law, for example, the many laws, although now increased by one (say, the international convention emerging over and above the national laws), do not effectively become one. A formal connective synthesis such as a unified or uniform law-text is simply not enough, in and of itself, to articulate the actual becoming-one of a diversity of law-worlds. Upon examination, such synthesis will reveal itself to be disjunctive and feature an attendant multiplicity of routes and permutations. Note, once more, that the disjunctiveness I discuss is not to be understood as implying the existence of monadic entities, but rather as allowing for a complex web of sophisticated intersections, each of them consisting in a singular assemblage between the non-local and the obstinately local. Even a determinedly peripatetic legal figure like 'proportionality', absent any convention or other agreement, demands to be resolved into an array of local assemblages traceable in significant part to local configurations of legal knowledge themselves featuring as cultural instantiations. [45] In Gunther Teubner's words, there is a 'fragmentation' harking back to 'contradictions between society-wide institutionalized rationalities, which [uniform] law cannot solve'.[46] Nor is this fact to be regretted. Difference is not deviance from some overarching paragon. And 'diversity is not the first step in an inescapable evolution toward uniformity or unity'; in effect, '[t]here is no ideal state of convergence or fusion toward which everything tends.'[47]

*

My observations on the ostensibly transnational, international, unified, or uniform law invite a complementary set of remarks on what would be

A Hellum and HS Aasen (eds), *Women's Human Rights* (Cambridge University Press 2013). Both books focus on the Convention on the Elimination of All Forms of Discrimination Against Women (CEDAW), a cornerstone of the international women's rights discourse, and analyze the Convention's differential transposition into local applications.

45 For an assiduous analysis, see A Marketou, *Local Meanings of Proportionality* (Cambridge University Press 2021).

46 A Fischer-Lescano and G Teubner, 'Regime-Collisions: The Vain Search for Legal Unity in the Fragmentation of Global Law' (2004) 25 Michigan J Int'l L 999, 1004.

47 B de Sousa Santos, *The End of the Cognitive Empire* (Duke University Press 2018) 39.

the globalized.[48] Owing to the work of sociologist Roland Robertson,[49] *glocalization* stands as a sophisticated answer allowing analysts to resist the simplistic view that so-called 'globalization' processes are dissolving local settings and structures, absorbing local lifeworlds more or less without further ado, and replacing those by a smooth and continuous identity or equivalence or commonality cutting across borders worldwide.[50] Even as there *is* a reconfiguration of spatial boundaries – a restructuration informed, incidentally, by a temporal process that the instantaneity of networked communication readily illustrates – glocalization, an analytically autonomous concept featuring a specific explanatory input, emphasizes how the compression of life manifesting itself on a planetary scale is not unfolding as sheer Americanization or occidentalization of any kind. Rather, in every locale there takes place a complex interaction between standardization and (inevitable) indigenization in the form of a seemingly infinite array of customized and differentiated assemblages, each construction ultimately singular. There is, then, the irreducibility of the glocal, because there is 'the irreducibility of idiom'.[51]

[48] I leave to one side the matter of historical sequentialism. But see eg, with specific reference to law, M Pitts and MJ Versluys (eds), *Globalisation and the Roman World* (Cambridge University Press 2015); D Kennedy, 'Three Globalizations of Law and Legal Thought: 1850-2000' in DM Trubek and A Santos (eds), *The New Law and Economic Development* (Cambridge University Press 2006) 19–73. For a thoughtful critique of Duncan Kennedy's text, see C Tomlins, 'The Presence and Absence of Legal Mind: A Comment on Kennedy's *Three Globalizations*' (2015) 78(1–2) L & Contemporary Problems 1. While the argument in favour of more comparative law would also prevail in this instance, I am deliberately avoiding a consideration of the so-called '*lex mercatoria*'. For a decisive demonstration regarding the fictitious character of this intellectual elaboration, see E Kadens, 'Order Within Law, Variety Within Custom: The Character of the Medieval Merchant Law' (2004) 5 Chicago J Int'l L 39; E Kadens, 'The Myth of the Customary Law Merchant' (2012) 90 Texas LR 1153; E Kadens, 'The Medieval Law Merchant: The Tyranny of a Construct' (2015) 7 J Legal Analysis 251; E Kadens, 'Convergence and the Colonization of Custom in Pre-modern Europe' in O Moréteau et al (eds), *Comparative Legal History* (Elgar 2019) 167–85.

[49] Eg: R Robertson, *Globalization* (Sage 1992); R Robertson, 'Glocalization: Time-Space and Homogeneity-Heterogeneity' in M Featherstone et al (eds), *Global Modernities* (Sage 1995) 25–54; R Robertson, 'Glocalization' in R Robertson and JA Scholte (eds), *Encyclopedia of Globalization*, vol 2 (Routledge 2007) 545–47; R Robertson, 'Situating Glocalization: A Relatively Autobiographical Intervention' in GS Drori et al (eds), *Global Themes and Local Variations in Organization and Management: Perspectives on Glocalization* (Routledge 2013) 25–36.

[50] For definitions (including an account of the term's roots in Japanese commercial strategy) and applications, see V Roudometof, *Glocalization* (Routledge 2016) 2–5 and 23–29.

[51] GC Spivak, *An Aesthetic Education in the Era of Globalization* (Harvard University Press 2012) 472. cf J Derrida, *Donner le temps*, vol 1: *La Fausse monnaie* (Galilée 1991) 76: '[T]he essential link of thought . . . to language . . . will never do without idioms.'

In crucial ways, 'globalization' must therefore not be understood as destroying or annihilating the local. Indeed, 'globalization' is not even to be configured as standing in opposition to local forces or as happening beyond them. Rather, the flow of 'globalization' finds itself being interrupted along its homogenizing trajectory as the globalizing is made to attend to a ramifying range of local processes with which it must blend or mix as a condition of its successful implementation in a particular place. The globalizing thus encounters the local with which it links through a complex intertwinement so as to produce heterogeneous configurations – glocalizing interlacings that, in fact, may prove so intricate as to make disentanglement of one facet from another impossible.

Consider the promotion of the common law's rule-of-law model, nowadays predominantly a US template . '"Global" entities such as international organizations, courts and expert bodies all interpret norms to differing degrees and defend these interpretations around the world . . . . Domestic actors, meanwhile, contest, reinterpret and reshape these norms and, in their turn, trigger reactions' – the deliberation and confrontation of norms constituting an important assertion of democratic rights and thus showing how 'localization is at least recognized as having the potential to produce outcomes of a more legitimate, more stable and locally more appropriate kind' (although one must allow for local objections issuing from dictators, corrupt officials, or war-lords).[52] In other words, '[t]he overall pattern . . . is that of a "feedback loop": international promoters begin by pressing for full adoption of global standards using a conditionality-oriented mode of interaction; in response to local interpretation and contestation, they shift to a more persuasion-oriented (and less transparent) style of interaction and allow more scope for discussion about local translation'.[53] The key, then, is local resonance; for there to be a normative fit, there must be a cultural match. In sum, 'every norm is made sense of in a specific socio-political context' – although, to be sure, no claimed match or absence of match occurs without translation processes being fashioned locally by power or interest.[54]

[52] L Zimmermann, *Global Norms with a Local Face* (Cambridge University Press 2017) 15 and 51.

[53] ibid 192. More precisely, 'translation from the "global" to the "local" takes place in three dimensions: translation into discourse, translation into law and translation into implementation': ibid 54.

[54] ibid 207. For further discussion of the theory and practice of comparative law with specific reference to the rule of law, see P Legrand, 'The Guile and the Guise: Apropos of Comparative Law as We Know It' (2021) 16 Asian J Comp L 155.

Illustrations of such arrangements – of iterations whereby the globalizing is moulded into local knowledge through translation – abound.

To expand the range of examples beyond law narrowly understood, contemplate Christianity and the strategies of local adaptation it has had to adopt in order to assert a presence in China.[55] Or envisage the English spoken in Singapore or India,[56] or think of 'Spanglish' in the United States.[57] These three linguistic configurations, for instance, show how the late-twentieth-century dissemination of the English language (the globalizing fact), far from leading to a monolingual world (as may superficially appear to be the case), has instead prompted the formation of many glocal articulations whereby local syntax and vocabulary (the local fact) have shaped 'English' into different 'Englishes' and have effectively turned 'English' into an array of singular linguistic arrangements (the glocal outcome). Consider also a Paris version of Starbucks, the coffeehouse – an apposite instance of the customization or singularization of a 'global' brand in order to appeal to the local market.[58] In addition, one can advantageously deconstruct the broadcast of the FIFA World Cup final. While the transmission may appear at first sight as the perfect example of 'globalization', given the planetarity and instantaneity of the game's diffusion on account of information technology communication, closer examination reveals that in each country the broadcast undergoes

[55] Eg: PTM Ng, '"Glocalization" as a Key to the Interplay between Christianity and Asian Cultures: The Vision of Francis Wei in Early Twentieth Century China' (2007) 1 Int'l J Public Theology 101.

[56] Eg: EC Eoyang, *Two-Way Mirrors: Cross-Cultural Studies in Glocalization* (Lexington 2005); HK Tong and LH Cheung, 'Cultural Identity and Language: A Proposed Framework for Cultural Globalization and Glocalization' (2011) 32 J Multilingual & Multicultural Development 55; S Bhaduri (ed), *Negotiating Glocalization: Views from Language, Literature and Culture Studies* (Anthem 2008).

[57] Eg: C Mar-Molinero, 'The Spread of Global Spanish: From Cervantes to Reggaetón' in N Coupland (ed), *Handbook of Language and Globalization* (Wiley-Blackwell 2010) 162–81.

[58] Eg: L Alderman, 'In Europe, Starbucks Adjusts to a Cafe Culture', *The New York Times* (30 March 2012) <www.nytimes.com/2012/03/31/business/starbucks-tailors-its-experience-to-fit-to-europeantastes.html> [on file]. An analogous observation can be made with respect to Coca-Cola, a brand arguably even more readily associated with the idea of globalization in the minds of many. I borrow from Kwame Appiah's: '[A]t a respectable funeral in the United States, you wouldn't serve Coca-Cola. At a funeral in Ghana, if you don't serve Coca-Cola, you are not at a respectable funeral. One could think of endless examples of this sort of thing. . . . In every case, there's a material thing that circulates, but what it is doing is different. And this is what we humanists do; we notice these things': KA Appiah and H Bhabha, 'Cosmopolitanism and Convergence' (2018) 49 New Literary History 171, 188.

local calibration in a number of significant ways. For example, as it circulates through local commentators speaking in local languages, the telecast showcases local celebrities being interviewed at half-time (this Italian superstar in Italy and that Brazilian celebrity in Brazil) and displays local advertising – even the planetwide sponsors' publicity being released in local languages.[59] It follows that there is more than one FIFA World Cup final in co-presence, each operating as a differential local instantiation and all being linked through what is branded as 'the' FIFA event.

I can enter a parallel claim as regards the Olympic Games, although in this case the salience of the local, or the local anchoring, finds itself heightened – thus challenging even more directly the homogenizing grid. If one examines any local production of the Games, one observes in short order that certain sports are given pride of place, for example, those that are most popular locally, with respect to which the local team has a particularly good chance of success, or in which the local team is fielding a high-profile athlete. Meanwhile, other sports find themselves, for all intents and purposes, being relegated to a supporting role – if they are not rendered nearly invisible altogether.[60] To continue with sports, cricket offers a case where the imprint of localism is particularly remarkable.[61] Picture a game between India and Pakistan. Not only does such contest show cricket to have been 'hijacked' from the English and made much more aggressive and spectacular in the process,[62] but it also reveals how, quite plainly, 'England ... is no longer part of the equation'.[63] Once more, it is not that glocalization is reducing the significance of space, quite to the contrary. It is rather that any simplistic binarism or dichotomy between the 'global' and the 'local' finds itself superseded in favour of glocal hybridity, of a hybridity *asserting the local*.[64]

[59] See generally F Foer, *How Soccer Explains the World* (Harper Collins 2004).

[60] See generally R Giulianotti, 'The Beijing 2008 Olympics: Examining the Interrelations of China, Globalization, and Soft Power' (2015) 23 European R 286.

[61] Another sporting example is ice hockey. See B Berglund, *The Fastest Game in the World* (University of California Press 2021).

[62] The term 'hijacking' is in A Appadurai, *Modernity at Large: Cultural Dimensions of Globalization* (University of Minnesota Press 1996) 108 and 113. See generally F Mustafa, 'Cricket and Globalization: Global Processes and the Imperial Game' (2013) 8 J Global History 318.

[63] Appadurai (n 62) 109.

[64] See Roudometof (n 50) 13–15.

Instead of the isomorphism that an unexamined view readily assumes, what effectively materializes in all these situations is *allomorphism* – not unity or uniformity, but fragmentation, that is, translation, acculturation, and differentiation. To be sure, the local has never been 'purely' local (whatever that adverb may have suggested), and local knowledge has always been constructed through outside influences. What is different as regards glocalization is that the relevant outside influence in the instances I discuss takes the form of an identifiably globalizing phenomenon. Note that in this regard, it would be reductionist to equate the globalizing with 'form' and the local with 'contents'. What rather takes place is that the entity undergoing dissemination is developing or growing through rhizome-like local connections that are always-already singular and partial. While one witnesses a certain epistemic anarchy as links may be produced with any local entity by way of an assortment of different assemblages, it remains that relevant glocal connections are undeniably set to happen. As they materialize, these arrangements attest to plurality across locales rather than affirm anything pertaining to identity, equivalence, or commonality. If you will, think in terms of 'the hyper-differentials that link our hyper-connectivities'.[65]

Percipiently theoretizing glocalization, Victor Roudometof marshals the conceptual metaphor of the 'wave' in order to convey the interaction between flows and places, thereby showing the mutually constitutive character of both notions.[66] Again, and importantly, the globalizing entity ascertainably exists, independently from any localization and ahead of any localization. There are, then, waves of 'globalization' spreading across the surface of the entire planet or most of it. Harnessing a second metaphor, Roudometof proceeds to explain what then happens locally through the idea of 'refraction'.[67] Asserting a specific wave-resistance capacity, each locality refracts the globalizing through its prism. Not unlike light that passes through glass radiates an entire spectrum,[68] the globalizing that passes through the prism of the local radiates a variety of singularities. The final outcome of the 'wave + refraction' process is neither a denial of the 'global' nor a disavowal of

[65] D Kadir, 'Comparative Literature in an Age of Terrorism' in H Saussy (ed), *Comparative Literature in an Age of Globalization* (Johns Hopkins University Press 2006) 69.

[66] Roudometof (n 50) 64.

[67] ibid 64–66.

[68] Should an image be helpful, the band Pink Floyd's 1973 record, *The Dark Side of the Moon*, deploys on its iconic cover the very phenomenon I describe. Any Internet search with the apposite keywords will immediately reveal the picture I have in mind.

the local, but the upholding of an operation, which is glocalization, and of a resulting condition, which is glocality. Lisbeth Zimmermann thus shows how the 1989 United Nations Convention on the Rights of the Child underwent 'a "back-and-forth" process',[69] that is, an 'interaction between external norm-promotion activities and domestic norm translation point[ing] to the formation of "feedback loops" in reaction to the activities of rule-of-law promoters'.[70] Indeed, 'UNICEF promoted full legal adoption of the [Convention] in Guatemala and an initial code of rights for children was enacted. In the second step, however, major contestation erupted and the code never came into force. UNICEF then revised its interaction strategy.'[71] In 2003, by way of 'third step', the Guatemalan Congress adopted a new law 'reshaping ... the [Convention] standards in line with a "family-based" approach to children'.[72] Zimmermann's research illustrates to excellent effect not only what happens, but what must happen, as a purportedly 'global' norm like the rule of law seeks to earn local recognition and respect, in practice, local legitimacy and efficacy.[73]

Inevitably, the entanglements I discuss very much involve a power relationship. And the dynamics at play – which may have to do with prestige, money, knowledge, or other resources – can ultimately favour the 'global' or the local. For example, some locales will prove more wave-resistant than others, or they will reveal themselves to be better able than others at 'breaking' the arriving waves.[74] In any event, however, the fabric of the glocal and the fact of the glocal's unceasing persistence, whatever be the intensity with which local knowledge avers itself, directly defeat all totalizing claims, not least the arguments purporting to sustain a full-scale diffusion and implementation 'as such' of some aspect or other of the disseminating model or the views supporting any idea along the lines

69 Zimmermann (n 52) 53.

70 ibid 61.

71 ibid 83.

72 ibid. Zimmermann notes that in the 2003 law '[t]he text [i]s marked by its use of a strong, family-based vocabulary and the various freedoms [a]re subject to a greater degree of parental oversight': ibid 113.

73 For corresponding conclusions on the basis of extensive fieldwork in Bangladesh, see T Berger, *Global Norms and Local Courts* (Oxford University Press 2017). Tobias Berger's captivating account demonstrates that for rule-of-law norms to harbour any hope of local purchase, as they travel from the desks of European Union bureaucrats to United Nations officials in Dhaka to local NGOs in the countryside and to the rural Bangladeshi themselves, there must take place an extensive translation process involving 'significan[t] alter[ation] [of] ... meaning': ibid 118.

74 Roudometof (n 50) 73–74.

of universality.[75] Such mystical narratives cannot withstand the relativization that the necessary fact of glocalization empirically visits on the legal. Along the way, through its insistence on a more actor-based perspective bearing on the 'global' reach of models, ideas, and practices – the planetary 'spreading'[76] – glocalization aptly emphasizes the central role of local agency.[77]

Still, I am not arguing glocalization's immunity to critique. For example, it may well be that through the familiarization or 'naturalization' that accompanies the localization of 'global' capitalism, resistance to neo-liberalism finds itself thwarted and the acceptability of this economic model fostered. In other words, it is arguable that in the way in which it resolves the tension between the 'global' and the local, glocalization can effectively abet 'global' commercial interests in their search for ever-expanding profits (even if this quest should be cast in terms of objectionable marauding leading to the decimation or replacement of local networks of micro-producers, intermediaries, and small retailers, no matter how conceivably inefficient).[78] Be that as it may, my basic

[75] cf J Nederveen Pieterse, 'Global Culture, 1990, 2020' (2020) 37 Theory, Culture & Society 233, 234: 'I have become more careful about using "global". In the sense of worldwide significance and influence – yes. In the sense of global convergence – no.' To refer to the pandemic that emerged in early 2020, '[i]t would be an aberration to think that the "post" pandemic will be a simultaneous event in Germany, China, the US, Zimbabwe, Bolivia and Uzbekistan': WD Mignolo, 'The Logic of the In-Visible: Decolonial Reflections on the Change of Epoch' (2020) 37 Theory, Culture & Society 205, 216. The 2020 pandemic, quite apart from revealing an extraordinary array of local (legal) differentiations vis-à-vis the 'global' phenomenon at stake (the spreading virus), suggests that economic interconnectedness and unceasing mobility have yielded to a more fragmented planet, a pattern that not even the virtualization of professional lives can challenge. Think glocalization writ large.

[76] B Czarniawska, 'Storytelling: A Managerial Tool and Its Local Translations' in GS Drori et al (eds), *Global Themes and Local Variations in Organization and Management: Perspectives on Glocalization* (Routledge 2013) 66.

[77] Insightful writings include HH Khondker, 'Globalisation to Glocalization: A Conceptual Exploration' (2005) 13 Intellectual Discourse 181; E Swyngedouw, 'Neither Global nor Local: "Glocalization" and the Politics of Scale' in KR Cox (ed), *Spaces of Globalization: Reasserting the Power of the Local* (Guilford 1997) 137–66. For revealing case studies, see GS Drori et al (eds), *Global Themes and Local Variations in Organization and Management: Perspectives on Glocalization* (Routledge 2013); B Barber, *If Mayors Ruled the World* (Yale University Press 2013); P Sigismondi, *The Digital Glocalization of Entertainment* (Springer 2012); B Helvacioglu, 'Globalization in the Neighbourhood: From the Nation-State to Bilkent Center' (2000) 15 Int'l Sociology 326. See also R Robertson (ed), *European Glocalization in Global Context* (Palgrave Macmillan 2014); D Hebert and M Rykowski (eds), *Music Glocalization* (Cambridge Scholars 2018).

[78] For this contention, see WH Thornton, 'Mapping the "Glocal" Village: The Political Limits of "Glocalization"' (2000) 14 Continuum 79, 81–82.

argument holds: since there is glocalization rather than 'globalization' and because every further instance of glocalization fosters demand for comparison across glocal outcomes, the ever-increasing planetary or near-planetary or part-planetary spread of legal models must entail more comparative law.

*

The range of comparative law must also depend on what is understood to qualify as foreign law. In this regard, it would no doubt be unhelpfully formalistic to make too much of the fact that, strictly speaking, *for the comparatist foreign law cannot exist*. No foreign law is retrievable beyond the comparatist's re-presentation of it and therefore not otherwise than as the comparatist's translation of it in the comparatist's language (this last term being mobilized in the broadest sense). Because the other law is told, and can only be told, in the discourse that the self employs as a means of self-expression, legal otherness is necessarily subjected to this particular manifestation of selfness. From the moment the comparatist ascertains what there is 'out there' as law, however, it is no longer foreign to him. And as long as what there is 'out there' remains foreign to the comparatist, he cannot identify it as law.[79] Otherwise said, only indecipherability allows the foreign to retain its foreignness, while only decipherment makes it possible for the foreign to appear as law. Because what is perceived as foreign law is instantaneously lost as foreign law, the expression 'foreign law' effectively stands as an oxymoron from the vantage point of the comparatist, not at all an insignificant realization to behold even as one wishes to move beyond such analytics.

Comparative law is informed by an engagement with the planet's legal disparateness, which it regards in principle as beneficial and as normatively relevant. Accepting that, because one's being exists in a world one is fated to incessant interpretation,[80] responding to the

[79] For a philosophical statement of this problematique, see J-L Nancy, *Etre singulier pluriel* (Galilée 1996) 101: '[T]he otherness of the other constitutes precisely that to which recognition itself prohibits access.' In Theodor Adorno's formulation, '[t]he interpretation of the given reality and its abolition are connected to one another': TW Adorno, 'Die Aktualität der Philosophie' in *Philosophische Frühschriften* (R Tiedemann ed, Suhrkamp 1973 [1931]) 338.

[80] I adapt M Merleau-Ponty, *Phénoménologie de la perception* in *Œuvres* (C Lefort ed, Gallimard 2010 [1945]) 671. Maurice Merleau-Ponty's observation is that one's being-in-a-world condemns one to meaning. I am reminded of Charles Taylor who, echoing Martin Heidegger and Hans-Georg Gadamer, asserts how '*Verstehen* is a *Seinsmodus*':

redoubtable summons of other laws and others-in-the-law, of other legal cultures and other cultures, of other law-worlds and other worlds – whose singular 'thereness', unbidden, intransigently and insatiably hails one, making a claim on one, a singularity inviting one's recognition and respect – the comparatist contests nationalizing and universalizing strategies alike. While it obtains on the premiss that the legal cannot justifiably remain at home, in its abode, abidingly, comparatism also disputes the possibility and opportunity of one-law-for-all, unity or uniformity entailing what is in principle the indefensible destruction of space's spatiality and of time's temporality. Since there can be no comparison outside the conditions of address of a self to an other, comparative law involves the appreciation, within one glance, of more than one law, one of the convoked laws in co-presence having to be *foreign* to the other, the (legally) foreign consisting not in a fixed or absolute form, but in what is not deemed one's own law – foreign law thus being seen to enjoy a negative identity.

Foreignness is therefore contingent: it depends upon conjuncture or situation, and any attempt at definition would prove wasteful. Imagine a Canadian academic having trained as a lawyer in Canada and having subsequently escaped to France in order to teach law at a French university. Quaere: has Canadian law become foreign to this jurist now that he has been away from Canada for more than twenty years without harbouring any appreciable interest in Canadian law during those two decades yet unavoidably being haunted (if unconsciously) by his early exposure to it? Is it helpful to contrast the straightforward case of the French lawyer vis-à-vis Canadian law? But what of a French lawyer claiming long-standing expertise in Canadian law? Would Canadian law be foreign to him? And does French law remain foreign to the Canadian academic I hypothesize given that he has been working in a French university for many years? Does it matter what courses he has been teaching? Could it be that both Canadian and French law are now foreign to him so that he could no longer claim any law as his 'own', so that he could no longer vindicate a self-in-the-law? But must one not always have an 'own' law – say, in the way one always has an 'own' language?

Now, envisage a Romanian jurist – say, my valued colleague and *compagnon d'armes* Cosmin Cercel – initially schooled in the law in his

C Taylor, 'Self-Interpreting Animals' in *Philosophical Papers*, vol 1 (Cambridge University Press 1985) 72.

native Romania, that is, socialized and institutionalized, epistemologized and encultured, into the law *there*. Could Cercel not legitimately embark upon the writing of a doctoral dissertation on Romanian law in the Communist era *as a comparatist* on the understanding that the totalitarian ideology that then visited Romanian legal culture is best understood as a disfiguring excrescence vis-à-vis 'Romanian' law, that it is accordingly foreign to 'Romanian' legal experience? Does the fact that the writing is taking place in French – in 'non-Romanian', if you will – make any difference to the conundrum of foreignness? Even if one were to allow Cercel's understanding of the foreign, as I confidently did,[81] surely one would have to draw the line at a German jurist writing on German law in English. Indeed, it seems difficult to accept that the language of inscription would suffice to turn a law otherwise not-foreign into a foreign one. Likewise, it is hard to think of a French analysis on French law written in the French language deserving to be acknowledged as comparative law on account of the fact that it would have articulated its critique through the staging of non-French characters.[82]

But what if a French jurist – having been socialized and institutionalized, epistemologized and encultured, in France into French culture, French legal culture, and French law – undertakes to devote a research project to the doctrine of originalism in the US Supreme Court's constitutional adjudication? Although this French jurist's text addresses exclusively US constitutional law, from beginning to end, I hold that it clearly prevails as a comparative investigation properly speaking. One easily supposes the formalist retort that 'a study of foreign law as such does not yet signify a comparison of law'[83] – that the work I postulate on US

[81] See CS Cercel, *Le Droit saisi par la politique: l'expérience communiste roumaine*, 2 vols (Ecole de droit de la Sorbonne, unpublished doctoral dissertation 2012). cf C Cercel, *Towards a Jurisprudence of State Communism* (Routledge 2018).

[82] I have in mind Montesquieu's pathbreaking *Lettres persanes*. Published anonymously in 1721 (for good measure, the name of the publisher was fictitious and the place of publication fake), this illustration of travel writing, then a rising genre, enjoyed huge success. Montesquieu has two Persians, Uzbek and Rica, undertake a nine-year journey in France (during which they mostly stay in Paris) and engage in a critical examination of French customs by way of a correspondence with relatives and friends in Persia numbering 161 letters. While Uzbek and Rica are evidently operating as comparatists, Montesquieu is not – unless one takes seriously the Orientalized sketches of Persian harem life he supplies along the way. See Montesquieu, *Lettres persanes* in *Œuvres complètes*, vol 1 (R Caillois ed, Gallimard 1949 [1721]) 129–373.

[83] K Zweigert and H Kötz, *Einführung in die Rechtsvergleichung* (3rd edn, Mohr Siebeck 1996) 6. This categorical approach boasts a long history. Eg: [E] Lambert, ['Rapport'] in Congrès international de droit comparé, *Procès-verbaux des séances et documents*, vol 1

constitutional law cannot be received as comparative, since it lacks a graphical comparison, because a comparison is not expressly present on the graphical surface of the text being inscribed on the page or the computer screen (that is, given that there is no section of the document explicitly compelling US law and some different law expressly to enter into a 'negotiation' with one another). Such rejoinder, I suggest, hardly deserves sustained consideration.

The empirical fact of the matter is that a French jurist who produces an essay on US constitutional law is generating a study that is inherently, thoroughly, and emphatically comparative. Every piece of US law information on offer within this text will have been processed or filtered, 'understood', by a French jurist having precedingly submitted to legal dressage in France. It will therefore have been distilled or clarified through this French jurist's incorporation or embodiment of the epistemological predilections attendant upon this singular legal training. The US constitutional law that will be inscribed as 'US constitutional law' in the essay I assume ought, on closer analysis, to be identified as something like 'US constitutional law through a French jurist's eyes'. Not only is the latter 'US constitutional law' bound to differ from the former, but it is, significantly, comparative to its core. In effect, *what could operate as a more comparative endeavour than a French jurist's writing on US law?*[84]

At the 'meremost minimum',[85] there is therefore comparative law to be had whenever a jurist proceeds to an *alternation* across laws or legal cultures, that is, whenever one's mind alternates between different laws or legal cultures, one of which is foreign to the other. *That much is clear.* Whether the alternation is explicit or tacit is irrelevant.[86] Unsurprisingly, Teemu Ruskola states the matter cogently: 'Comparative legal scholars . . . often insist on a distinction between the study of "foreign law" and the discipline of "comparative law" in a proper sense. The latter consists of the express comparison of two legal systems rather than

(LGDJ 1905) 29, where the author talks of 'the *necessity* to reject, outside of the domain of comparative law, . . . studies in foreign law' [my emphasis].

84 The idea that, say, J Bell, *French Legal Cultures* (Cambridge University Press 2001) or DP Kommers and RA Miller, *The Constitutional Jurisprudence of the Federal Republic of Germany* (3rd edn, Duke University Press 2012) would not qualify as comparative texts boggles the comparative mind.

85 S Beckett, *Worstward Ho* in *Company/Ill Seen Ill Said/Worstward Ho/Stirrings Still* (D Van Hulle ed, Faber & Faber 2009 [1983]) 82.

86 See H Collins, *Forms of Life* (MIT Press 2019) 65–68. Harry Collins draws on PL Berger, *Invitation to Sociology* (Penguin 1963) passim.

a mere description of foreign legal systems. However, it seems inescapable that the description of foreign law ... is always an instance of comparative law. Even in "mere description", the implicit point of reference is always one's own system, against which one compares the object culture.'[87] Yes.

I have one further observation, still as regards the need to resist any unduly formalist urge, and it is that one must withstand field fetishism, too. Comparisons-at-law happen where they happen, and they are emphatically not to be challenged as comparisons-at-law, because they are not published in the *American Journal of Comparative Law* or proclaimed before an assembly of the notorious International Academy of Comparative Law. Comparative law can appear in *The Translator*,'[88] and it can be spoken to the residents of a small *provençal* village.[89]

Now, comparative law's ubiquity raises the matter of language. In particular, whether the comparative is found to be emerging within transnational, international, or so-called 'global' schemes of legal governance, the comparatist will be pressed to grapple with a range of knotty issues pertaining to translation.

[87] T Ruskola, *Legal Orientalism* (Harvard University Press 2013) 34–35.

[88] Eg: P Legrand, 'Law's Translation, Imperial Predilections and the Endurance of the Self' (2014) 20 (3) The Translator 290.

[89] In the course of a Fondation Nancy Brown Negley residential fellowship at the Maison Dora Maar in Ménerbes, a small hilltop village in the Lubéron, Simone Glanert addressed local residents on the topic of comparative law and interpretation on 28 April 2016.

V

Borges's Challenge

The mountain exists, but one sees the mountain in words. In one's head, one says: 'It is huge'; 'It is beautiful'; 'It is white'; 'There is snow'. Without words, one cannot *see* the mountain. As one's world comes to designation or signification through language only, as there is no contact with one's world that is not linguistically mediated, as there are no non-linguistic situations or institutions, as all understanding is ultimately linguistic,[1] language emerges as a threshold problematique inevitably impacting research into foreign law, an elemental complex of issues that the comparatist must face and with respect to which he must position himself as he embarks on his foreign-law forays. Paradoxically, the comparatist-at-law's primordial tool also operates as his 'prison-house',[2] because he simply cannot eschew expression through language. (As was his wont, Samuel Beckett framed the epistemic tension I address by way of a succinct statement capturing at once the ineludible and carceral themes: 'What can you say, words it is, nothing else going.'[3])

[1] Eg: M Heidegger, *Einführung in die Metaphysik* (Niemeyer 1958) 11: '[F]or words and language are not shells into which things are only packed for spoken and written intercourse. In the word, in language, things only then become and are.' Indeed, Heidegger holds that '[o]nly where there is language is there world': M Heidegger, *Erläuterungen zu Hölderlins Dichtung* (Klostermann 2012 [1944]) 38. For an important argument making the claim for language as world-making, see E Danziger, 'The Eye of the Beholder: How Linguistic Categorization Affects "Natural" Experience' in S McKinnon and S Silverman (eds), *Complexities: Anthropological Challenges to Reductive Accounts of Social Life* (University of Chicago Press 2005) 64–80.

[2] Eg: F Jameson, *The Prison-House of Language* (Princeton University Press 1972). cf TW Adorno, *Metaphysik* (R Tiedemann ed, Suhrkamp 1998 [1965]) 107, where Theodor Adorno refers to 'the prison of language'.

[3] The quotation is an answer that Beckett gave Niklaus Gessner, his interviewer. For the transcript, revealing that Beckett spoke in French, see N Gessner, *Die Unzulänglichkeit der Sprache* (Juris 1957) 75. Gessner's appears to have been the first book devoted to the work of Beckett.

*

It ought to be a trite enunciation – *mais cela va mieux en le disant* – that a jurist purporting to work on foreign law must be able reliably to access source-materials in the source-language in which that foreign law exists – or so forcefully claims the philologist in me.[4] If one is to report creditably on Japanese law, one must be able to enjoy access – I mean *linguistic* access – to primary and secondary (legal) materials in Japanese. And if one is to compose a text on Qatari law, one must depend on primary and secondary (legal) materials in Arabic. Meanwhile, if one is to contribute a chapter on German law, one must be in a position to do so on the basis of a meaningful appreciation of primary and secondary (legal) materials in German. These three illustrations support my contention that, in terms of the most elementary intellectual and scholarly *integrity*, one simply cannot claim to be writing seriously on foreign law in the absence of any sustained consideration of (legal) materials in the relevant foreign language. In advance of empirical study, I harbour a strong sense that a professor of comparative literature would not even think of asserting expertise in Goethe if he could not read German or in Diderot if he could not read French. For reasons that are far from obvious, jurists have traditionally adopted a much more cavalier attitude concerning linguistic proficiency. Uwe Kischel's approach is typical as he writes that '[a]nyone who is interested in Japanese law but cannot at least read the Japanese language must resort to translations',[5] thereby suggesting that both types

[4] Otherwise, one runs the risk of facing the critiques that were justifiably addressed to HP Glenn, *Legal Traditions of the World* (2nd edn, Oxford University Press 2004). Eg: NHD Foster, 'Islamic Law as Tradition: Chapter Six of Legal Traditions of the World' (2006) 1(1) J Comp L 147, 150: 'In order to review the chapter [on Islamic law] without too many interruptions, only a few problems and mistakes have been mentioned. These are regrettably numerous, and range from straight errors to misapprehensions and distortions. It is difficult to understand why there are so many when they would have been easily spotted and remedied by someone with a knowledge of Islamic law and the Arabic language, and their sheer number means that the chapter cannot be recommended as an introduction to the subject.' See also BS Jackson, 'Internal and External Comparisons of Religious Law: Reflections from Jewish Law' (2006) 1(1) J Comp L 177, 180: 'Glenn's general strategy … in relation to the "talmudic legal tradition" is severely flawed – inevitably so, given the author's apparent lack of access to the primary sources.'

[5] U Kischel, *Rechtsvergleichung* (Beck 2015) 9. However, in the preface to the English version of his book, Kischel is suggesting differently as regards his own text. When he states that he wanted 'a translation that reads not like a translation', he appears to be considering translation as a lesser form of writing, what would therefore have been inadequate or insufficient for his book from his point of view. I refer to U Kischel, *Comparative Law* (A Hammel tr, Oxford University Press 2019) [ix]. cf Letter from S Beckett to B Rosset in *The Letters of Samuel Beckett*, vol 2 (G Craig et al eds,

of comparatists researching Japanese law (those who can read Japanese and those who cannot) are somehow operating on a level footing – if you can read Japanese, you go ahead reading it; and if you cannot, well, you go ahead not reading it. Such superciliousness deserves to be roundly condemned, because the matter of propriety that is at stake affects not only the comparatist's individual credit, but also the field's collective standing. I find it important to insist on this point: quite apart from the fact that the detrimental consequences on one's research of investigating Japanese law without more than a scrimption of acquaintance with the Japanese language lie like hidden land mines, to engage in this kind of perfunctory comparison is quite simply to do a major disservice to comparative law by effectively giving it a bad name, and it is therefore ultimately to undermine the attempts by fellow comparatists to earn recognition and respect for their field from the overall legal 'community'. In sum, enthusiasm and translations cannot be allowed to substitute for access to source-language (legal) materials – if, that is, one is aiming to be writing at all authoritatively on foreign law – and it therefore behoves the thoughtful comparatist to recall George Fletcher's fully warranted entreaty on the salient relevance of language for comparative law.[6] Let me add that one cannot permit collaboration with an 'informant' to parry one's lack of reading ability in the source-language.[7] (I have a sense that I am once more stating the obvious.)

Note that I am emphasizing access to primary and secondary (legal) materials. Specifically, I am not suggesting that a comparatist ought to

Cambridge University Press 2009 [11 February 1954]) 456, where Beckett chastises 'an irritating way of turning the unusual into the usual so that it won't read like a translation'.

6 Supra 67.

7 The idea that one would circumvent one's language deficiency – not to mention one's unwillingness to engage in fieldwork – by hiring a local surrogate to collect local data on one's behalf strikes me as being most unsatisfactory. In an e-mail dated 8 October 2020 [on file in a redacted version], a Brazilian colleague apprises me that he is personally acquainted with a young Brazilian academic whom a leading US law professor, claiming expertise in comparative constitutional law at a leading US law school, hired by the hour to fill in the blanks of a pre-drafted questionnaire on Brazilian law. These answers were later incorporated into the US law professor's monograph under the professor's signature. Without, it seems, any further verification, they infused the book's interpretations and conclusions. In time, the text was released by a leading US academic press without the surrogate's name being acknowledged anywhere in the book, the idea presumably being to hide the fact of local research assistance. My Brazilian colleague also mentions that a much garlanded professor of comparative constitutional law from another country later hired the same Brazilian reporter along analogous lines. Quaere: what epistemic warrant can proxy 'knowledge' command?

speak Japanese (or Arabic or German). In fact, since the possibility of exchange in a (more or less broken) third language can reasonably be expected, the added value of fluency in a foreign language is limited in terms of the conduct of meaningful comparative scholarship – which means that speaking four or five languages is hardly a useful badge of scholarly distinction within comparative law. (I deliberately leave to one side at this juncture the matter of writing skills except to remark immediately that for any comparatist-at-law, it has evidently become a huge benefit to be able to write in idiomatic English.) Even as I remain willing to reserve exceptional situations, readily devisable with a modicum of eccentric imagination, Jorge Luis Borges's question stands, tenaciously: 'You, who are reading me, are you certain to understand my language?'[8] Observe that Borges is not asking whether one can speak to him. Rather, his concern is to secure his reader's *understanding*. He is asking whether one can meaningfully *read* him.

*

Now, I find it crucial that the comparatist writing about Japanese or Qatari or German law in a different language – say, in English – should remind his anglophone readers that although they are reading him in 'their' language, they are reading about a foreign law that exists in a language different from 'theirs'. It is too easy – and much too dangerous from an epistemological standpoint – for the comparatist to attempt to design a horizontal space of indistinction where the Englishing of the various languages would effectively 'flatten' the differences across laws and override the cultural disparateness that there is, there, thus making all laws readily and equally available in some *Ursprache*, a calibration that would be anything but politically benign. As it happens, there are procedures that the comparatist is in a position to deploy in order to ensure that his anglophone readership cannot forget the presence of the foreign, especially perhaps when the foreign words herald enhanced idiomaticity. The parenthetical inscription in the source-language of the translated terms, on the occasion of their first occurrence in the body text, is such a useful strategy. For instance, one can write (in English) as follows: 'The French statute holds that the demonstration of religious belonging must have manifested itself "ostensibly" ("*ostensiblement*").'

[8] JL Borges, 'La biblioteca de Babel' in *Ficciones* (Alianza Editorial, 1997 [1944]) 98. Derek Attridge offers an interesting (and even more affirmatively sceptical) variation on Borges's theme: '[U]nderstand how little you understand me': D Attridge, *The Singularity of Literature* (Routledge 2004) 131.

Another course of action, of more capital significance, concerns the need to translate in such a way that the translation reveals itself as a translation. There are at least two crucial reasons justifying this approach. To track my illustration about the statute on religious belonging, I hold that not only does the comparatist-at-law require to do justice to the source-text in French, but he must remind his anglophone readers that the text they are reading in English is a translated text, that it is not the source-text itself. In this regard, to be *just* is more important than to be correct or exact – the latter goals being in any event inaccessible, since one is dealing in interpretation.[9] Soliciting his long-standing confidante and lover – a translator into English of Flaubert, Michel Tournier, Marguerite Duras, and other French authors – for a response to a draft translation he had penned, Beckett astutely remarked: '[A]ccuracy obviously secondary consideration.'[10] Bringing to bear the virtues of fairness and probity, the translator's ambition must indeed be justness – in French, *le mot juste*.[11]

*

Perhaps I can offer an illustration showing the kind of attunement that must inform the comparatist-at-law's translation work, the sort of sensitivity that must come into play in order to further the translator's aspiration to justness vis-à-vis the source-text. I refer to *L'Ecriture et la différence*, Jacques Derrida's first book, which appeared in 1967 a few months before *De la grammatologie*. In a chapter entitled 'Freud et la scène de l'écriture' ('Freud and the Scene of Writing'), a text that had initially been published in the literary journal *Tel Quel* the year before, Derrida addresses translation (*justement* . . .). For present purposes, I consider the transposition of Derrida's text from French to English. As I proceed, I abide by the following precepts. (While not all cases demanded such a significant investment as the instance I adduce by way of example, I did effortfully and fretfully craft my translations throughout *NCL* – a seemingly countless number of them – in line with the concerns I want my demonstration to emphasize.)

9 cf M Heidegger, *Heraklit* in *Gesamtausgabe*, vol 55 (MS Frings ed, Klostermann 1979 [1943]) 63: '[E]very translation is in itself already an interpretation.'

10 Letter from S Beckett to B Bray in *The Letters of Samuel Beckett*, vol 2 (G Craig et al eds, Cambridge University Press 2011 [14 November 1959]) 255.

11 For an argument in favour of just translation with specific reference to comparative law, see generally S Glanert and P Legrand, 'Foreign Law in Translation: If Truth Be Told. . .' in M Freeman and F Smith (eds), *Law and Language* (Oxford University Press 2013) 513–32.

While I have to consider common usage within the English language, I must above all try to do justice to the French inflexions that Derrida inscribed in his work. In my view, the translator's goal must therefore not be to create a thoroughly local text out of the foreign one, but instead to bring the local reader to the foreign text's foreignness – to get this reader to appreciate at all times that although he is reading in 'his' language, what he is reading remains foreign. Otherwise said, the translator must limit the extent of the de-localization of the foreign text. Once more, it is a matter of attempting to be just vis-à-vis the source-text, which is why I make demands on my anglophone reader whom I am inviting to read a foreignized English. I thus find myself firmly on side with Vladimir Nabokov: 'The clumsiest literal translation is a thousand times more useful than the prettiest paraphrase.'[12] Regard for the recognition of the other as other, for respect towards the other as other – such epistemic preoccupations having to animate all comparative work – must imply English forms that, although still ascertainable as understandable English, will not allow the reader to forget that he is reading a foreign language in English, will not permit him to escape the fact that he is 'negotiating' with a foreign-language text through translation. All along, translation must therefore allow the French to preponderate and not concede too much to English ways at the expense of the source-text.[13] Rather than assimilate or appropriate the foreign, instead of taming and integrating the foreign, the translator must effectively concede defeat, thereby allowing his intervention to be simultaneously strong and weak. Even as it is strong because it wrestles, courageously, with the source-language, translation must ultimately accept subordinating itself to foreignness. It must implement its inescapable weakness vis-à-vis the foreign. To approach the matter from another angle, some of the violence that is necessarily visited upon the source-text in the course of translation must be re-directed towards the host-language. It seems hard to overstate the significance of the issue – the deliberate foreignization of the translation is a key ethical/political motion giving its rightful prevalence to the

[12] V Nabokov, 'Problems of Translation: "Onegin" in English' (1955) 22 Partisan R 496, 496.

[13] I am thinking of how in seventeenth- and eighteenth-century France, translations that departed from the source-language with a view to being written elegantly in the host-language were derisively known as 'the beautiful unfaithful', or '*les belles infidèles*'. The expression is Gilles Ménage's. A learned linguist and historian, Ménage used it circa 1654 to challenge one of Nicolas Perrot d'Ablencourt's freewheeling translations. Instead of indulging 'the beautiful unfaithful', it befalls the translator 'to watch over the otherness of the other': J Derrida, *Le Toucher, Jean-Luc Nancy* (Galilée 1998) 218.

otherness being re-presented as a matter of recognition of its singularity and respect for its difference. Because the translative task is thoroughly interpretive,[14] crucially no translation (and none of *NCL*'s translations) can be objective or true. Applying objectivity or truth to translation would be like speaking of the velocity of a blanket or of the anger of a tree.[15] So, to Derrida, who writes as follows:

> Or un corps verbal ne se laisse pas traduire ou transporter dans une autre langue. Il est cela même que la traduction laisse tomber. Laisser tomber le corps, telle est même l'énergie essentielle de la traduction.[16]

The University of Chicago Press released the 'official' or authorized English translation of Derrida's book in 1978. It is the work of Alan Bass, a noted philosopher and practising psychoanalyst. As regards the passage that interests me, Bass's text runs thus:

> The materiality of a word cannot be translated or carried over into another language. Materiality is precisely that which translation relinquishes. To relinquish materiality: such is the driving force of translation.[17]

I suggest five observations to support the view that Bass's translation insufficiently accords with the epistemic responsibility to preserve foreignness in the host-language. To make my point differently, I contend that Bass is unduly concerned with writing in 'good' (or conventional) English and insufficiently preoccupied with attending to the adamant Frenchness of Derrida's text.[18]

First, while Derrida begins his statement with '*Or*', a conjunction linking the sentence I quote with his previous one – a word that, in this

[14] Eg: Heidegger (n 9) 63: 'Interpretation and translation are at their essential core the same.'

[15] For a compelling argument at the interface of translation studies and comparative law denying epistemic merit to objectivity or truth, see S Glanert, '"Aujourd'hui, maman est morte": traduction littéraire et droit comparé' (2020) 4 Revue Droit & Littérature 373.

[16] J Derrida, *L'Ecriture et la différence* (Editions du Seuil 1967) 312.

[17] J Derrida, *Writing and Difference* (A Bass tr, University of Chicago Press 1978) 210.

[18] Is it necessary to add that my preoccupation is not with Bass's competence? For observations regarding the meticulousness with which Bass acquitted himself of his interpretive/translative task, see B Peeters, *Derrida* (Flammarion 2010) 284. For 'anecdata' expressing the proximity (and therefore the ease of exchange) between Bass and Derrida and suggesting the well-informed character of Bass's interventions, see ibid 283–84, 512, 516–17, 524, and 688n3. Bass also translated Derrida's *Marges* (Editions de Minuit 1972); *Positions* (Editions de Minuit 1972) [hereinafter *Positions*]; and *La Carte postale* (Flammarion 1980).

context, could be translated as 'Now' – Bass ignores this coupling, in effect denying, in this instance at least, Derrida's famed 'building-block' approach to argumentation and rhetoric.

Secondly, '*un corps verbal*' becomes '[t]he materiality of a word'. Even someone who does not have French, I suggest, is readily able to appreciate that Bass moves well away from Derrida. In the sense in which Derrida is using it, the term '*verbal*' refers to what concerns the word (from the Latin '*verbum*', which means 'word'). Derrida's reference is to the chain of graphematic signifiers that constitute the text, the very inscriptions themselves, the marks on the page. Even as Derrida's French is insistently metaphoric, Bass's English wants to be more precise. In the process, not only is Derrida's French vocabulary being re-directed, but so is his allegiance to a certain philosophical style. Indeed, Derrida's philosophy adheres to a more literary discourse – not unlike, say, Nietzsche's or Martin Heidegger's; for its part, Bass's English readily evokes the British or US philosophical tradition and its analytical predilections (think Bertrand Russell or WVO Quine).[19] Along analogous translative lines, Derrida's '*l'énergie essentielle*' becomes 'the driving force' – another striking motion from abstraction to empiricalness.

Thirdly, Derrida writes that the '*corps verbal*' he is discussing '*ne se laisse pas traduire ou transporter*'. Specifically, he deploys '*laisser*' as a pronominal verb, which means that he must harness the impersonal reflexive pronoun '*se*'. Derrida's focus is thus squarely on that very '*corps verbal*' and on its 'own' refusal to allow itself to be 'translate[d] or transport[ed]'. If you will, Derrida emphasizes the '*corps verbal*''s very unwillingness to be displaced across languages – its intrinsic or structural reticence to relocation. For his part, Bass turns his attention away from the '*corps verbal*' towards the process of translation. Stressing operational limits, he holds of the '*corps verbal*' that it 'cannot be translated or carried over'. The restriction is no longer inherent to the '*corps verbal*' itself, to its immanent resistance to dislodgement across languages; instead, the matter becomes processual and pertains to the way translation operates, to what translation can – or cannot – achieve.

Fourthly, Bass lets go of the arrangement of French signifiers, that is, he does not copy French syntax and its placement of adjectives after nouns (as in '*un corps verbal*' or '*l'énergie essentielle*'). Presumably, Bass thinks that even as the situation of adjectives after nouns is standard usage in French, it has become archaic in English. But as he deviates from

[19] See L Venuti, *Translation Changes Everything* (Routledge 2013) 35–36.

Derrida's French syntax (as he writes '[t]he materiality of a word', 'the driving force'), Bass is anglicizing the source-text.[20]

Fifthly, Bass withdraws from the French text by refusing to conform to certain words or expressions ('*transporter*' becomes not 'transport', but 'carried over'; '*cela même*' not 'that itself', but 'precisely'; and '*laisse tomber*' not 'lets drop', but 'relinquishes').

I accept that Bass captures the tenor of Derrida's three-fold argument: that the chain of graphematic signifiers constituting the foreign text withstands reproduction in translation; that translation must therefore renounce such replication; and that this abdication is effectively the very gist of translation – in the sense at least that translation *must* concede a departure from the sequence of syllables that are inscribed as the foreign text. But I maintain that Bass's English text, in the end, features excessive ethnocentrism. Not only is there an unjustified loss of intratextual effects – the singular texture of certain dimensions of the source-text is forsaken in a number of important respects – but there is also an exorbitant forfeiture of intertextual effects as many of the singular evocations of the source-language within the source-text are sacrificed.[21] Even as every translation necessarily generates difference, Bass's translation produces the kind of difference that fails to do justice to Derrida's French text, that is unjust vis-à-vis it. For my part, I would, at this writing, translate Derrida's sentence in this manner:

> Now, a body verbal does not let itself be translated or transported into another language. It is that indeed ('*cela même*') that translation lets drop. To let drop the body, such is even the energy essential to translation.

As I translate, I attempt to reprise the foreign text as closely as I can, if at all possible to track it word for word,[22] one word at a time, without being too preoccupied with the disruption that I will provoke in my anglophone reader's readerly expectations. Again, my abiding concern must be to preserve a measure of the foreignness of the text in the host-language with a view to doing justice to the foreign text's singularity, to being just to its difference from the host-language – to ensure that foreignness therefore remains present within the host-text, that it inscribes

[20] See ibid 35.

[21] See ibid.

[22] cf J Derrida, *Qu'est-ce qu'une traduction "relevante"?* (L'Herne 2005) 22–23: 'So that one legitimately uses the word "translation" . . . , it must be that . . . the translation be *quantitatively* equivalent to the original. . . . [I]t is not a matter of counting the number of signs . . . , but of counting the *number of words*.'

a remainder, there. Once more, the pursuit of this goal must mean that my anglophone reader may well find himself discountenanced. I acknowledge this interference. Indeed, I *crave* such disturbance. In Lawrence Venuti's terms, the idea governing my comparative interventions is that '[i]n its effort to do right abroad, . . . translation practice must do wrong at home, deviating enough from native norms to stage an alien reading experience'.[23] (The expression 'do[ing] wrong at home' must be promptly qualified for '[t]he translator enriches his tongue by allowing the source language to penetrate and modify it'.[24]) Throughout, I operate in the realm of interpretation. To return to Derrida's sentence, I claim no objectivity or truth as regards my suggested translation, and I accept that other translations are feasible. Assuming an array of translations, it will ultimately fall to Derrida's anglophone readership to express a preference, to assess which translation it considers just, or at least more just than others, at any one time.

Some orthodox comparative law, if I may! Allow me two brief illustrations. In both cases, I reproduce the German source-text, which I draw from Konrad Zweigert and Hein Kötz's influential book. On each occasion, I also submit two English interventions, the first being Tony Weir's, appearing as Oxford University Press's 'official' or authorized translation, the second consisting of my own foreignizing recommendation.

> **Example 1**
>
> Die Lösungen der untersuchten Rechtsordnungen sind von allen systematischen Begriffen dieser Rechtsordnungen zu befreien, aus ihren nur-nationalen dogmatischen Verkrustungen zu lösen.[25]
>
> [Weir] [T]he solutions [comparatists] find in the different jurisdictions must be cut loose from their conceptual context and stripped of their national doctrinal overtones.[26]

[23] L Venuti, *The Translator's Invisibility* (3rd edn, Routledge 2018) 15–16. Venuti's work is substantially indebted to the late Antoine Berman's scholarship. Eg: A Berman, *L'Epreuve de l'étranger* (Gallimard 1984); A Berman, *La Traduction et la lettre ou l'auberge du lointain* (Editions du Seuil 1999 [1985]). For a compelling argument defending and applying Berman's ideas, see J Baillehache, *Le Désir de traduire* (Presses Universitaires de Rennes 2021).

[24] G Steiner, *After Babel* (3rd edn, Oxford University Press 1998) 67.

[25] K Zweigert and H Kötz, *Einführung in die Rechtsvergleichung* (3rd edn, Mohr Siebeck 1996) 43. Incidentally, I fundamentally disagree with Zweigert and Kötz's advice, which I would literally turn on its head so that the comparatist approaches legal solutions as instantiations of local legal/cultural discourse and seeks to make sense of them as such.

[26] K Zweigert and H Kötz, *Introduction to Comparative Law* (3rd edn, T Weir tr, Oxford University Press 1998) 44.

[PL] The solutions of the investigated legal orders are to be freed of all systematic concepts of these legal orders, to be unfastened out of their solely-national dogmatic incrustations.

Example 2

[D]er Rechtsvergleicher [muß sich] von seinen eigenen juristisch-dogmatischen Vorverständnissen und seinem eigenen kulturellen Umfeld lösen und sich 'neutraler' Begriffe bedienen.[27]

[Weir] [Comparatists] must cut themselves loose from their own doctrinal and juridical preconceptions and liberate themselves from their own cultural context in order to discover 'neutral' concepts with which to describe problems.[28]

[PL] [T]he comparatist must unfasten himself from his own juridical-dogmatic preconceptions and his own cultural context and must avail himself of 'neutral' concepts.

In these two instances, it must be clear that Weir's translations are English-language-oriented, that is, they seek to re-write the German text into elegant English, even if this strategy compels moving away from the German language (which Weir repeatedly does). For Weir, I surmise, the translator's goal is effectively to ensure that an anglophone reader forgets that he is reading a German text. As I explain, I beg to differ, and I argue that, on the contrary, the anglophone reader must be reminded at all times, through what one can style an 'agrammaticality effect', that he is reading a foreign text.[29] The reader must be made to listen, to hearken to foreignness. From my standpoint, such is the merit, in the formulations I devise, of expressions like 'the investigated legal orders', 'of these legal orders', and 'juridical-dogmatic'. The idea that I am deliberately implementing is very much to generate a 'friction' ('*heurt*'),[30] to strike a discordant note, to impede the habitual flow of the host-language so that the discontinuities on display will put the anglophone reader on notice that things are not normal, that it is not reading business as usual, so to speak. *In English, there must be the German remainder, the foreign*

[27] Zweigert and Kötz (n 25) 11. Again, I hold diametrically opposite views to Zweigert and Kötz's. The 'unfastening' they advise is neither possible nor desirable, and the 'conceptual neutrality' they seek can only pertain to the realm of fiction.

[28] Zweigert and Kötz (n 26) 10.

[29] L Bonoli, *Lire les cultures* (Kimé 2008) 98 [emphasis omitted].

[30] Lorenzo Bonoli refers, approvingly, to 'a *friction* that happens inside the horizon of a familiar sense but that manifests the existence of something that enters into contrast with that horizon and that comes to interrupt the comfort ensured by the "already known"': ibid 58.

unlost. Needless to add, in terms of the translations I suggest I am still operating interpretively – that is, neither objectively nor truthfully.

*

On the subject of writing, I am inclined to inscribe a few (additional) comments. Prudently allowing for exceedingly rare exceptions, it is fair to say that comparative law research attracting significant attention and discussion on the international scene is work circulating in English. (Even as I enter my modest caveat, I cannot in fact think of any counter-example.) While it is evidently the case that Italian comparatists debate comparative law scholarship published in Italian inter se or Portuguese comparatists comparative law scholarship released in Portuguese, such conversations are destined to remain largely local (which is not to say that they are devoid of interest, since it is evidently valuable for Italian or Portuguese comparatists to bring to Italy in Italian or to Portugal in Portuguese their insights into, say, US or Australian law). Nowadays, however, the existence of a broad international readership assumes an English text. Again, it is obvious that comparatists who enjoy writing proficiency in English therefore find themselves at a substantial advantage with respect to the dissemination of their scholarship. Still, as a matter of justness, comparatists writing in English have to trace their German, French, or Italian source-materials to the relevant source-language. To continue with the hypothesis of a text being prepared in English, I hold that every quotation hailing from a foreign language has to be translated into English and, preferably, made available in the source-language alongside the English translation, in one form or another – perhaps through insertion in a note (editorial word-limit permitting). Thus being provided with the source-text at his ready disposal, the reader can enjoy the opportunity to enter his own confrontation with it, if he can afford to do so from a linguistic standpoint and if he is keen to engage in this activity (which he may well prove to be regarding a specific issue or term of especial concern to him).

While the comparatist may find that there exists a published translation in English of the German, French, or Italian text that interests him, he should be very careful not to take such translation at face value (unless, of course, it is legally official, as would be the case, say, with a Supreme Court of Canada decision, which appears simultaneously and officially in English and French, both languages then being equal in law and equally law). Note in particular how the fact that a given English translation has been published under the auspices of a distinguished English or US university press, that it has been authorized, does not make it ipso facto authoritative and certainly not immune from critique. To be sure, the comparatist-at-law remains free to derive inspiration – and possibly close guidance – from the published translation in English, but he should painstakingly review it and not hesitate to enter whatever amendments he feels are necessary in order to be optimally just to the source-text. In other words, the comparatist-at-law should be actively disposed to formulate his own translation to substitute for the 'official' one (which is precisely how I have proceeded with *NCL*) for the sake of deploying enhanced justness vis-à-vis the source-text, recalling that no translation (even his proposed one) can eschew interpretive violence; that no translation (even his proposed one) is ever exact, correct, or accurate; and that no translation (even his proposed one) is ever definitive.

Throughout, the three-stage exercise in rigour that compels the comparatist to confine himself to source-materials he can read in the source-language; to invent his own translation of them (he finds the source-text, there, and fashions it in the host-language); and to divulge the source-quotation along with his translation of it, has the crucial benefit of keeping foreign-law research at once intellectually honest and trustworthy. I do not deny for a moment that the tracking of source-texts and the formulation of their just translations must require substantial time on the comparatist's part. I cannot see, however, how the significance of the issues involved can justify minimizing one's effort. Again, I want to substantiate my claim with an apposite illustration.

Arguably, the following excerpt – a capital hermeneutic insight for comparatists-at-law – is one of the most important statements in Hans-Georg Gadamer's *Wahrheit und Methode*, a book widely and justifiably regarded as a leading twentieth-century philosophical text: 'Es genügt zu sagen, daß man *anders* versteht, *wenn man überhaupt versteht*.'[31] I suggest that a just English translation might read thus: 'It suffices to say that one understands *differently, when one understands at all*.' As I see the matter, Gadamer's German sentence translates into English rather straightforwardly, in fact. The translative exercise, I think, calls for one notable observation only, which concerns the term '*überhaupt*', a word featuring a wide semantic reach. In this instance, it appears to me that '*überhaupt*' can legitimately be said to mean 'at all' as in the sentence 'Er hat überhaupt keine Ahnung', or 'He has no idea at all'.

[31] H-G Gadamer, *Wahrheit und Methode* (5th edn, Mohr Siebeck 1986) 302.

Forthrightness notwithstanding, the published French translation is unjust vis-à-vis the German text. It reads as follows: 'Il suffit de dire que, *dès que l'on comprend, on comprend autrement*.'[32] Leaving to one side the fact that the three French co-translators invert the two relevant passages in Gadamer's sentence and italicize both occurrences of the German verb '*verstehen*' even as Gadamer does so once only, the French passage somewhat strikingly distorts Gadamer's text. For Gadamer, whether there will ever be understanding remains doubtful. '[W]hen one understands at all', he writes, which means 'if ever one manages to understand in the first place', then, he claims, but only then, understanding will operate differently (say, from the text being understood and from other understandings of the text). In other words, Gadamer distinguishes between two sets of situations, one habitual and the other exceptional. For him, there are the usual instances, which is when there will be no understanding whatsoever, and there are those less ordinary cases, which is when there will be understanding. And it is specifically the latter occasions that hold Gadamer's interest (which makes sense, since there is arguably not so much to say about configurations where no understanding whatsoever arises). And what are the implications of the understanding that will materialize in the situations where there will be understanding? For Gadamer, such understanding will, perforce, operate singularly.

Meanwhile, the French text assumes that there will always be understanding along the merry way. It maintains that understanding will always emerge at some point – which is what the preposition '*dès*' indicates. A literal translation into English of the published French translation might read thus: 'It suffices to say that as soon as one understands, one understands differently.' But for Gadamer, again, the moment of understanding will mostly not even come to pass. In sum, the French translation ignores the German '*überhaupt*' in a way that is unjust to Gadamer's text. A just French translation might have rendered '*überhaupt*' by '*si jamais*' so as to read: 'Il suffit de dire qu'on comprend *autrement, si jamais l'on comprend*.'

For its part, the Italian text is likewise deficient, and it also does an injustice to Gadamer's writing – it also distorts Gadamer's argument – in one significant respect. In Italian, Gadamer's enunciation reads thus: 'È sufficiente dire che, *quando in generale si comprende*, si comprende

[32] H-G Gadamer, *Vérité et méthode* (P Fruchon et al trs, Editions du Seuil 1996) 318.

diversamente.'[33] Now, the Italian formulation '*quando in generale si comprende*, si comprende *diversamente*' can be transposed into English as '*when one understands in general*, one understands *differently*'. Once more overlooking the inversion, the objectionable terms are obviously the words 'in general', which are nowhere to be found in Gadamer's sentence. As with the French translation, the German '*überhaupt*' is misunderstood in a way that is unjust to Gadamer's text.

It is relevant to observe, I think, that Jean Grondin, one of the three French co-translators, and Gianni Vattimo, the Italian translator, were both Gadamer's dedicated students and are both considered foremost exponents of philosophical hermeneutics. In other words, neither Grondin and Vattimo's expertise in matters Gadamerian nor their loyalty to Gadamer's thought can reasonably be questioned. Nonetheless, it is the published English translation that comes closest, in my opinion, to doing justice to Gadamer's words. Joel Weinsheimer and Donald Marshall thus write in these terms: 'It is enough to say that we understand in a *different* way, *if we understand at all.*'[34] Still, Weinsheimer and Marshall unfortunately introduce the first person plural, twice, while Gadamer had elected to retain the third person impersonal throughout – perhaps after his mentor Heidegger, who makes conspicuous use of the expression '*das Man*' in his own writings.[35] And then, there is the addition of the term 'way' in the expression 'a *different* way' (the German word would be '*Weg*', which is not in Gadamer's work).

I claim that the francophone, italophone, or anglophone comparatist-at-law who would choose to rely exclusively on the French, Italian, or English version without devoting the time and effort necessary to verify the translation against the source-text would fail to appreciate that for Gadamer the emergence of an understanding is not in the least ordinary (contrary to what the published French text contends); fail to realize that Gadamer's focus was not understanding in general (contrary to what the published Italian text advocates); and fail to acknowledge that Gadamer did not write in the consensual language that the word 'we' implies (contrary to what the published English text indicates). Once more, my general contention is that while evidently convenient, published

[33] H-G Gadamer, *Verità e metodo* (German-Italian ed, G Vattimo tr, Bompiani 2019 [2000]) 615.

[34] H-G Gadamer, *Truth and Method* (2nd English edn, J Weinsheimer and D Marshall trs, Continuum 2004) 296.

[35] Eg: HL Dreyfus, 'Interpreting Heidegger on *Das Man*' (1995) 38 Inquiry 423; D Robinson, *Critical Translation Studies* (Routledge 2017) 113–23.

translations can prove deceptive, no matter how dependable they appear to be – either on account of the publisher's prestige, of the translator's eminence, or both.

*

I am concerned to offer one further reflection, if cursorily so, as regards linguistic competence and the practice of comparative law. It is silly to claim – an argument I have repeatedly seen or heard – that one cannot creditably compare laws unless one is able to read more than one language (I have already indicated the finite value of speaking abilities). This canard overlooks how it is quite possible for a US comparatist who is only able to read English to engage in significant comparative research featuring, say, the laws of Australia, Canada, and the United Kingdom. Likewise, a Spanish comparatist whose linguistic ability is confined to Spanish can profitably research the laws of Mexico or Argentina. To formulate the matter as crisply as I can, monolingualism and comparative law are not antithetical.

*

Against the backdrop of Borges's interrogation,[36] I maintain that translation is not an activity that can ever achieve mutual understanding across languages or allow two languages to reach agreement with one another. What a translator does, and all he can ever do, is to articulate linguistic difference. Indeed, 'translation is not at all destined to make difference disappear of which it is on the contrary the play: constantly it alludes to it, it conceals it, but sometimes by revealing it and often by accentuating it, it is the life itself of that difference'.[37] Note that difference is a structural component of every translation, a constitutive element that cannot be erased or overcome no matter how dedicated one's translative effort. In other terms, upon considering the two texts at hand – the source-text and the host-text – the translator requires to admit that the two forms of words must incessantly differ and that such must be the case notwithstanding his hardest work. At the outset, one must therefore resist thinking of the languages coming into the translation process in terms of ipseity, duplication, commonality, consensus, relation, alliance, consilience, reconciliation, and continuity (or, in French, '*mêmeté*'). Rather, translation demands the mobilization and application of ideas like distinction, dissensus, irrelation, discontinuity, mutation, transformation, seriality, addition, supplementation, and invention. In sum, identity is ever

[36] Supra 136.
[37] M Blanchot, *L'Amitié* (Gallimard 1971) 70–71.

breached, and '[e]quivalence is an interpretive fiction'.[38] For this reason, the distinguished analytical philosopher Willard Quine refers to 'sameness of meaning' as 'an ill-conceived notion within traditional semantics'.[39] Yes.

*

Since there can be no bridge or passage of any kind across languages,[40] because there can be no communication, say, between French and English or German and Italian – an instantiation of the cardinal fact that the self cannot be the other – a translator must dismiss even such a notion as 'dialogue', in effect, a stagnant cloud of obscurity.[41] Because 'there is something of the original text that no translation can touch',[42] the key operational word for a translator is rather 'monologue'.[43] What takes place as translation materializes is the co-existence of two monologues – and these monologues are involved in a negotiation at the translator's behest (it is the translator who is compelling the languages into interaction). In accordance with Leibniz's Law,[44] if there is more than one language or monologue in co-presence, there can no longer be identity (or *id*-entity), but there must be difference between them, irreducibly so.[45] This affirmation ascribes to translation its 'potential of active negativity'.[46] It 'make[s] the antagonisms of translation into vital forces, watchful forces, vigilant [forces], forces of misunderstandings that lead to consider nothing as definitively settled'.[47]

[38] D Robinson, *The Translator's Turn* (Johns Hopkins University Press 1991) 259.

[39] WV Quine, 'Indeterminacy of Translation Again' (1987) 84 J Phil 5, 10.

[40] See J Derrida, *La Bête et le souverain*, vol 2 (M Lisse et al eds, Galilée 2010 [2002]) 31.

[41] cf S Beckett, *Proust* in *The Grove Centenary Edition*, vol 4 (P Auster and JM Coetzee eds, Grove 2006 [1931]) 539: 'There is no communication because there are no vehicles of communication.' Not unlike 'globalization', the word 'dialogue' demands that comparatists-at-law attest to more circumspective use than heretofore. I do not exclude myself from the list of those who fell for insouciant harnessing over the many years. Eg: P Legrand, 'John Henry Merryman and Comparative Legal Studies: A Dialogue' (1999) 47 Am J Comp L 3.

[42] 'Table ronde sur la traduction' in J Derrida, *L'Oreille de l'autre* (C Lévesque and CV McDonald eds, VLB Editeur 1982) 152. The words are Derrida's.

[43] Eg: M Heidegger, *Unterwegs zur Sprache* (Neske 1959) 265: '[L]anguage is monologue'; it speaks 'lonesomely' [emphasis omitted].

[44] Supra 96.

[45] cf J Derrida, *Limited Inc* (E Weber ed, Galilée 1990) 253, where the author holds that difference is 'irreducible'.

[46] T Samoyault, *Traduction et violence* (Editions du Seuil 2020) 11.

[47] ibid 28. The movement away from dialogue (from mutuality or continuity) towards negotiation (towards misreading or interruption) is a departure from Gadamerian hermeneutics in favour of Derridean deconstruction. For an exploration of this key philosophical differend and a resolution earnestly supporting deconstruction's insights, see P Legrand, 'Derrida's Gadamer' in S Glanert and F Girard (eds), *Law's Hermeneutics: Other Investigations* (Routledge 2017) 144–67.

Meanwhile, the comparatist-at-law must heed the fact that no individual form of words can claim to be faithful to a source-text, to be loyally accounting for a source-text – which entails that comparative law must accept the empirical fact of untranslatability. Like Derrida, therefore, '[w]hat guides me is always untranslatability'.[48] And the further fact that also informs my comparison of laws is how 'we ... misunderstand the actual extent of our partial ... understanding'.[49] However, untranslatability and misunderstanding, which materialize as soon as a translation is attempted,[50] never prevent translation from actually taking place – and from multiplying, too (with all the attendant opportunities for further interpretive negotiation amongst translators and readers and therefore for the beneficial exploration of languages' boundaries).[51] Translation happens, incessantly, but it happens on every occasion as the possibilization of an actual impossibility – what *remains* an impossibility despite the fact that it is unceasingly happening.[52]

48 J Derrida, 'Du mot à la vie: un dialogue entre Jacques Derrida et Hélène Cixous' (Interview with A Armel) *Magazine littéraire* (April 2004) 26. The words are Derrida's. See generally E Apter, *Against World Literature: On the Politics of Untranslatability* (Verso 2013); SJ Levine and K Lateef-Jan (eds), *Untranslatability Goes Global* (Routledge 2018). Adde: B Cassin (ed), *Vocabulaire européen des philosophies: dictionnaire des intraduisibles* (Editions du Seuil 2004).

49 D Robinson, *Exorcising Translation* (Bloomsbury 2017) xiii.

50 Eg: 'Law' is not a translation of '*droit*' (how *could* 'law', which emerges in an idiographic legal culture such as England's, be a translation of '*droit*', the product of a nomothetic legal culture like that governing in France?). I develop an argument around the hiatus between 'law' and '*droit*' with specific reference to the work of Derrida in P Legrand, 'Jacques Derrida Never Wrote About Law' in P Goodrich and M Rosenfeld (eds), *Administering Interpretation* (Fordham University Press 2019) 105–46. cf JO Haley, *Law's Political Foundations* (Elgar 2016) 4: 'We have to take care what we call law. The lack of universally accepted definitions poses special problems for ... comparative law.' Alas, not all comparatists-at-law exhibit such wisdom. Eg: U Mattei, 'Three Patterns of Law: Taxonomy and Change in the World's Legal Systems' (1997) 45 Am J Comp L 5, 13n37: 'I do not wish to enter into the largely sterile and boring discussion of what can be considered law.' Note that to expose the limits of what translation can handle is also felicitously to reveal the limits of what 'translation-as-violation' can control, that is, of what imperial or colonial thought can subjugate. I borrow the compound expression from GC Spivak, *A Critique of Postcolonial Reason* (Harvard University Press 1999) 162.

51 Derrida offers an important argument about the virtues of 'misunderstanding, incomprehension, mistake': J Derrida, *Papier Machine* (Galilée 2001) 306. Eg: P Legrand (ed), *Common law d'un siècle l'autre* (Blais 1992). This book consists in original essays on the common law tradition by distinguished common law jurists writing in French and therefore translating the common law from English to French. Contributors include John Bell, JA Jolowicz, Neil MacCormick, Roderick Munday, Bernard Rudden, Geoffrey Samuel, and Tony Weir.

52 For a guide to the making of just translations with specific reference to comparative law, many of the conclusions running counter-intuitively to comparatists-at-law's unexamined

*

Translation is, perforce, an original creation – it is the first original, originally once more, if differently. Again, such difference obtains, because straightforward duplication across languages is beyond reach. In Derrida's words, 'for the notion of translation, one will have to substitute a notion of *transformation*: the regulated transformation of a language by another, of a text by another'.[53] He adds: 'We will not have been and have not been involved ever, in fact, in some "transportation" of pure signifieds that the signifying instrument – or the "vehicle" – would leave virginal and unbroached, from one language to another.'[54] Otherwise said, there can be 'no transportation without transformation'.[55] Observe that while the translator is writing a second original, he is inscribing an original of a peculiar kind, since this second original is not fully autonomous: it is an original that must emanate from the first original, that must be *of* it. There is play, then, inevitably so, but there is not free play.[56] Crucially, though, the idea of a second original assists in acknowledging the translator's agency, in recognizing the fact that the translator is a writer in his own *write* and in his own *re-write*.[57] To enunciate or enact a translation is *to do* something. Far from being neutral or anything of the kind, a translator's understanding, emphatically a '*participating* understanding',[58] is mired in contingency.

assumptions, see P Legrand, 'Mind the Gap! Translation of Foreign Law Is Not What You Think' (2021) 8 Revista de Investigações Constitucionais/J Constitutional Research 601.

53 Derrida, *Positions* (n 18) 31.

54 ibid. cf D Bellos and KL Scheppele, 'Translating Law Across Cultures and Societies: A Conversation with David Bellos and Kim Lane Scheppele' in E Mertz, S Macaulay, and TW Mitchell (eds), *The New Legal Realism*, vol 1 (Cambridge University Press 2016) 286: 'There is always something that changes in the course of translation because – you changed [the legal institution or legal idea] almost by definition when you moved it to a new place.' The words are Scheppele's.

55 B Latour, *Aramis ou l'amour des techniques* (La Découverte 1992) 104.

56 cf K Briggs, *This Little Art* (Fitzcarraldo 2017) 338: 'Some new thing starts to get made in the frame of againness; something that is *of the original*, yes, but that will extend beyond the reach of it, the purview of it, since it is being made by someone else, by me now.'

57 cf Derrida (n 42) 202: 'Translation is a writing, . . . it is a productive writing.'

58 R Bultmann, 'Das Problem der Hermeneutik' (1950) 47 Zeitschrift für Theologie und Kirche 47, 56.

VI

Outings

The questions of language and access to primary materials tally with another basic issue demanding consideration, that is, fieldwork, a term I borrow from anthropological research to claim that in order to write a creditable report on a foreign law, one must make one's way to the foreign location where that foreign law dwells. Consider Otto Kahn-Freund, writing a few years before his election as Professor of Comparative Law at Oxford: 'An American who wants to know what English, French or Chinese law is really like will have to go to England, to France or to China.'[1] If intellectual integrity must matter, as it evidently ought to do, I find it hard to vindicate another approach. Note that the journey does not in the least *guarantee* the production of reliability,[2] but it must stand, at least in principle, as an uncircumventable prerequisite towards the achievement of that goal. Within the field of comparative law, however, there is no ethos of fieldwork – unlike, say, the position that obtains in anthropology, where fieldwork is very much an authoritative and regulative rite of passage pertaining to the core and self-identity of the discipline, a hallmark practice. In particular, there is no institutional expectation within comparative law that early in one's career (or, for that matter, at a later stage), a comparatist will spend a year or two studying foreign law in a foreign country. In my experience, such displacements

1 O Kahn-Freund, 'Book Review' (1957) 67 Yale LJ 950, 950 (review of AT von Mehren, *The Civil Law System* [Prentice-Hall 1957]). I am pleased to assume that Kahn-Freund would have been aware how his view accorded with the most distinguished German literary lineage. cf JW von Goethe, 'Noten und Abhandlungen zu besserem Verständnis des West-östlichen Divans' in *Goethes Werke*, vol 1/7 (Böhlau 1888 [1819]) 1: 'He who wants to understand the poet/must go to the land of the poet.'

2 'Anecdatally', a French comparatist who had studied English law at a leading English law school for two years on a full-time basis hailed me in Paris on 7 December 1999 to ask why she could not find a discussion of estoppel in any of the English contract law textbooks that she had been researching.

continue to be sporadic at best. Over the course of one's academic career, the decision to travel or not to the foreign law's abode remains profoundly personal and very much turns on one's own self-acuity, on one's own idea of what constitutes reputable research (or, in the case of postgraduate students, on their dissertation supervisor's appreciation – some of my Paris colleagues thus discourage or prohibit foreign sojourns), not to mention, of course, the availability of funds. And although delocation might help to corroborate the comparatist's work in the eyes of some of his readers, the absence of it will clearly not prompt automatic invalidation.

I consider as distinctly odd the absence of any collective standards in comparative law whereby fieldwork would be regarded as a deeply inculcated aspect of professional culture and therefore assessed as an important value. In my view, such institutional laxity with respect to accountability is, frankly, unfathomable. While one can point to scholarly projects where fieldwork has readily imposed itself because of the specific topic at hand and been diligently pursued by dedicated comparatists-at-law,[3] there are many individuals who feel able to write on a foreign law, or to teach it, without having spent any meaningful time in the relevant foreign country either as a student or teacher. (Lest my reader should react incredulously, I hasten to add that *I have names*.) In my opinion, such nonchalance quite simply tarnishes comparative law's reputation. In fact, the situation is particularly disturbing, since for most comparatists-at-law fieldwork would hardly involve exotic pursuits such as a study of classroom-learning in the Waorani nation in the Ecuadorian Amazon or an investigation of trust in the Sulaymaniyah Governorate in the Iraqi Kurdistan. Rather, their on-site engagement with foreign law can be expected largely to consist of conversations with a few local colleagues (possibly within the framework of a seminar) on a university campus, sittings in local libraries, and visits to local academic bookshops in order to familiarize themselves with a range of law-texts and, one

[3] Eg: LK McAllister, *Making Law Matter: Environmental Protection and Legal Institutions in Brazil* (Stanford University Press 2008); M Lasser, 'Judicial (Self-)Portraits: Judicial Discourse in the French Legal System' (1995) 104 Yale LJ 1325. Tocqueville offers an illustration of fieldwork *avant la lettre*. Indeed, the two volumes of *De la démocratie en Amérique* released in 1835 and 1840 are based on a nine-month journey to the United States (and Canada) in 1831 and 1832. For a substantial diary revealing the many meetings Tocqueville held with local lawyers, officials, and politicians, see A de Tocqueville, 'Voyage en Amérique' in *Œuvres* (A Jardin et al eds, Gallimard 1991) 27–413.

hopes, with a certain assortment of what orthodox comparatists-at-law would regard as non-law-texts.

While allowing for the usual array of exceptional circumstances, I argue that the writing or teaching of foreign law must depend on a sustained encounter with that foreign law in its (relatively) stable site of occupation. The proliferation of electronic resources – for example, in the form of English translations of apex-court decisions or the complete text of law-review articles and monographs – does not meaningfully affect my claim. There is much more to a research visit in a foreign country than the sheer accumulation of 'black-letter' data. How, then, does fieldwork work in the field?[4] Although the following narrative purports to capture what would largely remain the characteristic physical deterritorialization exercise within comparative law when such move happens to take place, the story I offer also seeks to indicate how fieldwork can involve much more than shifting one's location for its own sake, how it must be envisaged as an intellectually productive way of being-in-the-foreign-law-world. In this sense, I straddle the age-old descriptive/prescriptive biarchy.

*

Imogene is a Canadian comparatist almost equally at ease in French as in her native English. Born in Montréal, she aspired to a stage less parochial and chose to pursue her university studies in Toronto. After a first degree in politics and international relations at the University of Toronto, she earned a law degree at the same institution. In time, she completed a year of postgraduate legal studies at a leading US, East Coast law school and proceeded to write her doctorate in law at LSE. Following her doctoral supervisor's footsteps, she then spent a year in the United States doing postdoctoral work at Berkeley under the guidance of two renowned experts in comparative constitutionalism. Subsequently, she began to teach law in Halifax, in Eastern Canada, where she has been based for

[4] I have derived particular assistance from A Cerwonka and LH Malkki, *Improvising Theory* (University of Chicago Press 2007); JD Faubion and GE Marcus (eds), *Fieldwork Is Not What It Used to Be* (Cornell University Press 2009); J Fabian, *Time and the Other* (Columbia University Press 1983); GE Marcus, *Ethnography Through Thick and Thin* (Princeton University Press 1998); J Clifford and GE Marcus (eds), *Writing Culture: The Poetics and Politics of Ethnography* (University of California Press 1986); P Rabinow, *Reflections on Fieldwork in Morocco* (University of California Press 1977); J Lunn (ed), *Fieldwork in the Global South* (Routledge 2014). There are many practical (or 'how-to') guides available. For a well-crafted illustration of this genre, see JE Marti, *Starting Fieldwork* (Waveland 2017).

the past six years and is now tenured. As part of a major Spanish transnational and transdisciplinary initiative on constitutional worlds into which she was recently co-opted (she happens to have excellent Spanish, and she visited the University of Granada for one academic year on a Canadian government fellowship), Imogene's current research project is to elucidate the law of the royal prerogative in a constitutional democracy with specific reference to the United Kingdom.

Imogene was pleasantly surprised to have been invited to join in this collaborative endeavour, and the fact that the head of the task force assigned her a research brief featuring the common law tradition in one of its most influential instantiations delighted her also. Although Spain is hardly Cambodia or Cameroon, Imogene likes the idea of a scholarly initiative originating from a country that remains a European outlier within the field of comparative law. Ideally, she would have been able to start her research earlier and would not have to submit her text so soon (she now has barely a few months left). And she would not be constrained by what she views as an unreasonable word limit. But she was told twice that these terms were to be strictly observed. So, 15 December and 12,000 words it shall be! For Imogene, the good news of the moment is that, with the Canadian academic year finally behind her, she can at last undertake her one-month research visit to Oxford. Fortunately, she has at her disposal a faculty research grant covering all her costs and therefore does not have to worry about financial support (she appreciates her good fortune, which not all comparatists-at-law with whom she is acquainted can likewise enjoy – she cannot help thinking of a French colleague marooned in the evermore impoverished French university system).

While Oxford city centre will be teeming with teenagers from all over the planet having enrolled in one of the numerous intensive summer programmes marketing more or less instantaneous proficiency in English, the libraries will be quiet as befits the Long Vacation. Having also spent the whole of July in Oxford three years earlier for her text on the reform of the British courts, Imogene knows the situation well. Contrary to what happened last time, however, she expects that on this occasion she can avoid the technical glitches that complicated on-site Internet access from her laptop computer. And, on the basis of her e-mail correspondence over the last few months, she is optimistic that this time, she will not have to cope with an unreasonable landlady and two crying babies. While she very much hopes that her administrative duties at her

Canadian university will not interfere with her Oxford research (she currently sits on two committees, including postgraduate studies), she ultimately values the fact that she can remain in easy electronic contact with her colleagues, not to mention her friends and elderly aunt back home. She realizes, of course, that her short visit will have little to do with immersion, which as far as she is concerned is just as well since she intends always to keep her head fully above the water line. (Imogene has long thought immersion a poor metaphor to describe the comparatist's travail.)

When, after a long journey featuring the usual vexations (which have definitely been increasing over the years), Imogene finally reaches Paddington Station, she learns that the next train to Oxford is delayed (the one after that having been cancelled). A Paddington 'café' may be an unlikely setting for epistemological musings but, as she pauses in the company of her tea and scone, Imogene cannot help thinking that her 'slate' is far from 'clean', so to speak. In other words, she is aware that she is very much coming to her research as a Canadian jurist. Moreover, what she understands of the royal prerogative largely concerns Spanish law. Indeed, she studied '*prerrogativas reales*' while at Granada. And for the past two years, she has been giving seminars on '*prerrogativas reales*' in her upper-year optional course on comparative constitutional law in Canada. At this stage, she cannot have a precise idea of how much this prior experience will influence her Oxford research. In fact, she suspects that even after her work has been completed she will remain unable to tell about the extent of that encroachment. However, having been sensitized by her mentors many years earlier to the centrality of epistemological issues regarding any investigation into foreign law (in this respect, her Berkeley postdoctoral advisers were perhaps even more emphatic than her LSE supervisor who, on account of his personal and educational English/US background, had already shown himself to be very insistent), she accepts that her Canadian legal education and Spanish legal specialization must entail the application of a cluster of specific prejudices (in the etymological sense of 'anterior judgements'). She discerns how these predispositions or predilections, this pre-understanding, cannot but colour to a certain extent at least her appreciation of the law of the royal prerogative in the United Kingdom. After all, it is *she*, and not someone else, who will soon be reading the law-texts on the royal prerogative in the United Kingdom and seeking to elucidate them through an exercise in ascription of meaning coming from *her*. In other words, she is conscious that any process of cognition is subordinated to a measure of recognition.

No doubt because of the biography she was reading on the flight from Canada, Imogene's thoughts soon focus on Marcel Duchamp, whom she has long admired. The possibility that Duchamp's ready-mades could be cognized as art when they were first exhibited – she has in mind the 1915 shovel or the 1917 urinal – depended on their being recognized (or, more accurately, *re-cognized*) as art. In other words, the process hinged on the existence of a pre-existing understanding of art into which Duchamp's work could somehow fit. Along these lines, Imogene is now reminded of a famous example of cognition-as-recognition involving one José de Acosta, a well-known sixteenth-century Spanish Jesuit and explorer. Her recollection is vague, and she would have to consult her notes. But she remembers reading an English translation of Acosta's account of his 'discovery' of the Americas while she was studying at Berkeley. In the relevant passage of his diary, Acosta is trying to make sense of llamas, which he does by effectively recasting this animal, then new to him, into the terms of the menagerie with which he was already familiar in Spain: 'sheep', 'calves', and 'camel[s]' (Imogene recalls '*carneros*', '*bezerros*', and '*camello[s]*'). Acosta, in effect, was doing precisely what Roy Wagner describes in a book she has been keeping at hand ever since it was recommended to her by her dissertation supervisor upon her arrival at LSE. According to Wagner, Acosta proceeded to 'inven[t] ... his own understanding'. More precisely, 'the analogies he create[d] are extensions of his own notions and those of his culture .... He use[d] the latter as a kind of "lever", the way a pole vaulter uses his pole, to catapult his comprehension beyond the limitations imposed by earlier viewpoints.'[5]

Imogene accepts that the comparative research she is about to undertake will likewise institute her 'own' pre-existing experience at some referential level or other. Again, though, she remains unsure that she can ascertain the full extent of the pre-existing epistemological baggage she is bringing to bear on her impending forays into UK law. Still, she feels that she must acknowledge the fact that her intuitions will inevitably be affected by her experiential pre-understanding albeit in ways that may well stay undefined and indeed undefinable – even as she tells herself that her insights cannot prove reducible to her prejudices. Be that as it may,

[5] R Wagner, *The Invention of Culture* (University of Chicago Press 1981) 12. José de Acosta (1539–1600) resided in Peru and Mexico from 1570 to 1587. The reference to Acosta's chronicles is to J de Acosta, *Historia natural y moral de las Indias* ([J]uan de Leon 1590) bk 4, ch 41, 293. Acosta's text initially appeared in English in 1604. For a re-translation into contemporary English, see J de Acosta, *Natural and Moral History of the Indies* (JE Mangan ed, F López-Morillas tr, Duke University Press 2002) bk 4, ch 41, 244.

she is determined to track this epistemological dynamic as closely as she can. Crucially, she thinks, such self-awareness ought to allow for a redress of the epistemological imbalance otherwise structuring the linkage between the comparatist, on one hand, and the law she has elected to study, on the other. Imogene maintains that epistemic introspection (no matter how bad human beings can be at self-knowledge) ought to act as critical self-monitoring with a view to qualifying any expression of power or authority over the foreign law that the comparatist is choosing to 'enframe', even if such hierarchization should be momentary only. Of course, her research will be ethnocentric (or juricentric) – it must be, since it is *her* research. But Imogene firmly believes that ethnocentrism (or juricentrism) can only be permitted within limits: it must be contained.

As Imogene knows well, one critical challenge for the comparatist is to resist anything like a 'yuck' reaction – the consideration of the other's norms as enormities – for even the laws that repulse one and incite one to withdraw in distaste or shock beseech understanding.[6] Granted, the law of the royal prerogative in the United Kingdom appears an implausible candidate for the kind of recoilment Imogene is now pondering – unlike, say, laws governing capital punishment for the mentally deficient, abortion for victims of rape, female circumcision, or religious attire at school. Even in such hard cases, Imogene is clearly of the view that it remains crucial for one to avoid engaging the other on the ground that one, unlike the hapless other, would somehow have access to the truth or that one could ascertain some universal that the benighted other would have missed. Indeed, she has a loquacious and argumentative personality, and she has on more than occasion made life publicly uncomfortable for her interlocutors when they seemed to fall so facilely for the assumption that the law of Canada or France or the United States ought somehow to be hurled to the rank of planetary referent. In fact, Imogene came to hold that revealing oneself to be voluble and opinionated in favour of the other is an important way of demonstrating recognition and respect vis-à-vis otherness, of attesting to the other that his otherness is being taken seriously – which is emphatically not to say that she readily indulges quietism. Once more, though, Imogene surmises that the ethical issues pertaining to the 'yuck' reaction are unlikely to

[6] For an apt warning against what he styles the 'yuck' reaction, see RA Shweder, '"What About Female Genital Mutilation?" and Why Understanding Culture Matters in the First Place' in RA Shweder et al (eds), *Engaging Cultural Differences* (Sage 2002) 222–26.

surface in the context of her study of the law of the royal prerogative in the United Kingdom.

On the train en route to Oxford, as Imogene is reflecting yet again upon how the play of the inescapably constitutive character of human agency in comparative research implies that the empirical material never simply gets collected or, to put the matter differently, as she is thinking about the way in which the comparatist is inevitably in-the-comparison, how each comparison is ultimately autobiographical, her thoughts spontaneously drift to the many late-afternoon conversations she had with her doctoral supervisor at the 'Balthazar' as he progressively managed to convince her to jettison the Cartesian dualism she had unwittingly inherited (and been taking for granted quite as unwittingly). The more she revisits these exchanges in her mind, the more she regards the fact that her supervisor had studied legal theory under a leading Heideggerian philosopher at Berkeley as one of the most significant strokes of good fortune in her intellectual life. To think where she would be without her supervisor having initiated her post-Cartesian turn! It is because of him that she ceased contemplating 'the law' as something that could be accessed, specified, and represented 'as such', independently of any individual intervening as representator. And there is more, because even as he was instructing her, Imogene's supervisor refrained from subjecting her to the dressage that her French fellow comparatist had to undergo as she was studying law in Paris. ('Dressage', which the French language spells *tel quel*, is actually Pierre Legendre's word – it is everywhere in his very many books to inform his sophisticated and justifiably acerbic critique of French legal education.) The fact is that not all processes of epistemologization unfurl identically, the variations in 'intensity' leading to the more or less profound incorporation or embodiment of the relevant epistemological matrix and therefore to a heightened or lessened plausibility of epistemic disobedience in reaction to the orthodox norms of governance within a scholarly field.

These days, Imogene is far more serene about her epistemological assumptions than she once was. Specifically, she has no compunction in maintaining that for any comparison even to get underway, the comparatist-at-law must already have adopted a constitutive account of the issues or laws under investigation – if an ever-modifiable one – and in defending the view that the warrantability of any comparison greatly depends on the interpretive velocity that such postulates afford. Still, Imogene has not forgotten the early reactions to her dissertation when it was made abundantly clear to her, certainly by various civil law professors, that her work was being apprehended as on-the-barricades scholarship. It was as if some of her fellow comparatists-at-law – the most vocal were a couple of stray Germans teaching in the United States – could not forgive her for having openly jettisoned any pretence at objectivity, for having squarely admitted her input in the collection of the data, in the interpretation of it, and in the fashioning of her argument. It was as if she had violated an institutional taboo by disclosing a major secret – that the data is not given – and by refuting any intimation of the purity of a legal interpreter's account of foreign law. What, her detractors seemed to be screaming? Was she not worried about affixing her name to ideas that called into question, as they saw it, the very worthiness of comparative research? If one could not, objectively, tell the truth about foreign law (*the* truth . . .), where did that leave comparative law scholarship? What were now going to be comparative law's *credentials*? To his credit, her supervisor proved most supportive in the face of these objections. That law-review article he wrote. . .!

Imogene has not at all forgotten about those early moments in her career. In fact, she still carries a sheet of paper with the jottings she made during a long and emotional telephone conservation with her mentor at the time. (She also has a PDF of this document on file, but she much prefers re-reading the notes she took long-hand on account of the *vivacity* they deploy.) Whenever she considers her scribblings, she continues to find them very empowering: 'Whatever people are willing to admit, fieldwork is a process of interpretive production'; 'You do not find knowledge, you produce information'; 'Look at your situatedness not as a predicament but as a generative influence upon your understanding, your interpretation, your making-sense'; 'There is no set of standardized techniques that every comparatist can be expected to implement irrespective of topic or country or of other circumstances'; 'In Oxford, the books are freely available, and they never leave the library. In Paris, the books are not freely available, and they readily get stolen or lost. This simple material difference will have an impact on your research. It will affect your conclusions. The law you state as foreign law is liable to differ depending on whether you researched it in Oxford or Paris. Learning cannot be fully divorced from your physical interaction with your material surroundings'; 'You have to be flexible, eclectic, audacious. You will have to improvise – and you will have to improvise your theoretical model, too, because the research you conduct and the results you engender along the way will, perforce, transform your assumptions'; 'Fieldwork has nothing whatsoever to do with the formulaic approach that the concept of "method" suggests'; 'The idea that there would be a programmable application with a calculable process!'; 'There is simply no single, generalized logic of inquiry'; 'Think experience, intuition, insight – think flair – not method'; 'Your authority over the foreign law you are studying is at once that of a witness to it, that of an investigator of it, and that of a fabricant of it'; 'Do not even aspire to a neutral account of foreignness'; 'Objectivity is a hoax'; 'Avoid "hoary" comparative law at all costs'; 'Above all, resist any infatuation with German-inspired conceptual and formal fundamentalism, no matter how much authoritarianism this model projects in seeking to impose itself'; 'Fight positivism. Fight spuriousness'; 'Knowledge? Does the information you are collecting about foreign law genuinely deserve to be styled "knowledge"? Is foreign law ever enough of an object vis-à-vis you – are you ever detached from it enough – so that there can be "knowledge"?'; 'There is this central paradox: you are at once too far and too close to be able to tell it as such – there is the gap that there must be between selfness and otherness and yet you are necessarily involved in the foreign law you are stating, it is inevitably your foreign law, if only because you are enunciating it in your language.' But the train is finally reaching Oxford.

After taking possession of what will be her living quarters for the next month in a Park Town semi-basement and quickly running some basic errands in nearby North Parade, Imogene, who is determined to optimize her research time in Oxford, is soon walking across the large park that will take her to the law library. Although she is happy to see the swans (they are very much a soothing part of the Oxford scenery), she pays little attention to them as she remains entirely focussed on her project: no time for the least foolishment. It occurs to her that while her 'slate' is not 'clean' – but then, there is simply no atheoretical way of researching foreign law – the law of the royal prerogative in the United Kingdom does not feature a 'clean slate' either in the sense that, not unlike her, it is also encumbered. In other terms, foreign law does not exist 'in the air'. Rather, it is grounded – very much so, in fact – and it is thus freighted with traces of history, philosophy, politics, and what not. In sum, even as she feels constrained by her personal and professional trajectory – as she feels encultured – Imogene reminds herself that she must remain fully alert to the fact that the law she is about to study is encultured, too. The image of the archive comes to her mind: the law of the royal prerogative in the

United Kingdom archives history, philosophy, politics, and so forth. Indeed, how could it not? How could history and politics, for example, not suffuse the law of the royal prerogative?

Climbing the steps of the St Cross Building, she tells herself that this hypercultural double bind is the greatest challenge she faces in the production of a persuasive account. To be sure, her text will have to forgo objectivity and eschew any intimation that it is telling anything like 'the truth' – even as she feels that she could exclaim, after Toni Morrison: 'I consider that my single gravest responsibility . . . is not to lie.'[7] Inevitably, her report will be the outcome of an interpretive configuration featuring uncircumventable structural indeterminacies (for example, she is who she is, and she is not who she is not). But her argument must be found convincing by her readers – who could decide, in fact, that it is poorly articulated, that the language of her interpretation does not 'fit' the language of the law as they (think they) know it. Even as she accepts that the merit of a scholarly exposition cannot ultimately be determined by the fiat of readers alone, Imogene finds it hard to minimize the impact of readerly reaction on the fate of her work: there is what she wants her text to mean, and then there is what her readership will *understand* her text to mean. There is the pivotal question whether her readership will agree to *move* with her text. In this way, Imogene finds that her work promises to operate not unlike a Broadway show: one cannot guess whether one has a 'hit' or a 'flop' until one has put the musical or the play before the audience. And, to track the Broadway example, it may matter to the show's reception whether it is associated with one of the entertainment industry's greatest names, whether as scriptwriter or actor. Likewise, Imogene appreciates that if she taught at Harvard, her writing would ipso facto prove more authoritative.

Incidentally, who will read her? Will fellow comparatists-at-law take an interest? What about the German colleagues who noisomely dismiss her scholarship as 'postmodernist', effectively, as 'unscientific' pussivanting? (Now, to think about what these 'black-letter' jurists know of continental philosophy . . .[8]) Will the British want to learn about their 'own' law as seen at an angle, that is, through the eyes of a Canadian

[7] T Morrison, 'The Site of Memory' in *What Moves at the Margin* (C Denard ed, University Press of Mississippi 2008 [1995]) 72. Toni Morrison's use of the verb 'to lie' puts Imogene in the mind of Damien Hirst's major 2017 exhibition in Venezia, 'There Lies the Truth', which made a deep impression on her.

[8] For assistance, see S Glendinning, *The Idea of Continental Philosophy* (Edinburgh University Press 2006).

constitutionalist with expertise in Spanish '*derecho constitucional*'? Will, say, Spanish constitutional experts care to learn about UK law? What about Mexican or Argentine jurists? Inevitably, much will turn on the fact that Imogene initially has to write her text in Spanish, because of the research group to which she belongs. This imperative pleases her as she is keen to show that comparative scholarship in law can take place – that it *must* take place! – in other languages than English. In this respect, she is immensely grateful that one of her Granada colleagues has kindly volunteered to edit her Spanish effort. (While her Spanish is outstanding, there is no way she would even consider a publication unless she had received a native speaker's warrant.) Evidently, though, she will have to produce an English version of her text – a task to which she will in fact have to devote herself sooner rather than later – with a view to ensuring the dissemination of her work. Whether one likes this development or not, it is a fact of every comparatist-at-law's life that in order to matter, comparative research must be available in English.

Imogene labours under no illusion as regards the translative challenges ahead with respect to the writing of UK law in Spanish, if only because she has long internalized Ortega y Gasset's observation that any translation is necessarily either 'deficient' or 'exuberant' vis-à-vis the source-text so that any idea of equivalence, of plain semantic duplication, must be excluded – a claim she saw vindicated, in language she thought persuasive, in a short and insightful book on differential analysis within comparative law that she came across in Canada, in French if you please, where the author observes that, inevitably, the otherness of other laws remains 'in part untranslatable'.[9] What happens, then, in the course of the displacement across languages is nothing less than an alteration of the foreign language and therefore *of the foreign law*. In effect, on account of the necessary disadjustment necessarily informing every translation, Imogene's Spanish text will operate a transformation of UK law (how to say 'House of Lords' in Spanish without modifying the semantic extension of the term? '*Cámara de los Lores*'?). In due course, when the time comes to rewrite her report in English, she will face other difficulties as her English text will take the form of a second 'original', if you will (albeit a second 'original' of a special sort inasmuch as this second writing endeavour will find itself largely constrained by the first) – not unlike the

[9] J Ortega y Gasset, 'La reviviscencia de los cuadros' in *Obras completas*, vol 8 (2nd edn, Alianza Editorial 1994 [1946]) 493; P Richard, *Le Jeu de la différence: réflexions sur l'épistémologie du droit comparé* (Presses de l'Université Laval 2007) 139.

way, then, in which *Waiting for Godot*, perhaps her favourite play, exists as a second 'original' as regards *En attendant Godot*. It is not, needless to add, that Imogene puts herself in Beckett's writerly league, but she has long felt deep admiration for the Irish playwright and, no doubt because she herself largely lives her life as an English-French bilingual author, she has long been fascinated by Beckett's aesthetics of translatedness, by the manner in which he refused to conceal the fact of translation, branded every translative intervention an inescapable failure, and compelled the host-language to a condition of 'becoming-other' thereby interrogating the hierarchy that has traditionally prevented translation from qualifying as creative writing in its own right, that has kept translation to a merely derivative status. Smiling to herself, Imogene recalls how Beckett referred to 'the usual wilderness of self-translation', what he called, in French, '*son petit enfer*' ('his little hell').[10]

For the time being, however, Imogene's linguistic preoccupations concern another issue. While writing an account in Spanish of the law of the royal prerogative in the United Kingdom will contribute to this law's delocalization, Imogene is aware that her motion will also emphasize the significance of the Spanish prism through which her research is being re-presented (while seemingly marginalizing her culturally determined Canadian 'filter' but, of course, never eliminating it altogether). It is obvious to her that it should not only be the foreign law that finds itself altered, because it must be made to fit the Spanish language, but that the Spanish language should also be transformed in order to adapt to the foreign law. In particular, she is keen not to eschew the formulation of Spanish neologisms as they prove necessary, if only because she feels strongly that her Spanish readership must never lose sight of the fact that it is reading about a foreign law – even if it is doing so in Spanish. While researching English law, she proposes to list the terms that she thinks may prove particularly hard to Spanishify.

As she installs 'Pomme', her ever-serviceable laptop computer, in the Bodleian Law Library, Imogene reflects that she has reached 'otherwhere'.[11] In order to optimize her research dividend, so to speak, she will now harness a variety of deeply ingrained personal qualities that she will combine, if often in indiscernible ways, with a diversity of acquired legal skills. At the minimum, Imogene feels that she is

[10] Letter from S Beckett to A Schneider in *The Letters of Samuel Beckett*, vol 3 (G Craig et al eds, Cambridge University Press 2014 [7 November 1962]) 513.

[11] W Shakespeare, *Henry VIII* (1613), act 3, scene 2.

marshalling a sound knowledge of the common law tradition conjoined with a certain familiarity as regards salient aspects of constitutional law in the United Kingdom – not to mention, of course, native fluency in English. Also, she is aware that she enjoys a pre-existing appreciation for the specific ways of the law library where she will be spending the next four weeks. And she has good reading habits inasmuch as she spontaneously favours close reading (in Imogene's experience, comparatists rarely consider their readerly ways to be an occupational risk – who asks oneself, what is that, to read foreign law?). These are important perquisites that, she thinks, are bound to impact her research beneficially.

Taking advantage of the fact that the library is almost empty at this late summer hour, Imogene undertakes to gather at her desk a first bundle of the available materials that she needs to launch her research. For her, 'available materials' include, above all, the library books and journals that she has previously identified through preparatory electronic research as being potentially relevant to her project. Of course, this process of ascertainment is hardly definitive, for Imogene was very much pressed for time when she sought to conduct her bibliographical investigation just before her departure from Halifax, and she had to content herself with a cursory exploration only. But she knows well that the Oxford library, quite apart from being a non-lending establishment, has long served as a 'legal deposit' institution (which, in this instance, means that it is legally entitled to request a free copy within one year of publication of any book released in the United Kingdom). From Imogene's point of view, these two felicitous facts greatly increase her chances of laying her hands on the law-texts she will eventually deem relevant for her work. (On the matter of hands, while she regularly researches online with the help of keywords, Imogene much prefers reading a document on paper, in a form featuring a solid existence. For one thing, she reckons that having a text in hand minimizes distraction. Meanwhile, she readily acknowledges that pixelation features the convenience of enhanced storability and searchability.)

As Imogene makes her way to the stacks, she finds herself addressing the variegated materialities with which comparatists-at-law mostly deal: books, books, and more books. To be sure, contingencies remain ineliminable, which means that Imogene must accept the presence of a serendipitous dimension to the acquisition of information on the law of the royal prerogative in the United Kingdom, no matter how thorough her research. What Imogene understands to be unsurpassable also – a constraint weighing heavily on her – is the finite character of her investigation on account of the limited time at her disposal and the strict word limit that she must honour. Trying her best to take these practical limitations in her stride, Imogene makes a point of prioritizing some of the more than sixty documents soon stockpiling at her numbered seat. But it is already closing time (she is emphatically not at Berkeley, where her preferred library was open through the night). While she is happy at the thought of enjoying her first Indian meal in Cowley, she would easily have stayed at her desk longer. At least, she can 'reserve' the books she has gathered until the next day thereby saving herself collection time upon her return. As she prepares to leave the law library, Imogene reflects on how such a seemingly trivial fact as opening hours is liable to carry material consequences in terms of the conduct of her research and, ultimately, to have an impact on her very conclusions – that is, well, on her very statement of the foreign law. Shuddering at the thought, she is soon on her way.

Early the next morning, Imogene resolutely faces the unspectacular, mostly repetitive, frankly humdrum, and above all solitary library life that awaits her as she engages in serious data-mining.[12] She promptly decides to make heavy use of the 2020 edition of the Smith textbook rather than rely on the 2015 version of the two-volume Jones text. As she implements this preference, she is aware that many British constitutionalists consider the latter treatise to be the more authoritative of the two. But, perhaps because of her Canadian legal education or on account of her personal proclivities, she feels more comfortable with a more recent work. After all, she is concerned that her readership, such as it will be, should deem whatever she writes about the law of the royal prerogative in the United Kingdom thoroughly reliable. Of course, she can do no more than offer her *interpretation* of UK law, but she wants that interpretation to be optimally persuasive (and certainly to eschew the pitfalls of *insensatae interpretationes*). In order to foster her readers' expression of confidence in her work, Imogene feels strongly that her report must be as current as possible (which means, incidentally, that she will have to address both the January 2017 and September 2019 'Brexit' decisions in the Supreme Court of the

[12] For a reflection on the comparatist's solitude, see JH Merryman, 'The Loneliness of the Comparative Lawyer' in *The Loneliness of the Comparative Lawyer and Other Essays in Foreign and Comparative Law* (Kluwer 1999) 1–12. Quaere: does the fact that the comparatist-at-law is feeling a sense of otherness in the place where he is researching help him to prove more sensitive to otherness in his work?

United Kingdom).[13] Presently, leafing through the relevant chapters of Smith's, Imogene immediately elects to begin the first section of her paper with a long quotation drawn from page 345. She also likes a shorter passage on page 222, but chooses to keep it for a footnote as she does not want to showcase this particular excerpt. (Incidentally, she is so pleased that she can do footnotes rather than be stuck with inconvenient endnotes.) Soon, Imogene is adamant that she will not so much as mention Thomas's 2017 critique published in what is clearly a lesser-known journal. Frankly, the esteem in which this article appears to be held baffles her anyway. As far as she is concerned, Thomas's rambling speculations are roughly as unhelpful as any 'argument' can seemingly get – as irrelevant 'as Firmament to Fin', to transpose imagery from Emily Dickinson's correspondence.[14] It is not that Imogene is against lesser-known journals, quite to the contrary. In fact, she proposes to give pride of place to two articles she read in journals that she did not even know existed until recently – thus confirming her long-standing intuition that the most revealing material can well emerge inadvertently.

If pressed to reflect on her strategy, Imogene would accept that she is at once affirming some information while repressing other. There is a leading anthropologist who puts the matter rather acutely when he writes that '[u]nderstanding is always a process of in-framing and out-framing', which means that there is unavoidably what one includes and what one excludes, the banned materials also remaining 'so open, so infinite in possibility'.[15] Yes: there is *triage*. Meanwhile, Imogene will never know what would have been the interpretive yield vis-à-vis her readership of the information that she chooses to omit from her report.

Evidently, Imogene will not confine herself to constitutional scholarship. In short order, she undertakes to digest the collection of twenty-six law reports that she has collected with a view to considering all leading judicial decisions including, of course, the 1610 *Case of Proclamations*. To be sure, she does not plan to make so much of the 1926 House of Lords judgment, but she is determined to scrutinize the 1904 case in the greatest detail, especially Lord Bloom's opinion. It remains to be seen

[13] *R (Miller) v Secretary of State for Exiting the European Union* [2017] UKSC 5; *R (Miller) v The Prime Minister* [2019] UKSC 41.

[14] Letter from E Dickinson to TW Higginson in *The Letters of Emily Dickinson*, vol 2 (TH Johnson ed, Harvard University Press 1958 [7 June 1862]) 408.

[15] V Crapanzano, *Recapitulations* (Other Press 2015) 196.

whether she will quote from Lord Fletcher's concurrence. It is not that Imogene is biased against what she styles 'secondary' opinions. Indeed, she very much likes Lord Brigham's concurring judgment in the 1944 *Brewer* case. However, Imogene would confess that she is not so at ease with dissents. In fact, although she has read at length on the matter, she has never been able to make those shifting articulations fall within her comfort zone (or, as her colleagues would say in Granada, '*en su salsa*'). It may well be, then, that she will mention two dissenting opinions – one by Lord Matthews in *Dyson* and the other by Lord Andrews in *Weller* – but she does not envisage doing very much with them. Looking at herself looking at foreign judicial decisions, Imogene observes that she is 'talk[ing] to [her] material, open to what is said to [her], but in the end *deciding* what is said to [her] as [s]he searches for consistency'.[16] Also, while busily making the countless micro-decisions that she is being required to take in order to frame her argument – an unscripted process whereby she is responding to the singularity of the foreign law that she is examining even as she is always-already investing the data with her critical theory – Imogene remains attentive to the heuristic hiatuses between structure and event that her research indicates such as exceptions, exemptions, or deviations.

In the process, Imogene reflects that qua comparatist-at-law she finds herself in an epistemic situation whereby she is able to wield immense interpretive and re-presentational power vis-à-vis foreignness. It is not an exaggeration to maintain that, even as she finds 'the law of the royal prerogative in the United Kingdom' in all these law reports now before her, she is simultaneously fashioning it as she re-enacts – or counter-enacts – that law in her own text, not least with a view to readerly intelligibility. She appreciates that the intelligibility she is seeking in order to benefit her readership can only find its warrant by way of her own intelligibility of the materials at hand. Now, since the self cannot be the other, her intelligibility of foreign law cannot be ad idem with the foreign law that there is, there. It follows that her intelligibility of foreign law simply cannot stand as a repetition of that foreign law. Instead, Imogene must generate an iteration of the foreign law under her scrutiny, which means that she has to be saying it anew, her enunciation thus featuring a necessary difference vis-à-vis it. Thanks to her dissertation supervisor, she has become able to envisage her epistemic circumstances

[16] J Vining, *The Authoritative and the Authoritarian* (University of Chicago Press 1986) 36 [my emphasis].

as an advantage – the opportunity to add interpretive value to foreignness – rather than a predicament.

Within days, in a resolute display of resistance to the familiarization or 'naturalization' of the research practices that comparative law's governing positivism has fostered, which she knows all too well, Imogene is walking down Holywell Street under a steady drizzle on her way to the main university library, where she plans to be spending perhaps as long as a week researching history and political theory monographs unavailable in the law stacks. Expressing her agency to engage in disciplinary promiscuousness in the manner that she proposes to implement – that is, if you will, making use of a self-awarded poaching license with a view to challenging the value-laden categorial and categorical system that orders orthodox comparative law's regime of research – Imogene, committedly indisciplined as she feels, nonetheless worries that she is headed for the sort of treacherous waters that could make her work institutionally vulnerable. And she is well aware that, no matter how handsomely she meets the negotiation and translation challenges that the crossing of disciplinary lines must entail, she is destined to face the kind of hostile reception from orthodox comparative law that she encountered when she published her doctoral dissertation in Switzerland. (In Switzerland . . . one of the most traditional legal cultures she knows! But then, she had this excellent Swiss friend who helped her make her way into a prestigious legal-theory series.)

On a whim, Imogene decides to stop at the Turf Tavern for tea, a good occasion for some thought-collection. It is clear to her that during her month in Oxford she is fabricating foreign law even as she finds it, there, before her. She is *inventing* foreign law (strange as the term may appear at first blush, this is precisely what she is doing in line with the two etymological meanings of the verb 'to invent': she is finding foreign law, and she is fashioning it for the purposes of her report). In effect, her fashioning is indissociable from her finding, since the very act of selection whereby she retains some sources of information and dispenses with others partakes of the making of the law that she will then inscribe into her study as 'the law'. Likewise, her fabrication cannot be separated from her enculturation. It seems that the only manner in which Imogene could disclaim any role for herself in the edification of 'the law of the royal prerogative in the United Kingdom' would be if somehow a text or series of texts ascertainably existed as 'the law of the royal prerogative in the United Kingdom' for every observer to see identically as such, and if that text or series of texts featured one possible meaning and one possible meaning only for every observer to harvest identically as such – without any need for any interpretation whatsoever. But since there is obviously no repository where 'the law of the royal prerogative in the United Kingdom' simply awaits harvesting and reproducing by the analyst and given that, being made of words, 'the law of the royal prerogative in the United Kingdom' cannot stand as a one-meaning text and therefore cannot resist interpretation (which it effectively *demands*), Imogene's input – a complex and ultimately intractable amalgam of personal inclinations and professional socialization, of enculturation and institutionalization, of *epistemologization* – is not only inevitable, but necessary: *interpretation requires her.* The implementation of an interpretive approach carries key epistemic consequences on account of the differential character of any interpretation, that is, the fact that the *interpretans* differs from the *interpretandum* and the further fact that different *interpretantes* will differ inter se. Daunting as the fact may appear to positivists assembled, one of these implications is, of course, indeterminacy (with apologies to the believers in *Rechtssicherheit* . . .).

Imogene is acutely aware that, being differently encultured, a different comparatist would be generating a different production of information from hers concerning the law of the royal prerogative in the United Kingdom. In fact, because there can be no self-overcoming of the self, Imogene has no doubt that ten different comparatists would invent ten different accounts, each offering a specific interpretive yield. In this respect, Imogene could never understand why some of her positivist colleagues assume that holding understanding to operate as a necessarily situated phenomenon should commit one to the view that all interpretations are equally valid, more or less irrespective of what anyone says. Rather, the straightforward point is that all interpretations being situated, some situated interpretations will prove interpretively more valid than other situated interpretations – at least in the eyes of certain interpreting readers, themselves being situated. In fact, it is fair to assume that if she had undertaken her research five years earlier or ten years later, Imogene would herself have fabricated her text differently so that the law of the royal prerogative in the United Kingdom she is currently ascertaining and will soon be inscribing would have differed – not only, then, because of legal developments, but also because of her own development. From her standpoint, her work is therefore destined to prove ever-provisional.

Be that as it may, Imogene is firmly convinced that the knower, the being-known, and the act of knowing – assuming a momentary willingness to think of the foreign-law information being amassed as 'knowledge' – are structurally intertwined within the interpretive configuration: both the comparatist and the foreign law are encultured, and both remain beyond any possible de-enculturation. Such an intricate cognitive situation bears frankly very little resemblance to the fictitious 'subject'-'object' dichotomy that informs positivism, which Imogene, ever since she was invited to undertake her philosophical turn well away from Cartesianism, has come to regard as a profoundly detrimental approach, if only because it suggests that the identification of foreign law and the ascription of meaning to it can apply objectively and take the form of a truth-identification process.[17] Again, Beckett leaps to mind: 'N[o] ... direct contact possible between subject and object.'[18] Pace Descartes, there is only so much one's (encultured) reason can achieve in its attempt to dominate a foreign law-world.

Imogene's train of thought leads her to think again about the fact of language proficiency – which, it occurs to her, actually makes a compelling argument against positivism. It must be clear that a comparatist coming to foreign law with limited foreign-language reading skills only will simply not have access to the range of materials that will be available to someone with the ability to read foreign law-texts in the language into which they have been written. And, once more, the ensuing statement of the foreign law will accordingly differ. This observation can also be applied to interpretive situations featuring an expert in a foreign legal culture (what some comparatists, but not Imogene, like to style a 'jurisculture'), on one hand, and a neophyte, on the other. The experience factor can legitimately be expected meaningfully to structure the collection and interpretation of information – and therefore the very enunciation of the foreign law to follow. In sum, since it seems hard to escape the conclusion that the research output – the form that the comparative account will finally adopt – must have something to do with the information that was initially collected and the interpretation that was then offered of it, the shape that foreign law will eventually be made to assume cannot be dissociated from the mindset that will have implicated itself in the investigation of foreignness in the first place (for instance, either bringing to bear linguistic fluency or not and either applying legal competence or not). Interestingly, positivism has never explained – not to Imogene's knowledge at any rate – how the

[17] Contra: L Alexander, 'Theory's a What Comes Natcherly' (2000) 37 San Diego LR 777, 778: '[O]ur situatedness is as immaterial to our theoretical enterprises as it is inevitable.'

[18] S Beckett, *Proust* in *The Grove Centenary Edition*, vol 4 (P Auster and JM Coetzee eds, Grove 2006 [1931]) 544.

comparatist's interpretation could intervene 'on' the foreign law without any trace whatsoever of the comparatist's positionality affecting the process. Is the comparatist not tasked with *making sense* of foreign law, a formulation evoking an inherent measure of input or invention? And is the making-sense not the work of the comparatist himself – *that very comparatist and not someone else* – coming to the foreign law? For Imogene, to maintain that her understanding is always-already situated is not only to acknowledge that she is inevitably bringing her prejudices to bear on her foreign-law research (a fact that implies, for example, the prioritization on her part of certain questions or emphases over others), but it is also to appreciate that her understanding of foreign law is inescapably taking place *through* the mediation of these prejudices. If you will, her appreciation must be the outcome of a filtering cognitive process (like Acosta's vis-à-vis the llamas).

As she slowly undertakes through various jottings to formulate the law of the royal prerogative in the United Kingdom as she discerns it, Imogene is very much aware that she depends on the views of individuals – for example, of British writers of textbooks or articles – whom she is willing to regard as local knowers although, frankly, it is not always plain to her how she assesses a particular author to be a reliable source of information in an area in which she herself, being from Canada, cannot act as an authority. It is rare that Imogene seeks to pursue the chain of epistemic command very far. In effect, in her urge to use information rather than verify it, a deficiency she acknowledges, Imogene usually fails to seek a 'first knower', that is, she *satisfices* – and she does so for obvious practical reasons.[19] Yet again, though, a crucial question resurfaces, seemingly forever nagging at her (not least in the kind of introspective interludes she is experiencing at the Turf): does the fact that so much information remains personally uninvestigated not imply that, once all is said and done, she will effectively be holding a *belief* about the law of the royal prerogative in the United Kingdom rather than have actual *knowledge* of it in the strict sense of the word?

Be that as it may, Imogene is fully aware that the information about foreign law she is acquiring is being gathered in an adventitious and messy agglomeration of ways – a fact, she thinks, that must argue in favour of prudence and humility as she assesses the effectivity of her ability to *know*. Again, all that the comparatist can deploy vis-à-vis

[19] cf H Collins, *Forms of Life* (MIT Press 2019) 20: '[T]here is nothing "objective" about judgments of trust.'

foreign law is an understanding of it that must be – that can only be – *her* understanding of it. And, if Hannah Arendt's cautionary note is to be heeded, one must agree – and Imogene most certainly concurs – that '[u]nderstanding is a complicated process … which never produces unequivocal results'; rather, it consists of 'an unending activity' operating 'in constant change and variation', and it is certainly not about 'having correct information'.[20] In other terms, understanding is an intrinsically fluid affair structurally fraught with indeterminacy. For Imogene, it is not at all that this configuration must nullify the value of the comparative enterprise, but it means that the comparatist must prove cognizant of the state of epistemic play – of the unavoidable interpretive leeway – within which her comparison is unfolding.

Having finally reached the Bodleian, duly spent a number of days researching history and political theory in the PPE Reading Room, then returned to the law library for yet more investigative work in the law stacks, Imogene must, in time, come to terms with the fact that her departure from Oxford already looms. She rejoices that her stay was not interrupted by correspondence from her law school or preoccupations that would have arisen from her private life (after all, *la vie continue* …). Even though she was able to devote herself optimally to her research during four very busy weeks, Imogene is fully conscious that she is leaving behind a host of remnants. But irrespective of how much time she could have had at her disposal, it would have been impossible for her to cover every single parcel of relevant information. No doubt on account of the impact that her supervisor's calming influence has long exercised over her, Imogene feels no particular anxiety as she accepts that her account of the royal prerogative in the United Kingdom can only ever prove partial, in both senses of the term: it is hers, and it is incomplete. Strictly speaking, the law of the royal prerogative in the United Kingdom is *unsaturable* – and Imogene has made her scholarly peace with this scholarly fact. Now, Imogene's quietude extends to the further scholarly fact that her re-presentation – her presentation anew, following upon the local presentation of the law she initially encountered – is fated to prove ephemeral: not only will the foreign law continue to develop, but other reports will in all likelihood appear and offer competing interpretations liable to carry over hers, certainly in the eyes of some readers.

Imogene notes with a tinge of regret that her Oxford month did not make it possible for her to establish communicative or collaborative

20 H Arendt, *Essays in Understanding* (Schocken Books 1994 [1954]) 307–8.

social processes (the idea, of course, not being the social ties in and of themselves, but the way conversations or possibly leisure activities can cement a professional connection and catalyze affect into productive bonds, for example, how social activities can be harnessed to facilitate the exchange of more honest information than what appears in print, which can then be leveraged into comparative 'capital'). However, the library and coffee room were basically deserted. Imogene realizes that in the absence of conversations, she does not have any anecdote to report, which she finds disappointing as she is firmly of the view that anecdotes can very much work as 'anecdata' by providing useful points of entry into more traditionally empirical information. But Imogene feels that she has honourably passed the test of intellectual strength and character that a month's research abroad inevitably involves. And she was fortunate in securing all the materials she wanted to gather ('being lucky is very important in fieldwork').[21] Also, she is pleased with the many books she bought at Blackwell's in the course of her repeated visits to what remains for her, along with Chicago's Seminary Co-op, the best academic bookshop on the planet.

On the train taking her back to London, Imogene can hear her supervisor's words: 'What does the comparatist do? *She writes.*' Imogene is acutely aware that there will be much more to her involvement in the making of the law of the royal prerogative in the United Kingdom than the identification and selection of materials she has just completed.[22] Now that her fieldwork has come to an end, that the archive has been mined, Imogene understands that she will be sitting alone for many quiet hours as she engages in the hushed tasks of reading, interpreting, and writing with a view to producing a report on the other law, an account of the other's law. Very soon – and certainly not later than in the days following immediately upon her return to Canada – she will be arranging to compose a first draft of her report on the basis of the notes she took and the photocopies or scans she made while in Oxford. Having long set the epistemic bar very high, Imogene is determined to articulate an intense interaction between her empirical research and her theoretical analysis even as she proceeds to instil some coherence, as she sees it, to her documentation.

[21] Collins (n 19) 43.

[22] cf C Geertz, *The Interpretation of Cultures* (Basic Books 1993 [1973]) 19: '"What does the ethnographer do?" – he writes.'

In no time – there is that deadline! – Imogene will be polishing her writing by choosing this word rather than that, this formulation instead of that, and this argumentative sequence over that. In addition, she will be deciding to italicize this passage, insert this sub-heading, indent this quotation (but not that one . . .), and opt for the 'pensiveness' of a comma or the 'pointedness' of a period.[23] Imogene readily acknowledges that her ultimate goal is to construct a narrative – a *narrative* – that will be found to be persuasive by her readership. (Once again, think of the Broadway show: '[W]hat counts as credible depends on the community in which it is presented.'[24])There is more, for her report must be deemed more convincing than other narratives from which she is seeking to distinguish herself. To this end, she is determined to eschew flat (and suffocating) positivist discursivism. What Imogene cannot avoid, however, if only because she knows that she is unable to circumvent this structural feature characterizing every single comparative report, is the rhetorical fictionalization of her account.[25] Besides, why would she resist the urge to sprucify her text with a touch of profluence?

Given the lack of expectation of any fieldwork at all within comparative law, Imogene is not presumed, perforce, to want to commit to any auto-ethnographic reflection. However, her supervisor – he of the Berkeley background! – has long impressed on her that an ethics of engagement is embedded even in what appear to be the most trivial fieldwork choices and strategies: there is quite simply no disinterested decision. And he has forcefully told Imogene that not only must she always share with her readership key introspective insights about the fabrication of her argument, but she requires, as a matter of scholarly probity, to present herself as a constitutive part of her text (*her* text . . .). Many years later, Imogene vividly recalls her supervisor's words: 'You want your research to be life-affirming, and you want it to be affirming *your* life.' Imogene is thus determined to ensure that her report should incorporate her thoughts on the descriptive and interpretive processes that she will have followed in 'working through' her inventory of materials, including the abrupt shifts or turns in direction that on-site experience will have provoked.

In the end, Imogene is keen that any close reading of her intervention on the foreign law-texts, her investigation-cum-inscription, should reveal

[23] A Piper, *Enumerations* (University of Chicago Press 2018) 26.
[24] Collins (n 19) 20.
[25] cf Crapanzano (n 15) 3: 'There is no ethnography . . . that is free of the fictional.'

how her work will have involved from beginning to end a course of *invention* of the law of the royal prerogative in the United Kingdom. Having found the law, having fashioned it with a view to achieving an optimal articulation of it, as she sees the matter, Imogene will now be writing it (a process entailing, of course, ever more fashioning, ever more invention). She is aware that the text she plans to style – somewhat conventionally, to be sure – 'The Law of the Royal Prerogative in the United Kingdom' ought, in all rigour, to be named differently. More appropriately, she would retain a title like 'My Very Best Interpretation of the Law of the Royal Prerogative in the United Kingdom at This Time on the Basis of the Materials I Have Come Across, of the Texts I Have Decided to Use, of the Arguments I Have Chosen to Mobilize, of the References I Have Elected to Retain, of the Quotations I Have Thought to Feature, and of the Words I Have Preferred to Deploy in Order to Account for What I Know Not to Be the Whole' – all of these determinations being indissociable in a meaningful sense from Imogene's enculturation. Not only would such a formulation prove suitably self-reflexive, but it would accord with Imogene's research ethos, which lustres ago compelled her to relinquish any claim to veridiction. The empirical fact of the matter is that the comparatist is actively at work in terms of the very structuration of the foreignness of foreign law. Comparison-at-law is *ars inveniendi*.

On her way to Heathrow, Imogene is thinking that immediately upon her return to Canada, there will be friends or colleagues to ask her whether her trip was worth all the effort (and the money). She has in mind a couple of fellow academics in particular who had openly suggested to her that digital technology made it possible to reach her results without leaving her computer station in Halifax. However, no matter how extensive the database (how enormous its storage capacity), how rich the hypertexts or intertextualities, how powerful the available electronic searches, how enabling the entire technological apparatus – irrespective of how accelerated the intellectual process can become – Imogene feels strongly that it continues greatly to matter for the comparatist to make her way to the place where the foreign law lives (pandemics notwithstanding). She has in mind the opportunity to observe the other law and the other-in-the-law at close range and in participatory fashion, the feeling of discomfort that one experiences as one confronts indigeneity, and the self-examination that a sense of estrangement can be expected to induce (at least in a responsive individual). Even if in a somewhat undefinable manner, being *there* still makes a difference, technological advances notwithstanding. Indeed, the reading of legal otherness that is possible on location continues profoundly to differ – and certainly not for the worse – from the e-reading that the architecture of a website invites. Of course, indexicality has value, but Imogene's point is that so does ecstasy (she means the exalted sense of emotion that engrosses the mind once one finds oneself *there*). No claim extolling the new norms of professionalization, no argument concerning the politics of knowledge – say, the dismissal of fieldwork as pertaining to idiosyncratic temperament or penchant, as some anachronistic remnant of 'old-school' ways – no contention in favour of the democratization of expertise can hide the fact that cyberspace and Oxford remain, quite simply, unconvertible. For Imogene, it is obvious that not even the digital revolution has managed to produce an algorithm for ethnographic research: no one can enter into the fully fledged, the deep or thick negotiation with otherness and otherness-in-the-law that comparative research must assume, by staring at one's computer screen for hours on end.[26]

[26] I am very much in Imogene's camp. During the sixteen years that I volunteered to direct the postgraduate programme in comparative law at the Sorbonne, from 2000 to 2016, I required that my French students spend six consecutive weeks abroad to research their thesis. Evidently, this time-span was much too short. But courses ran from October to March with final examinations taking place in June, a calendar that limited what was possible. Also, I had to bear in mind the financial constraints under which most of my students were labouring (the result of the absence of any publicly funded support structure combined with a decanal prohibition on the solicitation of private-sector assistance, the idea being to salvage, at student expense, the so-called 'dignity' of the French public university). At the very least, I was sending a clear message pertaining to theoretical and practical rigour: one cannot creditably research, say, the US law of class actions in a couple of Paris libraries. Over the years, the large majority of my students made their way to leading US law schools (all of which – from Berkeley to Harvard and from Yale to Stanford – generously agreed to welcome them gratis). Amongst the many implications of a research visit to a US law library was the key realization that the research process was literally infinite. Even as one had to deem one's research 'finished', because one's sojourn had come to an end and one had to address the impending departure of the aircraft, the wealth of available documentation on open shelves ensured that one saw for oneself, in the most material of ways, that one's work was in fact incomplete (a realization that might not have been so obvious if one had stayed in Paris and worked with the five books, two of them outdated, that would have been available in the Sorbonne law library). As I know from my better students' reports, their time in foreign libraries, brief as it was, also allowed them to experience the virtues of serendipity. There is more, for I heard about invitations to sit on lectures, join seminars, present on French law, attend a dinner at the Dean's home – not to mention common-room conversations with full-time students over coffee. It seems utterly superfluous to insist that not a single one of these events would have materialized if my French students had been content to research US law out of Paris, even assuming the local availability of the most powerful database. And then, there was the sheer delight and pride that my students felt upon their return to Paris: they had been elsewhere, they had been enriched, and they had survived. They were now

The plane has now begun its descent into Toronto, where Imogene must transfer. She already has visions of herself sitting at her desk, pressing her fingers on the keys while her eyes are scanning the screen, trying different words until she is satisfied that she has hit upon the ones matching the ideas she wants to express, every sentence a wager (often, the words she initially crafts reveal themselves to be quite different from what she thought – or half-thought – she wanted to say). And the words that will come to her will be the result of a process whereby she has invited otherness to impact upon the pre-existing configurations of her legal/cultural world – more precisely upon a legal/cultural world as it has found itself incorporated or embodied in a singular mind (hers) even as this mind can hardly be reduced to the work of 'culture', since one's mind is evidently more than an incorporation or embodiment of culture. And soon, over weeks of *Sitzfleisch*, Imogene will be 'producing' her 'own' otherness-in-the-law, a huge responsibility. But who gave her permission to re-present UK law anyway, to speak on behalf of UK law? Imogene cannot help but reflect on one of the many paradoxes governing the comparative intervention: that the comparatist exercises power over the other to the extent that she can actually shape the perception of otherness and indeed shape otherness itself, even as the other has not authorized her to do anything of the kind. As she is making it her abiding goal to attest to UK law's singularity, out of recognition and respect, in order to acquit her scholarly debt, as a matter of justice, Imogene will, principle of charitable interpretation *oblige*, do her very best to speak *for* the other – to provide deep or thick understanding of the reasons and misreasons informing the other's legal ways. Of course, she cannot forget that ultimately, regardless of how much earnestness she brings to her re-presentative endeavour, her interpretive mind can only work through her enculturation. (Not so long ago, she was re-reading some of Montaigne's essays, as she tries to do over two or three weeks once a year, when she came across a passage arguing this very point.[27] Now, Montaigne was writing more than 400 years ago . . .)

different. And one could tell they *liked* their enhanced selves. To move from students to colleagues, could Gunther Teubner have written his seminal comparative piece without leaving Frankfurt? Did it not make a difference that he was then teaching at LSE and interacting, on site, with other British academics, not all of them jurists? I refer to G Teubner, 'Legal Irritants: Good Faith in British Law or How Unifying Law Ends Up in New Divergences' (1998) 61 Modern LR 11.

[27] Montaigne, *Les Essais* (J Balsamo et al eds, Gallimard 2007 [1595†]) bk 2, ch 12, 565: 'Human eyes can perceive things only through the forms of their knowledge.' cf S Fish, *Doing What Comes Naturally* (Duke University Press 1989) 518: '[W]ere every preconception, acquired belief, assumed point of view, opinion, bias, and prejudice removed

Singularity, Imogene remarks to herself, is an odd tool-to-think-with, not least because the singularity of a foreign law points to the distinctiveness of it and even to a distinctiveness resisting thetic exposition. Yet, for a foreign law-text to be readable and scriptible, its singularity cannot be absolute (if the other were entirely other, he would prove inaccessible: he could not be read or written). It must follow that singularity has to be approached, if you will, as being absolutely non-absolute. In effect, UK law's singularity will be emerging through a re-fashioning of Imogene's self – through adjustments to her own singularity – so that her self is in a position to acknowledge otherness-in-the-law as it is bringing the foreign into meaningful existence.[28] For Imogene it is not just about valuing singularity, but it is a matter of *valorizing* it, that is, her comparative research, as she sees it, concerns enhancement of the other-in-the-law's value.[29] Yes: Imogene's commitment to difference is so resolute. Of course, Imogene is not deluding herself, and she fully appreciates that neither valorizing nor valuing pertain to objectivity. She remembers an article about empirical research concerning tomatoes: for a transporter, a good tomato is a firm one, while for the grower it is one that is cheap to produce, and for the consumer one that is tasty.[30]

Even as Imogene accepts that a map reproducing reality exactly would be of no interest, she finds it regrettable, as always when she is about to start writing with dedication, that she will fail to tell the whole foreign law. Of course, she well realizes that perception – one of the basic forms through which human beings connect to the world – is inherently amplifying. As she sees a cat on a bench (there is one right there, before her eyes, in the transfer terminal), Imogene says something like: 'There is a cat on the bench.' To be sure, she does not say that she sees part of a cat on part of a bench. Yet, this is precisely what she is seeing, because it is impossible for her, no matter what perspective she chooses, to see the whole of the cat or the whole of the bench. (Imogene reasons that it is, in fact, like her body: she never sees the whole of her, and yet she perceives herself as whole.) But discourse spontaneously re-presents the world in totalizing terms, and one readily forgets about the limitations that one

from the mind, there would be nothing left with which to calculate, determine, and decide.'

28 See D Attridge, *The Singularity of Literature* (Routledge 2004) 24.

29 Imogene read about the distinction between the two strategies in F Vatin, 'Valuation as Evaluation and Valorizing' (J Rogers and A Bidet trs), (2013) 1 Valuation Stud 31.

30 See F Heuts and A Mol, 'What Is a Good Tomato? A Case of Valuing in Practice' (2013) 1 Valuation Stud 125.

must inevitably accommodate – until, that is, these strictures manifest themselves with a vengeance in the form of the sheer realization of the structural inadequacy of one's writing in comparative law, some aspect or other of the foreign necessarily eluding the comparatist's thought and thus remaining mired in secrecy.[31] Imogene has little choice, then, but to accept Jacques Derrida's assertion: '[A]nalysis escapes by definition every closing and every exhaustive formalization.'[32] Analysis! Martin Heidegger explains that historically, for instance in its Greek sense, 'analysis' means unravelling, disassembling, dismantling. And he mentions the use of the word in the *Odyssey* to account for what Penelope did

[31] Being fond of the work of philosopher-cum-anthropologist-cum-sociologist Bruno Latour, Imogene recently came across his *Enquête sur les modes d'existence*. In this book, Latour asks his reader to imagine a mountain and a map of the mountain (on the clear understanding that – as Borges established many years ago through the shortest of short stories – there can be no perfect map, plotted at the scale of 1:1). From the perspective of the cartographer, it seems undeniable that there can be discerned a continuous chain of reference joining the mountain and the map into an assemblage. Think only of the surveying, the drawing, the captioning, and the printing. Any idea of straightforward dualism is therefore untenable. As the cartographer looks at his map, for instance, the fact of the mountain cannot be isolated from his evaluation of it. In other words, the drawing before the cartographer's eyes is *at once* the fact of the mountain and his evaluation of it. Fact and evaluation are entwined, there, on the map, and it would be impossible as one looks at the drawing to distinguish one from the other – there is what Martin Heidegger calls an 'essential togetherness' between the mind and the map: M Heidegger, *Identität und Differenz* (Neske 1957) 27. For the cartographer drawing and captioning his map, the mountain is no longer exclusively a brute object standing in front of him, obdurately 'out there' with an absolutely discrete existence (none of these observations, evidently, serving to deny the physicality of the mountain). No objectification, that is, no veridiction of the mountain *as such* is therefore possible. Incidentally, neither objectification nor veridiction can obtain no matter what topographical method the cartographer may have used. Still, it seems incontrovertible that the map simply does not exist in the same way as the mountain: each entity has its own mode of existence. What one therefore does not (and cannot) have, in Latour's terms, is 'a *maintenance* of the same upon the same': B Latour, *Enquête sur les modes d'existence* (La Découverte 2012) 119. In other words, 'however far they go, however well equipped they are, however fine the mesh, however complete their "coverage", however competent their operators, chains of reference can never in any way *substitute* themselves for what they know': ibid 94. Indeed, 'nothing less resembles Mont Aiguille than the map of Mont Aiguille': ibid 86. Accordingly, there arises the inescapability of differential co-presence. Think of Mont Aiguille as foreign law and of the map of Mont Aiguille as the comparatist's inscription. Here, too, there is – and there must be – differential co-presence, a fact that Imogene has to countenance, which she ultimately does (mostly . . .). The reference to Borges is to JL Borges, 'Del rigor en la ciencia' (1946) in *El hacedor* (Alianza Editorial 2009 [1960]) 119.

[32] J Derrida (with D Attridge), '"Cette étrange institution qu'on appelle la littérature"' in T Dutoit and P Romanski (eds), *Derrida d'ici, Derrida de là* (Galilée 2009 [1989]) 270. The words are Derrida's.

night after night.[33] Penelope … Imogene smiles to herself: quite the encouragement she needs!

Imogene's interior flight has landed in Halifax. The day after next, she will start writing. 'I am nothing, if not Criticall', Imogene bravely reminds herself.[34] Now, she puzzles, why does Iago's exclamation to Desdemona in *Othello* thus suddenly come to mind as she awaits the delayed delivery of her luggage? Could it be the lure of *integrity*?

[33] See M Heidegger, *Zollikoner Seminare* (M Boss ed, Klostermann 1987 [1965]) 148.
[34] W Shakespeare, *Othello* (1622), act 2, scene 1.

VII

For Indiscipline

Because the idea of fieldwork readily evokes anthropology, I am moved to note that I find it exceedingly difficult to hypothesize circumstances pursuant to which a comparatist – whether a law professor, law student, law reformer, judge, or practitioner – can dispense with at least a basic understanding of the foreign law's enculturation and still proceed to account creditably for foreignness. Even though the required depth of cultural appreciation will vary depending, say, on whether one is writing a doctoral dissertation or a three-page memorandum for one of the law firm's senior partners, no foreign-law research can be content strictly to obey 'a legalistic spirit', a strategy that effectively amounts to '[t]he use of comparative law . . . becom[ing] an abuse'.[1] For a familiar example of the perversion I envisage, recall Rudolf Schlesinger's examination of contract formation as he informs his reader that his comparative project is directed towards the formulation of an area of agreement across laws 'in terms of precise and narrow rules'.[2] (Having aptly described Schlesinger's enterprise as an application of – German – 'dogmatic legal science', the late John Merryman observed politely that in the common law tradition such endeavour is 'unusual in the extreme'.[3]) As an alternative to an understanding of law exclusively according to its artificial rule-ordered dynamics (an approach effectively narcotizing the

[1] O Kahn-Freund, 'On Uses and Misuses of Comparative Law' (1974) 37 Modern LR 1, 27.

[2] RB Schlesinger, 'Introduction' in RB Schlesinger (ed), *Formation of Contracts: A Study of the Common Core of Legal Systems*, vol 1 (Oceana 1968) 9.

[3] JH Merryman, 'Comparative Law and Scientific Explanation' in JN Hazard and WJ Wagner (eds), *Law in the United States of America in Social and Technological Revolution* (Bruylant 1974) 98 and 99. In the civil law tradition, jurists have long been 'intent on creating a comparative discipline on purely juridical . . . terms': M Koskenniemi and V Kari, 'A More Elevated Patriotism' in H Pihlajamäki et al (eds), *The Oxford Handbook of European Legal History* (Oxford University Press 2018) 996.

critical sense), I argue that the comparatist can hope to achieve a more significant discernment of legal ordering through enunciations that show law 'not merely [as] a system of rules to be observed, but [as] a world in which we live'.[4] As he ascribes meaningful meaning to law through his recognition of the enculturation of the legally foreign that exists, there, and as he accepts that nothing can be deeply or thickly interpreted without the support of a cultural narrative (featuring the idea of tradition if one is discussing a cultural manifestation arising over the long term or the very long term), the comparatist purposefully moves beyond subordination to law-texts in the habitual and constricting sense oh-so-familiar to Swiss experts in the Swiss law of *prescription* or to French experts in the French law of *aveu*.[5] Rather, the comparatist adopts a view of law as a cultural signifier that can variously involve, say, anthropological, economic, historical, linguistic, philosophical, political, psychological, or sociological signifieds. To adopt and adapt Marcel Mauss for comparative law's purposes (he, of course, had other concerns), each manifestation of the law can then be apprehended as something like a complete legal fact, a '*fait [juridique] total*'.[6] So that I can exemplify the complexity I discuss, I propose to rehearse my mad-cow illustration.

*

The first cases of so-called 'bovine spongiform encephalopathy' (BSE), a malady that precipitates the degeneration of the brain tissue of its victims, struck British cattle in 1986. In the late 1990s, when I first took a scholarly interest in this matter, the scientific 'community' had been struggling with the question of whether eating beef products contaminated with BSE might be linked to the deadly human illness called 'Creutzfeldt-Jakob disease' (CJD), a condition leading to the progressive deterioration of the brain. To this day, the specific cause of infection of individuals afflicted with CJD remains unknown although there is now strong evidence (and more solid evidence than was available in the 1990s) that the agent responsible for BSE is also responsible for one form of CJD in humans. The culprit, it appears, is neither a virus nor a bacterium but

[4] RM Cover, '*Nomos* and Narrative' (1983) 97 Harvard LR 4, 5.

[5] Michel Villey pithily captures a key epistemic inhibition characteristic of civil law jurisdictions in M Villey, 'Préface' in A-J Arnaud, *Essai d'analyse structurale du Code civil français* (LGDJ 1973) i: 'Jurists read jurists.'

[6] M Mauss, 'Essai sur le don' in *Sociologie et anthropologie* (Presses Universitaires de France 1995 [1925]) 274–75 and passim. Mauss, a sociologist, actually wrote of a '*fait social total*', 'a complete social fact'. It bears mentioning that Mauss's socio-anthropological work was resolutely comparative. See J-F Bert, *Le Courage de comparer* (Labor & Fides 2021).

a prion, that is, a protein reproducing itself without DNA or any other genetic material. Indeed, excess protein deposits have been found in victims' brains.

Now, what appears to be a straightforward scientific question was always-already much more than *that*. It was, for instance, an economic question. One has only to think of the financial impact on the farming 'community', if not on the British economy as a whole, when more than a third of the nearly twelve million head of cattle in England, Scotland, and Wales needed to be destroyed. And what of corn producers in the US Midwest who were exporting the grain required to feed British cows? Also, beef prices having plummeted in the mid-1990s, auction markets had closed, employees had lost their jobs at abattoirs, and shopkeepers in market towns like Hereford were suffering from the diminution of spending power experienced by people associated in diverse ways with the cattle industry.

In addition, this allegedly scientific question was also a political question, if only because the announcement of a possible connection between cases of human brain infection and BSE was made by Britain's Health Secretary in the House of Commons in March 1996, but also since, for a substantial sector of the British population, the ministerial declaration raised the matter of the trustworthiness of the Conservative government along with the inevitable doubts as to whether the political party in power had not self-inflicted irreparable political wounds on account of its (mis) management of the crisis (as we now know, the Tories were roundly defeated in the general election that took place in May 1997). Other political issues arose from the European Commission's decision in March 1996 to ban the export of British beef anywhere in the world for an initial period of six weeks. In the event, the prohibition lasted more than three years and was not lifted until August 1999. In France, the embargo endured until October 2002, while in the United States it continued until March 2020. Furthermore, a question of tradition was at stake. What of the British midday Sunday meal of roast beef and Yorkshire pudding? Simon Schama, the celebrated historian, reminds his readers that '[i]n the ebullient infancy of the British Empire, beef ... was an entire gastronomic constitution, the marrow of political freedom'; to this day, opines Schama, the cow remains 'the four-legged symbol of essential Britishness'.[7] Moreover, what was a scientific question was, of course, an ecological question, because the annihilation of even part of the British

7 S Schama, 'Mad Cows and Englishmen' *The New Yorker* (8 April 1996) 61 and 62.

herd could be expected to have a significant impact on the ecosystem given that the much-prized manicured English countryside is in important ways sustained by the grazing of cows and sheep (although it is also claimed that an overpopulation of cows is poisoning the topsoil). This purportedly scientific question was also a demographic question. On account of CJD's long incubation period (it is estimated to last between ten and twelve years), individuals afflicted in the 1980s were just starting to manifest symptoms in the 1990s. Under a catastrophe scenario, an important segment of the British population could have died in the early 2000s (over time, nearly 200 people died after having contracted BSE). And the scientific question was, abidingly, a legal question, not least because all the prohibitions and restrictions, whether in the European Community (as it then was), in the United Kingdom, or elsewhere took the form of statutes and regulations.

Thus, what initially appeared to be a strictly scientific question can rapidly be identified as *simultaneously* having been an economic, political, traditional, ecological, demographic, and legal question. My example wants to show how there simply cannot be any such thing as a neatly circumscribed, unalloyed scientific question that would exist in isolation from all other questions as they are studied in other fields of specialized knowledge such as economics, politics, or law. For the thoughtful analyst, the scientific question at issue is rather an imbroglio in the sense that it consists of an intricate assemblage of other questions that are ultimately inseparable and run across a whole sheaf of disciplines. If you will, mad-cow disease unabashedly crosses 'the borders of the great fiefdoms of critique'.[8] It is not as if it had an economic or political dimension that would somehow prove neatly detachable from the whole so as to avoid any risk of overlap with other questions that would be equally autonomous. Prions, the farmers' income, the Conservative government's re-election prospects, Sunday lunches, the countryside, and statutes are hardly commensurable. Yet, they are all, at once, composite or constitutive elements of the question of mad-cow disease. It may help to consider the question of mad-cow disease as a cube and think of the six facets as standing for the economic, political, traditional, legal, and other features of the problematique. Take away one facet, and there is no longer a cube. A cube, therefore, *is* its six facets. Likewise, the question of mad-cow disease *is* science, economics, politics, tradition, ecology, demographics,

[8] B Latour, *Nous n'avons jamais été modernes* (La Découverte 1997) 14. It must be clear from the body text that my debt to Bruno Latour reaches beyond this quotation.

law, and so forth. In other words, the question of mad-cow disease is thoroughly encultured. It is, integrally, completely, a *cultural* matter. Nor is this phenomenon unique to the question of mad-cow disease. To demonstrate my argument, I could easily introduce another illustration that was in fact contemporary to the BSE scandal. I am thinking of French nuclear tests in the South Pacific in 1995 and early 1996. The scientific question – was this series of tests necessary in order to refine the computer simulation models that would allow France to dispense with testing in future? – was inevitably a political question (that of France's defence policy), an economic question (that of the boycott of certain French products abroad, for example), an ecological question (that of the impact of the nuclear explosions on the ecosystem around the Muroroa and Fangataufa atolls), a historical question (that of the legitimacy of the French presence in the South Pacific), a legal question (that of the statutes and regulations monitoring the nuclear industry and authorizing nuclear testing according to specific modalities, not to mention the matter of compensation for illness or death on account of undue exposure to radiation),[9] and so forth.

Whether one is talking about British mad cows or French nuclear tests,[10] the seemingly scientific question under consideration is inescapably, in effect, an 'outrageous and heterogeneous collag[e]',[11] that is, literally, a monster. Indeed, my electronic *Oxford English Dictionary* defines a monster as a creature that is 'large, ugly, and frightening', an

[9] The debate regarding compensation remains current more than a quarter-century later. See the 'Muroroa Files' <https://moruroa-files.org/investigation/moruroa-files>, an investigative project by media outlets and environmentalist groups whose conclusions have also been released in book form as S Philippe and T Statius, *Toxique* (Presses Universitaires de France 2021).

[10] Even without the perspective that critical analysis demands, it is easy to see how the vaccines against the 'Covid-19' coronavirus, while obviously constituting a scientific question (think of their efficacy or the health risk they comport), also operate, at once, at the very least, as an economic question (consider the sums invested in research, on one hand, and the commercial losses having ensued from lockdowns that could now be averted, on the other), a political question (envisage the matter of logistical deployment from the standpoint of good governance), a geo-political question (because it is at war with Russia and since the United States bans vaccine exports, Ukraine, for example, decided to obtain its vaccines from China), an ideological question (there are millions of individuals who profess a staunch anti-vaccination stance), a religious question (the fact that some pharmaceutical companies used fetal cells in the course of research and development is rebarbative for many), and a legal question (if only because there must be approval from regulatory authorities in each country).

[11] J Law, 'Monsters, Machines and Sociotechnical Relations' in J Law (ed), *A Sociology of Monsters* (Routledge 1991) 18.

entity that 'combines elements of two or more . . . forms'. In my view, these characteristics accurately describe the two purportedly scientific questions I have considered. That *every* question is a compound of incongruous elements, a 'series of things at once rather heterogeneous and yet in a state of co-incorporation contaminating and teratological'[12] – that every question is inescapably, precisely, a hybrid, an interface or, figuratively, a monster – has long been apparent to anthropologists: 'Send [an ethnographer] to the Arapesh or to the Achuar, to the Koreans or to the Chinese, and you will get a self-same narrative to link the heavens, the ancestors, the shape of houses, the cultivation of yams, of manioc, or of rice, initiation rites, forms of government, and cosmologies'.[13] If anthropologists are accustomed to treat the questions they address not in isolation, but as incorporating a seamless web of further questions, if they are used to seeing in each question a multiplicity of questions taking them across fields of knowledge conventionally labelled as 'ethnology', 'history', 'politics', and 'sociology', such is not the case for jurists, who emphatically continue to engage in a purification exercise, to establish a partition between what they regard as two entirely discrete ontological zones: the law and the non-law. Applying (consciously or not) the time-honoured connection between 'order' and 'beauty' – think in terms of a machine's 'absolute purposiveness and reliability of motions, [its] extreme reduction of resistances and frictions, [its] harmonic interlocking of the smallest and the largest components'[14] – the basic idea is to keep things not 'large, ugly, and frightening', but 'compact, comely, and comfortable', that is, to stick to law-as-rules-and-the-authoritative-interpretations-of-rules-as-law.

For jurists, there are legal – strictly or purely legal – questions that only they, as jurists, can understand in the way they ought to be understood, that is, legally. There is, for example, such a (familiar) practice as 'legal thinking' or 'thinking like a lawyer'.[15] To the extent that jurists are prepared to

[12] J Derrida, 'Some Statements and Truisms About Neologisms, Newisms, Postisms, Parasitisms, and Other Small Seisms' in T Dutoit and P Romanski (eds), *Derrida d'ici, Derrida de là* (Galilée 2009) 227. This text was first published in English translation in 1989. On the occasion of the (posthumous) release of the essay in the French original, to which I refer, the editors observed that Derrida had wanted to maintain the English title: see ibid 223n1.

[13] Latour (n 8) 15.

[14] G Simmel, 'Soziologische Aesthetik' in *Gesamtausgabe*, vol 5 (O Rammstedt ed, Suhrkamp 1992 [1896]) 205.

[15] Eg: see E Mertz, *The Language of Law School: Learning to 'Think Like a Lawyer'* (Oxford University Press 2007); F Schauer, *Thinking Like a Lawyer* (Harvard University Press 2009). cf B Brożek, *The Legal Mind* (Cambridge University Press 2020).

concede that a given question could arise *also* as a philosophical, political, or sociological question – as a *cultural* question – they proceed to confine themselves strictly to what they choose to apprehend as the legal dimension of the matter. They regard the legal aspect of the question as discrete and somehow nimbly detachable from its other facets, which they are content to leave to philosophers, politists, or sociologists to consider. Although most of them would be hard pressed to advance a compelling theory of the 'distinctively legal',[16] jurists insist that they only do law. In my experience, this (unexamined) view of the lifeworld as consisting of law and non-law is particularly prevalent in the civil law tradition, where it remains a crucial epistemic consideration. Hans Kelsen's pure theory of law stands as the epitome of this model. For Kelsen, '[t]he Pure Theory of Law wants to present the law as it is' and '[o]nly positive law ... is given as a task to cognition', this exclusionary strategy being the exclusive way to 'true legal science'.[17] Civilians thus readily assume that their unique expertise lies in their ability to study legal rules, that is, rules that create, regulate, modify, or terminate legal relations. In the words of Merryman, given the adamant focus on 'scientism, system-building, conceptualism, abstraction, formalism, and purism', '[t]he result is a highly artificial body of doctrine that is deliberately insulated from what is going on outside, in the rest of the culture' (and certainly insulated also from the idea that law would exist as culture).[18] Civilians take the matter of specialization further still (and, one could say, carry artificialization further, too), because they erect hard barriers within the realm of law itself. There are, for instance, rigorous divisions arising between private law and public law or between civil law and commercial law – such delineations being apprehended so seriously that they are assumed 'to be scientifically derivable from objective legal reality'.[19] And it is on the basis of this categorial and categorical thinking that faculties are structured, chairs allocated, courses taught, doctoral dissertations supervised, conferences organized, journals published, and intellectual fiefdoms articulated. It is how academics interact inter se.

The jurists' distinction of law from other academic pursuits (not to mention their hierarchization of law above other discourses) and the

[16] I borrow the expression from P Selznick, 'Law: The Sociology of Law' in DL Sills (ed), *International Encyclopedia of Social Sciences*, vol 9 (Macmillan 1968) 51.

[17] H Kelsen, *Reine Rechstlehre* (Deuticke 1934) 16, 17, and 17.

[18] JH Merryman, *The Civil Law Tradition* (2nd edn, Stanford University Press 1985) 65. I deliberately refer to this edition, the last to have appeared under Merryman's signature. See also Koskenniemi and Kari (n 3).

[19] Merryman (n 18) 90.

compartmentalization of the so-called 'legal mind' itself are developments that can be explained historically. And these rationalizations refer, for example, to the rise of Italian universities in the late eleventh century, which 'provided an ambience where schoolmen, insulated from the messy details and responsibilities of legal practice, could indulge in the luxury of treating texts of classical antiquity with dispassionate erudition as objects of intellectual inquiry'.[20] Ultimately, however, the availability of a historical explanation to account for the fact that jurists came to regard law as a self-contained or closed system of knowledge in a number of European jurisdictions (and in Europe's former colonies around the planet) does not efface the fact that law, that any legal instantiation, is effectively at once a philosophical, political, or social – a cultural – phenomenon. It may well be that jurists do not want to internalize the information that any legal question exists as an interface or monster. But the refusal to come to terms with the law's worldliness does not lead the law's worldliness to vanish. If it accomplishes anything, the undue attachment to propositional knowledge only serves to accentuate the *décalage* between the law and the culture within which – and as which – it inevitably works. In the final analysis, the insistence on law's purity marginalizes the form of knowledge favoured by academics in law faculties by rendering it *unrealistic*, not unlike the way in which the handling of known variables in a highly controlled, aseptic laboratory cannot but remain spurious.[21]

Note that while I have emphasized the civil law's predilection for the purely legal, the common law tradition, too, is replete with 'doctrinal scholars', all individuals 'who aim to help the courts reach better decisions' and achieve their goal by way of 'a careful reading of the cases seeking to derive from them a coherent set of rules and principles already found in them, a task for which there is no need for any serious knowledge of history, economics, psychology, or philosophy',[22] the governing idea being that 'law is in some important sense autonomous from other disciplines',[23] that while 'other approaches, perspectives, or disciplines may provide observations *about* law . . . , they cannot contribute to the study *of* law'.[24] Otherwise said, 'there is a distinctive task for academic

[20] MR Damaška, *The Faces of Justice and State Authority* (Yale University Press 1986) 31.

[21] Eg: see B Latour and S Woolgar, *Laboratory Life: The Construction of Scientific Facts* (2nd edn, Princeton University Press 1986) passim.

[22] D Priel, 'Two Forms of Formalism' in A Robertson and J Goudkamp (eds), *Form and Substance in the Law of Obligations* (Hart 2019) 165.

[23] ibid 166.

[24] ibid.

lawyers ... [a]nd the task is legal'.[25] From a critical standpoint, Pierre Schlag holds that '[w]hat is involved, in short, is a kind of cognitive deficit'.[26] Indeed, '[t]he reduced cognitive possibilities are precisely how law becomes law'.[27] Specifically, there takes place 'the construction of endless legal mazes, the piling on of endless legal distinctions, the excruciating refinement of ever more precise doctrinal taxonomies. Legal actors and thinkers become prisoners of the small frame – captives of small thinking.'[28]

Perhaps unsurprisingly, then, when jurists have turned to the study of foreign law, they have readily replicated the narrow doctrinal techniques they had applied to their investigations of national law. In this respect, James Gordley's scholarly commitment is characteristic of the mindset informing orthodox comparative research. Not only does he exclaim that a comparison borrowing from sociology and history 'should not be confused with a description of ... the law',[29] but he writes, categorically and excludingly: 'I am concerned with *what the law [i]s*.'[30] However, neither statutes nor judicial decisions – to focus on two standard sources of law – can be helpfully regarded as strictly legal questions. Any legislative text or judgment lies, not at all unlike the scientific question I examined with respect to mad-cow disease, at the junction of the economic, the political, the social, and so forth, that is, any legislative text or judgment exists *as a cultural question*. This formulation is crucial: 'If we are to make headway in understanding legal studies as cultural studies and legal practice as cultural practice, then ... [t]he goal ... is to understand law not in relationship to culture, as if they were two discrete realms of action and discourse, but to make sense of *law as culture*.'[31] Consider the December 1993 decision of the British House of Lords, as it then was, in the case of *Cambridge Water*

[25] A Beever and C Rickett, 'Interpretive Theory and the Academic Lawyer' (2005) 68 Modern LR 320, 337 (review article of SM Waddams, *Dimensions of Private Law* [Cambridge University Press 2003]).

[26] P Schlag, *The Enchantment of Reason* (Duke University Press 1998) 140.

[27] ibid 144.

[28] ibid.

[29] J Gordley, 'When Is the Use of Foreign Law Possible? A Hard Case: The Protection of Privacy in Europe and the United States' (2007) 67 Louisiana LR 1073, 1077.

[30] ibid 1081 [my emphasis]. See also B Markesinis, 'Comparative Law: A Subject in Search of an Audience' (1990) 53 Modern LR 1, 13, where the author writes that '[c]ase law can reveal *what the law really is*' [my emphasis].

[31] N Mezey, 'Law as Culture' (2001) 13 Yale J L & Humanities 35, 36 [my emphasis].

Co Ltd v Eastern Counties Leather plc – a judgment I regularly teach my French students in Paris.[32]

The claimant company supplied with water a population of approximately 275,000. Meanwhile, the nearby defendant, a leather manufacturer, used a chemical solvent in the degreasing of its pelts. In the process, there occurred regular spillages of relatively small amounts of solvent on the concrete floor of the defendant's tannery. Not being readily soluble in water, they seeped into the soil below despite the surface being regularly washed. The solvent eventually reached the strata from which the claimant extracted its water through a borehole. In the event, the claimant was forced to stop using the borehole and dig another in order to preserve its supply of uncontaminated water. Some thirty years ago at this writing, the cost of these alternative arrangements was approximately one million pounds, hence the lawsuit. The House of Lords decided the case against the claimant.

This judgment raises, of course, a legal question in the technical sense. Not only is the decision an official pronouncement from an official judicial body, but it features the court's selection and interpretation of the various judicial precedents it deems relevant to the facts of the case as they have been ascertained in line with recognized procedural and evidentiary doctrines and to the extent that the sitting judges consider them material. But the judgment also represents a political determination, because Lord Goff, writing the main opinion, states that the matter of ascribing no-fault liability is one for the British Parliament rather than the courts. The judgment also makes an economic pronouncement, since by adjudicating against the water company the court is effectively forcing it to increase its prices, reduce its production costs, or lower its profits in order to cover its loss. As it engages in issues of distributive justice, the judgment also pronounces philosophically. Inevitably, the judgment involves an ecological question, too, because the House of Lords is, in effect, allowing water pollution to occur without any ensuing ascription of civil liability to the polluter. The judgment takes the form, then, of a *cultural* adjudication inasmuch as, through it, important aspects of a given model of local ordering come into view, not least the thought processes governing the English approach to legal epistemology. Clearly, the House of Lords decision in the *Cambridge Water* case is a monster. It is *monstrous*. Yes.

32 [1994] 2 AC 264.

Observe that this apprehension must also apply to a statute or to any legislative law-text. For instance, the adoption by the French government of a workers' compensation scheme towards the end of the nineteenth century illustrates an internalization by the law, without acknowledgement of pedigree, of a phenomenon that, quite apart from being technically legal (thus marking the passage from a fault-based to a strict-liability regime), is at once historical, ideological, political, sociological, and more – in one word, *cultural*. The 1898 French statute thus marks an inversion in the then balance of power, the effacement of a domination and possibly the advent of another, not to mention the emergence of a new vocabulary, in sum, an epistemological rupture characterized by a move away from the classical understanding of obligation towards notions of solidarity and re-distribution defining a profoundly new pattern of social regulation, what François Ewald calls 'a specific form of use of abstract technology by reference to an insurance fancy'.[33] In other terms, the 'technical' dimension is seen to consist of one side only of a multi-faceted geometrical figure rather than as constituting the whole of it. And, as is the case with a cube, the fact that all sides cannot be perceived at once does not ultimately prevent the (astute) observer from envisaging a side *as a side*.

Each law-text, perforce, generates a legal question. But, beyond being a manifestation of technical (or instrumental) thought, it also stands, inevitably, as an array of intertwined philosophical, political, social, and other questions (economic, epistemic, and so forth). Each law-text is thus thoroughly, monstrously *cultural*. Now, it can hardly come as a shock that a judgment or statute should manifest itself as an incorporative cultural form, since it is so obviously the case that a law-text, any law-text, far from existing 'in the air', is fabricated, made, indeed hand-made. It is produced, which means that it is a product. It is elaborated by men and women, who are culturally situated, who espouse a particular worldview that has been forged for them and transmitted to them so that it informs their cultural identity. As I refer to culture, I have in mind a framework of intangibles within which interpretive 'communities' operate and that exercises normative force over these 'communities'. In fact, a moment's reflection should persuade even the incredulous observer that the idea of a judge or legislator unconstrained by culture is untenable, that cultural transmission must therefore have a pervasive

[33] F Ewald, *L'Accident nous attend au coin de la rue* (Documentation française 1982) 125 [emphasis omitted]. See generally F Ewald, *L'Etat providence* (Grasset 1986).

impact on the adjudicative or legislative process. How could a judicial decision or statute not stand as a manifestation of the culturally determined mental constraints that judges or politicians bring to bear on the legal issue before them? How could a law-text operate apart from the culture of which it necessarily partakes? How could a law-text circumvent culture unlike other texts such as recipes, novels, or songs? How could a law-text not exist as culture?[34]

Although those who claim expertise in the law apparently wish to appear as not being impacted by other, allegedly exogenous discourses, it is the case that these further configurations, far from being external to law, are inevitably present within the law – indeed, that these *are* the law to the extent, at least, that they are 'transsubstantiated' into law as the law integrates them into a unique synthesis that produces a new, original output. I hold that within comparative law, then, what has traditionally (and pedantically) been envisaged as non-law, as the unthinkable, as that which is there but ought to be avoided as not being worthy of the jurist's attention, must no longer be what the comparatist elides, but what he deploys with a view to obtaining an enhanced interpretive yield out of the foreign.

The so-called 'non-law' – the negative of the law – must become a key element that focusses and validates legal analysis as law is seen also to exist *beyond* rules. Crucially, though, law has *always-already* been *impure*, if only because law has forever been powerless to exclude from itself what would not be itself. Emperor Justinian's sixth-century compilation can be seen as an early manifestation of willed boundary-speech in law, of the conventionalized way of 'talking law' or 'thinking like a lawyer'. The virtues of exhaustivity and autarky that Justinian claimed for his Digest found their expression in the enactment of a formal imperial prohibition against commentaries on it, an interdiction that proved unsuccessful.[35] In Justinian's wake, law specialists have sought to use the speech of law, more or less unthinkingly, as an exclusive explanatory resource. In the process, they have wanted to create distinct

[34] And yet, one can still come across the thoroughly embarrassing position that 'linking law to . . . cultural phenomena of a specific country would be impossible': JM Smits, 'The Harmonisation of Private Law in Europe: Some Insights from Evolutionary Theory' (2002) 31 Georgia J Int'l & Comp L 79, 81.

[35] For a prominent discussion of Justinian's prohibition, see F Pringsheim, 'Justinian's Prohibition of Commentaries to the Digest' in *Gesammelte Abhandlungen*, vol 2 (Winter 1961 [1950]) 86–106. For a more recent examination, see G Falcone, 'The Prohibition of Commentaries to the Digest and the Antecessorial Literature' (2014) 9 Subseciva Groningana 1.

ontological zones, both between law and the outside world and within law itself.

Again, though, one would be mistaken if one advocated that the local jurists' understanding of law must now move from a stage of purification to one of hybridization, that comparative law must now learn to overcome the distillation and purification process that has produced the autonomization of an allegedly internally consistent 'legal' sphere of meaning. Rather, it is that, despite continuous attempts at scientificization and technicization by academics in law faculties acting as the state's adjutants (at least, in the civil law tradition), miscibility has always-already informed law or legal analysis. It follows, to quote Michel Villey speaking of Kelsen's pure theory, that 'there is no philosophy that represents more perfectly what one must criticize'.[36] Despite the prevailing legalist creed, law has consistently been technique and *also* economics, philosophy, politics, psychology, sociology, and so on – *culture*! For Kent Greenawalt, there are no 'characteristically *legal* reason[s]'.[37] What is accordingly demanded of comparatists today is 'simply' to acknowledge that '[p]ositivism is a utopia',[38] that the jurists' attempt at producing a purely juridical configuration must be illusory.[39]

As he is invited to accept that the foreign law he is examining is the expression or re-presentation of a dominant cultural discourse and as he is tasked with ascertaining what discursive configurations in particular the law he is considering effectively incorporates or embodies (philosophical, political, or otherwise), the comparatist is not being asked to try to assimilate to the law something that would be exterior to it. On the contrary, he is required to attempt to escape his constricting (and willed) 'legal self',[40] to dedisciplinarize himself in a way in which the local jurist, irredeemably caught in the web of the anti-scholasticism characterizing the technical practice of law within his interpretive 'community', cannot readily do. In the apt words of David Sugarman, which accord with my own understanding (if in slightly differently accented language), one

[36] M Villey, *Leçons d'histoire de la philosophie du droit* (2nd edn, Dalloz 1962) 285.

[37] K Greenawalt, *Law and Objectivity* (Oxford University Press 1992) 199. See also Brożek (n 15) 3: 'Legal thinking is by no means special.'

[38] O Kahn-Freund, 'Introduction' in *The Institutions of Private Law by Karl Renner* (O Kahn-Freund ed, A Schwarzschild tr, Routledge & Kegan Paul 1949) 8.

[39] This illusion may, however, be important to the practice of law, that is, to law as it solves disputes and provides remedies. Stanley Fish's argument is thus that law can only assert its authority as a practice if it can proclaim its formal autonomy. See S Fish, *There's No Such Thing as Free Speech* (Oxford University Press 1994) 141–79 and 21–22.

[40] See Schlag (n 26) 126–40.

must 'direct attention away from questions about the effect of law on [culture] or even the effect of [culture] on law toward conceptualizing a more complex and interactive relationship between law . . . and culture. Instead of mutual influences between the two separate entities, this perspective sees the boundaries between law . . . and culture as so blurred that they are best perceived as participating in the same . . . field.'[41] The brand of intellectual versatility that must be expected of a comparatist-at-law – a teratology of learning – may recall what is demanded of an astronaut, who must know about piloting, engineering (electrical and otherwise), physics, astronomy, aerodynamics, geography, cartography, meteorology, chemistry (as regards combustion, at the very least), computer programming, and human biology, not to mention the need to have basic medical and pharmaceutical notions. (Comparatists-at-law who, like Konrad Zweigert and Hein Kötz, envisage comparative research as a scientific pursuit – a 'science pure' – ought to find this analogy gratifying.[42])

To argue that cultural processes and patterns are not epiphenomenal or derivative vis-à-vis the law and to promote the recognition of culture as an active principle, preceding, guiding, and channelling the legal – informing or animating it in its diverse manifestations – is to make a very important epistemological claim, to risk an exorbitant wager.[43] The expansive approach to comparison-at-law that I proffer, which harnesses culture as 'a theoretical tool for developing sensitivity for differentiation',[44] is significantly more exigent than the positivist perspectives that depend merely on rule-based explanations. I repeat: it is not that I am fetching the cultural from some realm outside the law and bringing it into law, but that I defend the argument that law is not

[41] D Sugarman and R Warrington, 'Land Law, Citizenship, and the Invention of "Englishness": The Strange World of the Equity of Redemption' in J Brewer and S Staves (eds), *Early Modern Conceptions of Property* (Routledge 1995) 126. I substitute 'culture' for 'society'.

[42] K Zweigert and H Kötz, *Einführung in die Rechtsvergleichung* (3rd edn, Mohr Siebeck 1996) 6. The expression I quote appears in French and without italics in the German text.

[43] Theoretical audacity extends to the contemplation of different discourses – irrespective of how hermetically sealed they appear to be vis-à-vis one another while they are seen to unfold within a given society – as so many local cultural instantiations. Different discourses, no matter how seemingly particularistic and mutually exclusive, are but different local cultural forms. Thus, Jean-François Lyotard makes the apt observation that different discourses can meet as different discourses within one world. See J-F Lyotard, *Le Différend* (Editions de Minuit 1983) 50–51.

[44] M Alvesson, *Cultural Perspectives on Organizations* (Cambridge University Press 1993) 120.

separable from culture, that culture constitutes a primordially constitutive dimension of law, that it imbues the law. Again, I propose that law exists *as* culture and that it can therefore only be *meaningfully* understood on cultural terms. As I formulate this claim, I remain aware how strongly positivists maintain that one ought to approach law as that only which is (legally) binding – a tautological understanding of the 'legal' that, despite being so forcefully asserted, remains but an interpretation and cannot therefore foreclose other readings such as mine. However, as the compound comparative enterprise that I herald unfolds, the comparatist willing to overcome the positivist passion for ignorance must be prepared to face various hurdles. Roland Barthes refers to 'very painful difficulties', a predicament that he details as follows: '[D]eliberations, decisions partial, difficult, tribulations of the will and of desire, doubts, discouragements, trials, blocages, obscurities [–] quite a - *peregrination*.'[45] Yes.

A threshold concern is that since the legal is cultural, not unlike weaving, management strategies, or birthday celebrations – Isaiah Berlin long ago stated the need 'to perceive that a certain type of legal structure is "intimately connected" with, or is part of the same complex as, an economic activity, a moral outlook, a style of writing or of dancing or of worship'[46] – cogent insights for comparatists-at-law are liable to emerge literally anywhere. For instance, consider the lessons one can learn as regards the work of the Supreme Court of the United Kingdom and the French *Cour de cassation* by reading the late George Steiner's confrontation of Shakespeare and Racine – Steiner being a literary critic who, needless to add, did not purport to make a point about comparative law:

> Shakespeare uses more than 20,000 different words; Racine a shade over 2,000. The difference is ontological. It declares two radically contrasting senses and sensings of the world. That of Shakespeare is prodigal, open-ended and fluid as the stream of life itself; the other aims at essence through abstention. Racine is of the family of Bach's partitas, of Giacometti's figures, spare as the wind. He is a minimalist of immensity, aiming at indispensability in each touch. Remove a couplet from *Phèdre* or *Bérénice*, and the tensed arch, the fugue of totally realised possibility, may

[45] R Barthes, *La Préparation du roman* (N Léger and E Marty eds, Editions du Seuil 2015 [15 December 1979]) 407–8. This book transcribes the lectures that Barthes delivered at the *Collège de France* in 1979–80.

[46] I Berlin, 'The Concept of Scientific History' in *Concepts and Categories* (H Hardy ed, Oxford University Press 1980 [1960]) 109.

collapse. Shakespeare is more often than not performed incomplete. His purpose survives rearrangements and merry or sinister follies of production. A play by Racine is a perfectly closed whole. One by Shakespeare is a script, brimful of variant possibilities, open to transformative innovation, always provisional. The images of man are almost antithetical.

... In Racine burns the supposition that there are orders of moral and intellectual clarity, of mortal *dignitas*, possible only ... when the contingent material world is excluded. No 'roaring hurricanoes', no woods on the march, no exits followed by bears. A naked stage ....

Shakespeare is tragi-comic in every fibre, as is our existence. He knows that someone is being born next to or even on a lower floor in the house of high death. That there is never only midnight or noon.... In an artifice of the absolute, Racine closes reality .... This closure ... crystallises the sum of being into one single instant .... The surrounding universe has been brought to a stillness....

This compaction empowers the unison of Racine's style. Shakespeare can be uneven, mixed, wasteful, inferior to himself, as is human nature.[47]

In effect, the resolution of the challenge arising from the infinite dissemination of relevance remains easily stated, even as it proves impossible to achieve: '[O]ne ought to read everything, study everything.'[48] Given the massive erudition – the superb omnivorousness – that is required for the sophisticated appreciation of foreign law-as-culture so as to avoid the production of half-learning, the only limits to the comparatist's bricolage

[47] G Steiner, *Errata* (Weidenfeld & Nicolson 1997) 34–36. cf M Edwards, *Racine et Shakespeare* (Presses Universitaires de France 2004) 61: 'The world for the reader of Racine is a formidable Order produced by a Reason that transcends in absolute fashion the folly of men. For the reader of Shakespeare, it is a profusion that is past understanding, like the leaves of summer or the sky nocturnal.' Likewise, French legicentrism can be evidenced not only through the civil code's prohibition of judicial law-making (art 5), but by way of paintings depicting Napoleon writing the code. I have in mind an 1812 portrait by Jacques-Louis David now at the National Gallery of Art in Washington (DC) as 'Napoleon in His Study' or Jean-Baptiste Mauzaisse's 1833 allegory where Napoleon, sitting on a cloud, is seen inscribing the French civil code on a stone tablet. This painting is on display at the *Musée national du Château de Malmaison* in Rueil-Malmaison, near Paris.

[48] The injunction is Michel Foucault's, which he articulated in the course of an interview with Raymond Bellour, later collected as 'Michel Foucault, "Les Mots et les choses"' in *Dits et écrits*, vol 1 (D Defert and F Ewald eds, Gallimard 1994 [1966]) 499. cf Steiner (n 47) 19: 'The informing context of any single sentence in, say, Flaubert's *Madame Bovary*, is that of the immediate paragraph, of the surrounding chapter, of the entire novel. It is also that of the state of the French language at Flaubert's time and place, of the history of French society, and of the ideologies, politics, colloquial associations and terrain of implicit and explicit reference, which press on, which perhaps subvert or ironise, the words, the turns of phrase in that particular sentence. The stone strikes the water and concentric circles ripple outward to open-ended horizons.'

are those arbitrarily imposed, either by himself or others (think of a deadline or a word limit, for instance). The fact of the matter is that no description is ever adequately deep and no interpretation sufficiently thick. If you will, the 'experience of understanding is always and *necessarily* open to further experience; it never completes itself'.[49] And no interpretation eschews further interpretation. Little wonder that, observing how '[d]etail could know no end',[50] Steiner should have recorded how '[he] felt a peculiar dread'.[51] '[P]ossessed by an intuition of the particular, of diversities so numerous that no labor of classification and enumeration could exhaust them',[52] convinced that '[t]he available indices of reality . . . could never be exhaustively comprehensive',[53] that 'no inventory, . . . however compendious, could ever be *complete*',[54] that '[t]here was simply too much to everything',[55] Steiner, one of the most eminent twentieth-century literary critics and comparatists, felt 'the fusion of delight and menace, of fascination and unease'.[56] I suggest that the comparatist-at-law can hardly do any better: *il faut se débrouiller avec cela*.

If anything, an even more major preoccupation arises from the fact that the comparatist is expected to conflate heteronomous disciplinary knowledge-claims, to incorporate or embody knowledge from other discourses into the law's construction of the world – that is, to operate a 'juridification' of (what has classically been perceived within law as) non-legal knowledge. Now that law-as-rules is being recast as law-as-culture, that 'what appeared to have traceable contours and a determinate content turns out in practice to be variously and unendingly interpretable',[57] it becomes necessary to raise the vexed matter of the comparatist-at-law's referential competence to marshal economic information (is he a trained economist?), to handle historical information (is he a trained historian?), to wield philosophical information (is he a trained philosopher?), to harness sociological data (is he a trained sociologist?), and so forth. At the outset, let me say emphatically that not every study engaging in the most cursory cross-referencing to

[49] RJ Bernstein, *The New Constellation* (Polity 1991) 307.
[50] Steiner (n 47) 5.
[51] ibid.
[52] ibid 3.
[53] ibid 4.
[54] ibid 3.
[55] ibid 4.
[56] ibid 2.
[57] MA Schneider, *Culture and Enchantment* (University of Chicago Press 1993) 26.

a sprinkling of allegedly non-law-texts must be seen as making a useful contribution to comparative analysis.

Even implementing what, concretely speaking, must inevitably be, at best, a programme of limited cultural investigations, the comparatist is doomed to intervene within law-as-culture as an ill-informed enthusiast, as someone who must gain vicariously from other scholars' experience so as to compensate for the limited range of his own, who will inevitably have to settle on other disciplinary 'communities' in order to achieve epistemological reliability. Because he must accept claims of authority made in other fields of intellectual endeavour, even though he does not know how reliable certain economic, historical, or philosophical statements happen to be, the comparatist-at-law is destined to fall for approximate assumptions and conclusions – a precarious position that should prompt him to heed DH Lawrence's warning to the effect that '[a] little knowledge is indeed a dangerous thing',[58] an exposed situation that ought to encourage him to cultivate a certain modesty even as he asserts with Correggio that he, too, is a painter.[59] Yet, neither the necessity nor the virtues of eclecticism can be in doubt, for *foreign law exists as culture*.[60] And the difficulties attendant upon the inscription of this fact as comparative research do not affect in any sense the empiricalness of the fact itself.

To be sure, I aim to encourage an intellectual practice based upon *movement*, that is, to foster a new pattern of interaction by the

[58] DH Lawrence, 'Etruscan Places' in *Mornings in Mexico and Etruscan Places* (R Aldington ed, Heinemann 1956 [1927–28]) 51.

[59] I lift the reference to A da Correggio from Montesquieu's foreword to *De l'esprit des lois*, where he mobilizes the painter's exclamation, '*ed io anche son pittore*': Montesquieu, *De l'esprit des lois* in *Œuvres complètes*, vol 2 (R Caillois ed, Gallimard 1951 [1748]) 231.

[60] For a defence of law's borrowing and derivation from other disciplines, see eg D Kennedy, *Sexy Dressing Etc* (Harvard University Press 1993) xi. See also D Kennedy, *A Critique of Adjudication* (Harvard University Press 1997) 15–16. While any comparative endeavour pertaining to the scrutinization of foreign law destined to combat the organization/dislocation of knowledge along disciplinary lines is in principle to be saluted, I maintain that not all undertakings are equally restorative. For example, I argue that the displacement of the locus of comparative research away from law-as-rules to law-as-economics, likewise featuring a comforting emphasis on (alleged) predictability and quantifiable accuracy, once again purports to omit the determining role of culture (although bounded rationality *is* encultured rationality). Judicial decisions, qua encultured narratives, are hardly creditably reducible to instantiations of rational-choice theory or utility maximization (not, of course, that these models themselves exist aculturally). For an excellent critique of law-as-economics with specific reference to comparative law, see G Watt, 'The Poverty of Economics and the Hope for Humanities in Comparative Law' (2014) 9(2) J Comp L 166.

comparatist with foreign law-texts as, restless and incessantly wayward, he finds himself once more drawn from the (disciplinarily) familiar into the (disciplinarily) strange. Because comparison belongs to the ontological condition of '*Unterwegssein*',[61] the comparatist-at-law must strive to leave his law faculty, his faculty office, his law library, his law databases, and himself-as-jurist, in his quest for an epistemologically significant encounter with the other-in-the-law. (If he is lucky, the walk from the law school to the central university library can prove very pleasant, the way it is at the University of San Diego.) In other words – and in a context where the discipline of law has proved to be 'quintessentially disciplinary and disciplining', the disciplinary and disciplining habitus of law thus 'play[ing] a coercive role in relation both to what counts as knowledge and with respect to the hierarchy of disciplines'[62] – the comparatist must assert himself as *indisciplined*. Although I introduced this term in my published work in 1995,[63] it took me many years, and many more conversations with my valued colleague, fellow-traveller, and friend Alexandra Mercescu, to appreciate that the recognition of foreign law's basic enculturation calls on the comparatist to commit to *indiscipline*, that is, to dedisciplinarization, rather than to interdisciplinarity. Let me enunciate the matter as forcefully as I now can: even as there is nothing that a jurist cannot consider legally (not unlike the manner in which there is nothing that a philosopher cannot envisage philosophically),[64] *the comparatist-at-law must not aspire to interdisciplinarity.*

Stanley Fish is proving insightful, it seems to me, when he argues that no matter how many references he imports from other disciplines, the jurist will never cease to work *as a jurist* – and will never begin to operate as an economist, a historian, or a philosopher. The jurist will always effectively be seeking to consolidate his argument as a matter of law. This

[61] M Heidegger, *Unterwegs zur Sprache* (Neske 1959). The German term suggests the condition of 'being-under-way'.

[62] P Goodrich, 'Intellection and Indiscipline' (2009) 36 J L & Society 460, 460, and 461. Elsewhere, Peter Goodrich underlines that this disciplinary quintessence cannot be appreciated without reference to religion. In effect, '[t]here is no discipline of law without the religious inculcation of the clerics, the early scriptoria or writing workshops that copied texts and authorized publications by pontifical and then later royal decree': P Goodrich, *Advanced Introduction to Law and Literature* (Elgar 2021) 11.

[63] P Legrand, 'Comparative Legal Studies and Commitment to Theory' (1995) 58 Modern LR 262, 272.

[64] Thomas Bernhard percipiently exclaims how '[t]he world is utterly, thoroughly legal': T Bernhard, 'Ist es eine Komödie? Ist es eine Tragödie?' in *Erzählungen* (Suhrkamp 2001 [1967]) 74.

strategy, Fish contends, pertains to appropriation or assimilation – to hierarchization, also – not to interdisciplinarity. Ultimately, 'the practice of importing into one's practice the machinery of other practices [does not] operate to relax the constraints of one's practice'.[65] Specifically, 'the shape [that terms and distinctions] appear in will always be relative to the socially constructed activity that has received them and made them its own'.[66] In other words, '[w]hile we attend to the content of our instruction, we are fundamentally but imperceptibly modeled by its form'.[67] The argument that one could be thoroughly self-reflective about this issue fails, since one cannot 'simultaneously operate within a practice and be self-consciously in touch with the conditions that enable it'.[68] Indeed, 'once the conditions enabling a practice become the object of analytic attention . . . , [one is] engaging in another practice (the practice of reflecting on the conditions of a practice [one is] not now practicing)'.[69] Fish's conclusion follows: 'Being interdisciplinary is more than hard to do; it is impossible to do.'[70]

The tractability of interdisciplinary competence (which is not constellatory omnicompetence) is, therefore, to resolve itself along Gayatri Spivak's lines: 'I am not erudite enough to be interdisciplinary, but I can break rules.'[71] Again, the goal must be *indiscipline*, not interdisciplinarity,[72] which means that the comparatist-at-law requires to adopt a negative attitude towards the ideas of discipline

65 S Fish, 'Being Interdisciplinary Is So Very Hard to Do' (1989) Profession 15, 19.

66 ibid. cf Fish (n 39) 221–22: '[T]he particular form in which materials from other disciplines enter the law will be determined by the law's sense of its own purpose and of the usefulness to that purpose of "foreign" information. . . . It is those purposes and not the purposes at the core of the quarried discipline that rule. . . . Law will take what it needs, and "what it needs" will be determined by *its* informing rationale and not the rationale of philosophy, or literary criticism, or psychology, or economics.'

67 R Terdiman, 'Structures of Initiation: On Semiotic Education and Its Contradictions in Balzac' (1982) 63 Yale French Stud 198, 221.

68 Fish (n 65) 20.

69 ibid.

70 ibid 19.

71 GC Spivak, *A Critique of Postcolonial Reason* (Harvard University Press 1999) xii.

72 For an extensive and rich defence of the argument from indiscipline within comparative law, see A Mercescu, *Pour une comparaison des droits indisciplinée* (Helbing & Lichtenhahn 2018). For a further claim with specific reference to the need to infringe disciplinary style, see A Mercescu, 'Change of Style, Change of Mind: Lawyers' Writing Manners' (2019) 15 Int'l J L Context 310. cf B Hutchinson, *Comparative Literature* (Oxford University Press 2018) 4: 'Comparative literature . . . constitutes an *in*discipline.' Adde: D Ferris, 'Indiscipline' in H Saussy (ed), *Comparative Literature in an Age of Globalization* (Johns Hopkins University Press 2006) 78–99.

and disciplinarization. In other terms, the comparatist-at-law must resist the institutionalization of canonical boundary-maintenance, that is, of discursive formations aiming to confine or cabin within hampering limits cognitive and rhetorical schemes of perception, appreciation, and intervention. He must (strenuously) object to the fact that these formalized configurations of knowledge-production have been shaped by epistemological assumptions or technologies, whose contingent demarcation criteria allowing for the delegitimation of certain theoretical discourses reputed to be order-threatening have long become mired in a power-related refusal of reflexivity (think of method). *Indiscipline is epistemic disobedience.* If you will, the comparatist-at-law must stage an *epistemic coup* within comparative law and resolutely engage in epistemic impertinences, wanderings, and roveries.

*

I claim that indifference to the fact of the existence of all law-texts as culture is primarily a remarkable indifference to thinking – and that such insouciance places an epistemological barrier in the way of the acquisition of meaningful information aiming at an improved understanding of foreign law. Now, the eclipse of culture, which requires to be envisaged in an important way as a historicity that is other than (and more than) the historicity of the comparing comparatists themselves, is not innocent in the sense that it would simply illustrate a lack of concern or neglect based on 'well-meaning sloppiness of thought'.[73] Even if the comparatist's agency manifests itself in important ways as the ever-unfolding outcome of a specific process of formation through institutions, norms, and conventions beyond his control – whereby his intent has found itself being disciplined, that is, chastised and instructed, which is another way of saying that the comparatist comes to law-texts haunted by his own spectres – who could naively believe that comparatists, in the end, naively believe in the autonomy of the rules that they purport to interpret? It is not excessive to envisage positivism's exclusion of culture from its economy, along with its concomitant re-inscription of itself topographically qua culture-less zone, as an act of violence (if masked), of systemic brutality (if hidden). What is unfolding is obviously not violence in the everyday, sociological sense of the word, for example, the visible and palpable violence of an aggression being perpetrated by one person upon another. But there is positivism's attempt – through a deployment of control, mastery, subordination, or

[73] *Holt v Markham* [1923] 1 KB 504 (CA) 513 (Scrutton LJ).

confinement – domineeringly to drive a wedge between the legal and the cultural, even at the risk of making the institutional precinct of the law, as designed by positivists themselves, appear uncannily disengaged from the lifeworld and so frighteningly conceptual.[74]

For orthodox comparatists-at-law, the main idea has been to generate an overall effect of *steadfastness* – and to do so basically at any epistemic cost. In fine, the comparative orthodoxy's only resort in order to contain the cultural threat has been to harness the institutional code whereby it is able to define law's disciplinary area disciplinarily, that is, to implement a strict application of the relevant disciplinary structures and declare culture out of bounds, deem it to be outside the law, *out-law* it.[75] Inasmuch as culture produces interpretive insecurity (and there is little doubt that the cultural has more to do with the flow of existence than with the statics of the conceptual), a positivist like Gordley will simply not accommodate it within the realm of the legal.[76] Here, lability is liability and, to return to Zweigert and Kötz, very much something from which positivism holds that it must 'release' itself.[77] Culture would therefore pertain to the worldly, but it would not concern law. Being expelled from law, being deemed not to have to do with law, thus allowing law to understand itself and be understood as strictly or purely legal, culture would not obstruct access to 'what the law is' – *die Sache selbst*. In other words, 'what the law is' would not find itself obscured on account of any

74 cf R Musil, *Der Mann ohne Eigenschaften* (A Frisé ed, Rowohlt 1978 [1930]) bk 1, s 62, 253: 'Philosophers are criminals, who have no army at disposition and therefore submit the world to themselves in such a way that they lock it into a system.'

75 Eg: see U Kischel, *Rechtsvergleichung* (Beck 2015) 229–38. After all, legal culture is 'not a demanding concept in the sense of its theoretical charge' (ibid 236). Indeed, it cannot be ascribed 'an exact definition' (ibid 231). Moreover, it is 'strongly tainted out of its socio-legal origin' (ibid 238). In other words, culture is at once realistic, indeterminate, *and* impure. One easily imagines the *Rechtsdogmatiker*'s distress. For further dogmatic dismissals of a compelling heuristic role for culture, because it cannot be defined crisply enough to assuage the positivist craving for reassurance, see J Basedow, 'Comparative Law and Its Clients' (2014) 62 Am J Comp L 821, 836n44; J Husa, *A New Introduction to Comparative Law* (Hart 2015) 3. Another illustration of the inability to operate an epistemic delinking from positivism is CJ Milhaupt and K Pistor, *Law and Capitalism* (University of Chicago Press 2008) 208: '[T]he open-ended concept of "culture" opens a Pandora's box of interpretive nightmares.' Adde: R Michaels, 'Two Paradigms of Jurisdiction' (2006) 27 Michigan J Int'l L 1003, 1017, where the author maintains that a comparative account 'must remain within the law without taking recourse to general societal culture, because culture and its relation to the legal rules and institutions are unclear'.

76 Supra 190.

77 Zweigert and Kötz (n 42) 11.

process of enculturation, either of the foreign law or the foreign law's interpreter. Again, positivism craves fixity of meaning – and the positivist dressage loathes anything remotely resembling ephemerality or mutability, two intrinsic characteristics of the cultural (which is never identical to itself).[78] Not only does positivism deny culture, however, but positivism is positivism only *in so far as* it denies culture – which is to say that it derives its very force at making decisions, at drawing lines, at stopping the movement of interpretive play or slack, at bringing interpretive latitude under house arrest, at producing certainty, and at generating predictability, *from this denial.* (Ironically, positivism fails to see that it also stands – inevitably – as a variation on the overarching theme of culturalism. How could positivism and positivists operate beyond culture? Far from consisting in the neutral configuration that it assumes itself to be, positivism operates as a technology of power committed to values such as clarity, immaculacy, indisputability, and systematization – a non-exhaustive, *cultural* enumeration.)

Involving the formulation of critical ideas about the complex connections between a foreign law and the polylogical world it inhabits, and that inhabits it, the entrenchment of the new practice of comparative law I recommend wants the comparatist to evade the deceptive raiment of conventions of re-presentation that, over time, have come to be regarded as appropriate within the field and imposed strict collective limits upon the forms of comparative discourse deemed acceptable. In particular, I contend that the comparatist must distance himself from national-positivist moulds and disrupt expected academic roles by humanizing his work and writing different articles and different books espousing forms of speech that have been viewed as unrealistic in the light of the highly conventionalized and seemingly ossified practice of comparative law still enduring in academic discourse – nowhere more so than in the context of the quadrennial meetings organized under the auspices of the infamous International Academy of Comparative Law. Considering the fact that some self-styled comparatists continue to feel able to devote more than 700 pages to an argument in favour of the commonality of European laws with respect to good faith in contractual relationships while ignoring a lead article by a leading scholar in a leading journal that develops a sophisticated indisciplined argument to the effect that

[78] cf J Derrida, *L'Autre cap* (Editions de Minuit 1991) 16: '[T]he specificity of a culture is not to be identical to itself.'

German and English laws on point differ and can only differ,[79] I must accept, however, that there is still a very long intellectual road to travel before orthodox comparative law moves from the surface to the interface in acknowledgement of the law-texts' and their law-words' cultural agency.

Observe that the stakes concern not only the comparatist's creditability – and, through him, that of comparative law in general – but also address an ethical preoccupation, since comparative law research must at all times strive to do justice to the foreignness of the foreign in all its intricacy, which must mean that the comparatist needs to circumvent disciplinary palisades for this reason also.[80] Significantly, the comparatist has a responsibility to the foreign law-text, which must be read and interpreted scrupulously. This responsibility – a word that suggests the idea of response (not in the sense of an instantaneous reaction, but as a considered rejoinder) – entails an exigent fidelity to the singularity of the foreignness of the law-text. Specifically, this loyalty implies the acknowledgement of the irreducibility of the foreign law-text's singularity – in particular, of its heterogeneity to texts in other laws.[81] It also demands the marshalling of protocols of rigorous argument, which must integrate the comparatist's own singularity, that is, allow for the fact that the comparatist-at-law is unavoidably speaking situationally.[82] (It matters that one is interpreting the French statutory prohibition on certain religious attire in public schools, say, as an Australian or Canadian rather than as a Swede or Dane.)

[79] See R Zimmermann and S Whittaker (eds), *Good Faith in European Contract Law* (Cambridge University Press 2000). The startling omission is G Teubner, 'Legal Irritants: Good Faith in British Law or How Unifying Law Ends Up in New Divergences' (1998) 61 Modern LR 11.

[80] I agree with H Marcuse, *One-Dimensional Man* (2nd edn, Routledge 1991 [1964]) 129: 'Epistemology is in itself ethics, and ethics is epistemology.'

[81] Eg: C Gallagher and S Greenblatt, *Practicing New Historicism* (University of Chicago Press 2000) 6: 'The task of understanding ... depends ... on an encounter with the singular, the specific, and the individual.'

[82] cf Letter from M Heidegger to K Löwith in D Papenfuss and O Pöggeler (eds), *Zur philosophischen Aktualität Heideggers*, vol 2 (Klostermann 1990 [19 August 1921]) 29: 'I actually work factically out of my "I am" – out of my spiritual, indeed factical origin – my environment – my life connections, from what is, from there, accessible to me as living experience, from that within which I live.' And Heidegger could well have added that he had no choice in the matter. In his autoportrait, Giorgio Agamben formulates the state of affairs succinctly: '[W]e cannot tear ourselves from ourselves nor abjure ourselves': G Agamben, *Autoritratto nello studio* (Nottetempo 2017) 31.

If one assumes the role of re-presentor of foreign law, one becomes indebted vis-à-vis the foreign: one owes it a just re-presentation. Note that there is thus an active dimension to the idea of responsibility. It entails a duty of vigilance, of lucidity. It is about lending an ear, for example. Crucially, the treatment of foreign law I foster requires hearkening to the law-text (according to the electronic edition of the *Oxford English Dictionary*, 'to hearken' variously means '[t]o apply the ears to hear', to 'give ear', '[t]o apply the mind to what is said', 'to have regard to'). In this respect, I heed Rudolf Bultmann, one of Martin Heidegger's colleagues and influential disciples, who advocates 'listening to [the] claim [of the text]'.[83] Along with Kierkegaard, who also enjoins the interpreter to listen – 'hasten, oh! hasten to listen'[84] – and who argues that '[e]verything ends with hearing',[85] and in line with Jacques Derrida, who agrees that 'it is indefatigably about the ear',[86] I find that when it comes to foreign law, there is a speaking-to-one at work, a '*Zuspruch*'.[87] Accordingly, it behoves comparatists-at-law to commit to the kind of comparative work that manifests itself as 'otology',[88] the goal being to move away from positivism's tautology. (What does the law say? The law says what the statute says. What does the statute say? The statute says what the judge says. What does the judge say? The judge says the law.)

In my view, comparative law's responsibility to singularity – to the foreign law-text's singularity and to the comparatist's singularity – is a demanding ethical act. Indeed, this standard of engagement is so onerous that, in the end, it cannot be met. For instance, the foreign law-text will be betrayed as what the comparatist says about its singularity must fall short of everything that he could be saying. In an important

[83] R Bultmann, 'Das Problem der Hermeneutik' (1950) 47 Zeitschrift für Theologie und Kirche 47, 65. See also M Heidegger, *Was heisst Denken?* (Niemeyer 1984 [1954]) 88: '[W]e are compelled, as soon as we set out upon a way of thought, to give specific attention to what the word says.'

[84] S Kierkegaard, 'Fire opbyggelige Taler' (Four Upbuilding Discourses) in *Atten opbyggelige Taler* (Eighteen Upbuilding Discourses) in *Samlede værker*, vol 4 (AB Drachmann et al eds, Gyldendal 1962 [1843]) 128.

[85] S Kierkegaard, *Papirer*, vol 1 (2nd edn, N Thulstrup ed, Gyldendal 1968 [1836]) s A235, 112.

[86] J Derrida, *Marges* (Editions de Minuit 1972) x. See also J Derrida, *Béliers* (Galilée 2003) 37–38: '[To keep] forever attention in suspense, that is to say, alive, awake, vigilant, ready to go down any other road, to let come, lending the ear, listening to it faithfully, the other word, hanging on the breath of the other word and of the other's word – right there where it could seem still unintelligible, inaudible, untranslatable.'

[87] M Heidegger, *Holzwege* (Klostermann 2015 [1950]) 369.

[88] J Derrida, *Politiques de l'amitié* (Galilée 1994) 410.

sense, then, the comparatist's signature inevitably attests to a form of violence being perpetrated on the foreign law-text; it stands as a countersignature. But this violence is very much the lesser violence, the violence that is less than positivism's regimented and regimenting evisceration of relevance. Again, note that the comparatist's responsibility to singularity is also a responsibility to the field of comparative law, a fragile spatio-intellectual configuration in need of all the epistemological commitment it can muster from its comparatists as it longs for intellectual creditability.

Meanwhile, as one assesses the structure of disciplinary governance within comparative law, it seems uncontrovertible that the *Kampfplatz* continues to be dominated by comparatists who approach foreign law as a sort of entity existing positively – meaning and all – apart from any cultural discourse, as a figure somehow living apart from culture, not to mention the fact that for orthodox comparatists comparatists-as-interpreters-of-foreign-law somehow exist apart from culture, too.[89] To be sure, even orthodox comparatists claim to understand that comparative law involves an interpretive shaping of the foreign material. However, effectively applying Cartesian dualism, the orthodoxy holds that the foreign 'in itself' pre-exists interpretation and continues to exist irrespective of interpretation. In other words, there is the foreign 'in itself', and there is the comparatist's subsequent interpretation of it – more or less accurate, more or less exact vis-à-vis the 'itselfness' of foreignness. Now, the appreciation of law as culture changes the coinage. While a sensible pathway to the foreign has to activate the latent ontology (of course, there is a foreign law-text, there), it must operate without emphasizing presence in the way the ontological narrative does (foreign meaning is not there – it does not exist 'in itself' – but is rather the outcome of an exercise in ascription coming from this-comparatist-interpreting-that-text). It follows that interpretation is not original

[89] A typical positivist move has been to restrict culture to context. Eg: Kischel (n 75) 187, where the author refers to the 'cultural context'. Unaccountably, the same book also advocates for 'Context Instead of Legal Culture': ibid 238. For my critique of Kischel's confusion regarding his treatment of culture, see P Legrand, 'Kischel's Comparative Law: *Fortschritt ohne Fortschritt*' (2020) 15(2) J Comp L 292, 321–28 (review article of U Kischel, *Comparative Law* [A Hammel tr, Oxford University Press 2019]). Adde: Husa (n 75) 3: 'Legal culture refers to . . . legal contexts.' For contrastingly sophisticated configurations, see generally L Rosen, *Law as Culture* (Princeton University Press 2006); Mezey (n 31). For an insightful and arrestingly pithy formulation of the problematique, see G Watt, 'Comparison as Deep Appreciation' in PG Monateri (ed), *Methods of Comparative Law* (Elgar 2012) 88: 'Culture grows law grows culture.'

(in the sense that it does not arise ex nihilo, but emerges out of a dynamic enmeshment between encultured comparatist and encultured text) and that it cannot capture anything like the originality of the foreign (since there is not *that*).

This set of observations leads me to draw on my own pedagogical experience in order to show how, concretely, law-as-culture can generate a significantly more pertinent interpretive yield than law-as-rules – how, indeed, law-as-rules forms an epistemological barrier to a deep appreciation of the foreign, what Gaston Bachelard called a 'counter-thought'.[90] While I often try to harness case studies, I appreciate that the logic of exemplarity is troublesome, and I accept that illustrations have their limitations (examples thus always seem over-determined or under-determined, that is, they never appear to *fit* the theoretical claim they are meant to sustain). In fact, illustrations can be said to act like theoretical shortcuts. Yet, an example is efficient. Specifically, then, I want to stage an instance of the epistemologically desirable situation that can obtain within comparative law if – to frame the matter in a binary way – a *culturalist* perspective rather than a positivist demeanour is brought to bear on the study of a foreign law-text in the classroom.

*

Imagine a group of twenty US law students, say, in Chicago, whom a comparatist invites to consider the 2004 French statute prohibiting 'attire' ('*tenues*') 'ostensibly' ('*ostensiblement*') demonstrating a religious belonging in public primary and secondary schools. Hailing as they do from a multicultural society, these students can reasonably be expected to harbour a certain number of prejudices (in the etymological sense of 'anterior judgements') regarding the way in which France is handling the matter of religious diversity in the public sphere. These US students' prejudices will vary, not least depending on each individual's enculturation. To be sure, most of these US students do not consciously harbour xenophobic or Francophobic inclinations (they enrolled in 'Comparative Law', after all!). However, their convictions, their world-view – in particular, their understanding of the significance of freedom of religion and freedom of speech – must turn, at some level of consciousness or other, on their relegation of the French practice to the realm of the unacceptable. From these US students' perspective, the French exclusion of teenage headscarf-clad Muslim women from the classroom partakes of an otherness that they themselves are required to deprecate in order for

90 G Bachelard, *Essai sur la connaissance approchée* (Vrin 1987 [1928]) 17.

them to sustain their own sense of their cultural selves. In other words, for the US students to be the sensible multiculturalists they want to be, they must form a view of the unsatisfactory character of the French statute: one cannot be a good US multiculturalist *and* accommodate the French statute's (intolerant) prohibition.

At this juncture, I ask my reader to imagine further that a class discussion is taking place under the guidance of a comparatist whose life experience allows for a sense of relativization that is arguably more sophisticated than his students'. As the US students bring to the conversation their experience or understanding of religious attire in the classroom, the comparatist, acting not as positivist but as *culturalist*, guides them to a close reading of the French statute that is informed by French history (including a long-standing tradition of state interventionism in religious affairs, not to mention nineteenth-century colonial forays), French politics (with specific reference to post-colonial immigration policy), French demographics (France is said to feature the largest Muslim population in Europe), French republican values (not least the matter of '*égalité*' as regards men and women, but also with respect to the earnest refusal to grant legal status to minorities and recognize minority rights), the French articulation of citizenship (featuring unswerving adhesion to the idea of national indivisibility and a forceful rejection of any modus vivendi along the lines of multiculturalism or communitarianism), the French conception of public schools as the principal vehicle for the institutionalization of students into French republicanism, French trust and faith in the state and the French demand for sustained state interventionism, French epistemology (notably, the reverence for statutes and the strong commitment to their uniform application nationwide correlating with abhorrence for local or exceptional regimes), and, yes, a measure of French anxiety or Islamophobia vis-à-vis the ever-growing Muslim presence on French territory (which is not to say that all French people think identically in this or in any other respect, for there is simply no such empirical homogeneity).

The comparatist, continuing to intervene as *culturalist*, proceeds to devise how these historical, political, and other questions have coalesced and morphed into the law-text, how they have become constitutive of the law-text as 'jurimorphs',[91] and how they have left their trace within the

91 Eg: K McGee, 'On Devices and Logics of Legal Sense: Toward Socio-Technical Legal Analysis' in K McGee (ed), *Latour and the Passage of Law* (Edinburgh University Press 2015) 61–92.

French statute – or, to approach the matter the other way, how the law-text can be traced to them. Even as he appreciates that he cannot aspire to polymathy and must therefore remain selective as regards the range of his cultural investigations, the comparatist's close-reading and indisciplined strategy has the huge merit of standing athwart the positivist's closed and disciplinary reading that would exclude culture from its analytical range and, to that extent at least, effectively seek to contain difference across laws (to eliminate history, politics, republican values, the configuration of citizenship, and so forth, is to efface so many instances of differentiation distinguishing US and French laws). In stark opposition to positivism's hypomnesis, culturalism thus makes possible a *hyper-reading* of the French statute, a reading of the traces lurking between the statute's lines, encrypted in the text's fabric, that the hyper-aware comparatist can see to be pertaining to the statute's *hypergraphy* rather than its perigraphy.[92] While positivism would readily regard all textual traces as non-law, as il-legal, culturalism engages in a re-signification of the law-text as hypertext and hyperlaw. Enhancively, tracing – in effect, culturalism's interpretive and therefore critical vector – ascribes new signifiance: it makes the law-text signify anew and more. If you will, on account of the compelling interpretive yield that it generates, tracing enables comparative law to disclose law at its *lawmost*.

In the light of the negotiation that can be expected to take place in class with two or three of the more inquisitive students or perhaps with a couple of students proving reluctant to accept what they perceive as an unconvincing narrative on the part of their teacher, it is possible that some US students – possibly not more than a small number of them – will begin to probe their own, encultured assumptions, and that they will start to make space for a new interpretation of the French exclusion that they had readily excluded from their understanding of acceptability. In other terms, these students may now observe how an appreciation of foreign law on the basis of superficial resonances leads to the other being cast, unjustly, as an imperfect version of the self.

It may well be that, in the end, the steps that can effectively be taken towards a new interpretation of the French approach that the comparatist stages in his US classroom will be few and slight. For example, it is quite possible that only a limited number of students will be willing to follow their teacher along the interpretive path he

[92] cf J Derrida, *Positions* (Editions de Minuit 1972) 87–88: '[T]he "text" does not reduc[e] itself . . . to the sensible or visible presence of the graphical or of the "literal".'

suggests. Still, one can envision that for some US students at least, the class discussion will prove an 'I opener',[93] so much so, in fact, that their intellectual and moral lives may possibly be permanently changed as a result. In the process, because it is now recognized and respected on account of the *culturalist* interpretation that has been supplied, the French practice ceases to be so readily unfathomable – or, at least, becomes unfathomable differently, that is, in a different sense of the word (it is no longer that it must be wholeheartedly condemned, but that it is to be regarded, say, as incongruous). After class discussion and under the guidance of the comparatist teaching the group as *culturalist*, the French statute's otherness is not any longer of the kind that must be readily deemed inadmissible, but of the type that now deserves to be understood. If you will, it has been made plausible. To put the matter more graphically perhaps, US students have managed to overcome their initial 'yuck' reaction.[94]

To be sure, there is nothing to indicate that US students have to agree with the French model. But at least – and this strikes me as being hugely noteworthy – the interpretive yield that the comparatist's *culturalist* interpretation will have introduced to them avoids any ready and reductive appropriation of the French statute to the local, US idea of discrimination or ostracism. Because the comparatist has given the differend a hearing in the course of his teaching, since he has attempted to make sense of the French statute in local, French terms, some at least of the US students' hostility will have subsided, some of their concern will have disappeared. The French model will no longer be so cavalierly dismissed. In other words, US law students will have learned to acknowledge the singularity of foreign textuality, to recognize otherness-in-the-law, perhaps to fashion a modicum of respect for a different approach to the matter of religious attire in public schools. If you will, although one can never fully release oneself from oneself,[95] US law students will have conceded a de-imperialization of the legal mind – of their legal mind – so that they no longer spontaneously see the French statute as an offence vis-à-vis what they tend to regard as the highly prized value of individualism. They can now glimpse how the wearing of a headscarf in a public school can be apprehended otherwise – say, as a normative refusal to

[93] S Beckett, *How It Is* (EM O'Reilly ed, Faber & Faber 2009 [1964]) 81.

[94] RA Shweder, '"What About Female Genital Mutilation?" and Why Understanding Culture Matters in the First Place' in RA Shweder et al (eds), *Engaging Cultural Differences* (Sage 2002) 222–26.

[95] Again, Agamben makes the point convincingly: supra 205n82.

integrate into the collective of French republicanism – and they can therefore show themselves to be wiser to the other, to be other-wise.

Note how I am not saying that the US students I hypothesize will have acquired a *knowledge* of French law – not, at least, in the strong sense of the word 'knowledge' – if only because what they 'know', far from being the outcome of their own research and reflection, is very much indebted to their teacher's re-presentation, which had to be singular (other comparatists would have suggested other interpretations), which could not be exhaustive (other information might have been conveyed), and which had to be interrupted (other practical considerations needed to be addressed). In any event, the teaching comparatist does not have 'knowledge' of otherness-in-the-law either.[96] Ultimately, I am minded to quote Maurice Merleau-Ponty, the influential phenomenologist: 'I do not *know* the others.'[97] At best, on account of their irreverent intellectual trajectory towards the French monologue, these US students will have made their way within echoing distance of their teacher standing at knowledge's edge.

*

In an essay on Virginia Woolf's *To the Lighthouse*, Gayatri Spivak observes at the outset that her critique is 'not necessarily an attempt to ... lead ... to a correct reading' of Woolf's novel.[98] Likewise, the comparatist in the classroom, as he engages in a *culturalist* interpretation of the French statute, is not seeking to produce a 'correct' reading of it, but rather to offer a compelling *interpretation* of the foreign law-text. (The idea of a correct reading must assume the existence of the-text-in-itself-and-its-meaning-in-itself, which interpretation would seek to harvest. But there is not *that*: there is neither text nor meaning in itself.) Incidentally, this is where ethics becomes relevant again: the comparatist as mediator must behave with integrity. His exploration must be passionate, of course, but also circumspect and flexible. Certainly, it must be innovative, but it has to intervene thoroughly and faithfully, too.[99] Yet, the comparatist's re-presentation very much remains his own,

96 Supra 172.

97 M Merleau-Ponty, *Le Visible et l'invisible* in *Œuvres* (C Lefort ed, Gallimard, 2010 [1964†]) 1693.

98 GC Spivak, *In Other Worlds* (Routledge 2006 [1987]) 41. cf Byron, 'Hints from Horace' in *The Complete Poetical Works*, vol 1 (JJ McGann ed, Oxford University Press 1986 [1831]) line 418, 304, where the poet refers to 'the paltry suffrage of "Correct"!'

99 cf J Derrida, *De la grammatologie* (Editions de Minuit 1967) 345: '[The reading] cannot legitimately transgress the text.' See also J Derrida, 'Fidélité à plus d'un' (1998/13) Cahiers

encultured intervention into French law – and it stands as his own, encultured re-presentation of French law (that is, his presentation anew and therefore necessarily different from the French law that there is, there, in France). In the course of this act of re-presentation, as he is making the existing French statute his focus of study and fashioning his own interaction with it – as he is *inventing* the French law-text – the comparatist is required to take any number of decisions, none of which heralds objectivity or truth, all of which are necessarily interpretive, all of which are the outcome of the negotiations he must conduct with the foreign law-text and with himself as he proceeds to deploy otherness – and that would take him forever to justify (to the extent that he could even become conscious of all the epistemic ramifications involved).

To assume that the US students I postulate welcome the French model, that they are now disposed to show themselves hospitable to the other, might be excessive. But these US students are no longer so riveted to themselves, some of their prejudices having been dismantled and the range of their appreciation expanded – all of which has valuable progressive political implications. In a way, the other has come along – the differend has emerged – to save the US students' selves from themselves. The US selves in the classroom thus find themselves emancipated from the facile view that the other must somehow be (colonially) appropriated to their categories, a salutary epistemological development. It is not that the French statute is now being envisaged objectively. It continues to be seen through US eyes, so to speak (not only is it still 'not us', but it also remains 'not US'). However, the US students have learned that as they read the French statute, what they see is not what they see (that is, there is much more to the statute than meets the eye). And they can now talk of the other without experiencing reflexive repudiation of otherness. In sum, the exercise in *culturalist* comparison is well worth the epistemic trouble.

In the meantime, positivism would be positively unable to foster this kind of responsibility, not least on account of its reductionist urge for the institution of equivalences or commonalities, but also because the sort of information that a positivist analysis would convey is quite simply incapable of generating a deep or thick understanding of foreign law. (The positivist cannot be sensible to the fact that foreign law-texts are freighted with culture's traces, that

Intersignes 221, 262, where the author observes that there is 'the law of the other text, . . . its injunction, . . . its signature'.

the traces are present within the text and as the text. He has no feel for tracing.) To be sure, French courts have had to circumscribe the semantic extension of the word 'attire' (in French, the open-textured '*tenues*') as they have had to analyze the scope of the term 'ostensibly' ('*ostensiblement*'). But how would an exclusive focus on, say, authoritative judicial interpretations of the statute – a characteristic illustration of the positivist approach – serve to foster an appreciation of the *profound* reasons informing the French way of thinking as regards the interface between religion, republicanism, and public schools? In a nutshell, US law students may well be made to examine all manner of French judgments on 'attire' and 'ostensibility', but none of this investigation will begin to reveal anything about the French conceptualization of schools (as distinguished from hospitals or airports) that makes it seem perfectly obvious to the French state that what needs to be done in order to eschew religion enjoying a visible foothold in society must above all assertively be done in public *schools*. The fact of the matter is that '[the] value [of rule-comparison] as a source of explanation … is small'.[100] And this is why, in addition to a consideration, say, of the relevant judicial decisions – as a jurist, one will evidently want to probe these materials, too – the comparatist intervening as *culturalist* will readily value supplementing his interpretation with the kind of cultural insights that will make it possible for US law students to ascribe some meaningful sense to the French experience rather than confining themselves and their understanding to dull descriptions arising from leading cases. To quote Hans-Georg Gadamer, the comparatist, by propounding a *culturalist* interpretation of the French statute, by introducing to his US students 'an opinion and a possibility that one brings into play and puts at risk',[101] makes it feasible for these US law students to 'other' themselves *jusque-là* – an outcome that a positivist reading of French law would never be able to achieve as sophisticatedly.

Beyond that development – and, again, on the firm understanding that there can be no expectation of a US agreement with the French standpoint (and that there is no need for such consensus either) – US students might want to militate in order to change the discourses

[100] Merryman (n 3) 89n20.

[101] H-G Gadamer, *Wahrheit und Methode* (5th edn, Mohr Siebeck 1986) 392. In German, 'to put at risk' is '*aufs Spiel setzen*', an expression allowing Gadamer to use '*Spiel*' ('play') twice and engage in … word-play. In this regard, the English language fails.

that inform the French statute and to which the law-text can be traced (say, the French conception of citizenship or minority rights). But for US students to have any chance of making an impact in whatever conversation they could have, say, with a French jurist, they must first be willing to recognize and, yes, respect the French approach. There is no significant opportunity for persuasion, it is clear to me, without such threshold valorization of otherness-in-the-law, which must turn on relevant cultural information being made available ab initio.[102]

Although I configure US students and French law on the basis of my own on-site teaching in the United States and France (comparatists are well advised to avoid discussing topics with which they are not ascertainably familiar), I am acutely aware that comparative law must multiply incursions of the kind that a few bold comparatists have been willing to initiate in legal cultures that, vis-à-vis the habitual jurisdictions, are at once outstanding and standing out.[103] There is, clearly, an imperative – ethically, politically – to move comparative law beyond the occidental confines that have classically

[102] I cannot resist further imagery. Assume that I am asked to describe the law school where the comparatist is teaching his US students. In times past, it used to be a family home until it was bequeathed to the university. I could talk about the type of stone or brick, the colour, the year in which the building was erected. This would be one possible description. Another approach would be to supplement this narrative, to add that the property used to be a private house inhabited by a wealthy family, to say a little about that family, to explain what that house meant to these people in terms of social status and respectability, and to recall in what circumstances it was bequeathed to the university and converted into a law school. In both instances, I am telling about the law school, but in the second case, I have sought to trace it to its historical or social – to its cultural! – constitutive features. My claim is that if one proposes to engage in meaningful comparative law so as to foster a deep or thick understanding of the foreign, one must aim to avoid talking strictly in stone-and-brick terms.

[103] Eg: T Ruskola, *Legal Orientalism* (Harvard University Press 2013); S Seppänen, *Ideological Conflict and the Rule of Law in Contemporary China* (Cambridge University Press 2016); LK McAllister, *Making Law Matter: Environmental Protection and Legal Institutions in Brazil* (Stanford University Press 2008); T Roux, *The Politico-Legal Dynamics of Judicial Review* (Oxford University Press 2018); P Nicholson and S Biddulph (eds), *Examining Practice, Interrogating Theory: Comparative Legal Studies in Asia* (Brill 2008); JL Esquirol, *Ruling the Law* (Cambridge University Press 2019); E Mérieau, *Constitutional Bricolage: Thailand's Sacred Monarchy vs the Rule of Law* (Hart 2021).

limited the reach of the field's research studies to a cluster of northern countries on either side of the Atlantic.[104] I am also thinking of the need for the comparative legal mind to work beyond the confirmed themes and assumptions.[105] In this regard, the matter of colonialism arguably demands particular attention.

[104] The requirement to expand comparative vistas beyond the 'usual suspects', so to speak, is not a challenge that is unique to comparative law. Eg: J Baggini, 'How to Compare Fruit' *The Times Literary Supplement* (25 May 2018) 9 (book review of S Golob and J Timmermann, *The Cambridge History of Moral Philosophy* [Cambridge University Press 2017]): 'The Middle East gets a bit part in this story, with two out of fifty-four chapters dealing with medieval Jewish and Islamic philosophy. On this account, moral philosophy has never existed in Asia, India, Africa or South America.' But see O Flanagan, *The Geography of Morals* (Oxford University Press 2017).

[105] Eg: R Noguellou and D Renders (eds), *Uber & Taxis: Comparative Law Studies* (Larcier 2018); K Roach (ed), *Comparative Counter-Terrorism Law* (Cambridge University Press 2015); K Pistor and O De Schutter (eds), *Governing Access to Essential Resources* (Columbia University Press 2016); IW Martin et al (eds), *The New Fiscal Sociology: Taxation in Comparative and Historical Perspective* (Cambridge University Press 2009); L Thio and JL Neo (eds), *Religious Offences in Common Law Asia* (Hart 2021); H Alviar García and G Frankenberg (eds), *Authoritarian Constitutionalism* (Elgar 2019); PG Monateri, *Dominus Mundi* (Hart 2018); D Marrani, *Space, Time, Justice* (Routledge 2018); M Cohen, 'Regulating Milk: Women and Cows in France and the United States' (2017) 65 Am J Comp L 469; I Petretta, 'The Question of Comparison' (2020) 68 Am J Comp L 893; D Bonilla Maldonado, *Legal Barbarians: Identity, Modern Comparative Law and the Global South* (Cambridge University Press 2021); K Brayson, 'Generating Comparison-in-Law: Embodied Epistemologies, For the Love of Knowledge' (2021) 8(2) Critical Analysis L 52. Now, *à quand* the first study in comparative 'genderfuck' law?

VIII

Decoloniality

On the understanding that coloniality can fairly be regarded as a 'psychoepistemic disorder plaguing modern forms of knowledge to the core', an 'obvious corridor through which knowledge about the [o]ther is transmitted' and through which knowledge is transmitted to the other,[1] I find that a major concern must be addressed within comparative law harbouring even greater significance than any argument in favour of more Vietnam and less Canada or more Kenya and less Germany. Beyond the obvious fact that one also wants more Indonesia and more Nigeria and the possibly less obvious fact that comparative law likewise needs more *ubuntu* (a philosophical term that had a decisive impact on South Africa's Truth and Reconciliation Commission), more *sumak kawsay* (an idea that made its way into the constitutions of Ecuador and Bolivia in 2008 and 2009, respectively), and more Andean *pachamama*,[2] beyond the further fact that the field requires non-Eurocentric critiques of Eurocentrism and of non-Eurocentrism alike, I refer to the epistemic demand consisting in the unravelling of the logic of coloniality that has conspicuously informed law's comparisons, for example, in the guise of universalizing and totalizing claims. Easily traceable to what is plausibly identifiable as the first 'institutional' comparative law monograph, Eduard Gans's multi-volume text on the laws of inheritance,[3] going as far back as Sepúlveda's 1550 argument in

[1] WB Hallaq, *Restating Orientalism* (Columbia University Press 2018) vii and viii.

[2] For an introduction to these various notions, all pertaining to 'the epistemologies of the South', and for the observation that they are not necessarily to be found in a pristine state, because they may well have been subverted by local political practice, see B de Sousa Santos, *The End of the Cognitive Empire* (Duke University Press 2018) 10. For a detailed treatment of '*ubuntu*', see L Praeg, *A Report on Ubuntu* (KwaZulu-Natal 2014).

[3] See E Gans, *Das Erbrecht in weltgeschichtlicher Entwicklung*, 4 vols (Scientia 1963 [1824]).

Valladolid,[4] 'already at work' in Cartesianism,[5] such contentious contentions have long ago assumed the character of standardized illusions prevalently informing the orthodox comparison of laws.

*

I borrow 'coloniality' from Aníbal Quijano, who coined this word as '*colonialidad*' to much acclaim, in order to refer to forms of colonialism that have survived the end of colonization.[6] Now, the deconstruction of coloniality, that is, the edification of decoloniality, allows one to see that instead of universals or totalities, there are, strictly speaking,

> words that project the North Atlantic experience on a universal scale that they themselves helped to create. North Atlantic universals are particulars that have gained a degree of universality, chunks of human history that have become historical standards. They do not describe the world; they offer visions of the world. They appear to refer to things as they exist, but because they are rooted in a particular history, they evoke multiple layers of sensibilities, persuasions, cultural assumptions, and ideological choices tied to that localized history. They come to us loaded with aesthetic and stylistic sensibilities; religious and philosophical persuasions; cultural assumptions ranging from what it means to be a human being to the proper relationship between humans and the natural world; ideological choices ranging from the nature of the political to its possibilities of transformation.[7]

[4] For discussions of the Valladolid disputation, see eg E Andújar, 'Bartolomé de las Casas and Juan Ginés de Sepúlveda: Moral Theology Versus Political Philosophy' in K White (ed), *Hispanic Philosophy in the Age of Discovery* (Catholic University of America Press 1997) 69–87; DR Brunstetter and D Zartner, 'Just War Against Barbarians: Revisiting the Valladolid Debates Between Sepúlveda and Las Casas' (2011) 59 Political Stud 733; F Castilla Urbano, 'The Debate of Valladolid (1550–1551): Background, Discussions, and Results of the Debate Between Juan Ginés de Sepúlveda and Bartolomé de las Casas' in J Tellkamp (ed), *A Companion to Early Modern Spanish Imperial Political and Social Thought* (Brill 2020) 222–51.

[5] WD Mignolo, *The Politics of Decolonial Investigations* (Duke University Press 2021) 470. Mignolo's claim is that '[i]f Descartes arrived at the conclusion "I think, therefore I am", it was precisely because . . . he just took for granted this: if you feel and know that you are humanitas, you most likely will not be concerned about *where* you do and think – you would assume that you inhabit the universal house of knowledge, the epistemic zero point': WD Mignolo, *The Darker Side of Western Modernity* (Duke University Press 2011) 99.

[6] See A Quijano, 'Colonialidad y modernidad/racionalidad' (1991) 13(29) Perú indígena 11 [on file].

[7] M-L Trouillot, 'North Atlantic Universals: Analytical Fictions, 1492–1945' (2001) 101(4) South Atlantic Q 839, 847. For a historical conspectus unveiling the geo-historical location of purportedly abstract universals and showing the development of the massive occidental epistemological machine promoting knowledge deemed superior to other knowledges elsewhere on the planet (thus suitably demonized), effectively making the planet into its

Even as Konrad Zweigert and Hein Kötz's orthodox comparatism aspires to 'a unitary concept of justice' harking back to 'natural law',[8] a universalizing and totalizing framework that a practice of comparative law as 'science pure' would make possible,[9] decoloniality helps one to discern that '[n]othing is less rational, finally, than the pretension that the specific cosmic vision of a particular ethnie should be taken as universal rationality, even if such an ethnie is called Western Europe [or Germany or German legal culture!] because this is actually [to] pretend to impose a provincialism as universalism'.[10] Decoloniality also makes it possible to appreciate that when James Gordley writes that he is 'concerned with what the law [i]s',[11] he is choosing to overlook the fact that '[d]ecolonially speaking, ontologies are cosmologies/epistemic creations': it is epistemology that prescribes ontology, that institutes it.[12] Indeed, '[e]pistemologies are always derived from cosmologies' – '[t]he Big Bang theory of the creation of the universe, for instance, is within Christian cosmology not within Islamic or Chinese cosmologies'.[13] Ultimately, 'ontology is an epistemological

object, and assuming the warrant of universalization on account of its self-proclaimed ascendancy, see WD Mignolo, 'The Decolonial Option' in WD Mignolo and CE Walsh (eds), *On Decoloniality* (Duke University Press 2018) 153–93. See also Sousa Santos (n 2) 39: 'There is no European universalism; there is rather a European foundational experience that, due to its overriding economic and military power, imposed itself on other foundational experiences existing in the world and thereby granted itself the prerogative of proclaiming its universal validity.' Adde: P Fitzpatrick, *The Mythology of Modern Law* (Routledge 1992) 65. A particularly important illustration of the movement I describe, perhaps the 'master epistemic code', concerns Christian cosmology, which proceeded to displace itself from being a local phenomenon to a would-be universal totality. I quote from Mignolo, 201. Capital constitutes another paramount example of European distension. Without capitalism, Eurocentrism would arguably have unfolded as just another ethnocentrism – hence Partha Chatterjee's insight: 'If there is one great moment that turns the provincial thought of Europe to universal philosophy, the parochial history of Europe to universal history, it is the moment of capital . . . . It is the narrative of capital that can turn the violence of mercantile trade, war, genocide, conquest and colonialism into a story of universal progress, development, modernization, and freedom': P Chatterjee, *The Nation and Its Fragments* (Princeton University Press 1993) 235.

8 K Zweigert and H Kötz, *Einführung in die Rechtsvergleichung* (3rd edn, Mohr Siebeck 1996) 3 and 44.

9 ibid 6.

10 A Quijano, 'Coloniality and Modernity/Rationality' (2007) 21 Cultural Stud 168, 177.

11 J Gordley, 'When Is the Use of Foreign Law Possible? A Hard Case: The Protection of Privacy in Europe and the United States' (2007) 67 Louisiana LR 1073, 1081. See also B Markesinis, 'Comparative Law: A Subject in Search of an Audience' (1990) 53 Modern LR 1, 13, where the author writes that '[c]ase law can reveal what the law really is'.

12 Mignolo (n 7) 135.

13 ibid.

concept',[14] which means that there is no law that meaningfully 'is' without an interpretive assignment of 'isness' by someone like Gordley – which means further that the meaningfulness of a law-text, as Gordley states it, is indissociable from an interpretive Gordleyization of the law.[15] In Gordley's account of the French law of '*erreur sur la substance*', there is not the French law of '*erreur sur la substance*' as such, but there is the French law of '*erreur sur la substance*' as Gordley interprets it (no doubt most sophisticatedly). And there can be nothing else.

From a decolonial standpoint, Zweigert, Kötz, and Gordley can readily be shown to be acting as mystifiers. Formulations like 'a unitary concept of justice' or 'the law as it [i]s', for example, or others yet such as 'scientific exactitude',[16] are so many confounding statements, all the more obfuscatory perhaps if they are inscribed in French, thus '*science pure*' or '*école de vérité*' (what could be more bewildering than assertions crafted in French in a German text?).[17] But these phrases effectively 'distrac[t] [one] from the tricks and designs of the enunciator'.[18] (Arguably, they are *meant* so to distract.) Decolonially speaking, however, there cannot be an enunciation without enculturation, not even Zweigert and Kötz's statements, not even Gordley's pronouncement. Consider Gordley. When he claims that there is 'the law as it [i]s' and that he, Gordley, can tell 'the law as it [i]s' as it is, he has the matter the wrong way around, for '[w]hat *there is* depends on how [h]e ha[s] been programmed to name what [h]e know[s]'.[19] For example, 'no continent named America existed to be discovered' without further ado.[20] And no cultural traces constituting the French statute on religious attire in public schools exist to be discovered without further ado either. Pace positivism, the French statute's meaning 'is' not. Rather, it is the French statute's interpreter who

[14] ibid. Martin Heidegger acknowledges that even 'the ontological investigation that [he] is ... conducting is determined by its historical situation': M Heidegger, *Die Grundprobleme der Phänomenologie* (F-W Von Herrmann ed, Klostermann 2005 [1927]) 31.

[15] cf G Agamben, *Signatura rerum* (Bollati Boringhieri 2008) 7: '[D]octrine can be espousing legitimately only the form of interpretation.'

[16] Zweigert and Kötz (n 8) 44.

[17] ibid 6 and 14. Both expressions appear in French and without italics in the German text.

[18] Mignolo (n 7) 144.

[19] ibid 148.

[20] ibid 184. Likewise, there is no atherosclerosis until the physician has diagnosed and named it. See generally A Mol, *The Body Multiple* (Duke University Press 2002). I propose a treatment of this question from the standpoint of comparative law in P Legrand, 'What Is That, to Read Foreign Law?' (2019) 14(2) J Comp L 294.

brings the law-text to meaningfulness as he *enacts* the cultural traces haunting the law-text through a phenomenon of encryption.[21] And the interpreter's enactment can only take the form of an encultured assertion, because the enactment ascribing meaning to the statute is *the interpreter's* enactment, and no interpreter exists beyond culture (no interpreter exists 'in the air').

Decoloniality, as 'it aims at altering the principles and assumptions of knowledge creation, transformation, and dissemination',[22] effectively calls for the deconstruction of the hegemonic character of colonial epistemology and of its controlling, managerial disposition with a view to (1) acknowledging that orthodox enunciations are not planetary representations or planetary renderings, but local institutions, the process of institutionalization manifesting itself through the 'doing' of the enunciations;[23] and (2) triggering an alternative manner of thinking and living. Along the way, decoloniality requires the deconstructor to focus squarely on the comparatist-at-law-as-knower, for it is he, for instance, who does the (colonial) doing, that is, it is he who holds the priority of science as rigorous and incontrovertible knowledge; who defends universalism as a configuration existing independently from enculturation; who promotes truth as a device existing to valorize a representation of reality that would be exclusively accurate; who supports disciplinary specialization along the lines of 'law is law' and 'philosophy is philosophy'; and who fosters a distinction between knower and known allegedly making objectivity achievable. It is he who peddles this mythological caravanserai. Yes.

I discern, then, a colonial attitude having implanted identifiable cognitive habits in the minds of orthodox comparatists-at-law and their disciples. Hiding behind the fig-leaf of 'convenient fictions',[24] these individuals are readily willing to forget that all theories and all conceptual frames (not least neo-liberalism or other discourses extolling an

[21] Annemarie Mol talks about the physician 'enacting' atherosclerosis: Mol (n 20) 32–33 and passim. See also Legrand (n 20) 293–94 and 300. cf RM Cover, '*Nomos* and Narrative' (1983) 97 Harvard LR 4, 4: 'No set of legal institutions or prescriptions exists apart from the narratives that locate it and give it meaning.'

[22] Mignolo (n 7) 145.

[23] cf ibid 151: '[R]epresentation . . . makes us believe that there is a world out there that can be described independently of the enunciation that describes it.' The two most influential critiques of such an epistemological strategy as, effectively, a rhetorical sleight-of-hand remain M Foucault, *Les Mots et les choses* (Gallimard 1966) and R Rorty, *Philosophy and the Mirror of Nature* (Princeton University Press 1979).

[24] Trouillot (n 7) 839.

enhanced commodification of the planet) are tenaciously encultured, that is, they are firmly ensconced in what is inevitably a local-knowledge arrangement (no matter how dilated), which means that any attempt to evoke or convoke transcendental tenets effectively mobilizes a colonial matrix of power intervening as a predatory approach to thinking, feeling, analyzing, knowing, living – and being-in-the-law and being-in-the-comparison-of-laws. Accordingly, I plead in favour of decoloniality as an attitude that would overcome and relativize the mindset ultimately inherited from the Renaissance and the Enlightenment, whereby both the thinking and the doing animating comparative law (the theory and the practice), which I regard as an assemblage rather than discrete configurations, are distortingly apprehended as being able to extirpate themselves – as being self-extirpable! – from any and all cultural belonging. (I hold that 'the detached individual self is only a fiction of the North Atlantic geography of imagination, an ideological by-product of the internal narrative of modernity'.[25]) And accordingly, too, I defend another way of theorizing the comparative, and I advance another strategy governing the implementation of comparison, which means that the colonial mindset and its impact on 'lived experience' (in the comparison of laws) – which, for instance, has been framing one's experience of difference as a phenomenon at once unproductive and discardable – must be *unlearned*.[26] In this regard, thoughtful comparatists-at-law can derive assistance from a leading anthropologist's critique chastising as 'utterly unsupportable' Zweigert and Kötz's view that a finding of difference or significant conflict across laws must mean bad comparative research.[27]

The forging of decolonial pathways that would overcome the violent epistemic tendency to dominate under the guise of various metaphysical conceits (such as the universal) implies, crucially, that the comparatist must train himself to *think-with* and *think-from* other peoples, other knowledges, and other laws – other cultures! – rather than simply think

[25] ibid 853. For a critique of selfhood as autonomy with specific reference to comparative law, see S Glanert, 'The Comparatist and the Illusion of Autonomy' in S Glanert, A Mercescu, and G Samuel, *Rethinking Comparative Law* (Elgar 2021) 31–60.

[26] For an important argument regarding the extent of coloniality's impact, see N Maldonado-Torres, 'On the Coloniality of Being' (2007) 21 Cultural Stud 240, 242.

[27] L Rosen, 'Beyond Compare' in P Legrand and R Munday (eds), *Comparative Legal Studies: Traditions and Transitions* (Cambridge University Press 2003) 505. The reference is to Zweigert and Kötz (n 8) 39, where the authors dismiss conclusions heralding 'differences or even total contradictions' and enjoin the comparatist-at-law then to start his investigations afresh.

about them (or, worse, think about them from a place imagined to be *above* them).[28] Moreover, as he proceeds to operate through an interpretive approach that manifests itself as a worthy response to otherness – that is prepared 'to take seriously the epistemic force of local histories'[29] – the comparatist-at-law is invited to cultivate a mode-of-being-in-the-comparison acknowledging that his own analytical frame is incorporated or embodied, which means accepting that the questions, reflections, and considerations that occupy him are themselves existence-based – in effect, to recognize, pace Descartes, that 'I am where I think'.[30] Only then do such epistemic configurations actively purport to transgress the colonial mindset and say no to totalizing validity-claims. Once the law-worlds beyond one's own are re-signified as genuine and signifying heterorealities, instead of being cast as realities awaiting appropriation to one's model effectively advocating for one-solution-fits-all – that is, much too often, *my*-solution-fits-all – it becomes possible to recognize and respect the other's law. In sum, it becomes plausible to envisage the other's law as a contribution to the emergence of new understandings from an alternative epistemic place of enunciation deserving critical consideration, that is, beyond colonial epistemology.

I claim that the comparatist must equip himself so as to overcome the cancellation of epistemic otherness in which the colonial-minded orthodoxy within the field of comparative law has long engaged. It is not, of course, that coloniality as one has known it can ever disappear completely. In this sense, the decoloniality that I promote is not so much the fully fledged absence of all coloniality as a process of sensing, thinking, interpreting, and living other-wise in the law and in the comparison – 'other-wise' as in 'differently from before' *and* 'in a way that is wise to the other'. Now, wisdom to the other can materialize, for example, in terms of the interrogatings, actionings, and understandings that will take place beyond 'a set of self-serving narratives' facilitating the deployment of epistemic power over other experiences of the legal – beyond all strategies purporting to apply epistemic power imperially, and all the more imperially the more differentiated the experience of the other appears to be in the eyes of

[28] A fine example of thinking-with and thinking-from is in RA Shweder, '"What About Female Genital Mutilation?" and Why Understanding Culture Matters in the First Place' in RA Shweder et al (eds), *Engaging Cultural Differences* (Sage 2002) 216–51.

[29] A Escobar, 'Beyond the Third World: Imperial Globality, Global Coloniality and Anti-Globalisation Social Movements' (2004) 25 Third World Q 207, 217.

[30] Mignolo (n 5) 80–81.

the comparing self.[31] In particular, comparative law other-wise prevents the articulation of foreign law as *lack* vis-à-vis one's 'own' law.[32]

To overcome the universalist or totalizing tendency is to surmount at once the marginalization of difference and the denial that difference is being marginalized (a disavowal that is typical of the colonial logic). And to differentiate – rather than imperially and imperiously bringing into equivalence or commonality – is precisely one of 'those actions [that] are at the very root of the critical task'.[33] It is to move the governing epistemology from an otherization of the stigmatizing type to one of the respectful kind whereby fragmented singularities are allowed to recover their name and their materiality. Vis-à-vis the orthodoxy that prevails within comparative law, decoloniality thus takes the form of 'the exercise of power within the colonial matrix to undermine the mechanism that keeps it in place requiring obeisance', and because '[s]uch a mechanism is epistemic . . . so decolonial liberation implies epistemic disobedience'.[34] Decoloniality disconnects from universalizing and totalizing schemes in order to reconnect with local knowledge. This passage operates at the level of cognition, of course, but it also harbours an affective or aesthetic dimension as it touches upon emotions and desires. For the comparatist-at-law, it is about leading one's life consciously, giving it form and direction through constant, probing attention to the local, an attitude existing in perceptible tension with the goals of an abstract configuration such as universalization or totalization heralding its long-institutionally-defined-and-simplified appraisals and pathways.

Even as I earnestly advocate for a theory and practice of decoloniality within comparative law, I must accept, lest I lapse into contradiction, that

[31] Mignolo (n 7) 110. cf Fitzpatrick (n 7) 65, where the author observes a connection between 'racialization' (that is, 'defining a savage Other') and the Enlightenment, the former discourse being 'woven into the very fabric' of the latter.

[32] Simply put, the ascription of 'lack' installs otherness as subordinate to selfness, thereby cancelling its legitimate status as genuine otherness. I oppose such hierarchization as unbecoming to comparative law 'other-wise'. Rather than a lesser experience – which the idea of lack assumes – the other must be seen to have a different one. See P Legrand, 'Book Review' (2013) 8(2) J Comp L 444, 450 (review of T Ruskola, *Legal Orientalism* [Harvard University Press 2013]). In reaction, Donald Clarke brings to bear a positivist mindset and misses my epistemic argument altogether. See D Clarke, 'Anti Anti-Orientalism, or Is Chinese Law Different?' (2020) 68 Am J Comp L 55, 60n19. cf D Chakrabarty, *Provincializing Europe* (2nd edn, Princeton University Press 2008) xii: 'No country . . . is a model to another country, though the discussion of modernity that thinks in terms of "catching up" precisely posits such models.'

[33] BE Harcourt, *Critique and Praxis* (Columbia University Press 2020) 155.

[34] Mignolo (n 7) 114.

decoloniality cannot assert itself in the guise of truth, truth being precisely one of the self-interested fictions that the doxa has been touting – recall Zweigert and Kötz's 'école de vérité'[35] – and that decoloniality is meant to interrupt and overcome, to 'le[t] . . . go'.[36] It is crucial that 'critical theory does not become a method for truth', that '[w]e . . . get beyond the idea that critical theory, as the unmasking of illusions, unveils the truth'.[37] Indeed, '[t]hat is precisely the problem: the claim to truth, the dangerous appropriation of truth, the will to truth'.[38] It follows that comparative law must oppose the 'power play' that any truth-regime effectively countenances,[39] no matter how obdurately stubborn its hegemonic contention proves to be.[40] Otherwise (or other-wise) said, then, I must accept that decoloniality can only offer itself as an epistemic opportunity.[41] It follows that 'decoloniality . . . cannot be a missionary imperative to control and dominate',[42] which means that '[n]o universal decoloniality can be mapped by one single local history and one single project'.[43]

Bereft of the argument from truth, it is then up to *me* to carry the decolonial comparative claim within the framework of any research. On each occasion, 'I have to be confident, convincing, and empowering'.[44] What remains the case every time, though, is that decoloniality as epistemological shift is an option that is explicitly political inasmuch as it wants to obviate the prevailing politics of validation of knowledge that would have one believe in positivism being able to warrant something like (universal) veridiction. Decoloniality operates to subvert global design – it is therefore unlike, say, Christianity, neo-liberalism, or Marxism – and it is earnestly confronting and rejecting these or other purported universals acting as fundamentalisms (or 'totalitarian totalities') ultimately arrogating to themselves an entitlement to governance of the planet.[45]

35 Zweigert and Kötz (n 8) 14.
36 Mignolo (n 7) 148.
37 Harcourt (n 33) 46.
38 ibid 505.
39 ibid 184.
40 cf ibid 220: '[T]he claims to truth always come back.'
41 See Mignolo (n 7) 115.
42 ibid 225.
43 ibid 231.
44 ibid 224.
45 ibid 147. To be sure, the argument from universalism can prove less strident, perhaps even seemingly reasonable. However, it is doomed to fail nonetheless. Consider the following 'anecdata'. On 28 May 2018, an interlocutor in São Paulo asked me if comparative law can address the problem of colour-blindness. I answered that it must be able to do so, that it simply cannot be the case that comparative law would be confined to topics

'[T]he mirage of universality of knowledge' notwithstanding,[46] then, '[e]very enunciation is local'.[47] While the argument for relativism – cultural, legal, or otherwise – is thus inescapable, because the facts as recorded by anthropologists regarding cultural diversity and enculturation compel one to conclude that relativism is intellectually irrefutable (such that 'right and wrong are not detached universals but are based on premises argued by actors grounded in institutions'),[48] there is no question of condoning an 'anything-goes' approach. Crucially, the relativist does not contend that all cultural or legal practices are equally valid, but rather asserts that no cultural or legal practice – not one's own, not anyone else's – is valid 'in any event' or 'come what may'. In sum, a relativist holds that every cultural or legal practice is apophantic. Such is the subversive or negative aspect of the relativist doctrine, which saves it from being re-framed as a universalist argument.[49] Indeed, critics cannot claim that relativism contradicts itself by entering an absolute proposition. After Theodor Adorno, the relativist claim is intrinsically subversive or negative rather than assertive, and no relativist enunciation can be other than relative to its enunciator's encultured ways, in any event. There is one more important reason why the relativism that I defend cannot be absolute, why it cannot put all worldly configurations on a level footing, certainly from the standpoint of the

along the lines of breach of contract, vicarious liability, and such like – which is, however, precisely how Zweigert and Kötz would have it. As the 'negotiation' continued, my interlocutor emphasized that the matter of colour-blindness is 'the same everywhere' – at least, this is what I heard him to be saying, this is the claim that I understood him to be making about what he seemed to regard as a necessary universal. Now, he was 'Black', and I was 'White'. I sensed that he had expertise, while I did not (I would later learn that he had conducted postgraduate work on colour-blindness at Harvard Law School). Still, no matter how sensible this presumption of universal identity might appear, I could not accept it. I replied that, in advance of empirical study, I must hold that colour-blindness could not be identical or mean something identical in France, Brazil, and the United States (I deliberately kept myself to national 'units', but I appreciate that colour-blindness is also unlikely to mean something identical in Nancy and Marseille, in Recife and Curitiba, in Stowe, Vermont, and Mobile, Alabama.) In short order, I found information suggesting that the late Brazilian sociologist Milton Santos agreed with me. Writing about his experience of having been a 'Black' person over four continents, Santos observed that in each location being 'Black' had meant differently: see M Santos, 'Ser negro no Brasil hoje' in *O país distorcido* (WC Ribeiro ed, Publifolha 2002) 157–61.

46 Mignolo (n 5) 3.

47 ibid 224.

48 ibid 220.

49 See eg BH Smith, *Belief and Resistance* (Harvard University Press 1997) 86–87. Such is Theodor Adorno's well-known position. See TW Adorno, *Negative Dialektik* (Suhrkamp 1966) 45–46.

comparatist-at-law: a model that would implement the juggernaut of imperialism or colonialism cannot deserve recognition or respect as if it were not so imperialist or colonialist.[50]

*

As I consider comparative law in its various institutional guises, I note, to borrow Walter Mignolo's felicitous form of words, that '[c]oloniality is not over, [that] it is all over'.[51] The challenge, of course, cannot be only the undoing of decoloniality. Rather, it must extend to the redoing of the field – the goal must be to pursue the *re-existence* of comparative law.[52] Just like '"taking hold" of the [colonizing] state was the fundamental task of *decolonization*',[53] comparatists-at-law must challenge the imposition of weasel terms like 'objectivity', 'truth', 'scientificity', or 'universality', with a view to 'decolonizing knowledge ... [so as] to liberate knowing and becoming what coloniality of knowledge ... prevents to know and become'; such is 'at this point the fundamental task of *decoloniality*'.[54] The idea is therefore to change the terms of the conversation in order to modify the contents of the conversation, that is, to delink the theory and practice of comparative law from the damaging narratives that have informed it through the insistent application of a positivist matrix of

50 Mignolo worries that cultural relativism should be 'blind to colonial[ism] and imperial[ism]', that it should 'mis[s] ... the power differentials': Mignolo (n 5) 223 and 226. While Mignolo's concern is legitimate, the ignorance he addresses is evitable.

51 Mignolo (n 7) 119. For an illustrative celebration of Europe's conquering and expansionist ways, of the export of 'civilization' to 'backward' territories, an encomium well embedded in the twenty-first century and thus offering substantial vindication of Mignolo's claim, see JC MacLennan, *Europa* (Pegasus 2018). For a reference to 'the old colonial reflex', see R Gildea, *Empires of the Mind* (Cambridge University Press 2019) 223. In this regard, one is minded to think of European museums exhibiting the spoils of wars waged against colonized peoples and rationalizing such displays as a great custodial and educational service to the planet. In effect, these museums are extending imperial violence into the present (while, of course, extracting economic gains from tourism in the process). To be sure, Europe is not the only imperial power warranting decolonial (and comparative) interest. For instance, consider KL Thornber, *Empire of Texts in Motion* (Harvard University Press 2009), where the author explores the dynamics between the Chinese, Korean, and Taiwanese literary worlds, on one hand, and Japan, on the other, with specific reference to the period between 1895 and 1945, that is, when the Japanese colonization of East Asia was in full pursuit. For a general treatment of the contemporary relevance of post-imperial legacies, see S Puri, *The Shadows of Empire* (Pegasus 2021).

52 See CE Walsh, 'Decoloniality in/as Praxis' in WD Mignolo and CE Walsh (eds), *On Decoloniality* (Duke University Press 2018) 120.

53 Mignolo (n 7) 136.

54 ibid.

power reeking of imperialism and colonialism.[55] Or, if you will, the idea is to foster decolonized interventions into foreign law that will provoke the decolonizing that must materialize in the name of the justice due to the other, not least for the sake of comparative law. Specifically, any strategy of recognition and respect will make an auspicious epistemic start if it acknowledges that it does not have objective access – and that it *cannot* have objective access – to anything like the truth about the other law or about the other-in-the-law, to the other law or to the other-in-the-law 'as it is'. To recognize and respect otherness does not mean (and *cannot* mean) to get otherness 'right', exactly – which is, in fact, precisely the assumption of supremacy that must be surpassed. Rather, I must accept that '[w]hat I am telling is not the truth, but an interpretation'.[56]

It follows that one must aim for a *just* interpretation, a reading of foreign law that wants to do justice to the other. I evoke the idea of aspiration advisedly, since if there will be interpretation, as there must be, there will necessarily be a failure to achieve *justice*, which can only figure as an ideal. Again, no encultured interpreter can tell an encultured foreign law objectively or truly, 'as it is'.[57] And every interpreter must acknowledge his inevitable interpretive input in the act of representation, better inscribed, then, as a *re-presentation*. Unavoidably affecting the foreign law that is his focus of study and decisively being shaped by it also, the critical theorist's reflexivity – the mental constructs he applies to his reading, the power dynamics he implements to shape the interpretive moment – resolutely prevent him from speaking in universal terms, hence Bernard Harcourt's exclamation: 'First, there are no universals.'[58] Crucially, thinking decolonially means thinking *differentially*, and it means acknowledging, accepting the *differential* character of one's thinking, whether vis-à-vis the foreign law – word will differ from world – or as regards other interpretations of foreignness.[59] Decoloniality is a contrarian plea both for enhanced 'thereness' (a more perceptive attunement to foreign law-as-culture) and for increased 'hereness' (a heightened discernment of the comparatist's implication as inventor of foreignness).

55 See ibid 144.

56 Harcourt (n 33) 28.

57 Eg: J Kramnick, 'Criticism and Truth' (2021) 47 Critical Inquiry 218, 234: 'The epistemic virtue of a given reading cannot be separated from its making of something that has never exactly existed before.'

58 Harcourt (n 33) 436.

59 For a survey on decolonial thinking and practice addressing more than forty artists or intellectuals and ranging over 120 pages or so, see H Copeland et al, 'A Questionnaire on Decolonization' (2020/174) October 3.

IX

The Same as the Different

Comparative law's predicament evinces itself in manifold ways, not least in the manner in which, in the large majority of law schools, it has not succeeded in casting itself as other than a suspect stratagem. The platitudinous condition of epistemic stasis that tends to inform the work of comparatists-at-law – think of the long-standing orthodox prioritization of equivalence or commonality animating the comparison of laws – cannot be foreign to that enduring, if deeply disappointing, state of affairs. For my part, I forcefully object not only to the illusoriness informing the epistemic orientation that postulates mimesis, but also to the consequential depreciation of difference across laws, a trivialization that appears on full display when Vicki Jackson releases a substantial book to make the case for '[c]omparability in the sense of *similarity*' in order, as I read her, to reassure a US constituency, notably its more conservative elements, that judicial references to foreign law are not to be feared. After all, or so seems to go her argument, foreign law is very much cognate with US law.[1] And I emphatically reject the orthodox implication that the equivalence or commonality that comparative law would be ascertaining should pertain to the objective production of true knowledge. Indeed, the claim from veridiction, to speak economically, hides the significance of the participative role that the comparatist necessarily plays from an epistemic standpoint as he frames and deploys his comparative endeavour and also obscures the impact of the theoretical premisses (and values) inevitably guiding the comparative work and just as inescapably qualifying whatever comparative conclusions are reached. Moreover, I refute the received view – a variation on the theme of the marginalization of differences across laws enjoying wide-ranging

[1] VC Jackson, *Constitutional Engagement in a Transnational Era* (Oxford University Press 2010) 178.

currency within comparative law – that the act of comparison operates dialectically, that it is condemned to oscillate between the ascertainment of equivalences or commonalities, on one hand, and the detection of differences, on the other, which is to say that it can be expected to find differences between entities that appear alike even as it can be presumed to track likenesses between configurations that seem different.[2] Now, whether comparatists-at-law approach comparison as a process aiming at the veridictive elicitation of equivalence or commonality across laws or as consisting, at will, either in the equation or distinction of the *comparanda*, I contest the prevailing devaluation of difference. I advance two principal claims to support my demurrer.

First, I mobilize Leibniz's argument – 'Leibniz's Law' – for the inevitability of differential co-presence in order to account for the fact that in *the co-presence of more than one law, which means that there is not one law only anymore, there cannot be equivalence or commonality and there must be difference between these laws.*[3] In Leibniz's words (which he wrote in French, as it happens), 'by virtue of insensible variations, two individual things could not be perfectly similar, and . . . they must always differ'.[4] At the very least, this analytical principle stands for the proposition that the diverse is necessarily 'other than' (that distinct entities are never exact replicas of one another, that is, if there is A and B, A is at least

[2] Eg: P Craig, 'Comparative Administrative Law and Political Structure' (2017) 37 Oxford J Legal Stud 946, 946: 'Study of comparative administrative law reveals commonality and difference between the systems studied. This is axiomatic and self-evident.' Paul Craig's approach, including his unwarranted sense of obviousness, is typical, which is why I refer to this excerpt in a strictly exemplary capacity. Let me add, however, that all that appears 'self-evident' in Craig's statement, in my view, is his supercilious understanding of the practice of research into foreign law. In passing, I find Craig's evocation of revelation problematic. The assumption that difference across laws is to be revealed minimizes the fact that the comparatist plays an active role in the articulation, construction, and edification of the differend – so much so that any stated difference is, in a meaningful way, *the comparatist's difference*. If you will, no difference can unfold without interpretation. To return to Craig, it is not enough to claim that '[s]tudy of comparative administrative law reveals . . . difference between the systems studied'; in effect, the comparative inquiry fashions difference, it *invents* it.

[3] I draw on J Derrida, *Memoires for Paul de Man* (2nd English edn, C Lindsay tr, Columbia University Press 1989) 15. The English translation was released before the French text and is more specific, hence this citation.

[4] GW Leibniz, *Nouveaux essais sur l'entendement* in *Die philosophischen Schriften von Gottfried Wilhelm Leibniz*, vol 5 (CI Gerhardt ed, Olms 1965 [1764†]) 49. This text was written in 1704. Leibniz expresses the idea in some of his other work, too. Eg: GW Leibniz, *Discours de métaphysique* in *Die philosophischen Schriften von Gottfried Wilhelm Leibniz*, vol 4 (CI Gerhardt ed, Olms 1965 [1686]) s 9, 433: '[I]t is not true that two substances resemble each other entirely.'

minimally something that exists as not-B). Alfred North Whitehead famously extended Leibniz's proposition to contend that '[n]o two occasions can have identical actual worlds' – his claim being that no matter how faithfully situation Y purports to mimic situation X, the fact is that when Y comes along, X has already taken place, which entails that event Y features as one of its constitutive elements the pastness of event X and therefore, if on that ground alone, differs from event X.[5] Both Leibniz and Whitehead are showing that, structurally, two laws thus differ and must differ from one another. Laws are separated by a differend, which is *what there is*, which is *what is the case*: 'In the beginning, difference, there is what happens, there is what has already taken place, *there*.'[6] This differend is embedded in the very factical 'there-isness' of the laws-in-co-presence.[7] As such, this differend is 'irreducible'.[8] And it remains irreducible no matter how orthodox comparatists-at-law yearn after its effacement.

Secondly, I maintain that samenesses or similarities, similitudes or semblances, resemblances or likenesses – equivalences or commonalities of all hues – *all* effectively pertain to the realm of difference, which is *all there is*, there, across laws. (In case it should be felt that a Latin formulation is needed at this juncture so as to inject suitable momentousness into my statement, let me solemnly assert, *omne simile est dissimile*.) In this crucial sense, I hold that a sound theory of comparison must interrupt any and all age-old routinized or ritualized dialectical claims: it must *negate* them. In other terms, and contrary to what so many comparatists reflexively contend, the comparison of laws is neither about similarities and differences nor about similarities or differences according to the whim of any given comparatist. In the absence of equivalences or commonalities across laws (cf Leibniz's Law supra), *there is and there can only be difference*. No matter how typical the statement, it is therefore erroneous to hold that '[a]ll comparative work involves the exploration of similarities and differences' – unless, of course, one means to say that one is writing about the exploration of small differences and of larger differences (which appears implausible).[9] Such, then, is precisely the kind

[5] AN Whitehead, *Process and Reality* (Free Press 1978 [1929]) 210.

[6] J Derrida, 'Deux mots pour Joyce' in *Ulysse gramophone* (Galilée 1987) 44.

[7] I borrow the word 'differend' from the English translation of J-F Lyotard, *The Differend* (G Van Den Abbeele tr, University of Minnesota Press 1988 [1984]).

[8] J Derrida, *Limited Inc* (E Weber ed, Galilée 1990) 253.

[9] D Nelken, 'Comparing Legal Cultures' in A Sarat (ed), *The Blackwell Companion to Law and Society* (Blackwell 2008) 119.

of basic fallacy prompting the urgent requirement for comparison-at-law to transform itself into *negative* comparison – and comparative law to change itself into *negative comparative law*: one must say no to any assumption that there is anything other than difference across laws. In particular, one must emphatically say no to the '*præsumptio similitudinis*',[10] the expression within comparative law of a nefarious delusion that '[t]here [is] nothing distinctively German, French or American about [German, French, or American judicial] decisions',[11] that 'the problem of whether a boy is liable for injuring a playfellow or a seller is liable for defects in his merchandise is analysed in much the same way in Hamburg, Montpellier, Manchester, and Tucson, or for that matter in New Delhi, Tel Aviv, Tokyo, and Jakarta',[12] or that 'Visigothic Spain, parts of post-mediaeval Germany and nineteenth century California could accept for a variety of reasons what is basically the same régime of matrimonial property',[13] all enunciations manifesting a 'tendency, primary, precipitous, to reduce everything to the similar and the homogeneous',[14] a propensity to settle for rough-and-ready conclusions ('much the same', 'basically the same') unbecoming to creditable scholarship, a penchant to establish a self-serving system of Rationality or Reasonableness that would be master of its own epistemic conditions in the ideological service of oneness-in-the-law.[15] Notwithstanding how

[10] K Zweigert and H Kötz, *Einführung in die Rechtsvergleichung* (3rd edn, Mohr Siebeck 1996) 39. Following upon Zweigert and Kötz, Uwe Kischel is keen to preserve the '*præsumptio similitudinis*' as a 'working hypothesis': U Kischel, *Rechtsvergleichung* (Beck 2015) 181.

[11] J Gordley, 'Comparative Legal Research: Its Function in the Development of Harmonized Law' (1995) 43 Am J Comp L 555, 563.

[12] J Gordley, *The Philosophical Origins of Modern Contract Doctrine* (Oxford University Press 1991) 1.

[13] A Watson, *Society and Legal Change* (2nd edn, Temple University Press 2001) 110.

[14] F Jullien, *Si près, tout autre* (Grasset 2018) 12. François Jullien is a leading sinologist whose comparative observations I find helpfully discerning. cf J Vining, *The Authoritative and the Authoritarian* (University of Chicago Press 1986) 65: '[T]he comparati[st] presumes similarities between different jurisdictions in the very act of searching for them.'

[15] The abiding ideological ambition is to achieve a unified law of civil procedure, a unified tort law, a unified administrative law, or – why not? – a unified planetary law. The express articulation of such ideas in Unidroit's *Principles of International Commercial Contracts*, an ostensibly comparative endeavour, is exemplary: 'The objective of the Unidroit Principles is to establish a balanced set of rules designed for use ... *irrespective* of the legal traditions and the economic and political conditions of the countries in which they are to be applied': Governing Council of Unidroit, 'Introduction' in Unidroit, *Principles of International Commercial Contracts* (International Institute for the Unification of Private Law 1994) viii, repr in 4th edn (2016) xxix [my emphasis].

imaginative orthodox comparative law's fantasizing, how domineering its wishful thinking, difference across more than one law remains what is the case, and the comparatist is simply not at liberty to deny this epistemic condition – indeed, '[w]ithout acknowledging differences, comparison is partisanship'.[16] Consider Hans-Georg Gadamer: 'Each [being] that shows itself necessarily distinguishes itself from an other being that shows itself. It separates itself from the other [being].'[17] And even '[t]he same lets itself be said only if difference be thought'.[18] Yes.

*

In his 'Seven Strictures on Similarity', Nelson Goodman, the influential US philosopher, percipiently remarks that '[s]imilarity, ever ready to solve philosophical problems and overcome obstacles, is a pretender, an impostor, a quack'.[19] There is nothing inherent about any form of semblance whatsoever. Rather, all equivalences or commonalities exist only as attributes that are affixed to some entity or other by an interpreter. It follows that the quality of 'being like' is contingent, and it means that very much must depend upon an array of facts including the circumstances within which the interpreter finds himself. A reference to Michel Foucault may assist: 'There is no resemblance without signature. The world of the similar can only be a marked world.'[20] Foucault's discerning realization is that it does not inherently pertain to any entity (say, to any law) to be like another entity (say, another law). Far from constituting an essential characteristic, equivalence or commonality is always attributed by an analyst or commentator. Hence, Foucault's enunciation that there is 'no resemblance without signature', that every resemblance bears the signature of an analyst or commentator. This is the

16 S Moyn, 'The Trouble with Comparisons' *The New York Review* (19 May 2020) <www.nybooks.com/daily/2020/05/19/the-trouble-with-comparisons/> [on file]. For a critical exploration of the bias that Samuel Moyn fittingly denounces, see P Legrand, 'The Guile and the Guise: Apropos of Comparative Law as We Know It' (2021) 16 Asian J Comp L 155. In this text, I am effectively inviting comparatists to heed Montesquieu, *De l'esprit des lois* in *Œuvres complètes*, vol 2 (R Caillois ed, Gallimard 1951 [1748]) 229: '[N]ot to regard as similar cases really different; and not to miss the differences in those that appear similar.'

17 H-G Gadamer, 'Hermeneutik auf der Spur' in *Gesammelte Werke*, vol 10 (Mohr Siebeck 1995) 160.

18 M Heidegger, '…dichterisch wohnet der Mensch…' in *Vorträge und Aufsätze* (Klostermann 2000 [1951]) 197. Already, Montaigne had been maintaining that '[r]esemblance does not so much make, one, as difference makes, another': Montaigne, *Les Essais* (J Balsamo et al eds, Gallimard 2007 [1595†]) bk 3, ch 13, 1111.

19 N Goodman, 'Seven Strictures on Similarity' in *Problems and Projects* (Hackett 1972) 437.

20 M Foucault, *Les Mots et les choses* (Gallimard 1966) 41.

sense in which Foucault affirms that 'the world of the similar can only be a marked world', that every resemblance carries the mark of an analyst or commentator. Thus, Goodman: '[S]uppose we have three glasses, the first two filled with colorless liquid, the third with a bright red liquid. I might be likely to say the first two are more like each other than either is like the third. But it happens that the first glass is filled with water and the third with water colored by a drop of vegetable dye, while the second is filled with hydrochloric acid – and I am thirsty.'[21] In effect, '[c]ircumstances alter similarities'.[22] Jacques Derrida contributes an important deconstructive intuition on this issue. Seeking to probe the term 'resemblance' with a view to generating heightened understanding, he observes that '[t]he way in which resemblances constitute or stabilize themselves is relative, provisional, precarious'.[23] Indeed, if equivalence or commonality is the product of an analyst's or commentator's interpretive input, one can expect this interpretation to depend on its interpreter (it is therefore relative to him), to be liable to amendment (for example, it may well be modified as the interpreter changes his mind over time on the basis of further consideration arising from the gathering of new information), and to be fragile (not least in the manner in which its success hinges on its reception by the interpreter's readers). Given the severely limited epistemic value of equivalence or commonality, Goodman is keen to draw attention to semblance's 'insidious' character.[24] He concludes that upon close reflection all attempts at explanation by way of the idea of similarity are abysmally deficient. Equivalence or commonality, quite simply, 'profess[es] powers it does not possess'.[25] Unsurprisingly, Goodman chastises 'our addiction to similarity'.[26]

To maintain that entity A (say, US judicial review or impeachment) is the same as entity B (say, the Mexican *amparo* or Brazilian 'impeachment') or that it is similar to entity B or that it resembles entity B or that it is like entity B – in sum, that it features an equivalence or a commonality with entity B – must mean, on every occasion, that entity A effectively differs from entity B, that it is singular vis-à-vis entity B. Again, *this is what is the case.* Only if entity A were identical to entity B would it not distinguish itself from entity B. But the only way in which entity A could

[21] Goodman (n 19) 445.
[22] ibid.
[23] J Derrida, *Politique et amitié* (M Sprinker ed, Galilée 2011 [1993]) 112.
[24] Goodman (n 19) 437.
[25] ibid.
[26] ibid 438.

be identical to entity B would be for entity A to be entity B.[27] If entity A were entity B, the very idea of a comparative study featuring entities A and B would become nonsensical. I insist that this logical demonstration is decisive for comparative law and that it is not dismissable as sophistry. Again, consider Derrida: '[T]o compare[:] ... there must be a difference permitting it.'[28] To compare, there has to be more than one entity in co-presence. It follows that the assignment of a 'compare and contrast' essay is, in fact, the setting of 'compare and compare' work or, if you prefer, of a 'contrast and contrast' task. The fact of the matter is that if a law is said to be the same as another or similar to another, if it is regarded as equivalent or common to another, there must be more than one law being addressed, which means, in line with Leibniz's cardinal insight, that there has to be difference across these laws. In Goodman's words, '[t]he flaw here went unnoticed for a long time, simply for lack of logical scrutiny'.[29] For those who would welcome immediate reassurance, I hasten to add that the contention concerning the necessary differend between entities A and B, the claim that all endeavours at 'equivalentization' or 'commonalization' must ultimately stand as so many restatements of differentiation, does not prohibit connections or even generalizations across the comparative compass. I return to this argument presently, with the benefit of an illustration involving a US comparatist looking at French law.

Difference being what there is, there, across laws, comparatists can hardly find scholarly refuge in confutation or abjuration, unwitting or blindness. The only worthy intellectual strategy vis-à-vis the differend-at-law is to accept that, in principle at least, difference must make a difference – which means that comparatists have to take a serious normative interest in the singularity of foreign law. Against the backdrop of incontrovertible empirical findings that, whether post-colonial or neo-colonial or indeed ex-colonial, contemporary societies are of diasporic 'communities' and migrant groups, of exiles and refugees, and that the planet is generally and increasingly of cultural interfaces and interconnections, many of them legal, comparatists-at-law (not to mention other jurists), pinching their nose if they must, bracing themselves if need be, require forcefully to engage with Walter Benjamin's 'now of knowability', that is, to accept that the moment has come to awaken to

[27] '[N]o two things have all their properties in common': ibid 443. Goodman adds that similarity is thus 'an empty and hence useless relation': ibid.

[28] J Derrida, *La Vérité en peinture* (Flammarion 1978) 429 [emphasis omitted].

[29] Goodman (n 19) 442.

otherness-as-difference.[30] In this regard, I salute Mary Ann Glendon's chastisement of Justice Stephen Breyer's widely circulated claim that '[j]udges in different countries increasingly apply somewhat similar legal phrases to somewhat similar circumstances', an unsubstantiated argument that she appositely discards as 'casual' and 'disquieting', an unverified contention that she properly rebukes as not doing justice to the complexity of 'comparability'.[31] (Note how the equivocation of Breyer's 'somewhat similar', a formulation he uses twice, recalls that of Gordley's 'much the same' and Watson's 'basically the same'.) Benjamin's cryptic expression thus points to the tension between an actuality (the fact of difference) and what remains for the time being a virtuality (the recognition of difference). I read the words as soliciting an ability henceforth to know what there is, there, what exists now, differentially or singularly. To apply Benjamin's statement to a foreign law – a law that is out-of-the-land, of the home-land, an out-landish law, a law that is outlandish also in the sense of being extravagant (etymologically, a wandering outside limits) or outrageous (that is, an *ultra-jus* or *outra-jus*) – it holds that it wants that law becoming ascertainable on its own terms, now.[32] Far from petrifying comparatists into the speechlessness too readily associated with otherness's estrangement or uncanniness, the acknowledgement of a legal heterotopia existing in advance of any makeshift togetherness (and resisting it, too) must serve to impulse a felicitous epistemic motion away from the production, propagation, and analysis of foreign law-texts that would be of the duplicative sort – worse, of the autotelic and self-authenticating variety, of the kind that ultimately and unabashedly clamours, 'here is my only elsewhere' (recall Jackson's view of foreign law, for instance).[33] I argue that the time is long

[30] W Benjamin, *Das Passagen-Werk* in *Gesammelte Schriften*, vol 6(1) (R Tiedemann ed, Suhrkamp 1982 [1927–40]) 591–92 [Convolute N9(7)].

[31] MA Glendon, 'Comparative Law in the Age of Globalization' (2014) 52 Duquesne LR 1, 16. Glendon refers to S Breyer, 'Keynote Address' (2003) 97 Am Society Int'l L Proceedings 265, 266. Justice Breyer's imprisonment of singular modes of being-in-the-law into superficial patterns of standardization prompts him to say also that there are to be found 'cross-country results that resemble each other more and more' and refer to 'growing institutional and substantive similarities' across constitutional laws: ibid 267. Justice Breyer's constitutional simplism is far from being an isolated occurrence of reductionism. Eg: J Greene, 'Rights as Trumps?' (2018) 132 Harvard LR 28, 36 and 132, where the author writes that different countries would be facing 'similar problems' or 'similar social, political, and legal challenges'.

[32] See S Weber, *Benjamin's -abilities* (Harvard University Press 2008) 168.

[33] I draw on N Melas, *All the Difference in the World* (Stanford University Press 2007) 1–43. 'Heterotopia' is indebted to M Foucault, 'Des espaces autres' in *Dits et écrits*, vol 4 (D Defert and F Ewald eds, Gallimard 1994 [1984]) 752–62. The quotation in the body

overdue for otherness's difference or singularity to be made to matter within comparison-at-law. Yes.

*

Otherness – the otherness legitimately soliciting recognition and respect – also exists within selfhood, a claim inviting a further reconsideration on the part of the comparatist-at-law, who has been inclined to favour a binary approach whereby the self is here, at home, and the other is there, abroad. Counter-intuitively, perhaps, there is more to foreignness than what would neatly confine itself to the tither side of the frontier, for the foreign is also present within local law, that is, within legal configurations asserting themselves as straightforwardly local. Even as national laws largely retain their country-centric character (instances and patterns of legal deterritorialization notwithstanding), no such law consists exclusively in a mononational narrative. Not even poetry – poetry! – is ensconced within a strictly local paradigm. Against TS Eliot's declaration that, because 'a feeling or emotion expressed in a different language is not the same feeling or emotion', 'no art is more stubbornly national than poetry',[34] and pace WH Auden's converging statement to the effect that 'poetry is the most provincial of the arts',[35] Jahan Ramazani, relying upon such matrixes as dates, occupation, and nationality, convincingly establishes that poetry has not remained immune to foreign influence and that it very much stands in fact as a cosmopolitan endeavour (not least in the cases of Eliot and Auden, one a US writer from Missouri who worked in England for forty years or so, the other an English writer from Birmingham who operated in the United States for more than thirty years).[36] To return to comparative law (which I never really leave), it is the case, for instance, that from Brazil to the United States and from Germany to Australia, comparatists have been addressing and assessing judicial decisions pertaining to local constitutional adjudication that bring foreign law into play, that elect to ascribe a certain normative role to certain foreign legal sources. The ensuing enmeshment, say, between US constitutional law and foreign law on account of the US Supreme Court having expressly referred to the European Court of Human Rights means that 'here' is no longer fully separable from

text is from S Beckett, *The Unnamable* (S Connor ed, Faber & Faber 2010 [1958]) 121. The reference to Jackson is at supra 229.

34 TS Eliot, 'The Social Function of Poetry' (1945) in *On Poetry and Poets* (Farrar, Straus & Giroux 2009 [1957]) 8.

35 WH Auden, 'Writing' in *The Dyer's Hand* (Faber & Faber 2012 [1963]) 21.

36 See generally J Ramazani, *A Transnational Poetics* (University of Chicago Press 2009).

'there'.[37] But this assemblage – like every composition combining some 'hereness' with a dose of 'thereness' – finds itself thoroughly located *somewhere*. As regards the US Supreme Court's decisions, they clearly exist within US law and as US law despite the European input. The other (in-the-law) thus dwells within the self (in-the-law), otherness becomes an element of selfhood, foreign law partakes of US law: difference's *everywhereness* extends to the self itself.

*

Any comparative enterprise, since it must assume more than one term of comparison and also a comparatist, requires to be envisaged as an interruption of totalizing thought. The idea that, in the face of the legally diverse, a situated comparatist-at-law should (want to) achieve a holistic synthesis that would be governed by Reason quite simply stretches epistemic creditability. Comparison is a practice of desublimation or defocalization: think impressionism or cubism, dodecaphonism or ragtime music. Through its stress on the discontinuity and localization of knowledge, as opposed to any idea of transcendental unity (effectively an expression of the alienated proclivities of the human imagination), comparison acts as a kind of schizophrenic not-all. Comparative law is thus possessed of an inherent contestatory energy: whether vis-à-vis the transcendental or indeed the local, comparison intervenes as a break or transgression rather than a mere annotative elaboration. In fact, the more vehement totalizing thought makes itself, the more the act of comparison must herald its own discontinuous or disruptive rhetorical valence, that is, its epistemic value. Otherwise (or other-wise) said, the more the comparison of laws must commit to yielding information about the contingent and specific character of legal rules, about the singularity of assumptions and practices – about difference. In order to concretize my claim, I suggest the following example from my classroom experience.

When I teach comparative law in the United States, I begin by asking my students to apprise themselves of three French documents: the 'headscarf' statute, the 'burkini' photograph, and the 'handshake' decision.[38] Not unlike the way in which Foucault marvels at Jorge Luis Borges's Chinese encyclopaedia and roundly pronounces on 'the stark

[37] Eg: *Lawrence v Texas* (2003) 539 US 558.

[38] What I style the 'headscarf' statute, without making any claim to impartiality, refers to the 2004 legislative prohibition against ostensible religious attire in French public primary and secondary schools. For the reference to the law-text, see Statute no 2004–228 of 15 March 2004 enframing, in application of the principle of laicity, the wearing of signs or attire demonstrating a religious belonging in public primary and secondary schools, art 1

impossibility of thinking *that*',[39] my US students soon declare that the French ways make no sense to them, that they themselves cannot think like *that* – although, unlike Foucault considering Borges, they do not detect 'the exotic charm of another thought'.[40] Instead, they see

<www.legifrance.gouv.fr/loda/id/JORFTEXT000000417977> [on file]. Meanwhile, the 'burkini' photograph points to a picture taken on 23 August 2016 and widely circulated on the Internet (eg: <www.independent.co.uk/news/world/europe/burkini-ban-swimwear-france-armed-police-nice-hijab-muslim-a7209091.html> [on file]). Pursuant to a 5 August 2016 municipal ordinance ('*arrêté*') taken by the mayor of Villeneuve-Loubet, near Nice, with a view to regulating swimwear on the beach by reference to the 'principle of laicity' ('*principe de laïcité*'), the image shows three male police officers ordering a woman to remove what they regard as excess clothing on the ground that her garments would carry a religious 'connotation' ('*connotation*'), thus contravening the terms of the law-text. For a thorough and thoughtful critique of the 'burkini' legal initiative, see K Brayson, 'Of Bodies and Burkinis: Institutional Islamophobia, Islamic Dress, and the Colonial Condition' (2019) 46 J L & Society 55. For its part, the 'handshake' decision concerns an 11 April 2018 judgment ('*arrêt*') by the *Conseil d'Etat*, the highest French administrative tribunal, confirming the government's withholding of French citizenship to a woman, because she refused to shake hands with two male officials, on account of her faith, during the public ceremony that the local authorities had elected to hold in order to mark the solemnity of the occasion, without there being any legal requirement for such an event to take place. See <www.legifrance.gouv.fr/affichJuriAdmin.do?oldAction=rechJuriAdmin&idTexte=CETATEXT000036791217&fastReqId=729319897&fastPos=1> [on file].

39 In Foucault (n 20) 7, the French philosopher begins thus: 'This book has its place of birth in a text from Borges. . . . This text quotes "a certain Chinese encyclopaedia" where it is written that "animals divide into: a) belonging to the Emperor, b) embalmed, c) tamed, d) suckling pigs, e) sirens, f) fabulous, g) stray dogs, h) included in the present classification, i) that agitate themselves like madmen, j) innumerable, k) drawn with a very fine camel-hair brush, l) et cetera, m) that have just broken the jug, n) that from afar seem flies". In the wonderment of this taxonomy, that which one reaches in one leap, that which, owing to the parable, is indicated to us as the exotic charm of another thought, is the limitation of ours: the stark impossibility of thinking *that*.' Borges originally published 'El idioma analítico de John Wilkins', the text that is drawing Foucault's attention, in 1952. It was later collected in JL Borges, *Otras inquisiciones* (2nd edn, Alianza Editorial 1997 [1974]) 154–61 [hereinafter *Inquisiciones*]. Wilkins (1614–72) was an Anglican clergyman and philosopher who attempted to frame a universal language. In his essay, Borges claims that Wilkins's classification, which appeared in print in 1668, reminds him of an ordering that Franz Kuhn (1812–81), a philologist and comparatist, allegedly attributed to a Chinese encyclopaedia that he styled, in Borges's words, the '*Emporio celestial de conocimientos benévolos*' ('The Celestial Emporium of Benevolent Knowledge'). The list that Borges unfolds might therefore be Kuhn's. However, in the absence of any evidence that Kuhn ever translated a Chinese encyclopaedia, the taxonomy is properly regarded as pertaining to Borges's imagination. The short story can be read as illustrating the singular enculturation of any attempt at the organization of information. For the list of Borges's encyclopaedic entries in Spanish, see Borges, *Inquisiciones*, 158.

40 Foucault (n 20) 7.

a doctrinaire and oppressive epistemological regime – frankly, colonial arrangements.

Now, what is the meaning of Foucault's 'that' as he writes of 'the stark impossibility of thinking *that*' in the passage I quote? It is fair to say that Foucault wants to inscribe a (tacit) contrast between 'that' and 'this', an opposition revolving around the idea of proximity. In a nutshell, 'this' is closer than 'that'. To say that I think like this, that I can think like this, refers to what is close to me, what is familiar, not necessarily intimate, but proximate. Contrariwise, the word 'that' implies a distance. Foucault's 'stark impossibility of thinking *that*' thus purports to indicate a distantiation, which the italics are presumably meant to accentuate (if you will, on account of the italics the 'that' would recede even further into the distance). The thought striking Foucault as being so strange is happening somewhere else. One could summarize the antithesis between 'this' and 'that' in terms of 'here' and 'there', that is, 'here' and 'elsewhere' (again, an italicized 'elsewhere' would be notionally located even further away).

I want to argue that there has been on the part of orthodox comparatists-at-law, upon being faced with a 'that' appearing to them as unfathomable or implausible, a spontaneous tendency to reframe it in more familiar language with a view to the other world making sense to them, somehow. Remember Gordley holding that the law in Jakarta (*that* law) is like the law in Tucson (like *this* law) or Watson maintaining that the law in Spain (*that* law) is like the law in California (like *this* law).[41] Within comparative law, 'that' has been destined to become 'this' (which, as it happens, is precisely the imperial or colonial motion). For instance, orthodox comparatists-at-law have been unwilling to content themselves with the singularity of otherness, a situation that would effectively prove epistemically unbearable to them. Rather, they have reflexively tried to tame otherness interpretively. To return to the headscarf, the 'burkini', and the handshake, a US comparatist-at-law can readily be expected to frame these situations on US terms, that is, by reference to US law: the three French examples I mention will therefore rapidly be re-signified as illustrations of affronts to freedom of religion or freedom of speech, as instances of insensitivity, intolerance, or, possibly, xenophobia. Effectively, the 'that' will thus find itself being reframed as a 'this'. Thus, Jackson: 'Many of our [US] constitutional rights and values – liberty, equal protection of the law, due process, freedom of expression – reflect not only specific decisions made in the United States, but also widely

[41] Supra 232.

shared commitments of many Western democracies.' In other words, the 'constitutional rights and values' in 'many Western democracies' (*that*) are in effect US 'constitutional rights and values' (*this*). That is this, and (epistemic) familiarity holds.[42]

To return to my three French illustrations, for the US comparatist-at-law – say, my US student – the foreign way facing him, that way of thinking, that thought to which it is initially impossible for him to ascribe any (meaningful) local meaning because it exists 'out there', stands as a challenge, a provocation, perhaps. Of course, his interpretive remit is ultimately to make sense of it. His spontaneous epistemic motion, so to speak, is therefore to appropriate or assimilate foreignness in order to tame its strangeness; it is instinctively to move the 'that' to a 'this'. What appears baffling can be recast in home language, in words that have meaning within the home culture (such as denial of freedom of religion or speech, intolerance, xenophobia, and so forth).[43]

However, as 'that' finds itself being restated in terms of 'this', it must be seen that the US comparatist's thought is effectively asserting itself imperially or colonially. It is, literally, taking hold of 'that', grasping it, seizing it, in order to re-enact it as 'this'. In the process, the comparatist's interpretation is erasing the 'thatness' of the 'that', it is eliding the singularity of the 'that' – which is not an accidental move at all, which is what is wanted. The comparatist deliberately engages in a form of epistemic violence towards the 'that' – an epistemicide, in fact. The 'handshake' case, to track this example, will thus no longer be a matter involving an individual's refusal to integrate into French republican values for reasons ranging from shallow caprice to dangerous subversion (which is the French understanding of the decision), but it will be re-signified as an encroachment on freedom of religion or speech. In the process, the US comparatist-at-law will have forced the other into his normative box so that he can (meaningfully) make sense of otherness on his terms, so that otherness can (meaningfully) make sense *to him*. All along, the US comparatist-at-law is erecting this/his analytic grid, this/his legal narrative, as the canonized, unquestioned, primordial taxon.

No matter how seemingly reasonable and habitual, how *established* within comparative law, such strategizing is highly objectionable, since it ultimately vindicates distortion of thought and undue ethnocentricity or,

42 V Jackson, 'Yes Please, I'd Love to Talk with You' *Legal Affairs* (July/August 2004) 45.

43 cf J Derrida, *Le Calcul des langues* (G Bennington and K Chenoweth eds, Editions du Seuil 2020 [c 1973]) 35: 'The ultimate cunning . . . to divert or skirt difference is the dialectical analogy that binds in resemblance.'

more specifically, invidious juricentricity. One is no longer accounting for the 'that' that there is, there, but for a 'that' that has effectively been pressured, interpretively, to fit into 'thisness' – in my example, to conform to the US comparatist-at-law's 'this' (think of an ipsative motion). Still marshalling my illustration, for the US interpreter of French law what the French are doing does not, in the end, pertain to 'integration into republican values'. From his standpoint, this is not what is happening, epistemically speaking. Rather, the three enunciations I mention (the statute, the photograph, and the judgment) are recast as attacks on fundamental rights. But 'the Other, if it is to be Other, cannot let itself be restricted to the Other *of* the Same', that is, 'the Other [can] never [be] merely the Other of my-Self'.[44] I argue that the US interpreter, if he is going to do justice to the differend across laws, to the singularity of the other law that is French law – and comparative law must emphatically be about interpretive justice – therefore requires to resist the impetuous motion from 'that' to 'this'. Intervening as comparatist-at-law, he must assert himself as *otherist* and thus withstand the imperial or colonial streak in his thought, that is, the inflexion in his interpretation that would readily seek to 'master' the other, that would fall for the classificatory impulse leading him to 'frame' the other into this category or subsume it under this label. The US comparatist-at-law must resist seeing French law through an epistemic order (conveniently) delivering it to him *on his terms*.

The empirical fact of the matter is that French legal culture and US legal culture are singular law-worlds, and the epistemic fact of the matter is that what there is between the two is the differend.[45] Think of French legal culture and US legal culture as epistemic 'islands' vis-à-vis one another.[46] It cannot be just, then, for the US interpreter to be content to 'filter' French legal thought through his own epistemic ways so that

[44] R Gasché, *Deconstruction, Its Force, Its Violence* (SUNY Press 2016) xv.

[45] cf Letter from RM Rilke to C Rilke in *Rilke Briefe*, vol 1 (Rilke-Archiv ed, Insel 1950 [2 September 1902]) 41: 'And there stand those stupid languages, helpless as two bridges that go over the same river side by side but are separated from each other by an abyss. It is a mere bagatelle, an accident, and yet it separates. . .' Rilke was writing about German and French.

[46] I refer to J Derrida, *La Bête et le souverain*, vol 2 (M Lisse et al eds, Galilée, 2010 [2002]) 31: '[B]etween my world and every other world, there is at the outset the space and the time of an infinite difference, of an interruption incommensurable with all the attempts at passage, at bridge, at isthmus, at communication, at translation, at trope, and at transfer that the desire for world or the want of world . . . will attempt to pose, to impose, to propose, to stabilize. There is no world, there are only islands.'

after the intellectual journey from Paris to Chicago, so to speak, upon arrival, there is effectively a taming of otherness taking place with a view to ensuring that otherness is constricted, that there is effectively not too much of it, that there is no surfeit of it. It cannot be just that the only otherness being allowed to complete the epistemic crossing would be the otherness that fits the interpreting culture's own understanding of its own world or of its own law-world. The other law simply cannot find itself being kept in epistemic check in this way. Quaere: how much of such epistemic tactics – this enforced 'equivalentization' or 'commonalization' – would have to do with the desire to protect the epistemic stability of the 'importing' model, to avoid anything that would prove too menacing or disturbing *to it*? To what extent are US interpreters of French law trying to protect US values? (Another, arguably less agreeable question, would be to ask to what extent are comparatists-at-law seeking to protect themselves – say, from making the indisciplined effort that ascription of meaningful meaning to thatness must demand?)

I claim, rigorously and vigorously, that the US comparatist-at-law must earnestly strive to do precisely the opposite of the tactics that the imperial or colonial paradigm invites. Quite apart from having to acknowledge that otherness-in-the-law will ultimately resist his understanding, that is, from having to accept, in advance of any actual comparison, his failure to comprehend otherness on account of the basic epistemic fact that the self cannot be the other, the comparatist-at-law must therefore proceed in reverse. (To be sure, the failure I mention cannot be total, since the other, not coming from outer space, cannot be *absolutely* other.) Even as the 'that' remains unavailable to him as fully fledged epistemic possibility – because, as a US interpreter who cannot jettison the complete range of the predispositions into which he has been encultured (these having been in-corporated or em-bodied and now being a constitutive part of his identity), he can never get to think the French way – he must attempt to bring the 'this' towards the 'that'. The idea must be to make sense of French thought by moving as closely as possible to the way in which the French themselves actually think – although the US interpreter appreciates that he cannot make thoroughgoing sense of French legal thought given that French legal thought ultimately exceeds what it is possible for him to think within 'his' culture. (Again, this failure fails to disqualify the comparative enterprise and confers critical surplus interpretive value to it.[47]) If you will, instead of

[47] Supra 81–82.

seeking to make the heterogeneous homogeneous to his world, my US law student must strive to make sense of the other's heterogeneity on its own terms – and to do so by reference to the principle of charitable interpretation, too, that is, by assuming the other to be making sense. 'That' thought, no matter how ultimately impossible for him, must now become inscribed by him as a possibility. Otherwise said, the impossible must become possible (if as impossibility) – pace Kant, who held that there is no justification in saying that one ought to do what one cannot do (the Kantian assumption being that 'ought' implies 'can'). Thus, the US comparatist-at-law must, as he purports to convey otherness-in-the-law in 'his' language, as he seeks to bring the foreign into narrative existence, let it continue to occupy a place that is epistemically different and indeed incommensurable vis-à-vis the one that he himself holds.[48]

This approach must assume a certain un-selfing of the self – which, even though it can only be feasible within limits,[49] is not in the least an insignificant expectation or banal achievement. Rather than arrange the other-in-the-law in line with the self's enculturation, the comparatist-at-law must attempt a measure of de-enculturation with a view to seeking to meet the other where he himself is dwelling, away from the self's epistemic comfort zone. To put the matter differently still, the comparatist-at-law must actively engage in a process of recognition of difference, of respect for it, of valorization of it, too – which effectively supposes a form of subordination of the self to the other (a way to countermand the habitual power dynamics). So as to prioritize the other over the self – again, not in the least a trivial intellectual commitment – the comparatist requires to step out of his law-world towards the other's, to prepare himself to intervene on behalf of the other, *whom he cannot count wrong.*[50]

As a matter of the justice owed to the otherness that the comparatist-at-law has now undertaken to disclose and discuss, on account of the indebtedness thereby arising vis-à-vis the other, the re-presentor (the one who is presenting the other anew, in 'his' language) must go *out of his way* so as to enter the discomfort zone. Moreover, he must take the other's

[48] I draw on E Hayward and C Gossett, 'Impossibility of That' (2017) 22 Angelaki 15.

[49] Eg: M Jackson, *The Other Shore* (University of California Press 2013) 5: 'It is not possible, of course, to simply walk out on yourself.'

[50] Eg: RA Shweder, '"What About Female Genital Mutilation?" and Why Understanding Culture Matters in the First Place' in RA Shweder et al (eds), *Engaging Cultural Differences* (Sage 2002) 216–51.

side and reveal the other benevolently (although I accept that the divulgence of the other's conception of governmentality-in-the-law, not to mention the elucidation of the underlying epistemic mesh, may prompt the comparatist to uncover and assert structures that disturb the other's self-understanding – in fact, a mark of the comparative advantage, of the autonomy that critical distance allows).[51] Always, though, '[he] must try to write in such a way that the language of the other does not suffer from [his]'.[52] It bears repeating that all along the comparatist-at-law can never gain access to foreignness 'from within' – to the foreign's foreignness – and that he should not even invest himself in trying to do so.[53] The comparatist's ambition must be, through a thinking-for-the-other, to achieve a '[c]oming-into-the-nearness of distance'.[54] Yet, there is no point in the self trying to become the other, an approach profoundly unbecoming to the comparative motion in any event, which demands the preservation of at least minimal critical space (the metaphor of immersion therefore proving so misleading). At best, the comparatist's foreign law will be a foreignness (or an otherness) that is formed at the epistemic interface between the comparative mind's application of power and the law-in-location that is its focus. The comparatist's foreign law can only be a *transactional* figure.

*

As regards the epistemic dynamics I defend, I find Emmanuel Levinas's theorization helpful. According to Levinas, as long as the perspective on the interaction between the self and the other remains ontological only ('I am I, and you are you'), the self will be unable fully to avoid an instrumentalization of otherness. This is why it is important to 'overthro[w] . . . the philosophical rank of ontology',[55] why it is necessary to accept that ethics exists before ontology, to be understood as something

[51] A good illustration of such a counter-intervention is the tracing of the German law of privacy to fascism. See JQ Whitman, 'The Two Western Cultures of Privacy: Dignity Versus Liberty' (2004) 113 Yale LJ 1151; JQ Whitman, 'On Nazi "Honour" and the New European "Dignity"' in C Joerges and NS Ghaleigh (eds), *Darker Legacies of Law in Europe* (Hart 2003) 243–66; JQ Whitman, 'Enforcing Civility and Respect: Three Societies' (2000) 109 Yale LJ 1279. Talal Asad calls Whitman's claim 'startling': T Asad, *Secular Translations* (Columbia University Press 2018) 33.

[52] J Derrida, *Points de suspension* (E Weber ed, Galilée 1992) 374.

[53] cf J Derrida, 'Hospitality, Justice and Responsibility: A Dialogue with Jacques Derrida' in R Kearney and M Dooley (eds), *Questioning Ethics* (Routledge 1999) 71: '[W]e never have any access to the other *as such*. That is why he/she is *the* other.' The words are Derrida's.

[54] M Heidegger, *Gelassenheit* (Neske 1959) 43.

[55] E Levinas, *Dieu, la mort et le temps* (J Rolland ed, Grasset 1993 [1976]) 11.

other than being, as something whose 'being' is 'otherwise than being', more fundamental than being, a pre-ontological privilege that lies beyond simple interpretation (which is fated to be always-already inadequate to the *interpretandum*, because it is differently situated). A 'structure . . . on which lean all others',[56] ethics considered primordially allows one to maintain, for example, that the self cannot simply 'be' a self. Instead, the self becomes a self through an egress out of selfness, that is, by way of a connection with the other: '[I am] *with respect* to all that is only because I am *out of respect* for all that is.'[57] Without the other, being does not have meaning as being. But the other is the foreign, which is not therefore '*under category*': the other must not be classified by the self in any of the self's categories.[58] Indeed, the other surpasses the idea that the self may have of him: there is 'excession'.[59] In effect, '[h]e is he *to whom* I speak'.[60]

Ethics does not express itself ontologically in the said (in the already-known, in what is), but rather 'in a saying that, in connection to being, is the exception'.[61] Because it is there, 'out of any characterization . . . for the ontological order',[62] which implies that the self cannot meet it through representation, the other calls on the self to unsay the said or enunciate a said otherwise. Short of the self eliminating the other, erasing the other's opposition to him (which is, in fact, another violent way of attesting to the otherness of the other),[63] the other presents himself in front of the self as a point of exteriority not fully reducible to the self, just like otherness is not transmutable as equivalence or commonality through the mediation of the self: 'The connection with [a]nother does not annul the separation.'[64] The other does not resist the self through force: he resists the self by being the other.[65] Therefore, the other sets

[56] E Levinas, *Totalité et infini* (Livre de Poche 2001 [1971]) 77.

[57] E Levinas, *Autrement qu'être ou au-delà de l'essence* (Livre de Poche 2001 [1974]) 188.

[58] Levinas (n 56) 65.

[59] See ibid 43. The other is an 'excession': E Levinas, *Entre nous* (Grasset 1991) 105.

[60] Levinas (n 56) 65 [my emphasis].

[61] Levinas (n 57) 18.

[62] ibid 32.

[63] The limitation on this strategy results from the fact that one can only efface what has first emerged. See J Derrida, *Adieu* (Galilée 1997) 160.

[64] Levinas (n 56) 281.

[65] cf A Machado, 'Juan de Mairena – Sentencias, donaires, apuntes y recuerdos de un profesor apócrifo' in *Poesía y prosa*, vol 4 (O Macrì ed, Espasa-Calpe 1989 [1936–39]) II, 1917: '*From the one to the other* . . . . All the labour of human reason tends to the elimination of the second term. *The other does not exist*: such is the rational faith, the incurable belief of human reason. Identity = reality, as if, in the end, everything has to be, absolutely and necessarily, *one and the same*. But *the other* does not allow [itself] to [be]

a radical existential demand, the power of which comes precisely from the fact that he is entitled to ask for justice and from the further fact that the imprecision of any such demand generates anxiety in the self, who is overwhelmed by the feeling that *he could do more, interpretively*.[66] The other thus compels the self to recognize the inevitability of otherness and to circumscribe the hold of the totalizing ontological form, to interrupt the language of ontology, to discontinue the said. The other constrains the self to a '[l]etting-be of the other in his existence'.[67] In the presence of the other, who comes to disturb solipsism, the self must mark a self-limit.

Under epistemic pressure, the self awakens from his 'dogmatic slumber'.[68] Anxiously, he realizes that he '[will] never be finished with the other'.[69] The late George Steiner thus refers to 'a fathomless depth of differentiation, of non-identity'.[70] But, because he is in the vicinity of the other, in a position to exercise a power over the other, for instance, by attributing a meaning to the other, the self reveals otherness's dependency, which through the other's moral demand understood by the self as a call, purports to generate other-oriented attention from the self to the other, a feeling of responsibility of the self for the other even. The self thus finds himself always-already *indebted* to the other.[71] It is a responsibility that does not depend on the kind of other there is or on the other's merits, the existence of which the other does not have to prove. Rather, it is a responsibility that is unconditional and always-already inscribed in the primordial connection with the other: 'The responsibility for the other cannot have begun in my engagement, in my decision. The unlimited responsibility in which I find myself comes short of my liberty, from an "anterior-to-any-memory" . . . , by excellence from the non-original . . . . The responsibility for another is the place where stands the no-place of subjectivity.'[72] One may object that there is nothing behind being, but

eliminate[d]: it subsists, it persists; it is the hard bone to crack on which reason leaves its teeth. [There is] what might be called the incurable *otherness* that the *one* endures.'

66 See G Steiner, *Errata* (Weidenfeld & Nicolson 1997) 1–5.

67 J Derrida, *L'Ecriture et la différence* (Editions du Seuil 1967) 202.

68 Levinas (n 56) 103.

69 Levinas (n 55) 184.

70 Steiner (n 66) 5.

71 See Z Bauman, *Postmodern Ethics* (Blackwell 1993) 74–81 and 85–92.

72 Levinas (n 55) 24. cf D Attridge, *The Singularity of Literature* (Routledge 2004) 127: 'We cannot deduce the obligation to the other from the existing world; the existing world – including the means by which any deductions could be made about ethics or responsibility – is premised upon an obligation to the other. Ethics, then, is the fundamental relation not just between subjects but also between the subject and its multiple others – a relation

this argument is, precisely, ontological, and it suggests that everything exhausts itself in ontology. Ethics, however, exists before being. As a non-gnoseological event, it is 'otherwise than being', it is even in advance of the a priori.[73] It is therefore to this engagement *for* the other – to a presence as an observing participant rather than as a participating observer, as an upstanding witness (although, aporetically, always-already 'idiomatic'[74]) of the authenticity of the worldly other, out of a preoccupation for justice towards otherness – that a phenomenology of the tacit solicits the comparatist-at-law to ascertain the other as other rather than seize hold of the other as has long been orthodox comparative law's strategy.[75]

The empirical fact of the differentiation of laws provides comparative law with its vital epistemic warrant while the configuration of pluralism as an enabling condition of thought supplies comparatists with a protocol of deterritorialized action emancipating them from local epistemic ways and foregrounding an interpellative ethics upon which all structures organizing the dynamics between self-in-the-law and other-in-the-law must be made to rest. Comparative analysis therefore manifests itself as a powerful political act: not only does it discern otherness, but it inscribes it to the point where what the comparatist writes constitutes the other's legal identity, at least beyond the territory where the other dwells (an identity that, therefore, can easily operate as a betrayal of otherness). This further fact reinforces the call for the voice of the other-in-the-law to be allowed to be heard. Because the crossing of boundaries also means the violation of boundaries, it is important to accredit the discourse of the other by permitting the other-in-the-law to be who he is in the law, in his law, on his law-terms. As a matter of the justice that is owed the other, because of this indebtedness, a fortiori when one arrogates to oneself the entitlement to tell the other's foreignness, the comparatist-at-law must engage with validity-claims made and accepted

that is not a relation and that cannot be named, for it is logically prior to relations and names, prior in fact to logic.'

73 See Bauman (n 71) 74–81.

74 J Derrida, *Le Monolinguisme de l'autre* (Galilée 1996) 116.

75 It is an objectionable feature of Gadamer's philosophical hermeneutics that it should expressly correlate understanding primarily with the understanding of oneself in the other and only secondarily with the understanding of the other *tout court*. See eg H-G Gadamer, 'Vom Zirkel des Verstehens' in *Gesammelte Werke*, vol 2 (Mohr Siebeck 1986 [1959]) 75. cf R Barthes, *Fragments d'un discours amoureux* in *Œuvres complètes*, vol 5 (2nd edn, E Marty ed, Editions du Seuil 2002 [1977]) 285: '[H]enceforth, of the other, not to want to seize anything.'

elsewhere on the basis of symbolic premisses guiding statements and actions, there, and taken as being either meaningful or apt, there. Specifically, throughout his inquiry, in recognition of the semiotically complex cultural material underwriting denotational textualization, the comparatist must address the matter of linguistic practices of singularization, that is, he requires to acknowledge linguistic otherness.

In the process, comparative law's traditional interest in posited law is shown to be of very limited epistemic significance. Taking the view that sense cannot securely be held to reside exclusively within the posited law, the comparison of laws wishes to critique posited-law-as-closed-normative-system. It aims to unwork 'the law' by determinedly unravelling it. Its task is thus interventionist. By challenging, by saying no to the objectification of foreign law that positivism assumes – the other's law would be sitting 'there', inertly, docilely awaiting harvesting by its comparatist – comparative law emphasizes an experience of disjunction. It seeks to aid the non-identical, which finds itself repressed by positivism's compulsion to emphasize identity (what is 'the' law, 'the' law 'as it is'?) and identification (the law in Jakarta is the law in Tucson, and the law in Spain is the law in California).[76] As it presses against the epistemic barrier that positivism has built, comparative law purports to supplant the impulsivity of artificial unity with the authenticity of multiplicity. It can therefore liberate one from the idea that familiar assumptions, rules, and practices are necessary, just, and unchallengeable. Through comparative law, legal agents put themselves in a position to realize that no epistemic arrangements (and certainly not one's own) can afford to be regarded as self-evident. In the way in which the development of the law and the achievement of justice demand that problems be approached and resolved in the light of information supplied by other disciplines (whether, for example, anthropology, economics, literary criticism, philosophy, or sociology), they command that an issue be examined with reference to the epistemic sensitivities prevailing in other jurisdictions.

Accordingly, comparative law must not be concerned with the dry juxtaposition of legal propositions issuing from a range of laws. Instead, it must preoccupy itself with the localization of law, that is, with the

[76] My reference to 'what the law is' is to J Gordley, 'When Is the Use of Foreign Law Possible? A Hard Case: The Protection of Privacy in Europe and the United States' (2007) 67 Louisiana LR 1073, 1081 ('I am concerned with what the law [i]s'). My source for Jakarta-as-Tucson is Gordley (n 12), and my mention of Spain-as-California is from Watson (n 13).

situation, the all-situation of a law as it dwells in its own epistemic setting. Because, being aware of comparative law's structural inability to grasp foreignness's *genius loci*, the comparatist wishes to elucidate foreign law optimally, to achieve or yield a deep or thick understanding of its being-in-a-world, since he wants to diagnose foreign law through a profound interrogation of its character (etymologically, to diagnose means to learn to know thoroughly and asunder), the comparison of laws is best effectuated by reading law-texts as expressions of the work of culture – of culture expressing itself legally – and therefore by securing pertinent anthropological, historical, linguistic, literary, philosophical, psychological, and sociological insights with a view to ascribing sophisticated meaning to law-texts that necessarily exist as law-texts-in-a-foreign-world, as worldly law-texts (no law-text exists out-of-a-world). Once more, the comparatist can only account in a meaningful way for how the law is constructed in a foreign jurisdiction through an indisciplined investigation, which often means that massive dedication is necessary to produce even small accretions in pertinent information.[77] (Still, the comparatist's erudition is usually not enough to allow him an escape from life at the intellectual margins of the legal academy.)

No comparison can be initiated without a comparatist taking the view that an investigation involving more than one law is worth making, that it has a lesson to teach. Unfurling his predisposed interpretation-enabling enculturation, the comparatist must then resist effectuating any appropriation of otherness to selfness, that is, any 'equivalentization' or 'commonalization', lest he should be silencing the other-in-the-law.[78] An earnest appreciation for the other's law-world requires the comparatist to surmount the reductionist urge to confine comparative analysis to the ascertainment of would-be equivalences or commonalities, say, in his account of statutes or judicial decisions across jurisdictions. Avoiding the pitfalls of essentialization, comparative law must rather address itself to *enculturation*, that is, to a framework of intangibles within which legal 'communities' operate and that exercises normative force over these 'communities' and that, over the long term, determines a certain legal configuration as a local referent (even though not completely and coherently instantiated). When one researches the law other-wise, when one reads a statute or judicial decision bringing to bear an other-oriented

[77] Supra 197–202.

[78] cf Jullien (n 14) 170: '[T]his "other" . . . is integrated . . . in a rationality that encompasses it: thereafter [it] is lost as other.'

response, one finds oneself being implicated in a matrix of inexhaustible singularity. The more one proceeds with the task, the more one finds oneself enmeshed in an experience of irreducibly complex, singular life-forms. The network of associative connections that energizes usage in any given law can be replicated into the comparative analysis only partly and then by virtue of periphrastic and metaphrastic manoeuvres that – not unlike the translation of a poem – inevitably transform the intensity, the evocative means, the formal autonomy of the other law. Once more, to accord difference priority is the only way for comparative law to take optimal cognizance of what is the case. Only in deferring to the non-equivalent, to the non-common, can the claim to justice proceed towards redemption.

In an age of so-called 'globalization' – which because it cannot be taken to have fostered a de-enculturation of law is effectively an era of glocalization – there is an urgent need to understand how foreign legal 'communities', including subaltern legal 'communities', think about 'their' law, why they think about 'their' law as they do, why they would find it implausible to think about 'their' law in any other way, and how their thought differs from others (including ours). Any urge for comparative law to stereotype knowledge through the elicitation of epigrammatic answers from foreign laws, not to mention any compulsion to construct prescriptive axiomatic patterns established through strict reference to the formalized elements of law and the simulation of a condition of unity or uniformity across laws (the orthodoxy's well-weathered ideological umbrella), is necessarily based on a repression of differences located in the local matrix within which any manifestation of posited law is inevitably ensconced. Ultimately, comparative law cannot detract from the relevance of Max Weber's guiding principle, an injunction he formulated 100 years or so ago and that continues to stand the thoughtful comparatist-at-law in excellent stead:

> A truly critical comparison ... would be just as rewarding as fruitful, naturally only when it does not hunt, in the manner of the presently fashionable constructions of general development schemes, for 'analogies' and 'parallels' as target, but on the very contrary, only if its goal is the working out of the particularity of each of the two developments [being compared], in the end-result such different developments, and thus of the circuit of the causal imputation of this different course.[79]

[79] M Weber, *Agrarverhältnisse im Altertum* in *Gesammelte Aufsätze zur Sozial- und Wirtschaftsgeschichte* (Marianne Weber ed, Mohr Siebeck 1924† [1909]) 288.

The comparison of laws is premised on a foreign law being capable of representation. But, whatever its intention, writing reflects a certain ideology and incorporates a certain poetics. Writing, since it necessarily intervenes at a time that is subsequent to experience, remains as a memory of that which cannot be restored as such. Observe that no act of 'reproduction' can overcome singularity, since any representation – in effect, then, a re-presentation – is tied in insuppressible fashion to ex post facto construction, even as the re-presenting statement purports most faithfully to account for what had been presented, there. In this sense, every comparison always-already involves a necessary transformation of the foreign law being investigated. While the comparatist reports on actual connections, he himself devises or invents them in 'his' language in order to make the situation under study amenable to (his) clarification and exposition. The comparatist's theoretical equipment thus allows him (and compels him) to eschew anything like objectivity or veridiction as he appreciates that his understanding is necessarily conditioned by the concrete cultural situation in which he himself is decidedly embedded and as he internalizes the fact that 'the (foreign) law' is also culturally inscribed. For this reason, too, and in order to restrain ethnocentric or juricentric violence, the comparatist-at-law must display tenacious scepticism towards alleged frameworks of commensuration across laws, and he must practice a healthy brand of legal relativism thus accepting that while contradictions or antagonisms may be noted and probed, it does not fall to him to resolve such conflicts through some sort of pseudo-synthesis reminiscent of Hegel's *die Nacht der Nächte*.[80]

By way of the deconstructive exigencies of a thought that allows the other-in-the-law to signify according to himself and his own obviousness – a thought that is, empathically and emphatically, *for* the other – the comparatist engages in self-distantiation from his own assumptions (which, then, no longer partake in 'truth'), proves interested in a variety of legal initiatives across laws, and shows himself keen to grasp the singular significance of these undertakings for given 'communities' so that his understanding not only of their world, but of his world is stronger and so that he lives more critically – the idea being that the self can become more explicit to itself only through the mediation of an other (which means that, in this sense at least, comparative law operates not

[80] cf V Crapanzano, *Recapitulations* (Other Press 2015) 266: 'I argue for a heuristic relativism – taking the part of the other, without necessarily accepting his or her position, in order to better understand the other's world and, one hopes, gain a perspective on one's own that will refine our understanding of both.'

unlike psychoanalysis). It remains, though, that the self can never fully overcome the epistemic partiality arising from the fact that interactions with foreignness are inherently asymmetrical and irreversible. In the end, comparative law thus features a constitutive aporia: it demands the public intervention of critical individuals who accept that, within the structural constraints set by the human interpretive apparatus, understanding of a law or an experience of law other than one's 'own' can only arise from thorough singularization and can therefore never emerge completely – given that epistemic areas are irrevocably irreconcilable, even though one articulates them in co-presence and acts as if one can effectively conciliate them.

Of course, differential analysis is not immune to travesty. But the fact that difference can be mobilized to operate divisively – that it can be impoverished through weaponization in a form of warfare, verbal or otherwise – cannot be regarded as controlling or disqualifying. To be sure, difference can be invoked to the disadvantage of those to whom it is applied as when it serves to place the distinctiveness of an individual or a 'community' in jeopardy through oppression or disavowal, exclusion or obliteration. Overt sexual or ethnic discrimination provide evident applications of this discursive strategy – as did imperial tactics of deliberate binarization which, as early as the sixteenth century, sought to establish well-known contradictory dualities along the lines of Christian/pagan, White/Coloured (think of 'Indians' or 'Blacks'), culture/nature, developed/undeveloped, civilized/uncivilized, all with a view to devaluing the knowledges and ways of life of colonized peoples. It remains that while a term like 'difference' may be used to foster not only a progressive project, but also a reactionary one, this fact cannot entail that the word would now become analytically unavailable. In any event, this kind of semantic affliction is hardly specific to difference (consider how the former *Deutsche Demokratische Republik* debased 'democracy').

The difference that is the case – the singularity – thus calls to be ethically experienced as an assertion of foreign selfness. It is that difference that provides the other with a vital capacity for epistemic action by enabling him to resist the erosion of boundaries between individuals, allowing him to elude misrecognition or banishment, permitting him to avoid violent confusion or confutation. Not only is difference therefore linked to the very matter of intelligibility (how could understanding come from indistinction?), but it is also connected to the possibility of social organization and survival of the foreign, for it aborts all possible totalization. It is this redemptive, empowering feature of difference – difference's responsive and responsible 'no' to appropriation, assimilation, or standardization of all hues – that I am committed to upholding through the practice of comparative law. I am therefore heeding Ludwig Wittgenstein, who is reputed to have exclaimed: '[M]y interest is in showing that things which look the same are really quite different. I was thinking of using as a motto for my book a quotation from *King Lear*: "I'll teach you differences".'[81] (I assume he had in mind meaningful differences, that is, differences that make a difference.[82]) Because 'discernment imposes to comparison the primary and fundamental search for difference',[83] since 'the comparative study of law cannot be a matter of reducing concrete differences to abstract commonalities',[84] I propose to do like Wittgenstein and teach differences also, if differently from him.

*

I easily relate to the Nietzschean insight that 'the annoying seeing-like and making-level is the mark of weak eyes'.[85] From the standpoint of political philosophy, I therefore refute consensus-driven forms of liberalism such as John Rawls's or Jürgen Habermas's, and I object to the idea underlying these theoretical frameworks to the effect that neither pluralism nor conflict deserve to be credited, that inasmuch as idiocratic configurations are deemed to be contradicting the goal of universalization they ought ultimately to be assimilated to unreasonable localizations of thought or even castigated as irrational claims. A remark by Joseph Raz strikes me as characteristic of liberalism's obsession with the irenic:

81 M O'C Drury, 'Conversations with Wittgenstein' in R Rhees (ed), *Recollections of Wittgenstein* (Oxford University Press 1984 [1948]) 157. The theatrical reference is to W Shakespeare, *King Lear* (1606) act 1, scene 4.

82 If my five-year-old daughter is watching me make coffee in the morning with a 'French press' and remarks that a few grains have spilled from my spoon, I can confidently tell her that I do not need to replace these grains and explain that in terms of the 'French press' I am using, the loss of these grains is indifferent. I can tell her that it does not matter whether I have these grains or not, that I will be making coffee just as well with or without the grains. Of course, strictly speaking, the inclusion or exclusion of these grains has an impact on the quantity of coffee I shall be making, and my interpretation cannot alter this empirical fact. But it is fine for me to ignore this difference as it is not meaningful. Literally, *it does not make a difference*. The fact that some differences can be interpreted as inconsequential or simply uninteresting usefully shows that there is nothing objective or true about difference.

83 Foucault (n 20) 69.

84 C Geertz, *Local Knowledge* (Basic Books 1983) 215.

85 F Nietzsche, *Die fröhliche Wissenschaft* (2nd edn) in *Digitale Kritische Gesamtausgabe* (G Colli et al eds, 2009– [1887]) <www.nietzschesource.org/#eKGWB/FW-228> III, s 228.

'I neither have argued nor will argue that our culture has the intellectual resources which make it possible, with good will and sympathetic imagination, to understand alien cultures. *I take it for granted that this is so.*'[86] Rather – and, I daresay, at once less arrogantly and more realistically – I argue that antagonisms are (and must be) an inescapable feature of the dynamics informing laws in co-presence,[87] not to mention the fact that they require to animate the further dynamics arising between these laws vis-à-vis the comparative law discourses that purport to account for them. And I claim that these antagonisms are ultimately unbridgeable and that one ought to appreciate the democratic virtues attendant upon such impassability, since only disagreement can be the opportunity for further debate and continued discussion.[88] It follows that I am thoroughly sanguine at the realization that there is no possibility of bringing together the plurality of paradigms in existence through any Rational or Reasonable – that is, authoritarian – resolution that would, inevitably partially, favour one scheme at the expense of all others.

In contradistinction to liberalism – which although it considers pluralism as a fact,[89] confines itself to a confirmation of multiplicity's existence with a view to overcoming it in short theoretical and practical order – I argue for (legal) diversity's primordial democratic desirability. I therefore reject unanimity or homogeneity not least, but not only, because I regard such 'agreements' as being constitutively dependent upon acts of exclusion and therefore as structurally fictitious (if there is exclusion, as there must necessarily be to allow oneness to emerge, any claimed accord is fallacious, someone's imposition masquerading as concurrence).[90] Instead, I defend difference as 'axiological principle'.[91]

86 J Raz, *Between Authority and Interpretation* (Oxford University Press 2009) 46 [my emphasis].

87 cf R Gagné, 'Regimes of Comparatism' in R Gagné et al (eds), *Regimes of Comparatism* (Brill 2019) 2: 'One way or another, comparatism is always a space of contestation.'

88 The case of extremism must be reserved (arguably, though, extremism must be reserved under any scenario). More interesting, I think, is the view that rivalry and violence arise from equivalence or commonality rather than from difference. Eg: R Girard, '"Ce qui se joue aujourd'hui est une rivalité à l'échelle planétaire"' (Interview with H Tincq) *Le Monde* (6 November 2001) 20: 'The error is always to reason within the categories of "difference", when the root of all conflicts is rather "competition", the mimetic rivalry between beings, countries, cultures.' The words are René Girard's. One need not subscribe to Girard's entire philosophical system to appreciate the percipient character of this observation.

89 See J Rawls, *Political Liberalism* (2nd edn, Columbia University Press 1996) 36.

90 See C Mouffe, *The Democratic Paradox* (Verso 2005 [2000]) 19.

91 ibid.

Liberalism's vaunted epistemic objectivity – consider Rawls's prioritization of the right over the good[92] – is ultimately the expression of a regime of political value, and it simply cannot be creditably presented or understood as being objectively dictated by Rationality or Reasonableness. To unravel its construction (that is, to identify the delineation between the deemed-acceptable and the reputed-unacceptable that must orient even the most tolerant or deferential pursuit of unification or uniformization) is to show that the alleged concord cannot intervene otherwise than as an assertion of power actively engaged in acts of marginalization.[93] In Chantal Mouffe's arresting words, '[c]onsensus in a liberal-democratic society is – and always will be – the expression of a hegemony'.[94] It is only through an act of power, therefore, that any epistemic 'objectivity' is maintained (I qualify the word advisedly), and the issue is always 'the creation of an "us" by the determination of a "them"' (moreover, that 'them' is our 'them', that is, it is a 'them' that arises as we observe and as we talk, through our words).[95] Otherwise said, the claim to objectivity (or to universalism – or, indeed, to truth) would effectively consist of a (castigatory) declaration by one comparatist-at-law, whose experience would necessarily be personal and partial, that all *other* experiences are, somehow, necessarily personal and partial.[96] Faced with such blatant contradiction, comparative law discourse must seek to integrate precisely the voices that Kantian liberalism and liberal rationalism purport to efface. (In this regard, I willingly acknowledge that there are rare exceptions to the typical strategy of erasure, which include Isaiah Berlin, John Gray, and Michael Walzer.)

As I approach the matter, the abiding challenge for comparative law is thus to articulate an epistemology recognizing and respecting the plurality of laws that there is, there, meaningfully (and charitably) expressing the legal differend that there is, there. Rejecting the (unexamined) idea that consensus should reflexively operate as epistemic *desideratum*,

[92] See Rawls (n 89) 173–210.

[93] See C Mouffe, 'Democracy in a Multipolar World' (2009) 37 Millennium: J Int'l Stud 549, 550.

[94] Mouffe (n 90) 49.

[95] C Mouffe, 'Deliberative Democracy or Agonistic Pluralism?' (1999) 66 Social Research 745, 755. See also P Cheah, 'The Material World of Comparison' in R Felski and SS Friedman (eds), *Comparison* (Johns Hopkins University Press 2013) 180: 'The ethical relation to the other ... is always a matter of power because it involves the capacity or ability to act or to do: to be generous, gracious, respectful, tolerant, or accepting of differences.'

[96] See B de Sousa Santos, *The End of the Cognitive Empire* (Duke University Press 2018) 38.

I argue for a comparatism that deliberately implements a strategy of emancipatory agonism with a view to remedying the violent epistemic banishments that orthodox comparative law has for so long conducted in its forceful (if counter-intuitive) attempts to restrict or deny legal pluralism. Again, think of Jakarta-as-Tucson or Spain-as-California.[97] I agree with Werner Menski that any comparative law project along the lines of universalism 'reflects an absence of ultimate respect for global diversity and only tolerates it as an interim measure'.[98] In this regard, Zweigert and Kötz's claim that 'differences ... are not relevant' and their correlative extolment of 'a unitary concept of justice' is typical and typically flawed.[99] And so is their simplistic (and frankly jejune) assertion that the

[97] I refer to Gordley (n 12) and Watson (n 13), respectively.

[98] W Menski, *Comparative Law in a Global Context* (2nd edn, Cambridge University Press 2006) 48.

[99] Zweigert and Kötz (n 10) 60 and 3. I do not want to suggest that Zweigert and Kötz (and Gordley and Watson) enjoy a monopoly on the kind of discourse that proclaims the impertinence of differences in comparative research across laws. Consider Uwe Kischel's intervention before the British Association of Comparative Law, at the University of Central Lancashire in Preston (UK), on 3 September 2019, as Geoffrey Samuel, then in attendance, helpfully reported it to me while I was teaching in California. In the course of the discussion that followed his speech, Kischel referred to the proposition 'a contract is formed with the meeting of the wills of the two parties' as an illustration of what he regards as a 'neutral' legal rule. At the minimum, as I understand the basic idea, such a legal rule, being intrinsically non-different, could be found to exist indifferently in any law or at least in many laws. In other words, a 'neutral' rule would be unencultured; it would exist as law *sans* culture. Of course, the contention that unification or uniformization would then be readily achievable could be expected to follow in short order. Both John Bell and Samuel replied to Kischel's claim regarding contract formation. In correspondence [on file], Bell indicates to me that his principal objection to Kischel was that the idea of the will is closely tied to German philosophy in general and to Kantian philosophy in particular so that it can hardly be claimed to be devoid of cultural baggage. For a detailed argument along these lines, Bell recommends G Rouhette, 'The Binding Nature of Obligations' (J Bell tr) in D Harris and D Tallon (eds), *Contract Law Today* (Oxford University Press 1989) 57–63. In separate correspondence [on file], Samuel mentions how he retorted to Kischel that the will has historically been foreign to the common-law way of approaching formation of contracts, a matter that common-law judges have traditionally considered from an objective rather than a subjective standpoint – that is, a question they have envisaged from a perspective that does not allow the will to play any significant normative role. Upon reading Samuel's explanation, I was promptly reminded of the very first case that I was tasked to read in my basic contract law course all these years ago. My excellent teacher at McGill University was Michael Bridge, and he had assigned *Tamplin v James* (1880) 15 ChD 215, a short late-nineteenth-century English decision involving the sale of real estate. In *Tamplin*, the court orders specific performance against the buyer even though he has made a mistake regarding the contents of the sale (on the basis of his personal acquaintance with the property, he thought that certain gardens came with the land when, in effect, they were not part of the sale). What is

significant for the court is not whether the buyer's will is ad idem with the seller's, that is, the court is not concerned with what the buyer had in mind or with how his mindset did not fit the facts of the contract so that he could invoke the doctrine of mistake in order to be excused from performance, which is what he wanted. Rather, the court's decision turns on a so-called 'objective' analysis. I recall Bridge: would a reasonable person have deemed the particulars of sale to have been clear? If so, such 'objective' assessment must prevail – again, irrespective of the actual buyer's actual will. Three judges of the Court of Appeal, confirming the single judge in Chancery, thus hold unanimously in favour of the seller and order specific performance against the buyer, who is thereby compelled to proceed with his purchase. It is key to note that the resolution of the dispute does not focus on the actual buyer's actual state of mind – the case does not emphasize his will. In sum, the making of an enforceable contract is seen to depend not on the agreement of two minds in one intention, but on the deemed meaning of a set of signs (the particulars of sale) external to the mind. I distinctly recollect Bridge expediting *Tamplin* (it was but one of the three cases we had to analyze in the course of an hour). Evidently, *Tamplin* pertained to elementary contract law. What students had to appreciate was that formation of contracts in the common law tradition was approached very differently from the way things were done in the civil law tradition, a model with which they had become acquainted in law school the year before (think Canada, think the civil law and common law traditions both occupying Canadian territory on account of imperial and colonial considerations, France and England having been successive conquerors). In further correspondence [on file], Samuel observes that the decision to marginalize the will in *Tamplin* is particulary remarkable since, being an action for specific performance, the matter was adjudicated in the *Chancery* Division (a decision later confirmed by *three* judges in the Court of Appeal). It is striking that even the law of equity – despite having been heavily influenced by canon law and Roman law – would refuse to attach significance to the will. Samuel also comments that *Tamplin* is hardly the most famous case making the legal argument it does. Specifically, he indicates the celebrated English Court of Appeal decision in *Carlill v Carbolic Smoke Ball Co* [1893] 1 QB 256. In Samuel's words, *Carlill* 'reinforces the point that contract is about the enforceability of an objective promise seriously made and supported by consideration. It reject[s] the idea that there must be subjective agreement between the company and Mrs C[arlill]'. Quaere: is Kischel's proposition 'a contract is formed with the meeting of the wills of the two parties' a 'neutral' legal rule? *Is any legal rule 'neutral', ever?* Even on the basis of cursory reflection, the answer to both questions must be resolutely negative. In the absence of neutrality there can only be partiality, that is, there can only be a rule that is partial to a certain world-view and that therefore exists singularly or differentially from other, foreign rules, themselves partial to other, foreign world-views. It follows that differences across legal rules, encultured as these necessarily are, can hardly be regarded as irrelevant. It also follows that any unification or uniformization agenda must rapidly become intractable. Meanwhile, I am surprised that the author of a massive textbook on comparative law, devoting some 150 pages to the common law tradition, should be oblivious to such a basic difference between the civil-law and common-law mindsets as the contrast I discuss here. See Kischel (n 10) 243–388. It appears that one is faced with a somewhat striking case of undue ethnocentric (or juricentric) projection, an epistemic embarrassment all too frequently weighting on the practice of comparative law. Kischel shows how comparatists hailing from the civil law tradition continue to try and mute even the most salient differences arising between the civil law and the common law. On this point, perhaps I may be so bold as to suggest P Legrand, 'European Legal Systems Are Not Converging' (1996) 45 Int'l & Comp LQ 52,

equivalence or commonality they herald can be expected to generate 'an increase in the general standard of living'.[100]

Accepting that power relations are ineliminable (there is no possibility of any knowledge being constituted without an act of power, no option of powerless knowledge),[101] the question becomes how comparatists-at-law can arrange the expression of (their) epistemic interventionism in a way that is compatible with the legal differend that there is, there, and in a manner that the numerous projects expatiating on the achievement of a unification or uniformization of laws radically fail to do. Otherwise put, 'how to establish this us/them distinction which is constitutive of politics in a way that is compatible with the recognition of pluralism'?[102] Acknowledging that a rational consensus across laws in co-presence is both impossible and unwarranted, I must, if I am, say, a Melbourne-based comparatist writing about the French statutory prohibition on attire ostensibly demonstrating a religious belonging in public

even though at this writing, in the light of what I shall euphemistically call later developments in European geo-politics, I would make my argument in stronger terms than I deployed a quarter-century or so ago. I am especially minded to recommend this reading to Kischel, since the pages he writes on the 'convergence debate' reveal him to be unaware of this publication: see ibid 666–78. I quote from ibid 670. For my extended critique of Kischel's book, see P Legrand, 'Kischel's Comparative Law: *Fortschritt ohne Fortschritt*' (2020) 15(2) J Comp L 292. As Alexandra Mercescu shares with me an excerpt from Robert Nozick's, I am struck how his words, while not written with totalizing comparatists-at-law in mind, uncannily apply to what I regard as totalitarian pursuits along the lines of Zweigert and Kötz et al. I refer to R Nozick, *Anarchy, State, and Utopia* (Basic Books 1974) xiii: 'All those things are lying out there, and they must be fit in. You push and shove the material into the rigid area getting it into the boundary on one side, and it bulges out on another. You run around and press in the protruding bulge, producing yet another in another place. So you push and shove and clip off corners from the things so they'll fit and you press in until finally almost everything sits unstably more or less in there; what doesn't gets heaved *far* away so that it won't be noticed. . . . *Quickly*, you find an angle from which it looks like an exact fit and take a snapshot; at a fast shutter speed before something else bulges out too noticeably. Then, back to the darkroom to touch up the rents, rips, and tears in the fabric of the perimeter. All that remains is to publish the photograph as a representation of exactly how things are.'

[100] Zweigert and Kötz (n 10) 3. cf M-B Dembour, 'Following the Movement of a Pendulum: Between Universalism and Relativism' in JK Cowan, M-B Dembour, and RA Wilson (eds), *Culture and Rights* (Cambridge University Press 2001) 73, where the author observes that 'the *prima facie* value of universalism is generally not contested'.

[101] Yet, there is 'the illusion that we could free ourselves completely from power': Mouffe (n 95) 753.

[102] Mouffe (n 93) 551.

schools,[103] operate in the name of emancipatory agonism, that is, resist the disqualification of French law as some sort of enemy of Rationality or Reasonableness whose (legal) solution to the matter of cultural integration would have to be eradicated in short order. To be sure, I need not settle for quietism, and I may well approach the French model as standing for a position that I hold I must dispute. But I must allow that France's entitlement to defend its local understanding of citizenship or republican values cannot be relegated to the ranks of obscurantist quests.

Otherwise said, I contend that comparatists-at-law must deploy an agonistic approach to otherness-in-the-law, that is, I plead for the instauration of a comparative mindset recognizing the conflictuality of the plural legal positions in co-presence, acknowledging the fact that there is no Rational or Reasonable solution to these conflicts, and attesting to the principled legitimacy of each differential claim as the expression of a local rationality. (Although charity *oblige*, I accept, of course, the possibility of mindlessness or utter irrationality.) Agonism thus defends both an entitlement to the non-universalizable character of singular laws and the expression of legal difference from the singularity of laws in the comparatist's account. It ensues that the other – in my illustration, the French – is not to be regarded as an enemy to be destroyed, but as an adversary. If you will, agonism militates in favour of the instauration of the differend as adversarial. I insist, with Mouffe: 'An adversary is a legitimate enemy.'[104] To return to the idea of charity, 'if we want to understand others, we must count them right in most matters'.[105] The principle of charitable interpretation thus becomes a necessary feature of every exercise in ascription of meaning. As he resists the projection of his beliefs unto the other, the comparatist-at-law accepts that he simply cannot countenance an articulation of difference that would disable the other's legitimate claim to rightness. The empirical fact of the matter is that there can be no Rational or Reasonable resolution of the conflicts between competing law-worlds – each insistently defending a different view of the good, each forcefully articulating a manifold of discourses and practices about what is right, each insistently excluding other possibilities. Pace Kant and other advocates of more or less abstract versions of universalism, it is key to appreciate that pluralism 'implies the

[103] The reference to the statute is at supra 237n38.

[104] Mouffe (n 95) 755.

[105] D Davidson, 'On the Very Idea of a Conceptual Scheme' in *Inquiries into Truth and Interpretation* (2nd edn, Oxford University Press 2001 [1973]) 197.

impossibility of the final reconciliation of all views',[106] which means that comparative law is destined to face the ineradicability of agonism. In this regard, Zweigert and Kötz's promotion of 'a unitary concept of justice' is disabling not only because this superficial idea blunts comparative acuity, but also on account of the fact that, within the field of comparative law, it protects the prevailing hegemonic epistemic order and its set of contingent power relations, which has been actively seeking to dilute local attachments to legal 'communities' in order to force laws away from their pluriversal setting into a universal model that can, in effect, never be – and that must never be if the different ways of life-in-the-law, instead of falling for a process of occidentalization (or is it Germanization?) – are to continue to express themselves with a meaningful voice.[107] Comparative law must therefore remain consonant with the fact that 'despite the overconfident claims advanced by the theorists of modernization and convergence', far from generating 'a cultural homogenization of the [planet]', what is naively called globalization has heightened the 'assert[ion] [of] the identity of cultural codes rooted in nations and ethnic groups'.[108]

In sum, I plead for a primordial reformulation of comparative law's understanding of consensus and a basic reconsideration of consensualism's assumed virtues, bearing in mind that the liberal rationalism of Rawls and Habermas is designed to achieve a stable conciliation through the deliberate silencing or exclusion of all that is deemed to be distinct from the view identified, by the liberal doxa itself, as consensual (or 'universal'). I ask that comparatists, through a profound transformation of their understanding of epistemic power relations, learn to view laws with an acute sense of agonistic recognition and respect. Incidentally, this approach corresponds to an understanding of the self as split, as lacking in essence, as being irreducible to a conscious, Rational or Reasonable ego. No self has a clear, stable identity that would be permeable to Reason, Rawls and Habermas notwithstanding.

Note that I favour the adoption of an agonistic inclination not only in scholarly venues like law reviews and conference settings, but also in official pedagogical situations such as the lecture hall and the seminar room – and through the myriad formal encounters in offices, meetings, and other events in which professional socialization and institutionalization within

[106] C Mouffe, *Agonistics* (Verso 2013) 130.
[107] Zweigert and Kötz (n 10) 3.
[108] D Zolo, *Cosmopolis* (Polity 1997) 135. I substitute 'planet' for 'world'. See generally V Roudometof, *Glocalization* (Routledge 2016).

comparative law takes place. I am arguing, if you will, for a new everyday comparative norm of conduct, a change in the ethics of comparative engagement to accommodate the singularity, that is, the granularity of the law. Incisively, Jonathan Culler asks, '[w]hat, in this newly globalized space, justifies bringing two or more texts together?'.[109] I answer: agonism. In this regard, it seems to me that Pheng Cheah articulates comparative law's existential paradox very well: '[I]n contemporary globalization, comparison … undermines the formation of a shared world even as it makes us more connected in unprecedented ways.'[110] Allow me to refer to Culler once more on the subject of the necessary operationalization of an alternative epistemic disposition against the comparative law that still believes in forcing contemporary legal diversity into the corset of a unified or uniform system. In particular, let me apply Culler's insight regarding the merits of 'instruction in otherness', his point being that the comparatist must offer 'vivid, compelling evidence of differences in cultures, mores, assumptions, values' with a view to 'mak[ing] otherness palpable and mak[ing] it comprehensible without reducing it to an inferior version of the same, as universalizing humanism threatens to do'.[111] Yes.

*

The argument from agonism can be deployed from another standpoint altogether. A 'triangle consisting of the comparati[st] and the two sides of the comparison that the comparati[st] puts into motion',[112] comparison names 'a mode of inquiry'.[113] The word 'inquiry' thus points not to something that would be there – a given or pre-given – but to something that has yet to be made or produced. Very much a cognitive operation, a constructing activity emanating from the mind trying to articulate the empirical, a bricolage, also a 'black box' not so easily susceptive to analysis, comparativity demands critical engagement, for only as one makes it more reflexive does one make it more creditable.

109 J Culler, 'Comparability' (1995) 69 World Lit Today 268, 268. Pace Culler, there is no 'globalized' space but rather a glocalized one.

110 P Cheah, 'The Material World of Comparison' in R Felski and SS Friedman (eds), *Comparison* (Johns Hopkins University Press 2013) 168.

111 J Culler, *Framing the Sign* (Blackwell 1988) 48.

112 M Xie, *Conditions of Comparison* (Bloomsbury 2011) 37. See also WD Mignolo, 'On Comparison: Who Is Comparing What and Why?' in R Felski and SS Friedman (eds), *Comparison* (Johns Hopkins University Press 2013) 99: 'Comparison is minimally a triangular business.'

113 R Chang, *Making Comparisons Count* (Routledge 2002) 1. See generally ibid 1–2.

Now, it is widely assumed that comparison is a trichotomous process: A is better than B, worse than B, or equal to B. For my part, I accept Ruth Chang's perceptive observation that these dynamics do not exhaust the comparative enterprise's conceptual arena, which must in fact be approached as a tetrachotomous framework. Before I say more about the fourth option – the one that comparative law must in fact embrace, in my view – let me develop how comparison is organized.

Since there can be no comparison *simpliciter* (every entity must be compared to another as regards a certain aspect), it follows that every comparison must proceed with reference to a third value.[114] For example, liberty and equality are comparable with reference to enhancement of justice within society. Meanwhile, '[i]f I tell you that an evaluative difference does not exist between Mozart and Beethoven with respect to musical talent, I have told you that Mozart and Beethoven are incomparable with respect to musical talent' (*for comparison assumes difference*).[115] A bald claim to the effect that a Camargue horse is better than a Porsche makes no sense. For this evaluation to hold, the Camargue horse and the Porsche have to be made to interact in one (interesting) aspect or other. Accordingly, a Camargue horse could be said to be better than a Porsche, because it is less costly or since it is capable of affection. Of course, the necessary third value must be such as will allow for a meaningfully evaluative comparison. To compare maple syrup and the number one thus requires to identify a third value that cannot be candour or zizz.

A third value consists of a value structure. By way of illustration, consider once more the 2004 French statute prohibiting attire ('*tenues*') 'ostensibly' ('*ostensiblement*') demonstrating a religious belonging in public primary and secondary schools.[116] This enactment offers an application of the constitutional principle of laicity ('*laïcité*').[117] Currently regarded in France as a constitutional pillar of French republicanism, the idea harks back to early-twentieth-century legislation on the separation between the churches and the state and in earlier guises to Enlightenment discourse. Moreover, it can be traced to the 1598 Edict of

114 See P Legrand, 'Foreign Law in the Third Space' (2012) 4 Juridikum 32.

115 Chang (n 113) 14.

116 The reference to the statute is at supra 237n38.

117 In France, laicity carries a local cultural nuance that secularism fails to convey. The French language also has words like '*séculier*' and '*sécularité*'. However, the French do not use these terms in matters concerning the churches and the state. In sum, there exists a specifically French version of secularism bearing a specific appellation.

Nantes and to fourteenth-century frictions between the French king and the Pope. Since the fall of 2004, when the 'headscarf' statute was initially implemented in sustained fashion, French newspapers have been reporting that students, principally Muslim girls refusing to renounce the *hijab*, have been expelled from school.[118]

Still in terms of the example I want to adduce, consider also the Supreme Court of Canada's 2006 unanimous decision allowing a twelve-year-old Sikh boy to wear his ceremonial metal dagger at school.[119] Imposing certain practical conditions relating to the use of this *kirpan*, the Court held that the absolute prohibition by the school board infringed the boy's freedom of religion and found that the interference effectively deprived him of his right to attend a public school. Even though the ban was motivated by a desire to ensure safety at school, it could not be warranted pursuant to the *Canadian Charter of Rights and Freedoms*. (Section 27 of the *Charter* officially recognizes multiculturalism as a Canadian constitutional value, the provision stating that the *Charter* must be interpreted consistently with 'the preservation and enhancement of the multicultural heritage of Canadians'.) The Court added that '[the prohibition was] disrespectful to believers in the Sikh religion and d[id] not take into account Canadian values based on multiculturalism'.[120] It found that 'accommodating [the plaintiff] ... demonstrate[d] the importance that [Canadian] society attache[d] to protecting freedom of religion and to showing respect for its minorities'.[121]

It seems hard to escape the view that the French and Canadian law-texts are worthy of comparison-at-law as they make different claims regarding 'religious attire in public schools'. It must be clear, then, that value pluralism need not entail incomparability. In fact, even in the face of irreducible plurality, a comparison can be meaningfully articulated if a third value can be identified, something which is done through a process of assignment. It is the comparatist himself who ascribes the third value, who constructs a connector that 'glues' the two discourses

118 Eg: *Le Monde* (21 October 2004) 1; *Le Monde* (22 October 2004) 12; *Libération* (18–19 December 2004) 15; *Le Monde* (30 April 2015) 8. While the earlier reports concern headscarves, the 2015 article explains that a fifteen-year-old female Muslim student was denied access to her public secondary school on two occasions, because she was wearing a black skirt deemed to qualify as 'ostensible' religious attire on account of its length.

119 *Multani v Commission scolaire Marguerite-Bourgeoys* [2006] 1 SCR 256.

120 ibid [71] (Charron J).

121 ibid [79] (Charron J).

'not-together' for (his) comparative purposes. And it is the third value that possibilizes the comparison. Now, despite the fact that the French and Canadians each have their own way of making a situation matter, a third value generating an interface between the French statute and *Multani* might be 'strategy of conduciveness to an orderly polity given the fact of a plural society' (rather than, say, 'strategy to optimize an efficient reduction of the trade deficit').

As I have indicated, every third value effectively consists in a value structure, which means that a third value features contributory values from the entities being compared. It is the contributory values that make the third value what it is (the third value is an iteration of aspects of each entity within the comparison, that is, it repeats each entity differently from itself – it iterates it). Envisage inclusiveness, which can reasonably be said to contribute to a 'strategy of conduciveness to an orderly polity given the fact of a plural society'. In other words, the more inclusive the legal strategy, the more likely it is to prove able to configure an orderly plural polity. (Of course, one should not overlook the fact that the French and Canadians are likely to approach the matter of inclusiveness from different perspectives. It may well be, for instance, that the French and Canadians would disagree as to whether the French statute is inclusive, the French presumably being of the view that it is, and the Canadians just as predictably opining that it is not – which goes to show, incidentally and importantly, that there is no such thing as Inclusiveness.) Another contributory value, which could be contemplated as making a lesser contribution to the strategy, might be clarity. In this regard, statutory terseness could be felt to operate more effectively than judicial prolixity. Throughout, the focus is squarely on differences across laws. Indeed, the concept of difference is so elementary within comparison that Chang calls the idea 'primitive'.[122] (Personally, I prefer to use the word 'primordial'.)

At this juncture, I fail to see how I could usefully refer to the French statute as being 'better than', 'worse than', or 'equal to' the Canadian judicial decision. Such an argument would misconceive comparability by presupposing that it must be scalar and that the processes of deliberation that engendered the French and Canadian law-texts had to be calculative in the strict sense of the term, a matter of adding and subtracting certain quantities of a certain value.[123] Challenging 'the widespread but

[122] Chang (n 113) 15.
[123] I closely track ibid 76.

unreflective assumption that the [t]richotomy [t]hesis is true',[124] there is a fourth possibility that Chang develops as the leitmotiv of her argument, which is to contend that although they are neither better nor worse than one another and not equally good either (logically, equality requires an absence of difference), the French statute and Canadian judgment exist *on a par.*[125] Note immediately that the concept of parity is at variance with that of equality: while equality implies 'zero difference', parity entails 'non-zero difference'.[126] It is against the basis of parity that difference can be ascertained, asserted, and justified. Parity shows how, in the face of incommensurability, the comparison – more accurately, a given comparatist's given comparison – holds.

Observe that parity accommodates preference. For example, while the French statute and the Canadian decision in *Multani* exist on a par, a comparatist can well prefer one to the other. From a French vantage point, the French statute will in all likelihood appear especially sensible to the extent that it inscribes an inverse correlation between French citizenship and religious visibility: *part of what it is to be French is to accede to the view that the deployment of religious belonging ought to be excluded from the public sphere, regardless of one's personal commitments.* Meanwhile, from a Canadian outlook, the Canadian judicial decision can be foreseen to look particularly attractive as it marks a direct correlation between Canadian citizenship and religious visibility: *part of what it is to be Canadian is to accede to the view that the deployment of religious belonging ought to be allowed in the public sphere, regardless of one's personal commitments.* Still, I accept the (evident) fact that there are people in France who are drawn to multiculturalism, and I admit that an argument for laicity could win some support in Canada – although one would expect the relevant proposition to have to be adjusted, or localized, so that it could resonate beyond the legal culture of whose practice it is the informing theory. What must remain fanciful, however, is the formulation of a contention vindicating one of the different claims in a way that would prove acceptable *both* to the French and Canadians, or the delineation of a postulation that would seem persuasive within *both* prevailing paradigms. In particular, one cannot reasonably imagine a situation where the French would

124 ibid 122.

125 See ibid.

126 cf Melas (n 33) 31: '[T]here is a "basis for comparison" . . . , but "no ground of equivalence" when it comes to the . . . analysis of . . . knowledge.'

understand the Canadian position on its own terms and according to its own justifications; then proceed to identify inadequacies in the Canadian view that the Canadians themselves would accept; and finally explain how, by resorting to the French model, these difficulties could be avoided in a manner that the Canadians would countenance. If you will, the French strategy pertains to Canada's unthought (itself ultimately a constitutive part of Canada's thinking).[127] And 'every culture has its own unthought implicit to its episteme, *irreducible* to the mode of the unthought of another culture'.[128] In my view, the example of the French statute and Canadian judicial decision convincingly shows how the comparatist must read across laws so as to create interpretive crises even as national lawyers read within laws so as to resolve them (the discipline of private international law standing as the epitome of this conciliatory impulse).[129]

Albeit from another angle, my analysis readily captures the epistemic argument that I have developed in favour of agonism as the idea of parity resists the kind of hierarchization simulating consensualism whereby one model effectively becomes a referent for others at the expense of others. Instead, parity means an entitlement for each model to exist in co-presence, if adversarially, that is, singularly or differentially. It follows that parity across laws must inform other-oriented comparison-at-law – or comparison other-wise. Percipiently, Samuel Beckett captures the enigmaticity of this situation as he refers to 'the simple and necessary and yet so unattainable proposition that their way of being we, [is] not our way and that our way of being they, [is] not their way'.[130] When the Canadian state is being a state dealing with religious attire in public schools, like France, the Canadian state's way of being *that* (a state dealing with religious attire in public schools) or the Canadian state's way of being a state that, like France, is dealing with religious attire in public schools or, in short, the Canadian state's way of being France as regards religious attire in public schools, is not France's way. This

127 cf R Visker, *Truth and Singularity* (Kluwer 1999) 395.

128 Xie (n 112) 44 [my emphasis].

129 See S Fish, *Doing What Comes Naturally* (Duke University Press 1989) 136–37. Making specific reference to comparative law, the late Rodolfo Sacco also draws the distinction between the two configurations I mention. See R Sacco, *Introduzione al diritto comparato* (5th edn, UTET 1992) 47. Incidentally, Sacco observes that 'comparison consists in measuring the differences that exist across a multiplicity of legal models': ibid 11.

130 S Beckett, 'The Capital of the Ruins' in *The Complete Short Prose* (SE Gontarski ed, Grove 1995 [1946]) 277.

position also carries in reverse concerning France vis-à-vis Canada. The French statute and the Canadian judgment thus exist on a par: they are *coeval*. I maintain that the singularity of the two laws and the attendant untranslatability across laws – there is no dialogue, and there is more than one monologue – require acknowledgement; indeed, they demand recognition and respect.

It must be clear that the French and Canadians are using different conceptions of 'orderly polity' – or rather, of what I, operating as comparatist, denominate as 'orderly polity'. For I am at work *inventing* an (unobjectivizable and untruthable) notion of 'orderly polity' through a 'thirding' of knowledge on account of which I can stage a forced negotiation between French and Canadian laws possibilitating my comparison. Observe how my notion of 'orderly polity' enacts my decision to compel French and Canadian laws into a negotiation that would not otherwise happen. It is not, obviously, that local manifestations of 'orderly polity' can be reduced to a figment of my imagination. Rather, it is that, in interpretive response to the information that I have garnered in the course of my research, in reaction to the particulars that I have chosen to retain out of the available concatenation of details arising from my scrutinization, I frame 'orderly polity' in my (encultured) way, according to my (encultured) ingenuity – to my (encultured) 'flair'[131] – in the humble realization that my (encultured) construction is refutable, at least to the extent that a more convincing argument can be found to carry over mine (or that I myself may later commit to an improved interpretation). And I must accept that my 'orderly polity' pertains to narrativity, for no reading of a law-text can be dissociated from a commentary on it. Since no account of foreign law is wholly free of narrativity, it follows that every report on foreign law is autobiographical, the expression of a *partial* point of view that, like every comparatist, I call mine (and that finds itself vying for influence with other partial observations by other comparatists).[132] Note that no amount of logic, precision, or clarity in the comparatist's record of foreign law – and certainly no so-called 'method' – can eliminate narrativity from his transcript, which is fated to remain an *incomplete* and *orientated* exposition. The more the comparatist 'keeps wanting

[131] J Derrida, *De la grammatologie* (Editions de Minuit 1967) 233.

[132] Because of enculturation, every report on foreign law is also autoheterographical.

to add just one more word, in the futile hope of making it all clear',[133] the more *storied* his rendition of foreign law becomes.

*

The matter of differential analysis of laws effortlessly segues into two further indispensable investigations regarding, first, the task of cultural critique and, secondly, the cultural agent of the critique himself – two additional threshold sets of considerations relating to the theoretical matrix within which I argue comparative law must operate and, indeed, two topics compelling further theorization at radical variance from the culture-less and agentivity-less framework that the Positivist Engine has been implementing as it has been exercising epistemic governance of the field, a socio-intellectual arena thus shown to remain woefully under-theorized.[134]

133 JH Miller, 'Zero' in J Wolfreys (ed), *Glossalalia* (Routledge 2003) 388.

134 In July 2018, I encountered a statement on the Internet to the effect that comparative law might be 'over-theorized' [on file], an unsupported assertion that I continue to regard with consternation. How would Lawrence Rosen react to such a flippant pronouncement? I refer to Rosen, supra 69. For my part, I find myself being reminded of the connection that Max Horkheimer famously draws between the 'hostility' to theory and the opposition to 'critical thought': M Horkheimer, *Traditionelle und kritische Theorie* (Fischer 2011 [1937]) 249. An observation from Theodor Adorno's also seems apposite: 'The not narrow-minded is [what is] represented in theory': TW Adorno, *Stichworte: Kritische Modelle 2* in *Kulturkritik und Gesellschaft*, vol 2 (R Tiedemann et al eds, Suhrkamp 2003 [1969†]) 763.

X

Comparatism Is Culturalism

My argument begins with jurists in general and then moves to comparatists-at-law in particular.

*

If jurists are to prove at all able to calibrate the power that culture holds over them, they must first show cognizance of the epistemic conditions pursuant to which they came into being as legal agents and appreciate that they are not acting freely while operating pursuant to the paradigm they apply. They must accept that their world-view is framed. Specifically, they must become aware that they are the product of a process of socialization and institutionalization, of *enculturation*, such that the scheme of apprehension they bring to bear upon their juristic doings is informed by determinants of their consciousness and behaviour that have been 'orchestrated' in advance of any intervention in the law on their part. (How happy or displeased legal agents are about the world-view into which they have been epistemologized is irrelevant for present purposes, my basic claim being that the world-view in question has come to cabin one's agency through a 'naturalization' process that strongly limits one's openness to alternative options.)

Although only after coming to enhanced discernment can legal agents reasonably hope to accede to a state of greater freedom, it is unlikely that they can ever reach full awareness given that the epistemic control over their inner lives may be so extensive and so profound. In any case, even increased realization may not be enough to dissolve social or institutional coercion, not to mention epistemological constraints. Unlike, say, neurotic repression, which can potentially be overcome through a struggle with oneself, neither society nor the institutional or epistemological complex can be abolished merely by changes in the legal agent's beliefs, since a combat with culture involves a fight with a phenomenon that ultimately lies beyond the self's volition and reach. In addition to a change in form of consciousness, a (long) course of political action may be required before, say, a certain institution actually stops restricting the intellectual freedom of the now hypothetically enlightened legal agent. Meanwhile, the newly found illumination I assume may well increase frustration by magnifying disappointment. At least, though, one can be rid of the compulsion to believe in the institution as a necessary fact, and institutional oppression may find itself delegitimized to this extent. How, then, does one move from a state of delusion regarding agential autonomy to a condition of amplified understanding with respect to the limits restricting self-determination? How does one make one's way from epistemic bondage towards release?

In advance of any answer, I wish to observe that the 'clarification', whether it should arise from the augmented knowledge of practices or magnified self-knowledge, is somewhat paradoxically likely to generate resistance from those it would benefit – say, academics or scholars of the law – given that legal agents believe in the legitimacy of their 'community' and derive gratification from participation in the life of their 'community' in a way that would be endangered by critical emancipation. In other words, legal agents may come to perceive that they acquired certain beliefs under compulsion, but they may well decide to abide by these 'convictions' nonetheless. (For example, they may elect to maintain the stance they were taught in their French law school that the *Cour de cassation* – the French supreme court in matters of private law – behaves objectively and apolitically, that is, 'scientifically', as they may choose to uphold the view that was instilled into them by their mentors that the *agrégation*, France's state-controlled qualifying examination for aspiring law professors, is an intellectually liberating rather than a soul-crushing experience.) Effectively, the decision thus being made entails the withholding of any challenge to the legitimatory institutional apparatus (particularly so in the light of the burdens that the abandonment and replacement of the opinions at stake would impose upon agents). One can thus appreciate how power, when it is exercised in the performative mode, may assert itself to quash an opportunity for relief from subjection.

Because culture and the ensuing enculturation process assume a single, fully integrated domain of cognitive authority, the development of an alternative perspective, of another world-view, requires cultural *differentiation*. There are probably many 'solutions' on offer to implement such a programme of relativization. With a view to estranging one's legal culture and one's culture, I have long found myself, for my part, being interpellated by one specific transgressive strategy. My personal and professional itineraries – not least the fact that I have taught law on a full-time basis in four different countries for a minimum of three years on each occasion – show that I have considered this approach as offering a meaningful promise of epistemic deliverance. I refer to comparative law. In this regard, however, I have been facing an important difficulty inasmuch as the orthodox theoretical model on offer within the field of comparative law to inform one's practice does not meaningfully assist one's research into foreign law, a lack of relevance that I have had occasion to ascertain for myself when I have had to make sense of foreign law in the context of the full-time teaching positions I have been occupying in England, the Netherlands, and France.

Irrespective of the implacable injunctions comparative law's orthodoxy has been directing at me,[1] I have not felt, for instance, that I could ever detach myself from my cultural background as I came to the study of foreign law, and I have not thought it made any sense to uproot foreign law from its cultural background as I was conducting my examination of it. Indeed, the epistemological challenges I faced in the foreign countries where I worked presented themselves in exactly the opposite way. For example, it was obvious to me that I had to contend with my own enculturation as I sought to appreciate foreign law on its own terms as much as was reasonably feasible, just as it was evident to me that I had to understand the foreign law's enculturation in order to make any meaningful sense of whatever law-text I was investigating. Equally clearly, I could never convince myself that to confine my comparative intervention to the examination of a posited foreign law would allow me to reveal anything of *significance* about that foreign law's existence even as the bulk of the comparative endeavours before me were firmly ensconced within the positivist enterprise. Typically, these undertakings were devoted to the juxtaposition of results in the search for what I regarded (and continue to regard) as narrow, dubious, and deceptive employability in terms of what would be envisaged (profoundly mistakenly, in my opinion) as the ready utility of epigrammatic foreign-law snippets aiming to show the laws' ultimate equivalence or commonality.

[1] Eg: K Zweigert and H Kötz, *Einführung in die Rechtsvergleichung* (3rd edn, Mohr Siebeck 1996) 11 and 43: '[T]he comparatist must unfasten himself from his own juridical-dogmatic preconceptions and his own cultural context'/'The solutions of the investigated legal orders are to be freed of all systematic concepts of these legal orders, to be unfastened out of their solely-national dogmatic incrustrations.'

It would be disingenuous at this point not to offer an illustration of the brand of scholarship I condemn for its lack of an intellectually rewarding theoretical framework, its pursuit of an agenda favouring range over depth or thickness of coverage, its formulaic insistence on law as consisting only of legislative enactments and (reported) judicial decisions (with occasional doctrinal texts), its unwillingness to engage in anything beyond the most superficial exercise in indiscipline, and its almost total absence of critical insight.[2] The comparative study I propose to critique, which appeared in a prominent comparative law journal, concerns abortion in francophone jurisdictions.[3]

The three co-authors address French law – which they regard as the cornerstone of their analysis – in one and a half pages. Luxembourg is explored in one paragraph and Belgium in just over a page. 'Other Francophone Countries' are discussed in sixteen lines, while 'Hybrid Francophone States' are treated in slightly less than a page. This congeries of dryly reductive reports is almost exclusively preoccupied with references to extant legislated texts, although three Belgian decisions are briefly summarized. The twenty-two page 'comparative' survey that follows is organized around topics such as 'definition [of abortion]', 'grounds for abortion', 'procedural conditions', and so forth. It also consists in a descriptive account of the posited law as the co-authors understand it with frequent, if cursory, reference to legislative materials and occasional inclusion (without discussion) of judicial decisions. Some mention of scholarly commentaries deemed apposite completes the digest – even as introductory texts and entries in encyclopaedias better suited to harried practitioners than to academics interested in serious comparative scholarship simply cannot be regarded as adequate substitutes for the much richer examinations published in the indigenous languages. (All in all, it seems that the selection of the secondary literature had at least as much to do with its

[2] As I develop this argument, I am painfully aware that some of my early work is open to the rejoinder that it is itself guilty of a positivist emphasis on rules. I am thinking of various publications that I authored before permanently leaving Canada – which I deliberately refrain from indicating (and *tant pis* for the citation index). My *historia calamitatum* would show that I was once fashioned into an obedient positivist, in touch with 'truth', and therefore insouciant. In my abjected life, I had not yet read Pierre Schlag's scathing and judicious indictment of positivism's deleterious ways. See P Schlag, *The Enchantment of Reason* (Duke University Press 1998).

[3] See BM Knoppers et al, 'Abortion Law in Francophone Countries' (1990) 38 Am J Comp L 889.

ready accessibility at the local law library as with its intrinsic merit.) I quote typical passages:

> Morocco is the only country considered in this study where there is a positive requirement that the husband give his consent to the abortion. (The footnote specifies the source of this obligation as royal decree no. 181–66 of 1 July 1967 modifying article 453 of the penal code.[4])
> Unlike the other countries looked at in this section, the Belgian legislators have determined that it would be excessive to punish someone whose actions had, in fact, brought no result (i.e., where the child survives the attempt). (The footnote adduces an entry in a leading multi-volume encyclopaedia devoted to Belgian law in general.[5])

A brief protocol and a shorter conclusion inform the reader that '[a] multitude of conflicting factors make legislating in this area supremely complex' and that '[e]ven when ... liberalization is achieved through the decriminalization of abortion ..., it is rendered meaningless when procedural or geographical constraints make access difficult or impossible'.[6] Neither of these banal statements is further substantiated by any critical consideration of relevant data. I wish to emphasize that, in its approach to comparative law, this text affords one illustration inter very many aliases rather than an isolated occurrence.[7] In other words, I am individuating this article on account of its representative character and not because of its idiosyncrasies. It is the case, however, that while the particulars of this study are in no way exceptional, the survey proves especially demonstrative

[4] ibid 912.

[5] ibid 917.

[6] ibid 889 and 920.

[7] Lest it be thought that I harbour ulterior motives in directing my reprobation at a specific contribution, I should disclose the main features of the elementary selection process I implemented. I first decided to confine my search to journals published in English given that I am myself writing in this language. I then opted to make my choice out of the American Journal of Comparative Law, arguably the leading periodical in the field. I subsequently determined to examine the volume for the year 1990 – a 'round' number allowing for a 'safe' thirty-year critical distance (twenty seemed too close, forty too remote). Before I opened the annual bound volume, I had formed the view that I would consider the first ten articles listed under 'Index of Titles'. As I perused the index, I retained the text most obviously 'comparative' to me in terms of its design. Interestingly, I thought, this article happened to address a topical and controversial question of great social and political significance, that is, of meaningful cultural import. It thus had the potential readily and strikingly to illustrate the gap between what could be achieved by comparatists approaching their research with responsible, respondent sensibility, and what I intuited had effectively been done in this instance. Incidentally, while I focussed on a law-review article, I could also have introduced a book, since very many of the monographs or textbooks produced under the banner of 'comparative law' tend to be epistemologically deficient also.

of the instrumental voracity that orthodox comparative law can disclose and the kind of embalming narrative it can pursue.[8] It also reveals comparative law's existential paradox: not enough of it (there is a dearth of comparative work vis-à-vis what remains stubbornly local legal analysis), but too much of it (there is a surfeit of insistently positivist comparative legal analysis still).

In sum, I required another model to replace what I had come to regard, in relatively short order, as the profoundly impoverished scheme on offer from the orthodoxy within the field of comparative law. I therefore resolved to fashion an alternative approach to the acquisition of foreign legal information that would tally with my 'fieldwork' experience, so to speak, in England, the Netherlands, and France (to which I could easily add, beyond these three foreign venues where I held full-time teaching posts, the long list of countries in which I assumed visiting professorships over many years). In brief, I would focus on 'the modalities of the production and reception of law as legal meaning'.[9] This insight suggested an investigation into legal discourse, but it also intimated an inquiry into a further discourse that had produced the legal discourse, a kind of meta-discourse, if you will. I took the view that it was through the articulation of such meta-discourse with the legal discourse that I could profitably ascribe meaning to foreign law in the sense of deep or thick meaning (as opposed to surface or thin meaning). It followed that I had to acquire detailed and creditable information on the historical, linguistic, philosophical, political, psychological, and social discourses informing the law – that is, on the *cultural* commitments underlying and determining the foreign law-texts, whose traces lurked between the lines of the law-texts themselves, encrypted in the texts' fabrics. How else could I survive in the law, let alone situate myself as a *connected critic*, in the diverse foreign countries where I dwelled?

[8] The brand of reductionism I discuss prompts me to refer to the Internet, which is emphatically not to be regarded as a strictly vehicular form wholly transparent to the texts it delivers. In other words, as the materiality of foreign law-texts gets pixelated over a screen, both the textuality of the foreign and the reading of that textuality are affected. Although electronic diffusion advantageously allows for planetary dissemination of foreign law, this process assumes production of the material in the guise of web-oriented content – which means that a foreign judicial decision, for instance, often finds itself *gauged*, that is, summarized and translated into English. As a result, the tendency to content oneself with snippets of information-in-translation and the attendant illusion of understanding are liable to manifest themselves even more baldly than was the case before the Internet became omnipresent. Meanwhile, the tension between access *to* information and distortion *of* information is genuine. Otherwise put, the imperative for the comparatist to guard against shallowness and resist the urge to satisfice is, if anything, stronger than ever.

[9] P Goodrich, *Legal Discourse* (St Martin's 1987) 211.

*

There was never any question of losing the law from sight, because it was always the law that I aimed meaningfully to understand. (I was trained as a jurist and a lawyer, was I not?) But I formed the view, on account of my general interaction with foreignness and because of discussions with foreign colleagues, that the foreign law-texts I was considering were culturally saturated – indeed, how could it realistically be otherwise? Along the way, I refuted the idea of the necessary foreign law-text (since matters were different across laws), just as I rejected the view of the accidental foreign law-text (since difference could not reasonably be said to have to do with chance). I held that each meaningful foreign law-text – yes, even texts in the field of commercial law,[10] a subject I taught for years – featured significant cultural embeddedment (that is, the engrainment happened in a manner that signified, that carried meaning). To be sure, this intricate cultural complex was not any more 'given' than the foreign law itself and would, just like the foreign law itself, require to be interpretively elucidated by interpreters such as myself, all of us encultured.[11] The recognition or legitimation or sanction of any law-text within a given foreign legal 'community' or society at large – in other words, the law-text's authoritativeness – depended, at least in part, on its adherence to the cultural expectations that had developed over time in a specific place, possibly over the *longue* or *très longue durée*. In other words, the foreign law-text had to harbour certain cultural insignia in order to register on the culturograph of a legal 'community' or society. Would an anonymous Supreme Court judgment running to half a page without any references to earlier decisions be recognized as a *judgment* in England? Would a highly personalized *Cour de cassation* judgment running to eighty pages with dozens of references to earlier decisions be recognized as a *judgment* (or '*arrêt*') in France? Now, even if I had not understood that my attempt to characterize certain of the peculiarities of English or French legal discourse was also a political project, the

[10] Eg: B Kozolchyk, *Comparative Commercial Contracts: Law, Culture and Economic Development* (2nd edn, West 2018).

[11] cf J Culler, *Framing the Sign* (Blackwell 1988) ix: '[T]he opposition between an act and its context seems to presume that the context is given and determines the meaning of the act. We know, of course, that things are not so simple: context is not fundamentally different from what it contextualizes; context is not given but produced; what belongs to a context is determined by interpretive strategies; contexts are just as much in need of elucidation as events; and the meaning of a context is determined by events.' While I would not talk of 'context' – it is not that there is culture around the law, but that *law exists as culture* – the gist of Culler's observation holds, hence my quotation.

resistance I soon met within comparative law as I began to retrench from positivism would have promptly reminded me of this abiding fact.

As a foreigner teaching and researching law in England, the Netherlands, or France, I was involved in an interminable act of comparison.[12] It was clear to me that if I was going to engage in the counter-positivist close reading of law-texts I had in mind and that I felt creditable comparativism demanded, I had to marshal a set of appropriate appliances. Where to find them given orthodox comparative law's fatally flawed material? I had to look elsewhere – that is, in other fields. I did so. After having read scores of books and articles, I felt able to articulate two sets of implements, which I thought could sustain my comparative enterprise. (I insist that there was no epiphany, but rather a lengthy trial-and-error process unfolding over a number of years, at once an exhilarating and distressing experience.)

First, I identified what I have been calling, after Michel Foucault, the archaeological or genealogical dimension of the comparative motion, which I thought required to be addressed in terms of key notions such as culture and otherness. Secondly, I ascertained the epistemological argument, which involved a recourse to Jacques Derrida's deconstruction (with a few important insights from Hans-Georg Gadamer's hermeneutics), tracing, and flair. Interestingly, some of my readings brought me into contact with academics whose work, unlike the example on abortion laws I mention, purported precisely to attest to the enculturation of law as they searched for its meaningful meaning. Consider Gerald Bruns's forceful statement: '[T]he law … is not a system … but … a heterogeneous cultural practice.'[13] Crucially, I was now able to appreciate that the brand of comparative law

[12] Even if I limited my research strictly to English, Dutch, or French law, the fact that I came to the relevant law as a foreigner compelled me to comparison, since I processed – and indeed could only process – every law-text that I encountered through my encultured frame of reference, which was not English, Dutch, or French.

[13] GL Bruns, 'Law and Language: A Hermeneutics of the Legal Text' in G Leyh (ed), *Legal Hermeneutics* (University of California Press 1992) 33. Accord: S Fish, *There's No Such Thing as Free Speech* (Oxford University Press 1994) 193. See generally eg L Rosen, *Law as Culture* (Princeton University Press 2006); PW Kahn, *The Cultural Study of Law* (University of Chicago Press 1999); G Watt (general ed), *A Cultural History of Law*, 6 vols (Bloomsbury 2019). See also eg W Gephart, *Recht als Kultur* (Klostermann 2006). Having been coerced to publish a book by the director of the research institute into which I had been co-opted against my will during my years of teaching in the Netherlands, I very reluctantly produced my own effort: P Legrand, *Fragments on Law-as-Culture* (Tjeenk Willink 1999). To style this book an *erreur de jeunesse* is perhaps unduly harsh, but I am not proud of it (not least because I never received the promised proofs so that I could not correct the publisher's many mistakes) – and I hide my copies in the basement of my secondary residence.

I had in mind, and the paradigmatic shift that this configuration seemed to entail vis-à-vis the pattern to which orthodox comparatists had accustomed me over a decade or so, could be revealingly cathected to signal and influential contributions 'less interested in the psychology of individual minds or in the constitution of a universal human nature than in the … shared understandings and ideals that make up the [legal] culture of a society'.[14]

Where was the meta-discourse that interested me and that I regarded as capital? Where was *culture* to be found? And what was the character of its connection with the law? What did it mean to contend that law existed as culture, that law was effectively *law-as-culture*? Did culture actually – and somewhat mechanically – cause the law to be what it was? Or were the dynamics at work more complicated, more subtle, too? While the answers to these questions remained fuzzy, I could identify rough parameters to guide my exploration. Without claiming unity of form or anything like systematicity, I could discern, for example, various regularities emerging in the range of the discursive legal formations that I was encountering. All English judgments I read thus appeared to attach great importance to facts and indeed seemed to make the enunciation of the law dependent upon the particular reading of the facts they retained. Interestingly, this normative construction did not seem to obtain in France, where the *Cour de cassation* appeared more preoccupied with upholding the conceptual coherence of the law – to dispel errors of logic – more or less over against the facts. Upon close reading, the justificatory strategies deployed by the courts disclosed other contrastive patterns, too.

In my search for elucidation, I certainly did not take the view that there existed a repository of knowledge that would supply me with 'the' answer to any of my interrogations. For one thing, I was well aware that there were many different interpretive voices expressing themselves around me. When I taught in the north-west of England in the early 1990s, for instance, I only had to walk down the corridor to meet the gamut of positivist, Marxist, critical, structuralist, and postmodern views. Of course, none of these theoretical stances would account identically, say, for the English statute on privity of contracts.[15] I could never be in any doubt, therefore, about the range of theoretical models on offer. Through this heterogeneity, some voices inevitably carried more authority than others within the 'communities' of academics, lawyers, and

[14] RM Unger, *Law in Modern Society* (Free Press 1976) 5.

[15] Contracts (Rights of Third Parties) Act 1999, ch 31.

judges – some re-presentations, and some contestations also, were better received. Be that as it may, I could appreciate that whatever theoretical scheme I would adopt would not prove uncontroversial and would find itself being disputed, perhaps vehemently, by some of my colleagues, English or otherwise. I insist that I never deluded myself into believing in the existence of any consensual 'internal' agreement within the various legal 'communities' where I worked. In sum, it never occurred to me to essentialize, say, Englishness or Frenchness. As I considered the privity-of-contract statute, for instance, I never assumed that the answers to the issues detaining me had to involve information uniquely English, essentially English, that would not be found anywhere else on the planet and would accordingly be beyond the reach of anyone not born and bred in England. But I did take the view that the answer to my concerns about the privity statute could not be found in Brazil or Sweden. I had to look within England, being aware, of course, that what were now (or, more accurately, what I now took to be) the English ways – say, English legal culture – could well prove the result of an assimilation or amalgamation of practices having been imported and adapted from other jurisdictions. Be that as it may, if the posited law held any interest for comparatists – if, say, the study of the liability of municipal officers or aspects of inheritance law held any meaningful interest for comparatists-at-law – it had to be in terms of the way legal culture manifested itself through these rules and as these rules. Contrariwise, the identification of foreign law as a set of legal rules, and its reduction to *that*, presented insufficient intellectual interest.[16] (After all, if I needed information regarding an Italian legal rule, I would do much better to turn to an Italian lawyer than approach a US comparatist.)

Observe that I am not arguing that the posited dimension of the law is irrelevant. For a jurist or lawyer, this contention would seem very silly. Of course, it matters, for example, how judicial decisions are interpreting the wording of a statute. And as a comparatist coming, say, to English contract law, I imperatively require to mobilize a sound understanding

[16] cf LM Friedman, 'Book Review' (1979) 6 British J L & Society 127, 129 (review of A Watson, *Society and Legal Change* [Scottish Academic Press 1977]): 'The idea of spending a lifetime of study on some pitiful handful of cases about horses that kick at a stable-boy, or dogs that tear up the roses – that this could or should be at the heart of legal scholarship – strikes me as almost bizarre.' For a measure of the road yet to be travelled, contrast M Bogdan, 'On the Value and Method of Rule-Comparison in Comparative Law' in H-P Mansel et al (eds), *Festschrift für Erik Jayme* (Sellier 2004) 1233, 1242: '[Rule-oriented comparisons] are . . . a very useful and scientifically rewarding enterprise, requiring the use of sophisticated and advanced research methods.'

of the relevant doctrinal issues (which, in this specific instance, I have long been able to do on account of the excellent teaching that I received from Michael Bridge). My claim is rather that the comparative endeavour cannot be allowed to stop where it begins, that is, it cannot be permitted to renounce the pursuit of deep or thick understanding once it has covered the 'black-letter' law – which must rather be regarded as a springboard towards a more elaborate interpretation. Crucially, while positivism must exclude culture in order to be positivism, culturalism can afford to include a positivist component and remain culturalism. In the process, culturalism shows itself to be counter-hegemonic rather than offer a substitutive hegemonic discourse. Operating non-hegemonically, it addresses the positivist hegemony obliquely.

When the time came to prepare my classes for my English, Dutch, or French students, I had to accept that the theoretical texts on offer within comparative law did not operate along the lines of law-as-culture and could not help me. Except for a few, very few, notable instances, comparatists had been steadfastly confining themselves to the very identificatory and reductive processes that I was keen to surpass – and what choice did I have but to engage in resolute surpassing if I wanted to ascribe meaningful meaning to foreign law-texts? As a result, there was very little by way of scholarly materials that I could mobilize for my archaeological/genealogical and deconstructive/hermeneutical endeavours. If I wanted to abide by my ambition to pursue *understanding*, an aspiration that still inspires my work many years later,[17] I would have to plough a new furrow with a view, primordially, to overcoming any form of flattening of foreignness's singularity, entangling the cultural and the legal, deploying the legal as cultural, enacting the entity 'law-as-culture'. This would be comparative law *other-wise* – a different brand of comparatism resolutely attuned to the singularity of the different otherness-in-the-law.

For a quarter of a century or so at this writing, I have unceasingly been arguing against orthodox comparatists that comparative law requires a different episteme and another ethics – in short, an alternative intellectual politics. Elements of this *paradoxical* programme – an argument designed to circumvent the doxa – first appeared in print in England in the mid-1990s. The ways of our institutional worlds being what they are, I proceeded under the assumption that the battle for another comparative law would in all likelihood confine me to a somewhat marginal itinerancy at the edge of the field (no matter how bevelled). And, as I had expected,

[17] Eg: P Legrand, 'Foreign Law: Understanding Understanding' (2011) 6(2) J Comp L 67.

the bulk of orthodox comparatists-at-law have been content to ignore my writing or disparage it, thus confirming my intuition that one cannot blithely purport to be disrupting the basic epistemological security system prevailing within the field.[18] (Think of a wire barrier, floodlit, and dog-patrolled.) To say the very least, my attempt at epistemological consciousness-raising was received as indecorous. In response, I could simply have left comparative law and, rather than obstinately inscribe my counter-signature whenever I had the opportunity to do so, have made my intellectual life elsewhere – as one erstwhile comparatist-at-law whose critical work I discuss in *NCL* proceeded to do. (I could have continued as a commercial-law specialist, for instance – incidentally, a much more lucrative pursuit.) Instead, plausibly for a range of identifiable biographical reasons, I have been standing firmly at the periphery of comparative law, where I have come to feel somewhat strangely at home. There, I have been forging my work as a point of pressure on the orthodoxy, and I have been incessantly promoting a different paradigm. As far as the field of comparative law is concerned, the anti-positivist position, the pro-culturalist stance that I defend remains a staunchly minoritarian view, if an *irritating* one.[19]

I do not deliberately mean to inflame the paternal law, as if to ensure that it is still there. I do not care for Oedipal games or for what Georges Bataille, referring to Icarus's pathological desire to be struck, termed 'subterfuges Icarian'.[20] I am neither making a neurotic plea for punishment nor engaging in a paranoid demand for *Ordnung*. I have no deliberate wish to become a 'puerile victi[m]', a 'contemptible victi[m] of incomprehension and general brutishness'.[21] I do not intentionally favour 'outraged provocation having as a goal to attract on myself

[18] At times, orthodox behaviour has proved caricatural enough to attract scholarly attention, thus confirming the fact that being ignored or denigrated can lead to another form of academic existence. Eg: G Watt, 'Comparison as Deep Appreciation' in PG Monateri (ed), *Methods of Comparative Law* (Elgar 2012) 83; M Siems, 'Book Review' (2008) 12 Edinburgh LR 334, 335 (review of E Örücü and D Nelken [eds], *Comparative Law: A Handbook* [Hart 2007]). (Having noted the latter text for present purposes, I would not want to be taken to endorse the statistical apprehension of the matter of relevance that it features. I firmly believe that calculative reason does not deserve to be debased in the way it is in this argument.)

[19] For the claim that my work 'irritates the . . . consensus of comparativists', see G Teubner, 'Legal Irritants: Good Faith in British Law or How Unifying Law Ends Up in New Divergences' (1998) 61 Modern LR 11, 14.

[20] G Bataille, 'La "vieille taupe" et le préfixe sur dans les mots surhomme et surréaliste' in *Œuvres complètes*, vol 2 (Gallimard 1970) 109.

[21] ibid 104.

a brutal and immediate retribution'.[22] I am not eager to be tweaked by Hein Kötz or spanked by James Gordley.[23] To be sure, I do aim to undo the (epistemological) law of comparative law. And I do want to be much more than a deferential comparatist. Yes. Still, I have never sought to engage in polemical denunciation for its own sake. To be sure, I propugn a model, but I refrain from procacity. As I apprehend the transgressive character of my work to be tracing a fracture within the symbolic order that brands itself 'comparative law',[24] my ambition has been to intensify, with all the scholarly integrity I could muster, the awareness of the limits that comparative thought – or foreign law – owes to its encultured conditions of production and to get rid of the illusion that comparatists – or foreign laws – operate free of epistemic limits.

My contrarian challenge, then, is to the effect that the comparatist cannot remain fixated on foreign law as a strictly ruleful entity and pretend to be construing foreign law-texts in a detached or neutral manner, thereby providing what would be descriptively validating reports about the foreign that could claim objective appreciation or true understanding. Contrarianism thus questions comparative-law's overly choreographed or patterned practices, and it enables a clearer, if disconcerting, awareness of the restricted reach of these scenarios, which can only generate reified, lifeless information. The fact is that the indisciplined stance that allows value, intensity, and meaning to be caught in the comparative work can be seen as blurred theoreticist hypostatization only from within seemingly secure, decisive disciplinary enclosures advocating unalloyed diremption. And this fearful view of indiscipline obscures new articulations that are most suitable for addressing basic questions that themselves cut across disciplines such as the connection between a text and its (mnemic and material) traces. In so far as the instrumentalization of comparative law has been experienced as requiring boundary-setting and positioning theory to be a largely superfetatious pursuit, my programmatic call for a lucid theoretical undergirding of comparatism and for epistemic humility, too – an interpellation that neither laments nor mourns the loss of securities

22 ibid 103. In suggesting 'skilfu[l]' deliberateness on my part, Basil Markesinis is presumably surrendering to projection: B Markesinis, *Comparative Law in the Courtroom and Classroom* (Hart 2003) 159.

23 I follow H Foster, *Compulsive Beauty* (MIT Press 1993) 112.

24 I draw on H Foster, *The Return of the Real* (MIT Press 1996) 157.

that were always illusory in any event – may be interpreted as a return of the repressed.[25]

Comparative law other-wise is also – let me recall – a protest against plenitude, a resistance to a hubris of sufficiency that would have local law (most often, still, national law) revel in its self-adequacy. As an exercise in epistemic disobedience, in epistemic liberation, too, as an intervention purporting to delink the study of law from the positivist matrix having aggressively informed it – an 'enabling violation'[26] – comparison otherwise thus signifies *horror pleni*. Of course, from the vantage point of the formal order of the positivist whole, it partakes in chaos – at best in the sense of *Kunstchaos*[27] – inasmuch as it proclaims the inacceptability of totalization. Through its effectuation of the principle of *varietas*, by way of its emphasis on the discontinuity and delocalization of information as opposed to anything like a unitary body of objective or true knowledge, comparatism acts as a kind of schizophrenic not-all. It is, in fact, the prevalence and vehemence of totalizing thought itself that confers on the act of comparison its disruptive – its *radically* disruptive – rhetorical valence or violence. An appreciation for the profoundly subversive or counter-hegemonic character of comparative studies must therefore assume an awareness of the reach of totalizing thought. In this regard, I claim that totalization is very much the dominant cognitive thread, at least since the Enlightenment purported to develop a coherent body of thought aiming at the production of rational universals, that is, since it 'sought to produce describable constants out of [what it perceived to be] the morass of idiosyncrasies . . . whose terms seemed to legitimate nothing beyond absolute hedonism and libertinism'.[28]

Orthodox comparatists-at-law having transposed positivism from its national confines in order to deploy across borders the only epistemic model they knew and loved, comparative law stands as a field where the dominant idea assumes a cognitive path stretching from the comparatist's initial ignorance about foreign law to his acquisition of a total knowledge of it, a process somehow unfolding independently of any

[25] See P Legrand, 'The Return of the Repressed: Moving Comparative Legal Studies Beyond Pleasure' (2001) 75 Tulane LR 1033.

[26] GC Spivak, *A Critique of Postcolonial Reason* (Harvard University Press 1999) 371.

[27] The idea is that of a skilful chaos, a chaos produced by thought, a chaos that is the outcome of scholarly or philosophical reflection as opposed, say, to brute or crude chaos. The German term is in F Schlegel, *Kritische Schriften und Fragmente*, vol 2 (E Behler and H Eichner eds, Schöningh 1988 [1798]) 146.

[28] D Simpson, *Situatedness* (Duke University Press 2002) 5.

cultural setting (either the comparatist's or the foreign law's). If you will, the images in the cave are replaced by clear vision, a vision that is at once straightforward, transparent, and unified. According to this world-view, the reticence to embark on a quest for grounded certainty, for achievable objectivity and truth, amounts to blind confusion in the old myths or wilful epistemic unrest. In other words, the only worthwhile cognitive search becomes that of aiming for ever more totalizing perception resting on ever firmer grounds of knowledge. Anything other than the pursuit of *guaranteed* integral knowledge smacks of a pernicious anti-philosophy reminiscent of the advocacy of Plato's Gorgias.

But not even an idealization of cognitive form can creditably claim its independence from ethical/political orientations. Thus, comparative law's orthodox *Weltanschauung* also heralds a politics, which at the very least evinces a love of order and stability, ultimately a preference for authority and arguably for some authoritarianism, too. Indeed, Descartes's stigmatization of custom, education, and social pressure at the beginning of his *Discours de la méthode* is not at all innocent. In this respect, the conjecture I defend is, I think, expressible in cursory language: totalizing thought (and the instrumental rationality on which it rests) is ultimately repressive, and comparison, if understood as not-positivism, can intervene to counter its dominance. Comparison, as I see it, can be the response of 'lifeworld' to 'system'. In other terms, I am saying it cannot be the case that our only options are rational universality or arbitrary force. While the persistently enveloping presence of totalizing thought within the orthodoxy currently cabins comparative law to the margins of academia, I remind my reader that margins have been very important historically. In early occidental print culture, for example, all the analysis or commentary would be written in the margins.

With the turn to comparative law other-wise, an entire research paradigm is being superseded. Specifically, the desire to scientize the comparative enterprise about law (to '*faire science*' of it) and the further ambition to constitute practitioners and judges as the only interlocutors who matter are being challenged. The notion of scientificity that I target, loosely modelled on a certain objectifying (and largely unexamined) idea of science, attaches the utmost importance to the gathering and analysis of information. However, while it wishes to evoke scientissimous comparatists, it stands as misplaced (and mesmeric) scientism. Now, comparative law other-wise no longer reduces the comparatist-at-law to one dominant part only – that of compiler or reproducer of data – in a manner obscuring or excluding other, more vital roles such as meaning-maker, critic, and intellectual.[29] As it insists on the shallowness of any confinement of comparative law to positivism and the unsustainable epistemology that informs this ideology (and that has sought, for instance, to denigrate culture as a legitimate area of investigation), comparative law other-wise emphasizes how comparison intervenes as a cultural practice, as an experiential practice, as a critical practice, too, researching foreign law that exists as culture also. Comparative law other-wise therefore stands as a promise. It purports to be edifying, that is, it professes to be constructive. It seeks to rehabilitate law-as-culture, to restore the merit of local knowledge on the understanding that there is simply no foreign law (or no comparatist) without a minimal local colour, taste, or twang, without a singularizing grain linking it (or him) to a particular place. Comparative law other-wise, acknowledging the singularity of the (encultured) comparatist, wants to do justice to the singularity of (encultured) foreign law. Not in the least nihilistic (I am as a matter of principle *for* foreign law and *for* the comparison of laws), not fundamentally sceptical (I emphatically advocate epistemological realism), arguably 'fortif[ying]',[30] comparative law other-wise, my negation of comparative-law-as-we-know-it, as it stretches the logic of non-contradiction, is simultaneously deconstructive (it exposes and dismantles the epistemic inanities long perpetrated by comparative law's orthodoxy) and reconstructive (it activates and releases reparative, newly confident, more rewarding epistemic possibilities). I mobilize, so to speak, 'two hands, two gazes, two hearings. Together at once and separately.'[31] And I make clear, again, that deconstruction intervenes as a protocol of reading that simply cannot be equated with destruction or demolition. Observe that there are many passages in Derrida's philosophy, often overlooked – not least by his detractors – to the effect that deconstruction, the movement that has become so closely associated with his name, segues into reconstruction (the word 'deconstruction' features 'construction', not 'destruction').[32] In effect, deconstruction pertains to the kind of scrutiny and audacity allowing for optimized epistemic circumstances. When deconstruction comes to comparative law, there can be no way around it; rather, the comparatist has to work through it.

[29] cf I Stengers, *La Volonté de faire science* (Les Empêcheurs de penser en rond 1992).

[30] S Beckett, 'Rue de Vaugirard' in *Poèmes* (Editions de Minuit 1999 [1946]) 16: '[T]hen [I] start again fortified/by a negative irrecusable.'

[31] J Derrida, *Marges* (Editions de Minuit 1972) 75.

[32] Eg: see J Derrida, *Psyché*, vol 2 (2nd edn, Galilée 2003 [1985]) 389.

Meanwhile, there are those who prefer to announce 'the end of comparative law' (2007), who write 'comparative law is not dead – or, is it?' (2012). And there are others still who claim that 'there is increasingly little need for comparative legal expertise'. Indeed, it is argued, '[w]ho needs to read a scholarly comparison of legal institutions in India and the United States when one can simply incorporate an Indian legal thinker into one's project collaboratively?'. In sum, or so goes the conclusion, 'comparative scholarly moves seem somehow beside the point, irrelevant, *uninteresting*'. And it is therefore time to shift from comparison to collaboration (2015). What to say? I know very well, of course, the institutional pressures that impel a law teacher in the anglophone world, more so in the United States than anywhere else, to rush to the naming of ever-newer paradigms in the hope of having such denominations promptly attach to one's own name – to arrogate to oneself the privilege of naming and to be in a position to implant one's naming, meaning that one is then able effectively to manage knowledge. But summarily to execute an entire field without, it seems, allowing for any significant possibility of redemption, of re-existence, all for the sake of institutional novelty or, more accurately, in order to validate one's institutional standing through novelty? While the argument's reach remains unclear, I assume that it is limited to the field of comparative law, and that it is not militating against the value of comparison as a primordial cognitive motion – what Saint-Simon has in mind, for example, when he writes that '[a]ll operations of the human mind reduce themselves to comparisons';[33] or what Michel Foucault is thinking when he holds that 'comparison . . . is required for almost all knowledge';[34] or what Wael Hallaq reckons when he considers that the absence of comparison is 'a debilitating dead weight for understanding'.[35]

It should be obvious that in order to flourish, if such be the ambition, 'collaboration' does not require the razing of comparative law (or of 'comparative scholarly moves'). In fact, it appears that if collaboration is to yield creditable information about a foreign legal culture or law-text, the experience of the informant must be open to probing. To return to the 'Indian legal thinker', whose easy enrolment into a research endeavour would seemingly cancel any need for comparative scholarship, who, I ask, if not a Brazilian, French, or US scholar familiar with Indian legal

[33] [Saint-Simon], 'Quelques opinions philosophiques à l'usage du dix-neuvième siècle' in *Œuvres choisies de C-H de Saint-Simon*, vol 3 (Van Meenen 1839 [1825]) 219–20.

[34] M Foucault, *Les Mots et les choses* (Gallimard 1966) 66.

[35] WB Hallaq, *Restating Orientalism* (Columbia University Press 2018) 15.

culture, would be in an optimal position to consider the Indian experience being narrated by the Indian legal thinker himself and to do so with the necessary critical discernment? It is not in the least cavillous to contend that there is only so much self-introspection that the Indian legal thinker can (be expected to) achieve. And it is not unreasonable to maintain that the necessary meaningful critique must therefore materialize from the vantage point of critical distance. When it comes to transcultural analysis (which, again, any translegal analysis must emphatically be), I agree with Sanford Budick that 'critical distance' is 'a vital phenomenon'.[36] Given the need for comparative evaluation to supplement the Indian legal thinker's own account of Indian legal culture, it is apt to observe, on the basis of a charitable (or empathetic) assessment of comparative law, that the ideas of construction and reconstruction should be recommending a more productive approach to comparative analysis and holding that such enhanced comparatism is possible. It is not to strike an unduly Pollyannaish tone to maintain that the good comparison thus remains highly meritorious,[37] to defend the view that the good comparison continues to provide a most valuable scholarly resource, any whimsical interest in collaboration notwithstanding. There is, I contend, much merit in undertaking a shipwreck operation to rescue a poignant ruin from epistemological waywardness. It is very much worth clinging to the wreckage.[38] Yes.

In my view, the most formidable hurdle to any healing of the theorized practice predominantly obtaining within the field of comparative law remains, of course, the idea of totality that, because it connotes autarky and exhaustivity, autotelism and autoreferentiality, would literally relegate comparison to the realm of irrelevance. Once there is the whole or the all – *le tout, das Ganze* – there is nothing other than *that*. In the absence of any residue, what would the comparison be *with*? If there is totalization, comparison is *hors jeu*. This means that any perspective *on* the whole, because it can only be exterior *to* the whole, must deny or

[36] S Budick, 'Crises of Alterity: Cultural Untranslatability and the Experience of Secondary Otherness' in S Budick and W Iser (eds), *The Translatability of Cultures* (Stanford University Press 1996) 14.

[37] Eg: T Ruskola, *Legal Orientalism* (Harvard University Press 2013).

[38] The three texts I address are, sequentially, MM Siems, 'The End of Comparative Law' (2007) 2(2) J Comp L 133; P Zumbansen, 'Transnational Comparisons: Theory and Practice of Comparative Law as a Critique of Global Governance' in M Adams and J Bomhoff (eds), *Practice and Theory in Comparative Law* (Cambridge University Press 2012) 187; A Riles, 'From Comparison to Collaboration: Experiments with a New Scholarly and Political Form' (2015) 78(1–2) L & Contemporary Problems 147.

subvert wholeness. Accordingly, my thesis is that any comparative endeavour requires to be apprehended as an interruption of totalizing thought. Comparison thus becomes a practice of fragmentation, of mutilation even. (Envisage also the connection between the comparatist and the masochist: do they not both challenge the integrity and integrality of holism?[39])

To be sure, then, comparative law must also earnestly resist being indentured to totalizing myths and methodologies 'from within', including normalizing, harmonizing, closure-seeking, exhilarating, self-satisfying, pleasure-bearing narratives.[40] As orthodox comparatists preach a condition of unity or uniformity across laws, they trivialize or deny the epistemological difficulties necessarily attendant upon re-presentation that prove especially acute with respect to the transcultural research that translegal investigation entails. In their urge to operationalize contingency, orthodox comparatists focus on the signifier (although conveniently leaving the matter of language to one side) to the virtual exclusion of any concern of significance for deep or thick meaning, for the reason why the law does what it does in the way in which it does. The doxa overwhelmingly adopts a form of projective reprocessing in which the 'voice' or the perspective of the other-in-the-law is not effectively heard or addressed. Rather, otherness finds itself being assimilated into a discourse – the self's – that is reduced to a monologic or narcissistic account unwilling to respect manifestations of resistance to obliteration. This is why unifying or uniformizing ideology intent on sweeping away undesirable elements can most legitimately appear terrifying, no matter how chaste it sounds. But the empirical fact of the matter is that the other within the comparison is always in excess of the self – and therefore of all totalization (and certainly of any totalization that the self might want to

[39] Interestingly, there can also be identified a close connection between the comparatist and the fetishist in that they both engage in a form of transgressive idolatry by investing an entity with value (say, foreign law for the comparatist). By ascribing value to foreign law (something that a local lawyer would not do), the comparatist fetishizes the foreign. Indeed, the usage of the word 'fetish' involves a discrepancy between those who believe in the fetish entity (say, the comparatist believing in the foreign law) and those who, looking at the fetish entity from the outside (thus, local lawyers operating from their local base and confining their vistas to the local law), judge the fetishist deluded. As Wendy Steiner underlines, though, '[t]he fetishist's error supposedly lies in the habit of fetishizing per se, but in fact it consists in choosing the "wrong" fetishes': W Steiner, *The Scandal of Pleasure* (University of Chicago Press 1995) 81. In other words, local lawyers are fetishists, too, except that they fetishize local, not foreign law.

[40] See Legrand (n 25).

enact). Not only does otherness effectively disqualify any self-pretence at a totalization that would embrace it (after all, the other inevitably keeps a secret), but it implies limits to the self as totality: otherness dooms the self, the comparing self, to unachievement. And such is another important epistemological tenet pursuant to which the self is invited to acknowledge his epistemic subordination to the other.[41] Meanwhile, the vain character of the unifiers' or uniformizers' strategy deserves to be roundly exposed.[42]

Also, comparative law other-wise seeks to rescue comparative-law-as-we-know-it from its detractors on all sides – from positivists (including empiricists), who discern dilettantism; from transnationalists, who perceive obsolescence; from feminists or other progressists, who see a lack of political awareness; from (most) conservatives, who fear subservience to the foreign; and from (many) liberals, who worry about relativism. Communitarians, too, are prone to regard the comparative venture as inadequately value-oriented. With so many enemies, comparative law needs friends. The defence that I offer as *NCL*, heartfelt and robust, wants to be an attempt at vindication. As I seek to revisit the orthodox assumptions, I find it important to mention, once more, that the orthodoxy can hardly escape responsibility in the lacklustre academic fortunes of the discipline that it has incessantly been piloting.

*

— *A Questioner* (*Q*): So, you are doing this? You are really launching a frontal attack on established comparative law?

— Well, I have been writing against comparative law's orthodoxy for many years so the 'attack', as you call it, is a line of argument I instigated a long time ago. I am not sure this monograph's contentions are any more 'frontal' than the claims I have been advancing in other publications.

[41] Consider three statements issuing from Derrida's: '[N]othing essential will be done if one does not let oneself be summoned . . . by the other': J Derrida, 'Fidélité à plus d'un' (1998/13) Cahiers Intersignes 221, 233; '[T]he other is the other only if its otherness is absolutely irreducible': J Derrida, *L'Ecriture et la différence* (Editions du Seuil 1967) 154; 'One must keep watch on the otherness of the other': J Derrida, *Le Toucher, Jean-Luc Nancy* (Galilée 2000) 218.

[42] For a persuasive argument that there is under-appreciated economic value in local legal differentiation and singularization, see eg PB Stephan, 'The Futility of Unification and Harmonization in International Commercial Law' (1999) 39 Virginia J Int'l L 743.

— *Q*: But why put yourself in such a vulnerable position? Why risk alienating so many colleagues?

— Basically, I look at the issue as a matter of scholarly integrity. I am not out to alienate anyone, and I am certainly not in the business of hurting anyone's feelings. My concern is ideas, and my ultimate preoccupation is the scholarly standing of comparative law and of comparatists-at-law. I have no interest in polemicizing with anyone, in all likelihood a thoroughly ineffectual strategy. Having said this, I readily confess that I find the monophony of comparative law's positivism extraordinarily frustrating. Such epistemological narrowmindedness upsets me – and it saddens me, too. I am minded to quote a French poet, René Char, whose writing I greatly value: 'To escape from orthodoxies. Their conduct is atrocious.'[43] While I appreciate that positivism's exequy is unlikely to materialize imminently, I think it is crucial for me to do what I can in order to torpedo the positivist agenda in comparative law. And I hold that percussive writing may help to attract attention to the problem, to the magnitude of the problem, by making pertinently impertinent claims. *Silere non possum*. Now. . .

— *Q*: Let me interject. I think it is important to examine what a complaint can achieve. Do you think your critique will help comparative law?

— I can assure you that I am not labouring under any illusion. But I think it would be good if my book helped generate a crisis within the field. I think it would stand comparative law in very good stead.

— *Q*: But who wants a crisis? A crisis is disruptive. No one likes a crisis.

— I am firmly of the view that a crisis can be a very fruitful epistemic moment, and I am firmly of the view, too, that a full-blown epistemological crisis in comparative law is way overdue. Think about it: the selfsame (German) book has been acting as the governing text within the field for forty years or so. And now, a new (German) book has come along effectively claiming the mantle of governing text for itself, but wholeheartedly endorsing practically every major epistemological claim that the earlier text has been making all along. In other words, there is this impermutability. As far as one can tell, comparative law – certainly in terms of its orthodoxy – appears doomed to continue at an

[43] R Char, 'A une sérénité crispée' in *Recherche de la base et du sommet* in *Œuvres complètes* (J Roudaut ed, Gallimard 1983 [1952]) 755.

epistemological standstill for the foreseeable future. Such long-term hegemony cannot be intellectually healthy. It is, in fact, intellectual atrophy. So, I accept that I am making some epistemic trouble, but I hold that I am making good trouble (I have in mind an activist/resistant magazine by that name). It is high time for comparatists-at-law seriously to think about thinking and to take a good look at looking.

— Q: Unless, of course, the dominant model is a good one. If the dominant model works well, does it not make sense that the new German text you are mentioning – I assume you mean Uwe Kischel's – should be praising it?

— But it is not at all good, and it does not work at all. Little wonder, in fact, that comparative law lacks academic standing. The dominant model is fundamentally flawed in a significant number of ways. It is very, very impoverished epistemologically. And I would add 'inevitably so', because the (German) jurists who articulated it basically never left the (German) law-box. They readily talk about objectivity, neutrality, truth; they discuss method, science, what have you, without any insight from other disciplines, no insight whatsoever, nothing. In effect, their writing appears to be giving expression to their (German) hunches. I am exaggerating, but you could be at your local *Wirtshaus*.

— Q: *Wirtshaus?*

— The German pub, if you will.

— Q: And the crisis you invite would build to a greater truth?

— No, this is not about truth at all. Comparative law's ambition must be to fashion better epistemic equipment in order to conduct more meaningful research into foreign law so as to yield more sophisticated interpretations of foreignness. Truth – or any model of veridiction – has nothing to do with this intellectual endeavour. It is not *true* that a young Muslim woman must be allowed to wear a headscarf at her local public school according to the dictates of her faith (the Canadian position), and it is not *true* that she must be prohibited from doing so (the French position). What we have – what comparatists-at-law must address – is an interpretive clash, a conflict of interpretations. And there is no argument – not the Canadian claim, not the French contention, and certainly not the comparatist's thesis – that is not the enunciation of an encultured conviction. It is about culture, not truth. As a comparatist-at-law coming to the Canadian and French arguments, I am therefore not in a position to assert truth. I repeat: truth is irrelevant.

— *Q*: I reckon that you would not want to be advancing faddish concerns. Presumably, faddishness would be doing a disservice to comparative law. Is it not faddish to dispense with truth, for instance? I am thinking of 'post-truth' and all that.

— As anyone who knows me will readily confirm, I am not in the least a faddish kind of individual. But then it is easy for the lazy or the fearful to dismiss a critique by designating it under a deliberately controversial or unattractive label, to call it 'faddish' or 'fashionable', for example. I see this exclusionary strategy being deployed regularly. You categorize someone's work as 'postmodern', for instance, and you thereby manage to trigger immediate reactions that can range from the suspicious to the inimical on the part of individuals who have only the vaguest acquaintance with the texts and tenets of the so-called 'postmodern' (and who fail to realize that postmodernism, like any 'post', is always a before, too). As often as not, the author of the repudiation does not know much more than his hapless readers.

— *Q*: And you think the comparatists who have been promoting the model you are challenging, who have invested their reputation in it, and who have done well institutionally out of it, you think such individuals would now be prepared to abandon it?

— Again, I am not naive, and I can readily see your point. To be sure, there is nothing more threatening to the status quo than an alternative epistemological paradigm that is cogently argued. However, I hold fast to a couple of basic convictions. First, I think there are comparatists who are operating in good faith (not all of them do, of course). And if these comparatists are shown the flaws of the model they have been defending (often for no other reason than the fact that they were taught to defend it), I think they can reasonably be expected to feel awkward at the thought of continuing to promote a demonstrably broken model. Secondly, I think there are many comparatists, especially younger ones like postgraduates, who are in search of a model. To show these new or aspiring comparatists that the orthodox model is profoundly defective is, I think, a very important goal to pursue. In fact, you could say that it is rather an urgent task to undertake – once more, then, an undertaking long overdue. To put the matter in different language, I am writing for people who realize that they have to break with the doxa, who are perhaps already in the process of breaking with the doxa. And, of course, I am writing for postgraduates who do not know the doxa (or who are not aware that they have been introduced to the doxa).

— Q: You have been called '*l'homme de la différence*'. Is this a fair account of your project?

— I cannot imagine engaging a comparison that does not involve moments of very intense looking as a conscious, reflective, curious looker, attempting to describe everything in a deep or thick way, and trying to leave nothing out, going as far as vision can tell. Otherwise, I am deeply convinced that I have not dealt with the foreignness of foreign law. To defend such an approach is an ethical/political move. It is, very much so. Therefore, I do not want to go anywhere until I have seen everything that foreign law has to show me. I accept that I cannot see *everything*, of course. But I firmly resist coming to foreign law to take only what accords with the narrative I have chosen to affirm or to reconfigure foreign law (say, 'functionally') so that it fits my agenda – my abiding commitment to intellectual integrity prohibits that kind of 'gerrymandering'. To be sure, I will have to make decisions. When someone is faced with a lot of something (a lot of textual traces, for example), one has to enter choices regarding what one will discuss, what one will emphasize. But it remains that foreign law cannot be subject to alteration under the pressure of a comparatist's world-view. Every foreign law harbours an entitlement to differ (not unlike every human being, in fact). I have lived a career affirming this idea. I can recognize and respect even a minor difference, because even a minor difference can signify: it can herald a predilection or a predisposition. I take it as being incontrovertible that every foreign law demands to be read in the light of its singularity (again, very much like every human being). My comparative law is a deeply empathetic project. And then, there is the comparatist's difference, for no two comparatists will read foreign law identically. Every comparison gives evidence of a given comparatist's intervention, of a given comparatist's personality. Often, it flaunts it. So, there is difference intervening in this respect also. And I would add that the comparatist also harbours an entitlement to differ in terms of his reading of foreign law. In sum, the foreign law's difference is legitimate and so is the comparatist's differential reading of foreign law. This is the gist of my argument. Like Adorno, I operate under the sign of the rigorous consciousness of non-identity, which is the key message he conveys through his deployment of 'negative dialectics': non-identity across laws and non-identity across comparatists – and, of course, non-identity across laws and comparatists (the comparatist can never tell foreign law as such). I repeat: no comparative account can reproduce foreign law identically to the foreign law that there is, if only because no account can tell foreign law exhaustively. And this means that difference also informs the narrative dynamics, another instance of non-identity.

— *Q*: On reflection, do you really think the various guises in which you claim difference to be appearing cannot be overcome? This would seem such a defeatist approach.

— You cannot make two comparatists behave identically vis-à-vis foreign law. And you cannot make a comparative account be identical to the foreign law that it is addressing. You simply cannot make these identities happen. And you cannot make a law identical to another law through unification, uniformization, harmonization, or whatever. Comparative law has to come to terms with the epistemological limitations that are inherent to the comparative endeavour. For one thing, comparative law must forgo its ambition to reach a consensus across laws (or across comparatists, for that matter). Instead, it must allow the dissensus to express itself through an agonistic – that is, an adversarial – staging. It is the incessant negotiation and renegotiation of this tension that makes comparison epistemologically worthwhile. This is why I operate largely *sans* Hegel. The issue is not Hegel's incorporation of radical differentiation – of contradiction and its virulent power of interruption – into a theory of knowledge, which I salute. Rather, what is problematic is Hegelianism's ultimate reconciliation of opposites into a unitary synthesis. In my view, such an outcome is neither possible nor desirable, and this is where I side with Adorno's negative dialectics – hence, obviously, *NCL*.

— *Q*: *NCL*?

— *Negative Comparative Law*. The abiding goal must be to make comparative law into a *regio dissimilitudinis* without, needless to add, Augustinian overtones. It is about saying no to the orthodoxy's epistemology. Evidently, the word 'negative' must not be understood to mean pessimistic or demoralizing. Rather, it wishes to indicate refusal of consent, opposition, rejection, dissent. Not unlike photography, it conveys the idea of a reverse impression – specifically, then, of a reverse comparative law, of an other comparative law, of comparative law otherwise.

— Q: By saying no to objectivity and to truth – which is what you forcefully do and repeatedly, too – you seem willing to countenance every comparatist's subjectivity working its way into the comparative analysis?

— Every comparative analysis requires a particular stance towards the foreign, and every comparative analysis – every single one – assumes a certain frame of mind. For me, the crucial thing is to find a way to open oneself to the foreign law-text and the textuality of that text – to what that text is existing as (and I argue that it is existing as a concatenation of cultural traces, as a cultural precipitate). To be sure, orthodox comparative law discourages this appreciation, which it regards as too 'subjective' (not a word that I would use, but a term that orthodox comparatists would use and indeed do use). To them, the approach that I discuss (what I style 'tracing') is not methodical. It is not scientific. It does not qualify as *Wissenschaft*. And that is exactly right, I daresay: of course, it does not! As a comparatist, I am trying to open myself experientially to the maximum degree to the foreignness of the law and to draw forth from the foreignness-at-law that there is, there. I am trying to become attuned to what the foreign has to tell me and to do it justice in my re-presentation of it, in the way in which I proceed to present foreign law anew (that is, through my own lenses – which, of course, are far from being strictly my own, since I am emphatically a cultural product).

— Q: Can I interrupt?

— Let me just say a little more about traces, because they are key. If comparative law will ever manage to escape from the throes of positivism's epistemology, it will be through tracing. The traces are built into the foreign law: they exist, they are there. Every foreign law-text is freighted with them, that is, every foreign law-text transports the burden of them. Accordingly, they ought to elicit an interpretive reaction from the comparatist. Again, it is a matter of justice vis-à-vis foreignness. One of my stock examples may help. Take the 2004 French statute on religious attire in public schools. Along with many other analysts, as I read between the lines of the statute, as I decipher what has been encrypted in the text's fabric, I see traces of Islamophobia (indicating, at the very least, a fear of Islam). French courts will not address this matter, because it does not pertain to the 'black-letter' dimension of the law-text. But the comparatist, I claim, must do so. Without this tracing exercise, the comparatist is doomed to a superficial and inadequate understanding of the statute. In fact, Islamophobia, even though it is never expressly mentioned, arguably stands as a pillar of the statute. It is emphatically not outside the law-box, then. Rather, it stands as one of the very underpinnings of the law-box, which only an excavation (or a deconstruction) will allow to elucidate. Through the trace, fine-grained ascription of significance becomes possible. Note – and this point is crucial – that the traces are not injected into the statute by the comparatist. They partake of the statute, and the comparatist is coming to find them, there, in order to fashion them into his interpretation. In other words, the comparatist is drawing the traces out of the text. But he does so as an encultured being. The comparatist's seeing or perceiving (of the traces) is a bodily or embodied activity. There is simply no disembodied seeing or perceiving. Ultimately, then, the comparatist's body and the foreign law-text are profoundly (and intricately) intertwined. There is certainly no such dynamic as a 'subject' here and an 'object' there, nothing like this crude and obsolete Cartesianism. Rather, it is about two enculturations – the comparatist's and the foreign law's – effectively entering into a negotiation with a view to meaning-making. I emphasize that we are dealing with a negotiation. What we have are two monologues: the comparatist is speaking his language, and so is the foreign law. If you will, comparative law is about squaring that circle.

— *Q*: I am not sure I can follow you all the way. Surely, the texts of the law are, well, about law. I mean... I do not want to sound more Kelsenian than I have to, but surely lines must be drawn to delineate the law. I mean... The law cannot be everything.

— You claim that the law cannot be everything! Well, let me respond in this way. I maintain – most reasonably, I like to think – that foreign law is inherently worldly, structurally so, that it is permeable to the world, and that its worldliness is therefore constitutive of the legal as it exists (and, of course, I contend that foreign law permeates the world in its turn and that it is therefore constitutive of the world as it exists in its turn). I am sure you and I can agree that no law hangs in the air, so to speak. If we accept that there is the law's worldly embeddedness – if we agree that the law is grounded – the idea that the law's worldliness would somehow not count as law, that it would be somehow excluded from the legal equation, that it would not pertain to any deep or thick analysis of the legal, not belong to comparative *law*, this idea, then, strikes me as hopelessly reductionist (and, also, as unacceptably self-interested from the positivist standpoint). I simply cannot accept such a distorting and opportunistic account, which is precisely the one being peddled by positivists, whose contention is that they are lawyers, they do law, and they are concerned with what the law is, only. One of my former French colleagues at the Sorbonne – a rather high-profile academic figure in his day – is on record as holding that when it comes to law, 'scientific rigour' must entail the elimination of 'all sociological, political, or technological dregs that burden and deform it'.[44] It is hard to imagine how one could frame in starker terms the position that negative comparative law aims to overthrow. Indulge me an analogy with painting, which I think can help.

— Q: Painting? Are you not pushing the envelope?

— Try me. Take *Le Serment des Horaces*, Jacques-Louis David's famous late-eighteenth-century painting (I came across it at the Louvre in January 2020 when I went to see the exhibition in honour of Pierre Soulages.) In David's painting the characters are dressed in a certain way and not in another. Why? And the characters, who are three brothers – a piece of information that I hold from my acquaintance with the Roman legend that inspired David – are saluting an individual who is clearly their father, a gesture that obviously carries a certain meaning, which itself must have something to do with geography (where is the salute happening?) and temporality (when is the salute happening?). And the meaning of this salute to the father cannot be dissociated from certain facts about elementary family structures governing at the place where the salute is performed and at the time when the salute is performed. And then, there is the gender issue, which must also connect with space and time, with geography and chronology. While the painting distinctly showcases the three brothers' virility in the forefront, it also features a weeping woman at the back. There is more. Think of the patriotic claim that infuses the scene. Even as this information pertains to what I shall style 'culture' (I am thinking, notably, of the dress code, the display of allegiance to the father, the projection of virility, and the abiding loyalism), can any analyst actually maintain that these cultural traits or cultural traces – if you will allow the term – are not 'in' the painting,

[44] G Timsit, *Thèmes et systèmes de droit* (Presses Universitaires de France 1986) 92.

that they do not exist 'as' the painting, 'as' part and parcel of the painting? Surely, the information that I indicate cannot reasonably be said to be elsewhere! It is harnessed and activated by the painting itself. Of course, the deference shown to the father pertains to a discourse having to do, let us say, with family mores. But the discourse has now morphed into the painting so that it has become, properly speaking, a constitutive part of it: the discourse exists as the painting (or the painting exists as the discourse). Now, why would a painting feature its worldliness in this way and not a text? Why would the painting's worldliness emerge as a constitutive part of the painting's meaning while a text's meaning would somehow be immune to its own embeddedness in a world? If you examine this distinction, you will see that it makes no sense whatsoever. In other words, the ascertainment of the meaning of the painting or text – including the foreign law-text – both involve an elucidation, a bringing-to-light, of the worldly information that constitutes these artefacts as painting and text – or as foreign law-text.

— *Q*: Could you offer another example from law, briefly?

— Very well. Is it conceivable that the majority opinion in *DC v Heller*, the 2008 US Supreme Court decision recognizing a constitutional right to keep and bear arms at home, would not harbour traces of conservatism, of individualism – that these ideological fundamentals would not be constitutive building-blocks of the decision, if tacitly so, that the judgment could not be traced to these ideological ingredients that would undergird the decision? If you are going to conduct a meaningful comparative analysis of this law-text, I cannot see how you can conceivably omit this tracing exercise and pretend that the judgment consists exclusively in a purely exegetical interpretation of the US Constitution. And the ideological components I mention cannot reasonably be said to be located elsewhere than in the judgment. They are a constitutive part of the judgment, and a crucial one at that. They support the judgment, and as the judgment's support they are firmly within the 'law-box' (I mean, the cement structure underneath the building is part of the building!). They are political or philosophical discourses that have morphed into the judgment, that are encrypted within the judgment, which is therefore very much to be understood as a cultural precipitate. They have become the judgment, they now *are* the judgment.

— Q: And you think this is the kind of book that will succeed in vindicating your theoretical ambitions? Yours is rather an intimidating text in a number of ways. Your writing demands a great deal from its readership.

— I make no apology. It is the book that I think had to be written, certainly at this particular juncture. It is high time that comparative law should escape from the image of an easy practice that so many comparatists have been promoting for so long – the general idea being, it seems, that if you sprinkle your research with a few references to foreign laws, then you have engaged in comparative law. Along the lines of 'the more, the merrier', many comparatists seem to think that comparatism, even if it 'levels down' in the way I indicate, should nonetheless be encouraged. The epistemological debasement that such delibations cause to happen can be quite extraordinary, actually. For example, you have the leading text in the field not saying a single word about translation. It is, literally, as if translation was not a difficulty for comparatists. Think about it: we are addressing comparative law, and there is silence on the issue of translation! Meanwhile, you have comparatists writing about foreign laws whose languages they cannot read – which is another basic epistemological problem. The list of such major epistemological issues is a very long one. Another illustration leaps to mind: you have a seasoned comparatist encouraging his colleagues to manipulate the data so that laws can be made to look equivalent or common and can therefore appear more readily 'unifiable' or 'uniformizable'. This comparatist uses the very word 'manipulation' (actually, he refers to manipulation that would be 'well-meaning' – now, talk about an oxymoron!). Astonishingly, this outrageous statement has met with general indifference within the field (or is it that comparatists feel this author's honesty to be carrying over his tactics?). And then you have the co-authors of the leading text in the field imagining, with engaging modesty, that method had now culminated inside their own heads, that their method was the only method, and that their method had to be applied in its pure form (the word 'pure' is actually theirs). And it is also the leading text in the field that calls private law 'the main area' ('*[die] Hauptdomäne*') within comparative law.[45] Where does that statement leave the practice of comparative law in the United States or Canada, for example, where constitutional law is emphatically the principal subject-matter within the

[45] Zweigert and Kötz (n 1) 3.

law? I mean... such under-theorization is astonishing! So I have sought to deploy an alternative composition with a view to supplanting the orthodoxy's bromides. I readily refer to my work as bricolage, the key idea being that it unfolds as a conjunctive space, a space where various disciplines conjoin in order to make comparative law intellectually stronger.

— Q: Is there not a risk of over-theorization, though? Again, your material can prove pretty heavy going, some might even say highfalutin.

— I find it interesting that you should use the word 'highfalutin', because the entire project revolves around the idea of modesty. I have not wanted to inject an ounce of pomposity into my argument, the point being exactly the opposite: to fight the arrogance that has been on display within comparative law for so long. I have in mind the idea that the comparatist would be able to conduct research that is pure, that he could do so objectively, that he could achieve exactitude, that he could access truth – all this epistemic nonsense. It is high time for comparatists-at-law to operate a lucid registration of their epistemic limits, to lower their epistemic sights. Meanwhile, comparative law is nowhere near having to address over-theorization. At this juncture, comparative law urgently requires more comparatism, not less, so as to generate the epistemological rupture that is in order; it needs more thinking about comparison, about what it means to compare.[46] But this thinking must be serious thinking, well-informed thinking, the sort of thinking that draws assistance from other disciplines in order to address the relevant epistemic issues with the intellectual sophistication they require.

— Q: Are these interdisciplinary demands realistic?

— I am evidently not asking that the comparatist-at-law should become a fully fledged philosopher or a trained linguist, a pedigreed historian or a certified anthropologist. But I do hold that from the moment one acknowledges that law is worldly, that one accepts how law is embedded in a world – and how could anyone honestly deny this fact? – one has to bring the law's worldliness into one's explanatory matrix. And this means that one has to prove indisciplined in the sense that one must disobey the disciplinary injunctions to the effect that a jurist should be doing 'pure'

[46] cf R Gagné, 'Regimes of Comparatism' in R Gagné et al (eds), *Regimes of Comparatism* (Brill 2019) 2: 'Comparatism is reflexive comparison. . . . [It] includes a reflection on the process of comparison.'

law only, or words to that effect. I am not saying that it will be easy for the comparatist to bring philosophical or sociological materials into comparative law. But I am claiming that one does not have the choice if, of course, one is prepared to engage in the kind of beneficial comparative research that will actually seek to answer the question 'why?' – why is that foreign law doing things in a certain way and not otherwise? Why is it proceeding differently from our law? And then, there is the matter of doing justice to foreign law's worldliness, of attempting to tell the foreign law-text as it is, of coming as close to that ambition as is reasonable. There is that abiding epistemic responsibility befalling comparatists.

— Q: So, justice – as you see it – depends on eclecticism?

— I am the comparatist, I am the one who is intervening within foreign law. It is therefore for me to figure out what foreign law is up to. I might be right, or I might be wrong – such is life in the realm of interpretation. But it is my job to try and work things out optimally, and my task is to deploy the utmost energy towards this interpretive end, to do so from the inception of my research to the termination of my writing. I am the one having to make sense of what is going on, and a major interpretive vehicle for accomplishing that task is to trace the law to its constitutive historical, philosophical, political, or sociological facets, that is, to recognize and respect law as the cultural statement that it is. If you are willing to approach it with a view to meaningful elicitation, foreign law will promptly take you out of law as positivists have framed it and show you the actual complexity of the legal. The comparative challenge then becomes the ascertainment, understanding, and articulation of what is necessarily a singular foreign law. In this regard, the tracing exercise that I herald and indiscipline go hand in hand.

— Q: You talk about the singularity of foreign law. What about legal transplants?

— As you well know, this is a long-rehearsed debate arising from the fact of an extraordinarily ill-chosen metaphor. Let me, then, answer your question in this way. When someone like James Gordley asserts that as regards liability for bodily harm or the sale of defective goods, the law is 'much the same' in Jakarta, Tel Aviv, Montpellier, and Tucson, he appears to be saying at the very least that there are 'fundamentals' (my word) that one can identify in these various laws, that bring these various laws together in a significant way, so much so, in fact, that what differences one can also observe become secondary and can safely be relegated to the side of the comparative argument. But this claim can only be formulated from within a squarely positivist framework. Contrariwise, if you accept that the legal is meaningfully informed by the cultural, that the legal can meaningfully be traced to the cultural – that law exists as culture – the very idea that the law in Jakarta and the law in Tucson would be 'much the same' becomes implausible. Dissemination or diffusion processes across laws – which do exist and have indeed been proliferating – change nothing whatsoever to the fact of singularity. Wherever it 'lands', a circulating law has to 'localize' itself if it is to enjoy the slightest chance of taking root. And such 'localization' must imply a 'fit' with local culture, to make the point rapidly. A transplant suggests identity: that geranium from the small blue pot into the larger brown pot or that heart from Mary into Jane. Law in motion does not operate in that manner at all. It must transform itself along the merry way – which is a crucial fact that the image of the 'transplant' obscures completely. Transportation implies alteration. Law travels – of course, it does. But it does not travel *as such*. Actually, my attack on Alan Watson's metaphor has met with a favorable reception from readers who understand the claim I am making. But let me refrain from listing these endorsements.[47]

— Q: You argue that the comparatist invents foreign law. This appears an excessive contention. Do you expect to persuade anyone?

— I am confident we can agree that, on examination, the comparatist implements a research process consisting of two major steps. First, the comparatist finds foreign law in the library (or elsewhere). It is there, in the statutes and judicial decisions, in the textbooks and law reviews. It pre-exists him. It faces him. It is there *before* him – right there, on the shelves (or in the databases, on a computer screen). Secondly, once the comparatist has the foreign law in front of him, whether in the form of paper or electronic documents, he proceeds to design it for reporting purposes. For example, he chooses to emphasize this statutory provision rather than that, he decides to insist on this judgment rather than that, he elects to include this quotation from a certain law-review article rather than that quotation from another law-review article. Note that on each

[47] For a sample, see P Legrand, 'Kischel's Comparative Law: *Fortschritt ohne Fortschritt*' (2020) 15(2) J Comp L 292, 324–27 (review article of U Kischel, *Comparative Law* [A Hammel tr, Oxford University Press 2019]).

occasion there takes place an assertion of epistemic power on the part of the comparatist inasmuch as the selection of materials – and, indeed, of words – forecloses other materials and other words, and therefore other understandings. Musil has one of his characters exclaim (Diotima, I think it is): 'As soon as we speak, doors are closing.'[48] Take the matter of words. There is a difference between choosing to write that a judgment is 'unconvincing' and that it is 'poorly reasoned', and you are not inviting identical appreciations from your readership. Every comparative intervention, then, constantly moves between constatation and performance – there takes place what Derrida calls an 'infinitely rapid oscillation'.[49] Finding and designing are co-constitutive and inseparable. Now, 'to find' is one meaning of the verb 'to invent', an admittedly forgotten meaning, and 'to design' is the other, more current meaning of the verb 'to invent', which connotes the idea of crafting. 'Invention' therefore captures, economically and optimally, the complexity attendant upon comparative research (a complexity that the serious comparatist cannot deny). In effect – and this is Derrida's contention – 'one must today reinvent invention',[50] that is, one must revisit the meaning of 'invention' so that one accepts that the comparatist's intervention is properly speaking an invention, so that one appreciates the formulation 'the comparatist invents foreign law' therefore to be making very good sense.

— Q: And what are the reactions to your claims?

— I must confess that I very rarely pay attention. As far as I can tell, responses vary widely. In France, where I am based (strictly for personal rather than professional reasons, I hasten to add), to the extent that there is anything qualifying as a 'reaction', the prevailing attitude is predictably hostile. In fact, the French contributor to the *Oxford Handbook of Comparative Law* has expressly complained that my brand of indiscipline is too complicated for her. Not only did this lame (and, frankly, embarrassing) statement grace the first edition, but the author saw fit to repeat it in the second edition nearly fifteen years later. Even after so much time, this person remains overwhelmed – evidently a structural problem pertaining to her socialization and institutionalization into the law. But in France, the concern to keep things simple and to forgo any investigation of the worldly dimensionalities of foreign law is a very significant

[48] R Musil, *Der Mann ohne Eigenschaften* (A Frisé ed, Rowohlt 1978 [1930]) bk 1, s 105, 504.
[49] J Derrida, *Psyché*, vol 1 (2nd edn, Galilée, 1998 [1984–86]) 25.
[50] ibid 37.

preoccupation. I wish I could say that such a hollow assertion as the *Oxford Handbook*'s is unrepresentative, but precisely the opposite is the case. Sad as it is to be making this point, on this occasion French comparatists-at-law get precisely the spokesperson they deserve. Meanwhile, whatever French law professors may think, philosophical reflections on the self/other dynamic or thoughts issuing from translation studies on the merits of a foreignizing translation cannot remain extraneous to understanding what it means to investigate and interpret foreign law; they are essential to the comparatist's sense-making. (Incidentally, allow me to emphasize this point, since we were just talking of invention. The comparatist's remit is to make sense of foreign law: to *make* sense.) I do not see myself as claiming any prodigious insight. I would say that I am mostly being receptive to the complexity of the matter of comparability. As I have had occasion to write, comparison is not for the faint of heart.

— *Q*: Are you not taking the matter too seriously, though? Is there not something to be said for being a little more relaxed about these questions?

— I trust you are not suggesting that there is anything wrong with approaching scholarship seriously. I am certainly prepared to accept that I take comparative law very seriously. But then, I had a very serious dissertation supervisor! Of course, I take it seriously! I do it every day. I do it many hours a day. I am like a professional violonist, if you will. I need to practice daily, for hours on end. I see no other way. In Sylvia Plath's correspondence, there is a letter where she writes that 'everyday, one has to earn the name of "writer" over again, with much wrestling'.[51] Well, I suggest substituting 'comparatist' for 'writer'. It is indeed about 'earn[ing]' and 'wrestling'. Now, I am prepared to accept that my personality has something to do with my earnestness (it is hard to imagine how this would not be the case). I have never been light-hearted in matters of the mind, and there are personal reasons that I think I can identify to account for this state of affairs. But leaving to one side both the people who influenced me and my idiosyncrasies, the fact is that the epistemological stakes are pretty high when it comes to comparative law. I mean, if you are prepared to pitch the issue at a somewhat philosophical level, what is at stake is nothing less than the dynamic between the self and the other, in particular between the self's law and the other's

[51] Letter from S Plath to AS Plath in *The Letters of Sylvia Plath*, vol 1 (PK Steinberg and KV Kukil eds, Faber & Faber 2017 [2 October 1956]) 1261.

law. If you bring in the pressures towards universalization (which would effectively erase local singularity) and the opposite pressures in favour of nationalism (which would effectively cancel transnational motions), you can see that comparative law readily takes the form of a pressing ethical/political commitment. Seriousness is complicated, you see, and you can (and must) take comparative law very seriously without taking *yourself* too seriously.

— Q: Are you saying that comparative law is political?

— It evidently is. The very idea of going 'comparative', so to speak, is profoundly political. And then, every comparative intervention is thoroughly political, too. It is political to work on China rather than Germany. It is political to work on freedom of speech rather than breach of contract. It is political to work as a positivist or culturalist, to deploy one particular toolbox instead of another. It is political to work in French rather than English (or to stop writing in French in order to publish in English). And the comparison is political also as regards the results that the comparatist wants to achieve (for example, the unification or uniformization of laws, the critique of local law by way of foreign law, the critique of foreign law, or whatever). Comparative law is necessarily and obviously political in a number of extraordinarily significant ways. Meanwhile, the leading textbook in the field expressly denies the political fabric of comparative law – or, more accurately perhaps, it is expressly arguing that comparative law should be kept well away from politics. So, here is another of the doxa's epistemological blind spots that I am challenging.

— Q: But you said that the leading textbook in the field is a German text. Surely, you would expect German writers to contest the political character of comparative law.

— Of course, I would. But then, we need to ask ourselves whether the German way of thinking about the law can reasonably pretend to make itself into a planetwide point of reference for the theory and practice of comparative law. After all, German legal epistemology features very singular assumptions.

— Q: So, your argument in this book cannot work to persuade a German constituency?

— The situation strikes me as being more complex than you suggest. I can think of some German jurists, of a few German comparatists, who have become very critical of German legal epistemology, who have been able to engineer their epistemic emancipation, if you will. Do you want a name? I have in mind Günter Frankenberg, for example. I am also thinking of Simone Glanert, whose work on Goethe could simply not have been written out of a German law faculty and indeed began in the United States, many years after she had permanently left Germany, and later continued in England.[52] In fact, the thought of such indisciplined work would not even have occurred to her in Germany. Paradoxically, the fact of teaching in Germany would have prevented the emergence of work on Goethe! Incidentally, this process of emancipation can happen *hic et ubique terrarum*. If I think about Italy, for instance, Piergiuseppe Monateri's name springs to mind. So, as you can see, epistemic determinism is not absolute. Ultimately, however, I hold that such exceptions are, well, exceptional. The very large bulk of European comparatists, to focus on this particular constituency, apply to the comparison of laws the extraordinarily narrow Kelsenian or Kelsenian-like model that they had drilled into them during their initial and national law-school years – and they do so, whether they realize it or not. They may think they have unfettered themselves through the taking of an interest in foreign law, while they are in effect carrying their national mindset in their epistemic luggage and transposing it willy-nilly to the study of foreign law. The late French philosopher Jacques Derrida coined the expression 'false exits' to refer to such circumstances,[53] and I think these two words aptly capture the point that I am making.

— *Q*: You seem to be saying that there is a German issue for comparative law. Is there also a French issue or an Italian issue? Is there a US issue?

— Yes, there is clearly a German issue, and if you have met the Hamburg crowd you must know exactly what I mean. Contrariwise, there is no French issue at all, if only because there is basically no French presence within comparative law on the international scene, none whatsoever, really. You have two or three comparatists teaching in France who do have a scholarly impact internationally. But, as it happens, they were not born in France: they work in France, but they are not from there. The case of US comparatists (or comparativists!) is more intricate. If you are

[52] See S Glanert, 'Goethe's Challenge' (2013) 8(2) J Comp L 288.

[53] Derrida (n 31) 162.

based, say, at Yale or Stanford, you can, in principle at least, harness your institutional aura to achieve an important measure of academic influence. And, presumably, you have access to significant resources to assist you in this process. Empirically speaking, however, there are many leading US institutions that do not feature a leading comparatist at all. Either they do not have anyone, or they have someone who somehow remains less significant within comparative law than one would expect to be the case. There are no doubt excellent reasons to account for this state of affairs, but in the United States comparative law very much remains a fringe academic endeavour.

— Q: But does France not have a strong comparative law tradition? Is it not the case that the leading text in the field used to be French?

— I would certainly not speak of a 'strong tradition'. There is emphatically no 'tradition' of comparative law in France, and it follows that there is patently not a 'strong' one. On the French academic scene, comparative law remains a most eccentric (and excentric) pursuit, and it was never more than that. Interestingly, I think, the two most famous French comparatists were never affiliated to any academic institution (and certainly did not think of themselves as comparatists and even less as comparatists-at-law). I have in mind Montesquieu and Tocqueville. Now, it is a fact that in the late 1960s and throughout most of the 1970s a French comparatist teaching at the Sorbonne – one of my institutional predecessors, then – established his book as the leading text in the field. These days, however, the only comparative-law scholarship issuing out of France that carries any intellectual weight internationally is the work of a small handful of comparatists who, while being based in France, are not from France.

— Q: So, even though you are based in France, as you say, you do not expect French comparatists to read your book?

— Frankly, I think that when it comes to comparative law, the French academy is so profoundly invested in positivism of the narrowest kind (not to mention its commitment to well-known and enduring parish-pumpery) that I cannot imagine how anyone would sustain an interest in an argument like mine (which is one of the reasons why I stopped publishing in French a number of years ago). Having said this, I suppose there will be one or two exceptions. There usually are. Still... How many times have I had to tell postgraduate students contemplating an academic career in France that, if they were to work on the sort of topic that had piqued their attention in the context of my postgraduate teaching, and if they were to approach that topic in the kind of critical and indisciplined manner that I was advocating, they would never be able to teach in France. On occasion, some of my very, very best students have refused to allow themselves to be discouraged and have maintained their dedication to their preferred theme, which is very much to their credit. But I had not been wrong: despite holding a Sorbonne doctorate, having won a major academic prize, and having had their dissertation released by a major law publisher, they all teach outside of France. I could offer many more examples of the French intellectual retrenchment I address.[54] Geoffrey Samuel, who has excellent first-hand knowledge of French law faculties on account of the fact that he visited at a large number of them, often recurrently, over very many years, says that 'the situation in France is particularly grim'.[55] Yes, 'grim' is the word.

— *Q*: Positivism and culturalism are irreconcilable, then?

— Briefly, if I may! Vis-à-vis positivism, there is, clearly, the culturalist advantage, and there are at least two reasons why this is the case. First, culturalism is more encompassing than positivism. While a positivist analysis must exclude culture from its remit (if not, it fails as positivism), culturalism can easily accommodate a positivist point of entry into the investigation of foreign law. Culturalists have no difficulty asking how courts have interpreted the relevant statute, for example. But they refuse to stop there, they are determined to move to other and bigger interpretive questions. While positivism sidelines culture altogether, culturalism does not exclude positivism: it comes to it obliquely, if you will. Secondly, it is the case that ultimately positivism is a form of culturalism. I mean: positivists do not live outside culture. To commit to positivism is emphatically to devote oneself to the pursuit of certain values. And values cannot reasonably be said to exist beyond culture. Unbeknownst to positivists, then, they are culturalists, too!

— *Q*: You reject universalism. But what do you make of international law's universals? I am thinking of article 38 of the Statute of the International Court of Justice, which includes in the list of sources of

[54] See G Samuel and P Legrand, 'A Conversation on Comparative Law' (2020) 15(2) J Comp L 371, 378.

[55] ibid 378.

international law 'the general principles of law recognized by civilized nations'.

— My succinct answer is that these so-called 'general principles' are a legal fiction. International lawyers may choose to behave as if such 'general principles' existed, but not even a collective fantasy can change the reality of local differentiation and singularity – of glocalization, if you will. 'Res judicata' does not mean identically in Brazil and Norway, no matter how fervently international lawyers may want equivalence or commonality. Think comparative international law.

— Q: Is this debate between positivism and culturalism not a narrow, pointless discussion? Should comparatists not have a bad conscience about it?

— I must remind you that I am *responding* to Zweigert and Kötz, Kischel, and others – a situation not devoid of invidiousness. What should one be doing? Should one be giving these comparatists-at-law free rein, because they are making a narrow and pointless positivist claim? If one bears in mind that law features especially strong 'disciplinarity' (that it carries particularly forceful normative value), such abdication simply cannot be. One has to do one's scholarly duty, if you will, and one has to object, to say no to the narrow and pointless argument that – let us not forget – has somehow governed the field of comparative law for decades. If one cares for one's craft, one must say no and express oneself vigorously, too. In the process, one can possibly hope to pitch the comparative conversation at a higher level of sophistication.

— Q: Very well, but your proposed theoretical framework must still address the question of its usefulness.

— I readily concede that comparative law will not help with the development of meteorological configurations that can predict the connection between the level of carbon dioxide in the Earth's atmosphere and the planet's surface temperature; and that it will not assist either with the improvement of mRNA-vaccine technology; and that it will not facilitate nematology. But since you want to talk about usefulness, let me ask you: what could be more useful within comparative law than to *understand* foreign law, irrespective of what one wants to do with it (import it for law reform's sake, study it to enhance one's critical knowledge, mobilize it to deepen one's awareness of foreignness, or whatever)? In every case, it must be a threshold requirement that one should be able to make sense of foreign law in a meaningful way. Vis-à-vis positivism, my model – a model that says no to an array of positivist assumptions – can yield considerably enhanced understanding of foreignness. So, yes, negative comparative law is useful. It is so very useful that it is *necessary*.

— *Q*: And what about the fact that aspects of your argument work for national law, too? Take your claim about invention. If one follows your understanding of the term, one could say that national lawyers find-and-fashion the national law; that a national law-text does not feature a meaning as such; and so forth.

— In a number of crucial ways, a critique of comparative law is ultimately a critique of law, which suggests that the connections or resonances you mention must be expected. While foreignness is comparative law's specific issue, this matter does not detract from the fact that whether foreign or local, law remains about texts, texts about words and traces, words and traces about meaning, meaning about interpretation, interpretation about interpreters, and interpreters about enculturation.

— *Q*: By way of final question, how disappointed will you be if the book fails to make headway?

— I simply cannot bring myself to care about the matter of impact. In any event, whatever headway *NCL* proceeds to achieve can only happen over the long term, arguably not in my lifetime (unless I live to be as old as Gadamer, perhaps!). Meanwhile, there will be what Beckett styles the 'gratifyingly hostile reviews'.[56] But, to quote Beckett once more, '[o]ne is what one is and one's work what it is and the concern with approval small'.[57] I have long discerned much wisdom in these few words. Meanwhile, I am extremely grateful to my publisher, to my commissioning editor, and to my copy editor for their vote of confidence in my work. Perhaps they deserved better. I mean perhaps they merited a more standard text that would be warmly received in the way innocuous, non-disruptive statements tend to be.

[56] Letter from S Beckett to B Rosset in *The Letters of Samuel Beckett*, vol 4 (G Craig et al eds, Cambridge University Press 2016 [9 April 1974]) 366.

[57] Letter from S Beckett to M Hutchinson in *The Letters of Samuel Beckett*, vol 3 (G Craig et al eds, Cambridge University Press 2014 [14 February 1957]) 25.

— Q: I cannot resist a further question. Is it not arguable that comparative law is an intellectual pursuit featuring a past rather than a future – and a fraught past at that given a somewhat dubious intertwinement with imperialism and colonialism?

— I am moved to make a number of points. I do not deny for a moment the imperial or colonial streak within comparative law, and it is clear to me that comparatists have to make themselves aware of this predicament and undertake to try hard to overcome it. All this language about there being laws that are better than others, about there being truth, about there being 'a unitary concept of justice',[58] all the talk about universalism, too, all these formulations reek with an imperial or colonial predilection. And it is, of course, crucial for comparative law urgently to move beyond this mindset. Incidentally, the post-imperial and post-colonial motions I encourage are also meant to overcome the obsolescence of Cartesianism.

— Q: But there is this famous passage where Descartes promotes comparison! If memory serves, he writes: 'It is good to know something of the customs of various peoples so as to judge ours more soundly, and that we do not think that everything that is against our ways is ridiculous and against reason, as are in the habit of doing those who have seen nothing.'[59]

— Fine words! But it remains that Cartesianism is a philosophical project inherently imperialist and colonialist. The evidence in support of this critique abounds. Suffice it to say that Descartes aspired to 'a universal language', and there is little chance that he had in mind Swahili.[60] On the matter of imperialism and colonialism, though, comparative law cannot stand alone in the dock. Take positivism, the very positivism that would be strictly apolitical, entirely pure, and wholly scientific. Well, Kimberley Brayson shows very convincingly how positivism, despite its much-vaunted claim to neutrality, is clearly the ideological foundation on which state-building has proceeded since the 1648 Treaty of Westphalia.[61] Positivism stands as the legal instantiation of the

[58] Zweigert and Kötz (n 1) 3.

[59] Descartes, *Discours de la méthode* in *Œuvres philosophiques*, vol 1 (F Alquié ed, Garnier 1997 [1637]) I, 573.

[60] Letter from Descartes to Mersenne in *Œuvres de Descartes*, vol 1 (2nd edn, C Adam and P Tannery eds, Vrin 1987 [20 November 1629]) 81.

[61] See K Brayson, 'Positivism and the Peace/Power Dialectic: Feminist Reflections in a Transnational Age' in L Siliquini-Cinelli (ed), *Legal Positivism in a Global and Transnational Age* (Springer 2019) 215–52.

nation-state and therefore of the idea of 'one legal truth' and therefore, inevitably, of the imperialist and colonial agendas. As regards the future, let me refer to Brayson's work again, since she makes the point most cogently. It seems incontrovertible that we live in an era of pluralism and that, if anything, fissiparity is set to continue, indeed to expand. Now, positivism and its idea of 'one legal truth' is, quite simply, inadequate to the contemporary reality of pluralism. Positivism's unitary conception of law must be about exclusions that are, in effect, discriminations and injustices. On reflection, such development is hardly surprising. How could a seventeenth-century legal model remain relevant nearly 400 years later given a vastly different transnational landscape? In terms of the demands of the moment, positivism falls very, very short. Meanwhile, the discipline that is par excellence attuned to local diversity is comparative law – I have in mind, of course, a depositivized and decolonized comparative law. Incidentally, globalization – so-called 'globalization' – only serves to reinforce comparative law's relevance. The more laws disseminate across the planet, the more local assemblages there are. Since every disseminating model must 'connect' with local ways in order to operate locally, there is an obvious role to play for comparative law in making sense of these various assemblages, all of them necessarily different from one another. If you will, the scene is agonistic rather than irenic, dissensual instead of consensual. And the contention I address is a sign of life! The idea that comparative law would be dead or about to die rests on a conception of comparison as a formalist and imperatorial enterprise. But this configuration is at once extraordinarily impoverished and profoundly treacherous.

*

The philosopher and literary critic Walter Benjamin famously wrote that '[c]onstruction presupposes destruction'.[62] With Derrida's assistance, I propose to reformulate this statement and argue that construction rather assumes *deconstruction*, which itself heralds reconstruction.[63] To quote Derrida: 'How could you reconstruct anything without deconstruction?'[64] Having been pressed to define the movement that had become so closely associated with his name, Derrida, wanting to

[62] W Benjamin, *Das Passagen-Werk* in *Gesammelte Schriften*, vol 5(1) (R Tiedemann ed, Suhrkamp 1982 [1927–40]) 587 [Convolute N7(6)].

[63] Supra 285.

[64] J Derrida, 'Hospitality, Justice and Responsibility: A Dialogue with Jacques Derrida' in R Kearney and M Dooley (eds), *Questioning Ethics* (Routledge 1999) 77.

resist the kind of formulaic description that, in his eyes, would mortgage his critical capability, offered a clarification consisting of a brief formula, whereby he sought to capture the basic heteronomic gesture to which he was committed: '*[P]lus d'une langue*, that is, both more than a language and no more of *a* language.'[65] Understood in this way, deconstruction's primordial relevance for comparative law cannot be in any doubt (which does not entail that in order to articulate his sense of being in the world and of foreign law being in the world, too, the comparatist must adopt an extreme deconstructive position: what matters is the appropriation and adaptation from deconstruction of certain key ideas).

The epistemological project governing research into foreign legal cultures or law-texts thus demands a strategy of dismantlement – of dishabiliment – of legal discourse. Once more, this is hardly for pleasure's sake, but because only such unravelling can expose the ideological claims that both the foreign legal cultures or law-texts themselves, and the analyses of these legal cultures or law-texts produced as 'comparative law', are effectively propounding. And only such disassemblement can reveal the arguments that both the foreign legal cultures or law-texts themselves, and the analyses of these legal cultures or law-texts produced as 'comparative law', are seeking to disable on account of their ideological undertakings. In this crucial sense, deconstruction must intervene as the leitmotiv informing my 'comparative law other-wise', as this different practice of comparison purports to deploy itself in resistance to the dominant view, that is, as it decides resolutely to answer no to the orthodoxy – for instance, in the face of the orthodoxy pressing epistemological contentions that it claims would pertain to sheer description,[66] such description somehow being inscribed 'without critical evaluation'.[67] Abidingly, comparative law other-wise is clear: no description, no matter how purportedly purely constative and 'scientific', can ever remain *flat*, that is, no description can ever fully eschew a prescriptive (and encultured) dimension – no description can ever be

65 J Derrida, *Memoires for Paul de Man* (2nd English edn, C Lindsay tr, Columbia University Press 1989) 15. The words '*plus d'une langue*' are added to the English version and inscribed in French, which is why I deliberately refer to the English text.

66 Eg: J Gordley, 'When Is the Use of Foreign Law Possible? A Hard Case: The Protection of Privacy in Europe and the United States' (2007) 67 Louisiana LR 1073, 1081 ('I am concerned with what the law [i]s'); Bogdan (n 16) 1237 ('The basis of any meaningful rules-oriented comparative legal work is, of course, the obtaining of correct information about the rules to be compared'); Zweigert and Kötz (n 1) 44, where the co-authors make a claim for 'scientific exactitude'.

67 Zweigert and Kötz (n 1) 42.

a *description*.[68] Inevitably, the comparatist dwells within the comparison, and the comparison is *his* comparison. And if there is positivist concern that the comparatist's presence within the comparison should make description erratic, let me claim that for a comparison to be erratic is only problematic if it is erratically erratic, not if it is inspiredly or inspiringly erratic, not if it is meaningfully erratic.

[68] 'Method' is not the way to tame the difficulty I address. Consider J Law, *After Method* (Routledge 2004) 5: '[M]ethods, their rules, and even more methods' practices, not only describe but also help to produce the reality that they understand.' Adde: ibid 143: '[M]ethod does not "report" on something that is already there.' With specific reference to comparative law, consider Simone Glanert's powerful indictment of method in S Glanert, 'Method?' in PG Monateri (ed), *Methods of Comparative Law* (Elgar 2012) 61–81.

XI

This Comparatist, Even

Looking beyond the wilfulness, curiosity, and concern that can be expected to inform an inclination for otherness and bearing in mind that 'comparative legal work will remain difficult . . . especially for those lacking a pre-disposition towards accepting difference',[1] one can advantageously ask about the agency that allows one, in time, to exit one's status as the local jurist that one would have initially become and transform oneself into a comparatist, whether consistently or sporadically, that is, change into someone taking it upon oneself to validate the imputation of normative significance to other laws and other legal cultures, inquire into the singularity of others-in-the-law, and attempt meaningful ascription of meaning to foreignness along the way. Who is this individual who would be dealing in difference across laws? Why would one thus put oneself in danger of marginalization at the hands of one's local legal 'community' in a manner that most other jurists around one obviously do not seem prepared to risk? (I have in mind an esteemed US comparatist-at-law, a colleague and friend, who tells me – this is February 2019 – how he 'get[s] a lot of flak' from the people around him on account of his comparative scholarship.) After all, one can hardly change the tendencies of institutional legal gravity, which will keep proving localistic and persist in entailing that one's investment of (ethical) energy towards the invention of a normative role for otherness-in-the-law to play locally will largely fail to be valorized within one's local legal 'community' at large. (Is it excessive to discern in this local defiance

[1] W Menski, *Comparative Law in a Global Context* (2nd edn, Cambridge University Press 2006) 30. In the passage that follows, I draw on EA Povinelli, 'The Will To Be Otherwise/The Effort of Endurance' (2012/111) South Atlantic Q 453. Elizabeth Povinelli herself relies on Michel Foucault.

a measure of occasional jealousy in response to the comparatist's international standing?)

Given that comparatism is a generally available practice, why is an individual in particular adopting it and not others? Why is an individual, thus showing himself willing to bear the burden of this differentiating activity as it preoccupies itself with the laws' singularity, engage in this new kind of focussed effort to re-coördinate his habits of mind, while many more jurists who would be capable of doing so do not follow suit? (Without appearing unduly uncharitable, one would also want to ask why it is that there are jurists who, obviously lacking the general cultural disposition and the specific linguistic competence, nonetheless feel attracted to comparatism and determine to rebrand themselves as comparatists.) And why is it that an individual, whether skilled or not, who is amenable to interaction with the foreign, does not feel a sense that he is believing and behaving unjustifiably as all signs point to the incidental or uncreditable character of his enterprise from a local institutional standpoint? What personal experience explains such preparedness to withstand relegation from the academic mainstream (I am a US academic specializing in US contract law in the United States) to the intellectual periphery (I am a US academic specializing in Italian '*diritto dei contratti*' in the United States)? Why a readiness to experience what the late John Merryman aptly styles '[t]he loneliness of the comparative lawyer'?[2] Why the transformative move by, say, this Brazilian jurist from the possible to the actual even as another Brazilian jurist, who could also proceed comparatively, makes an earnest show of tacit or express resistance? Why him and not her? Why me, us, and not them? Is it about one having encountered, perhaps fortuitously, favourable comparative circumstances within a given society or legal 'community'? And what would these be? Are there historical moments that, in one's personal or professional life, can be ascertained as having been actively conducive to the manifestation of the comparative vocation – if this is what is indeed at stake? And what characteristics would these junctures have harboured? Is it about a mentor who would have exercised an abiding influence on one? And how relevant is displeasure or frustration with one's 'own' law – or

[2] JH Merryman, 'The Loneliness of the Comparative Lawyer' in *The Loneliness of the Comparative Lawyer and Other Essays in Foreign and Comparative Law* (Kluwer 1999) 1–12. I observe that Merryman struck this saturnine chord even as he taught at Stanford Law School for more than six decades, by all accounts (including the *US News and World Report*'s!) a premier centre for legal sophistication where, I assume, there would have prevailed, on the whole, a resolutely anti-parochial attitude.

with one's life-in-the-law, or perhaps with one's life *tout court*? Meanwhile, how much of the attraction to otherness could be usefully explained by a special predilection on the individual's part, an idiosyncrasy? To pursue the idea of the calling, what is it precisely about the foreign that would interpellate one? What is it about another law or legal culture that would prompt in one the sentiment of being solicited? And once the self-in-the-law has crossed the threshold towards the foreign, are there predictable limits to the deployment of a thought purporting to break the vestryish grasp on one's *mentalité*? How much of the feeling of responsibility or entitlement to report on other laws or others-in-the-law can ascertainably be traced to the society within which the self-declared comparatist lives or to the legal 'community' into which he has been socialized or institutionalized, that is, epistemologized, encultured? Consider the possibilities: an old imperial power, a former colony, a bilingual or bicultural country, and so forth. And while it evidently matters that one was trained as a French or Dutch jurist,[3] how much does it count and in what ways – what difference does it actually make?

*

Against the backdrop of these interrogations as intriguing as they are diverse, I turn to my circumstances in the belief that while one may not be able to explain the work through the life, one can certainly not explain it apart from the life. Although it cannot be an easy task to elucidate scraps – or shreds – out of the entanglement that I am pleased to style 'my life', I do not deliberately seek to fashion ex post patterns of intelligibility or anything along the lines of a *Wunschautobiographie*. Specifically, as I recount aspects of my story – at this writing, I contend that events happened as I have collated them – I do not feel the impulse to ascertain a linear account that would somehow mean I have lived coherently and well. Moreover, I am disinclined to concede that my narrative is the product of a consistent and fully dependable memory. In fact, I maintain that my text, faithful as it adamantly tries to be, is necessarily untrustworthy.

*

I hold documentary evidence that I was legally born to francophone parents in Montréal (Canada), and I can establish that, for the first twenty-three years of my life, I was domiciled in that metropolitan area, in various francophone neighbourhoods – Montréal being a place

[3] cf R Gagné, 'Regimes of Comparatism' in R Gagné et al (eds), *Regimes of Comparatism* (Brill 2019) 12: 'Each manifestation of comparatism belongs to an epistemological horizon.'

where '[d]ifference is at the very core of cityhood'.[4] Two manifestations of the many quotidian ways in which difference forcefully intervened in the life of a young francophone *Montréalais* in the 1960s and 1970s would make a lasting impression on me.

The first assertion of difference that I have in mind pertains to the attempt to distinguish francophone culture in Québec from French culture in France. Montréal being a remote outpost within an occidental cultural configuration whose cores are in locations like New York, London, or Paris, intercourse with eminent cultures could only be awkward. Most complicatedly, perhaps, the acquisition of a Québécois cultural identity required the implementation of a critical approach vis-à-vis the French colonial referent in cultural matters, that is, the practice of a differentiation strategy from Frenchness. (The colonial theme always-already marked my education. I was in primary school, and my French-books-from-France included characters like 'Léo' and 'Sabine', these first names then being unknown in Québec. And I have long remembered a rebus puzzle that featured a drawing of water ripples with a small island, where a sign reading 'Léman' had been planted. The answer was evidently 'lake', except that such lacustrine obviousness was completely lost on an eight-year old francophone kid from Québec who had never heard of 'Lac Léman', arguably the most famous pond in francophone Europe.) To summarize, one of my secondary-school instructors, in a bold display of decolonial assertiveness, taught me Marie-Claire Blais alongside Balzac and Marcel Dubé next to Molière – both Blais and Dubé, of course, giving pride of place, in their different ways, to the local *parlure*. The fact that the presence of Blais and Dubé on the reading list meant that there would be no time for Proust and Racine was seemingly not regarded as problematic or, if you will, the cultural cost of differentiation was deemed well worth paying in order to escape the cultural arrogance or condescension then steadfastly issuing from imperial Paris (not least through the authoritarian persona of a general-turned-politician).

The other affirmation of difference to which I could not fail to be alerted at an early stage comes from the fact that Montréal is a bicultural and bilingual city. In my youth, the '*Révolution tranquille*' had not yet run its course, and in many important respects francophones, although numerically majoritarian to a significant degree in Québec, still lived on the outskirts of society. Certainly, the world of commerce and finance was almost exclusively under anglophone control, the French language

[4] S Simon, *Translating Montreal* (McGill-Queen's University Press 2006) 19.

being cast as the useless tongue of illiterate labourers. When my mother took me shopping with her all the way from our soporific northern district across the bridge to downtown, it was as if we had passed a border. Although I would not then have been able to formulate the matter in such terms, Montréal's bustling existed for me along the lines of the beyond. I recall being elated, every time. For my mother, though, the situation was infinitely more challenging, and no doubt somewhat threatening also, because she suddenly had to overcome the cultural oppression to which the large francophone 'community' remained subjected at the hands of the much smaller, but substantially wealthier, considerably better educated, and noticeably more influential anglophone population. In paradoxical manner, the bridge, even as it symbolized access to more sophisticated territory, heightened my sense of how different my mother and I were from the people who lived on the tither side of it, sharpened my realization that we did not belong to that other world.[5] The bridge emphasized the fact that we were from elsewhere – not only geographically or socio-economically speaking, but, much more significantly, I think, culturally and above all linguistically. As it purported to allow the connection, the bridge inscribed the differentiation. On the other side of it, where the anglophone other vigorously marked its presencing, my mother would swiftly become alien, 'unhomed'.[6]

How, then, did Rachel Vanier – one of six children to a widowed *maîtresse d'école* in the working-class district of Villeray – negotiate her colonized position, her situation of deemed cultural inferiority, once we had reached the neon lights? Courageously, I now reflect, she would approach 'communication' with the staunchly (and, often, provocatively) unilingual anglophone saleswomen at Eaton's, Simpson's, or Morgan's (Ogilvy's was too far west, too anglophone chic for us) by opiniatedly attempting to speak their language, even as she knew she could never get *there*, that she would at best manage to stutter in some kind of 'fake' English making her sound benighted – even as she understood that she would necessarily *fail*. In (her) other words, my mother resolutely asserted her non-native language in the knowledge that her 'English' would differ from the English being obstinately spoken by the saleswomen. Effectively confronting the military and political fact of the English conquest of Nouvelle-France, she sought to step out of

[5] cf M de Certeau, *L'Invention du quotidien*, vol 1 (2nd edn, L Giard ed, Gallimard 1990) 188: 'There is everywhere the ambiguity of the bridge: alternately, it welds and it opposes insularities.'

[6] HK Bhabha, *The Location of Culture* (Routledge 1994) 9.

herself, and out of her dissident and dissonant history also, in order to do things otherwise and, I would say, other-wise (that is, in a way that sought to be wise to the otherness of the individuals with whom she had to contend).

Living in Montréal not only made difference-consciousness inescapable, then, but it endowed the fact of cultural/linguistic singularity with immense value. Even though 'we', Québec francophones, were treated as inferior by 'them', whether the French-from-France or the anglophones – even though 'we' were the victims of antagonism and discrimination *squared* – there was no sense that 'we' wanted to mimic 'them', to be like 'them', to be 'them'. I cannot recall, for instance, that there was any intimation that we wanted to speak French-from-France or English instead of the local dialect. To be sure, however, 'we' wanted our very own 'French' to be recognized and respected (whether vis-à-vis France, which was my secondary-school teacher's point when he selected Blais over Proust, or at Eaton's and Simpson's). In other terms, 'we' wanted our entitlement to difference vindicated, not disavowed or sublated. In fact, it was precisely because the singularity of the Canadian francophone 'community' – its historico-politico-social differentiation, its *cultural* specificity – belatedly sought recognition and respect that it would emerge/survive as author of its agency, in possession again and anew of its own narrative (although surrounded by nearly 250 million anglophones to the south, west, and east). As of the late 1960s, Canadian francophony would finally raise its cultural profile in earnest, on occasion dramatically so, all the while responding to the seemingly relentless anglophone urge towards appropriation and assimilation. As 'a form of cultural reinscription that moves *back to the future*',[7] as an act of cultural enunciation and self-assertion, specifically against all local anglophone attempts at colonial containment, Canadian francophones were in effect actively re-enacting their past – the time when, before France's surrender to England in 1760, local francophony had been meaningful instead of anomalous. As this enterprise proved successful in a number of ways from the mid-1970s onwards, it vindicated the motif of group particularity to the point where no Canadian francophone who is at all socially aware can ignore the strong political emphasis that has been afforded group particulars in Canada over recent decades. Now, such consideration has arisen largely out of a sense of basic deference for francophone difference having lately been cast as enriching and enabling (although I would not deny for

[7] ibid 252.

a moment that what indications of recognition and respect proceeded to express themselves, if intermittently and grudgingly, also participated in tactics aiming to cabin francophone nationalism and circumvent political independence for Québec). But more must be said about the life of the mind in francophone Canada.

*

Writing on 'French Canada' in a noted comparative study, the distinguished politist Louis Hartz remarked on 'the incapacity of the people to assume Enlightenment responsibilities'.[8] Over the long term, this phenomenon helps to account for the dearth of intellectual activity that analysts have repeatedly noticed amongst Québécois. Referring specifically to francophone Québec, one commentator thus asks: 'How does one become an intellectual? By falling at the outset under the spell of books, thereafter by crossing the Atlantic'.[9] Unsurprisingly, the Québécois thinker has been termed a 'mimetic [i]ntellectual' on account of his dependency upon foreign ideas.[10] His practice has even been castigated as 'followism'.[11] Indeed, one observes a general tendency to abide by 'ready-to-think',[12] which means that, to retain an illustration from sociology, after studying in Europe for a few years 'the temptation could be great upon returning [to Québec] to occupy a position straightaway legitimate through making oneself on location the interpreter, the delegate, or the intellectual representative of Althusser, of Poulantzas, of Touraine, or of Bourdieu'.[13] This situation means that in francophone Québec one 'accede[s] to the position of intellectual only on the basis of putting oneself into exteriority in relation to one's originary identity'.[14] It also entails that the Québec intellectual 'represents himself a popularizer, introducer, synthesizer, always subjected to the risk of being a "weathervane" according to fashion and incapable of elaborating an indigenous thought'.[15] In sum, 'the Québécois intellectual cannot escape, so to speak, his genetic condition, that of hailing from a dependent

[8] L Hartz, *The Founding of New Societies* (Harcourt, Brace & World 1964) 30.

[9] A Lacombe, 'Les intellectuels québécois dans leur mémoire au XXe siècle, de Lionel Groulx à Gérard Pelletier' in M Brunet and P Lanthier (eds), *L'Inscription sociale de l'intellectuel* (L'Harmattan 2000) 278.

[10] M-H Soulet, *Le Silence des intellectuels* (Saint-Martin 1987) 71.

[11] ibid.

[12] ibid.

[13] ibid.

[14] ibid 70.

[15] ibid 71.

society'.[16] It has been said that the foremost characteristic of a francophone Québec intellectual is 'the impossibility to think for oneself alone'.[17] This fact has prompted one scholar to note that examples of the lack of a critical tradition in Québec could easily be multiplied.[18] Another commentator refers squarely to 'the anti-intellectualism that has marked Québécois history'.[19]

Two other series of observations appear pertinent. First, the state of affairs that I describe has been unfolding within the wider configuration of 'a certain New World anti-intellectualism',[20] which privileges commodity forms located somewhere between the technical and the popular. To quote Allan Bloom speaking of the United States, '[o]ne need not have read a line of philosophy to be considered educated in this country'.[21] Bloom's observation can apply to Canada in general and to francophone Québec in particular. In sum, practical competence carries. What matters is 'insuring a lucrative living by the mere fact of a diploma that is not a mark of scholarly achievement'.[22] Secondly – and this point is significantly more specific to francophone Québec – no intellectualism is possible without the self-effacement of the individual thinker before the francophone 'community' considered as a whole.[23] Concretely, this necessary adhesion to the collective, which is effectively an attachment to the emancipation of francophone Québec, means that no critique of francophone endeavours or initiatives can be seriously entertained. Perhaps an anecdote can make the point more vividly than a lengthy argument. Upon hearing of my published work critical of various structural aspects of the 1994 Québec civil code, a very good friend – an

[16] ibid. See also P-A Linteau, 'Un débat historiographique: l'entrée du Québec dans la modernité et la signification de la Révolution tranquille' in Y Bélanger et al (eds), *La Révolution tranquille quarante ans plus tard: un bilan* (VLB Editeur 2000) 29: 'Québec is a typical borrowing society, which proceeds through imitation and adaptation.'

[17] Soulet (n 10) 71.

[18] See G Caldwell, 'La fonction critique de l'intellectuel québécois est-elle en voie de disparition?' in M Brunet and P Lanthier (eds), *L'Inscription sociale de l'intellectuel* (L'Harmattan 2000) 356.

[19] M Fournier, 'L'intellectuel, le militant et l'expert' in M Brunet and P Lanthier (eds), *L'Inscription sociale de l'intellectuel* (L'Harmattan 2000) 28. This observation excludes Québec's anglophone 'community'.

[20] Y Lamonde, 'L'époque des francs-tireurs: les intellectuels au Québec, 1900-1930' in M Brunet and P Lanthier (eds), *L'Inscription sociale de l'intellectuel* (L'Harmattan 2000) 211.

[21] A Bloom, *The Closing of the American Mind* (Simon & Schuster 1987) 378.

[22] ibid 369–70.

[23] See Soulet (n 10) 60–71.

experienced lawyer, a seasoned teacher at Bar school, and a well-travelled woman – retorted (in French): 'But how can you criticize us in this way? We are so small' ('*Nous sommes tout-petits*'). Needless to say, the 'us' and the 'we' referred to the francophone 'community' in Québec understood as an indissoluble cluster somehow deserving a form of immunity from critique on account of its demographic vulnerability before the much larger anglophone North America.

Commentators have noted how the Québec intellectual is spontaneously 'gregarious', and how in fact 'he identifies himself only through the *We*'.[24] He is an 'apparatus intellectual', a phenomenon 'excluding . . . all dissidence through singularity'.[25] A people having historically feared for its survival, it seems, can only envisage collective rather than individual freedom. The cultural obsession with victimization, this *mentalité de siège*, prompted a leading French law professor having spent a year in a Québec university to write of '[a] culture on the defensive'.[26] Obviously determined not to offend his hosts, he asked in the most polite terms (which could mask neither astonishment nor scepticism): 'Can a law, no matter which, treat itself to the luxury of shunning a solution for the only reason that it is inspired by such or such foreign example?'.[27] I could effortlessly submit many illustrations of obdurate francophone chauvinism,[28] but suffice it to say that in my personal experience Québec is a rare place where bilingualism may actually carry a stigma, where speaking English in addition to French may be considered along the lines of treasonable activity. As far as I can tell, even Belgium does not take bilingual matters this far.

In my case, the noxious cultural assemblage consisting of an assertive anti-intellectualism and a stultification of individualism – a committed provincialism in the most parochial sense of the term – was compounded by the fact that I was born to an ardently philistine family and, notably, to a forcible browbeater of the archetypal ilk whose idea of education consisted of instilling in his two sons obsequious acquiescence to his moneyed views and mercenary values (his autocratic strategy worked according to plan in one instance, a forbidding case of replication *avant*

[24] ibid 71.
[25] ibid 61.
[26] C Atias, *Savoir des juges et savoir des juristes: mes premiers regards sur la culture juridique québécoise* (Centre de recherche en droit privé et comparé du Québec 1990) 15. Christian Atias was referring to legal culture.
[27] ibid 33.
[28] Eg: P Legrand, 'Comparative Contraventions' (2005) 50 McGill LJ 669.

Dolly vindicating Hegel's most famous vignette of the dialectic and allowing me a useful marker to gauge my success by reference to how much my life differs from my sibling's). Not only were there no books at home apart from a few airport novels (including, of course, the novel *Airport*), not only was I *never* taken to a symphony or jazz concert, to a ballet or contemporary dance event, to a play or singing performance, to an exhibition or book fair, but there was *never* the slightest encouragement to take the slightest interest in any intellectual or indeed cultural endeavour whatsoever. Quite to the contrary, I was actively and consistently discouraged from engaging in pursuits of the mind, all of them bar none roundly stigmatized as inconsonant with the production of wealth.

Intellectuals and artists, I was repeatedly and violently told, were but 'parasites' ('*des parasites*'), the general assumption being, I now think, that writers or teachers, musicians or actors, were enjoying state-of-the-art health care and well-paved roads even as their low incomes and lower taxes made them undeserving of these social benefits.[29] Such abhorrence of intellectualism and artistry, two words I can safely use in their widest affordances, was perhaps not wholly unusual for a man having come of age in the 1950s in a Montréal working-class neighbourhood (there is a family secret around the fact that this individual had to contend with a slump in living standards at the age of five and spend the rest of his childhood and teenage years in my mother's impoverished part of town – they met at the local outdoor skating rink – even as his father was a judge, a prestigious position in Québec on account of English law having imposed its institutional model as of the late eighteenth century). Yet, the aggressive reaction I witnessed more than once vis-à-vis the slightest intellectual or artistic inclination very much stood at the extreme end of the boorishness spectrum. I was still stuck in the patriarchal abode pondering the workings of shame when, towards the end of my first year of law school, I was spotted with the expensive criminal law textbook I had bought with my meagre savings, because my teacher was ineffectual and I needed help. (Having been denied tenure, a rare situation, the individual in question would be dismissed at the end of the semester.) I heard the relentless scold expressing genuine anger: 'You do not mean to build yourself a library, do you?' ('Tu ne vas quand même pas te monter une bibliothèque?'). I had acquired *one* law-book. Much

[29] cf D Trudeau, 'Grand parleux, p'tit faiseux' (1984) 26(3) Liberté 3, 8: 'Despite the raising of educational levels in contemporary Québec, the intellectual is still considered as a being sterile and marginal.'

more seriously, of course, I had transgressed the monocratic anti-scholastic edict. A library! The very idea…

Seconding the view that academics were useless individuals otherwise unemployable, my mother readily joined her toxic husband in castigating the idea of a university life. She, too, tried to countermand my ambition to become a law teacher and attempted to hold me to a petty local law practice working as '*le fils de*…' – and 'at the same law-firm as…', if you please. Despite the considerable patriarchal amassment of wealth that resulted from the arrangement of diverse corporate mergers and acquisitions, a prosperity that was proudly paraded over the years, it was crystal clear that I could not hope to secure the least fraction of the financial assistance I required in order to pursue postgraduate work and be able to contemplate engaging in the academic career to which I aspired. In fact, augmentation of wealth was matched by a correlative increase in cupidity. Most fortunately, I was able to secure a major scholarship allowing me to continue my studies. (Incidentally, the astoned commissar's reaction upon learning of my success – I obtained what easily ranks as the most prestigious student bursary available in academia – was to ask if I would be paying tax on the honour. In the 120-year history of this distinction, has any other recipient ever been posed such a *stupid* question?) As far as I can tell, my retort to my parents' energetic condemnation of academic endeavours has been to immerse myself in the realm of ideas as soon as I could, secure half a dozen university degrees in three countries, make my life as a law teacher as of my late twenties and soon proceed to do so in Europe, an ocean away, and build myself a library through the acquisition of thousands of books (which I buy the way others purchase penny candy). In time, perhaps by way of further distantiation from the bullying anti-intellectualism to which I had been treated for two stifling, smothering decades, my scholarly work would take a resolute theoretical turn and seek evermore intellectual knowledge in the form of ever more detailed intellectual answers to ever more profound intellectual questions. (I have come to take resarciation to such lengths that I now theorize theory, and I compare comparisons.)

I went to law school in Montréal (for my parents, it was quite simply *inconceivable* that I should attend university anywhere else) without harbouring the slightest interest in law and, although I hailed from legal lineage, without having the least acquaintance with law either, because not the slightest transmission of information had ever happened. (On induction day, I asked a perplexed classmate – 'didn't you tell me you come from a family of lawyers?' – whether I *really* had to buy the Québec civil code. It was not on any course-list of compulsory materials, it was expensive, and I was as poor as a church mouse.) In short, I went to law school, because my upbringing and my upbringers did not allow me any choice whatsoever in the matter. Although, allowing for three (anglophone) exceptions, the teaching at McGill University in the 1980s was mostly remarkable for its thoroughly pedestrian approach to law, this institution featured an original and intensive comparative curriculum whereby, over a period of four years, one was made to learn about the civil law and common law traditions in parallel. A typical lecture on the civil law of obligations in the *magister dixit* mode by a law professor trained in France would therefore be succeeded later in the day by an interactive course on common law constitutional theory taught by an Oxford-educated academic, perhaps an Englishman, focussing either on House of Lords cases dealing with parliamentary sovereignty or on the thought of Dicey and Jennings. The two (colonial) 'streams' were very clearly delineated as were the epistemologies that students had to deploy.[30] If I experienced difficulty understanding '*erreur sur la substance*', I went to read Jean Carbonnier's exposition of the subject-matter in his famous French *précis*. Meanwhile, if I failed to appreciate the fine points of the distinction between constructive and resulting trusts, I read or re-read the leading English precedents and *Hanbury and Maudsley's Modern Equity*. The idea was to prepare students for the practice of law anywhere in Canada (while Québec is in important ways a civil law jurisdiction, the rest of the country belongs firmly to the common law world). For my part, I therefore found myself being introduced from my earliest law-school days, unbeknownst to me, into comparative law and into the necessary realization of the profound differences across laws and legal cultures. (Interestingly, I find, I never said to myself that I would become a comparatist, but from the very beginning of my law-school experience this is the only form of legal knowledge I encountered.)

Before long, I would be hired as a research assistant to work at McGill's then new (and strikingly empty) comparative law centre. Coinciding with this further process of institutionalization, I started to spend evenings and weekends researching an argument that advocated for the transposition of a French precept on precontractual disclosure to the law of Québec. Although this text was later published and subsequently made

[30] This situation has changed in favour of courses claiming to 'integrate' civil law and common law materials. Anyone interested in this mishmash or in the vagaries of McGill's comparative curriculum in general will be pleased to know that there is no shortage of descriptive (and self-congratulatory) publications on the scholarly market.

its way to a Supreme Court of Canada opinion, I now regard it as the somewhat stupefying result of the relentless (colonized) extolment of French law to which I had been subjected in one of my first-year courses. (Incidentally, the position I held at the comparative law centre was one of three part-time jobs I kept during my law-school years. Combined with various grants and awards, my revenues, such as they were, made it possible finally to get away from the patriarchal habitation I despised at twenty. To be sure, my girlfriend and I had to operate in survival mode for a number of years – in addition to her university studies in biochemistry, she worked the night shift a few times a week at Canada's main telecommunications company. But survive we did.)

These four years of early apprenticeship in the law were followed by four more years of immensely rewarding advanced legal studies in Oxford and Paris. Obviously, if one is a Canadian jurist desperately wishing to graduate from Canada in order not to leave life untried, it very much helps to be devoting oneself to foreign law. But I took the matter one important step further. Building on my early exposure to comparative law, I formed the view that foreign law ought to be seen as carrying a significant and indeed crucial measure of intellectual and normative purchase for academics, lawyers, and judges operating locally – or, to articulate the matter differently, I resolved that it was necessary to relativize the overdetermination of any local legal referential repertory, whether in terms of concepts, categories, definitions, and so forth. When I arrived in Oxford in the early 1980s to engage in the writing of a postgraduate dissertation, I therefore found myself being directed towards the chair of comparative law, whose occupier was then Bernard Rudden. Two years later, still very much bringing to bear a comparative mindset, I would interrupt my Oxford studies and enrol in a postgraduate degree in French private law ('*droit privé*') at the Sorbonne, where I was the only foreigner amongst thirty French students or so. Jacques Ghestin, the leading French contract law professor of the day, had designed the programme to suit his academic interests and was its very 'hands-on' director. Out of my English and French escapades, I would in time obtain four degrees, including two doctorates.

With his unmistakable Gaullian allure, Ghestin made a strong impression on me. When I took his postgraduate courses in the mid-1980s, he was at the height of his scholarly fame, and he cumulated an impressive number of senior administrative roles at the Sorbonne. A prolific writer, he aimed to fashion a comprehensive theory of French 'contract law' ('*droit du contrat*'). To this end, his lectures would effortlessly range from the normative implications of an obscure certification on food products emanating from some low-level government agency to the French reception of Kant's theory of the will at the turn of the nineteenth century. My clear recollection is that my classmates and I felt we were witnessing path-breaking legal scholarship unfolding on a weekly basis before our dazed studenty eyes. I had never been exposed – certainly not in my McGill civil law courses – to what then struck me, quite simply, as very ingenious legal thinking. One day, I bumped into a former McGill classmate, who was also doing postgraduate work in Paris. He happened to be the son of one of the civil law professors who had taught me back in Montréal, which is why I was more than a little surprised when he wondered aloud why it was that we had not been treated, in Québec, to the rich intellectual life that had become our daily fare at the Sorbonne. However, it is impossible to mention the Sorbonne without evoking how extraordinarily decrepit it all was. The material facilities were dilapidated beyond anything I would have thought possible, if it had ever occurred to me to turn my attention to this issue in advance of my arrival in Paris. The antiquated Sorbonne law library particularly sticks to mind. The collection was kept in firmly closed stacks, and the ordering of a book, which could only be done at certain times of the short day, involved a process so bureaucratically inefficient that only the French, I assume, could have devised it. When all went well, it would take an hour or so before the book would finally appear (unless, of course, the *magasinier* had collected the wrong one, not an infrequent situation given the intricate, insistently non-Deweyian call numbers). And, of course, one could only order so many books at a time and on any given short day.

My Sorbonne year was but a break from my Oxford degree, which remains my most consequential postgraduate enterprise. The academic standards were very high, and I know of more than one contemporary who, having invested years of hard labour into the writing of their dissertation, failed the *viva*. I still carry discernible traces of the deep influence that my Oxford supervisor exercised over me during the four years when he loomed so large in my life in the course of the 1980s. (Anyone interested in physiognomy ought to think George Bernard Shaw.) Rudden was frighteningly bright, and he could be commensurately harsh and abrasive. He had been elected to the Oxford chair of comparative law in 1979 over Alan Watson, who later left the United Kingdom permanently for the United States and in fact never recovered from his defeat. (I know: he told me twice, first in 1996 and again in

2006.) Rudden held the position for twenty years until he withdrew in 1999, before reaching the age of compulsory retirement. (I cannot resist adding that the extraordinary institutional abasement of the chair of comparative law at Oxford since the early 2000s is a distressing sight to behold.)

A high-toning don of the 'old school' and in many ways a characteristic Oxbridge eccentric, Rudden once informed me that he was firmly committed to the 'Oxford' method, otherwise known, he explained, as the 'mushroom' method: 'You put your student in the dark. You feed him shit. And you watch him grow.' (I use quotation marks most advisedly.) Many years later, I met a McGill law graduate who had also written his dissertation at Oxford and had encountered Rudden in the context of a pedagogical initiative featuring four optional meetings on postgraduate research and writing that the Law Faculty had scheduled to assist students working towards higher degrees. (The idea that these sessions would have been entrusted to Rudden continues to strike me as peculiar in the extreme as I would have been hard-pressed to name a less student-friendly teacher.) By then a professor of law at a leading English university, my colleague recalled Rudden vividly: 'He used to scare the living daylights out of me', a view he had formed on the basis of the most minimal interaction with him while attending a handful of optional research-and-writing seminars. For my part, I had to submit 'copy' to my supervisor every single Thursday by 5:00 p.m. and meet with him every single Friday at 9:30 a.m. for almost four years. (I distinctly recall Rudden's acid reply when I informed him that I would be away for a month to take advantage of a unique opportunity to spend time in Africa, the only occasion I treated myself to an extended holiday break during my Oxford years. Without so much as turning away from his computer screen, he muttered 'I thought you wanted to be an academic'. At least, I was spared the flinty stare.[31])

Once I had earned my Oxford degree and a few calming years had passed, Rudden and I managed to forge a dynamic – the word 'relationship' somehow seems ill-adapted – pursuant to which we kept in touch and regularly met in various countries. Crucially, he helped me to break free of the disconcertingly unillumined Canadian academic culture into which I had been inducted upon my return from Europe by fulsomely

[31] Upsetting as it was, this incident does not qualify as the worst moment I experienced during my Oxford years. This distinction must go to the time when Rudden, muttering 'Is that it?', contemptuously and irascibly threw my weekly essay on the floor. Was my supervisor having a particularly bad day? Was my piece of writing in such a particularly bad way?

supporting my application to a teaching position in England. (Did it help that I was trying to be hired as a comparatist at a law school in North West England where Harry Lawson, Rudden's mentor, had taught after retiring from the chair of comparative law at Oxford?) And touchingly, I still think, he later produced a generous review of the first edition of the French primer on comparative law that I released in 1999, an appreciation he wrote in French and had published in France.[32] To my everlasting pride, Rudden referred to my text as 'an essay original and audacious'.[33] The man from Brasenose noted a 'brazen approach', and he emphasized the singularity of the argument by observing that it was 'very much [my] own' (and that it was anything but 'a boring summary of received ideas').[34] For my part, I did for Rudden what former supervisees can do to express gratitude to their adviser: I invited him to the schools where I taught, initiated the award of a major academic honour to him, contributed a chapter to his *Festschrift*, and crafted appreciative dedications. However, I absented myself from the commemorative service in the fall of 2015.

Although I was never in a position to appreciate Rudden's expertise on Soviet or Russian law, which had been the focus of his doctorate, I heard more than one specialist (in more than one country) express the utmost respect for his learning. While I was his student at Oxford, Rudden completed a detailed study of the legal regime that had governed the New River Company, a corporation established in 1609 – the oldest commercial enterprise in England – with a view to supplying water to the City of London (which the municipality could not get from the

[32] P Legrand, *Le Droit comparé* (Presses Universitaires de France 1999). The book went through five editions, being thoroughly rewritten along the way, and enjoyed a print run of 12,000 copies. In 2015, upon publication of the fifth edition, I withdrew. From the start, this editorial venture had proved greatly disappointing in a number of significant respects. Even formal apologies in writing from the chief executive officer (or '*Président du Directoire*') could carry so much redemptive value only, and even the commiseration of esteemed colleagues in various countries could offer so much moral sustenance only. In time, the editorial situation steadily worsened so much so that by 2015, it had reached a level of idiocy particularly egregious even by claustral local intellectual standards. For the benefit of my incredulous reader, let me mention, by way of illustration, how the series editor vetoed a parallel between comparative law and comparative literature on the stated ground that 'law has nothing to do with literature' ('le droit n'a rien à voir avec la littérature') in utter ignorance, of course, of the law and literature movement that has been in institutional existence for decades, not to mention its more recent 'droit et littérature' instantiation. In sum, the thought of any further commitment to this project became, quite simply, unsupportable [correspondence on file].

[33] B Rudden, 'Book Review' (2000) Revue internationale de droit comparé 275, 275 (review of P Legrand, *Le Droit comparé* [Presses Universitaires de France 1999]).

[34] ibid.

Thames, because the river was far too polluted). A reviewer in the Cambridge Law Journal called the 400-page text 'extremely scholarly'.[35] For his part, one of the leading British legal historians of the day, Brian Simpson, pronounced the book 'an important contribution to the history of legal forms of capitalism'.[36] I harbour not the slightest doubt that both assessments are indisputably sound. Even if some of Rudden's highly original work was duly printed,[37] in the typical style of traditional Oxford much stayed unpublished. Personally, I have derived the greatest benefit from Rudden's insights into various theoretical issues pertaining to comparative law that caught his academic fancy over the many years. An example of his singular brand of (inedited) comparative scholarship, which easily finds its place in this narrative, concerns what one may style the 'corrective virtues' of comparative law. In my language, I refer to comparatism's contrarianism.

The background to the text I have in mind is as follows. During the 1980s and 1990s, Rudden would take advantage of his regular visiting professorship at Cornell Law School to conduct occasional seminar presentations in the United States or Canada. In advance of each intervention, he was in the firm habit of circulating a two-page synopsis of the argument he proposed to maintain. When he accepted the invitation I extended on behalf of the Canadian law school where I was occupying my first teaching position and generously agreed to spend a week in residence in October 1988 (his only demand had been that Nancy could accompany him) – a decision I chose to interpret as a nod of encouragement to a former postgraduate student holding his initial academic post at a bottom-of-the-ladder institution – Rudden delivered the counterblast that I want to address. The two sheets of paper, featuring the inscription 'Fall 1988', are typed in 'Courier', which reminds me of the

35 AJG Cummings, 'Book Review' (1987) Cambridge LJ 199, 199 (review of B Rudden, *The New River* [Oxford University Press 1985]).

36 AWB Simpson, 'Book Review' (1986) 4 L & History R 486, 488 (review of B Rudden, *The New River* [Oxford University Press 1985]).

37 Eg: B Rudden, 'Matter Matters' in T Endicott et al (eds), *Properties of Law* (Oxford University Press 2006) 367–79; B Rudden, 'The Gentleman's Agreement in Legal Theory and in Modern Practice' (1999) 2 Euro R Private L 199; B Rudden, 'Things as Things and Things as Wealth' (1994) 14 Oxford J Legal Stud 81; B Rudden, 'Torticles' (1991–92) 6–7 Tulane Civil L Forum 105; B Rudden 'Equity as Alibi' in S Goldstein (ed), *Equity and Contemporary Legal Developments* (Hebrew University 1992) 30–45; B Rudden, 'For the First Gravedigger' (1984) 100 LQR 540. For an extensive bibliography, see '*Opera Ruddeniana*' in P Birks and A Pretto (eds), *Themes in Comparative Law: In Honour of Bernard Rudden* (Oxford University Press 2002) 289–96.

massive computer Rudden had had installed for him in the Oxford law library's so-called (and now defunct) 'Typing Room', where he worked all day, every working day. As far as I could discern, he was the only law don regularly using a computer in the mid-1980s. And even if I am in error, there could not have been more than a small handful of Oxford law teachers having taken the technological turn at that early juncture, then a quirky motion.

*

Rudden's claim thus shows how one of comparative law's many intellectual advantages is to act as a corrective to scholarly over-interpretations, for instance, in situations where a new theoretical model purports to offer an alternative to the usual doctrinal reading of the law. In its eagerness to overcome the received interpretation, the innovative understanding may prove unduly enthusiastic, comparative law then being potentially in a position to curb the excessive conclusions on offer. Rudden's illustration concerns a publication issuing from the critical legal studies movement, which throughout the 1970s and 1980s developed within US law schools as a foremost intellectual current expressly committed to the promotion of political positions one associates with the left. The example involves *Hadley v Baxendale*, a leading English case regarding the matter of contractual damages. I envisage Rudden's argument as an excellent example of the merits of the comparative counter-signature.

In its 1854 judgment, the English court held that

> [w]here two parties have made a contract which one of them has broken, the damages which the other party ought to receive in respect of such breach of contract should be such as may fairly and reasonably be considered either arising naturally, i.e., according to the usual course of things, from such breach of contract itself, or such as may reasonably be supposed to have been in the contemplation of both parties, at the time they made the contract, as the probable result of the breach of it.[38]

In an in-depth study of the decision, Richard Danzig, a prominent adherent of critical legal studies, drew an arresting conclusion: 'Arising squarely in the middle of the "industrial revolution" and directly in the midst of the "Great Boom" of 1842–1874, *Hadley* v *Baxendale* was a product of these times.'[39] In order to understand the case, said

[38] *Hadley v Baxendale* (1854) 156 ER 145 (Exch) 151 (Alderson B).

[39] R Danzig, '*Hadley* v *Baxendale*: A Study in the Industrialization of the Law' (1975) 4 J Legal Stud 249, 259.

Danzig, one had to appreciate 'the industrial and legal world out of which it came and for which it was designed'.[40] Danzig's argument was readily accepted amongst critical scholars, and references to his article have featured prominently in critical legal studies literature. A representative endorsement is distinguished legal historian David Sugarman's: '[T]he ... work of Richard Danzig ... provides strong ... evidence in support of ... the conceptual restructuring of the foundations of modern contract law and its close ... relationship with the needs of the judiciary and entrepreneurs.'[41] However, intervening from the vantage point of comparative law, Rudden convincingly demonstrates that Danzig's interpretation is unpersuasive. Far from being a peculiar English development flowing from the Industrial Revolution, the *Hadley v Baxendale* doctrine can be traced to French law, which itself traces it to Roman times. Rudden's compelling comparative statement deserves to be reproduced *verbatim*, if at some length:

> In the English case of 1854, counsel and the judges were reading to each other from an American book: Theodore Sedgwick's *Treatise on the Measure of Damages*, NY 1847. For the passages relied on in court and repeated (without attribution) in the judgment, the American author's main sources are the works of the French writers Domat (1625–96) and Pothier (1699–1772), and the distillation of their views in the Code Napoleon #1149–51 (1804). Pothier's account is largely based on a 16th-century Latin treatise on Damages by the French jurist Dumoulin (Molinaeus) who, in turn, discusses critically many earlier writers including Cino da Pistoia (Cynus), a 14th-century professor at Bologna and judge at Rome. As primary source material, Dumoulin is using a printed, and Cino a manuscript, annotated edition (the Great Gloss) of the Roman texts (*Corpus Juris Civilis*), assembled by the Florentine, Accursius (1185–1263). This edition surrounds with the notes and commentary of the 11/12th-century Law School at Bologna (founded by Irnerius about 1087) the texts published in Istanbul (then Constantinople) by a Slav (the Emperor Justinian) in 530–3. The medieval discussion deals at length with the Damages Act 530 promulgated at Constantinople by Justinian in order to settle the controversies among the jurists of Rome in the 2nd and 3rd centuries, above all in their writings on the remedies of buyer and seller; as authorities for their views these jurists are citing their predecessors back to the days of the Republic. Extracts from their opinions, assembled and edited in the *Digest* part of the *Corpus Juris*, were published on

[40] ibid.

[41] D Sugarman, 'Book Review' (1980) 7 British J L & Society 297, 306 (review of MJ Horwitz, *The Transformation of American Law, 1780–1860* [Harvard University Press 1977]).

> December 16 533, to come into force in that form on December 30. From these texts it appears that the Roman lawyers were debating contract damages some two thousand years ago. It is submitted that the modern rule in *Hadley* v *Baxendale* is a distant, but direct, product of their opinions. And of nothing more.[42]

Danzig's argument in favour of the spatial and temporal particularization of a given contract doctrine thus fails as (callid) comparative law shows the development in question to have spanned more than thirteen centuries and, through the reception of Roman law over a large part of the occidental world, to have been disseminated (*not transplanted*) in various laws via processes of local adaptation.

Rudden's insight prompted me to teach my students how comparative law can act as a check on allegedly innovative theoretical claims in a different fashion, too. Instead of revealing an anachronism (such as Danzig's argument), comparative law can disclose an anachorism. In the 1990s, at a time when feminist jurisprudence was decisively asserting itself as a preponderant intellectual force, Leslie Bender argued that common law's refusal to acknowledge a duty to rescue reflected the prevalence, within the common law tradition, of values such as individualism, personal freedom, and autonomy, all of them typically associated with masculinity. A feminist perspective would, for its part, foster values characteristically linked with women like compassion, responsibility, co-operation, and solidarity. And the operationalization of these feminine values ought spontaneously to lead common law courts to recognize a duty to rescue.[43] Now, if one were to compare the legal treatment of the matter of the duty to rescue in England – where, as elsewhere in the common law world, it is habitually not recognized – with the position in France, a civil law jurisdiction located 'next door' where, pursuant to the doctrine of 'fault through abstention' ('*faute d'abstention*'), one can be held liable for not acting in a situation where it would have been deemed appropriate to intervene,[44] one should be led, in the light of Bender's feminist reasoning, to the following conclusion: English law embraces values said to be typically male, while French law illustrates values

[42] B Rudden, 'The Rule in Hadley v Baxendale: Some Notes on Ancestry' (1988) [unpublished] (on file).

[43] L Bender, 'A Lawyer's Primer on Feminist Theory and Tort' (1988) 38 J Legal Education 3, 33–36. See also L Bender, 'An Overview of Feminist Torts Scholarship' (1993) 78 Cornell LR 575, 580–81.

[44] Eg: G Viney, *Traité de droit civil*, vol 4: *Les obligations: La responsabilité: conditions* (LGDJ 1982) nos 452–56, 540–47. I deliberately refer to the treatise that was the leading French textbook in the relevant field at the time of Bender's publications.

characteristically identified as female. Such a profound ideological gap, however, could only appear most surprising, since there is nothing to suggest that French law has historically proved less patriarchal than English law. Much more plausibly, a comparative argument reveals the fragility of Bender's explanation and leads one to conclude that feminism cannot draw the relatively easy equation it has sought to propound between common law doctrine and masculinity. The simple fact of the matter is that France, an influential jurisdiction within the civil law tradition, is, as French feminists would no doubt emphatically argue, at least as much governed by the values of masculinity as England. Yet, French law has no difficulty in acknowledging liability for failure to rescue. In this instance, comparative law rescues (!) the feminist claim from its armisonous reading of the common law by showing that another law, arguably as androcentric as the common law, reaches an opposite conclusion with respect to the duty to rescue.

*

Upon completion of my legal studies, and leaving to one side my brief sojourns at a couple of Montréal corporate law firms (which allowed me in short order to confirm *everything* I suspected and feared about lawyers' quaestuary ways and the practice of law's philargyry), I soon embarked on an academic career, which initially took me to the common law tradition, then to a so-called 'mixed' jurisdiction (as if there were pure ones...), back to the common law, and subsequently to two civil law countries. While fashioning these two juristic versions of myself as common law lawyer and civilian – a kind of *Doppelgänger* phenomenon that even prompted me to join both common law and civil law Bars – I have held full-time positions in four countries and visiting posts in thirty countries or so and at certain institutions on more than ten or fifteen or twenty occasions, very often for weeks or months at a time. In the process, I have taught common law in French to common law audiences (in Canada and England), common law in French to civil law audiences (in France, Switzerland, and Egypt), common law in English to common law audiences (in Canada, England, Ireland, Australia, Singapore, and the United States), common law in English to civil law audiences (in a wide range of European jurisdictions, China, Indonesia, Brazil, and Qatar), civil law in French to common law audiences (in Canada and England), civil law in French to civil law audiences (in France and Canada), civil law in English to common law audiences (in Canada, England, Ireland, Australia, Singapore, and the United States), and civil law in English to civil law audiences (in a number of European jurisdictions and Canada). It is therefore my own life-in-the-law – that of someone without a mother-law who is free to imagine oneself as either common law lawyer or civilian, a jurist who was never locked inside the claustrophobic overdetermination of one law, a law teacher who has constantly straddled two leading legal traditions – that informs my comparative work and provides me with a few basic intuitions and premisses concerning comparative interventions.

*

The mass displacements of population, whether forced or not, with which one has had to become acquainted over recent decades suggest that exile may no longer qualify as an event within the range of abnormal human experience. Still, one does not cast oneself adrift without excellent reason. In my case, I abandoned my 'home life', because what was available to me in Canada simply did not deserve to be called *home* or *life*. For me, as a result of my suffocating upbringing and education, exile has therefore meant (and, to a considerable extent, continues to signify) an exhilarating liberation beyond anything I had even imagined feasible.[45] Nearly forty years after I first left Québec to study at Oxford, I continue to marvel at the fact that I could *escape* a world so poor in spirit, so petty, and so forgettable. But the acquisition of this freedom has come at a very high price (not least exheredation, *somme toute*). Importantly, my circumstances have prompted me to experience a double bind, which I now know I shall never be able to surmount completely. To reiterate the point, even before I departed Canada I had a less-than-confused sense of living in a sub-intellectual environment. Finding myself in England and France, my sentiment that Canada was without an intellectual tradition of significance, and my profound conviction that I myself had failed to acquire intellectual sophistication, found themselves vindicated. Whether at Blackwell's or Vrin's, whether sitting in Rudden's office in the Oxford law library or listening to Ghestin at the Sorbonne, I faced incontrovertible evidence: intellectually speaking, the place of my birth was at best bland and much more plausibly mediocre. As an individual, as a 'cultural product' issuing from that location, I could not reasonably be hoping to fare meaningfully better. Such painful appreciation of the dismal shortcomings of the Canadian academic scene persuaded me that a teaching career in Canada would

[45] I am thinking of Vladimir Nabokov's 'syncopal kick': V Nabokov, *Speak, Memory* in *Novels and Memoirs 1941–1951* (B Boyd ed, Library of America 1996 [1947]) 573.

only generate considerable intellectual suffering – an intuition that I was able to confirm within a mere four years. (I thought the Canadian academic scene so dismal that, despite my strongest moral and conceptual reservations, I had made the wrenching resolution to go into full-time practice, which I was under contract to enter on 1 July 1991. As fate would have it, though, on 28 May I received an offer to hold a lectureship at a law school in North West England and thus found myself being saved *in extremis* both from practice and from Canada. Fie upon Canadian law firms and their enclosing, stunting, warping cubicles!) Reflecting many years later on the acute *honte culturelle* I had experienced as a recent Oxford and Sorbonne graduate returning whence I had come in order to attempt a life of the mind in Québec, I realized that my situation was far from unique.[46]

A highly respected journalist in francophone Québec throughout the 1950s and 1960s, André Laurendeau thus referred to his two years at the Sorbonne by noting how 'intense' his intellectual life had been in a society 'better structured, so much richer' than his native Québec.[47] He thought in terms of 'the great intellectual adventure'.[48] But Laurendeau, like many others, had decided to settle in Québec after all. To be sure, he had 'the feeling of conceding a sacrifice'.[49] He knew that 'by accepting to return home, he [was] amputating himself of a part of [himself]'.[50] Years later, Laurendeau acknowledged occasional 'bitterness' and confessed that '[s]till some scars re-open themselves sometimes'.[51] For his part, David Lewis, a distinguished Montréal politician who was prominent on the Canadian scene in the 1960s and 1970s, recounts in his memoirs how, after three years of law studies

[46] On the subject of *honte culturelle*, I keep good company. In Pierre Carles's film *La Sociologie est un sport de combat* (Buena Vista Home Entertainment 2001), Pierre Bourdieu admits that hearing someone speak with a pronounced Béarn accent, which reminded him of his rural roots in South West France, would put him to shame. He readily acknowledges that as an intellectual and sociologist, he should not be reacting in this way. But he also notes that he simply could not overcome his strong feelings. Jacques Derrida tells of an analogous experience: 'I would like it so much that no publication shows anything of my "Algerian French". . . . I am not proud of this, I do not make this into a doctrine, but there it is: an accent, no matter what French accent it is, and above all the strong meridional accent, appears to me incompatible with the intellectual dignity of public speech': J Derrida, *Le Monolinguisme de l'autre* (Galilée 1996) 77–78.

[47] A Laurendeau, *Ces choses qui nous arrivent* (Hurtubise HMH 1970) 141.

[48] ibid.

[49] ibid 142.

[50] ibid.

[51] ibid 142 and 141.

at Oxford, he 'struggled with a serious temptation to remain in England'.[52] Along analogous lines, the leading political scientist Léon Dion described his Québec homecoming, after his years of further studies in France and England, as a 'traumatizing experience'.[53] Faced with the loss of 'a cultural ambiance that . . . had dazzled [him]',[54] he felt a 'disarray human and intellectual'.[55] As a Montréal child, I had occasion personally to experience this distress at close range, albeit in a way that I was then unable to recognize or express into words.

The tormenting hector's only sibling, his elder sister Aline – a kind, generous, educated, cultured, and cosmopolitan woman – remained single. Having earned herself a Canadian government music scholarship, she spent five years in Paris – this would have been circa 1956 to 1960 – at a time when the uncontested supremacy of Roman Catholicism in Québec would have made it extraordinarily difficult for a young francophone woman in her twenties to go abroad on her own. While in Paris, Aline followed various programmes of musical instruction at the Conservatoire, where she was trained as a musicologist (a theorist of music), notably under the great Olivier Messiaen. But my aunt was an eclectic mind, and she also attended lectures by Merleau-Ponty and Bachelard at the Sorbonne. After her death in 1995, I even found in her extensive library an original edition of Michel Villey's *Le Droit romain* in the celebrated '*Que sais-je?*' series duly annotated in her hand (not to mention books by Adorno, Beckett, Duchamp, Giacometti, Klee, and other 'marginal' writers). My aunt moved in artistic circles, and she counted as her friends Paul-Emile Borduas – the Québec painter who had authored the 1948 pamphlet *Refus global* – and Pierre Alechinsky, of CoBrA fame. (I own a large Alechinsky litograph, '*Trois-quarts de veille*', bearing a warm dedication to Aline Legrand.) Upon her return to Québec, Aline devoted her career to art criticism. She worked as a producer of literary and musical programmes at the Canadian Broadcasting Corporation (CBC), except for a two-year spell in the early 1980s as director of the *Centre culturel canadien* in Paris. (Pierre Trudeau, the prime minister of Canada, whom Aline had briefly dated in her twenties, appointed her. I assisted Trudeau as a speechwriter in the late 1980s, and I recall a conversation with him over a Japanese dinner when he fondly remembered the Aline of his youth.)

[52] D Lewis, *The Good Fight* (Macmillan 1981) 75.

[53] L Dion, *Québec 1945–2000*, vol 2 (Presses de l'Université Laval 1993) 168.

[54] ibid 167.

[55] ibid.

Aline's Montréal apartment featured books, more books, and yet more books – at least, this is how I recollect it. There were books lining the walls in Aline's study. There were books along the walls in the living room (the many oversized art books were there, and I often turned their pages for a long time – even as they could hardly stay open on my laps). There were books from floor to ceiling in the den. There were books all around the dining room. And there were books lining the walls of the long corridor leading to her bedroom as far as my young eye could see. (In all likelihood, my mind is conflating images from two different apartments she occupied over the years – but then, 'so wide appears/The vacancy between me and those days'.[56]) In the rare spaces where there were no books, one could find a painting or other art work. (I recall a dark canvas *à la* Soulages, my aunt explaining with a broad smile that it was entitled '*Neiges*'.) On the substantial coffee table, Aline always kept newspapers such as *Le Monde*, *The Times*, *The New York Times*, and Maurice Nadeau's *La Quinzaine littéraire* (these are the ones I can still visualize). She would buy them from one of the very few newsagents then selling foreign papers in downtown Montréal. Sometimes, I would accompany her to claim these evocative titles, which the shop had piled for her. I have a vivid image of one of these walks: we were braving a blizzard. I would have been ten or so.

In my constricted world, my aunt was unique – no one else I knew had books and paintings on her walls, no one else I knew read foreign newspapers, and no one else I knew spoke French as elegantly as she did. No one else I knew was an *intellectuelle* or even came remotely close. What I could not tell as a child was how she missed Europe and France so terribly, how she had left her heart at '10, rue des Ecoles, Paris V^{e}'. As she progressively moved into a life of paranoia and reclusion, we became estranged. But when she died, I learned that a decade or so earlier she had discreetly bought herself a studio apartment in Paris, where she returned two or three times a year.

As far back as I can remember, it was evident to me that I, too, was going to study at the Sorbonne and live in the *Quartier latin*. I arrived in law school, at McGill, firmly thinking along those lines. In the event, I was deflected to Oxford on account of a series of extraordinary circumstances culminating in the implausible obtention of a most famous scholarship specifically attached to that university. (Again, I absolutely required

[56] W Wordsworth, *The Prelude* in *The Thirteen-Book Prelude*, vol 1 (ML Reed ed, Cornell University Press 1991 [1799]) 2.28–29, 125.

a substantial award to finance my postgraduate studies – indeed, I needed a merit-only benefaction, because in the 1980s one could still be denied on account of parental wealth even though one lived by oneself and one's parents did not contribute a cent to one's welfare. Incidentally, a loan was out of the question, since I would have had to provide a surety.) I would eventually arrange to suspend my Oxford studies so as to spend an academic year at the Sorbonne (although I soon realized there was no way I could afford to live anywhere on the *Rive gauche*) – a sojourn that coincided, as it happened, with Rudden's visiting appointment at the same institution. (I actually had him as a teacher in one of my Paris courses, and my sense was very much of being under surveillance.[57])

While I like to think that my cultural experience in Europe, first in Oxford and later in Paris, would have resembled Aline's of thirty years earlier, I ultimately took a very different decision from her. Instead of returning to Québec, I chose to live in Europe permanently, relegate my impoverished Québécois self to the background as much as was feasible, and eliminate abjection from my life. Although 'the issue is between me

[57] Although the dynamic between us remained practically as asymmetrical as any intellectual interaction could possibly be, the fact that we were now in Paris gave me a linguistic edge. On a number of occasions during his teaching visit, Rudden asked me to review lectures he had written in French. Most importantly, he promptly 'invited' my participation in the drafting of a French article effectively opposing Ghestin's theoretical model on contract law, which revolved around the ideas of justice and utility. Eg: J Ghestin, 'L'utile et le juste dans les contrats' Dalloz 1982 Chron 1. Contributing typical common law and English pragmatism, Rudden's critical retort drew on economic analysis to emphasize what he perceived to be the inefficiency of Ghestin's claims. See B Rudden, 'Le juste et l'inefficace: pour un non-devoir de renseignement' (1985) Revue trimestrielle de droit civil 91. Not only was Rudden challenging the gist of Ghestin's grand theory of French 'contract law', but he was doing so with specific reference to the matter of pre-contractual information, which had become Ghestin's favourite law-reform initiative and a cause with which his name was closely associated. For a review of Ghestin's many publications on point at the time, see P Legrand, 'Pre-contractual Disclosure and Information: English and French Law Compared' (1986) 6 Oxford J Legal Stud 322. Somehow, Rudden had managed to get his objection printed in the leading French law review and have it published just before the end of his academic visit. Ghestin was not amused. By then, he knew that I was Rudden's student and proceeded to tell me, no doubt expecting that I would relay the message, how inappropriate it was for a guest to behave in such confrontational manner ('ce n'est pas convenable' were Ghestin's exact French words). Apart from earning myself an express acknowledgement in the *Revue trimestrielle de droit civil*, my editorial effort eventually led to a Paris dinner when, in short order, I was ordered to order rabbit, my first *lapin à la moutarde*. Whenever I think of how my Oxford and Sorbonne worlds clashed all these years ago, I readily find this conflict corroborating my agonistic view of comparative law.

and the culture which has formed me',[58] which means that the refusal of accommodations with the lamentable fact of my pre-European self is essentially a private question, I can say that I had become adamant not to be a Québécois like Laurendeau, Lewis, Dion, or my dear aunt, who had all returned to a miserable, dreary place to sink deeper into their natal track. For my part, I was not going to massacre myself in that way. I urgently wanted an existence featuring a bigger 'I', something else rather than something less. The time had come to answer the call of responsibility, to open my consciousness towards possibility, to listen to the voice emerging from within, to resurrect the assassinated self that I carried within me.[59] Stern action was required. Like Stephen Dedalus, I would enact my own *non serviam*.

For all my resolve, exile remained anything but trivial. This event was not the easy decision that, decades later, it may appear to have been; rather, it was an emotionally and intellectually exorbitant determination, since for all its promise it enacted the dislocation of a world. I was unmooring myself even as I knew that no one breaking rank with francophone Québec could expect to enjoy complete impunity. (I have already referred to the substantial cost I incurred on account of my departure. But there were other penalties also such as the jettisoning of ten years of scholarly publications having to do with Québec law on the basis of which I had made a local name for myself.) Now, even as I sought in earnest to take leave of my imposed, *quétaine* self so as to uncover and release what I considered to be my authentic, intellectual self, I realized that I could not wipe the slate clean. Still, I was confident that I would loosen the stranglehold of the coarseness I readily associated with my Québec years. Fortunately, there remains a measure of plasticity to one's cognitive equipment, which allows for longing and permits striving – despite culture bearing so heavily on one and colouring even the most intimate aspects of one's experience. To be sure, I knew that I would struggle in vain to eradicate Québec from my life. Although I had to accept that enculturation does not dissolve under the pressure of wishful thinking and that I would always have to carry within me the bleak embers of my youth, I could reasonably hope to tame some at least of

58 J Berger, 'Speech on Accepting the Booker Prize for Fiction' in *Selected Essays* (G Dyer ed, Pantheon 2002 [1972]) 254.

59 The allusion is to Beckett: 'I have always had the feeling that there was in me an assassinated being. … I had to find this assassinated being again. Try and give it life again': C Juliet, *Rencontres avec Samuel Beckett* (POL 1999 [1973]) 15. In this interview with Charles Juliet, Beckett spoke in French.

such fatefulness.[60] From an epistemic standpoint, I was moving resolutely away from the crutches that belongingness and docility appeared to afford. Not unlike Jacques Derrida, I was proclaiming '*Je ne suis pas de la famille*' ('I am not one of the family'), both literally and metaphorically.[61] Against the familial disqualification of ideas, the parochial regimentation of thought, and the provincial subordination of the mind, I would affirm my commitments to intellectuality, independence, and individuality. Henceforth, I would think, but I would not think – or indeed work – collectively. Not only would I resist being caught in the net of ideology or co-opted into any form of *bien-pensance*, I would eschew submission. Well away from any tribal instinct, I would stand for resistance and contention, recalcitrance, and opposition. (Having overcome more than two decades of remorseless cruelty precisely through the deployment of defiance, I had form.) In sum, I would now bear the solitary burden of intellectual survival.

Alas, I could not make my move so quickly, and after Oxford and Paris I first had to return to Canada for four years. At the time, I experienced an acute 'Ibarra' effect, which confirmed forthwith my decision to deterritorialize myself for good.[62] In the early 1990s, having been offered an exciting teaching opportunity in North West England, for which I remain immensely grateful, I finally settled in Europe. The Bodleian and the *Bibliothèque nationale de France* would now be where I researched, and

[60] cf S Beckett, *The Unnamable* (S Connor ed, Faber & Faber 2010 [1958]) 36–37: 'What I speak of, what I speak with, all comes from them. . . . It's of me now I must speak, even if I have to do it with their language, it will be a start, a step towards . . . the end of madness, the madness of having to speak . . . of things that . . . they have crammed me full of to prevent me from saying who I am . . . and from doing what I have to do . . . . How they must hate me! Ah a nice state they have me in, but still I'm not their creature . . . . I'll be myself, in the end.'

[61] J Derrida and M Ferraris, *Le Goût du secret* (A Bellantone and A Cohen eds, Hermann 2018 [1993]) 34. The words are Derrida's.

[62] In *Noli Me Tangere*, a Filipino novel originally published in 1887 in Berlin during the Spanish occupation of the Philippines, a prelude to the Philippine Revolution of 1896, an acknowledged masterpiece of Filipino literature and source of great nationalist pride known locally as 'the Noli', José Rizal has Don Crisóstomo Ibarra return home to the Philippines after spending almost seven years in Europe. But Ibarra has been seized by 'the devil of comparisons': he is now unable to look at the botanical garden of Manila without remembering wistfully the botanical gardens of Europe, 'wealthy and well-kept', to be found in countries that invest 'much determination and much money so that grows a leaf and opens its calyx a flower'. I quote from J Rizal, *Noli Me Tangere* (M Russotto ed, Biblioteca Ayacucho 1982 [1887]) 51. In one of his famous novels, Milan Kundera discusses '*Entfremdung*' ('estrangement') as 'the process during which what has been close to us has become foreign': M Kundera, *Les Testaments trahis* in *Œuvre*, vol 2 (F Ricard ed, Gallimard 2016 [1993]) 877.

the London and *Quartier latin* bookshops where I browsed (and bought!). The decision to launch a new career in Europe – I was then in my early thirties – was bold and would prove professionally momentous. It would also have huge personal implications ranging from the worst imaginable to the best conceivable (all falling beyond the scope of this narrative).

*

As an academic in England, I had much cause to observe that the discernment of the insignificance of my legal education was still *becoming.* Seemingly every discussion with the colleagues with whom I taught in the North West, some of them remarkably clever – I have in mind Costas Douzinas, Peter Goodrich, Geoffrey Samuel, and David Sugarman – heightened my feeling of ineptness, every reading of their publications making things worse. Yet, with full 'exilic insolence',[63] I aimed to raise myself to European intellectual standards. However, because '[t]he past is never dead', indeed '[i]t's not even past',[64] I soon had confirmation that I would never be 'English' or 'French' in the way individuals who had been socialized and institutionalized into the law in England were English and in the manner people who had been socialized and institutionalized into the law in France were French. At least, I was managing not inconsequential de-quebeckicization. In effect, I was destined to operate within a 'third culture' – neither completely English or French, of course, nor fully Québécois anymore – that would feature its own originality, its peculiar marginality, and its precariousness also. I would be *different.* And I would also be different, because I would later move to occupy a research chair in comparative legal cultures in the Netherlands and then, after five years, relocate to France.

My displacements across cultures – the implementation of an 'ascetic code of willed homelessness'[65] – have profoundly marked my appreciation of comparative law. Initially as a student and then as an academic, I had to make sense of legal materials in jurisdictions other than the one where I had been socialized into the law and institutionalized into deference for the law. Having to contend with the disaggregation and disintegration of my formerly mostly cohesive if inconsequential self – 'a disfaction, a désuni, an Ungebund'[66] – I required to fashion a new recital in order to address the differend that I faced in the midst of my alternative legal

[63] J Kristeva, 'L'autre langue ou traduire le sensible' (1998) 52 French Stud 385, 388.
[64] W Faulkner, *Requiem for a Nun* (Vintage 2011 [1951]) 73.
[65] EW Said, *The World, the Text, and the Critic* (Harvard University Press 1983) 7.
[66] S Beckett, *Dream of Fair to Middling Women* (E O'Brien and E Fournier eds, Arcade 1992 [1932]) 138.

circumstances. When I arrived in a new country, I found myself on each occasion being in a different position from local lawyers, who must spend much of their time engaging in acrobatic conceptual pirouettes with a view to reconciling various documentary materials in order to identify 'the law' on a particular point at a particular moment. For my part, I confronted another task, a more elementary challenge also, since I had to ascribe basic meaning to the posited law that I encountered. Now, 'making sense' of the law certainly meant that I could not content myself with observing it (or with observing myself observing it). I had to strive for *appreciation*.

One frame of understanding readily suggested itself, for it was the model with which I was familiar on account of my early years of legal studies, that is, positivism – according to which law is law, and everything else is everything else. I would now say that it was the frame of understanding into which I had initially been *indoctrinated*, I would now call it something like a Cartesian or neo-Kantian or Kelsenian mindset, and I would now see this disposition for the eminently ideological and political project that it is. While in England, the Netherlands, and France – not to mention my incessant travels throughout continental Europe over the many years – I have repeatedly encountered positivists. These colleagues present 'the law' as an entity objectively and authoritatively given, any attempt to go beneath, behind, or beyond the law-texts in order to situate them within a matrix other than that of the technical process of their production being roundly condemned as not law and as something less serious than law, unworthy of law. Not only is there *scientia juris*, but there is *scientia scientarum*. Perhaps, ultimately, this lawyerly smugness and this contempt for other brands of knowledge – this attempt to cancel other knowledges on account of their allegedly 'unscientific' character (whatever that word may have meant) – reminded me too much of my old world for me to be able to feel the least bit comfortable with this paradigm. In the back of my mind, I could distinctly hear someone proudly boasting – the clangour of vulgarity triumphant – that in his ten, twenty, or thirty years of practice, he had not needed anything beyond the civil code and the Securities Act, the only two texts he kept in his bare office. Perhaps because of such inanity, I felt I had a privileged insight into the positivist mindset. I sensed that I could possibly devise what a positivist allegiance effectively betrayed, that is, a disposition along the lines of insecure strictness deriving its sustenance from the mastery of a limited range of technicalities and the correlative denigration of forms of knowledge ranging beyond its angustate worldview. In other terms, I experienced the 'law-is-law' paradigm as a cosmology based on authority and closure, on denial and repression, on obtuseness and unsophistication – all these familial and familiar attitudes. I was not impressed. Admittedly, Europe was exposing me to a particularly crude version of the legal model. Be that as it may, for my part I certainly did not want to wallow in this kind of obscurantist philodoxy. I simply did not care for dogmatic pronouncements of the type 'the law is this' and 'the law says that'. No matter how purportedly sophisticated – and I am readily willing to concede the intellectual acumen of an HLA Hart or a Neil MacCormick – the positivist approach could not persuade me. It was simply not satisfactory for me. I had had well enough of the authoritarian paradigm, of being told what was what and that was that. I simply could not marshal the obedient disposition – the faith[67] – that positivism assumed on the part of its adherents. I wanted answers to my questions. I wanted to know *why* the law was this way rather than that, *why* the law said this rather than that. Instead of any proclivity for acquiescence, I sought to implement a decidedly inquisitive inclination.

Quite apart from these estimations, I found it impossible to understand what positivism expected me to see when, coming to the matter as a Canadian jurist, I found myself reading an English statute or a House of Lords decision. I certainly could not perceive any statement that appeared *necessary*. I could not spot any *objectivity* and, frankly, I could not identify any *truth* (and I certainly did not sense that there could exist any *method* allowing access to objectivity or truth). As I had often felt as a child or teenager, I was of the view that the answer to the law-text's singularity must lie out-of-disciplinary-bounds. Indeed, the interpretation for the foreign law's encultured singularity must be located where discipline did not permit me to go, where the decision to go notwithstanding disciplinary interdiction would attract chastisement (etymologically, a discipline is a whip). The answer had been effectively out-lawed, relegated beyond law's borders (these frontiers having been drawn by positivists themselves). In sum, I was convinced that the meaning of legal rules, to adapt a passage from Peter Winch's, 'depend[ed] entirely on their belonging in a certain way to a system of ideas or mode of living'.[68] I thought it was precisely these 'ideas' or this 'mode of living' that positivists were trying to exclude from the legitimate

[67] One of the staunchest advocates of 'scientific' positivism explicitly mentions the connection between 'law', on one hand, and 'religion' and 'dogmatic theology', on the other. See H Kelsen, 'The Pure Theory of Law' (1934) 50 LQR 474, 490.

[68] P Winch, *The Idea of a Social Science* (2nd edn, Routledge 1990) 108.

range of legal investigation. And I felt strongly that it was these very 'ideas' and 'mode of living' that were crucially relevant to any understanding that wished to move beyond platitudes along the lines of 'the reason why this is not negligence is because there was no duty of care, and the reason why there was no duty of care is because the parties did not stand in a proximate relationship, and the reason why the relationship was not proximate is that the judge says it was not'.

For me, as I tried to make sense of English law 'from the outside', so to speak, it was obvious that I needed to grasp the cultural preconditions of law's possibility in order to ascribe significant meaning to the Englishly legal. I took the view – the most sensible view, I thought – that whatever I might be prepared to style as 'knowledge' of foreign law had to be anchored in the life of the world where the foreign law dwelled. How could law's foreignness reasonably be assumed to be detached or detachable from its worldliness? By excluding so-called 'non-scientific' data from the realm of pertinence, positivism was leaving me bereft of information regarding the most revealing aspects of foreign law. In assuming that every meaningful aspect of legal 'reality' could be subsumed under a finite series of objective or true statements pertaining to so-called 'scientific' propositions and categories, positivists in effect abandoned whole areas of legal life to randomness (at the very least, to the vagaries of doctrinal construction). Against such a woefully impoverished cognitive outlook, EP Thompson's exasperated utterance, an exclamation I had come across during my Oxford years, appeared unimpeachably judicious:

> I found that law did not keep politely to a 'level' but was at *every* bloody level; it was imbricated within the mode of production and productive relations themselves (as property-rights, definitions of agrarian practice) and it was simultaneously present in the philosophy of Locke; it intruded brusquely within alien categories, reappearing bewigged and gowned in the guise of ideology; it danced a cotillon with religion, moralising over the theater of Tyburn; it was an arm of politics and politics was one of its arms; it was an academic discipline, subjected to the rigour of its own autonomous logic; it contributed to the definition of the self-identity both of rulers and of ruled; above all, it afforded an arena for class struggle, within which alternative notions of law were fought out.[69]

In fact, foreign laws do not feature serendipitous collections of attitudes, modes of expression, forms of reasoning, preferences, skills, and

[69] EP Thompson, *The Poverty of Theory* (Merlin 1995 [1978]) 130. Tyburn was a village in Middlesex close to where Marble Arch currently stands. It is recorded in the Domesday Book, and it was the main place of execution for London until 1783.

rituals (no matter how 'scientifically' labelled). Rather, anything from emotional responses to approaches to problem-solving to the solutions themselves can be connected to the operation of 'integrative mechanisms' – understood here as pathways to the internalization and 'naturalization' of ideas – that law-makers (in the broadest sense) acquire by way of personal habituation or tutored experience through latent neuropsychic states of readiness embedded in particular cultural configurations.[70] Law-texts thus arrive on the law-scene always-already cathected to a cognitive environment, which forms the *cultural* framework within which they can deploy themselves legally, the idea of an acultural legality being a contradiction in terms. Although each law-text can act as a unit of focal awareness in its own right, the elements are linked to each other – they 'fit' – to the point where the cultural framework features characteristic patterns of significance liable to discernment by an attentive observer, even if the interconnections can be very complex or only loosely identifiable.

And legal agents such as comparatists also come to the study of law as encultured beings – another fact that positivism has been keen to obliterate. Indeed, cultural patterns exercise a deep influence over legal agents' lives, so that they will not be easily renounced, many of them not effectively being open to relinquishment. In Pierre Legendre's apt words, 'the unconscious too is a jurist'.[71] The cultural patterns weighing on the comparatist's reading and interpretation of law-texts are widely shared within 'communities' (there are *French* comparatists, and there are *US* comparatists) – although allowance must be made for the fact that individual mental structures are also built over time on the basis of different personal reactions to certain learning events and on the basis of different learning events. (My observations on culture must not be taken to mean, then, that enculturation consists simply in passive exposure. Human activity is not so blindly conditioned. It is purposive. There is always at work a measure of intentionality, but it is an encultured intentionality.) Talk of cognitive schemas that would be shared and

[70] For general arguments to the effect that culture and biology are inextricably intertwined (and refutations of the view that the mind would not be culturally constrained), see eg DH Lende and G Downey (eds), *The Encultured Brain* (MIT Press 2012); BE Wexler, *Brain and Culture* (MIT Press 2006); PJ Richerson and R Boyd, *Not by Genes Alone* (University of Chicago Press 2005); LJ Kirmayer et al (eds), *Culture, Mind, and Brain* (Cambridge University Press 2020).

[71] P Legendre, *L'Empire de la vérité* (Fayard 1983) 21.

sanctioned by a 'community' of legal agents begs the decisive question of what is to be regarded as a 'community'. And 'communities' can be individuated by reference to various criteria (vis-à-vis China, for instance, Europe can stand as a 'community'). From a legal and comparative perspective, however, I hold that 'communities', certainly within an occidental setting, can most helpfully be organized primordially with respect to the decisive historical fact of reception or non-reception of Roman law, which connects to what legal agents, in an epistemic way that they will often not have expressly articulated, take to be sensible motives for action, cogent or persuasive arguments, relevant considerations, adequate epistemic principles, and so forth. Bearing in mind that no rigorous definition of anything is ultimately possible and that notions can only be understood in their interdefinability, allowing also for constitutive contradictions and the effects of heterogeneous signifying practices from 'within' and keeping to a Eurocentric frame, there are, thus, civil law jurisdictions, a label referring to 'communities' of legal agents partaking in the Romanist, nomothetic tradition, and there are also common law jurisdictions, whose 'communities' pertain to the English, idiographic tradition.[72]

*

In France, where I have been holding my main institutional affiliation for more than two decades at this writing, '*droit comparé*' remains, strictly speaking, an illegal pursuit within the legal academy inasmuch as it is not sanctioned by any of the three legally recognized '*concours d'agrégation*' in private law, public law, and legal history – I refer to France's state-run qualifying examinations for accession to law

[72] The list of studies analyzing the differences between the common law and civil law traditions is long even as the extant comparative work, distinguished as it can be, has arguably only barely scratched the proverbial surface. For a rewarding examination of the two different epistemologies, see O Kahn-Freund, 'Introduction' in *The Institutions of Private Law by Karl Renner* (O Kahn-Freund ed, A Schwarzschild tr, Routledge & Kegan Paul 1949) 8–16. For my own effort, see P Legrand, *Pour la relevance des droits étrangers* (IRJ Sorbonne Editions 2014) 119–240. Observe that the move from one legal tradition to another is as fraught as that from one language to another. And whether one is addressing legal tradition or language, perfect substitutability is not a possibility. Eg: E Kadens, 'Convergence and the Colonization of Custom in Pre-modern Europe' in O Moréteau et al (eds), *Comparative Legal History* (Elgar 2019) 167–85. Nor is consensus between, say, Christianity, Judaism, and Islam – or, for that matter, between Buddhism, Confucianism, and Hinduism. But see, for a thoroughly Rawlsian (and just as thoroughly unsustainable) argument advocating for the possibility of agreement along these religious lines, A Ferrara, *The Democratic Horizon* (Cambridge University Press 2014) 67–87 and passim.

professorships.[73] Now, if one accepts that the comparison of laws is meant structurally to address difference and if one allows that difference is a political and philosophical question devoid of any rightful place in the French intellectual and legal landscape (because of the Constitution's proclamation that France is 'indivisible' ['*indivisible*'], an individual's or a group's claim for the recognition of difference can readily be deemed illegal),[74] the local institutional banishment of '*droit comparé*' makes much sense. '*Droit comparé*' is therefore fated to remain *sans papier*, undocumented. In France, where I am '[a] lot alone but not lonely',[75] the enduring challenge is to earn the *right* to compare laws.[76]

[73] In the absence of private law-faculties in France, state interventionism boasts a long history. In the seventeenth century, professors of French law, who were established in all law faculties as of 1679, were appointed by the Crown, sometimes directly by the King himself. See LWB Brockliss, *French Higher Education in the Seventeenth and Eighteenth Centuries* (Oxford University Press 1987) 40–41. The entire French university system continues to exist exclusively as an arm of the state.

[74] cf F Cusset, *French Theory* (La Découverte 2003) 346.

[75] Letter from S Beckett to D Mendel in *The Letters of Samuel Beckett*, vol 4 (G Craig et al eds, Cambridge University Press 2016 [15 September 1967]) 95. To quote the passage in full, Beckett also says: 'Better have it like that.' Yes. And, I am minded to add, not least with a view to optimizing scholarly integrity. For a reflection on solitude not as fate, but as an experience of cognitive enhancement actively initiated, as a 'technique of the self', see T Macho and S Rashof, 'Alone With Oneself – Solitude as Cultural Technique' (2021) 26 (1) Angelaki 9. 'Technique of the self' is, of course, traceable to M Foucault, 'Les techniques de soi' in *Dits et écrits*, vol 4 (D Defert and F Ewald eds, Gallimard 1994 [1982]) 783. Problematically, the standard English translation is 'technologies of the self'. Eg: M Foucault, 'Technologies of the Self' (F Durand-Bogaert tr) in LH Martin et al (eds), *Technologies of the Self* (University of Massachusetts Press 1988) 16–49.

[76] The enduring challenge also concerns the right to compare laws *sans* proselytization. The inclination to confuse the study of foreign law and the comparison of laws with imperialism or colonization thus figured most prominently in the report of the *Secrétaire général* (in effect, the executive director) to the annual meeting of the French *Société de législation comparée* on 18 December 1995, in Paris, which I attended by invitation. The account consisted of a tally of the year's official journeys correlated with the chances that France enjoyed of seeing French law serve as a model for reform in various countries such as Lebanon, Colombia, or elsewhere. This most peculiar agenda emerges even more vividly from a 21 December 1998 letter by François Terré, a French law professor and erstwhile candidate to the *Société*'s presidency, which its author circulated to the membership and which came to my attention (I never joined the *Société*). In this document, Terré bemoans 'the so very dark times that French law's influence in the world is experiencing today' and contends that the *Société* has 'a role to play not only for the upholding, but for the return of the influence of [French] legal culture in the countries of Eastern Europe that are requiring it earnestly; within the [European Community]'s institutions in order to suggest models preferable to those constantly produced by Brussels institutions only; with and through all those in the Near East who wish the development of French influence; without

*

I am very pleased that the power of negation has asserted itself stubbornly enough to interrupt the epistemic sovereignty that had assumed full control of my old existence and to permit the construction of a heterogeneous intelligibility. Yet, I remain haunted by the deprivation of a decent intellectual upbringing – and I readily adopt and adapt Beauvoir's exclamation: 'J'ai été floué'.[77] Nor have I overcome the catastrophic self-image I first experienced at Oxford and that resurfaced during my teaching years in North West England. Because the damage runs deep,[78] I still regard myself as a renegade or, at the 'meremost minimum',[79] as someone who conquered intellectuality 'by breaking and entering'[80], who will always be en '*porte-à-faux*' vis-à-vis Europe (the French expression being an obliging Sorbonne colleague's, as if I needed reminding).[81] Along the way, I continue to temper my revolt largely through my readings and writings, which I persist in wanting to make more and more unlike what I was taught in

forgetting, of course, [France's] role in French Africa or in Asia – not only in the states of the old Indochina – as well as in the South Pacific' [on file]. Well away from such a thoroughly objectionable ethnocentric or juricentric stance, profoundly unbecoming to comparative law, I published an argument in France in favour of a greater role for (genuine) comparative analysis in French legal education. See P Legrand, 'Notes inspirées par une gêne persistante à l'égard de la fascination exercée par l'habitude, l'autorité, la loi et l'Etat dans les facultés de droit françaises' (1998) Revue trimestrielle de droit civil 303. See also Legrand (n 32) 62–71.

77 S de Beauvoir, *La Force des choses* in *Mémoires*, vol 2 (J-L Jeannelle and E Lecarme-Tabone eds, Gallimard 2018 [1963]) 380.

78 cf Letter from S Beckett to A Schneider in *The Letters of Samuel Beckett*, vol 3 (G Craig et al eds, Cambridge University Press 2014 [19 November 1963]) 582: '[T]he strange thing . . . , whatever it is, that gives us the strength to live on and on with our wounds.'

79 S Beckett, *Worstward Ho* in *Company/Ill Seen Ill Said/Worstward Ho/Stirrings Still* (D Van Hulle ed, Faber & Faber 2009 [1983]) 82.

80 A Ernaux, *L'Ecriture comme un couteau* (Stock 2003) 34. There is much in Annie Ernaux's ethnobiographical studies of her trans-sociological experience that applies, *mutatis mutandis*, to my own case – and this is no doubt why I have long felt close to her intellectual quest. Contrary to me, though, Ernaux engages in a rehabilition of her past and, specifically, of her parents. There is another respect in which Ernaux's experience differs significantly from mine as the sentiment of guilt at having betrayed her family is a principal motif informing her work. Both conciliatory motions may have to do with the fact that although her parents could not understand Ernaux's urge to pursue further studies, they ultimately encouraged and supported her. For my part, I experienced steadfast aspersion, disparagement, and denigration.

81 In line with the siderating legal patriotism that obtains in French law schools, the institutional decision appears to have been made to 'tolerate' me. For documentary proof, see C Jamin and D Mazeaud (eds), *L'Harmonisation du droit des contrats en Europe* (Economica 2001) [i].

Québec.[82] (But I engage in other forms of struggle, too.) Most fortunately, I easily harness enough resolution every day to keep pursuing my idiosyncratic 'third culture': I write minor legal scholarship, which is regularly featured by some of the leading journals and principal publishing houses on the international scene; I teach small groups of students at some of the world's major law schools. I am *different*.

Critically, I remain in exile. Now, I harbour no particular wish to exult in the celebration of an extravagant and costly condition, and I recognize that there is 'the executive value of exile'.[83] Indeed, my experience shows me that despite the confounding character of displacement, homelessness can, in time, be mobilized as vocational energy, thus allowing for a productive reconstitution of one's identity markers. Like Edward Said, Vilém Flusser observes how the exile's initial alienation can thus change into a sense of capacitation on which the migrant is then in a position to capitalize. In fact, Flusser came to regard nomadism as intellectually *desirable* on account of the incessant transformations in perspectives that this condition provoked in him.[84] At this writing, against the backdrop of an exile spanning thirty years or so, I wholeheartedly concur.

Whenever I engage in introspective and retrospective observations, I feel no remorse as regards my decision to leave Québec. For my part, *l'exil vaut le voyage*. With the rarest exceptions (for example, Nicholas Kasirer's appointment to the Supreme Court of Canada), I do not take any interest in developments from the distant country. I am reminded of Nietzsche, who compares the faculty of forgetfulness to a well-performing digestive system.[85] I am far less sanguine, however, about my decision to move to the Sorbonne in 2000 instead of accepting a pressing invitation to join a leading, 'top-three' US law school that came to me simultaneously (the Dean was so eager that he promptly addressed, over the telephone, the advantages of purchasing on-campus real estate). Yet, on the whole, I find merit in Vladimir

[82] Again, I observe a significant difference with Ernaux, who famously resorts to '*l'écriture plate*' (or 'flat writing') in order to blunt her self-willed alienation from her past. For my part, I can hardly wait to experience with ever more exacting writing in order to mark with ever-greater sharpness the break with my Québécois circumstances.

[83] Said (n 65) 8.

[84] Eg: see V Flusser, 'Exil und Kreativität' in *Von der Freiheit des Migranten* (Europaïsche Verlagsanstalt 2013 [1984]) 103–9.

[85] See F Nietzsche, *Zur Genealogie der Moral* in *Digitale Kritische Gesamtausgabe* (G Colli et al eds, 2009 [1887]) <www.nietzschesource.org/#eKGWB/GM-II-1> II, s 1.

Jankélévitch's remark that '[o]ne must not squander one's repentance'.[86]

The irritant that I am to orthodox comparative law remains, by birth, a Québec francophone, a Québécois, who is also a colonized francophone, someone who speaks the language of the first acknowledged colonizers of Québec, of those masters and schoolmasters, of those other francophones.[87] In this regard, I am very mindful of Derrida's experience of otherness-in-language as he observes, thinking at once of his Algerian roots and of metropolitan French as his native tongue, 'I have one language only, it is not mine'.[88] But I am also a francophone teaching at the Sorbonne, the most established academic institution within the planetary francophone 'community'. (As a professor of law at the Sorbonne, I accept that I carry a privilege, which shows that even within negative comparative law there is what one cannot negate.) And the Québécois that I continue to be does not speak French in the way my Parisian colleagues speak French. For a Québec francophone in Paris, to speak the French that one speaks is once more, although differently from when one was still marooned in the colony, to speak in a foreign language, in the language of the other – which entails that one relinquishes 'Parisian recognition', 'forever desired and desirable',[89] a forfeiture that also has to do, of course, with the familiar French diffidence towards foreignness and the no less habitual French *hauteur* vis-à-vis cultural colonies. I could say more. Having been thrown into *québécitude* by birth, I am also a Canadian, but not a Canadian in the way my Toronto-born colleagues can be Canadian. While to be Canadian is to find oneself on the intellectual periphery of the planet, to be Québécois is to be on the intellectual periphery's periphery. And there is more. As a Québécois and as a *Montréalais*, I am also North American (in fact, I have never been more consciously North American than since I moved to Provence), although my North Americanism is neither that of anglophone Canadians nor that of Canada's southern neighbours. I am *different*.

86 V Jankélévitch, *La Mauvaise conscience* in *Philosophie morale* (F Schwab ed, Flammarion 1998 [1966]) 172.

87 As of 1760, Québec was colonized by the British, too, but this is, literally, another story. cf J Gracq, *Nœuds de vie* (B Boie ed, Corti 2021† [before 2007]) 75: 'The marks of the ancient link of subjection between colonizers and colonized . . . remain indelible on both sides.' A geographer and a historian by trade, Gracq was a foremost twentieth-century French writer.

88 J Derrida, *Mémoires* (Galilée 1988) 13.

89 L Gauvin, 'Traversal of Languages' in C McDonald and SR Suleiman (eds), *French Global* (Columbia University Press 2010) 420.

*

My principal academic identity, then, has been that of comparatist – which is not unlike saying that I am afflicted with *mania comparativa*. For me, being a comparatist is a way of leading my conscious life, giving it form and direction through constant and probing questions of the kind that exist in perceptible tension with the ambitions of a strictly nationalist lawyer following conventional career paths, pursuing accredited institutional goals, and seeking accepted performance appraisals. Living life as a comparatist also entails a constant objection both to the propensity to claim universalism or globalization and to the inclination to foster unification or uniformization. As the comparatist takes part in the foreign and allows foreignness to partake of him – as he indulges this two-way libidinal investment – the epistemic stakes are always very high in any work he does: comparison is eminently a (heteronormative) site for the expression of a strong ethics and politics. More specifically, I am a comparatist-at-law, which means that, both in my teaching and research, I concern myself with foreign law, that is, with the comparison of laws (as distinguished, on one hand, from materials strictly limited to aspects of local law and, on the other, from a comparison focussing, say, on nineteenth-century novels or contemporary religions or medieval political regimes). Comparative law is my field of scholarly endeavour, a label that refers to the somewhat rigid division of intellectual labour based on an epistemology of difference prevailing within the academy (and suggesting, incidentally, a degree of internal intellectual coherence – of cohesion – *within* the group of comparatists-at-law easily liable to be exaggerated).

It should be clear that one cannot simply choose to be a comparatist-at-law and that one cannot simply assume that the statements one makes will readily enter comparative legal discourse. How, then, can one produce assertions that are appreciated as having the status of legitimate comparative information by those who are already behaving as comparatists-at-law and are already recognized as such? How does one become a comparatist-at-law in the eyes of the order of dominance within a field like comparative law, where the entry conditions are weak and the cross-control low? How did I become a comparatist-at-law, and how did I become the comparatist-at-law that I am? Another way, I think, to formulate this last pair of questions is as follows: how did I come to be consecrated as a comparatist-at-law within the field of comparative law, that is, by other comparatists-at-law who, at some earlier stage, were also inducted as comparatists-at-law within the field of comparative law before later finding themselves in a position to pass judgement in their turn? As I attempt an answer, I find it essential to bear in mind that, even though orthodox comparatists-at-law like to confine the political realm to a site that would lie somewhere beyond or beneath law, thus purporting to be preoccupied exclusively with law-understood-as-purely-the-non-political, the matter of ascription of professional competence – which evokes the idea of a self-distilling and self-policing process at work within the field – emphatically addresses the politics of recognition. The institutional dynamics whereby certain writings are elevated to the rank of respectable comparative legal work according to 'silent norms of pertinence' to the point where they may find themselves inscribed on the compulsory reading list, while others are made 'to sink back into the murmur of mere prose', does not, and cannot, succeed in concealing the hierarchy of powers at work within the field.[90]

Before all else, I argue that any assertion of being-as-a-comparatist-at-law on my part must have assumed – in ways not necessarily identifiable – a measure of alienation of self to a discursive authority spoken by established comparatists, the *insiders*, who were exterior to me and pre-existed me. In order to fashion myself as a comparatist-at-law, that is, so as to be recognized as a comparatist-at-law by those who held it in their gift to bestow something like official sanction unto me (for example, by inviting me to write for the journals they edited or soliciting my participation at the conferences they organized), I had to alienate myself, to an appreciable extent, to a discourse exterior to me (the idea being that once I had internalized that discourse's norm, I would become the vehicle of my own subjugation). If you will, I had to allow that discourse's signifying practices to seize hold of me. The fabrication of my identity qua comparatist-at-law therefore depended upon a threshold voluntary submersion of my individual identity. I wish to draw attention to this arresting paradox: I could only become the 'I' that I ultimately became through initial interaction with 'non-Is', that is, by way of others who prevailed over me, epistemically speaking. The making of my professional autonomy, or the creation of a space where I came to be able to assert an idiosyncratic institutional presence as comparatist-at-law, could only happen after I had accepted to subject myself to the normalizing work of the discursive matrix established by the interpretive 'community' established within 'my' field. This means that I could only constitute my

[90] EW Said, 'Opponents, Audiences, Constituencies, and Community' (1982) 9 Critical Inquiry 1, 12, and 25–26.

self-as-comparatist-at-law through others and the power of others. This also entails that I could only fashion my self-as-comparatist-a-law by *institutionalizing* myself.[91] One can draw an analogy with language, a framework that exists before one's birth, into which one is then thrown, and which one eventually makes one's 'own': it finds one more than one finds it.

Of course, I am I and, pace Rimbaud, *je ne suis pas un autre*. However, it is the case that the comparatist-at-law I have become was defined, certainly for an initial period of time, through a destruction or repression or negation of his self (arguably, then, another manifestation of the negative). A different way to frame the issue would be to say that in order to gain the institutional recognition I craved, I had to exhibit a false self.[92] There is a clear sense in which the more actively I sought an opportunity to emerge as an acknowledged comparatist-at-law, the more I had to be willing to undergo an effacement of my authentic self. The closer I positioned myself to the established ideal or model or norm of behaviour (the image of the 'safe' comparatist as understood by the executive directors of professional societies within the field or as envisaged by editors of journals and collections of essays or as contemplated by conference organizers of all ilk), that is, the more I proved willing to allow my self to be seemingly overtaken by the authoritative comparative discourse, the better chance I stood of being recognized. Contrariwise, the more I insisted on preserving the integrity of my self – the more singular I decided to remain, say, out of sheer critical obstinacy – the less occasion I had of ever becoming a recognized comparatist-at-law.

I find it important to insist that I have never been the passive recipient of an ascribed identity, the mere incorporator of orthodox professional reflexes in the guise of dispositional structures. To a certain extent, at least, I have always been actively (and incessantly) engaged in the making and re-making of my own identity as comparatist-at-law. While the power of discursive authority would discernibly act on me (and continues, in certain ascertainable respects, to make me subordinated to it and its domination), it has also *made* me – and, in this sense, I have deliberately been working towards the construction of my identity (on the understanding that this activity can never completely circumscribe

[91] Eg: Legrand (n 57); P Legrand, 'Judicial Revision of Contracts in French Law: A Case-Study' (1988) 62 Tulane LR 963; P Legrand, 'The Case for Judicial Revision of Contracts in French Law (and Beyond)' (1989) 34 McGill LJ 908.

[92] For a meditation on false selfhood, see P Gabel, *The Desire for Mutual Recognition* (Routledge 2018).

the authoritative discourse that fulfils a regulatory role within the field by setting the limits between what is acceptable and what remains unacceptable comparative law). I have therefore been the active principle of my own alienation (and, in this way, 'power' can be seen to have intervened, at once, repressively and productively). Indeed, I remain the willing principle of my alienation, since I value being a good comparatist-at-law and I value being recognized by other comparatists-at-law (at least by the few that I myself value) as being a good comparatist-at-law – as being as good as them, perhaps. And, of course, the process of consecration requires on my part a threshold recognition of the order that bestows it; it calls on me to apply a measure of scholarly *bienséance* or good comparative manners vis-à-vis that order, if not squarely within it. I knew at an early stage that I could only achieve the goal of accreditation if I were to be installed in the legitimate language of established comparatists and their schemes of cultural intelligibility: recognition demanded normalization. Thus did the epistemic doxa introduce itself into my intentions, even the most seemingly lucid ones.[93]

My more-than-unconscious desire to enter the field, my more-than-unconscious aspiration to acceptance within the field – my disposition and my *croyance* – have therefore compelled me to contend with the dissociation of my self that the disciplinary power at work within the field engineered. As I find myself empowered (I am a comparatist-at-law now),[94] I witness my disempowerment (I am de-personalized now, for I am in many significant ways a comparatist-at-law-like-*them*, writing in *their* journals and speaking at *their* conferences). As a comparatist-at-law, through a certain assimilation of the field's *acquis historique* at any rate, I am inhabited by the scholarly world that I inhabit. My knowledge of the field has therefore not developed through the dynamics of

[93] I follow P Bourdieu, *Méditations pascaliennes* (Editions du Seuil 1997) 166.

[94] Astonishingly, what I would have readily assumed had come to qualify as an incontrovertible fact appears to remain in doubt. See A Harding, 'The Legal Transplants Debate: Getting Beyond the Impasse?' in V Breda (ed), *Legal Transplants in East Asia and Oceania* (Cambridge University Press 2019) 14, where the author describes me as 'a legal theorist with an interest in comparative law'. The fact that this claim is made in a conspicuously self-serving setting hardly detracts from its incongruity. For the record, then, let me assert my institutional position: on the basis, at the very least, of indisputable scriptural evidence spanning more than forty years at this writing, I am a comparatist, specifically a comparatist-at-law, with a long-standing interest in theoretical issues broadly understood pertaining to the comparison of laws broadly understood. Accordingly, perhaps I can legitimately style myself a comparative law theorist, the way someone else would be, say, a music theorist.

exteriority that a knowing consciousness might hold in the face of an object of study. Rather, my comparative thought is, in important respects, structured by the field itself: I have in-corporated the field *within me* – I embody it, my body is the memory of it – and I have in-corporated my self *into it*. But the matter is even more complicated, because I have not simply been a docile or arrident agent (as the French saying goes, *ce n'est pas le genre de la maison*), and I have also earnestly (and energetically) worked *against* the field. This observation prompts me to raise further epistemic issues, if cursorily.

How much could I resist the normalizing injunction – the totalizing production of individuals having metamorphosed into totalizing persons through their transformation qua fully fledged comparatists-at-law – so that, through the liberation of a repressed individuality, I would fail to be completely constituted by the field? Could I overcome discursive hegemony? How much of my individuation could survive the socialization and institutionalization processes? To what extent could I supplant the symbolic violence wrought by the dominant discourse within the field (observe that there *is* a complicity between discourse and violence, if only on account of the imposition of the discrimination between comparatists and non-comparatists I just outlined)? What enfranchisement was ultimately possible? What resistance – understood here as a manifestation of *freedom* in the strong sense of the term – could I offer? To what extent could I re-claim the singularity of my self, or jettison my false self, given the field's enculturation process? Did I want to? Does it still matter?

There is another problematique arising. Is my theorization at all able to structure the field of comparative law in its turn? How far can it go in the exercise of influence given that 'in the realm of culture and of thought each production exists not only to earn a place for itself but to displace, win out over, others'?[95] Can my resistance lead to a re-articulation of the predominant discursive matrix within the field? In other terms, can I operate a subversive re-territorialization of the discipline?[96] In this respect, I argue that, yes, I can modify the cognitive terrain within comparative law, the mechanics and workings of the field, the principles governing vision and division (between what is acceptable and what is not), the theories, and the concepts. I claim that, in time, I can go beyond

[95] Said (n 90) 11.

[96] For a key reflection on the dynamics between power and resistance, see M Foucault, *La Volonté de savoir* (Gallimard 1976) 126–27. The significance of this passage, it seems to me, cannot be exaggerated.

the space that, historically, has defined the social possibilities of the comparatist-at-law-as-subject and his work of construction of foreign-law-as-object. I am an agent of change, and I can do *something* to change epistemological governance from my heterodox place within the field of comparative law. And I am in fact confident that I can affect the prior epistemological axiomatics in a manner reaching beyond minor adjustments. I believe in what Pierre Bourdieu labels a '*pouvoir-être*'.[97] Also, I accept, with Michel Foucault (more French theory!), that the main goal today must be to refuse what we are and instead build what we could be.[98] But I am not labouring under a delusion, and I know that the legitimation of a critique that calls into question the framework of assumptions having served established comparatists-at-law so well can only prove a long and circuitous path.[99] For this reason, I do not minimize the exclusionary tendencies to be marshalled by established members within the field (which can then genuinely be termed a discipline, that is, an array of rules for the regimenting of scholarly behaviour, for mental and moral training, too). Absent any particular susceptibility to compunction, Edward Said aptly refers to 'guild solidarity that dangerously resembles a religious consciousness'.[100]

In particular, I can easily envisage that *NCL* itself – even as it specifies its marginal or peripheral ethics and politics addressing the destitution of the orthodoxy – might be framed in terms of confrontational hostility so that it can then be more easily discredited. I can also contemplate that the text might be branded as 'difficult' – a term to imply, perhaps, that it is written by a 'difficult' person, that is, by someone who can be regarded as an anomaly and therefore as dismissible. I can also imagine how the argument might be declared irrelevant. Now, any ascription of irrelevance hides complex, unstated evaluations. Does irrelevance not effectively gesture towards the idea of epistemological adversity? In other terms, does it not mean difference? Does 'this book is irrelevant' not signify 'this book is inadequate to my conditions for seriousness'?[101]

97 Bourdieu (n 93) 258.

98 See M Foucault, 'Le sujet et le pouvoir' in *Dits et écrits*, vol 4 (D Defert and F Ewald eds, Gallimard 1994 [1982]) 232.

99 For a blunt expression of this idea, see LM Friedman, 'Book Review' (1979) 6 British J L & Society 127, 129 (review of A Watson, *Society and Legal Change* [Scottish Academic Press 1977]): 'If a person spends his life embroidering and decorating some little swatch of material, it is no use telling him he has wasted his time on a useless rag.'

100 Said (n 90) 17.

101 I follow GC Spivak, *The Post-colonial Critic* (S Harasym ed, Routledge 1990) 134.

As they contrast with the mainstream convictions conforming to the general interests of the doxa, alternative conceptions occupy a very precarious position. In the so-called *Prison Notebooks*, surely an altogether different configuration, Antonio Gramsci aptly attaches two 'determinate necessities' to any claim seeking to replace 'the old conceptions of the world', which I readily make my own: '[N]ot tire ever of repeating [one's] own arguments', and 'work incessantly to elevate intellectually' the individuals to whom the challenge is directed.[102] While I am certainly not alone in wishing to move from my assigned place, the question as to why I, rather than someone else, would seek openly to reject the governing ideology, expressly to contest the dominant political valency rather than mould myself into it – as so many of my fellow comparatists are only too eager to do (so many Danish, Dutch, Finnish, German, Italian, Swedish names rush to mind) – can only be rooted in my singular experience (which, inevitably, is also a singularly limited experience), in my singular existence, which, ultimately, must hark back to my childhood and the positioning and trajectory it prompted – although this point is not meant to suggest any blind loyalty to the doctrine of infant determinism.[103]

In other terms, my basic premiss is that my location broadly understood has an epistemically salient impact on the knowledge-claims I make, that these contentions are incorporated or embodied and therefore perspectively situated. As Richard Rorty puts the matter in typically Heideggerian (and Derridean) form, '[w]e have to start from where we are'.[104] Not only, then, are others and other laws situated, I, too, am encumbered with a concrete enculturation (including an epistemologization). By situating myself, I am situating my knowledge, a motion that I regard as valuable, if only on account of the heightened transparency that such exercise allows.[105] Having said this much, I cannot be permitted to forget that what I may wish to style my 'individuality' integrates sets of assumptions that are the outcomes of socialization and

[102] A Gramsci, *Quaderni del carcere*, vol 2 (V Gerratana ed, Einaudi 1975 [1932–33]) 1392.

[103] Still, I concur with Alasdair MacIntyre that '[o]ne remains imprisoned by one's upbringing': A MacIntyre, 'On Having Survived the Academic Moral Philosophy of the Twentieth Century' in F O'Rourke (ed), *What Happened in and to Moral Philosophy in the Twentieth Century?* (University of Notre Dame Press 2013) 31.

[104] R Rorty, *Contingency, Irony, and Solidarity* (Cambridge University Press 1989) 198 [emphasis omitted]. cf Beckett (n 60) 12: '[W]hat I say, what I shall say, if I can, relates to the place where I am, to me who am there.'

[105] For a compelling exploration of the rhetoric of situatedness, see D Simpson, *Situatedness* (Duke University Press 2002) 192–247 and 19–57.

institutionalization processes, of an epistemologization, having constituted me into the comparatist-at-law I have become. It is this enculturation that, to a significant extent, predetermines any intellectual strategy I may deploy, even in the absence of any brute causal connection to any specific experience from childhood or adulthood.

So, I hold that the intelligence is always affiliated, and I maintain that all comparatists-at-law have to answer the call of probity and *explicitly* include themselves, their lives, and their 'moment' in their research. Because he is – structurally so – a protagonist in the tale he tells (no author of an account on foreign law is *scriptor absconditus*), the comparatist must consider and reveal his own investment in the narrative he is weaving. *Wertfreiheit* being as unattainable as it is unattractive (what point a view from nowhere?), the comparatist must not only observe foreign law, but *he must also observe himself observing foreign law.* Otherwise said, even as he undertakes to make sense of the foreign, he must harness his experience of his enculturation to make sense of what he is doing – which means that the comparatist-at-law must submit his predispositions or predilections, his prejudices or pre-judgements, to a rigorous critical examination along the foreign way in order to try and understand the makings of his fated-to-fail appreciation of foreignness. As the comparatist wanders towards foreign law, he must wonder about the cognitive parameters within which his wandering is unfolding.

For instance, when a comparatist comes to the French statute on religious attire in public schools hailing from a multicultural society, this provenance cannot but matter in terms of the ensuing reading/interpreting/understanding/reporting process. Unlike Konrad Zweigert and Hein Kötz, I do not accept that enculturation ought to be jettisoned,[106] and I do not allow that it is jettisonable in any event. And unlike Zweigert and Kötz, I do not regard enculturation as a liability. Rather, I hold that enculturation is a crucial source of interpretive empowerment even as it operates as a constraint on every interpretation. (It is because he is familiar with the figure of the US judge that a US comparatist can ascribe a measure of meaning to the French *juge* and not mistake him for a priest, politician, or plumber. And this is a key epistemic fact although, since the US judge is bound to haunt the

[106] Eg: K Zweigert and H Kötz, *Einführung in die Rechtsvergleichung* (3rd edn, Mohr Siebeck 1996) 11 and 43: '[T]he comparatist must unfasten himself from his own juridical-dogmatic preconceptions and his own cultural context'/'The solutions of the investigated legal orders are to be freed of all systematic concepts of these legal orders, to be unfastened out of their solely-national dogmatic incrustrations.'

comparative investigation, the US comparatist is doomed to fail in his attempt to achieve fully fledged understanding of the French *juge*.) However, the exercise of the power I address commands epistemic vigilance. In particular, it dictates to the comparatist-at-law that he let his readership know how he is aware of some at least of the constitutive and productive epistemic postulates informing his research and subsequent report (other premisses admittedly not pertaining to the realm of full consciousness while nonetheless quietly ministering over the research and compositional strategies) – the idea that such research or report could somehow exist autonomously from these pre-judgements not resisting examination.[107] I haunt my comparisons, and I haunt them with the haunting that haunts me. And my haunting – both the one that imposes itself to me, whether I am aware of this fact or not, and the one that I inflict unto foreign law-texts, whether consciously or not – is inseparable from any promise of epistemic justice vis-à-vis otherness that I can maintain. Behold the beholder!

*

I have worked long enough in academia to evince acute awareness that the personal must not be seen to partake of the elaboration of scholarship, which is thought to be pertaining, and properly so by those who continue to believe in objectivity and truth, to the realms of detachment and impartiality. References to the self are readily taken to belong to the dominion of affect and thus best confined to poems and novels. The devaluation of the 'I' as not comporting any scholarly pertinence is perhaps felt in an especial way in law, where the sanctity of justice must exclude, it is assumed, the full range of individual proclivities. (In French law schools, this obfuscation adopts the form of an outright prohibition on writing in the first-person singular; in this respect as in others, the private and public spheres are not to meet, except in the *Tribunal des conflits* where they are, in fact, confirmed in their purportedly ontological separateness.)

'Perhaps the clue to the whole affair is its ghostliness', says Beckett.[108] Yes. *What* haunts me? And *what* haunting do I carry within me, as me, then to haunt the foreign law that I invent – that I find materially and proceed to fashion interpretively? As I have engaged in this exercise in

[107] See generally P Legrand, 'Foreign Law as Self-Fashioning' (2017) 12(2) J Comp L 7.

[108] S Beckett, *Proust* in *The Grove Centenary Edition*, vol 4 (P Auster and JM Coetzee eds, Grove 2006 [1931]) 637.

'hauntology',[109] I have satisfied myself that to formulate a point of view about my point of view as regards the theoretical and practical settings within which my comparative interventions have been taking place is neither a surrender to narcissistic self-gratification (and certainly not to autohagiography, either) nor to the indulgence of undue irreticence. I can see for myself, of course, that within the field of comparative law such exercise in self-lucidity as I have proposed to articulate is rare,[110] and I realize that this anamnesis may cost me symbolic capital, a loss of creditability that I am fully prepared to risk as I maintain that my inquiry about comparative law's cognitive limits cannot be an inquiry without cognitive limits. Yet, it seems important to emphasize that I do not understand space or time as directly and fully determining meaning. It would be crudely reductionist, for example, to argue that *because* I hail from francophone Québec, *therefore* I value difference. My claim is at once more subtle and complex, and it concerns the fact that (spatial or temporal) positionality impels interpretation, that it drives or informs imputation of meaning – not, again, that it compels meaning by way of a facile cause-and-effect dynamic.

[109] This felicitous neologism is Derrida's: J Derrida, *Spectres de Marx* (Galilée 1993) 31 [emphasis omitted].

[110] But see eg R David, *Les Avatars d'un comparatiste* (Economica 1982); GP Fletcher, *My Life in Seven Languages* (Mazo 2011); Merryman (n 2) 1–12. For my part, I have long held an interest in autobiography. See eg P Legrand, 'Questions à Rodolfo Sacco' (1995) Revue internationale de droit comparé 943; P Legrand, 'John Henry Merryman and Comparative Legal Studies: A Dialogue' (1999) 47 Am J Comp L 3. cf P Richard, *Le Jeu de la différence: réflexions sur l'épistémologie du droit comparé* (Presses de l'Université Laval 2007) 85, where the author observes that the work of the comparatist-at-law 'is destined to teach us as much on the comparatist as on the national law that is the focus of the comparison'. I find it interesting that even such an arch-positivist as Hans Kelsen should have written not only one, but two autobiographies. These 1927 and 1947 texts are available as 'Selbstdarstellung' and 'Autobiographie' in H Kelsen, *Werke*, vol 1 (M Jestaedt ed, Mohr Siebeck 2007) 19–27 and 30–91. For an excellent account, see M García-Salmones Rovira, *The Project of Positivism in International Law* (Oxford University Press 2013) 157–97. While on the subject of legal autobiography, I would be remiss if I did not mention the eagerness with which I read Allan Hutchinson's captivating and sensitive exercise in intellectual introspection. See AC Hutchinson, *Law, Life, and Lore* (Cambridge University Press 2018). Further afield, I observe that there is a fascinating argument, relying on substantial archival work, tracing Descartes's concern with objectivity and truth to his personal experience of authoritarianism, that is, connecting Cartesian veridiction with social rank or status rather than rationality or scientific inquiry. This political state of affairs led the philosopher to leave France for the Netherlands from 1629 to 1649. See HJ Cook, *The Young Descartes* (University of Chicago Press 2018).

*

The comparatist is inevitably injecting autobiographical elements into his reading of foreign law, which are inextricably woven into the foreign law that he is re-presenting and which, given their primordiality, cannot be dissociated from that foreign-law-as-re-presented. The epistemic fact of the matter is that as he researches foreign law, as he assembles the details that he has retained into a new formation, the authorial self textualizes itself: it inscribes itself – it writes itself – into the text on foreignness, it disseminates itself throughout the text and therefore through the foreign-law-as-re-presented, if often in barely discernible ways although, I maintain, the orientational features of the self's intervention, as they structurally issue from the place of utterance, carry effects that are in principle ultimately disclosable. If you will, 'every interpretation involves a degree of self-interpretation embedded in a stream of action'.[111] Note that the integration between foreign law and the comparatist's self runs deeper than co-extension, which assumes separability, measurability, divisibility, and identifiability. It is not that selfhood and texthood parallel or succeed each other, but that they tessellate each other, that they mingle – an arrangement that can prove conspicuous,[112] but also appear furtive,[113] not to say veiled.[114] Complicatedly, the persistence of the self, the irreducibility of the self's presence within the work on foreign law, must be seen to qualify the critical or emancipatory potential of any foray into the foreign. No examination of foreign law can therefore be celebrated as the unqualified antidote to localism that has been assumed. The comparatist is always-already directing his study towards a substratal

[111] DN Rodowick, 'The Value of Being Disagreeable' (2013) 39 Critical Inquiry 592, 608.

[112] Eg: J Gordley, *Foundations of Private Law* (Oxford University Press 2006) 239: '[C]ivil law systems are more inclined to allow one to recover for any infringement of dignity and reputation. . . . The reason, I believe, is a difference in the way these rights are regarded.' The words 'I believe' openly reveal a personal proclivity inserting itself into the account of foreign law.

[113] Eg: ibid 258: 'To my mind, many of the differences would disappear if American courts would agree that there are clear cases in which a disclosure which hurts someone is of little or no value to the public, and if civil law courts would agree that the press should be able to print matters which harm no one, even if they contribute little or nothing to public education.' The words 'To my mind, many of the differences would disappear' surreptitiously disclose a dissatisfaction with the judicial decisions having been considered. Again, this disagreement becomes an integral part of the report on foreign law.

[114] Eg: ibid 230: 'One can see a remarkable degree of continuity in the civil law.' The words 'a remarkable degree of continuity', while presented assertorily, effectively consist in a personal interpretation of the materials that the comparatist has elected to consider. Once more, the comparatist's input finds itself integrated into his report on foreign law.

end, which is *the edification of his self.* At the most rudimental level, the comparatist is driven by desire. The facilitating and structuring disposition of the drive carries a transfer of psychical energy, whether it be directed to the assuagement of a lust for learning, the making of a favorable impression on one's peers, the opportunity to establish oneself as an authority (or at least an inescapable reference), the fostering of certain ethical and political values to which one is committed, the amelioration of one's chances of promotion, or *whatever else.* Whether one appreciates this fact or not, every comparatist is engaging foreign law in a manner that is, basally, self-relating or first-personal, that is aimed at the betterment of the self, of *his* self. Thus, the fulfillment of desire is not a matter of objective reality: it does not depend on an object, it is not object-oriented or intransitive. Rather, desire turns on one's capacity to satisfy oneself: it pertains to pleasure. Desire is for-oneself – a condition that obtains even if the comparatist deliberately eschews any attempt at subordinating, domesticating, and reducing the foreign law-text that he is reading with a view to fitting it within his own presupposed model. The drive – the text-drive – towards foreign law being the expression of a desire, even when the self is attempting to think as if *he* were the other, selfhood's self-interest assumes precedence over otherness.

The haunting presence of desire within the captured and subsequently stated foreign law – again, I claim that desire cannot not haunt every possible cognizance or expression of foreign law – must be seen as a fatal impediment to the achievement by positivism of its abiding ideal, which stands as the pure description of the law in force as pure law. The comparatist's report thus gathers the self and the other even as the two terms continue to prove distinctive, indeed irreconcilable (the self cannot be the other or vice versa). If you will, *the account reconciles the irreconcilable.* In other words, even the connection between self (the comparatist) and other (the foreign law-text) that the report allows cannot avoid the insistent disconnection between the two interacting terms: the conjunction cannot erase the disjunction. As the boundary between self and other is shattered, as the habitual *idea* of the boundary between self and other finds itself smattered, there takes place a '[c]risis of the *versus*'.[115] In sum, the comparatist's exposition, because it issues from the comparatist's situation and is therefore '*ex* position', is not resolvable as the foreign law-text only – or as the comparatist only (evidently, the comparatist cannot do what he wants with foreign law: there is *that* foreign

[115] J Derrida, *La Dissémination* (Editions du Seuil 1972) 35.

statute or judicial decision, *those* words, *there*, to constrain him). Nor is the text on foreign law such as to reveal where, within it, the presence of foreignness begins and that of comparatism ends. Otherwise said, there takes place a queering of the binary, 'a calling into question of the very nature of two-ness, and ultimately of one-ness as well. . . . One is too few, two is too many'.[116]

*

Briefly revisiting the differentiating and differentiated comparative law that I have produced and promoted over time by way of my up-by-my-bootstraps intellectual operation (comparative law as comparative legal studies), reflecting upon the singular trajectory I have just staged and that cannot have been foreign to the fabrication of my comparative law – *comparative law other-wise* – I note how my displacements have been the expression of an inner journey that started with profound discontentment. If a pointed (and, I hope, not unduly amplifying) summary be allowed, then, I observe that my life-in-the-law builds on an early experience of law and comparison as co-constitutive and of comparison and difference as co-constitutive, too. For its part, my distrust in any form of aggrupation finds expression, I think, in the fact that my work inscribes discernible propensions to resist belongingness and integration, to withstand authority and conformity, to contest amalgamation and consensus. Not least because of the self-reliant ways informing my comparatism (I learned early that I could not take any support for granted, least of all the support I ought to have been able to take for granted), the work I publish acknowledges 'the first personal singular and a fortiori plural pronoun',[117] the 'I, . . . of whom I can't speak, of whom I must speak'.[118] In other words, my scholarship does not claim for itself anything along the lines of impartiality, neutrality, or objectivity. And it certainly does not arrogate for itself any entitlement to be proclaiming the truth. I resolutely and serenely discard such epistemic fallacies.

Whether over breakfast or late-evening drinks in his Trinity rooms, Tony Weir, not hesitating to name names, would castigate comparatists who live 'above their intellectual income'. Still in the felicitously negative vein, then, my scholarship flouts superficial arguments or

[116] K Barad, 'Quantum Entanglements and Hauntological Relations of Inheritance: Dis/continuities, SpaceTime Enfoldings, and Justice-to-Come' (2010) 3 Derrida Today 240, 251.

[117] S Beckett, *Company* in *Company/Ill Seen Ill Said/Worstward Ho/Stirrings Still* (D Van Hulle ed, Faber & Faber 2009 [1980]) 41.

[118] Beckett (n 60) 123.

unsophisticated texts (not least when they fall for the conniving promotion of shallow epistemology or the simplistic advocacy of homogenization, whether of the descriptive or prescriptive type) and scoffs at its own marginalization.[119] (While I can articulate rage on the page regarding comparative scholarship's willingness to compromise rigour and although I show little preparedness to countenance what I identify as mediocrity – in this regard, I can readily draw on my early years of consuetude with a rich medley of discord and obloquy easily to express forceful disagreement with pugnacity – I feel nothing but the utmost placidity with respect to the shunning of my work.) My comparatism refuses crude calculative thought.[120] It objects to the brute instrumentalization of the mind and the wholesale technical-managerial control of the law. Not least because it heralds a taste for difficulty and effort, for

[119] However, I hold that '[c]omparatists should support the members of the profession who are taking the greatest intellectual risks, those who fit together unaccustomed bodies of work in ways not predicted by our ready-to-hand theoretical vocabularies, because it is these and not the ones doing "safe" comparisons who will advance inquiry': H Saussy, 'Comparative Literature: The Next Ten Years' in UK Heise (ed), *Futures of Comparative Literature* (Routledge 2017) 28.

[120] I am heartened to learn of the World Bank's overdue concurrence. After releasing seventeen annual *Doing Business* reports from 2004 to 2020 (see <www.doingbusiness.org/en/doingbusiness>), each publication purporting to offer a comparative ranking of local regulatory environments according to an 'ease-of-doing-business' index featuring ten indicators ranging from 'dealing with construction permits' to 'getting electricity' to 'resolving insolvency' (I refer to the 2020 report), the World Bank announced on 16 September 2021 that it was ceasing publication. See <www.worldbank.org/en/news/statement/2021/09/16/world-bank-group-to-discontinue-doing-business-report>. Unsurprisingly, given their hubristic commitment to the canon of numeration, the reports' global governance strategy had long been challenged from many angles. Eg: KE Davis and MB Kruse, 'Taking the Measure of Law: The Case of the Doing Business Project' (2007) 32 L & Social Inquiry 1095; T Krever, 'Quantifying Law: Legal Indicator Projects and the Reproduction of Neoliberal Common Sense' (2013) 34 Third World Q 131; A Perry-Kessaris, 'The Re-co-construction of Legitimacy of/Through the Doing Business Indicators' (2017) 13 Int'l J L Context 498; S Schueth, 'Winning the Rankings Game: The Republic of Georgia, USAID, and the Doing Business Project' in A Cooley and J Snyder (eds), *Ranking the World* (Cambridge University Press 2015) 151–77. For my critique, see P Legrand, 'Withholding Translation' in S Glanert (ed), *Comparative Law: Engaging Translation* (Routledge 2014) 208–19. Alexandra Mercescu captures a key aspect of these demurrers as she explains how the reports always-already failed to take law seriously, how the rankings consisted in an exercise in exclusive and exclusionary economics, how the World Bank's foray into law was, in effect, 'a mere detour, a pretext' to vindicate economics '"doing business" as usual': A Mercescu, 'Quantifying Law? The Case of "Legal Origins"' in S Glanert, A Mercescu, and G Samuel, *Rethinking Comparative Law* (Elgar 2021) 267.

in-depth and wide-ranging probing, for meticulous argumentation and writing (one of my abiding preoccupations being to hide the inferiority of the place whence I hail), my comparatism is never accomplished, and it is never finished – no matter how indefatigable the comparatist at the wheel. Even as it fervently wishes '[s]omehow at any price to make an end',[121] *my comparatism is not done.* And it is not simply that there is still something to be written about the other law – as there inevitably must be given foreignness's unsaturability – but it is also that there will be someone writing about my comparative writing, thereby prolonging my analysis, extending it beyond my interpretive control, too. Indeed, I read foreign law, I deconstruct it, and I write a text about it. But my exercise of interpretive power will generate another such exercise in interpretive power, which will now focus on my writing. And this work on my work will, in time, give rise to more work on that work about my work – without there being any ascertainable end (or beginning) to this process.[122]

*

So, in Paul Celan's arresting formulation, 'I sing before strangers'.[123] Although the page will never be turned and affliction always endure, there are moments when, not unlike André Gide's character in *L'Immoraliste*, '[I] confuse not to be any more with never having been'.[124] As I persevere on the open-ended surface traversed by exile – nothing less than the question of *living on* is at stake – this ambiguity strikes me as a good omen, at least on sunny *provençal* days.

*

It remains to mention the prompting of a US colleague who, on the occasion of a conversation in Chicago in February 2017, forcefully

121 Beckett (n 117) 40.

122 cf J Derrida, '*Scribble*: pouvoir/écrire' in W Warburton, *Essai sur les hiéroglyphes des Egyptiens* (L des Malpeines tr [1844], Aubier 1977) 34: 'Each time that a code is disclosed, decrypted, published, the mechanism of power produces another one' [emphasis omitted]. Derrida adds that '[t]here is always overwriting and one can only analyze it . . . by further adding to it': ibid 13. Imagine the comparatist overwriting foreign law, and his overwriting being overwritten by another comparatist, whose own overwriting. . .

123 P Celan, 'Nachtstrahl' in *Gesammelte Werke*, vol 1 (B Allemann and S Reichert eds, Suhrkamp 1983 [1952]) 31.

124 A Gide, *L'Immoraliste* in *Romans et récits*, vol 1 (2nd ed, P Masson ed, Gallimard 2009 [1902]) 657.

maintained that I owed the field of comparative law an account of my circumstances. Even as I remain unconvinced that I have incurred such indebtedness, and despite the fact that ultimately 'all expatriatings remain singular',[125] I have been willing to ascribe merit to my fellow comparatist's argument in favor of a measure of disclosure, undertake the voyage into the past, and affront 'the stubbornness of memory'.[126] Like Peter Goodrich, then, I have wanted to refute 'the censure of embodiment, of name and practice [which] serves only to impoverish scholarship by desiccating the text'.[127] As a comparatist, I practice the archaeology of ways of 'knowing' (foreign law-texts); and I have now engaged in 'the archaeology of the archaeology of ways of knowing'.[128] Still, as I have sought to explore 'the archive of my institutional experience',[129] 'the intimate politics of judgment within the institution of law',[130] I have remained aware that '[s]uch a project does not conform to the convention that zones academic knowledge as belonging to the public genre of products and their marketability'.[131]

After Beckett, 'I have tried to reflect on the beginning of my story',[132] and I have sought to explore in words the recesses of the self even as I forgo the idea of a unified and stable self. I do assume the self's existence, however, and I thereby locate my autobiographical task within the realm of minimal realism despite having forsaken a detailed philosophical investigation of the matter. While I would not go as far as Roland Barthes and claim that '[a]ll of this must be considered as if spoken by a character in a novel',[133] I cannot deny that I have necessarily injected surplus 'continuity' value in my narrative although I tried very hard to resist such embellishment. And notwithstanding that I have actively avoided the purposeful destabilization of fact and fiction, I must accept that the aestheticization of violence or cruelty is in all likelihood inevitable. At any rate, I have attempted to proceed

[125] Derrida (n 46) 113.
[126] V Flusser, *Bodenlos* (Bollmann 1992†) 53.
[127] P Goodrich, 'Laws of Friendship' (2003) 15 L & Literature 23, 26.
[128] B de Sousa Santos, *The End of the Cognitive Empire* (Duke University Press 2018) 4.
[129] Goodrich (n 127) 26.
[130] ibid.
[131] ibid.
[132] S Beckett, *Malone Dies* (P Boxall ed, Faber & Faber 2010 [1956]) 14.
[133] R Barthes, *Roland Barthes par Roland Barthes* in *Œuvres complètes*, vol 4 (2nd edn, E Marty ed, Editions du Seuil 2002 [1975]) [577].

without the taint of conceit or vindictiveness. I am left, I find, with one abiding thought – perplexity – that is Beckett's also: 'Strange task, which consists in speaking of oneself.'[134] In fact, the ever-serviceable Beckett, who left Ireland to settle in France, summarizes my life's double bind exceedingly well: 'It is suicide to be abroad. But what is it to be at home, . . . what is it to be at home? A lingering dissolution.'[135]

[134] Beckett (n 60) 22.

[135] S Beckett, *All That Fall* in *All That Fall and Other Plays for Radio and Screen* (E Frost ed, Faber & Faber 2009 [1957]) 6. A variation on the autobiographical theme is, of course, novelization. See eg GP Fletcher, *The Bond* (Hart 2009). Based at Regina University, an Ivy League school on New York's Upper West Side, the distinguished author's main character, Adam Gross, specializes in comparative law. One is introduced to Gross as he is readying himself to teach an intensive course on US legal culture scheduled before the beginning of the semester for an LLM class consisting of over 200 foreigners. As he addresses a crowd featuring inter alia a German student in search of dogmatics, a French student thinking of the judge as a Montesquieuan mouthpiece, and an Israeli student staunchly defending the secularist cause, Gross discusses the differences between the civil law and common law traditions. Across the chapters, one follows Gross's musings on constitutionalism, religion, philosophy, and history which, comparatism *oblige*, embrace Latin America, Europe, and the Middle East, not to omit his reflections on language (interestingly, he assents to a student's view that 'French words used to explain common law terms . . . are artificial . . . like a computer language': ibid 13). The narrative gives pride of place to pedagogical strategy, academic freedom, political correctness, collegial life (and its inherent tensions), and the vexed topic of abortion – a fixture on the US legal scene. Gross, an erudite and cosmopolitan scholar who does not fail repeatedly to notice a female student's 'very pretty feet' (ibid 94) and likes to display his contempt for paperwork, is to be credited for affording one an insight into the life of a US law school, the teaching of comparative law and its accoutrements, and tango. It can be a small step from dance to composition, and it is fitting that the final words of this essay should circle back to my Oxford supervisor. Next to the Bodleian Law Library, there is a small and old cemetery. If one is walking from the city centre, one can detour through the heteroclite array of headstones in order to reach the library. In what must have been an awkward social moment, I once met Bernard Rudden on the street as we were heading to our respective library desks, his on the upper floor, mine on the lower. In the event, we walked together for a few minutes. Near our destination, I was told to enter the graveyard. My guide proceeded to explain that he always took the footpath across the cemetery and was in fact planning to be buried there so that he could haunt the law library. Although he does not now rest in the Holywell Cemetery, I nonetheless experienced the haunting Rudden had heralded as I spoke in the law building on 7 and 8 March 2022. I cannot know what he would have thought of his Oxford student having metamorphosed into an Oxford guest speaker. Nor can I devise how he would have reacted to my two interventions. But I am free to imagine that he would have been more pleased than surprised. The generous invitation was the Centre for Socio-Legal Studies' Florian Grisel and Linda Mulcahy.

XII

The Negative

Finding support in Plato's *Sophist*,[1] in Aristotle's *Metaphysics*,[2] and in Aquinas's commentary on Aristotle's *De interpretatione*,[3] a view holds the ontological, epistemological, psychological, and grammatical priority of affirmatives over negatives. Compare 'Simone has two horses' (one knows what Simone has) to 'Simone does not have two horses' (one does not know what Simone has). While the positive contention points to an identifiable state of affairs, to what circumstances precisely does the negative enunciation correspond? Observe that even as an assertion introduces a proposition into the discourse, negation, in its 'chief use',[4] in its 'most common use',[5] directs itself at a proposition that is already in the discourse. Not only, then, is the negative statement less informative and harder to process, but it is parasitic. If the analysis were to stop here, negation would find itself in danger of being cast as largely fallow. But more must be said in order to do justice to the complexity of negation, a concept that, despite 'the repeated attempts over the centuries to liquidate or tame it – negation as positive difference, as dissimilarity or

[1] Eg: *Plato's Sophist* (S Bernadete tr from Greek, University of Chicago Press 1984 [c 360 BCE]) 238c, 29: '[I]t's possible neither to utter correctly, nor to say, nor to think "that which is not" alone by itself, but it is unthinkable, unsayable, unutterable, and unspeakable' [hereinafter *Plato's Sophist*].

[2] Aristotle, *The Metaphysics* (H Tredennick tr from Greek [1933], Harvard University Press 1968) bk 3, 996b8, 105: 'For while there are many ways of understanding the same thing, we say that the man who recognizes a thing by its being something knows more than he who recognizes it by its not being something.' Aristotle lived from c 384–c 322 BCE. It is notoriously difficult to date his works, especially perhaps the *Metaphysics*.

[3] *Aristotle on Interpretation: Commentary by St Thomas and Cajetan* (JT Oesterle tr from Latin, Marquette University Press 1962 [1269–72]) bk 1, lesson 8, 17a9, 3, p 64: 'The affirmative enunciation is prior to the negative.' Cajetan completed St Thomas's text in 1496.

[4] O Jespersen, *Negation in English and Other Languages* (Høst 1917) 4.

[5] AJ Ayer, 'Negation' (1952) 49 J Phil 797, 799.

incompatibility, as falsity, as an admission of epistemic impoverishment, as the speech act of denial' – has shown extraordinary 'resilience in surviving these attacks', to the point where 'negation qualifies as the Rasputin of the propositional calculus'.[6]

The manifestation of a semantic opposition, whether through inconsistency, contrapuntality, contraposition, contrariety, contradiction, disagreement, dissent, denial, rejection, or cancellation, negation is, effectively, differentiation.[7] It means, therefore, more than the mere absence of something. It is a force, and it is productive: '[N]egations … are … generative of things.'[8] Indeed, a negation ('the desk is not white'), '[being] less directly related to fact just in so far as [it] is less specific',[9] can have a much broader range of meaning than an affirmation ('the desk is white') – hence what Herbert Marcuse styles 'the freedom of negative thinking',[10] a view accounting for the position that 'negations are superior to assertions'.[11]

Negation, while dependent upon positive statements of specific kinds, thus following a predetermined route delineated by prior claims, paves the way to a higher affirmation by dismissal of the lower; in this crucial sense, 'negation is the origin of assertion'.[12] It follows that affirmation and negation are not mutually exclusive, but rather feature a complex tension. Through the constructive power it heralds, negation is a form of language carrying epistemic value: for instance, it enables the uncovering or elicitation of what the prior affirmation has hidden or erased. Within comparative law, for example, negation makes it possible to appreciate that the orthodoxy has not articulated a defensible epistemological model; that positivism does not do justice to the singularity of foreign laws; that there is no unity or uniformity that would challenge the opportunity of comparison within allegedly transnational, international, or global configurations; that the foreign is not translatable; that the

[6] LR Horn and H Wansing, 'Negation' in *Stanford Encyclopaedia of Philosophy* (2020) <https://plato.stanford.edu/entries/negation/> sub-s 1.2.

[7] Eg: *Plato's Sophist* (n 1) 257b–258e, 53–56.

[8] [Proclus Lycaeus], *The Six Books of Proclus on the Theology of Plato*, vol 1 (T Taylor tr from Greek, Selene Books 1985 [1816]) bk 2, ch 10, 137–38. Proclus lived from 412–85. The 'Platonic Theology' is a late work, possibly Proclus's last.

[9] Ayer (n 5) 815.

[10] H Marcuse, *One-Dimensional Man* (2nd edn, Routledge 1991 [1964]) 227.

[11] *Proclus' Commentary on Plato's Parmenides* (JM Dillon ed, GR Morrow and JM Dillon trs from Greek, Princeton University Press 1987) bk 6, s 1074, 427. The 'Parmenides' is a text from Proclus's middle age, that is, from the mid-fifth century.

[12] ibid, bk 7, s 1208, 553.

foreign is not representable; that a disciplinary approach cannot disclose the foreign; that a formalistic appreciation of the foreign yields no meaningful information about it; that comparison cannot confine itself to what have long been the usual (occidental) laws; that the differend across laws cannot be ignored or effaced; that an exhaustive disclosure of the foreign is impossible; that the foreign cannot be understood; that an objective statement of the foreign is impossible; that a true statement of the foreign is impossible; that the foreign cannot be accessed as such though any method. The (non-exhaustive) enumeration of these various instantiations of negativity shows the crucial relevance of deconstruction to the process of comparison: '[N]egative knowledge *is* deconstruction.'[13] By way of amplification of this claim, consider the following application: 'Deconstruction amounts to the epistemological gesture of falsifying the pretensions to truth and completeness of all totalizing principles and the approaches rooted in these principles. Deconstruction *utters* these negative insights *about* the unifying instances.'[14] Hence, no doubt, Samuel Beckett's declaration: 'What I liked in anthropology was its inexhaustible faculty of negation.'[15] It follows, importantly, that deconstruction's is uncompromisingly a *subversive* politics undermining the received discursive frame, that is, 'a disturbance, displacement, or disruption of the status quo ... that retains enormous potential for resisting the self-assurance of any hegemonic discourse or practice' (such as positivism).[16]

The fact that one cannot compare (say, because the self cannot access the other) does not mean that one must not compare, quite to the contrary. (Think translation: the impossibility of the endeavour cannot be allowed to compromise the requirement for the practice.) Beckett refers to 'the clash between can't and must',[17] which is precisely where the (contrarian) comparatist-at-law takes his stand. In Herbert Marcuse's *Negations*, the authors of the foreword to the reprinted edition thus observe that

> *Negations* is ... not a negative book but a call to action, a thinking that involves an affirmation of thinking and of life and a hopefulness that knows also that hopefulness without negation – an awareness of what must be negated and the risks of that task – is naive. ... [T]o affirm life,

[13] R Gasché, *The Wild Card of Reading* (Harvard University Press 1998) 27.
[14] ibid.
[15] S Beckett, *Molloy* (S Weller ed, Faber & Faber 2009 [1955]) 37.
[16] D Wills, *Matchbook* (Stanford University Press 2005) 13.
[17] L Shainberg, 'Exorcising Beckett' (1987/104) Paris R 100, 103. Lawrence Shainberg is recalling a remark that Beckett would have made in conversation.

> one must engage in a process of negating what *is*. Because only through this negating of what is can one find determinate possibilities of development, progress, freedom.[18]

I agree, and I resolutely apply these words to negative comparative law.

Negativity, then, is not simply the opposite of positivity: it is not only nothing rather than something. Negative discourse is not no more than discourse negated. Complicatedly, negation features a positive potentiality. In time, negation wants to become the alternative determination, the new affirmation.[19] If you will, negation is thus an initiative aiming to cause its own supersession. Such is 'the power of negation',[20] 'the power of negative thinking'.[21] Negative comparative law therefore stands as the 'not-yet' (not unlike, then, the Blochian '*Noch-nicht*'): it exists today, and it *must* exist today, so that it will not be necessary some day – and the more empowering or capacitating its claim proves to be, the more it is effectively accelerating its own demise.[22] (Transgression, in effect, always comes with a time stamp: Duchamp was once controversial, as was Monet, but who would be scandalized nowadays?)

Now, consider photography. Any correctly exposed but undeveloped film bears a latent image. The processing of the film reveals and makes permanent this image in the form of a negative.[23] (I leave to one side

[18] S Böhm and C Jones, 'Foreword to the 2009 Edition' in H Marcuse, *Negations* (MayFly 2009 [1968]) xv. Deconstruction, too, affirms life. Eg: J Derrida, *Apprendre à vivre enfin* (J Birnbaum ed, Galilée 2005) 54.

[19] See generally LR Horn, *A Natural History of Negation* (University of Chicago Press 1989); JL Speranza and LR Horn, 'A Brief History of Negation' in DM Gabbay et al (eds), *Handbook of the History of Logic*, vol 11 (North-Holland 2012) 127–74. For an extensively researched intellectual history of the considerable role that the negative has long assumed within (occidental) philosophical thought, see D Heller-Roazen, *No One's Ways* (Zone 2017). See also H Wansing (ed), *Negation* (De Gruyter 1996); S Hüsch et al (eds), *Negative Knowledge* (Narr Francke Attempto 2020); MJ Kurrik, *Literature and Negation* (Columbia University Press 1988); S Weller, *A Taste for the Negative* (Legenda 2005).

[20] Marcuse (n 10) 65.

[21] ibid 13.

[22] Critical analysis is optimally valid in its immediate, historical setting. Consider Max Horkheimer and Theodor Adorno's 1969 preface to the second edition of their *Dialektik der Aufklärung* initially released in 1944, a foremost example of critique, where the authors insist on the 'temporal core' of their work: M Horkheimer and TW Adorno, *Dialektik der Aufklärung* (Fischer 2002 [1969]) [ix].

[23] The English astronomer and polymath John Herschel, also an experimental photographer, first suggested the terms 'negative' and 'positive' to refer to the different states of the photographic image: J Herschel, 'On the Chemical Action of the Rays of the Solar Spectrum on Preparations of Silver and Other Substances, Both Metallic and Non-Metallic; and On Some Photographic Processes' (1840) 130 Philosophical Transactions of the Royal Society of London 1, s 8, 3. Many histories of photography

digital photography, where there is nothing that corresponds either to a film or negative – which is not to say that there is not exposure, no matter how brief.) Over time, negatives have assumed various forms, starting with the paper negative (from 1840 to the 1860s), then advancing to the collodion negative (from 1851 to the 1890s), and moving to the gelatin dry plate negative (since 1885).[24] Always, the negative has been employed to produce positive prints. In other words, out of the negative, an integral part of the image-making process, out of the chemical development of a camera image, there has emerged the material reality of the photograph. Indeed, a potentially infinite amount of copies can be made from a single original negative.[25] Not only, then, is the negative productive, but it is necessary on the way to the manifestation of the positive print; otherwise said, no positive image stands alone, and every positive image is dependent upon, or suspended to, a prior negative. And once the positive image has come into being, the negative has effectively outlived its primordial usefulness. I envisage negative comparative law along analogous lines – not, then, as making an arrogant bid for timelessness, but as entering a modest claim for timeliness.

(I discern other resonances between the photographic and the comparative gazes. As of the 1840s, the camera became part of the imperial and colonial paraphernalia along with the gun and the Bible. Operating under the immense umbrella of imperialism or colonialism, the camera would ensure that nothing remained hidden from the controlling authorities, even if force had to be deployed to allow the recording of imagery. Observe that one 'shoots' with a camera, a choice of verb aptly acknowledging the obdurate kinship of photography and epistemic violence. To deploy one illustration only, envisage how, during the French war on Algeria from 1954 to 1962, the French military compelled people in the Kabylia region of Northern Algeria to be photographed for identification purposes. Marc Garanger's photographs thus include approximately 2,000 forcibly unveiled women.[26] As the language of visual domination

are available. For a particularly thoughtful perspective, see R Kelsey, *Photography and the Art of Chance* (Harvard University Press 2015).

[24] See S Kennel, *In the Darkroom* (Thames & Hudson 2009) 58–59, 24–27, and 44–45.

[25] Susan Sontag notes that 'there is a large qualitative difference between . . . prints made from the original negative at the time . . . that the picture was taken . . . and subsequent generations of the same photograph': S Sontag, *On Photography* (Farrar, Straus & Giroux 1977) 140.

[26] See M Garanger, *Femmes algériennes 1960* (Atlantica 2002). See generally C Naggar, 'The Unveiled: Algerian Women, 1960' (1990/119) Aperture 2.

denied these women the right to remain unseen, it visited injury and degradation – injustice – unto them through sheer assertion of power. To my mind, the imperial or colonial photographer's practice of assimilation and appropriation very much echoes the way in which orthodox comparative law has been instrumentalizing and distorting foreign law in order to make it fit its preconceived ideological patterning.)

*

A precision seems apposite in order to obviate the predictable rejoinder. While I would not be so presumptuous as to suggest that anyone should devote hours upon hours to a reading of my published work, the fact of the matter is that if one is willing to take a genuine interest in my scholarship, one will readily recognize that my writing is not at all defeatist or pessimistic – not in any way crepuscular. Having accepted the empirical fact of the spatialization of law, I have long committed myself to the *valorization* of foreign law. I have steadfastly argued that, normatively speaking, foreign law *matters*. What could ever be termed defeatist or pessimistic – what could ever be called *fellifluous* – about such ideas? Do these undertakings not express the deployment of epistemic generosity or empathy towards the foreign? And how could this expression of interest for other laws – this show of recognition, this manifestation of respect – be said to be despondent? How could attention to the singularity of other laws, to the singularity of the situatedness of other laws, of the enculturation of other laws, qualify as dejection?

I also defend the view that, instead of hiding behind such weasel words as objectivity, truth, or method, the comparatist-at-law must carve his own path to foreign law and make his own decisions about foreignness, all the while accepting that he will miss some questions, on one hand, and that further issues will remain unanswerable to him, on the other, not least on account of the conflict of enculturations, so to speak, between his own and the foreign law's. Is my advocacy in favour of the comparatist-at-law's assumption of cognitive responsibility and of his acceptance of his cognitive limits defeatist or pessimistic? It simply cannot be, not for a moment; if anything, I am pleading for an improved, an optimized comparative law. Let me, then, rather call my appreciation of comparative interventions 'idealistic' in the sense that I defend the comparative law that I would ideally like to see unfolding. In other words, it is a conception of comparative law I hold as a model for comparatists that prompts me to negate comparative law's orthodox epistemology.[27]

In this regard, one of my principal claims is that comparison-at-law must overcome its long-standing epistemic credulity and become aware, at the minimum, how the comparisons that take place are necessarily informed and coloured by the encultured comparatists fashioning them, on one hand, and how these comparisons inevitably face serious epistemic constraints restricting what can be accomplished cognitively, on the other, not least because the foreign is itself encultured and therefore situated in beyondness vis-à-vis the comparing mind. A thoughtful comparatist-at-law must want to acknowledge and factor into his research and into his comparison both realizations – the fact of a 'constrained agency', so to speak, and the further fact of an embedded otherness-at-law that structurally remains at one remove from him. Ultimately, my argument is thus about making one's research into foreign law – one's comparison – intellectually creditable. To return to the earlier point, surely, to militate for epistemic creditability is not to be defeatist or pessimistic. Instead, it is to demonstrate a keenly confident commitment towards comparison-at-law so that this practice be (finally) treated as a worthy intellectual enterprise. Again, my contention is not at all that one ought not to be studying foreign law. As it happens, I have devoted most of my academic life to foreign law! But one must appreciate that, epistemically speaking, there are the epistemic parameters that there are – there is the limited agency on the part of the comparatist that there is, there is the avoidless enframement of foreign law that there is, and there is the ineludible distance between the two entities that there is.

Crucially, as Susan Sontag deftly indicates in her book *On Photography*, one must accept that '[a]ll possibility of understanding is rooted in the ability to say no'.[28] Sontag's claim is not confined to technique. It is about a way of being in the world – and it can easily be harnessed to encourage a way of being in the field of comparative law, a way of working as a comparatist-at-law. To rephrase: if a comparatist wants to *understand* what it is to research foreign law, to compare laws,

[27] cf I Turgenev, 'Reminiscences of Belinsky' in *Literary Reminiscences* (D Magarshack tr from Russian, Farrar, Straus & Cudahy 1958 [1869]) 137: 'Belinsky was as much an idealist as a negationist: he negated in the name of his ideal.' Ivan Turgenev (1818–83), a Russian novelist, playwright, and translator, was writing about Vissarion Belinsky (1811–48), a Russian literary critic.

[28] Sontag (n 25) 23.

he has to say no to comparative law's orthodoxy as it claims both that comparison must be objective and true (which is disabling) and that comparison can be objective and true (which is misleading). Consider Jacques Derrida's arresting formulation, a statement that the English language cannot translate from the French: 'Il y va d'un certain pas.' In this sentence, the word '*pas*' stands at once for three ideas at least: 'it is a matter of an assured negation', 'it is a question of taking a certain step' (towards the assertion of negation), and 'it is about proceeding at a definite pace' (on the way to negation).[29]

*

Orthodox comparative law takes as its epistemically unexamined starting-point a fallacious model of the comparative dynamics pursuant to which consciousness, on one hand, and the worldly foreign legal cultures or law-texts, on the other, would have solidified into a thing-like polarity. I challenge this dualist appreciation, an excessively binary understanding of comparative law featuring a 'subject' and an 'object'. Such a configuration being the hallmark of positivism in general, and of legal positivism in particular, it behoves a culturally attuned comparatist to question the basic positivist assurances. I further reject the positivist idea that an entity that is (allegedly) the 'subject' can so identify itself with another entity that stands (allegedly) as the 'object', so that one would effectively be looking at a tautological situation, that is, an articulation where the subject's account of the object could take the form of becoming wholly and fully congruent with that object, an identical superimposition.

The fact of the matter is that (if one can momentarily indulge continuing to speak in these inadequate terms) no 'subject' can make himself ad idem with an 'object', no 'subject' can become the 'object' of one's knowledge: recall that the self cannot be the other. Such identification between thought-in-world-here and law-in-world-there being unachievable, it must follow that no mind's account of a foreign world can possibly qualify as objective or true (method notwithstanding). What the comparing mind perceives as the foreign world is inevitably not the-foreign-world-as-it-is, but the-foreign-world-as-the-mind-sees-it. And the process of 'seeing' cannot not involve the seeing mind. No 'seeing', then, can pretend to exist on a separate plane from the seeing mind's beliefs, preconceptions, biases, or preferences, which entails that the idea of an uncritical affirmation of givenness (of foreign law) cannot be

[29] J Derrida, *Apories* (Galilée 1996) 23 [emphasis omitted].

sustained. Every 'seeing' assumes an always-already-in-place enculturation, and the 'seeing' performance is at once enabled and constrained by that very enculturation – which is my argument about there being 'constrained agency', an agency that is enframed (which is evidently not to say that there is no agency at all, a stance that would be grotesque). Incidentally, the fact that the identification I address proves unattainable must not be taken to mean that one ought to entertain the contrary idea of a thoroughgoing dissociation between mind and world, another unsustainable postulation. While the comparing mind cannot be so close to the foreign world as to be able to identify with it (it is never close enough), it is not so far away from it as to be in a position to offer a fully detached view either (it is never far enough).

In the matter of understanding understanding, to understand something (or someone) is not – and cannot be – objectively to understand what that entity truly is or says. *Understanding can emphatically not be an event of truth.* On account of human finitude, because of enculturation – which features such intrinsic epistemic characteristics as encumbrance, contingency, and thrownness (most obviously, perhaps, one is thrown into a language) – and contrary to the Cartesian dream heralding the mind's autonomy from world and the mind's agentive supremacy over world,[30] any event of understanding simultaneously stands as an event of concealment, because one always comes to the act of appreciation with prejudice, with pre-judgement. Understanding necessarily happens in culture, which is a fact immediately preventing anything like knowledge of being-in-itself (to the extent that this expression harbours any defensible meaning). Indeed, any view of foreign law is an interpretation and any interpretation is perspectival – which means, ultimately, that there is never *knowledge* of foreignness. Because the comparatist who sees is being restricted by language, since language exercises a controlling role over 'seeing', there is, strictly speaking, no possibility of representational thinking of foreign law. Far from consigning what it sees, the seeing mind co-signs it.

Again, without falling for the opposite extravagance and contending for a mere inversion, that is, for the integral autonomy of the 'object' vis-à-vis the 'subject' or the integral supremacy of the 'object' over the 'subject', of the foreign world over the mind, I want to defend a radicalization of the foreign world's *resistance* to the mind, and I wish

[30] cf J Lacan, *Ecrits* (Editions du Seuil 1966 [1953]) 421: 'He is autonomous! That is quite a good one.'

to do so in the name of a persistent difference ultimately preventing any epistemic reconciliation. The fact that the foreign world withstands its wholesale absorption by the mind approaching it means that the mind's sovereignty over it must be limited. Note that as I emphasize the resistance of the foreign world, I do not defend the idea of the affirmation of the given. There is no foreignly given, and all is interpretation. This realization means that I salvage a key role for the comparing mind. However, the mind cannot do better than disseminate and recommend its interpretation of the foreign world. To continue with the matter of scattering, I do not agree that the interpretive drive must be stabilization and consensus. Rather, I favour negotiation and controversy. To be sure, I accept that encounters across difference may prompt an escalation of the differend through accrual of identity and attendant enhanced awareness of the divide – a phenomenon akin to Gregory Bateson's schismogenesis. As I wrest the principle of negation from the affirmative yearning for reconciliation or (Hegelian) *Versöhnung*, I very much regard the differential outcome as an opportunity. Pursuing the shattering of Hegel's goal of a harmonious finale by holding open what philosophical affirmation wanted to close, I deploy critical leverage against the harmonistic reach of comparative law that, by giving effect to a 'rationalized rage at the non-identical', autocratically fails to preserve the other's otherness and falls for the kind of epistemic injustice – of epistemicide, really – that comparison must emphatically resist accommodating.[31]

In other terms, there is, at the minimum, a serious problem about the comparatist's appreciation of his epistemic self that demands urgent attention. Even as he cannot achieve complete reflective distance from himself or deploy a fully unobstructed view of his own identity, the comparatist-at-law needs to improve upon his understanding of who he is, of what he does, and of what he is able to do – a strategy that must include the fashioning of an alertness both to his agency and cognitive limits. Crucially, the comparatist-at-law must make himself aware that there is simply no transcendental apperception that can exist apart from his culturally embedded condition of being-in-the-world. One cannot de-enculture oneself. (Even as one can step out of oneself by means of thought, one cannot leave oneself behind.) Despite the fact that thoroughgoing self-transparency is illusory, I hold that the comparatist can improve his insight into the interpretive conditions that govern his

[31] TW Adorno, *Negative Dialektik* (Suhrkamp 1966) 34.

understanding of himself and, therefore, his understanding of the foreign law-world – such understanding, perforce, taking the form of culturally conditioned understanding, that is, a not-understanding.[32] The comparatist is fated to attempt an understanding of the structure of understanding from within the structure of his understanding: there is no non-interpretive understanding of one's interpretive circumstances, so that what enhanced awareness emerges will be culturally conditioned, too: any other view pertains to metaphysics (or wishful thinking).

As the theory emanating from a comparing self must inevitably be situated or local, the question arises as to whether one's theory (and if so to what extent), as simultaneously enabled and constrained by one's enculturation, can provide guidance for other comparatists emerging from different enabling/constraining horizons, perhaps engaged in a different institutional pursuit. In other words, an important challenge – and a key question for me and my theoretical work – is to ask how much, if at all, can a theory detach itself from the encultured circumstances out of which it has emerged. How efficacious or consequential can one's (obviously contestable) theory become? For myself, if I did not think that my equipment or implements could be helpful to someone else's comparative theorization and practice, I would not have assembled *NCL*. But I remain acutely aware that my argument can only issue out of my singular experience in the law, that is, I am very conscious of my mind's inherent referential strictures (at least, I am keenly sensitive to a number of them). And I realize that my personal inclinations and professional socialization, my enculturation and institutionalization, my epistemologization, are at profound variance with, say, Konrad Zweigert and Hein Kötz's or Uwe Kischel's. It remains that there simply cannot occur an identity between the comparing mind and the foreign law-world in Germany any more than anywhere else.

*

I like to think that the main ideas I defend – that law exists as a cultural manifestation; that research into foreign law or the comparison of laws has nothing whatsoever to do with a scientific endeavour (that *Rechtswissenschaft* is no more about science than the horoscope is about astronomy); that more than one law cannot be identical, which means that they must therefore differ; that every report on foreign law cannot be but a particular comparatist's interpretation thereof; and that

[32] cf J Joyce, *Finnegans Wake* (R-J Henkes et al eds, Oxford University Press 2012 [1939]) 444: 'I overstand you, you understand.'

no comparatist can produce an exact representation of foreign law, that is, an objective or true account of it, because, well, it is *a comparatist* producing the report – I like to think that these ideas, then, pertain to good common sense informed by basic exigencies pertaining to rigorous and creditable thought. Far from foretelling the collapse of comparatism in law, *NCL*, as it argues against an overcommitment to epistemic fallacies and global postulates operating at a very problematic remove from the phenomenal world of singular law-texts, is an enthusiastic call to arms, an entreaty to *committed*, to *dedicated negativity*. Yes. If I may be so audacious as to express the way in which I imagine comparatism, I want comparatists to operate within sensible epistemic parameters – in particular, to internalize both their agency and the limited interpretive reach of any expertise, no matter how sophisticated, that they may harbour with respect to the (encultured) foreign. Also, I want comparatists purposefully to argue in favour of the normative relevance of foreign legal cultures or law-texts locally (foreignness being a necessary component of comparativity, however those institutionally deemed to be in a position legitimately to make such determination care to understand the foreign).

Not only must comparatists accept the indeterminacy of *their* forays, of *their* analytics, of *their* interpretations, of *their* reports – all being structurally or endemically unsettled – but the comparatists' readers (often fellow comparatists) must themselves appreciate that the comparative texts they are reading are intrinsically indeterminate. For instance, as I read a comparative account of French law (let us say, a report pixelated by a US comparatist), I must accept that what appears as definite, as having been resolved, has effectively been settled in a specific way as a result of selections made or options exercised by a specific 'settlor', a specifically encultured 'settlor' – bearing in mind that every word and every reference is an act of (encultured) choice. If you will, foreign law has been configured through a text and as a text, but it has been enunciated *after a fashion*. As I read the account on offer, it is incumbent upon me to challenge the binaries and boundaries that have channelled the fashioning of the foreign even as the words, sentences, and paragraphs that are being presented to me apparently feature clarity, consistency, coherence, and even as they seemingly purport to convey the irenic air that befits the (allegedly) strictly descriptive, the (allegedly) rigidly duplicative. Since it seems fair to say that texts are the primary mechanism of diffusion of information about foreign law and of dissemination of comparative narratives, the kind of attunement I mention is crucial. No matter how authoritative the comparative text he is reading, a reader is always reading someone's interpretation of a foreign law or legal culture.

Both the comparatist interpreting a foreign law or legal culture and the reader of the comparatist's account of the foreign, then, are tasked with undoing the graphical hegemony of the written word so as to elicit what lurks between the lines, what fills the blanks, what is encrypted in the text's fabric (etymologically, a text is a fabric – think textile). In other terms, the comparatist and his reader are both summoned to trace the foreignness that they make into their focus of study to its constitutive features. Initially, the comparatist would trace the foreign law-text, say, to its historical, ideological, or political threads. Later, the reader coming to the comparatist's text would trace it to the comparatist's epistemic investment (his predispositions, his biases, his ambitions, his desires). Note that in both cases, it must be clear that the texts at issue are constructed or fabricated, which is precisely what a positivist approach to them readily obliterates, because from such standpoint the (unsurmountable) interpretive contingencies I address do not count as a matter of law. As he says no to this obscurantism, no to the masquerade of description, no to the charlatanism of objectivity, no the chimera of truth – and no to the mirage of method – the comparatist recognizes that no reading of foreignness and no writing on foreignness can be, can ever be, a disinterested practice, that it is always, always-already, that it must be, that it can only be, the expression of an act of power by the comparative mind coming to foreignness. (An analogous remark concerns the reader of the comparatist's text: his reading is not innocent either.)

Committed or dedicated negativity is therefore an instance of epistemic militancy. It heralds a disposition resolutely embracing hyperawareness as a strategy of epistemic responsibility vis-à-vis the texts that govern the foreign and as regards the texts issuing from the comparative intervention that the comparatist-at-law will write with a view to accounting for the foreign. Even as the claim for enhanced sensitivity invests the individual with a sense of control of both the self and the foreign world, it must be remembered that what 'knowledge' is claimed is inevitably encultured, which means that it is ultimately at variance from the foreignness that there is, there: the direct gaze of the comparatist-at-law upon foreignness *is* fatefully obstructed, the challenge being to limit the extent to which otherness is made to fit into one's priorly formed epistemic grid. As I propose to restore the comparatist's critical agency and his crucial modesty, I hold that comparative law must include within the comparison an account of the comparatist's own situation: it matters that Zweigert and Kötz, the co-authors of the exasperatingly creaky and dogmatic model assuming epistemic governance over comparative law, are German or, at least, that they studied law in Germany and were socialized, institutionalized, and epistemologized – that they were encultured – in Germany (nationalism remains as deeply pervasive as it is officially disavowed amongst comparatists, a tacit but vast determinant of so much comparative work). As the comparatist scrutinizes foreign law, his scrutiny deserves and requires to be scrutinized in turn. The point, then, is not cynicism, but a wide opening of the comparatist's epistemic vistas with a view to greater integrity and more sophisticated response – even if this heightened honesty and enriched record must entail a (lucid) foregrounding of the epistemics of indeterminacy and provisionality, of interpretive leeway, of *play*.

*

One could say that comparatism's signal contribution to social theory is the prioritization of the 'More-than-One' over the One. Not only does a comparative treatment make for a more sophisticated consideration of well-nigh any subject-matter, not only is comparison 'what will make our cosmopolit[ical] arguments stronger, and our strength more cosmopolit[ical]',[33] but it provides for 'instruction in otherness: vivid, compelling evidence of differences in cultures, mores, assumptions, values' – and, to borrow from Jonathan Culler's, '[a]t [its] best [it] make[s] otherness palpable and make[s] it comprehensible without

[33] B Robbins, 'Chomsky's Golden Rule' in R Felski and SS Friedman (eds), *Comparison* (Johns Hopkins University Press 2013) 206. I have substituted 'cosmopolitical' for the author's 'cosmopolitan'. 'Cosmopolitism' distinguishes itself from 'cosmopolitanism' as it reclaims the polyphonic deconstruction and reconstruction of the planet through recognition of the heterogeneous cultural entities that inhabit it and by way of an expression of respect towards them. Meanwhile, cosmopolitanism, a variation on the theme of universalism, pursues a policy of one-world convergence and suggests that such integrative formation should be privileged over a differentialist sociality. Specifically, all human beings are regarded as equal members of one single community (etymologically, 'cosmopolis' evokes a planetwide body politic). 'Cosmopolitanism' is typically associated with Kantianism. In a famous 1795 essay, Kant articulated a '*jus cosmopoliticum*' as a guiding principle to help achieve enduring peace. Eg: C Corradetti, 'Kant's Legacy and the Idea of a Transnational *Jus Cosmopoliticum*' (2016) 29 Ratio Juris 105. See generally U Beck, *Der kosmopolitische Blick* (Suhrkamp 2004); KA Appiah, *Cosmopolitanism* (Norton 2006). Making due allowance for the structural inadequacy of binary categorizations, cosmopolitism resonates with comparative law – or ought to do so – while cosmopolitanism evokes the international law project.

reducing it to an inferior version of the same, as universalizing humanism threatens to do'.[34] In this sense, '[t]o introduce a comparativist viewpoint . . . enhance[s] the democratic spirit'.[35] Yes. 'Whatever disruption, anxiety, or competition it brings, [comparison] is an economy that ultimately serves the development of the human spirit and the establishment of the common good.'[36] Yes. Still, no matter how oppositional it may have appeared to be vis-à-vis local law, the orthodox comparatist project has remained trapped within the trajectory of positivist power, which is why comparative law as it has been not-theorized and practised is what must now be brought to crisis with a view to treating foreign law-texts and legal cultures – every law-world offers its singular reading of life-in-the-law – chiefly as opportunities for producing information about the cultural question that these texts were meant to answer locally and about what these answers have subsequently been authoritatively interpreted to mean locally.[37] In sum, the comparatist must be fully invested in the idea that he must account for foreign law as it exists, in all its traceable complexity, even as he must lose faith in the idea that he can account for foreign law as it exists, in all its traceable complexity.

What aspiration am I pursuing as I urge comparative law towards the negative space, as I contend that '[e]verything really reduces itself to thinking rigorously the negative'?[38] I seek nothing less than a new mode of comparative being. It is not, then, that I purport to 'chill' comparative law. Rather, it is that I want to 'freeze' heedless comparison-at-law. I believe in comparative law. *Of course, I believe in comparative law.* But I can only believe in a comparative law that appreciates how, even as it is deployed, it is necessarily unfolding as an epistemic aporia (one must tell *the foreign*, one cannot tell *the foreign*/one must *access* the foreign, one cannot *access* the foreign).[39] I can only believe in serious

[34] J Culler, *Framing the Sign* (Blackwell 1988) 48.

[35] GC Spivak, *An Aesthetic Education in the Era of Globalization* (Harvard University Press 2012) 298.

[36] P Cheah, 'The Material World of Comparison' in R Felski and SS Friedman (eds), *Comparison* (Johns Hopkins University Press 2013) 180.

[37] There is a reference to orthodox comparative law as 'atheoretical' in J Hill, 'Comparative Law, Law Reform and Legal Theory' (1989) 9 Oxford J Legal Stud 101, 112.

[38] M Merleau-Ponty, *Le Visible et l'invisible* in *Œuvres* (C Lefort ed, Gallimard 2010 [1964†]) 1695. cf Alain, *Propos sur les pouvoirs* (F Kaplan ed, Gallimard 1985 [19 January 1924]) s 139, 351: 'To think is to say no.'

[39] cf S Beckett, *The Unnamable* (S Connor ed, Faber & Faber 2010 [1958]) 134: 'I can't go on, I'll go on.'

comparative law that deploys itself as play.[40] I can only believe in a comparative law that, even as it makes sense of the astonishing complexity of the foreign, makes epistemic sense, too.

*

'The artist is active, but negatively.'[41] Given '[t]he centrality of negativity for comparative practices',[42] so is the comparatist comparing laws.

*

I find it helpful to supply further information about *NCL*'s title.

The Strong Programme in the sociology of scientific knowledge issued mainly from the Science Studies Unit at the University of Edinburgh in the 1970s. David Bloor is widely recognized as the movement's leading proponent, his 1976 *Knowledge and Social Imagery* being regarded as a key text within a list of publications, either by him or other participants, that is nothing short of plethoric.[43] In time, the Strong Programme informed in significant respects the then emerging field of science and technology studies (STS). I do not mean, of course, to apply every tenet of the Strong Programme to comparative law, if only because comparatists emphatically not being biochemists (Zweigert and Kötz's parallel with 'molecular biology' notwithstanding),[44] many correlations do not obtain. But there is a cluster of basic epistemic assumptions that fully warrant transposition – hence my explicit reference.

Decisively, the Strong Programme is a response to what it considers deficient theorization regarding the production of scientific knowledge. For Strong Programme scholars, no intellectual endeavour purporting to gather scientific knowledge can be detached from the sensory and intellectual conditions informing the process of acquisition. In particular, one must accept that any human-initiated research, no matter how purportedly scientific, is at all times structurally bounded by the researcher's

[40] For a sedulous discussion of serious play, see P Legrand, 'Jameses at Play: A Tractation on the Comparison of Laws' (2017) 65 Am J Comp L [Special Issue] 1, 110–20.

[41] S Beckett, *Proust* in *The Grove Centenary Edition*, vol 4 (P Auster and JM Coetzee eds, Grove 2006 [1931]) 637.

[42] K Postoutenko, 'Preliminary Typology of Comparative Utterances' in A Epple et al (eds), *Practices of Comparing* (Bielefeld University Press 2020) 57.

[43] See D Bloor, *Knowledge and Social Imagery* (Routledge & Kegan Paul 1976; 2nd edn, University of Chicago Press 1991). See also eg B Barnes, *Scientific Knowledge and Sociological Theory* (Routledge & Kegan Paul 1974); DA MacKenzie, *Statistics in Britain 1865–1930: The Social Construction of Scientific Knowledge* (Edinburgh University Press 1981); B Barnes et al, *Scientific Knowledge* (University of Chicago Press 1996).

[44] K Zweigert and H Kötz, *Einführung in die Rechtsvergleichung* (3rd edn, Mohr Siebeck 1996) 13.

senses, on one hand, and by the beliefs of the collectivity within which the researcher is operating, on the other. Because of such inescapable over-determination, it follows that no information being produced as scientific knowledge can ever be deemed certain or warranted. If you will, all such information is generated at an angle. The least fragment of information is innerved by the intrinsic fallibility of the researcher's sensory experience and of his faculty of understanding. No researcher is therefore in a position to establish the full independence of any of his 'findings' from his socialization, institutionalization, or epistemologization, from his enculturation. The intertwinement is too intimate to allow for any dissociation of 'object' from 'subject' – in effect, the enmeshment is too intricate to justify the use of these 'classical' markers.

In sum, the Strong Programme abjures the implied separation of culture and scientific practice. Instead, it maintains that enculturation is an independent factor and 'knowledge' a dependent outcome. It follows that a researcher is unable to foster any truth that would not be contingent, that would not bear the mark of his enculturation. And this conclusion must entail in turn that the researcher is unable to produce any truth at all (irrespective of any method being deployed to that end). Otherwise said, in the quest for ascription of meaning to the information that is gathered, truth cannot act as an explanatory resource. Meanwhile, those who wish to maintain the value of truth are effectively compelled to mobilize faith – and the attendant authoritarianism (recall how the Roman Catholic church used to burn heretics – 'able-to-choose' reprobates, according to Greek etymology – in the name of truth). With a view to making sense of the ascertainment of certain 'knowledge' as being superior to other, the Strong Programme also considers the connections between research-production and research-reception.

In addition, *NCL*'s title refers to 'weak thought'. I lift the expression from Gianni Vattimo's philosophical work.[45] At the outset, it is important to indicate that what Vattimo styles 'weak thought' ('*il pensiero debole*') has nothing to do with a weakness of thinking. Who, indeed, would want to encourage *that*? Vattimo's key insight concerns the requirement for thought to accept its strictly interpretive character. In other words, thought must recognize that it is incapable of relying on

[45] See G Vattimo and PA Rovatti (eds), *Il pensiero debole* (Feltrinelli 2010); D Antisani, *Le ragioni del pensiero debole* (Borla 1993); S Zabala (ed), *Weakening Philosophy* (McGill-Queen's University Press 2007).

sure epistemic foundations – for example, that it cannot base itself on objectivity, truth, or method – in a way allowing it to reach epistemically unassailable conclusions. Weak thought acknowledges that it cannot achieve fixity of meaning. The best that thought can do – and this is how it is 'weak' – is to *interpret* a world or worldly entity (such as a foreign law-text or legal culture). Now, no matter how sophisticated an interpretation manages to be – and some interpretations are very rich – no interpretation, whatever the interpretation, can access a world as it is and produce textual evidence about it that would replicate that world as it is and therefore feature incontrovertible evidence of that world as it is. No interpretation can account for a world or worldly entity (such as a foreign law-text or legal culture) as it is. No interpretation can transform itself into a truth-statement. To turn this enunciation around, veridiction does not – and cannot – pertain to interpretation.

Thought, then, is 'weak' to the extent that it can only operate within interpretive limits. It is 'weak', because there is only so much it can accomplish in terms of telling foreignness 'as it is'. Otherwise said, there is an impossibility for language – *an interpretation consists of language* – to duplicate a world as it is, because language is always-already positioned and will therefore inescapably consider a world at an angle. Language simply cannot process a world 'as it is', and it is its destiny to transform any purportedly stable, unwavering (textual) entity as it proceeds to address it, to interpret it (thus, the comparatist's language vis-à-vis foreign law). Since no interpreter can produce an interpretive correspondence with a world under investigation that would correlate with it identically, the (Cartesian) dominion of reason over world is a fiction.

Indeed, 'weak thought' holds that there is no objectivity, but that there is rather a horizon within which thought must operate; that there is no givenness (no data), but that there is rather understanding from a certain standpoint; that there is no neutrality, but that there is rather a predilection or predisposition; that there is no recovery of meaning, but that there is rather production of meaning; that there is no description, but that there is rather an inscription; that there is no restitution of meaning, but that there is rather a differentiation of meaning; that there can be no absolute affirmation, but that there must rather be the expression of a committed preference; that there can be no consensualism between the *interpretandum* and the *interpretans*, but that there must rather be a suspension of any agreement; that there can be no peremptory ascription or imposition of meaning, but that there must rather be persuasive interpretation and negotiation; that there can be no undue epistemic violence under the guise of objectivity, truth, or method, but that there must rather be a transaction – the lesser violence.

And then, I mix. I defend a strong 'weak thought', that is, a strong theory and practice of 'weak thought', a 'weak thought' asserting itself in strong language. The contradiction that *NCL*'s title seems to suggest is therefore apparent only. It is highly pertinent to want to strengthen 'weak thought',[46] not least within comparative law, which is in dire need of theoretical and practical *enforcement*.

[46] To be sure, the strengthening of 'weak thought' is also meant to generate a weakening of 'strong thought', an attenuation of the thought that has proclaimed itself to be strong, for example, to be objective and true, to be methodical, to be 'scientific'.

XIII

The Negative, Applied

It will not have escaped the attentive analyst that the 2004 French statute prohibiting 'ostensibl[e]' ('*ostensibl[e]*') religious attire in public primary and secondary schools is, well, about schools rather than airports, hospitals, or museums.[1] For a French court aiming to interpret the word 'schools' ('*les écoles, les collèges et les lycées*'), this legislative predilection hardly demands to be justified. Indeed, while French judges set themselves the institutional and interpretive charge of ascribing normative meaning to the relevant statutory term, they need not ask themselves – and will, in fact, refrain from wondering – why schools instead of another institution. By contrast, the discerning comparatist-at-law must emphatically address this question if, of course, he proposes to ascribe deep or thick meaning to the French statute, if he is pursuing comparative research with a view to generating a significant interpretive yield regarding foreignness – which, I argue, he must in principle want to do.

A threshold requirement for the conduct of the kind of elucidating inquiry liable to produce a *meaningful* report (a report full of meaning) on the French statute is for the comparatist to accept that his work involves *making sense* of a legislative text that is (inevitably) thoroughly encultured. To be sure, the word 'schools' is culturally freighted and is being deployed by the French legislature as a culturally freighted word. (Observe that I mobilize 'schools' as a convenient shorthand to capture the idea of pre-university public educational institutions – my foreignizing English translation of the French statute's '*les écoles, les collèges et les lycées publics*', even as I appreciate that the word '*lycée*',

[1] Statute no 2004–228 of 15 March 2004 enframing, in application of the principle of laicity, the wearing of signs or attire demonstrating a religious belonging in public primary and secondary schools, art 1 <www.legifrance.gouv.fr/loda/id/JORFTEXT000000417977/> [on file].

for example, is properly untranslatable.) Such enculturation entails that there is infinitely more to the term 'schools' than the letter or graphical surface of the statute might suggest. Positivism would, of course, squarely contradict this assumption. However, exegetical and formalistic ways are not at all suited to the brand of comparative investigation that I regard as compelling.

Because 'the' meaning of the word 'schools' is not, the comparatist must himself *enact* a meaning.[2] And in order to do so justly, he must elicit the relevant cultural encumbrances as so many constitutive elements of the law-text, unlike the aseptic view of the legal that orthodox comparatism has traditionally been peddling. Accordingly, the comparatist must prove himself determined to abide by a sophisticated appreciation of textuality and thus purport to *invent* – that is, find-and-fashion – articulable traces constitutively haunting the foreign law-text through infinitely complex networks of enmeshment, traces structurally partaking of the foreign law-text as the law-text that exists, there. Such is comparatism other-wise: a different comparatism from the model that has long prevailed within comparative law, a comparatism that tries to do re-presentative justice to the other law-text, that resolutely attempts to manifest interpretive wisdom vis-à-vis otherness-in-the-law, *a conjuration of the haunting of foreign law-texts*.

As the comparatist proceeds, he is himself acting as an encultured being, which means that his intervention into foreign law will inevitably be influenced by his own cultural freighting. For instance, what the comparatist says of 'schools' will turn on how much information he holds about France and French culture (that is, his work will be contingent on his pre-understanding of foreignness). The comparatist's account will also have something to do with how easy it is for him to access authoritative documentation on French schools, not least texts in the French language (and, correlatively, his report will hang on how much effort he is willing to expand on researching sources that are not so easily accessible – which, in turn, will concern how rigorously he was instituted into comparative law and how much time he has at his disposal).

Most significantly, the shape of the comparatist's probe will hinge on his preparedness to trace the law-text to its cultural fabric on the understanding that such tracing, which effectively consists in archaeological or genealogical work, must produce an indisciplined assemblage of

2 See P Legrand, 'What Is That, to Read Foreign Law?' (2019) 14(2) J Comp L 294.

information to supplement the extant statutory text, the authoritative judicial decisions, and the recognized doctrinal commentary. No matter how excellent, though, the comparatist's report must pertain to interpretation rather than veridiction – because any tracing necessarily does, any tracing being a singular comparatist's singular tracing of a singular foreign law-text. And the account that the comparatist-at-law inscribes must be his (encultured) interpretation rather than a statement instantiating objectivity or truth. It is unequivocally *his* response to foreignness that the comparatist is enunciating, not anyone else's (and certainly not some hypothetically neutral commentator's). Moreover, tracing is inherently critical – both in the sense that it is the comparatist himself who chooses the traces he is to elicit out of the range he can discern, and it is the comparatist himself who then follows a particular tracing itinerary until he decides to interrupt it.[3] But critique can also legitimately take the form of an express demurral to the legal commitments suffusing the foreign law-text under scrutiny.

Provided it abides by the principle of charitable interpretation and does not therefore dismiss the other-in-the-law as irrational or demonstrate contempt vis-à-vis him, on condition also that it attests to a genuine effort at understanding the other law's 'thereness' on its own terms, such oppositional interpretation pertains to the comparative *advantage*, to what distance allows and warrants – to what is, in sum, one of the very raisons d'être of comparative law. While ethnocentrism or juricentrism (say, as regards the French statute, one's Canadian multicultural inclination or one's sentiment as a colonized Québécois) must be kept steadily in check, it is legitimate that the comparatist's life experience, as it informs his rejoinder to foreignness, should possibly clash with the *Lebenswelt* of the law-text under examination. Subsequently, the comparatist's readership or audience, applying a suitably prudent (even wary) disposition, will adjudicate on the interpretive merits of the critical comparatism on display.

Note that the tracing culturalist at no time steps out of the law-box. Rather, the comparatist remains well inside the law-box throughout the interpretive process. To pursue the archaeological or genealogical metaphor, he is earnestly digging within the law-box to ascertain the threads that have (been made to) come together in order to constitute the French statute. Bringing to bear an aesthetics of suspicious reading, he is

[3] For a detailed exploration of tracing, see P Legrand, 'Siting Foreign Law: How Derrida Can Help' (2011) 21 Duke J Comp & Int'l L 595.

meticulously deconstructing the legal construction in place. If you will, the comparatist is excavating the law (contrariwise, think of positivism as leaving foreignness *unexcavated*). To transpose an excerpt from Samuel Beckett's, the comparatist-at-law is 'drill[ing] one hole after another' into the foreign text 'until that which lurks behind . . . starts seeping through', on the robust understanding that 'there [is no] reason why that terrifyingly arbitrary materiality of the word surface should not be dissolved'.[4] To the extent that they would want to resist tracing, cast it as counter-law rather than accept it as the hyperlaw that it is, perhaps denigrate it as some form of contemplative speculation mired in unjustifiable paralegal roundaboutations and divagations, orthodox comparatists-at-law would be contesting *what has always-already happened*,[5] for *the law-text has always-already been constituted through a myriad instances of jurimorphing*.

By way of illustration of the form that a habile tracing exercise can adopt as a matter of comparative law and the kind of revealing foreign information that tracing can elucidate as it engages in the task of making-sense, I suggest a vignette on 'schools' with specific reference to the French statute I am addressing. No more than a sketch, my report shows how information that orthodox comparatists would readily exclude as non-law assuredly and crucially belongs to the law – how it partakes of the very gist of the law, perhaps of the law's core of cores, because the French statute derives its very institutional pertinence from the very fact of the cultural reach of schools within France. (If schools did not mean what they mean in France as a matter of cultural fact, there would simply not have been promulgated into force a 2004 French statute on laicity.) As I embark upon my illustrative tracing of the legislative term 'schools' to its cultural fabric, at no point am I therefore in any way digressing from the law, never is the information I gather such as deserves to be relegated to the law's context, as warrants to be outlawed. From the perspective of comparative law, it is not at all that there is a cultural context surrounding the statute; it is rather that the statute exists as culture, that the statute exists as a cultural statement, that

4 Letter from S Beckett to A Kaun (V Westbrook tr) in *The Letters of Samuel Beckett*, vol 1 (MD Fehsenfeld and LM Overbeck eds, Cambridge University Press 2009 [9 July 1937]) 518. Widely known as the 'German Letter', this document exists only as a corrected draft. Beckett wrote it in German himself. I adopt Viola Westbrook's translation.

5 cf J Derrida, *La Voix et le phénomène* (Presses Universitaires de France 1967) 95: 'The living present springs forth on the basis of its non-self-identity . . . . It is always already a trace.'

the statute exists as an instance of French culture expressing itself legally (rather than, say, architecturally, literarily, or culinarily).

*

Without further ado, let me maintain that it appears unreasonable not to agree with Robert Paxton, to refer to a particularly distinguished exponent of French culture, that the 2004 French statute is '[a] law [that] was unmistakably aimed at the Muslim *foulard*, or headscarf',[6] that this legislative text must therefore be read as denying French citizens who adhere to Islam the right publicly to express their faith, at least within schools. To be sure, the French commentariat readily tends to deny this denial and defend the statute's 'absolute neutrality' in religious matters.[7] But only wilful blindness, it seems, can overlook the fact that the implementation of the 2004 statute aiming to homogenize the public sphere along non-religious lines and purporting to draw an impermeable divide between the public and private realms was expressly favoured by a governmental task force, the Stasi Commission, which was just as expressly established in the wake of the *Conseil d'Etat*'s advisory opinions,[8] most prominently that of 27 November 1989,[9] and its adjudicative decisions on complaints against the state in cases such as *Kherouaa*, of 2 November 1992,[10] and *Yilmaz*, of 14 March 1994,[11] all of these asseverations having had specifically to do with the presence of Islamic headscarves in public

[6] RO Paxton, 'Can You Really Become French?' *The New York Review of Books* (9 April 2009) 54. While Paxton mistakenly dates the French statute to 1994, he is evidently discussing the 2004 law-text.

[7] P Weil (with N Truong), *Le Sens de la République* (Gallimard 2015) 75. In France, Patrick Weil's opinion is exemplary.

[8] On 3 July 2003, French president Jacques Chirac named Bernard Stasi, French ombudsman ('*Médiateur de la République*'), as Head of an ad hoc 'Commission on the Consideration of the Application of the Principle of Laicity Within the Republic' ('*Commission de réflexion sur l'application du principe de laïcité dans la République*'). See Decree no 2003–607 of 3 July 2003 Bearing Creation of a Commission Charged With Conducting a Reflexion on the Application of the Principle of Laicity in the Republic <www.legifrance.gouv.fr/codes/texte_lc/JORFTEXT000000236506/2003-07-04> [on file].

[9] *Conseil d'Etat*, Section of the Interior ('*Section de l'intérieur*') no 346893 (27 November 1989) Advisory Opinion 'Wearing of Islamic Headscarf' ('*Avis "Port du foulard islamique"*') <www.rajf.org/spip.php?article1065> [on file]. I refer to a leading administrative-law journal for a reliable transcript as the *Conseil d'Etat*'s official website does not feature advisory opinions from the 1980s.

[10] Dalloz 1993 J 108, with a note by G Koubi.

[11] Dalloz 1995 J 135, with observations by B Legros.

schools.[12] (No doubt perplexingly from a foreign vantage point, the *Conseil d'Etat* is at once the provider of advice to the state regarding the legality of statutes and France's supreme administrative tribunal in litigation against the state in the guise of one or other of France's numerous public institutions.)

The *Conseil d'Etat*'s various pronouncements were widely criticized in France, especially in conservative circles, for having been unduly accommodating vis-à-vis religious pluralism,[13] hence a conservative president's decision to establish a commission of inquiry (under the leadership of a loyal senior civil servant) and entrust it with the power to make recommendations, which the panel did by advocating for prohibitory legislation.[14] Let me emphasize, then, that notwithstanding a widely circulating local stance holding firm to a contrary view, it is open to the comparatist-at-law, after mobilizing compelling empirical evidence, to ascertain the existence of a sequential link between the pronouncement of liberal institutional statements on Islamic dress at school, the reactive assertion of conservative values at the highest political level, the striking of an impromptu committee, the group's recommendation in favour of an interdicting statute, and the promulgation into force of a law-text precisely to this countermanding effect. Such is the position I (committedly) defend.

*

As the favoured vehicle of long standing to channel state intervention with specific reference to the constitution of citizenship and the promotion of republican ideology, that is, as regards the fabrication of Frenchness, the school occupies 'a preponderant place' in France, so much so that the role of the school within French society is said to

[12] For a thorough and insightful examination of these opinions, see ET Beller, 'The Headscarf Affair: The Conseil d'Etat on the Role of Religion and Culture in French Society' (2004) 39 Texas Int'l LJ 581.

[13] For variously disapproving reactions, see eg J Rivero, 'L'avis de l'Assemblée générale du Conseil d'Etat en date du 27 novembre 1989' (1990) 6 Revue française de droit administratif 1; G Koubi, 'De la laïcité à la liberté de conscience: le port d'un signe d'appartenance religieuse' (1990/3) Petites affiches 6; J Minot, 'A propos de l'affaire du foulard' (1990) 43 Revue administrative 32; J-C William, 'Le Conseil d'état et la laïcité' (1991) 41 Revue française de science politique 28; E Altschull, *Le Voile contre l'école* (Editions du Seuil 1995); D Le Tourneau, 'La laïcité à l'épreuve de l'islam: le cas du port du "foulard islamique" dans l'école publique en France' (1997) 28 Revue générale de droit 275.

[14] In a report submitted on 11 December 2003, the Commission advocated for the enactment of a prohibitory statute on laicity at school. See <www.ladocumentationfrancaise.fr/var/storage/rapports-publics/034000725.pdf> [on file] (hereinafter Stasi Report).

represent 'an unprecedented social fact'.[15] According to the Stasi Commission, '[t]he first venue for the learning of republican values is and must remain the school'.[16] Otherwise put, the republican responsibility of the school is '[t]o teach France' so that at school, 'the nation becomes the framework and the finality of all learning, from history to morality, from botany to the rules of politeness'.[17] Indeed, it is 'a distinctive feature' of the French model that 'the state's interest in instilling culture in its citizens is considered an ever-present party to any conflict over conduct in the public schools. This is no mere civic education in the Anglo-American vein. Rather, in France, the state, not the parent, is seen to have the ultimate responsibility to educate a child.'[18]

Such conception of school education makes the schoolteacher – in French, the '*instituteur*'/'*institutrice*', that is, the person who 'institutes' or 'educates into the institution' – the most important agent of the state in the national acculturation enterprise, itself one of the state's most significant political and epistemological endeavours.[19] As early as 1794, Napoleon established the *Ecole normale supérieure* – one of France's so-called '*grandes écoles*' (literally, 'great schools') – in order that the state could itself train teachers who, as civil servants, would then reliably foster state ideology in state schools.[20] Between 1880 and 1912, four more specialized 'normal schools' ('*écoles normales*') were created (a 'normal school' is meant to distil an institutional model, an institutional norm).

To this day, all schoolteachers graduating from a training school (there are now 'lesser' ones also) are invested with a legal mandate known as a 'mission of public service' ('*mission de service public*'): to educate the French people into republicanism, which must actively entail the reduction of individual difference or singularity to common national experience. In the words of French historian Mona Ozouf, the schoolteacher

[15] M Blanchard and J Cayouette-Remblière, *Sociologie de l'école* (La Découverte 2016) 3 and 11. Making specific reference to France, Cécile Laborde adverts to 'the centrality of education to the republican project': C Laborde, *Critical Republicanism* (Oxford University Press 2008) 49. For a notable historical panorama of the role of the school in France, see E Weber, *Peasants Into Frenchmen* (Stanford University Press 1976) 303–38. See also Laborde (supra) 49–55.

[16] Stasi Report (n 14) 51.

[17] A-M Thiesse, *Faire les Français* (Stock 2010) 70 and 73.

[18] Beller (n 12) 612.

[19] Eg: see Weber (n 15) 303. See generally M Ozouf, *L'Ecole de la France* (Gallimard 1984); J Ozouf and M Ozouf, *La République des instituteurs* (Editions du Seuil 1992); F Mayeur, *Histoire générale de l'enseignement et de l'éducation en France*, vol 3 (Perrin 2004).

[20] See RJ Smith, *The Ecole Normale Superieure and the Third Republic* (SUNY Press 1981).

must 'striv[e] to . . . make [students] alike' (the French word is '*pareils*', a term that connotes identity).[21] Along the way, the state is effectively using the school to disable the edification of any potential critique, to defuse any possible rebellion against its institutional model. It has thus been cogently observed that the schooling process is destined 'to . . . "bastion" the [French] Republic' – that is, to allow for the building of an intellectual fortress protecting the state from attack or assault.[22] The highly prized character of their patriotic duty, joined with their status as civil servants (a valued and respected social role in France), confers on schoolteachers undeniable moral authority within French society. (Perversely, there is arguably an inverse correlation between ascendancy and salary. The fact that the pay is low – below Organization for Economic Co-operation and Development (OECD) average[23] – suggests a vocational streak that translates into moral purchase.) In his 1913 book *L'Argent*, Charles Péguy, the celebrated humanist, called schoolteachers 'black hussars', thus making implicit reference to Hungarian soldiers reputed for their efficacy and devotion, and wrote admiringly that the *Ecole normale supérieure* appeared to be 'an inexhaustible regiment' that was like 'an immense governmental depot of youth and civic-mindedness'.[24]

From the French official standpoint, the goals of the republican pedagogical project, which involves the 'diffus[ion] [of] a corpus of objective knowledge' about the republic[25] – in effect, knowledge *deemed* objective – are 'at once emancipatory and regulatory'.[26] While students must obviously be supplied with the tools destined to ensure the acquisition of a degree of intellectual autonomy, they also find themselves, paradoxically, as having their individuality disciplined into unconditional obedience to the nation-state – the mainstream (and counter-intuitive) French idea being that this process is to be apprehended as unfettering: 'The school liberates through closing and through

[21] M Ozouf, *Composition française* (Gallimard 2009) 105.

[22] J-F Chanet et al, 'Comment faire des Français?' in A de Baecque and P Deville (eds), *Mona Ozouf* (Flammarion 2019) 182. The words are Jean-François Chanet's.

[23] See Organization for Economic Co-operation and Development, *Education at a Glance 2020* (2021) 388 <https://read.oecd-ilibrary.org/education/education-at-a-glance-2020_69096873-en#page390> and 391 <https://read.oecd-ilibrary.org/education/education-at-a-glance-2020_69096873-en#page393>.

[24] C Péguy, *L'Argent* (Gallimard 1932 [1913]) 26.

[25] C Laborde, 'On Republican Toleration' (2002) 9 Constellations 167, 170.

[26] J Surkis, *Sexing the Citizen: Morality and Masculinity in France, 1870–1920* (Cornell University Press 2006) 18.

regulating.'[27] In other words, the governing assumption is that through school, students are mercifully freed from whatever differential or singular circumstances – 'vaguely felt as evil'[28] – that might otherwise have affected the moulding of their educated selves into republican values. Meanwhile, they are corralled into a space of edification opened for them by the state on the state's own terms, with a view to becoming, in principle, within the public sphere at least, but reflective surfaces mirroring state ideology.

Intervening as comparatist-at-law, I claim that any deconstruction of the 2004 law-text – in particular, any re-signification orchestrated from a comparative angle – must be conducted in the light of two critical paramount observations. First, French republicanism is 'singularly ill-suited to look positively on contemporary demands for the recognition of cultural and religious differences in the public sphere'.[29] Consider the eminent politist Philippe Raynaud, who maintains that the 2004 legislative ban is 'an interdiction that is founded on the necessity to protect children or teenagers from a propaganda or a proselytism incompatible with the serenity of a public education'.[30] Even allowing for the deep-seated enculturation within which (and through which) Raynaud exists in the French world – in France, laicity incontestably pertains to the realm of culture[31] – it appears unduly expedient for this commentator to cancel religious identity, to reject 'a continuity between the interiority and the exteriority of the person',[32] and to proceed to do so in the name of 'serenity', as if religious allegiance and tranquillity were irrevocably antithetical values that could not countenance any form of conciliation whatsoever. Be that as it may, Raynaud's sub-text could hardly be clearer: the classroom must uniformly look the way classrooms used uniformly to look in the joyous era of '*la douce France*' (think Charles Trenet in 1947).

27 C Kintzler, *La République en questions* (Minerve 1996) 72.

28 V Descombes, *Le Même et l'autre* (Editions de Minuit 1979) 16.

29 Laborde (n 15) 4. Laborde, a French politist who initially trained in France, readily acknowledges that her critique of the French model only became possible on the basis of 'the Anglo-American liberal philosophy [she] became acquainted with in the rigorous and inspiring atmosphere of British universities': ibid v.

30 P Raynaud, *La Laïcité* (Gallimard 2019) 201. See also P Cabanel, 'Le principe de laïcité à l'école' in R Letteron (ed), *La Laïcité dans la tourmente* (Sorbonne Université Presses 2019) 172.

31 See M Miaille, *La Laïcité* (3rd edn, Dalloz 2016) 309–11.

32 P Mazet, 'La construction contemporaine de la laïcité par le juge et la doctrine' in J Baudouin and P Portier (eds), *La Laïcité, une valeur d'aujourd'hui?* (Presses Universitaires de Rennes 2001) 278.

Secondly, because '[t]he French educational system . . . is very strongly centralized',[33] since the school is apprehended as 'an enterprise of civic integration',[34] and given France's normative 'refus[al] to recognize cultural diversity within the public space',[35] French students are reputed legally entitled to be spared any meeting at school with a headscarf-clad female classmate (or, much less plausibly, with a male fellow wearing a turban or kippah), the French state's correlative duty being to shield French students from any such aggravation. Public discourse thus leaves no room whatsoever for anything other than 'the [French] concept of privatized religious practices and the code of non-conspicuous dress . . . as universally acceptable expressions of modern life and . . . [a] narrative of the world within which [France] is anchored as the firm, normative center'.[36] Indeed, '[French] citizenship is conceived as an indivisible whole the legitimacy of which expresses itself in a direct relationship of the citizen with the state',[37] which entails that the state 'refuses any kind of official recognition of minorities as such, where individuals are identified with a minority group . . . for the purposes of state action (whether redistributive or affirmative)'.[38] On account of France's 'apocalyptic crusaders',[39] even the idea of 'tolerance for

[33] Blanchard and Cayouette-Remblière (n 15) 63.

[34] B Nabli, *La République identitaire* (Editions du Cerf 2016) 28.

[35] D Schnapper, *La République aux 100 cultures* (Arfuyen 2016) 83.

[36] G Frankenberg, *Comparative Law as Critique* (Elgar 2016) 143. I substitute 'French' and 'France' for 'Western' and 'the West'. As it expresses itself within a comparative framework, Günter Frankenberg's critique is an apt reminder that there have been a number of noteworthy comparative discussions embracing the French statute. Eg: JW Scott, *Sex and Secularism* (Princeton University Press 2018)[hereinafter *Sex and Secularism*]; ES Hurd, *Beyond Religious Freedom* (Princeton University Press 2015); AC Korteweg and G Yurdakul, *The Headscarf Debates* (Stanford University Press 2014); JW Scott, *The Politics of the Veil* (Princeton University Press 2007); JR Bowen, *Why the French Don't Like Headscarves* (Princeton University Press 2007).

[37] Schnapper (n 35) 10. Recall that the Constitution expressly proclaims the French republic to be 'indivisible' ('*indivisible*'): <www.legifrance.gouv.fr/loda/id/JORFTEXT000000571356/> art 1.

[38] A Favell, *Philosophies of Integration* (2nd edn, Palgrave 2001) 71. Adde: P Legendre, *Jouir du pouvoir* (Editions de Minuit 1976) 70: 'Nothing is . . . more foreign to [French] nationalism than a non-unitary world tolerating particularisms.' Both the *Conseil d'Etat* and the *Conseil constitutionnel*, the body entrusted with the task of constitutional review, have stated repeatedly that group or collective rights are incompatible with the French constitution. Eg: *Conseil d'Etat* (30 October 2001) *Syndicat national des enseignements du second degré (SNES)* <www.rajf.org/spip.php?article465xxx> [on file]; *Conseil constitutionnel* no 99–412 (15 June 1999) *Charte européenne des langues régionales ou minoritaires* <www.conseil-constitutionnel.fr/decision/1999/99412DC.htm> [on file]; *Conseil constitutionnel* no 91–290 (9 May 1991) *Loi portant statut de la collectivité territoriale de Corse* <www.conseil-constitutionnel.fr/decision/1991/91290DC.htm> [on file].

[39] Frankenberg (n 36) 145 [capitals omitted].

veiling' gets no traction at all.[40] Nor does a fortiori the argument favouring 'a woman's right to culture'.[41] Quite to the contrary, the French attitude 'deepens the polarity between self and other'.[42]

Because of French republicanism's hermetism in response to the stipulations of pluralism and its dogmatism in the extolment of monism, the comparative perspective – the comparative advantage – makes it possible, significantly, for an interpreter who is evaluating the French project from a critical (and multicultural and colonized) distance to contend that '[t]he ban on the hijab in schools ... cannot be defended on any of the main grounds presented by official republicans'.[43] Even as the French state's position assumes that the public space, otherwise known as the 'republican space',[44] must remain the state's exclusive preserve so that it can occupy the entire ideological terrain and thus convey its republican message without any competition from an intellectual and spiritual counter-power such as Islam,[45] the comparatist is well placed to maintain that 'the demand that Muslism schoolgirls take off their headscarf is, in almost all contexts, wrong'.[46] (While I am pleased to quote Cécile Laborde, a shrewd analyst of French republicanism, I find the word 'wrong' to be problematically absolutistic, and I would rather encourage the deployment of more relativistic terms such as 'exaggerated' or 'excessive'.) From a comparative slant, the French state's determination not to allow its political postulates to be questioned out of an allegedly unimpeachable concern for the constitutional precept of 'equality' ('*égalité*') deserves critical scrutiny.

At this juncture, I find it important to insist that comparative analysis must not withhold critique on the ground that comparatism ought somehow to be confined to a strictly descriptive remit. Even leaving to one side

40 ibid 147.

41 See LL Veazey, *A Woman's Right to Culture* (Quid Pro Books 2015) 31–44, where the author discusses specifically French legislation on religious symbols. Linda Veazey castigates '[French] law's disproportionate impact on the symbols and dress of Muslim women' and observes that 'Muslim women's right to express their identity ... through dress was curtailed in a manner which would [not] impact ... Muslim men': ibid 44.

42 Frankenberg (n 36) 148.

43 Laborde (n 15) 14. Observe that even a foreigner who has lived and worked in France for many years can operate at a distance.

44 Weil (n 7) 110.

45 Eg: Chanet et al (n 22) 195, where reference is made to 'the public space, that is to say, in France, the space of the state'. The words are Pierre Birnbaum's.

46 Laborde (n 15) 14. The reservation addresses Turkey, 'where the wearing of hijab has been widely interpreted as the powerful and visible symbol of an Islamist onslaught on the secular republic': ibid 265n56. For a critique such as I invite in the body text by a prominent comparatist-at-law, see Frankenberg (n 36) 117–64.

the fact that a 'strictly descriptive' enterprise pertains to the realm of fiction, I cannot discern any persuasive argument why the comparatist-at-law should censor himself and avoid, say, a reprobatory response to foreignness as long, of course, as he manages to bring to bear a charitable interpretive disposition towards foreign law, that is, recognize and respect the fact that there is a rationality at work within foreignness rather than the unfolding of some sort of mental disorder. Also, I repeat that it is key for the comparatist-at-law to keep his enculturation on a tight epistemic leash.

*

What Günter Frankenberg has termed a programme 'geared toward conquering the covered woman and unveiling her in the public sphere' has been exacerbated by the fact that the French state has somehow appropriated gender equality as a republican value so that the wearing of a headscarf at school has come to be seen not only as an intolerable religious indicator, but also as an unacceptable sign of female oppression – such conclusion apparently not being influenced by the fact that, amongst French women declaring themselves to be Muslim, as many as thirty-five per cent say they wear either the hijab or the niqab.[47] Along the way, there appears to have been but the scantiest appreciation for the complexity of the processes of identity construction that Muslim women bring to bear on their sartorial decisions.[48] Consider anthropologist Talal Asad's observations regarding the work of the Stasi Commission:

[47] See J Fourquet, *L'Archipel français* (Editions du Seuil 2019) 164. The figure I mention is from 2016. Jérôme Fourquet indicates that it was twenty-four per cent in 2003: see ibid. My quotation is from Frankenberg (n 36) 150.

[48] This lack of understanding is hard to separate from the fact that the Stasi Commission heard only two young hijab-wearing women and did so late in the course of its proceedings, that is, on the occasion of the very last day of auditions. See M Belbah and C de Galembert, 'Dialogue avec l'absentionniste de la Commission Stasi: entretien avec Jean Baubérot' (2008/68) Droit et société 237, 246. A member of the twenty-strong Stasi Commission, Baubérot was alone in not voting for the report; he abstained. The widely held view in France that Islam, and Islamic dress in particular, systematically effectuates the patriarchal oppression of women is deftly rebutted in E Bucar, *Pious Fashion* (Harvard University Press 2017), where the author, deconstructing simplistic stigmatization, persuasively illustrates how, rather than express servile obedience to religious orthodoxy, the clothing worn by Muslim women engages with a range of aesthetic values as it displays local commitments to social distinction and self-empowerment. For different studies asserting the variety of re-signification processes at work and the ensuing intricacy of identitarian issues, see eg L Abu-Lughod, *Do Muslim Women Need Saving?* (Harvard University Press 2013); A Al-Saji, 'The Racialization of Muslim Veils: A Philosophical Analysis' (2010) 36 Philosophy & Social Criticism 875, 892–93; L Abu-Odeh, 'Post-colonial Feminism and the Veil: Considering the Differences' (1992) 26 New England LR 1527, 1535–36; H Adelman, 'Rights and the *Hijâb*: Rationality and Discourse in the

> [S]olicitude for the 'real' desires of the pupils applied only to girls who wore the headscarf. No thought appears to have been given to determining the 'real' desires of girls who did *not* wear it. It is conceivable that some of them secretly wanted to wear a headscarf but were inhibited from doing so because of what their non-Muslim French peers and people in the street might think or say. Or that unconsciously they simply desired to be 'modern'. Appearance alone was sufficient for the Commission: the absence of a headscarf worn in public means the person concerned has no desire to wear it. 'Desire' – the root of agency – is not definitively discovered, but semiotically constructed.[49]

Meanwhile, 'the explosive concoction of feminist or secularist liberation fantasies combined with a republican modernization agenda and an [I]slamophobic imaginary, which radicalizes the colonial obsession with unveiling, uncovering and unmasking',[50] has prompted both the deepening of laic interventions at school and their expansion beyond the public sphere. Specifically, a fifteen-year-old female Muslim student was denied access to her public secondary school on two occasions on account of the fact that she wore a black skirt deemed to qualify as 'ostensible' religious dress because of its length.[51] And, in the *Baby Loup* case decided in June 2014, the French *Cour de cassation* upheld the dismissal of a private day-care centre's female assistant director who had been employed for over ten years. The sanction for 'grave fault' ('*faute grave*') arose because the employee had insisted on wearing a headscarf at work on account of her religious

Public Sphere' (2008) 8 Human Rights & Human Welfare 43, 48; AK Wing and MN Smith, 'Critical Race Feminism Lifts the Veil?: Muslim Women, France, and the Headscarf Ban' (2006) 39 UC Davis LR 743, 757–71; M Zalnieriute and C Weiss, 'Reconceptualizing Intersectionality in Judicial Interpretation: Moving Beyond Formalistic Accounts of Discrimination on Islamic Covering Prohibitions' (2020) 35 Berkeley J Gender, L & Justice 71; C Killian, 'From a Community of Believers to an Islam of the Heart: "Conspicuous" Symbols, Muslim Practices, and the Privatization of Religion in France' (2007) 68 Sociology of Religion 305, 312–15; R Kapur, *Gender, Alterity and Human Rights* (Elgar 2018) 120–50; N Cox, *Behind the Veil* (Elgar 2019) 188–202.

49 T Asad, *Secular Translations* (Columbia University Press 2018) 53.

50 Frankenberg (n 36) 148.

51 See C Chambraud and S Graveleau, 'Crispation à l'école sur les jupes longues' *Le Monde* (30 April 2015) 8. For further reports, see eg A Hardy, 'Jupe longue au collège: le vrai du faux' *Journal du dimanche* (30 April 2015) <www.lejdd.fr/Societe/Religion/Jupe-longue-au-college-ce-qu-il-s-est-vraiment-passe-730316> [on file]; AJ Rubin, 'French School Deems Teenager's Skirt an Illegal Display of Religion' *The New York Times* (29 April 2015) <www.nytimes.com/2015/04/30/world/europe/french-school-teenagers-skirt-illegal-display-religion.html> [on file].

convictions.[52] Already, in 2010, a statute had been enacted prohibiting face covering in public.[53] And in April 2021, pronouncing on further law reform, the Senate (the French parliament's upper-house) voted to prohibit parents volunteering to accompany students during school excursions from wearing 'ostensibl[e]' religious attire (effectively targeting Muslim mothers); allowing public swimming pools to ban the 'burkini'; and prohibiting minors from wearing 'ostensibl[e]' religious attire anywhere in the public sphere.[54] In a searing autobiography, Kaoutar Harchi, a young Muslim female sociologist and writer, expressing both anger and fear, unsurprisingly exclaims how French Muslim women feel 'in their deepest [selves]' that there is a 'war [from] within' being waged against them and how they experience being 'publicly targeted'.[55]

As 'the denial of free will on the part of women and girls wearing modest dress' proceeds apace in France,[56] as the governance strategy on display continues to implement a rule-based (or nomothetic) approach rather than allow for facticity (or idiographics) to carry any normative value,[57] as '*faith in the state*' eschews any serious reconsideration of

[52] For an extensive examination of the decision, see S Hennette-Vauchez and V Valentin, *L'Affaire Baby Loup ou la nouvelle laïcité* (LGDJ 2014). The expression '*nouvelle laïcité*' ('New Laicity') purports to capture the semantic and ideological enlargement of laicity to the sphere of private relations that *Baby Loup* illustrates.

[53] Statute no 2010–1192 of 11 October 2010 Prohibiting the Concealment of One's Face in the Public Space <www.legifrance.gouv.fr/loda/id/JORFTEXT000022911670> art 1 [on file]. I find it noteworthy that, making specific reference to this law-text, one of France's foremost writers – admittedly a particularly well-travelled one – castigates 'the drifts of this provincialism': JMG Le Clézio, *Quinze causeries* (Gallimard 2019) 46. For thoughtful observations, see G Baldi, '"Burqa's Avenger": Law and Religious Practices in Secular Space' (2018) 29 Law & Critique 31.

[54] The vote concerned Statute no 2021-1109 of 24 August 2021 Reinforcing Respect for the Principles of the Republic <www.legifrance.gouv.fr/loda/id/JORFTEXT000043964778/>. See <https://www.assemblee-nationale.fr/dyn/15/textes/l15b4078_projet-loi#>. The Senate's amendments ultimately did not make their way into the statute. I address the matter of the 'burkini' supra 239.

[55] K Harchi, *Comme nous existons* (Actes Sud 2021) 105, 105, and 107.

[56] Frankenberg (n 36) 146.

[57] By way of contrast, English law typically operates idiographically rather than nomothetically. In *R (SB) v Governors of Denbigh High School* [2007] 1 AC 100 (HL), a female student wanted to wear a full Islamic dress (or *jilbab*), which was inconsistent with the school's uniform policy in a context where the uniform had been designed to take into account Muslim beliefs given that eighty per cent or so of the students were Muslims. Lord Bingham, delivering the main opinion of the House of Lords, emphasized how '[i]t is important to stress at the outset that this case concerns a particular pupil and a particular school in a particular place at a particular time': ibid 107. (Quaere: how much more idiographic can a judgment get?) He added: 'It would in my opinion be

France's political project (the terrorist attacks that took place in Paris in January and November 2015 and in Nice in July 2016 having only served to reinforce reliance on the state),[58] there emerges a key line of interpellation (although it appears to be anything but compelling in the eyes of French analysts), which political theorist Wendy Brown expresses in terms that deserve quotation:

> If successful [occidental] women are not free to veil, are not free to dress like men or boys, are not free to wear whatever they choose on any occasion without severe economic or social consequences, then what sleight of hand recasts their condition as freedom and individuality contrasted with hypostasized tyranny and lack of agency?[59]

Brown adds: 'What makes choices "freer" when they are constrained by secular and market organizations of femininity and fashion rather than by state or religious law?'[60] She further observes: 'To acknowledge that we have our own form of compulsory feminine dress would undercut this identity of superiority: we *need* fundamentalism, indeed, we project and produce it elsewhere, to represent ourselves as free.'[61]

Or, one might say, occidentals require to produce desexualization elsewhere in order to uphold sexuality as an acceptable identity marker

irresponsible for any court, lacking the experience, background and detailed knowledge of the head teacher, staff and governors, to overrule their judgment on a matter as sensitive as this': ibid 117. Lord Hoffmann agreed: 'These are matters which the school itself was in the best position to weigh and consider': ibid 125. To return to the French framework, it features seemingly inevitable complexity. In the course of three fieldwork studies, Christophe Bertossi thus shows how even in such highly institutionalized spheres as those of the army and the hospital, French official public discourse has adapted its response to pragmatic imperatives. See C Bertossi, *La Citoyenneté à la française* (CNRS Editions 2015) passim.

58 P Legendre, *Fantômes de l'Etat en France* (Fayard 2015) 219. Pierre Legendre also refers to 'the ingrained belief that *French laicity* be, in principle, a *universal democratic panacea*': ibid 212. In this regard, it bears mentioning public intellectual Régis Debray's view that a French citizen can be proud that his country has been able to 'concretize a regulatory idea of universal value': R Debray and D Leschi, *La Laïcité au quotidien* (Gallimard 2016) 150. In advance of empirical study, anyone who has lived in France over the last twenty years or so can easily confirm how such pride is widely held within the French citizenry irrespective of its factual merit (the French approach *evidently* has no claim whatsoever to universalism). Incidentally, Debray and Leschi purport to offer a guide-book explaining the practical resolution to various conflicts arising on a daily basis on account of the upholding of laicity in France. For another such 'instruction manual', see J Baubérot, *Petit manuel pour une laïcité apaisée* (La Découverte 2016).

59 W Brown, *Regulating Aversion* (Princeton University Press 2006) 189. I substitute 'occidental' for 'American'.

60 ibid.

61 ibid.

for themselves. Joan Scott, the distinguished historian of France, thus holds that the free expression of sexual desire whereby, absent religious constraints on her attire, the Muslim woman would now become a self-conscious sexual agent, effectively secures her (occidental) subordination to man since sexual emancipation – or the liberation of the sex drive – proceeds to perpetuate the sexualization of women in a way that benefits males. The gender asymmetry and inequality that the Muslim woman would be escaping is therefore preserved, if in another guise.[62] To enunciate this claim more concretely still, in a country like France the non-Muslim majority must brand Islamic dresswear for women as fundamentalist so that, meanwhile, by contrast, it can re-signify its deeply sexualized dress code for women (featuring skin-bearing and shapely clothes) as other than an imposition – as, indeed, a freedom for women to reveal their body advantageously. In effect, then, the ascription of fundamentalism is anything but disinterested as it provides the (male) majority with an alibi allowing it to recast its views on female clothing in the public arena as other than constraining.

In addition to these questions and observations, one can legitimately wonder whether the idea of Frenchness as it currently stands – an 'arrogative republicanism' partaking of a heady absolutist heritage of uncompromising centralization and of the myths of Revolutionary citizenship and laicity,[63] 'insist[ing] heavily on an adhesion to exalted political values',[64] and prompting a correlative disavowal of the empirical fact of French society's heterogeneity – is having significantly more impact than fostering the ever-greater embitterment of the exasperated 'non-citizens' of the *banlieues*. An astute politist like Laborde has contributed a perspicuous critique regarding 'the risks of state oppression involved in the imposition of a conception of the good life as self-determination or autonomy' and has flatly decried '[French] republican paternalism' as 'fail[ing] to respect the agency of those women it claims to emancipate in the name of an elitist, decontextualized and imperialist conception of individual autonomy'.[65] Historian Laurence De Cock's view is convergent: 'A tendency is asserting itself more and more in the school: to

62 See Scott, *Sex and Secularism* (n 36) passim.

63 F Khosrokhavar, 'Le djihad et l'exception française' *The New York Times* (19 July 2016) <www.nytimes.com/2016/07/19/opinion/le-djihad-et-lexception-francaise.html> [on file].

64 ibid.

65 Laborde (n 15) 101, 147, and 147. For Laborde's full critique of the idea of liberty with specific reference to 'female agency', see ibid 101–48.

transform laicity into a repressive tool.'[66] For her part, Falguni Sheth maintains that the transparency being legally implemented is 'a demand for "unfamiliar" strangers to present themselves as familiar, or at least, as unthreatening to the dominant, homogenous population – not merely through sincerity and collegiality, but through submission and obedience'.[67] According to Sheth, '[t]he cooperative Muslim female subject must illuminate herself as having crossed over to the 'light side': the side of illumination, enlightenment . . . . Only when she can illustrate her crossover via her appearing transparent, can she be recognized as having been truly liberated – in short, a good female, mildly feminist, liberal subject.'[68]

*

The French defence of the 2004 statute goes to remarkable lengths. For instance, a member of the Stasi Commission claims how '[i]t is not absurd to think that most Muslim families were relieved' on account of the enactment of the 2004 statutory prohibition.[69] Moreover, there is the view pertaining to France's *mission civilisatrice* that France's destiny is to teach others. Not only, then, is the French law-text to stand as 'an example' for Europe,[70] but it is rhapsodized as a 'very attractive' scheme 'worldwide'.[71] It is, in fact, claimed to be the legal arrangement 'of the future'.[72] Needless to say, there appears to be little French realization that, even as laicity continues to be promoted as a central element of the national republican programme of fully fledged cultural assimilation, 'French society . . . is . . . disintegrating under the pressures of globalization and cultural pluralism' so that 'immigrants (and their children) [a]re asked to bear the burden of keeping alive an ideal of Frenchness on behalf of an insecure French . . . fearful of losing [their] national identity'.[73] Unsurprisingly, it is very hard to discern the slightest French political space for the implementation of a 'politics of non-domination' – a 'negative politics of non-domination' – that would

66 L De Cock, *Ecole publique et émancipation sociale* (Agone 2021) 172.

67 FA Sheth, 'The Veil, Transparency, and the Deceptive Conceit of Liberalism' (2019) 9 philoSOPHIA 53, 53.

68 ibid 67.

69 Weil (n 7) 81. Is it unfair to discern in this enunciation (which fails to draw on any factual support) a characteristic illustration of self-projection so that Weil's statement would effectively stand as an expression of Weil's own relief?

70 Raynaud (n 30) 226.

71 Weil (n 7) 118.

72 ibid.

73 Laborde (n 15) 227.

accept the headscarf in schools with a view to removing obstacles to civic participation, to membership in the citizenry through 'the normalization and mainstreaming of Franco-Muslim identity'.[74]

*

What have I done?

Ever since I engaged with law, my most constant interest has concerned the foreign. In terms of my scholarly commitments, nothing remains as absorbing and yet as incomprehensible to me, at once so very near and so distant, as foreign law. Assiduously, I devote myself to the texts of the other-in-the-law, and I attempt to respond (not react) to their singularity, their idiom, as they precede me. I try to do justice to the other-in-the-law and the other law even as I force foreign law-texts into a negotiation with my counter-words, with my counter-signature. But I can only proceed responsibly – ethically – by bringing to bear my 'own' singularity. Of course, what I style my 'own' singularity has very much to do with the socialization and institutionalization patterns – the enculturation (not least the epistemologization) – into which I was thrown or, later, allowed myself to be thrown. Since I read, interpret, and understand singularly, I read, interpret, and understand differently – which means that my reading, my interpretation, and my understanding, no matter how intrinsically worthy, are fated to stand at some variance both from the foreign law-text and from other readings, interpretations, and understandings of the foreign law-text. I have come to terms with the structural, empirical fact of this non-coincidence, of this contretemps. Specifically, I have accepted that my reading, my interpretation, and my understanding must be out of joint vis-à-vis foreignness.[75] Also, I have deferred to the fact that since I can neither claim objectivity nor truth, my work is doomed to the production of indeterminacy – my readership having to assess, in its own encultured ways, whether my proposed indeterminacy is more convincing than the other indeterminacies on offer. (I can easily imagine that a German jurist will approach the matter of my argument's persuasiveness differently from, say, an Australian reader.) In sum, I came to the 2004 French statute with keen curiosity and genuine enthusiasm even as I felt the need for epistemic humility and interpretive realism. While positivism features a dearth of positionality (the positivist is not an observer of the

[74] ibid 230, 252, and 252.

[75] For an opportune exploration of the motif of disjointedness, see J Derrida, *Spectres de Marx* (Galilée 1993) passim.

positivist-as-interpreter and even less an observer of the positivist observing the positivist-as-interpreter), I have consistently sought to maintain an aculeate disposition in order to obviate situational ignorance – an epistemic predicament liable to delude me into thinking that I had been engaging in veridiction.

Along the comparative way, I could not escape the perpetration of two salient acts of epistemic violence on the French statute. First, I had to ascribe meaning to the foreign law-text (note that I ascribed meaning *to* the text, because meaning is not to be found *in* the text). Otherwise said, I had to make sense of the text – I had to *make* sense (*I* had to make sense). Secondly, I had to effect closure. Accordingly, I enforced a limit on a process (reading/interpretation/understanding) that could have continued endlessly for foreign law is unsaturable (there is simply no paraphrase able adequately to convey the entire semantic extension of the words that it is rewording). To be sure, the self-declaration that my treatment of the other's law must come to a halt at a given stage cannot dispense with a certain arbitrariness. And my decision to interrupt my investigation at a certain point rather than another features consequences as I must acknowledge, for instance, that various aspects of the foreign law-text's will therefore remain hidden from me, that the other's law will thus keep a secret from me.[76] There simply cannot be an interpretation,

[76] cf J Derrida, *Schibboleth* (Galilée 1986) 50: '[T]here is a secret there, in the background, forever shielded from hermeneutic exhaustion.' For his part, Edouard Glissant writes that there is not only a right to difference, but moreover a 'right to opacity', which is 'not imprisonment in an autarky impenetrable, but subsistence in a singularity non-reducible': E Glissant, *Poétique de la relation* (Gallimard 1990) 204. According to Jacques Derrida, the opacity – what he styles the secret, which etymologically means 'separation, dissociation' – qualifying the possibility of full transparency raises, of course, '[t]he risk of a misunderstanding': J Derrida, *Papier machine* (Galilée 2001) 398 and 306. However, Derrida observes that if a text was so clear as to be immediately fully understandable, there would be no room left for the interpreter to intervene, to inscribe his own signature. The negotiation that varied interpretations make possible, and indeed encourage, affords an occasion for a refinement of one's views and one's understanding, that is, for an enhancement of one's appreciation of otherness. Ultimately, the fact that there is more than one interpretation in co-presence makes every interpreter into a sharper analyst. Consider the opportunity that the text offers the interpreter to express himself as a matter of hospitality: the text makes itself hospitable to the interpreter's reading and the interpreter's writing (or voice). See J Derrida and M Ferraris, *Le Goût du secret* (A Bellantone and A Cohen eds, Hermann 2018 [1994]) 38–39. The passage is Derrida's. Christine Elgin thus remarks on '[t]he value of disagreement for a community of inquiry': CZ Elgin, *True Enough* (MIT Press 2017) 117. This idea is already in Baudelaire. See [C] Baudelaire, 'Mon cœur mis à nu' in *Journaux intimes* in *Œuvres complètes*, vol 1 (C Pichois ed, Gallimard 1975 [1887†]) s 42, 704: 'The world works only through Misunderstanding.' cf S Beckett, *The Unnamable* (S Connor ed, Faber

no matter how inventive or playful, how audacious or complicated, no matter how *prying*, that would do justice to the full meaning of foreign law. As I proceeded indisciplinedly to investigate the French statute, I found myself constantly oscillating between a 'tightening' of the law-text's semantic extension so as to render interpretation more secure, with the attendant danger of a correlative stultification of otherness, and a 'loosening' strategy with a view to enhancing the expression of otherness in exchange for more indeterminacy regarding imputation of meaning. I maintain that an absolute choice in this regard is absolutely impossible: there is at once an unresolved and unresolvable tension. Yet, I felicitously escaped the stasis that would characterize mimesis, if such were to be the comparatist-at-law's epistemological remit. Instead, there being no 'given' that is not a culturally constituted textuality that I constitute anew out of my enculturation, I had to contend with the epistemic risks attendant upon interpretive creativity and the demands of interpretive responsibility.

What, then, have I done?

Eschewing any pretence at mere description in favour of a resolutely opinionated, assertive, and critical stance – which is not to deny that even the most descriptively descriptive description also constitutes a form of critique – I have sought to bring to bear a genuine comparative perspective on what remains for me foreign law. (Even as I appreciate that, strictly speaking, 'foreign law' cannot exist for me, I have acted as if it can.) And I have painstakingly documented my argument. Was I thinking of Vladimir Nabokov, who liked 'footnotes reaching up like skyscrapers to the top of this or that page so as to leave only the gleam of one textual line'?[77] At any rate, I left the law library for the main library more than once.

I have read much more than appears from these few pages. But I have been very selective as I retained some arguments (say, a qualitative claim like the social status of the teacher) and not others (for instance, quantitative information regarding how many teachers there are in France). Likewise, I elected to refer to certain authors and publications rather than others. What influenced my countless decisions to read these monographs and not others or these articles and not others? Primarily, I have

& Faber 2010 [1958]) 37: 'Dear incomprehension, it's thanks to you I'll be myself, in the end.' I advocate for a *principled* misunderstanding – that is, an acknowledgement that misunderstanding exists within comparative law as a matter of principle and that this is a good thing, too.

77 V Nabokov, 'Problems of Translation: "Onegin" in English' (1955) 22 Partisan R 496, 522.

been swayed by the substantive contentions I had come to associate with particular writers (most often through further readings) and by the way in which I thought these reasons provided insights that I found more pertinent than others, that supported my own interpretations or inflected them in ways I thought incisive. I know I also considered the author's credentials, say, his institutional affiliation or his publisher's academic standing (being well aware, however, that such indicia of authoritativeness need to be addressed with great prudence). I then proceeded to identify some passages, whether very brief or longer, that I wanted to partake of my text as quotations. And I arranged to weave those excerpts into my narrative with a view to optimal seamlessness (occasionally deciding not to keep a quotation after all or perhaps truncate it).

Along the way, I set both a tenor and a tone, a course of thought and an accent. My decision to mobilize Frankenberg and Laborde, for example, to refer to their work and quote from their publications at some length, bolstered what I had decided would be the interpretive inclination of my vignette. (To be sure, when I write that 'I had decided' to follow a certain line of interpretation, I refer – let me repeat – to an encultured 'I', a socialized, institutionalized, and epistemologized 'I'.) And my decision to write, say, that a certain contention 'fails to draw on any factual support' – words that I could have omitted – indicates my attempt to invite my reader not to subscribe to the view being defended.

The elections I made about the materials, quotations, and wording that I sought to bring into *play* are literally innumerable.[78] (These choices include the key decision to refer to texts in French, which I have sought to translate other-wise on what I hope are just terms even as I know that some words are untranslatable or, to write it like Celan, '*unübertragbar*' – literally, 'un-carry-over-able'.[79] Of course, my translations are neither objective nor true in the sense in which they would be the unique, uniquely fixed, uniquely stable, and uniquely acknowledged translations of the French texts. In fact, objectivity or truth is as inapplicable to translation as would be the words 'serene' or 'kind' by reference to a carpet or cucumber. In other terms, the search for objectivity or truth is the pursuit of an imaginary goal thoroughly exogenous to the translative inquiry.)

[78] Play is a salient and serious motif within comparative law. It '*includes* the work of meaning': J Derrida, *L'Ecriture et la différence* (Editions du Seuil 1967) 382. For a detailed consideration, see P Legrand, 'Jameses at Play: A Tractation on the Comparison of Laws' (2017) 65 Am J Comp L [Special Issue] 1, 110–20.

[79] P Celan, *Der Meridian* (B Böschenstein and H Schmull eds, Suhrkamp 1999 [1960]) 75, 145, and 158.

Note that the integration between the translator's self and the source-text runs deeper than co-extension, which assumes separability, measurability, divisibility, or identifiability. It is not that selfhood and texthood parallel or succeed each other, but that they tessellate each other, that they mingle to the point of indissociability. Otherwise said, the translator proceeds to a selfing of the source-text (and of the host-language). The translating self textualizes itself: it inscribes itself – it writes itself – into the source-text (or into the host-language), it marks the text (or the language) so that a translation is ultimately resolvable as a quest for the expressive self.

Throughout the very many drafts in the course of which I constructed an argument deconstructing the statutory word 'schools' ('*les écoles, les collèges et les lycées publics*'), I pursued one goal only: as a comparatist, I wanted to offer a persuasive interpretation of the 2004 French statute with specific reference to the meaning of the law-text. In the absence of any textual 'is-ness', I could not tell the text as it is. At best, I could tell it as I honestly interpreted it without, needless to add, transgressing it.[80] To be sure, I started from the statute, therefore not at all ignoring the posited law. But I was unwilling to be content with textuality's graphical surface. Within a text, presence is not graphical only. It is more complex, and it comprises enciphering. In this regard, it did not matter to me that the statute does not expressly say 'given that pre-university public educational institutions are the primordial vector of republican values'. Crucially, as the interpreter includes the traces lurking between the statute's lines, encrypted in the text's fabric, he is still operating *sub specie scripturarum*.

Out of the many epistemic assumptions I deployed, two deserve emphasis. First, basing myself on the fact that normality – *especially* normality – is culturally freighted (public educational institutions instantiate normality in France), I implemented the view that the construct 'French legal culture' makes sense in the light of my research topic. Of course, the contours of the 'unit' will vary according to the comparative intervention at stake. In other terms, the location of culture depends on the specific question of concern to the comparatist-at-law. For example, the legal culture at issue might be that of Corsica, of commercial courts in France, or of the fishery in Marseille.[81] In each case, the scales of the comparison

[80] cf J Derrida, 'Fidélité à plus d'un' (1998/13) Cahiers Intersignes 221, 262, where Derrida refers to 'the law of the other text, . . . its injunction, . . . its signature'.

[81] For a detailed investigation of the fishery in Marseille, see F Grisel, *The Limits of Private Governance: Norms and Rules in a Mediterranean Fishery* (Hart 2021). Adde: F Grisel, 'How Migrations Affect Private Orders: Norms and Practices in the Fishery of Marseille' (2021) 55 L & Society R 177.

will influence what will count as data or hold as interpretive material. But the 'unit' can also be – and will often be – coterminous with French lawyers as a whole, that is, with the group of legal agents who, if you will, are French citizens (in other words, to write rapidly, who are 'French') or who practice law in France – although even notions like citizenship or practice can hardly claim impermeable intellectual borders and are not to be envisaged as totalizing structural formations.

French legal culture exists, then, as does French cheese. And this is the case even as one can easily imagine circumstances pursuant to which one will want the unit to be more precise so that one addresses *chèvres* or, more specifically still, *chèvres au lait cru*. But it remains easy to imagine that in given situations it shall make sense to address French cheese *tout court* – as distinguished from, say, Italian, Dutch, or English cheese. To return to law, the decision by a comparatist-at-law to emphasize one specific manifestation of culture only (say, the transmission of republican values through 'schools') cannot be taken as denying the legitimacy of cultural analysis.[82] Any research endeavour must ultimately contend, no matter how sorrowfully, with the matter of boundedness: there will be

[82] For positivism, however, culture is a contravention of rational logic since law must persist in being plain, clean, pristine. Law has to be conceived as bare, pure, essential even. As naked presence, it can only be confined to its own-nature and indulge its relentless habit of self-definition (the commentator says the law after the judge saying the law after the statute saying the law after the constitution saying the law) with a view to controlling the past, the present, and the future by evoking a transcendental power. In the process, the jettisoned cultural apparatus is left devoid of any intellectual significance and effectively reduced to the expression of 'atavistic "tribal" instincts': HK Bhabha, *The Location of Culture* (Routledge 1994) 250. Because positivism is obsessively in search of knowledge that is technically utilizable, culture simply does not register on the professional scale. For the positivist, positivism and culturalism are unredeemably incompatible. Positivism thus posits the deposition and the disposition of culture. Eg: R Michaels, 'Two Paradigms of Jurisdiction' (2006) 27 Michigan J Int'l L 1003, 1017, where the author maintains that a comparative account of foreignness 'must remain within the law without taking recourse to general societal culture, because culture and its relation to the legal rules and institutions are unclear.' (I am unclear as to what this passage means – and I have read *Finnegans Wake*.) Closure, of course, is the condition of positivism. Eg: P Schlag, *The Enchantment of Reason* (Duke University Press 1998) 140: '[T]o be really good at "doing law", one has to have … a stunningly selective sense of curiosity.' Adde: P Goodrich, 'Law-Induced Anxiety: Legists, Anti-Lawyers and the Boredom of Legality' (2000) 9 Social & Legal Stud 143, 147 (review of Schlag supra), where the author, referring to 'legal non-knowledge', observes that 'both structurally and sociologically law does not know the objects of its regulation'. Without positivism's fixation of boundaries, there could be no positivism. But what is necessary for the positivist system to behold is also fictitious: the discarded cultural alternative continues to operate in depth with the inevitability characteristic of the return of the repressed.

tears in the web of information. Otherwise, one finds oneself having to contend with the predicament of inutility, which Borges strikingly illustrates through the briefest of stories. There was an empire where the art of cartography had been developed to such perfection that the map of a single province occupied a whole town, and the map of the empire a whole province. In time, these enormous maps no longer satisfied, and the college of cartographers established a map of the empire the size of the empire, which coincided with it point for point. Subsequent generations reflected that this inflated map was useless, and they abandoned it.[83]

Secondly, I have eschewed method and its doctrinarian propensities. Indeed, '[i]t is important to recognise that comparison is not a method or even an academic technique; rather, it is a discursive strategy'.[84] In lieu of a consecution of precepts that would lead to a more or less inevitable outcome, my comparison has emerged through experience – or 'flair'[85] – which I have incessantly adjusted along the way, unceasingly seeking to make it more *just*. The absence of any '*οδος*' ('*odos*') has involved the much higher levels of self-consciousness that come with one's assumption of responsibility, with one's *response* to the foreign – at once bold and companionate, sustaining and contingent, a rejoinder through an invention (a finding-and-fashioning) of the foreign. No-method comparative law is evidently no excuse for sloppiness. There are protocols, as I style them, or 'directions for use'.[86] For the sake of intellectual and scholarly integrity, they require the comparatist-at-law to have 'a clear strategy for gathering evidence',[87] to engage in 'the attentive reading of texts, the reference to the original, patience, slowness'.[88] They also demand that the notes be authoritative and current, incisive and pertinent – which I have ensured they are.

[83] See JL Borges, 'Del rigor en la ciencia' in *El hacedor* (Alianza Editorial 2009 [1946]) 119. For a set of observations also reaching the conclusion that the key to a map's success lies in its differentiation from the world, see B Latour, *Enquête sur les modes d'existence* (La Découverte 2012) 86.

[84] B Anderson, 'Frameworks of Comparison' *London Review of Books* (21 January 2016) 18.

[85] J Derrida, *De la grammatologie* (Editions de Minuit 1967) 233.

[86] J Derrida, *La Dissémination* (Editions du Seuil 1972) 303: 'No method: this does not exclude certain directions for use.'

[87] E Darian-Smith and PC McCarty, *The Global Turn* (University of California Press 2017) 130.

[88] J Derrida and M Ferraris, *Le Goût du secret* (A Bellantone and A Cohen eds, Hermann 2018 [1994]) 59. The words are Derrida's.

Now, there is no doubt in my mind that I have been engaging in a comparative intervention even though my focus has been on French law only. In this respect, the fact that I offer a (long) note on English law is irrelevant, and my study would be just as comparative without it. But have I understood French law? No, I have not. And I have not, because I could not. And I could not, since the self cannot be the other, which means that the location of the foreign is – and must be – beyond epistemic grasp (I mean the very foreign that makes the comparative discourse of interest).[89] Certainly irreducible to calculable determinants,[90] the foreign escapes anyone's ability to recount it *as such*. 'I feel kept at word's length.'[91] What I wrote is not French law; it is my reading, my interpretation, and my understanding of French law: it is 'French law'.

*

Perhaps a convenient point of departure for a further exploration of the key matter of understanding is to consider an excerpt from Patrick Glenn's *Legal Traditions of the World*, where the author, in a manner that well exemplifies the orthodox view within the field of comparative law, assumes – particularly once different laws from different locations have been Englished within a space where disparateness now morphs into seeming linguistic equivalence or commonality – that there can be understanding across laws or legal cultures and that such understanding is ultimately uncomplicated. Writing with reference to Russian law, Glenn holds thus: 'If you are a western lawyer with no previous experience of Soviet or socialist law, there are no major conceptual problems in understanding it.'[92] I profoundly disagree. (I so easily imagine how the late Bernard Rudden, whose expertise lay precisely in

[89] cf Derrida (n 80) 226: 'One does not have access to the here-now of the other.' For an extensive investigation of understanding within comparative law, see P Legrand, 'Foreign Law: Understanding Understanding' (2011) 6(2) J Comp L 67.

[90] For a critique of the epistemological assumptions informing comparative law by numbers, see P Legrand, 'Econocentrism' (2009) 59 U Toronto LJ 215. For a thoughtful objection to the nefarious influence of law-as-economics generally on comparative law, see G Watt, 'The Poverty of Economics and the Hope for Humanities in Comparative Law' (2014) 9(2) J Comp L 166.

[91] Letter from S Beckett to N Rawson in *The Letters of Samuel Beckett*, vol 4 (G Craig et al eds, Cambridge University Press 2016 [14 February 1976]) 422.

[92] HP Glenn, *Legal Traditions of the World* (5th edn, Oxford University Press 2014) 348. Glenn's book is replete with such foolish observations. Since they address understanding, a few of his remarks on translation can be helpfully quoted. For Glenn, understanding across languages generally speaking does not appear to raise challenging issues. '[E]ven in our own language', he writes derisively, '[s]ome people, and professors, are just

Soviet or Russian law, would have responded to such a jejune declaration.) My decades of comparative law scholarship prompt me to maintain that the understanding Glenn assumes possible on the comparatist's part simply cannot be made to happen (even assuming fluency in the Russian language – which, in Glenn's case, is an unduly generous concession, since he did not have that skill). What is on display in Glenn's text, I find, is but the pathological, irrational, and ultimately paralyzing illusion of mastery or control over otherness, which can only be assumed and enunciated because a comparatist is prepared to elide, smother, reject, or disavow any limits on the epistemological reach of the self's understanding – an arrogance that effectively harbours the makings of an imperial or colonial mindset. Instead, I easily side with Ludwig Wittgenstein who, talking about someone offering an explanation and remarking that an explanation must always beget a further one, exclaims: '[I] still don't understand what he means, and never shall!'[93] I discern much intellectual integrity in this humble admission.

The empirical fact of the matter is that the comparative mind, which is structurally operating at a distance from foreign law – again, the self cannot be the other – is only capable of coming so close to foreignness. If you will, the inadequacy of the comparison has always-already begun, because of an otherness that outstrips all possible access and holds the

impossible to understand': ibid 49. In any event, he opines, superficially, that '[t]he translation industry in the world stands as testimony to [the fact of translatability]': ibid. And he submits a flippant pronouncement to the effect that '[i]f you don't like translations, ... you can always learn the other language': ibid. In response, James Whitman understandably writes that '[l]overs of serious scholarship are sure to dislike this book', 'a poorly executed, self-indulgent piece of work': JQ Whitman, 'A Simple Story' (2006/4) Rechtsgeschichte 206, 206. I feel bound to record that in June 1997, having been invited to assess Glenn's typescript in order to break a deadlock between two reviewers, I wrote to Christopher Rycroft, a commissioning editor at Oxford University Press, that 'the design of [Glenn's] project is fundamentally misguided and epistemologically flawed'. I added that '[t]his book was doomed to be derivative and superficial'. Moreover, I commented that 'even if one was to accept the merits of [this] brand of comparative scholarship, it remains that this *particular* book is poorly structured, poorly written, and poorly researched'. Specifically, I pronounced that '[b]y and large, the text is convoluted and rambling' [on file]. A lady from the press later contacted me by telephone to ask if publication as a student text rather than under the scholarly 'Clarendon' imprint would address my concerns (which, she appeared to concede, were not completely devoid of merit). Evidently, Oxford University Press was determined to publish that book, and it did, and it apparently proved a good marketing decision since it underwent five editions in less than fifteen years – and, at the end of the day, a publisher is not the Red Cross.

93 L Wittgenstein, *Philosophical Investigations* (4th German-English edn, PMS Hacker and J Schulte eds, GEM Anscombe et al trs, Wiley-Blackwell 2009 [1946–49]) s 87, 45e.

comparatist-at-law, at best, to adjacency or alongsideness.[94] *While the comparatist never ceases to cross the border, he never arrives on the other side.* Call it a question of *vergency.*[95] And if the comparative mind is then going to report on what it will have encountered, it will only be able to do so by mobilizing the stock of available words in the language in which the account is now finding itself couched, these words being, structurally, quite simply unable to capture the infinite complexity of foreign law typically unfolding in a foreign language. Even if he were to coin new words so as to ameliorate his interpretive yield, the comparatist would still have to use extant prefixes or suffixes – which means that he would continue to be faced with the structural problem I address. This difficulty from the standpoint of representation is nothing less than primordial: both the comparative mind and the comparatist's words are fated to fall short of otherness and therefore to short-change otherness (and to change it by falling short of it). Being inherent to the way in which mind and words operate, these limitations cannot be remedied, which means that *there must be failure.*[96] Through the use of 'his' mind and of 'his' language, the comparatist-at-law denies himself the very possibility of access to the foreign. But what else can he do? On account of thrownness, he must operate with 'his' mind and language, and there is no denying such fact.[97]

Envisage further the fraught correlation between word and world. To be sure, the consideration of this dynamic boasts influential antecedents, not least Beckett's *Watt.* In his singular novel, Beckett unfolds an epistemological claim to the effect that despite the porousness of any borders between self and world, the self's language is ultimately unable to make referential contact with world – thus, the word 'pot', Watt's utterance,

[94] cf M Heidegger, *Sein und Zeit* (Niemeyer 2006 [1927]) 239: 'We . . . are at most always only "nearby".'

[95] See P Legrand, 'The Verge of Foreign Law – With Derrida' (2010) 1 Romanian J Comp L 73. For her part, Gayatri Spivak refers to 'a patient and provisional and forever deferred arrival into the performative of the other': GC Spivak, *Death of a Discipline* (Columbia University Press 2003) 13. cf Letter from S Beckett to MM Howe in *The Letters of Samuel Beckett*, vol 1 (MD Fehsenfeld and LM Overbeck eds, Cambridge University Press 2009 [13 December 1936]) 397: 'It has turned out indeed to be a journey from, and not to, as I knew it was, before I began it.'

[96] cf Beckett (n 76) 133: '[T]hat's all words, they're all I have, and not many of them, the words fail, the voice fails.'

[97] cf J Derrida, *Hospitalité*, vol 1 (P-A Brault and P Kamuf eds, Editions du Seuil 2021 [1996]) 213, where Derrida observes that although 'I am certainly at home in my language', yet 'I remai[n] paradoxically a guest, a host, a foreigner welcomed in his home' – which means, concretely, that I cannot do whatever I want with 'my' language.

cannot *name* Mr Knott's 'pot'.[98] Otherwise said, the signifier's significatory capacity is intrinsically limited, so much so that a word cannot account for a world (even as a world is seen to be constitutive of a self rather than extending outside of it as Cartesianism has been unpersuasively contending): signifier and signified ultimately fail to coalesce. It follows that instead of the comfortable conjunction positivism unexaminedly expects and assumes, one must accept an exigent disjunction – a conclusion that must obtain notwithstanding any manifestation of intentionality to the contrary. Call it a theory of the rupture. As 'a word is not the expression of a thing, but the absence of this thing',[99] in effect, 'the division, the disjunction, *is the relation*'.[100] Otherwise said, there is 'a relation of relationlessness',[101] an *irrelation* – say, between the comparatist and the foreign law. And such irrelation is structural. Vis-à-vis (the foreign law's) 'world', the empirical fact of the matter is that (the comparatist's) 'word' is missing something (a letter, at least). *Mind the gap!*

Limitations on the power of reference as it expresses itself through language – '[i]t is the world of words that creates the world of things'[102] – must also inevitably mark the comparative investigation and, to paraphrase Blanchot (supra), the comparatist's words are not the expression of foreign law, but stand for the absence of foreign law. Given that language operates as a site of ontological disclosure – because of the basic 'linguisticality' of thought[103] – and since no experience is amenable to the circumvention of language, the comparatist must contend with his structural inability to establish a stable referential relationship between his words and the worldly foreign law that his words wish to inscribe. It

[98] See S Beckett, *Watt* (CJ Ackerley ed, Faber & Faber 2009 [1953]) 67.

[99] M Blanchot, *La Part du feu* (Gallimard 1949) 68.

[100] J Derrida, *Mémoires* (Galilée 1988) 110. cf F Ponge, 'La pratique de la littérature' in *Méthodes* in *Œuvres complètes*, vol 1 (B Beugnot ed, Gallimard 1999 [1961]) 678: 'I think that these two worlds [the world of words and the external world] are watertight, that is to say, without passage from one to the other. One cannot pass.' In French literature, the idea that language silences the object readily evokes Mallarmé's thought on the flower: 'I say: a flower! And … there arises … the one absent from all bouquets': [S] Mallarmé, 'Avant-dire au "Traité du verbe" de René Ghil' in *Préfaces* in *Œuvres complètes*, vol 2 (B Marchal ed, Gallimard 2003 [1945]) 678.

[101] R Jaeggi, *Entfremdung* (Suhrkamp 2016) 20 [emphasis omitted]. Rahel Jaeggi devotes an entire chapter to this problematique. See ibid 20–70.

[102] J Lacan, *Ecrits* (Editions du Seuil 1966 [1953]) 276.

[103] cf D Davidson, 'On the Very Idea of a Conceptual Scheme' in *Inquiries into Truth and Interpretation* (2nd edn, Oxford University Press 2001 [1973]) 185: '[S]peaking a language is not a trait a man can lose while retaining the power of thought.'

follows that the process of textualization, that is, the strategy whereby the comparatist effectively attempts, often in a hesitant, stuttering way, to convert foreign life-in-the-law into words, into the words that are available to him within 'his' language, can best be approached as a necessarily compromised effort. Even as the comparatist strives, often exhaustingly so, to foreignize his text in order loyally to account for the foreignness of foreign law, he is effectively, and not at all insignificantly, fashioning a text that very much textualizes his 'own' self-in-the-law.

Note that the comparatist's presence within the language of the comparison goes beyond the fact that he operates in 'his' language and concerns the further fact that within 'his' language, he proceeds to select 'his' preferred words. Indeed, the words that the comparatist harnesses to tell the foreign are very much his words of choice. Because these words are the comparatist's selection out of the words available to him within 'his' language, words within which the comparatist dwells, words that haunt him, they are words that he will now haunt as he marshals them towards the expression of his comparative narrative. And this haunting *squared* is one further reason why, irrespective of any assertion of intentionality to the contrary and no matter how insightful the comparative study at hand, the comparatist's presentation of foreign law cannot be a faithful representation of it. In Wittgenstein's parlance, a statement can be taken to represent foreign law except that it lacks what it must have in common with foreign law in order to be able to *represent* it.[104] At best, then, the comparatist's report will consist just of a re-presentation and, one very much hopes, of a just re-presentation. Therefore, the comparatist's words, because they are of 'his' language, but also since they attest to his discursive partialities, will necessarily fail the foreignness of the law that the comparing mind decides to inscribe. *C'est ainsi.* Yet, electing not to heed this epistemic fact, orthodox comparatists (like Glenn) consistently behave as if access to foreign law is possible and as if foreign law is available as such then to generate supposedly ad idem reporting. For my part, as I was investigating the French statute and writing on the edge of it, I remained aware at all times that Frenchness (had to) lay beyond my understanding.

The abiding ethical/political exigence for me as I researched the French statute and purported to write about it was to make the other-in-the-law

[104] I draw on Wittgenstein's *Tractatus*: L Wittgenstein, *Tractatus Logico-Philosophicus* (German-English edn, CK Ogden ed and tr, Routledge 1981 [1922]) s 4.12, 79. I refer to the first paragraph.

present, even as I knew that I could not make the other-in-the-law present. Observe that the interpretive logic at work is not that of either presence or absence, but of *both presence and absence*: the foreign law that is the focus of the comparative study is at once present and absent. The foreign is 'out there', in France, but it is not 'in here', in the comparatist's text. The aporia – etymologically, the absence of passage (*a/poros*) – cannot be avoided, and any movement aiming for a coincidence between self-in-the-law and other-in-the-law would be futile: the distance is irreducible, and whatever *irrelation* the comparatist fashions with foreign law, he must articulate from the space of this interruption. In this crucial sense, in the way in which it features such inherent representational limit, this structural inability to overcome the fissure between the self's language and the other's law, the comparatist's intervention upon foreign law stands as a primordial *negative*: it cannot make full contact; rather, it undoes the foreign that it is meant to uphold as it compels it to manifest itself through comparative speech. But just as in photography positive prints appear out of a negative, rewarding insights into the foreign may be generated out of the negative comparative account. There is at work a power-effect (think of a performative scenography): the word produces a world, and propositions (about foreign law) enact a 'reality' (said to be 'foreign law'): a form of 'out-thereness is accomplished or achieved',[105] a form, then.

I find it important to insist that a key consequence of the intervention of a singular interpretation of a singular law-work – this singular assemblage of interacting singularities – concerns the structural impossibility of any possible interpretive guarantee. The comparatist-at-law has no choice: he must compare along with this in-built insecurity rather than chase the vain hope of ascertaining something like the stable meaning of a text that would exist more or less immovably within it and that he could then reproduce just as solidly in his own interpretive work.[106] It is not, therefore, that the comparatist cannot connect at all with the legal singularity that there is, there, but that his irrelation pertains to a correspondence that must find itself interrupted.[107]

105 J Law, *After Method* (Routledge 2004) 38.

106 Eg: J Derrida, *Béliers* (Gallimard 2003) 45: 'The certainty of a reading assured would be the first inanity.'

107 The move to irrelation may appear radical, but there is no choice. Indeed, 'I do not see any possibility of relationship, friendly or unfriendly, with the unintelligible': Letter from S Beckett to T McGreevy in *The Letters of Samuel Beckett*, vol 1 (MD Fehsenfeld and LM Overbeck eds, Cambridge University Press 2009 [16 September 1934]) 227.

What takes place thus shows how the comparatist's interaction with the foreign is not structured through affirmative statements that would mirror or represent it, but by way of assertions that are necessarily at variance from the existential actuality of the foreign. What unfolds is effectively a non-accordance, an irrelation – hence a forceful negative. Note, crucially, that it is this very irrelation that saves the other from appropriation or assimilation and ultimately allows him to remain as other: '[T]he [o]ther is only other precisely because I am effectively without relation with it.'[108] And since the comparison of laws assumes more than one law, the irrelation I address is, in effect, ensuring the structural safeguarding of comparative law – arguably not an unworthy cause!

I require to enter a few additional reflections. The recognition of a foreign law's singularity – the comparatist's response to what is the case – has nothing to do with a kind of ghettoization of legal knowledges gesturing towards the essentializing assumption that a foreign legal culture is to be deemed co-extensive with one territory only and that such foreign legal culture can therefore stand for that one territory and its people only (and correlatively that no other territory and its people could have anything whatsoever to do with that legal culture). And the idea of legal singularity does not suggest an alignment of the politics of location with the identitarian enclaves that one readily associates with identity politics. Also, I accept that a thoroughly singular law would be, strictly speaking, unreadable. Even as I am addressing a ciphered singularity, I am therefore never concerned with a pure singularity (I happily leave *Reinheit* to Kelsen).[109] What happens, complicatedly, is that 'the singularity irreplaceable and untranslatable of the unique is iterable'.[110] It can be restated, but with a difference; and each restatement, being a given comparatist's iteration, is singular.

It is Tocqueville who wrote that 'without comparisons to make, the mind does not know how to proceed'[111] – a statement I am tempted to

[108] F Jullien, *Si près, tout autre* (Grasset 2018) 161.

[109] cf D Attridge, *The Singularity of Literature* (Routledge 2004) 63: 'Singularity is not *pure*; it is constitutively impure.'

[110] J Derrida (with D Attridge), '"Cette étrange institution qu'on appelle la littérature"' in T Dutoit and P Romanski (eds), *Derrida d'ici, Derrida de là* (Galilée 2009 [1989]) 262. The words are Derrida's.

[111] Letter from A de Tocqueville to E de Chabrol in *Correspondance à divers* in *Œuvres complètes*, vol 17 (F Mélonio and A Vibert eds, Gallimard 2021 [7 October 1831]) 108. cf TS Kuhn, 'The Trouble with the Historical Philosophy of Science' in J Conant and

paraphrase as follows: without a critique to make, my mind does not know how to proceed.[112] I have thus engaged in a critique of the French model of religious governance with a view to promoting the politics of pluralism and defending the decolonization of thought – the delinking of comparatism from imperialism or colonialism – as, I am intimately convinced, befits an other-wise vigilant comparatist.[113] Such critique cannot be about sententiously teaching the other-in-the-law the error of his ways, and it cannot be about instituting oneself as referent either. Moreover, it is not destined to encourage the French model to converge with others and in time dissolve itself into some sort of uniform configuration in line with Konrad Zweigert and Hein Kötz's argument to the effect that comparative law's future lies in a giant leap backwards returning us to where we were more than 300 years ago, to a period that they identify as the 'era of natural law' ('*Zeit des Naturrechts*').[114] Instead, my critique purports to exercise what I regard as my entitlement qua comparatist-at-law to question certain assumptions – ideological, epistemological, and so forth – while realizing and accepting how the postulates I am addressing are (singularly) encultured, and how I myself am operating from the standpoint of a (singularly) encultured self.

My comparative analysis of the 2004 French statute is, structurally, inadequate. There was more to say, and I could have written more. Perhaps I could have attempted to specify the distinctive meanings of '*collèges*' and '*lycées*'. And I might have been able to elucidate further the semantic extension of '*les écoles, les collèges et les lycées publics*' by making reference to the German '*öffentliche Grundschulen, Mittelschulen und Gymnasien*' (although, while seemingly transparent and agreeable, this German translation raises insuperable problems and ultimately unfolds *monologically*). I must accept that, structurally, *der Vergleich hinkt*.

J Haugeland (eds), *The Road Since Structure* (University of Chicago Press 2000 [1992]) 115: '[I]n [the] absence [of the Archimedean platform], comparative evaluation is all there is.'

112 cf Letter from S Beckett to G Duthuit in *The Letters of Samuel Beckett*, vol 2 (G Craig et al eds, Cambridge University Press 2009 [11 August 1948]) 95: 'Nothing for me will ever be sufficiently against.'

113 For guidance, see WD Mignolo, *The Politics of Decolonial Investigations* (Duke University Press 2021) 458.

114 K Zweigert and H Kötz, *Einführung in die Rechtsvergleichung* (3rd edn, Mohr Siebeck 1996) 44.

*

I have articulated a constitutive engagement with foreign law rather than any dualist detachment from it. I have intervened performatively: I have found the other law and fashioned it into 'my' words (the very English words that I have chosen to tell French-law-in-French, *these words* and not others), I have invented it – I have actively made sense of it. My wordy arrangement, while it does not seek to dispense with statutes and judicial decisions, boldly twists itself out of positivism. To be sure, it remains fragmentary rather than totalizing, but it has no choice. And it is a self-portrayal rather than a withdrawal, and there is no option in this regard either, for I am thoroughly in the comparison and in the comparative text, indiscerptible from both configurations. While it is not a matter of simplistically identifying a given statement as straightforward self-portrayal, the fact of the matter is that no assertion can convincingly be said to have safely escaped all autobiographical input. Incidentally, I would also be advancing this claim if I had written on the French civil code's provisions on termination of contract or if I had expounded on the rights of minority shareholders under French law. In these instances, too, I would be thoroughly and indiscerptibly in the comparison and in the comparative text. *Where else could I be?*

Instead of entrapping ideas like method, objectivity, and truth, this clanking caravanserai erringly and eerily suggesting the existence, the accessibility, and the reproducibility of the 'is-ness' of foreign law (as in the phrase 'what the law is'), I claim that comparatists-at-law indisciplinedly require to acknowledge law as culture, culture as trace, and trace as law – a virtuous epistemic circle, indeed. As a matter of justice, I have therefore tried to offer a just interpretation of foreign law. Along the way, I have confirmed yet again that as he approaches foreignness, the comparatist cannot separate himself from his enculturation and that the foreign law-text is also inseparable from its enculturation. I have also confirmed that the comparatist-at-law is separated from the foreign law-text so that he never accesses it: he remains at a necessary distance from otherness-in-the-law and is therefore confined to an interpretation of it, his task being to yield the most felicitous response possible (the separation, though, not being so thoroughgoing as to prevent any making-sense whatsoever). I have therefore confirmed a comparative intervention as consisting in the intertwinement of three separations, two that cannot be and one that must be. Pace positivism, which assumes that the comparative mind and the foreign can agree, I have confirmed that ultimately the motif of separation – a key variation on the theme of negative comparative law – irremeably informs the theory and practice of comparison-at-law.[115]

Inventing – finding-and-fashioning – French religious governance from within the epistemic irrelation and through an indisciplined, playful, and rhizomatic tracing eschewing impeccably gridded configurations, in effect inscribing 'my' French law, I have found it critically important interpretively to emphasize local incoherences (and not simply the obvious ones[116]). Consider two further non-quietist observations from the comparatist-as-culturalist's coign of vantage. First, given that French constitutional law purports to insulate the churches from the state and the state from the churches – the official separation between these institutions harking back to early-twentieth-century legislation – how can the state justify its assertive immixtion into the practice of the Muslim faith? Secondly, the oft-expressed legislative ambition being to favour the integration of individuals into French society, how is the exclusion of religious Muslim students from schools conducive to that goal?

[115] My theoretical commitments suffuse my work on foreign law even if I do not expressly think about them on the spur of the comparative moment and although I only tend to formulate them at length either ex ante or ex post. To capture this modus operandi, Derrida helpfully articulates the idea of 'distracted theory': J Derrida, *Psyché*, vol 1 (2nd edn, Galilée 1998) 9.

[116] J-L Bianco, 'Jean-Louis Bianco: "La laïcité est un trésor républicain"' (interview with I Bonet) *La Provence* (28 November 2020) ii: 'Laicity is universal.' The words are Bianco's. Bianco chaired a now defunct consultative body tasked with advising the government on matters of laicity from 2013 to 2021.

XIV

My Equipment

While I have no intention of honing comparative law to a fine utilitarian edge (nor to indulge gadgeteering), I hold that the comparatist is *homo faber* to the extent at least that he must choose his contrivances (through which he devises himself as comparatist-at-law) to fit in the tool-box he will have acquired from a fine online travel shop. For my part, whenever I embark on fieldwork I carry a kit comprising a dozen implements or so.

My devices include a large, state-of-the-art, multi-tasker differentiator (the high-end model easily recharges through my laptop so I can always have it at hand in a fully operational condition). When I activate the deconstructive programme, my differentiator proceeds to a critique of the foreign law under scrutiny. As I trigger the culturalist key, it re-signifies law-texts in terms of law-as-culture. If I launch the comparative application, my differentiator promptly singularizes foreignness. I also have a textograph (effectively achieving as regards texts the decomposition that a spectrograph attains for light). I invested in the ultra-sensitive, fine-point appliance featuring an innovatory detector, which optimizes discernment of textual haunting between the lines – of enciphering – and is therefore best for elucidating the mnemic and material textual tracery.

An indisciplinator, I have long come to realize, is necessary for the conduct of any meaningful cultural interpretation.[1] While all brands

[1] Indiscipline connects with singularity – a link that Samuel Beckett's customary perspicuousness allowed him readily to grasp (if in different language). Bringing to bear his interest in utensils (a further point of convergence with my work, then), Beckett has one of his characters exclaim how within a panoply of jadges, each measurer tells the matter at hand differently, every disciplinary assay an exercise in singularization. I refer to S Beckett, *Endgame* (R McDonald ed, Faber & Faber 2009 [1958]) 31–33: 'It was an extra-ordinarily bitter day, I remember, zero by the thermometer. … It was a glorious bright day, I remember, fifty by the heliometer ……. It was a howling wild day, I remember, a hundred by the anemometer. … It was an exceedingly dry day, I remember, zero by the hygrometer.' Observe how each disciplinary appreciation changes the 'day' being

boast an easy-to-handle dial greatly simplifying disciplinary motions or passages (either to one or more than one other discipline apart from law), I recommend the purchase of an integrated compass in order to facilitate orientation on unfamiliar disciplinary terrain, which can present awkward epistemological topography, vicissitudes ranging from tenebrous abysses to steep escarpments. In addition, I deem it important to take along a translator of the foreignizing type. Even if it is definitely more difficult to handle than the usual sort, it tends to generate just results by producing the most other-directed translations. I always bring with me a heavy-duty charitabler (indeed, my research experience suggests exigent mobilization of charitable interpretation).

And, of course, I make certain that I have a negator, too. I prefer the ultra-forthright version although it inevitably comes at a cost. The value combination, admittedly not so easy to deploy, allows the comparatist variously to say no to purity (of law or legal theory); no to translatability (of foreignness); no to understanding (of foreignness); no to method (in research); no to objectivity (in interpretation); no to truth (in interpretation); no to exactitude or correctness (in interpretation); no to the idea of one right meaning (in interpretation); no to representation (in interpretation); no to equivalence or commonality (across laws); no to 'transplants' (of laws); no to the assumption of a better law; no to universality; and no to what would be globalization, unification, or uniformization (of laws).[2]

I remain open to the acquisition of new gear. A few years ago, I bought an inventor. It works like a spell checker and searches my report on foreign

'described'. However, there is no 'description', and each disciplinary evaluation is *constitutive* of what is said to be the 'day' that there is, there. Each discipline singularizes the 'day'.

[2] At this juncture, the most recent negator on the market is the '*Vivitur ingenio*', which displays on a small screen the main reasons justifying its engagement in negation with respect to any specific issue. For example, the caption negating method currently reads as follows (there are regular updates): 'Arguably a sanitized choice masking a conservative normativity (in the sense at least of a fear of change and of a worry about contingency), in effect the imposition of a stagnant cloud of obscurity, the hardcore positivist canonization of method deceptively heralds a kind of predictability, which is also a mark of rigidity – at any rate, a linearity – even as comparative research's meanderings pertain to convolutions and intricacies, to circumlocutions and intermittencies, to deviations and irregularities. Undeniably, "[m]ethod . . . is a system for offering more or less bankable guarantees. It hopes to guide us more or less quickly and securely to our destination, a destination that is taken to be knowledge about the processes at work in a single world. It hopes to limit the risks that we entertain along the way": J Law, *After Method* (Routledge 2004) 9. But such ill-considered clockworkiness remains deceivingly blind to the structurally winding and twisting character of any pathway to foreignness and to the no less structural secretness that the foreign is fated to harbour before the comparing mind.'

law to detect all textual manifestations of allegedly impersonal, impartial, neutral, objective, or true formulations that would shroud my input in the fashioning of the foreign law-text and in the fabrication of my account of it. I indulged the most expensive configuration (the 'Take EpRep' – which, according to the glossy brochure, stands for 'Take Epistemic Responsibility'). Not only does this design identify the concealments, but it substitutes first-person singulars throughout the writing.[3]

I have a few more elementary instruments such as a Swiss-army knife, which allows me to cut through the epistemic nonsense without further ado. Also, I always keep a whistle on me – the closest I come to the deployment of what could potentially be regarded as an apotropaic contraption. I knew a distinguished Cambridge comparatist-at-law who used the strident sound to gain his students' attention. For myself, I find it helpful to blow the whistle on diverse epistemic howlers. (Sporadically, perhaps because of the loud noise, I have been able to procure a readership and secure its interest or even its adhesion.) To be sure, I have a passport and, notwithstanding that I lay claim to being a resolutely heliotropic comparatist, I do not forget my umbrella – unlike Nietzsche, perhaps.[4]

[3] To return to Beckett's narrative (supra), it is important to appreciate that none of the statements he propounds is objective or true. To call the day 'extra-ordinarily bitter' or 'glorious[ly] bright' or 'howling wild' or 'exceedingly dry' is, each time, to offer a reading of it, an interpretation, which is also an intervention. On every occasion, Beckett's character is 'meaning in'. The day is not inherently 'howling wild' or 'exceedingly dry' so that everyone would be left merely to harvest these conclusions and agree to them. Only a reading, an interpretation, an intervention, can make the day 'howling wild' or 'exceedingly dry'; can make sense of it as 'howling wild' or 'exceedingly dry'; can invent it (find it/fashion it) as 'howling wild' or 'exceedingly dry'. And other readers or interpreters or interveners might well regard the day as not 'howling wild' or not 'exceedingly dry', that is, they might disagree with the reading or interpretation or intervention that is being submitted to them. Take someone who was raised in Provence, where the famed *mistral* can blow at very high speed for a week, if not longer. For this person, in the light of where he has lived – of where he has been encultured – the Beckettian day might well fall quite short of being 'howling wild'. Because fixity of meaning is not an option, there will plausibly arise a misunderstanding between, say, a *Provençal* and a resident of halcyon San Diego – a dispute that may well generate an enriching confrontation about the characteristics concerning a 'howling wild' day. (Contrariwise, if both readers or interpreters or interveners readily agree that the day is either 'howling wild' or 'not howling wild', no beneficial conversation will ensue.) See P Legrand, 'What Is That, to Read Foreign Law?' (2019) 14(2) J Comp L 294.

[4] See F Nietzsche, 'Nachgelassene Fragmente' in *Digitale Kritische Gesamtausgabe* (G Colli et al eds, 2009 [1881]) <www.nietzschesource.org/#eKGWB/NF-1881,12> s 12. In English, Nietzsche's entry in his notebook reads 'I have forgotten my umbrella'. (One has to be mindful of the quotation marks.) cf J Derrida, *Eperons* (Flammarion 1978) 103–13.

XV

Appreciation

The omnium gatherum of words, statements, quotations, arguments, speculations, facts, and 'anecdata' that I gleaned, amassed, assembled, wrote, constructed, edited, and curated – the 'gnoseological and aesthesic reconstitutio[n]' that I style *NCL*[1] – attests how 'one cannot be a self on one's own',[2] how autobiography is also autoheterography. Beyond acknowledging my dues to the many authors whose publications I expend in the body text or notes – a signal that the thoughts I bring into play in *NCL* are unfathomably and ultimately obliged to scholars who wrote before me – I want to inscribe further specific expressions of gratitude even as I recognize how '[t]he number of lives that enter our own is incalculable'.[3]

*

I am glad to emphasize my profound intellectual debt to my late mentor from the University of Oxford, Professor Bernard Rudden. His incisive mind, demanding scholarship, exacting prose, and abiding integrity set virtuous standards I have long strived to attain. Rudden once told me that the comparatist is a ceaseless digger who, although he occasionally finds something that glisters, rarely strikes gold. In an important sense, the essays that I have collected as *NCL* celebrate both the dark good fortune of the mining itself and the irredeemable foundering (I write in order to portray a foreignness I know will forever elude me), the incessant challenge as I '[f]ail again' being to '[f]ail better'.[4]

Differently, Peter Goodrich, a rare kind of humanist whom I met at an optimally opportune professional juncture for me, has made a pronounced

1 WD Mignolo, *The Politics of Decolonial Investigations* (Duke University Press 2021) xxi.
2 C Taylor, *Sources of the Self* (Harvard University Press 1989) 36.
3 J Berger, *Here Is Where We Meet* (Vintage 2006) 161.
4 S Beckett, *Worstward Ho* in *Company/Ill Seen Ill Said/Worstward Ho/Stirrings Still* (D Van Hulle ed, Faber & Faber 2009 [1983]) 81.

impression on my work for nearly three decades. No doubt unbeknownst to him, his inspiration is an integral part of these texts – although I hasten to enter the usual disclaimer lest he find himself saddled with any or all of the variations on the general theme of my *non-savoir* that I have fashioned as *NCL*. On the understanding that '*how to see* always means *what to notice*' and that to be shown '[h]ow to see, in short, is normative',[5] Rudden and Goodrich, each in his own eccentric and excentric way, convoyed an arduous education (*educare*, *e-ducare*: to lead out of – for example, to lead out of dismaying unlearnedness). They both encouraged a difficult exertion of the mind that might otherwise have remained inchoate. In the process, they communicated an empowering sense of permission and promise. In neither case have I felt the anxiety of influence.

*

It took an inordinately long time for the precipitate that is *NCL* to form. Over the more-than-one lustre during which it was actively in suspension, I found myself very fortunate that Catalina Avasilencei, Steven Calabresi, Cosmin Cercel, Laurence Claus, Erin Delaney, Michael Devitt, Georgina Firth, Clint Francis, Daniel Hachem, Clea Hance, Josh Kleinfeld, Anna Menzel, Alexandra Mercescu, Roderick Munday, Michael Palmer, Michael Ramsey, Michael Rappaport, Daniel Rodriguez, Geoffrey Samuel, Maimon Schwarzschild, Ricardo Spindola, Rafael Valim, and Franz Werro (*polúmētis*) should have so generously imparted their friendship to me in forms *diverses et variées*, all of them trusting and thus highly meaningful – an amicable confederacy whom I relieve forthwith of any complicity in my enueg.[6] Throughout the composition, Alexandra, Franz, and Maimon maintained an affable, extensive, and enriching correspondence that I have greatly cherished.

My deepest appreciation is for the person closest to me, who effectively allowed me to move into technicolour away from an existence set to be lived in greyscale, who has been the animating force of this endeavour and is justly its dedicatee. She has immensely enhanced my life as she has immeasurably improved *NCL*. Not only has her steadfast love (her *grenzenlose Liebe*) informed the long journey, not only has she adamantly argued in favour of this enterprise long before I glimpsed a trajectory (was she incited by the crisp, early-morning, summery Corsican air?), not only has her persistent inducement given me much of the impulse and

[5] M Tamen, 'Interpretation and Resistance' (2012) 18 Common Knowledge 208, 211.

[6] I had occasion to express my thankfulness to Geoffrey Samuel in P Legrand, 'Foreign Law as Self-Fashioning' (2017) 12(2) J Comp L 6, 6n*.

energy I needed to launch, pursue, and realize this project (I kept wondering if the planet genuinely needed one more protest), not only has her extraordinary patience allowed me repeatedly to express my incredulity regarding the merits of this scriptitious venture, not only has she sustained me at several points that I perceived as moments of *blocage* in my *bricolage*, not only has she consistently accepted with remarkable abnegation the extravagant solitude I required in order to bring this undertaking to a stage that could reasonably pass as readiness-to-publish (the gift of time is inestimable), but she has sharpened very many of the arguments I deploy – whether she agrees with me or not. In fact, there is hardly a printed page that she does not haunt, and many of *NCL*'s sentences feature a significant trace of hers. It is not only, then, that she has not left my voice unchanged, but that without her this work would never have moved to inception, let alone completion. It is no exaggeration at all to say that quite simply, this book would not have been released – and the wound from so long ago that ultimately explains the articulation and writing of my critique would not have borne this fruit. To my *Camarguaise*, then, *danke*.

*

The prevailing (and seemingly ever-worsening) monetization or commoditization of scholarship – the corporatization of the university – inclines me to insist that *NCL* was written without the benefit of any institutional subsidy whatsoever (without absurd application forms, then): no fellowship, no bursary, no grant, no stipend, no award, no endowment, no scholarship, no sponsorship: *nothing*. Nor was it advantaged through any academic leave, whether paid or unpaid. I produced this text on my own time, and I did so on my own (dazzling) Apple laptop computer, having bought my own books, entered my own subscriptions to journals, magazines, or newspapers, and paid my own Internet charges. I conducted all of my research and verified all of my references by myself without any undergraduate or postgraduate help.

To be sure, I relied on selfless librarians to secure many documents that would otherwise have remained out of my reach, and I am keen to extend heartfelt thanks in particular to Sarah Reis, *bibliothécaire extraordinaire* at the Northwestern University Pritzker School of Law in Chicago, whose deft, benevolent, and copious assistance readily exemplifies for me the US idiom 'above and beyond'. Crucially,

I was able to count on Sarah's succour while in Chicago, but also when I found myself more than 7,000 km away. Inna Muradyan and her Legal Research Center team at the University of San Diego School of Law also deserve commendation for their indispensable help. (How many hundreds of 'Circuit' books did USD librarians deliver to me over the years?) Generally speaking, my precious US affiliations allowed an unceasing convocation of digital resources that proved pivotal to the fabrication of *NCL*.[7]

Other than that, and in the most practical of manners (not only, then, in theoretical terms), the configuration of my claims concerning research into foreign law and with respect to the comparison of laws has taken the form of a substantial experience in delocalization and relocalization as I have repeatedly (and most rewardingly) left my *provençal* phrontistery to teach and lecture – often for prolonged periods of time – in locales as diverse as Australia, Brazil, China, Denmark, Egypt, Finland, Greece, Hungary, Indonesia... Poland, Qatar, Romania, Singapore... (to track the alphabet). Each of these numerous excursions has supplied me with intellectual oxygen, and my gratefulness to my many hosts continues unbounded.

*

The preceding sentence easily segues into the following cluster of reflections. On an admittedly less than agreeable note, I find it important to observe in print, to *record*, that these essays were written notwithstanding the fact that my principal institutional affiliation is to a French university, which means that, in France, I have been teaching (and preparing and grading) eight different courses every academic year; that, in France, I do not have an office (I conduct my pedagogical ministrations in cafés); that, in France, I do not have any teaching, research, librarious, or secretarial assistance whatsoever; that, in France, I do not have access to the least travel resources; and that, in France, I have no entitlement to periodic sabbatical leave. (I overlook what else my French law school is too impoverished to supply, but there is much more: think computer, printer, stationery...) Let me repeat, then, that these essays were written

[7] I would be remiss if I did not credit San Diego law deans Daniel Rodriguez, Kevin Cole, and Stephen Ferruolo; Northwestern law deans Daniel Rodriguez, Kimberly Yuracko, Jim Speta, and Hari Osofsky; and Cambridge programme director Roderick Munday for their sustained expression of confidence in me and my work. Their extremely meaningful and sustained support has been paramount.

despite the fact that my main professional connection is to the French university system – where, incidentally, the overall condition of comparative law is nothing short of an outrage to the very idea of scholarship.[8] The texts I have foregathered as *NCL* therefore stand as so many tokens of resistance to a scholastic configuration that, in the ways I evoke but in many others also, appears specifically designed to thwart its professoriate's life of the mind. (While besmirching is unseemly, the preposterous must be denounced.)

There is more, for I have had to contend with what François Cusset, a prominent French literary critic, identifies as '[a] tenacious tradition of intellectual isolationism', which he styles 'French cultural isolation'.[9] For his part, the German philosopher Peter Sloterdijk, although committedly francophile,[10] observes that 'France has become the most hermetic country in the world, [so that] even Tibet is of a total transparence in relation to [France]'.[11] In the end, I cannot be surprised that after more than twenty years of teaching '*droit comparé*' in Paris, I have come to the firm conclusion that the local significance of this undertaking features the

[8] I am aware of four graduates issuing from the comparative law programme that I directed at the Sorbonne over more than fifteen years who are actively pursuing a career as full-time academics specializing in what I would (and what they might not) name 'negative comparative law'. Three of these former students teach in England, one in Romania. Note that the significance of 'sunk costs' in academic life should not be undervalued. To frame the matter succinctly, every established professor has a large stock of reading notes, ready-to-hand interpretations, and written materials that he has painstakingly accumulated over years of study and publication. Any noteworthy challenge to the canon threatens the devaluation of such fixed assets. The rational response of the establishment is to seek to preserve the worth of its intellectual capital even if it is hopelessly obsolete. The disputants pursue opposite interests as they aim to peripheralize the incumbents and promote intellectual operations within a given field on the basis of an alternative set of epistemic endowments. As established professors fight to maintain their relevance, they readily retrench and just as willingly proceed to exclude perceived antagonists – the erection of a line of defence materializing particularly assertively within strongly conservative academic structures. In France, '*droit comparé*' thus remains as static as it has long been and continues to be mired in the marginalizing snares of secondary-school-style *culture générale*, while a new generation of Sorbonne-educated comparatists, all of them determined to take foreign law seriously, work abroad. I draw on D Riley, 'Notes on the Curriculum' (*Sidecar*, 7 October 2021) <https://newleftreview.org/sidecar/posts/notes-on-the-curriculum>.

[9] F Cusset, *French Theory* (La Découverte 2003) 336.

[10] Eg: P Sloterdijk, *Mein Frankreich* (Suhrkamp 2013).

[11] P Sloterdijk, 'La France est une exception psycho-politique, une bulle préservée' *Libération* (5–6 August 2006) 31.

kind of relevance I imaginatively associate with lectures on 'The Thought of Simone de Beauvoir' in Khartoum or on 'Oceanography' in La Paz. Indeed, how could comparative law, which structurally addresses the more-than-one, carry any pertinence in France where 'the phantasm of the One charges the whole of the political with its furious, archaic, and terrorizing energy'?[12]

Quite apart from the haughty disdain incessantly and intransigently shown towards foreign laws and languages, I have had to face very inadequate information technology in a country that persists in its decidedly anachronistic modes – *un pays en voie de sous-développement*, in fact. (At least the French university rescued me from any danger of reluctant accommodation to the ways of academe.)

These essays are survivors; they have survived what texts hardly survive.

*

Jean d'Aspremont graciously extended *NCL* the hospitality of the Cambridge Studies in International and Comparative Law series and actively supported my submission in a number of significant ways, not least through excellent advice and welcome encouragement in the course of steady and engaging correspondence. At Cambridge University Press, I was most fortunate to be able to count on Tom Randall's fairness and efficiency – on his courtesy and diligence, on his consideration and professionalism – throughout the exacting editorial process. I find it difficult to imagine how much more solicitude an author can legitimately expect from his commissioning editor.

There is the *difference* a copy editor makes. I have formed considerable esteem for Joseph Shaw's incisive advice on grammatical and syntactical improvements to the typescript. Perhaps because copy editors are inexistent in France, where publishers are in effect printers, I am particularly sensitive to the fact that Joseph should have lavished so much of his expert attention over so many weeks on the meticulous amelioration of my essays. Not only am I beholden to him for the indelible – and invariably tactful – stamp he has put on *NCL*, but I owe him for so magnanimously indulging my *travail en charrette*. And a '*travail*', dare I add, *NCL* very much claims to be in Michel Foucault's compelling sense of the term: '*Travail*: what is susceptible of introducing a significant

[12] R Dadoun, *La Psychanalyse politique* (Presses Universitaires de France 1995) 31.

difference in the field of knowledge at the price of a certain effort for the author and the reader.'[13]

My Project Manager at Integra Software Services, Akash Datchinamurthy, steered the metamorphosis of the typescript into a ready-to-print document with consummate skill. Moreover, he showed me great kindness, and I shall long remember his benevolence.

*

Now, it cannot be injudicious to adjourn *NCL* by exclaiming: 'Forsi altro canterà con miglior plectio.'[14]

[13] M Foucault, 'Des travaux' in *Dits et écrits*, vol 4 (D Defert and F Ewald eds, Gallimard 1994 [1983]) 367 [my emphasis].

[14] M [de] Cervantes, *El ingenioso caballero Don Quijote de la Mancha* (1605) <https://es.wikisource.org/wiki/Don_Quijote,_Primera_Parte:_Cap%C3%ADtulo_LII> pt 1, ch 52 [on file]. A sentence drawn from Ludovico Ariosto's *Orlando Furioso*, a 1516 Italian chivalric epic whose final version appeared in 1532, this excerpt ends part 1 of Cervantes's *Don Quijote*. (Part 2 would not be published until 1615.) Actually, Cervantes misquotes Ariosto's text, which reads '[F]orse altri canterà con miglior plettro' (30.16.8) and could be translated into English as 'Perhaps other people will sing with a better plectum'.

Supplement

'A text . . . is at the same time the condensation of a history scarcely delimitable. But this condensation of history . . . remains . . . indissociable from an event *absolutely* singular, a signature *absolutely* singular, and therefore also of a date, of a language, of an inscription autobiographical.'[1] What ascertainable circumstances, then, does this exercise in amplification herald, this supplement in the sense in which Jacques Derrida understands the term, that is, a text come from within *NCL* even as it is written after completion of *NCL* and grafted on to *NCL* in extremis?[2]

At the heart of the story must appear wintry Chicago, where I am relievingly, delightedly, and obligedly spending an extended period of time as I devote most of my waking hours over a number of weeks to the proofreading and indexing of *NCL*. While it remains feasible to inscribe a few interventions still, endmost marks that I envisage as just-in-time further edifications suddenly evidently *indispensable*, the pagination issuing from the excellent typesetting cannot be disturbed in the least and therefore acts as a material stricture inflexibly circumscribing the range of possible emendation. The idea of this addition thus arises as an act of ultimate resistance to the confoundingly structural character of a text's incompletude, years of incessant research and writing (and rewriting) notwithstanding. And on account of the indulgence of a most gracious commissioning editor, I find myself presented with the unexpected opportunity to respond to further contentions at once new and familiar, to impart to *NCL* a modicum of enhanced currency, in effect to iterate negativity's deconstructive and reconstructive counter-signature,

[1] J Derrida (with D Attridge), '"Cette étrange institution qu'on appelle la littérature"' in T Dutoit and P Romanski (eds), *Derrida d'ici, Derrida de là* (Galilée 2009 [1989]) 262. The words are Derrida's.

[2] See J Derrida, *De la grammatologie* (Editions de Minuit 1967) 308.

also to defer a little longer the moment when this entire composition must finally stop. Although the predicament concerning textual unfinishedness, not to mention the attendant cognitive vexation and affective disarray, is arguably liable to haunt every writing, it occurs to me that a comparatist, because of the sense of unacquitted indebtedness he experiences towards the foreign that he has elected to re-present for his own reasons – I refer to the justness and the justice owed foreignness – feels this disappointment uniquely.

*

Principally, perhaps, I understand law as necessarily a cultural enunciation; I defend law's condition as existing differentially; and I invite interpretive deference towards law's entitlement to difference, that is, recognition of it and respect for it. Meanwhile, the Similarization Enterprise – the Mimesis-Making Machine, the 'Triple M' Engine – harbours no interest in singularity and, for ideological reasons occasionally fathomable, persists in the peremptory pursuit of appropriation, assimilation, and totalization. Consider Holger Spamann's empirical study on judges.[3] This research – which contends that '[c]ommon and civil lawyers do not think differently after all'[4] – claims for itself 'an unusually high degree of realism'.[5] However, it is in fact, certainly from a comparative standpoint, profoundly *unrealistic* to sample 300 judges or so hailing from seven jurisdictions and to stage all of them to be sitting on the self-same court, all of them to be implementing the self-same law of procedure and the self-same law of evidence, all of them to be adjudicating on the self-same case, and all of them to be basing their decision on the self-same set of documents (allowing for translation in various languages) subsequently to conclude that, well, they proceed to think about the matter at hand in the self-same way. Given the design of an 'experiment' seemingly devised so that self-sameness should beget self-sameness, was any other outcome reasonably expectable? On reflection, it seems hard to think of a more *unrealistic* arrangement than this kind of epistemic strait-jacketing, all these sameness clauses summoning a highly artificial non-comparative setting, a typical occurrence of the doctor's doctoring effectively confirming Emanuele Lugli's insight: '[S]ameness is never a product of measuring; you need to believe in it before any

[3] H Spamann et al, 'Judges in the Lab: No Precedent Effects, No Common/Civil Law Differences' (2021) J Legal Analysis 110.

[4] ibid 112.

[5] ibid 113.

measuring is even undertaken.'[6] Recall how the anticipatory belief that Lugli identifies has long been the focus of Joseph Vining's critical epistemology: '[T]he comparati[st] presumes similarities between different jurisdictions in the very act of searching for them.'[7]

Spamann could have spared himself considerable aggravation and presumably saved substantial money by replacing his contrived equations and diagrams (in any event lying beyond the comprehending reach of one of his co-authors at least) by comparing, say, a French *Cour de cassation* decision in Civ 3d, 17 December 1997, and the House of Lords judgment in *Fitzpatrick v Sterling Housing Association* with specific reference to – how to name the issue in language that might speak to an empiricist whose research is apparently informed by the compulsive urge to scientificize comparative law? – the 'judicial sanguinity' coefficient as regards the normative indeterminacy arising from semantic vagueness.[8] To attempt more empirical resonance, the two cases that I indicate optimize comparability on account of the ascertainably close analogy between both arrays of material facts. Moreover – further balm to the empirical heart – the two judicial pronouncements were issued contemporaneously (specifically, within sixteen months of each other). Plausibly, to paraphrase Spamann, one can therefore legitimately refer to 'an unusually high degree of [comparability]' (supra). Needless to add, in these two instances French and English judges are dealing with very different sets of documents, which themselves correlate with very different local institutional, procedural, and evidentiary models. A meticulous examination of the two judicial law-texts featuring both the textual graphical surfaces and the textual traces encrypted (or enciphered) in the texts' respective fabrics would therefore have readily emphasized *what is the case*: the French epistemological commitment to nomothetics and the English epistemological predilection for idiographics. I continue to think that Geoffrey Samuel, a quintessential common law lawyer (as anyone who knows him will readily attest) and a comparatist whose comparatism includes years, nay decades of first-hand acquaintance with French legal culture on account of having held innumerable visiting professorships in France, frames the matter exceedingly well: unlike the standpoint that obtains in the civil law tradition, in the common law 'legal reasoning is a matter, not of applying pre-established legal rules as

6 E Lugli, *The Making of Measure and the Promise of Sameness* (University of Chicago Press 2019) 215.

7 J Vining, *The Authoritative and the Authoritarian* (University of Chicago Press 1986) 65.

8 Dalloz 1998 J 111; [2001] 1 AC 27.

such, but of pushing outwards from the facts'.[9] Observe that the two epistemic dispositions are irreducibly irreconcilable. Indeed, there is incommensurability, which means that in the absence of any meta-language 'one must necessarily prefer one conception to the other'.[10]

The agonistic delineation of the epistemological contrast I address would have saved Spamann from his awkward mimetical allegation, which unjustly 'imprison[s] someone [in effect, both the investigated judges and the interpreting comparatists] in a false, distorted, and reduced mode of being'.[11] I refer to the fact that quantification, a reduction of the intricate texture of the law to its elements deemed numerically effable only, stands as a crude materialism striking discernibly Faustian overtones. (Ironically, even as they pretend to stigmatize culture, Spamann's submissions very much represent a staunch cultural statement in their own right.) By way of arresting imagery, Gary Watt captures the ethical and political stakes – quite apart from the indigence of the economic thought on display – at once cogently and pithily: 'Perhaps it does not matter, micro-economically speaking, that a bridge was built by slaves, provided it stands; but we should not stand for such a bridge.'[12] By way of ancillary benefit (benefits matter to economists!), the comparison I suggest would have prevented Spamann from expressly aligning himself with Patrick Glenn's *Legal Traditions of the World*,[13] a trivializing undertaking that a dozen leading comparatists or so compellingly discredited in a leading comparative-law journal.[14]

Comparative law is about *seeing* things, not *seeing things* – and what is the case, given more than one legal tradition in co-presence, is (a Leibnizian) epistemic difference across legal traditions. To close on a

[9] G Samuel, *Epistemology and Method in Law* (Dartmouth 2002) 104. If I may be excused for hawking my own wares, I am moved also to note P Legrand, 'Alterity: About Rules, For Example' in P Birks and A Pretto (eds), *Themes in Comparative Law: In Honour of Bernard Rudden* (Oxford University Press 2002) 21–33. M Cohen, 'Ex Ante Versus Ex Post Deliberations: Two Models of Deliberations in Courts of Last Resort' (2014) 62 Am J Comp L 951.

[10] P Schlag and AJ Griffin, *How to Do Things with Doctrine* (University of Chicago Press 2020) 115.

[11] C Taylor, 'The Politics of Recognition' in A Gutmann (ed), *Multiculturalism* (Princeton University Press 1994) 25.

[12] G Watt, 'The Poverty of Economics and the Hope for Humanities in Comparative Law' (2014) 9(2) J Comp L 166, 189.

[13] HP Glenn, *Legal Traditions of the World* (5th edn, Oxford University Press 2014).

[14] See NHD Foster (ed), 'A Fresh Start for Comparative Legal Studies?' (2006) 1(1) J Comp L 100; BS Jackson, 'Internal and External Comparisons of Religious Law: Reflections from Jewish Law' (2006) 1(1) J Comp L 177.

suitably empirical note: the difference there is, there, is as overwhelmingly real as the proverbial tax bill, one's ideological preference for ascription of equivalence or commonality notwithstanding.

Along converging similarizing lines, although without the gongs and gyres pertaining to empirical legal studies, Steven Calabresi's authoritative monograph maintains that '[i]t can now be said that France has full fledged judicial review of the constitutionality of laws and of executive actions to the same degree as . . . the United States does',[15] in other words that '[i]n 2021, US style judicial review . . . [is] present in . . . France'.[16] As I read his monumental text, a further illustration of a sustainedly loquacious comparative constitutional law discourse, I hold that it is Calabresi himself who, sovereignly and momentously, simultaneously ascribes the togetherness that he proclaims and effaces the differences that, as a matter of what is the case given more than one constitutional law in co-presence, must make the French model irreducibly singular.[17]

[15] SG Calabresi, *The History and Growth of Judicial Review*, vol 2 (Oxford University Press 2021) 178.

[16] ibid vol 1, 317.

[17] For a thoughtful argument that I locate squarely within differential comparatism, see D Halberstam, 'How Europe Brought Judicial Review to France' in R Albert (ed), *Revolutionary Constitutionalism* (Hart 2020) 239–63. Interestingly, Daniel Halberstam's text expressly styles itself as a reply to B Ackerman, *Revolutionary Constitutions* (Harvard University Press 2019), which brings to mind the review where Jeremy Waldron addresses Bruce Ackerman's own similarization strategy. I refer to J Waldron, 'Quibbling, Wrangling' *London Review of Books* (12 September 2019) 11–12 and 14: 'Sometimes, . . . it seems that Ackerman's narratives are held together by nothing much more than similarities that happen to occur to him. De Gaulle was like George Washington: they both faced hardship and won military victories. We are supposed to be struck by the fact that de Gaulle endured political setbacks by retreating to Colombey-les-Deux-Eglises, while Washington could retreat to Mount Vernon. Alcide de Gasperi, leader of the Christian Democrats in Italy, was like [Nelson] Mandela in having defied a repressive regime; [FW] de Klerk was like General Jaruzelski. And so on. . . . In a batty moment, [Ackerman] even compares the authority of the unelected supreme leader of Iran . . . with that of the justices of the US Supreme Court, inasmuch as both "claim the right to safeguard the regime's fundamental values when they are endangered by popularly elected institutions".' To return to the singularity that I ascribe to the French constitutional review process (supra 93–94), I am minded to add a further (intangible) difference along the lines of 'indicia of constitutional earnestness'. On 23 February 2022, both the *Assemblée nationale* and the Senate validated three appointments to the French *Conseil constitutionnel*, such legislative confirmation a mere formality. In line with the letter of the Constitution, one nomination was the President's (he chose an elderly minister with a minor portfolio, an individual without any legal background whatsoever who had made a career as a secondary school teacher in history and geography); one was the President of the *Assemblée nationale's* (he selected a former chief prosecutor who, four years earlier, had overseen the decision to close the file concerning a corruption investigation against him); and one was the President of the Senate's (he picked the person who had been

Even as I contest Calabresi's invisibilization of French singularity – one of comparatism's uncircumventable conflicts of interpretations thus left to the adjudication of readers thereby entrusted with the task of assessing the interpretive yield of two opposite analyses – I salute how his imposing work makes three significant contributions to the comparative agenda. First, *History and Growth of Judicial Review* shows a commitment to the normative value of foreign law even as, at this early February 2022 writing, countries ranging from Hungary to the United Kingdom, from the United States to Brazil, and from Poland to India indulge forms of retrenchment vis-à-vis foreignness (or, like Russia in Ukraine, engage in the most bellicose and expansionist neo-nationalism). Secondly, the book demonstrates how conservative values – Calabresi is a prominent Republican on the US scene – can accommodate a dedication to foreign legal studies. As conservatism makes further inroads into the political life of the United States, the Calabresian alliance with comparatism in fact becomes all the more consequential for comparative law. Thirdly, the two volumes confirm the autobiographical character of the comparatist-at-law's work. In my opinion, the epistemological noteworthiness of this book's three brave achievements can hardly be overstated, which is why, on 3 December 2021, *une fois n'étant pas coutume*, I agreed to join a group of distinguished constitutionalists, most of them comparatists, to discuss Calabresi's comparative constitutionalism – my assigned remit, the chapter on France.

In the course of my ten-minute presentation (although online and speaking from various countries, the panelists were *in the United States*), I addressed Calabresi's convergence thesis as regards the French and US models of constitutional review and contended that there is a self-fashioning dimension to his position, a stance that he himself promptly confirmed in his immediate reply to my argument. Strangely, I thought, given Calabresi's endorsement, Tom Ginsburg then proceeded, strenuously and stentoriously, to declare how he found my views 'offensive' and to insist that, since 'we are scholars', it could not be that 'positionality' mattered 'more' than 'ideas'. Leaving to one side the fact that I have never thought, said, or written that 'positionality' prevails over 'ideas' – my standpoint is that autobiography inevitably informs comparative scholarship in ways pertaining to indissociability rather than hierarchization – I was not-stunned to observe that well into the twenty-first century there are senior academics who still take strong exception to the affirmation that their scholarship would not be immune to

his chief of staff from 2014 to 2017). Quaere: how *seriously* does France take constitutional law (and constitutional justice)?

authorial situatedness, who hold fast to the view that their *work* (their *surveys*, their *figures*, their *diagrams*) would somehow not be *their* work (*their* surveys, *their* figures, *their* diagrams). Conversant as I am with the indigence of the orthodoxy's intellectual ways within the field of comparative law (along the lines of the 'gift' that keeps 'giving'), the ossification of the governing epistemic configuration remains a cause for perplexity.

*

Not every comparison is dipped in a monotonous palette of watery beiges and drab browns. A fine differential analysis, Florian Grisel's *The Limits of Private Governance* thus probes at length the impact of glocalization on private ordering with specific reference to the centuries-old fishery commons of Marseille, a large port town not far from Arles.[18] Elsewhere, echoing Sherally Munshi's arguably precursive voice,[19] a few comparatists have been embracing decoloniality.[20]

[18] F Grisel, *The Limits of Private Governance: Norms and Rules in a Mediterranean Fishery* (Hart 2021).

[19] See S Munshi, 'Comparative Law and Decolonizing Critique' (2017) 65 Am J Comp L 207.

[20] Eg: E Mérieau, 'Area Studies and the Decolonisation of Comparative Law: Insights from Alternative Southeast Asian Constitutional Modernities' (2020) 51 Int'l Q Asian Stud 153; L Salaymeh, 'Decolonial Translation: Destabilizing Coloniality in Secular Translations of Islamic Law' (2021) 5 J Islamic Ethics 250; K Brayson, 'Generating Comparison-in-Law: Embodied Epistemologies, For the Love of Knowledge' (2021) 8(2) Critical Analysis L 52; GR Borges, *Hermenêutica jurídica descolonial: a revisão dos paradigmas interpretativos em direção à descolonialidade* (Faculdade de direito da Universidade de São Paulo, unpublished *'livre-docência'* dissertation 2022), where Guilherme Borges castigates the 'ethnojuricide' (*'etnojuricídio'*) that European determinedness visited on Brazilian originality (ibid 6–7 and 184–87). He opposes this metropolitan geo-politics of knowledge that took the form of the pernicious epistemic grafting unto local legal *conhecimento* of a European rationality deemed superior and imposed oppressively through a colonial and racist mindset (without any seeming appreciation, incidentally, for the fact that 'legal transplants' are properly impossible). As he argues in favour of a *'descolonial'* interpretive paradigm – the Portuguese term being deliberately retained to distinguish the Brazilian experience (ibid 194) – Borges wants to redeem the demotion of local knowledge. In order to overcome the naturalized character of this disqualification, he invites all local jurists to practise an epistemology of suspicion so as to 'unravel' (*'desvendar'*) the foreignness that has sedimented itself into Brazilian legal culture although not according with Brazilian reality (ibid 206). If you will, the idea is for every Brazilian jurist to operate a 'decolonial filter' (*'filtro descolonial'*) as a form of resistance to European epistemological hegemony (ibid 207). While Borges convincingly demonstrates that a 'decolonial turn' (*'giro descolonial'*) must advene (ibid 205), the challenge is daunting. Consider how it has indeed been observed that 'a large part of the content of Latin American law textbooks consist of an agglomeration of long textual citations of international doctrine, a collage that limits the role of local legal scholars to that of a commentator of cited foreign authorities. … The style of theoretical analysis tends to be that of a ventriloquist: local spokesmen for legal theories from Europe or the United States abound': C Rodríguez-Garavito, 'Remapping

In particular, boldly and sophisticatedly, Kimberley Brayson's theoretical and indisciplined contribution to comparative law's negative future – or so I choose to interpret her work – advocates for the epistemic value of a brand of experiential 'knowledge', of 'knowledge'-as-experience, that would be neither acultural nor patriarchal and accordingly purports to relocate the comparative endeavour beyond its historically impairing colonial and gendered logics commandingly masquerading under the guise of shibboleths like impersonality or objectivity or truth, Reason or unitarity or universalism.[21] And Brayson's earnest plea for a revisitation of comparative law's seminally imperial texts and textualities, for a properly subversive re-signification of significance, for an invention and re-invention of denotation and connotation, cannot be thwarted by what would be positivism's steadfast defence of fixity of meaning or permanency of interpretation. Recall Jorge Luis Borges: '[I]t is possible to affirm that each reading of a book, that each re-reading, each memory of that re-reading, renews the text. The text, too, is the changing river of Heraclitus.'[22] Through the articulation of a vehement 'no' to the orthodoxy's epistemic petrification, comparative law's grammatologic can indeed be *renewed*. Yes. When, as with Brayson's argument, negativity refutes the established model of epistemic governance, when negativity eloquently protests that it does not want to be like *that*, negativity operates as a '*resource*', indeed.[23]

Law and Society in Latin America: Visions and Topics for a New Legal Cartography' in C Rodríguez-Garavito (ed), *Law and Society in Latin America* (Routledge 2015) 3. Jorge Esquirol pointedly remarks that 'the deep engagement in European transnationalism is one of the sources of legal failure in the region': JL Esquirol, 'The Latin American Tradition of Legal Failure' (2011) 2 (1) Comp LR 1, 9 <www.comparativelawreview.unipg.it/index.php/comparative/issue/view/7> [on file]. Adde: L Salaymeh and R Michaels, 'Decolonial Comparative Law: A Conceptual Beginning' (2022) Rabels Zeitschrift 166. While I do not allege that only the colonized can legitimately advocate for decoloniality, it would be naive to ignore the matter of creditability. In this regard, applying a charitable disposition, as is my wont, I find it *implausible* that a director of a research centre that has long stood as an epitome of the imperial and colonial institutional attitude within comparative law, a German comparatist who has expressly proclaimed oh-so-essentially that 'German doctrinal scholarship will always be superior to that of other countries' (supra 116n29), should be rebranding himself as a reliable *décolonisateur sans peur et sans reproche*. In an e-mail dated 25 February 2022 [on file in a redacted version], a distinguished US comparatist and esteemed Chicago colleague, making express reference to this article, claims 'relentless virtue signaling'. Now, I cannot bring myself to find *that interpretation* implausible.

21 I refer to Brayson (n 20).

22 JL Borges, 'La poesía' in *Siete noches* (Fondo de cultura económica [Mexico] 1980 [1977]) 102.

23 J Derrida, *L'Ecriture et la différence* (Editions du Seuil 1967) 381.

And negativity deploys itself as a considerable resource in the way in which it informs a compelling critical counter-narrative hailing from the South that foregrounds comparative law's historical contribution (think Montesquieu and Maine) to the construction of the imperial or colonial legal mind and to the elaboration of a contemporary political economy of imperial or colonial legal knowledge – not unlike, then, the discipline of anthropology.[24] Asserting law to be thoroughly encultured and acknowledging the writing of comparatism as inseparable from autobiographying, Daniel Bonilla Maldonado eschews the positivistic understanding of the legal pursuant to which, ultimately, there would be 'true law' in Europe or North America and 'religion or politics', 'not really law', in Asia or Africa.[25] Perhaps two brief excerpts can afford an appreciation of Bonilla Maldonado's bracing subversiveness: 'When we examine law as culture, we therefore examine ourselves', and '[u]nderstanding law is understanding who we are as individuals and collectivities'.[26] Recall the threshold interrogation that animates *NCL* – '"[H]ow not to be governed *like that*, by them, in the name of these principles, with a view to such objectives and by the means of such processes, not like that, not for that, not by them?"'[27] – and as this book's argument goes full circle, let me commend Bonilla Maldonado for ingeniously bringing to bear intriguing epistemic insights on the exigent deconstruction and reconstruction of the rancid positivist comparative-law project.[28]

[24] D Bonilla Maldonado, *Legal Barbarians: Identity, Modern Comparative Law and the Global South* (Cambridge University Press 2021).

[25] ibid 114.

[26] ibid 4.

[27] This excerpt belongs to the quotation from Foucault's that I mobilize as *NCL*'s epigraph. The reference is at supra 45n134. Allow me what must be a conclusive illustration of the epistemic governance that demands the compelling resistance I herald in *NCL*. In September 2018, half a dozen self-styled comparatists-at-law met as a Sorbonne committee in order to deny a top (and ascertainably impecunious) postgraduate law student a modest scholarship that would have helped to finance the writing of his comparative doctoral dissertation on transitional justice. The explicit ground for the refusal was that *forgiveness is not a legal concept*.

[28] Incidentally, one would do very well to apprise oneself of the imperial and colonial mindset that René David – he of *Les Grands systèmes* (supra 57n29) – applied to the writing of a civil code for Ethiopia that he had been commissioned to draft in the late1950s: see Bonilla Maldonado (n 24) 117–26. Even acknowledging French hubris – an empirical rather than a misogallic claim – David's comparatism vis-à-vis Ethiopia is an epistemic wonder to behold.

INDEX OF MATTERS

It is Isaac Disraeli, an early-nineteenth-century British scholar and father to the famous Prime Minister, who may well hold the distinction of having lavished the greatest praise on indexers: 'I, for my part, venerate the inventor of indexes; and I know not to whom to yield the preference, either to Hippocrates, who was the first great anatomiser of the human body, or to that unknown labourer in literature, who first laid open the nerves and arteries of a book.'[1]

My vote goes to Hippocrates. Be that as it may, the construction of an index features a brand of interpretive input that distinguishes it from anatomy. In particular, this index very much stands as my own artisanal design after I (easily) resolved to eschew a professional or digitized configuration. The predictable advantages and inconveniences therefore inform this exercise in *invention*.

*

[1] I D'Israeli, *Miscellanies; or, Literary Recreations* (Cadell and Davies 1796) 196.

INDEX OF NAMES

This list does not tabulate citations deployed strictly for illustrative purposes. I have in mind the following referential scenario:

The territory of science is also a cultural space.

Eg: K Chemla and EF Keller (eds), *Cultures Without Culturalism: The Making of Scientific Knowledge* (Duke University Press 2017); K Knorr-Cetina, *The Manufacture of Knowledge: An Essay on the Constructivist and Contextual Nature of Science* (Pergamon 1981); B Latour and S Woolgar, *Laboratory Life: The Construction of Scientific Facts* (2nd edn, Princeton University Press 1986); A Pickering, *Constructing Quarks: A Sociological History of Particle Physics* (University of Chicago Press 1984).

For further examples of omissions along these lines, see 69n88; 154n4.

*

CAMBRIDGE STUDIES IN INTERNATIONAL AND COMPARATIVE LAW

Books in the Series

167 *Negative Comparative Law: A Strong Programme for Weak Thought* Pierre Legrand

166 *Detention by Non-State Armed Groups under International Law* Ezequiel Heffes

165 *Rebellions and Civil Wars: State Responsibility for the Conduct of Insurgents* Patrick Dumberry

164 *The International Law of Energy* Jorge Viñuales

163 *The Three Ages of International Commercial Arbitration* Mikaël Schinazi

162 *Repetition and International Law* Wouter Werner

161 *State Responsibility and Rebels: The History and Legacy of Protecting Investment Against Revolution* Kathryn Greenman

160 *Rewriting Histories of the Use of Force: The Narrative of 'Indifference'* Agatha Verdebout

159 *The League of Nations and the Protection of the Environment* Omer Aloni

158 *International Investment Law and Legal Theory: Expropriation and the Fragmentation of Sources* Jörg Kammerhofer

157 *Legal Barbarians: Identity, Modern Comparative Law and the Global South* Daniel Bonilla Maldonado

156 *International Human Rights Law Beyond State Territorial Control* Antal Berkes

155 *The Crime of Aggression under the Rome Statute of the International Criminal Court* Carrie McDougall

154 *Minorities and the Making of Postcolonial States in International Law* Mohammad Shahabuddin

153 *Preclassical Conflict of Laws* Nikitas E. Hatzimihail

152 *International Law and History: Modern Interfaces* Ignacio de la Rasilla

151 *Marketing Global Justice: The Political Economy of International Criminal Law* Christine Schwöbel-Patel

150 *International Status in the Shadow of Empire* Cait Storr

149 *Treaties in Motion: The Evolution of Treaties from Formation to Termination* Edited by Malgosia Fitzmaurice and Panos Merkouris

148 *Humanitarian Disarmament: An Historical Enquiry* Treasa Dunworth

147 *Complementarity, Catalysts, Compliance: The International Criminal Court in Uganda, Kenya, and the Democratic Republic of Congo*
Christian M. De Vos

146 *Cyber Operations and International Law*
François Delerue

145 *Comparative Reasoning in International Courts and Tribunals*
Daniel Peat

144 *Maritime Delimitation as a Judicial Process*
Massimo Lando

143 *Prosecuting Sexual and Gender-Based Crimes at the International Criminal Court: Practice, Progress and Potential*
Rosemary Grey

142 *Capitalism As Civilisation: A History of International Law*
Ntina Tzouvala

141 *Sovereignty in China: A Genealogy of a Concept Since 1840*
Adele Carrai

140 *Narratives of Hunger in International Law: Feeding the World in Times of Climate Change*
Anne Saab

139 *Victim Reparation under the Ius Post Bellum: An Historical and Normative Perspective*
Shavana Musa

138 *The Analogy between States and International Organizations*
Fernando Lusa Bordin

137 *The Process of International Legal Reproduction: Inequality, Historiography, Resistance*
Rose Parfitt

136 *State Responsibility for Breaches of Investment Contracts*
Jean Ho

135 *Coalitions of the Willing and International Law: The Interplay between Formality and Informality*
Alejandro Rodiles

134 *Self-Determination in Disputed Colonial Territories*
Jamie Trinidad

133 *International Law as a Belief System*
Jean d'Aspremont

132 *Legal Consequences of Peremptory Norms in International Law*
Daniel Costelloe

131 *Third-Party Countermeasures in International Law*
Martin Dawidowicz

130 *Justification and Excuse in International Law: Concept and Theory of General Defences*
Federica Paddeu

129 *Exclusion from Public Space: A Comparative Constitutional Analysis*
Daniel Moeckli

128 *Provisional Measures before International Courts and Tribunals*
Cameron A. Miles

127 *Humanity at Sea: Maritime Migration and the Foundations of International Law*
Itamar Mann

126 *Beyond Human Rights: The Legal Status of the Individual in International Law*
Anne Peters

125 *The Doctrine of Odious Debt in International Law: A Restatement*
Jeff King

124 *Static and Evolutive Treaty Interpretation: A Functional Reconstruction*
Christian Djeffal

123 *Civil Liability in Europe for Terrorism-Related Risk*
Lucas Bergkamp, Michael Faure, Monika Hinteregger and Niels Philipsen

122 *Proportionality and Deference in Investor-State Arbitration: Balancing Investment Protection and Regulatory Autonomy*
Caroline Henckels

121 *International Law and Governance of Natural Resources in Conflict and Post-Conflict Situations*
Daniëlla Dam-de Jong

120 *Proof of Causation in Tort Law*
Sandy Steel

119 *The Formation and Identification of Rules of Customary International Law in International Investment Law*
Patrick Dumberry

118 *Religious Hatred and International Law: The Prohibition of Incitement to Violence or Discrimination*
Jeroen Temperman

117 *Taking Economic, Social and Cultural Rights Seriously in International Criminal Law*
Evelyne Schmid

116 *Climate Change Litigation: Regulatory Pathways to Cleaner Energy*
Jacqueline Peel and Hari M. Osofsky

115 *Mestizo International Law: A Global Intellectual History 1842–1933*
Arnulf Becker Lorca

114 *Sugar and the Making of International Trade Law*
Michael Fakhri

113 *Strategically Created Treaty Conflicts and the Politics of International Law*
Surabhi Ranganathan

112 *Investment Treaty Arbitration As Public International Law: Procedural Aspects and Implications*
Eric De Brabandere

111 *The New Entrants Problem in International Fisheries Law*
Andrew Serdy

110 *Substantive Protection under Investment Treaties: A Legal and Economic Analysis*
Jonathan Bonnitcha

109 *Popular Governance of Post-Conflict Reconstruction: The Role of International Law* Matthew Saul

108 *Evolution of International Environmental Regimes: The Case of Climate Change*
Simone Schiele

107 *Judges, Law and War: The Judicial Development of International Humanitarian Law* Shane Darcy

106 *Religious Offence and Human Rights: The Implications of Defamation of Religions*
Lorenz Langer

105 *Forum Shopping in International Adjudication: The Role of Preliminary Objections*
Luiz Eduardo Salles

104 *Domestic Politics and International Human Rights Tribunals: The Problem of Compliance*
Courtney Hillebrecht

103 *International Law and the Arctic*
Michael Byers

102 *Cooperation in the Law of Transboundary Water Resources*
Christina Leb

101 *Underwater Cultural Heritage and International Law*
Sarah Dromgoole

100 *State Responsibility: The General Part*
James Crawford

99 *The Origins of International Investment Law: Empire, Environment and the Safeguarding of Capital*
Kate Miles

98 *The Crime of Aggression under the Rome Statute of the International Criminal Court*
Carrie McDougall

97 *'Crimes against Peace' and International Law*
Kirsten Sellars

96 *Non-Legality in International Law: Unruly Law*
Fleur Johns

95 *Armed Conflict and Displacement: The Protection of Refugees and Displaced Persons under International Humanitarian Law*
Mélanie Jacques

94 *Foreign Investment and the Environment in International Law*
Jorge E. Viñuales

93 *The Human Rights Treaty Obligations of Peacekeepers*
Kjetil Mujezinović Larsen

92 *Cyber Warfare and the Laws of War*
Heather Harrison Dinniss

91 *The Right to Reparation in International Law for Victims of Armed Conflict*
Christine Evans

90 *Global Public Interest in International Investment Law*
Andreas Kulick

89 *State Immunity in International Law*
Xiaodong Yang

88 *Reparations and Victim Support in the International Criminal Court*
Conor McCarthy

87 *Reducing Genocide to Law: Definition, Meaning, and the Ultimate Crime*
Payam Akhavan

86 *Decolonising International Law: Development, Economic Growth and the Politics of Universality*
Sundhya Pahuja

85 *Complicity and the Law of State Responsibility*
Helmut Philipp Aust

84 *State Control over Private Military and Security Companies in Armed Conflict*
Hannah Tonkin

83 *'Fair and Equitable Treatment' in International Investment Law*
Roland Kläger

82 *The UN and Human Rights: Who Guards the Guardians?*
Guglielmo Verdirame

81 *Sovereign Defaults before International Courts and Tribunals*
Michael Waibel

80 *Making the Law of the Sea: A Study in the Development of International Law*
James Harrison

79 *Science and the Precautionary Principle in International Courts and Tribunals: Expert Evidence, Burden of Proof and Finality*
Caroline E. Foster

78 *Transition from Illegal Regimes under International Law*
Yaël Ronen

77 *Access to Asylum: International Refugee Law and the Globalisation of Migration Control*
Thomas Gammeltoft-Hansen

76 *Trading Fish, Saving Fish: The Interaction between Regimes in International Law*
Margaret A. Young

75 *The Individual in the International Legal System: Continuity and Change in International Law*
Kate Parlett

74 *'Armed Attack' and Article 51 of the UN Charter: Evolutions in Customary Law and Practice*
Tom Ruys

73 *Theatre of the Rule of Law: Transnational Legal Intervention in Theory and Practice*
Stephen Humphreys

72 *Science and Risk Regulation in International Law*
Jacqueline Peel

71 *The Participation of States in International Organisations: The Role of Human Rights and Democracy*
Alison Duxbury

70 *Legal Personality in International Law*
Roland Portmann

69 *Vicarious Liability in Tort: A Comparative Perspective*
Paula Giliker

68 *The Public International Law Theory of Hans Kelsen: Believing in Universal Law*
Jochen von Bernstorff

67 *Legitimacy and Legality in International Law: An Interactional Account*
Jutta Brunnée and Stephen J. Toope

66 *The Concept of Non-International Armed Conflict in International Humanitarian Law* Anthony Cullen

65 *The Principle of Legality in International and Comparative Criminal Law*
Kenneth S. Gallant

64 *The Challenge of Child Labour in International Law*
Franziska Humbert

63 *Shipping Interdiction and the Law of the Sea*
Douglas Guilfoyle

62 *International Courts and Environmental Protection*
Tim Stephens

61 *Legal Principles in WTO Disputes*
Andrew D. Mitchell

60 *War Crimes in Internal Armed Conflicts*
Eve La Haye

59 *Humanitarian Occupation*
Gregory H. Fox

58 *The International Law of Environmental Impact Assessment: Process, Substance and Integration*
Neil Craik

57 *The Law and Practice of International Territorial Administration: Versailles to Iraq and Beyond*
Carsten Stahn

56 *United Nations Sanctions and the Rule of Law*
Jeremy Matam Farrall

55 *National Law in WTO Law: Effectiveness and Good Governance in the World Trading System*
Sharif Bhuiyan

54 *Cultural Products and the World Trade Organization*
Tania Voon

53 *The Threat of Force in International Law*
Nikolas Stürchler

52 *Indigenous Rights and United Nations Standards: Self-Determination, Culture and Land*
Alexandra Xanthaki

51 *International Refugee Law and Socio-Economic Rights: Refuge from Deprivation*
Michelle Foster

50 *The Protection of Cultural Property in Armed Conflict*
Roger O'Keefe

49 *Interpretation and Revision of International Boundary Decisions*
Kaiyan Homi Kaikobad

48 *Multinationals and Corporate Social Responsibility: Limitations and Opportunities in International Law*
Jennifer A. Zerk

47 *Judiciaries within Europe: A Comparative Review*
John Bell

46 *Law in Times of Crisis: Emergency Powers in Theory and Practice*
Oren Gross and Fionnuala Ní Aoláin

45 *Vessel-Source Marine Pollution: The Law and Politics of International Regulation*
Alan Khee-Jin Tan

44 *Enforcing Obligations* Erga Omnes *in International Law*
Christian J. Tams

43 *Non-Governmental Organisations in International Law*
Anna-Karin Lindblom

42 *Democracy, Minorities and International Law*
Steven Wheatley

41 *Prosecuting International Crimes: Selectivity and the International Criminal Law Regime*
Robert Cryer

40 *Compensation for Personal Injury in English, German and Italian Law: A Comparative Outline*
Basil Markesinis, Michael Coester, Guido Alpa and Augustus Ullstein

39 *Dispute Settlement in the UN Convention on the Law of the Sea*
Natalie Klein

38 *The International Protection of Internally Displaced Persons*
Catherine Phuong

37 *Imperialism, Sovereignty and the Making of International Law*
Antony Anghie

36 *Principles of the Institutional Law of International Organizations*
C. F. Amerasinghe

35 *Necessity, Proportionality and the Use of Force by States*
Judith Gardam

34 *International Legal Argument in the Permanent Court of International Justice: The Rise of the International Judiciary*
Ole Spiermann

33 -

32 *Great Powers and Outlaw States: Unequal Sovereigns in the International Legal Order*
Gerry Simpson

31 *Local Remedies in International Law* (second edition)
Chittharanjan Felix Amerasinghe

30 *Reading Humanitarian Intervention: Human Rights and the Use of Force in International Law*
Anne Orford

29 *Conflict of Norms in Public International Law: How WTO Law Relates to Other Rules of International Law*
Joost Pauwelyn

28 -

27 *Transboundary Damage in International Law*
Hanqin Xue

26 -

25 *European Criminal Procedures*
Edited by Mireille Delmas-Marty and J. R. Spencer

24 *Accountability of Armed Opposition Groups in International Law*
Liesbeth Zegveld

23 *Sharing Transboundary Resources: International Law and Optimal Resource Use*
Eyal Benvenisti

22 *International Human Rights and Humanitarian Law*
René Provost

21 *Remedies against International Organisations*
Karel Wellens

20 *Diversity and Self-Determination in International Law*
Karen Knop

19 *The Law of Internal Armed Conflict*
Lindsay Moir

18 *International Commercial Arbitration and African States: Practice, Participation and Institutional Development*
Amazu A. Asouzu

17 *The Enforceability of Promises in European Contract Law*
James Gordley

16 *International Law in Antiquity*
David J. Bederman

15 *Money Laundering: A New International Law Enforcement Model*
Guy Stessens

14 *Good Faith in European Contract Law*
Reinhard Zimmermann and Simon Whittaker

13 *On Civil Procedure*
J. A. Jolowicz

12 *Trusts: A Comparative Study*
Maurizio Lupoi and Simon Dix

11 *The Right to Property in Commonwealth Constitutions*
Tom Allen

10 *International Organizations before National Courts*
August Reinisch

9 *The Changing International Law of High Seas Fisheries*
Francisco Orrego Vicuña

8 *Trade and the Environment: A Comparative Study of EC and US Law*
Damien Geradin

7 *Unjust Enrichment: A Study of Private Law and Public Values*
Hanoch Dagan

6 *Religious Liberty and International Law in Europe*
Malcolm D. Evans

5 *Ethics and Authority in International Law*
Alfred P. Rubin

4 *Sovereignty over Natural Resources: Balancing Rights and Duties*
Nico Schrijver

3 *The Polar Regions and the Development of International Law*
Donald R. Rothwell

2 *Fragmentation and the International Relations of Micro-States: Self-Determination and Statehood*
Jorri C. Duursma

1 *Principles of the Institutional Law of International Organizations*
C. F. Amerasinghe

For EU product safety concerns, contact us at Calle de José Abascal, 56–1°,
28003 Madrid, Spain or eugpsr@cambridge.org.

www.ingramcontent.com/pod-product-compliance
Lightning Source LLC
LaVergne TN
LVHW052019200926
848481LV00005B/1529

* 9 7 8 1 0 0 9 0 5 4 8 6 7 *